EARTH ◆ SCIENCE

Fourth Edition

Leonard Bernstein ◆ Martin Schachter ◆ Alan Winkler ◆ Stanley Wolfe

Stanley Wolfe
Project Coordinator

About the Cover: Earth science is the study of Earth and its history. The images of Glen Canyon and Lake Powell in Utah and dripping water represent some of the things you will be learning in this book. Erosion caused by water helped to create Glen Canyon. The rock layers of the Canyon provide Earth scientists with an opportunity to study the geologic history of this region of North America. What do you think are some of the other things you will study in Earth science?

Staff Credits: Amanda Aranowski, Doug Bauernschmidt, Melania Benzinger, Karen Blonigen, Sarah Brandel, Katie Colón, Barbara Drewlo, Daren Hastings, Helen Higgins, Mariann Johanneck, Becky Johnson, Mary Kaye Kuzma, Vivian Lemanowski, Charles Luey, Mary Lukkonen, Paul Ramos, Dan Ray, Marie Schaefle, Christopher Tures, Mike Vineski, Sue Will

ISBN-13: 978-0-7854-6763-2
ISBN-10:   0-7854-6763-7

7 8 9 10 11 V0UD 19 18 17 16 15

1-800-321-3106
www.pearsonschool.com

Acknowledgments

Science Consultants

Gregory L. Vogt, Ed.D.
Associate Professor
Colorado State University
Fort Collins, CO

Stephen T. Lofthouse
Pace University
New York, NY

Laboratory Consultants

Sean M. Devine
Science Teacher
Ridge High School
Basking Ridge, NJ

Vincent R. Dionisio
Science Teacher
Clifton High School
Clifton, NJ

Reading Consultant

Sharon Cook
Consultant
Leadership in Literacy

Internet Consultant

Janet M. Gaudino
Seventh Grade Science Teacher
Montgomery Middle School
Skillman, NJ

ESL/ELL Consultant

Elizabeth Jimenez
Consultant
Pomona, CA

Content Reviewers

Sharon Danielsen (pp. 320-321, 334-335)
Site Manager
Darrin Fresh Water Institute
Rensselaer Polytechnic Institute
Troy, NY

Art DeGaetano (Chs. 12, 13)
Associate Professor
Cornell University
Ithaca, NY

Ivan Dmochowski (pp. 364-365)
Helen Hay Whitney Postdoctoral Scholar
California Institute of Technology
Pasadena, CA

Marian B. Jacobs Ph.D. (Chs. 1, 2, 3, 4)
Columbia University
New York, NY

Dr. Charles Liu (Chs. 5, 7, 8, 16, 17, 18)
Astrophysicist
Department of Astrophysics and Hayden
   Planetarium
American Museum of Natural History
New York, NY

Terry Moran (pp. 30-31, 152-153, 202-203)
Moran Research Service
Harvard, MA

Dr. Nathan M. Reiss (Ch. 11)
Professor Emeritus
Department of Environmental Sciences
Rutgers University
New Brunswick, NJ

Dr. Gerald Schubert (Ch. 11)
Department of Earth and Space Sciences
University of California—Los Angeles
Los Angeles, CA

Dr. Dirk Schulze-Makuch (Chs. 9, 10)
Department of Geological Sciences
University of Texas at El Paso
El Paso, TX

Seth Stein (Ch. 6)
Professor
Geological Sciences
Northwestern University
Evanston, IL

Hugh P. Taylor, Jr. (Chs. 14, 15)
Robert P. Sharp Professor of Geology
Division of Geological and Planetary Sciences
MS 100-23
California Institute of Technology
Pasadena, CA

Dr. Raymond C. Turner (Chs. 14, 15)
Alumni Distinguished Professor Emeritus of Physics
Department of Physics and Astronomy
Clemson University
Clemson, SC

Todd Woerner (pp. 84–85, 172–173, 268–269, 412–413)
Department of Chemistry
Duke University
Durham, NC

Teacher Reviewers

Peggy L. Cook
Lakeworth Middle School
Lakeworth, FL

Claudia Toback
Consultant/Mentor
Staten Island, NY

Contents

Scientific Skills and Investigations Handbooks

UNIT 1 **INTRODUCTION TO EARTH**

Big Dipper

Appendices

Earth Science Features

Hands-On Activity

Web InfoSearch

What are scientific skills?

People are naturally curious. They want to understand the world around them. They want to understand what causes earthquakes and where is the best place to search for useful minerals. The field of science would probably not exist if it were not for human curiosity about the natural world.

People also want to be able to make good guesses about the future. They want to be able to track severe storms such as hurricanes and to find ways to protect their homes against flooding.

Scientists use many skills to explore the world and gather information about it. These skills are called science process skills. Another name for them is science inquiry skills.

Science process skills allow you to think like a scientist. They help you identify problems and answer questions. Sometimes they help you solve problems. More often, they provide some possible answers and lead to more questions. In this book, you will use a variety of science process skills to understand the facts and theories in Earth science.

Science process skills are not only used in science. You compare prices when you shop and you observe what happens to foods when you cook them. You predict what the weather will be by looking at the sky. In fact, science process skills are really everyday life skills that have been adapted for problem solving in science.

▶ 1 NAME: What is the name for the skills scientists use to solve problems?

▲ **Figure 1**
Scientists use science process skills to understand how gravity affects the way crystals grow and materials mix, how caves form and change, how the land is built up and then torn down, and what Earth's place is in the universe.

Contents

1 Observing and Comparing

2 Classifying Data

3 Modeling and Simulating

4 Measuring

5 Analyzing Data and Communicating Results

6 Making Predictions

1 Observing and Comparing

Making Observations An important part of solving any problem is observing, or using your senses to find out what is going on around you. The five senses are sight, hearing, touch, smell, and taste. When you look at a pebble and feel its smoothness, you are observing. When you observe, you pay close attention to everything that happens around you.

Scientists observe the world in ways that other scientists can repeat. This is a goal of scientific observation. It is expected that when a scientist has made an observation, other people will be able to make the same observation.

2 ▶ LIST: What are the five senses?

Comparing and Contrasting Part of observing is comparing and contrasting. When you compare data, you observe the characteristics of several things or events to see how they are alike. When you contrast data, you look for ways that similar things are different from one another.

▲ **Figure 2** River and glacial cut valleys look similar. However, you can see many differences from the valley floor.

3 ▶ COMPARE/CONTRAST: How are valleys carved by running water and valleys carved by glaciers similar? How are they different?

Using Tools to Observe Sometimes an object is too small to see with your eyes alone. You need a special tool to help you make observations. One tool that scientists use to observe is the seismograph. A seismograph detects earthquakes by measuring the vibrations of Earth's crust.

▲ **Figure 3** Seismologist checking a seismograph

4 ▶ INFER: Besides detecting earthquakes, what other use does a seismograph have?

Hands-On Activity

MAKING OBSERVATIONS

You and a partner will need 2 shoeboxes with lids, 2 rubber bands, and several small objects.

1. Place several small objects into the shoebox. Do not let your partner see what you put into the shoebox.
2. Cover the shoebox with the lid. Put a rubber band around the shoebox to keep the lid on.
3. Exchange shoeboxes with your partner.
4. Gently shake, turn, and rattle the shoebox.
5. Try to describe what is in the shoebox without opening it. Write your descriptions on a sheet of paper.

Practicing Your Skills

6. IDENTIFY: What science process skill did you use?
7. IDENTIFY: Which of your senses was most important to you?
8. ANALYZE: Direct observation is seeing something with your eyes or hearing it with your ears. Indirect observation involves using a model or past experience to make a guess about something. Which kind of observation did you use?

2 Classifying Data

Key Term

data (DAYT-uh): information you collect when you observe something

Collecting and Classifying Data The information you collect when you observe something is called **data.** The data from an experiment or from observations you have made are first recorded, or written down. Then, they are classified.

When you classify data, you group things together based on how they are alike. This information often comes from making comparisons as you observe. You may classify by size, shape, color, use, or any other important feature. Classifying data helps you recognize and understand the relationships between things. Classification makes studying large groups of things easier. For example, Earth scientists use classification to organize the different types of rocks and minerals.

5 EXPLAIN: How can you classify data?

Hands-On Activity

ORGANIZING ROCKS

You will need 15 pebbles of different colors, textures, and shapes.

1. Lay the pebbles out on a table. Classify the pebbles into two categories based on texture: *Smooth* or *Rough*.
2. Look at the pebbles you classified as smooth. Divide these pebbles into new categories based on similar colors.
3. Repeat Step 2 for the pebbles you classified as rough.

Practicing Your Skills

4. ANALYZE: How did you classify the pebbles? What other ways could you classify the pebbles?
5. EXPLAIN: Why is a classification system useful?

3 Modeling and Simulating

Key Terms

model: tool scientists use to represent an object or process

simulation: computer model that usually shows a process

Modeling Sometimes things are too small to see with your eyes alone. Other times, an object is too large to see. You may need a model to help you examine the object. A **model** is a good way to show what a very small or a very large object looks like. A model can have more details than what may be seen with just your eyes. It can be used to represent a process or an object that is hard to explain with words. A model can be a three-dimensional picture, a drawing, a computer image, or a diagram.

6 DEFINE: What is a model?

Simulating A **simulation** is a kind of model that shows a process. It is often done using a computer. You can use a simulation to predict the outcome of an experiment. Scientists use simulations to study everything from the insides of a volcano to the development of a tornado.

▲ **Figure 4** This student is discovering how volcanoes are created through successive layers of erupted lava.

7 DEFINE: What is a simulation?

4 Measuring

Key Terms

unit: amount used to measure something

meter: basic unit of length or distance

mass: amount of matter in something

gram: basic unit of mass

volume: amount of space an object takes up

liter: basic unit of liquid volume

meniscus: curve at the surface of a liquid in a thin tube

temperature: measure of the amount of heat energy something contains

Two Systems of Measurement When you measure, you compare an unknown value with a known value using standard units. A **unit** is an amount used to measure something. The metric system is an international system of measurement. Examples of metric units are the gram, the kilometer, and the liter. In the United States, the English system and the metric system are both used. Examples of units in the English system are the pound, the foot, and the gallon.

There is also a more modern form of the metric system called SI. The letters *SI* stand for the French words *Système International*. Many of the units in the SI are the same as those in the metric system.

The metric and SI systems are both based on units of 10. This makes them easy to use. Each unit in these systems is ten times greater than the unit before it. To show a change in the size of a unit, you add a prefix to the unit. The prefix tells you whether the unit is larger or smaller. For example, a centimeter is ten times bigger than a millimeter.

PREFIXES AND THEIR MEANINGS	
kilo-	one thousand (1,000)
hecto-	one hundred (100)
deca-	ten (10)
deci-	one-tenth (1/10)
centi-	one-hundredth (1/100)
milli-	one-thousandth (1/1,000)

◀ Figure 5

8 ▶ IDENTIFY: What are two measurement systems?

Units of Length Length is the distance from one point to another. In the metric system, the basic unit of length or distance is the **meter.** A meter is about the length from a doorknob to the floor. Longer distances, such as the distances between cities, are measured in kilometers. A kilometer is 1,000 meters. Centimeters and millimeters measure shorter distances. A centimeter is 1/100 of a meter. A millimeter is 1/1,000 of a meter. Figure 6 compares common units of length. It also shows the abbreviation for each unit.

SI/METRIC UNITS OF LENGTH	
1,000 millimeters (mm)	1 meter (m)
100 centimeters (cm)	1 meter
10 decimeters (dm)	1 meter
10 millimeters	1 centimeter
1,000 meters	1 kilometer (km)

▲ **Figure 6**

Length can be measured with a meter stick. A meter stick is 1 m long and is divided into 100 equal lengths by numbered lines. The distance between each of these lines is equal to 1 cm. Each centimeter is divided into ten equal parts. Each one of these parts is equal to 1 mm.

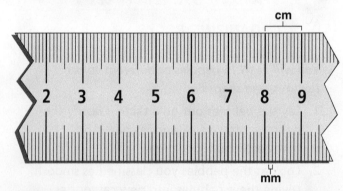

▲ **Figure 7** A meter stick is divided into centimeters and millimeters.

9 ▶ CALCULATE: How many centimeters are there in 3 meters?

Measuring Area Do you know how people find the area of the floor of a room? They measure the length and the width of the room. Then, they multiply the two numbers. You can find the area of any rectangle by multiplying its length by its width. Area is expressed in square units, such as square meters (m^2) or square centimeters (cm^2).

Area = length × width

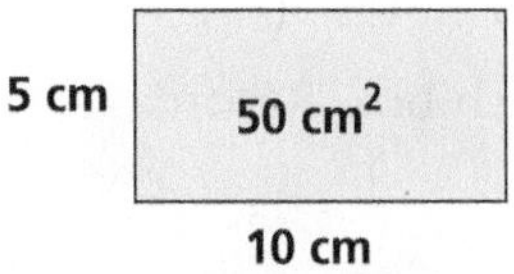

5 cm | 50 cm² | 10 cm

◀ **Figure 8** The area of a rectangle equals length times width.

10 CALCULATE: What is the area of a rectangle 2 cm × 3 cm?

Mass and Weight The amount of matter in something is its **mass.** The basic metric unit of mass is called a **gram (g).** A paper clip has about 1 g of mass. Mass is measured with an instrument called a balance. A balance works like a seesaw. It compares an unknown mass with a known mass.

One kind of balance that is commonly used to measure mass is a triple-beam balance. A triple-beam balance has a pan. The object being measured is placed on the pan. The balance also has three beams. Weights, called riders, are moved along each beam until the object on the pan is balanced. Each rider gives a reading in grams. The mass of the object is equal to the total readings of all three riders.

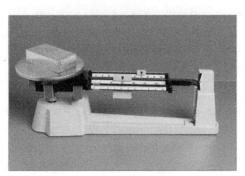

◀ **Figure 9**
A triple-beam balance

Mass and weight are related; however, they are not the same. The weight of an object is a measure of Earth's pull of gravity between Earth and that object. Gravity is the force that pulls objects toward the center of Earth. The strength of the pull of gravity between two objects depends on the distance between the objects and how much mass they each contain. So, the weight changes as its distance from the center of Earth changes.

11 IDENTIFY: What instrument is used to measure mass?

Volume The amount of space an object takes up is its **volume.** You can measure the volume of liquids and solids. Liquid volume is usually measured in **liters.** Soft drinks in the United States often come in two-liter bottles.

A graduated cylinder is used to measure liquid volume. Graduated cylinders are calibrated, or marked off, at regular intervals. Look at Figure 10. It shows a graduated cylinder. On this graduated cylinder, each small line is equal to 0.05 mL. The longer lines mark off every 0.25 mL up to 5.00 mL. However, every graduated cylinder is not calibrated in this manner. They come in different sizes up to 2,000 mL, with different calibrations.

Always read the measurement at eye level. If you are using a glass graduated cylinder, you will need to read the mark on the graduated cylinder closest to the bottom of the meniscus. A **meniscus** is the curve at the surface of a liquid in a thin tube. A plastic graduated cylinder does not show a meniscus.

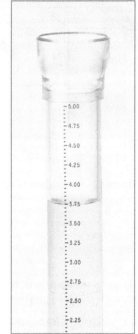

▲ **Figure 10** This glass graduated cylinder shows a meniscus.

The volume of solid objects is often measured in cubic centimeters. One cubic centimeter equals 1 milliliter (mL).

Look at Figure 11. Each side of the cube is 1 cm long. The volume of the cube is 1 cubic centimeter (cm³). Now, look at the drawing of the box in Figure 12. Its length is 3 cm. Its width is 2 cm. Its height is 2 cm. The volume of the box can be found by multiplying length by width by height. In this case, volume equals 3 × 2 × 2. Therefore, the volume of the box is 12 cm³.

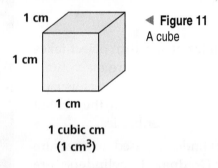

◄ **Figure 11**
A cube

1 cubic cm
(1 cm³)

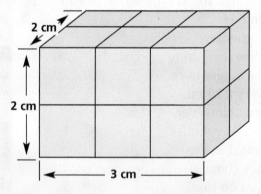

▲ **Figure 12** The volume of a box equals length times width times height.

$$V = L \times W \times H$$

If you have a box that is 10 cm on each side, its volume would be 1,000 cm³. A liter is the same as 1,000 cm³. One liter of liquid will fill the box exactly.

 CALCULATE: How many milliliters of water would fill a 12 cm³ box?

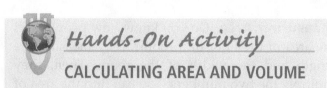

Hands-On Activity

CALCULATING AREA AND VOLUME

You will need 3 boxes of different sizes, paper, and a metric ruler.

1. Measure the length, width, and height of each box in centimeters. Record each measurement in your notes.

2. Calculate the volume of each box. Record each volume in your notes.

3. Find the surface area of each box. Record each area in your notes.

Practicing Your Skills

4. ANALYZE: Which of the three boxes has the largest volume?

5. CALCULATE: How many milliliters of liquid would fill each box?

6. ANALYZE: What is the surface area of the largest box?

Temperature **Temperature** is a measure of the amount of heat energy something contains. An instrument that measures temperature is called a thermometer.

Most thermometers are glass tubes. At the bottom of the tube is a wider part, called the bulb. The bulb is filled with liquid. Liquids that are often used include mercury, colored alcohol, or colored water. When heat is added, the liquid expands, or gets larger. It rises in the glass tube. When heat is taken away, the liquid contracts, or gets smaller. The liquid falls in the tube. On the side of the tube is a series of marks. You read the temperature by looking at the mark on the tube where the liquid stops.

Temperature can be measured on three different scales. These scales are the Fahrenheit (F) scale, the Celsius (C) scale, and the Kelvin (K) scale. The Fahrenheit scale is part of the English system of measurement. The Celsius scale is usually used in science. Almost all scientists, even in the United States, use the Celsius scale. Each unit on the Celsius scale is a degree Celsius (°C). The degree Celsius is the metric unit of temperature. Water freezes at 0°C. It boils at 100°C.

Scientists working with very low temperatures use the Kelvin scale. The Kelvin scale is part of the SI measurement system. It begins at absolute zero, or 0K. This number indicates, in theory at least, a total lack of heat.

COMPARING TEMPERATURE SCALES			
	Kelvin	Fahrenheit	Celsius
Boiling point of water	373K	212°F	100°C
Human body temperature	310K	98.6°F	37°C
Freezing point of water	273K	32°F	0°C
Absolute zero	0K	−459.67°F	−273.15°C

▲ Figure 13

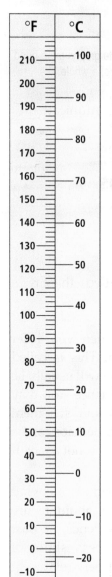

◀ Figure 14 The Fahrenheit and Celsius scales

Hands-On Activity

READING A THERMOMETER

You will need safety goggles, 2 beakers, a heat source, ice, water, a wax pencil, a ruler, and a standard Celsius thermometer.

1. Boil some water in a beaker.
   ⚠ CAUTION: Be very careful when working with heat. Place your thermometer in the beaker. Do not let the thermometer touch the sides or the bottom of the beaker. Wait until the mercury rises as far as it will go. Record the temperature.

2. Fill a beaker with ice water. Place the unmarked thermometer into this beaker. Wait until the mercury goes as low as it will go. Record the temperature.

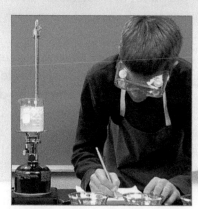

▲ STEP 1 Record the temperature of the boiling water.

Practicing Your Skills

3. IDENTIFY: What is the temperature at which the mercury rose as high as it would go?

4. IDENTIFY: What is the temperature at which the mercury went as low as it would go?

13▶ NAME: What are the three scales used to measure temperature?

5 Analyzing Data and Communicating Results

Key Term
communication: sharing information

Analyzing Data When you organize information, you put it in a logical order. In scientific experiments, it is important to organize your data. Data collected during an experiment are not very useful unless they are organized and easy to read. It is also important to organize your data if you plan to share the results of your experiment.

Scientists often organize information visually by using data tables, charts, graphs, and diagrams. By using tables, charts, graphs, and diagrams, scientists can display a lot of information in a small space. They also make it easier to compare and interpret data.

Tables are made up of rows and columns. Columns run up and down. Rows run from left to right. Tables usually show numerical data. Information in the table can be arranged in time order. It can also be set up to show patterns or trends. A table showing wind speed can reveal the effects the speed of wind will have on land. Figure 15 shows a table of gases in the atmosphere.

GASES IN THE ATMOSPHERE	
Gas	Percentage
Oxygen	21
Carbon dioxide	0.04
Nitrogen	78
Water vapor, helium, and other gases	0.02
Argon	0.94

▲ **Figure 15**

Graphs, such as bar graphs, line graphs, and circle graphs, often use special coloring, shading, or patterns to represent information. Keys indicate what the special markings represent. Line graphs have horizontal (x) and vertical (y) axes to indicate such things as time and quantities.

14 ▶ EXPLAIN: How do tables and graphs help you analyze data?

Sharing Results When you talk to a friend, you are communicating, or sharing information. If you write a letter or a report, you are also communicating but in a different way. Scientists communicate all the time. They communicate to share results, information, and opinions. They write books and magazine or newspaper articles. They may also create Web sites about their work. This is called written **communication**.

Graphs are a visual way to communicate. The circle graph in Figure 16 is showing the same information from Figure 15. The circle graph presents the information in a different way.

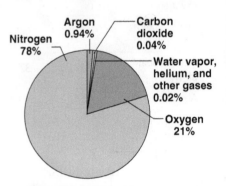

▲ **Figure 16** Circle graphs are a good way to show parts of a whole.

15 ▶ LIST: What are some ways to communicate the results of an experiment?

6 Making Predictions

Key Terms
infer: to form a conclusion

predict: to state ahead of time what you think is going to happen

Thinking of Possibilities When you **infer** something, you form a conclusion. This is called making an inference. Your conclusion will usually be based on observations or past experience. You may use logic to form your statement. Your statement might be supported by evidence and perhaps can be tested by an experiment. An inference is not a fact. It is only one possible explanation.

When you **predict,** you state ahead of time what you think will happen. Predictions about future events are based on inferences, evidence, or past experience. The two science process skills of inferring and predicting are very closely related.

16 ▶ CONTRAST: What is the difference between inferring and predicting?

How do you conduct a scientific investigation?

By now, you should have a good understanding of the science process skills. These skills are used to solve many science problems. There is also a basic procedure, or plan, that scientists usually follow when conducting investigations. Some people call this procedure the scientific method.

The scientific method is a series of steps that can serve as a guide to solving problems or answering questions. It uses many of the science process skills you know, such as observing and predicting.

Not all experiments use all of the steps in the scientific method. Some experiments follow all of them, but in a different order. In fact, there is no one right scientific method. Each problem is different. Some problems may require steps that another problem would not. However, most investigations will follow the same basic procedure.

1 ▶ DESCRIBE: What is the scientific method?

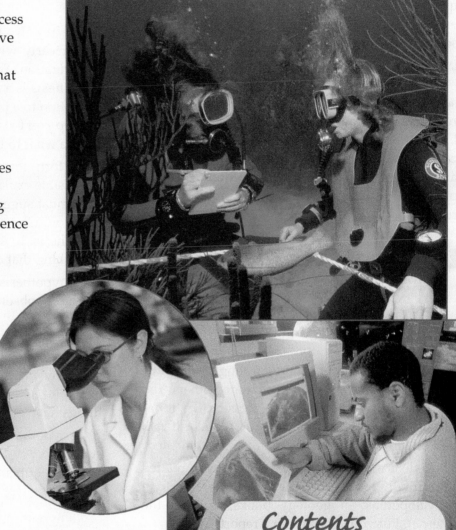

▲ **Figure 1** Scientists use the scientific method to guide experiments.

Contents

1 Identifying a Problem and Doing Research

Starting an Investigation Scientists often state a problem as a question. This is the first step in a scientific investigation. Most experiments begin by asking a scientific question. That is, they ask a question that can be answered by gathering evidence. This question is the reason for the scientific investigation. It also helps determine how the investigation will proceed.

Have you ever done background research for a science project? When you do this kind of research, you are looking for data that others have already obtained on the same subject. You can gather research by reading books, magazines, and newspapers, and by using the Internet to find out what other scientists have done. Doing research is the first step of gathering evidence for a scientific investigation.

 IDENTIFY: What is the first step of a scientific investigation?

BUILDING SCIENCE SKILLS

Researching Background Information Suppose you notice that a river running through your town looks brown on some days and clear on others. You also notice that when the river turns brown, it has usually rained the day before. You wonder if rain and the brown color of the river water are related.

To determine if the river water color is related to rainfall, look for information on rivers in encyclopedias, in geology books, and on the Internet. Put your findings in a report.

▲ **Figure 2** Water in river after a heavy rain.

2 Forming a Hypothesis

Key Terms

hypothesis: suggested answer to a question or problem

theory: set of hypotheses that have been supported by testing over and over again

Focusing the Investigation Scientists usually state clearly what they expect to find out in an investigation. This is called stating a hypothesis. A **hypothesis** is a suggested answer to a question or a solution to a problem. Stating a hypothesis helps to keep you focused on the problem and helps you decide what to test.

To form their hypotheses, scientists must think of possible explanations for a set of observations or they must suggest possible answers to a scientific question. One of those explanations becomes the hypothesis. In science, a hypothesis must include something that can be tested.

A hypothesis is more than just a guess. It must consider observations, past experiences, and previous knowledge. It is an inference turned into a statement that can be tested. A set of hypotheses that have been supported by testing over and over again by many scientists is called a **theory.** An example is the theory that explains how living things have evolved, or changed, over time.

A hypothesis can take the form of an "if…then" statement. A well-worded hypothesis is a guide for how to set up and perform an experiment.

DESCRIBE: How does a scientist form a hypothesis?

BUILDING SCIENCE SKILLS

Developing a Hypothesis If you are testing how river water and rainfall are related, you might write down this hypothesis:

Runoff is one cause of the river water turning brown.

Your hypothesis is incomplete. It is not enough to link water color and rainfall. You need to explain what materials make the river water brown and how rainfall causes those materials to get into the water. Revise the hypothesis above to make it more specific.

3 Designing and Carrying Out an Experiment

Key Terms

variable: anything that can affect the outcome of an experiment

constant: something that does not change

controlled experiment: experiment in which all the conditions except one are kept constant

Testing the Hypothesis Scientists need to plan how to test their hypotheses. This means they must design an experiment. The plan must be a step-by-step procedure. It should include a record of any observations made or measurements taken.

All experiments must take variables into account. A **variable** is anything that can affect the outcome of an experiment. Room temperature, amount of sunlight, and water vapor in the air are just some of the many variables that could affect the outcome of an experiment.

▶ DEFINE: What is a variable?

Controlling the Experiment One of the variables in an experiment should be what you are testing. This is what you will change during the experiment. All other variables need to remain the same. In this experiment, you will vary the type of earth.

A **constant** is something that does not change. If there are no constants in your experiment, you will not be sure why you got the results you did. An experiment in which all the conditions except one are kept constant is called a **controlled experiment.**

Some experiments have two setups. In one setup, called the control, nothing is changed. In the other setup, the variable being tested is changed. Later, the control group can be compared with the other group to provide useful data.

▶ EXPLAIN: Explain how a controlled experiment is set up.

Designing the Procedure Suppose you now want to design an experiment to determine what makes river water brown. You have your hypothesis. You decide your procedure is to construct a slightly tilted model of the river, the town, and the land upstream from the town. You will send water down the river and measure the color and clarity of the water. Next, you will create artificial rain and again check the color and clarity of the water.

Does it matter how much rain you add to your model? Does it matter how heavy the rainfall is? Does 3 inches (7.5 cm) of rainfall in 5 minutes have the same effect on your model as 3 inches in 1 hour?

In designing your experiment, you need to identify the variables. The amount of water and the rate at which you apply it to your model are variables that could affect the outcome of your experiment. Another important variable for your experiment is the steepness of the river. To be sure of your results, you will have to conduct your experiment several times. Each time you will alter just one variable while keeping the other variables just the same.

Finally, you should decide on the data you will collect. How will you measure the color and clarity of the water of the river? You might make a color chart that you lower into the river water to see how the sediment in the water changes its color.

The hands-on activity on page 12 is an example of an experiment you might have designed.

◀ **Figure 3** In your experiment, you will elevate the trays with books to test soil runoff.

▶ EXPLAIN: How do constants and variables affect an experiment?

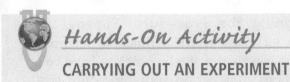

Hands-On Activity

CARRYING OUT AN EXPERIMENT

You will need 2 styrofoam meat trays from the grocery store, garden soil, grass sod, 2 plastic drinking glasses, 2 books, sprinkling can, scissors, and water. You should wear an apron and safety goggles.

1. Cut a small drain notch from the center of one end of each tray.
   ⚠ CAUTION: Be careful when using scissors.

2. Fill one tray with about a 1-inch layer (2.5 cm) of garden soil. Leave 2 inches (5 cm) of the notched end of the tray empty of soil.

3. Fill the second tray with a layer of sod except for 2 inches at the end with the notch.

4. Place the notched end of each tray at the edge of a table so that the trays extend over the edge a short distance.

5. Elevate the other end of the trays with books.

6. Label the cups *Soil* and *Sod*.

7. Sprinkle the soil tray with water. Keep sprinkling until the water runs off the surface of the soil and pours out the notch drain. Collect a glass of runoff water.

8. Repeat Step 7 with the sod tray.

Practicing Your Skills

9. OBSERVE: How much water did you have to sprinkle on the soil tray in order to collect a full glass?

10. OBSERVE: How much water did you have to sprinkle on the sod tray in order to collect a full glass?

11. COMPARE: Which glass had the dirtiest water?

12. EXPLAIN: What caused the difference in water clarity in the two glasses?

13. INFER: What would be the best way to reduce soil runoff in rivers?

4 Recording and Analyzing Data

Dealing With Data During an experiment, you must keep careful notes about what you observe. For example, you might need to note how long the rain fell on the trays before water began running off. How fast did the water run off each tray? This is important information that might affect your conclusion.

At the end of an experiment, you will need to study the data to find any patterns. Much of the data you will deal with is written text such as a report or a summary of an experiment. However, scientific information is often a set of numbers or facts presented in other, more visual ways. These visual presentations make the information easier to understand. Tables, charts, and graphs, for instance, help you understand a collection of facts on a topic.

After your data have been organized, you need to ask what the data show. Do they support your hypothesis? Do they show something wrong in your experiment? Do you need to gather more data by performing another experiment?

7 LIST: What are some ways to display data?

BUILDING SCIENCE SKILLS

Analyzing Data You made the following notes during your experiment. How would you display this information?

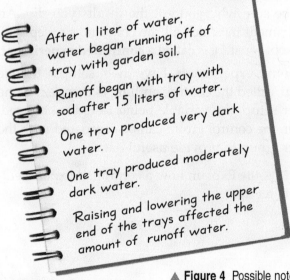

▲ **Figure 4** Possible notes

5 Stating a Conclusion

Drawing Conclusions A conclusion is a statement that sums up what you have learned from an experiment. When you draw a conclusion, you need to decide whether the data you collected supported your hypothesis. You may need to repeat an experiment several times before you can draw any conclusions from it. Conclusions often lead you to ask new questions and plan new experiments to answer them.

8 EXPLAIN: Why might it be necessary to repeat an experiment?

BUILDING SCIENCE SKILLS

Stating a Conclusion Review your hypothesis statement regarding the effect of surface material on rainwater runoff. Then, review the data you obtained during the experiment.

- Was your hypothesis correct? Use your observations to support your answer.
- Which surface reduced soil runoff better?

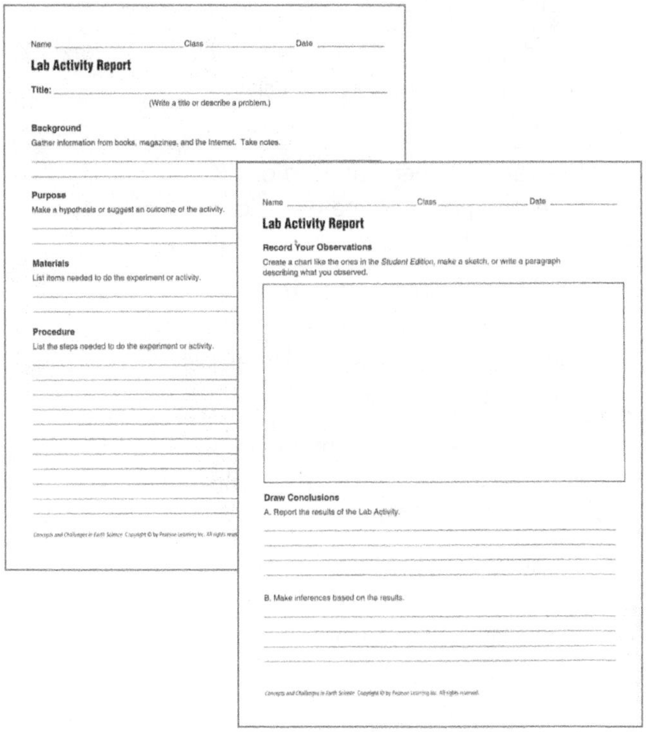
Name ______ Class ______ Date ______

Lab Activity Report

Title: ______ (Write a title or describe a problem.)

Background
Gather information from books, magazines, and the Internet. Take notes.

Purpose
Make a hypothesis or suggest an outcome of the activity.

Materials
List items needed to do the experiment or activity.

Procedure
List the steps needed to do the experiment or activity.

Name ______ Class ______ Date ______

Lab Activity Report

Record Your Observations
Create a chart like the ones in the *Student Edition*, make a sketch, or write a paragraph describing what you observed.

Draw Conclusions
A. Report the results of the Lab Activity.

B. Make inferences based on the results.

▲ **Figure 5** Throughout this program, you may use forms like these to organize your lab reports.

6 Writing a Report

Communicating Results Scientists keep carefully written records of their observations and findings. These records are used to create a lab report. Lab reports are a form of written communication. They explain what happened in the experiment. A good lab report should be written so that anyone reading it can duplicate the experiment. It should contain the following information:

- A title
- A purpose
- Background information
- Your hypothesis
- Materials used
- Your step-by-step procedure
- Your observations
- Your recorded data
- Your analysis of the data
- Your conclusions

Your conclusions should relate back to the questions you asked in the "purpose" section of your report. Also, the report should not have any experimental errors that might have caused unexpected results. For example, did you follow the steps in the correct order? Did an unexpected variable interfere with your results? Was your equipment clean and in good working order? This explanation of possible errors should also be part of your conclusions.

9 EXPLAIN: Why is it important to explain possible errors in your lab report?

BUILDING SCIENCE SKILLS

Writing a Lab Report Write a lab report to communicate to other scientists your discoveries about soil runoff. Your lab report should include a title, your hypothesis statement, a list of materials you used, the procedure, your observations, and your conclusions. Try to include one table of data in your report.

LAB SAFETY

Working in a science laboratory can be both exciting and meaningful. However, you must always be aware of safety precautions when carrying out experiments. There are a few basic rules that should be followed in any science laboratory:

- Read all instructions carefully before the start of an experiment. Follow all instructions exactly and in the correct order.

- Check your equipment to make sure it is clean and working properly.

- Never taste, smell, or touch any substance in the lab that you are not told to do so. Never eat or drink anything in the lab. Do not chew gum.

- Never work alone. Tell a teacher at once if an accident occurs.

Experiments that use chemicals or heat can be dangerous. The following list of rules and symbols will help you avoid accidents. There are also rules about what to do if an accident does occur. Here are some rules to remember when working in a lab:

 1. Do not use glass that is chipped or metal objects with broken edges. Do not try to clean up broken glassware yourself. Notify your teacher if a piece of glassware is broken.

 2. Do not use electrical cords with loose plugs or frayed ends. Do not let electrical cords cross in front of working areas. Do not use electrical equipment near water.

 3. Be very careful when using sharp objects such as scissors, knives, or tweezers. Always cut in a direction away from your body.

 4. Be careful when you are using a heat source. Use proper equipment, such as tongs or a ringstand, when handling hot objects.

 5. Confine loose clothing and hair when working with an open flame. Be sure you know the location of the nearest fire extinguisher. Never reach across an open flame.

 6. Be careful when working with poisonous or toxic substances. Never mix chemicals without directions from your teacher. Remove any long jewelry that might hang down and end up in chemicals. Avoid touching your eyes or mouth when working with chemicals.

 7. Use extreme care when working with acids and bases. Never mix acids and bases without direction from your teacher. Never smell anything directly. Use caution when handling chemicals that produce fumes.

 8. Wear safety goggles, especially when working with an open flame, chemicals, and any liquids.

 9. Wear lab aprons when working with substances of any sort, especially chemicals.

 10. Use caution when handling or collecting plants. Some plants can be harmful if they are touched or eaten.

 11. Use caution when handling live animals. Some animals can injure you or spread disease. Handle all live animals as humanely as possible.

 12. Dispose of all equipment and materials properly. Keep your work area clean at all times.

 13. Always wash your hands thoroughly with soap and water after handling chemicals or live organisms.

 14. Follow the ⚠ CAUTION and safety symbols you see used throughout this book when doing labs or other activities.

Chapter 1 The Structure of Earth

▲ **Figure 1-1** Earth as seen from space

This is an image of Earth created by an artificial satellite in space. Artificial satellites are sent into orbit for many purposes. For example, some satellites are used to study our planet and other objects in space. They help us to map Earth's surface and determine the size and shape of Earth. They also are used to study the land, oceans, and air. Computers can be used to reveal even more detail.

▶ The satellite image in Figure 1-1 shows some physical features of Earth. Which ones can you identify?

Contents

1-1 What is Earth science?

Objective

Identify and describe the four main branches of Earth science.

Key Terms

Earth science: study of Earth and its history

specialist (SPEHSH-uhl-ihst): person who studies or works on only one part of a subject

The Study of Earth Science The three major fields of science are Earth science, life science, and physical science. **Earth science** is the study of Earth and its history. It is also the study of changes on Earth and Earth's place in the universe.

As seen from space, Earth is much more than rock and soil. In fact, the most obvious features are the clouds and oceans. In addition, our environment is not just land, water, and air. Rather, it is air interacting with land, land interacting with water, water interacting with air, and so on.

Earth science is like a jigsaw puzzle made up of four pieces. Each piece of the puzzle is a main branch of Earth science. The four main branches of Earth science are geology, oceanography, meteorology, and astronomy. Together, they make up the field of Earth science. Look at Figure 1-2 below to learn something about each of the four main branches.

▷ IDENTIFY: What are the four main branches of Earth science?

Specialists in Earth Science A **specialist** is a person who studies or works on only one part of a subject. This one part of the subject is called a specialty.

There are many Earth science specialties. Most Earth scientists are specialists. For example, some oceanographers study only waves and tides. Others study the makeup of ocean water. Still others study the ocean bottom or deep-sea vents.

▷ DESCRIBE: What is meant by a specialty?

BRANCHES OF EARTH SCIENCE

Geology
Geologists study the forces that shape Earth. Some careers in geology are mineralogist, volcanologist, and soil conservationist.

Oceanography
Oceanographers study Earth's oceans. Underwater photographer and marine biologist are just two of the many careers in oceanography.

Meteorology
Meteorologists gather information from around the world about conditions in the atmosphere. Some careers in meteorology are weather observer and weather forecaster.

Astronomy
Astronomers study the universe beyond Earth. Rocket scientist and astronaut are careers in this field.

▲ Figure 1-2

The Importance of Earth Science Earth science is an important part of our everyday lives. The observations and discoveries made by Earth scientists affect us in many ways.

For example, weather information is collected by Earth scientists called meteorologists. Meteorologists are able to give early warnings about severe storms such as hurricanes and tornadoes. Storm warnings can help save lives and limit property damage. Geologists help locate oil and coal supplies. These fuels are used to heat homes, run cars, and generate electricity. Oceanographers study the ocean and map currents. These help in containing oil spills and the cleaning of polluted waters.

Exploring space and experiments done in space have led to new medicines and technologies. They have also led to improvements in radios, televisions, and telephones. The development of the space shuttle led to improvements in fire-resistant materials.

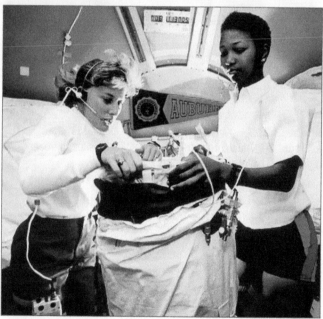

▲ **Figure 1-3** Astronauts carry out Earth science experiments in space that help us on Earth.

▶ EXPLAIN: Why is the study of weather important to our lives every day?

☑ CHECKING CONCEPTS

1. The study of Earth and how it changes is called _____.

2. A mineralogist studies the branch of Earth science called _____.

3. The study of Earth's oceans is called _____.

4. The study of space is part of the branch of Earth science called _____.

5. Another name for a weather forecaster is a _____.

💡 THINKING CRITICALLY

6. CLASSIFY: In which field of Earth science would you study each of these subjects?
   a. coral reefs   d. the planet Jupiter
   b. the Grand Canyon   e. soil quality
   c. hurricanes

7. ANALYZE: What is one way, other than weather, in which the study of Earth science affected you today?

Web InfoSearch

Earth Science Careers Choose an Earth science career from the ones that are mentioned in Figure 1-2 or another one that you have heard about.

SEARCH: Use the Internet to find out more information about the career you chose. How much education is required? What tools are generally used on the job? What is the average salary for a person who has some experience? What fields of study in this career would interest you most? What on-the-job activities would you enjoy most? Start your search at www.conceptsandchallenges.com. Some key search words are **Earth science careers, meteorology, geology, oceanography,** and **astronomy.**

◀ **Figure 1-4** As a geologist, you might study rock formations like this one.

1-2 What are the main parts of Earth?

The Lithosphere A **sphere** is a round, three-dimensional object. Earth is spherical in shape. The prefix *litho-* means "stone." The solid part of Earth is called the **lithosphere.** The ground you walk on is part of the lithosphere. Mountains are raised parts of the lithosphere. Valleys, found between mountains, are low areas of the lithosphere.

The lithosphere includes the continents as well as the land under the oceans. Continents are very large landmasses. The seven continents found on Earth today are shown in Figure 1-5.

▶ NAME: What is the solid part of Earth called?

The Hydrosphere The part of Earth that is water is called the **hydrosphere.** The hydrosphere includes all of the liquid water and ice on Earth. Saltwater makes up about 97 percent of Earth's water. Most of the saltwater is found in the oceans. There are three major oceans on Earth: Atlantic, Pacific, and Indian. These are all interconnected to form one large world ocean. The remaining 3 percent is freshwater. Freshwater is found mostly in rivers, lakes, glaciers, and the polar ice caps.

▲ **Figure 1-6** Much of the freshwater on Earth is found frozen in glaciers. This glacier is in Alaska.

▶ NAME: List the bodies of saltwater that are shown in Figure 1-5.

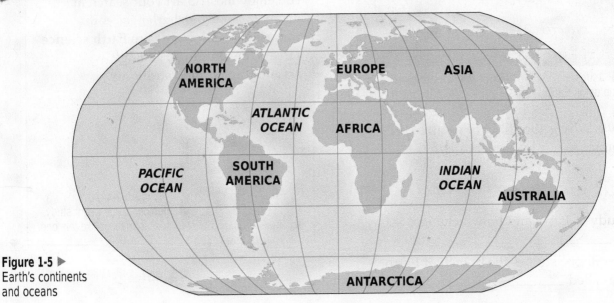

Figure 1-5 ▶
Earth's continents and oceans

NORTH AMERICA — EUROPE — ASIA — ATLANTIC OCEAN — AFRICA — PACIFIC OCEAN — SOUTH AMERICA — INDIAN OCEAN — AUSTRALIA — ANTARCTICA

The Atmosphere The envelope of gases surrounding Earth is called the **atmosphere.** The air you breathe is part of the atmosphere. Nitrogen and oxygen make up most of the atmosphere. Organisms need these and other gases to live. The atmosphere also helps protect living things by blocking harmful rays given off by the Sun. These rays, called ultraviolet rays, cause sunburn, skin cancer, and eye damage.

 IDENTIFY: What are the two main gases in Earth's atmosphere?

✓ CHECKING CONCEPTS

1. The ground you walk on is part of the _____.

2. The air you breathe is part of the _____.

3. The _____ includes rivers, lakes, and oceans.

4. Earth is a round, three-dimensional object known as a _____.

5. Saltwater makes up about _____ percent of the hydrosphere.

6. There are _____ continents on Earth.

7. There are _____ major oceans on Earth.

💡 THINKING CRITICALLY

8. INTERPRET: Use Figure 1-5 to answer the following questions:

   a. Which is the smallest continent?

   b. Which is the largest continent?

9. ANALYZE: Draw a pie graph that shows the percentages of saltwater and freshwater on Earth.

BUILDING READING SKILLS

Using Prefixes Prefixes are word parts that appear at the beginning of words. Prefixes have consistent meanings. Knowing the definition of a prefix can help you figure out the meaning of a particular word. Two prefixes that are used often in this lesson are *litho-* and *hydro-*. Find out the meanings of these prefixes. (Hint: *Litho* is defined in this lesson.) Then, figure out and write down the definitions of the following words that use these prefixes: *hydroelectric, hydrologist, lithology,* and *lithographer.* Circle the part of the definition that relates to each prefix. Put each word in a sentence.

 Integrating Life Science

TOPIC: biosphere

LIFE ON EARTH

The part of Earth that supports all living things is called the biosphere. Parts of the lithosphere, the hydrosphere, and the atmosphere make up the biosphere.

 The biosphere is a very narrow zone. You may think living things are almost everywhere. Some kinds of clams live in deep-sea vents on the ocean floor. Some spiders live high in the atmosphere. Bacteria are found deep in the crust. The biosphere extends 8 to 10 km into the atmosphere. Yet compared to the entire volume of Earth, the part where life exists is very small.

Thinking Critically Why do you think life is found only in the biosphere?

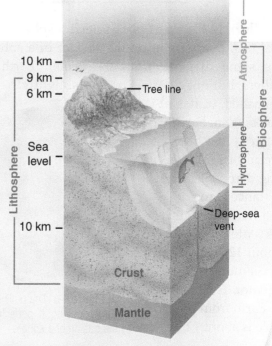

▲ **Figure 1-7** The biosphere is the part of Earth where life exists.

1-3 What is the structure of Earth?

Modeling Earth's Layers
HANDS-ON ACTIVITY

1. Cut a hard-boiled egg in half with the shell still on it.
   ⚠ CAUTION: Be very careful when working with sharp objects.

2. On three small pieces of paper or self-stick labels, write "Yolk," "White," and "Shell." Tape the papers to three thin straws or coffee stirrers or fold the self-stick labels around them. Use the straws or stirrers to label each part of the egg.

THINK ABOUT IT: Like the egg, Earth has a core, material around the core, and a thin but hard outer skin. Which parts of the model are like Earth's outer skin, middle, and core?

STEP 2

Objective
Describe Earth's major parts: the crust, the mantle, and the core.

Key Terms
crust: solid, thin outer layer of Earth

mantle (MAN-tuhl)**:** thick layer of earth below the crust

core: innermost region of Earth

A Slightly Flat Sphere A perfect sphere has no real top. Every point on the surface of a sphere is the same distance from the center. Earth is a sphere, but not a perfect one. It is slightly squashed, or flat, at its poles. Also, Earth bulges out a little around its middle. The diameter is the distance across a sphere through its center. Earth is about 12,756 km in diameter at the equator. The diameter of Earth from pole to pole is about 12,713 km.

▲ **Figure 1-8** The outline of Earth does not fit perfectly into the outline of a sphere.

▶ EXPLAIN: How is Earth not a perfect sphere?

Earth's Crust What is below Earth's surface? Like the hard-boiled egg above, Earth has three basic layers: the crust, the mantle, and the core. The **crust** is the thin, outer layer of Earth. It forms the upper lithosphere. Beneath the oceans, the crust is 5 to 10 km thick. Beneath the continents, the crust is 25 to 50 km thick. The thickest crust is beneath mountains.

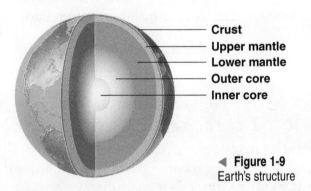

- Crust
- Upper mantle
- Lower mantle
- Outer core
- Inner core

◀ **Figure 1-9**
Earth's structure

▶ CONTRAST: How is ocean crust different from continental crust?

Earth's Mantle The layer of Earth beneath the crust is called the **mantle.** Earth's mantle ranges from about 1,800 to 2,900 km down. More than two-thirds of the mass of Earth is in the mantle.

The lithosphere includes all of the crust and the upper part of the mantle. Below this, the rock flows like a very thick liquid. Most of the mantle is made up of rock that flows very slowly.

▶ OBSERVE: Where is the mantle located?

Earth's Core The innermost region of Earth is the **core.** Scientists think that the core is made mostly of iron. The core has two parts. The outer core is liquid. It is about 2,250 km thick. The inner core is solid, with a radius of about 1,300 km.

THE LAYERS OF EARTH	
Layer	Thickness
Crust	5–70 km
Mantle	2,900 km
Outer Core	2,250 km
Inner Core	1,300 km

▲ Figure 1-10

 CALCULATE: Which is thicker, the mantle or the two core layers combined?

☑ CHECKING CONCEPTS

1. The crust is thickest beneath _____.
2. The core is made mostly of _____.

3. You can stand on Earth's layer called the _____.
4. The diameter of Earth at the equator is about _____ km.

💡 THINKING CRITICALLY

5. SEQUENCE: Arrange Earth's layers in order, from thickest to thinnest.
6. ANALYZE: A drilling rig can go down only 6 km. Where would you set it up to drill into the mantle? Why?
7. INFER: Which layer of Earth includes the continents?

BUILDING MATH SKILLS

Calculating The radius, or *r*, of Earth is the point measured from its center to its surface. Use the formula below to find the approximate circumference, or *C*, of Earth. Pi, or π, is equal to approximately 3.14. $C = 2\pi r$.

 How Do They Know That?

EARTH IS A SPHERE

For thousands of years, people believed Earth was flat. This seemed logical. If you stand in a field or sail on the ocean, you can see for many kilometers. Everything appears flat. About 2,500 years ago, around 500 B.C., the Greek philosopher Pythagoras suggested that Earth was a sphere. His idea was probably based on observing the night sky. The heights of stars in the sky varied, depending on where you stood on Earth's surface. The Moon appeared to be round. Possibly, Earth had the same shape.

Many years later, another Greek philosopher, Aristotle, supported Pythagoras's theory. While observing lunar eclipses, Aristotle noted that a curved shadow fell on the Moon. He believed this to be Earth's shadow. Aristotle concluded that Earth was round.

Today, pictures from space show us that Earth is indeed a sphere.

Thinking Critically How did Pythagoras's observation of the heights of stars support his theory?

▲ Figure 1-11 Pythagoras (about 580 B.C. to about 500 B.C.), Greek philosopher and mathematician

1-4 What are maps?

Objectives

Explain why a globe is the most useful type of Earth map. Describe what happens when the round Earth is shown on a flat map.

Key Terms

globe: three-dimensional model of Earth's surface

map: flat model of Earth's surface

distortion (dih-STOR-shuhn): error in shape, size, or distance

Globes A **globe** is a three-dimensional model of Earth's surface. A model is something that represents a real object such as a ship or an airplane. A globe correctly shows the shapes and sizes of features on Earth. For this reason, a globe is the best model of Earth. Most globes, however, are too small to show much detail. Larger globes are too big to handle. Imagine trying to carry a globe to school every day!

◀ **Figure 1-12** Globes are good models of Earth's surface. However, they can be hard to carry around.

▶ **DEFINE:** What is a globe?

Maps A **map** is a flat model, or drawing, of Earth's surface. It is two-dimensional. There are many kinds of maps.

Some maps show the whole Earth. Other maps show only part of Earth. Maps that show a small part of Earth can show more details than maps that show more of Earth.

Maps can show many different things. They can show the locations of and distances between places on Earth. Some maps show city streets. Other maps show buildings in a town. Some maps even show the weather or types of soil in an area.

▲ **Figure 1-13** Navigation systems in cars display maps that help you find your way in a strange city.

▶ **IDENTIFY:** What features are shown on maps?

Distortion When a round surface such as Earth is shown on a flat map, errors occur. If the shapes on the map are correct, the distances may be wrong. If the distances are correct, the shapes may be wrong. These errors in shape, size, or distance are called **distortions.** Nearly all maps have some distortions. Maps of smaller areas have fewer distortions.

▲ **Figure 1-14** Maps can vary in how much detail they show.

▶ **COMPARE:** Which would have more distortions, a map of the United States or a map of Florida? Explain.

1. A map is a _____ model of Earth.
2. The best model of Earth is a _____.
3. Errors on a map are called _____.

THINKING CRITICALLY

4. EXPLAIN: Why is a globe the best model of Earth?
5. HYPOTHESIZE: When would a flat map be more useful than a globe?
6. APPLY: Globes and maps can be used to find the distances between different places. Maria wanted to know how far it was from her house to her friend's house in the next town. She tried to use a globe to find out. Why might Maria have a problem using a globe to find the distance between the two towns?

BUILDING SCIENCE SKILLS

Modeling and Comparing Using an 8½ × 11-inch sheet of paper, make a map of your classroom.

1. Measure 2 cm from each edge of the paper to draw the walls of the room.
2. Fold the paper into quarters and then open it. Use these folds as guides.
3. Draw as many objects as you can in each part. Draw where you and your teacher sit.
4. Have a classmate locate places in the room on your map. Does your map have distortion? Indicate where in your map any distortion might be and why.

Science and Technology

EARTH-OBSERVATION SATELLITES

▲ **Figure 1-15** This satellite image shows Salt Lake City in Utah.

Landsat is the oldest U.S. land-surface observation satellite system. The satellites orbit from pole to pole. They use remote sensing to collect information about Earth's surface. Remote sensing is the ability to gather information about an object or event without actually being in physical contact with it. A *Landsat* satellite can provide images with great detail. Images from *Landsat* have been used to map wildfire hazards in Yosemite National Park, track lava flows in Hawaii, and observe population growth in large U.S. cities.

The National Aeronautics and Space Administration, or NASA, launched the first *Landsat* satellite more than 30 years ago. Before it was retired, it had recorded over 300,000 images. Since then, at least six more *Landsats* have been launched. Most of the launches were successful.

Other observation satellite systems are *SarSat* and *NavStar*. *NavStar* is made up of 24 satellites that orbit Earth over different areas. The system is used today to keep track of airplane traffic. It is also used to help during search and rescue missions. *SarSat* is an international search and rescue satellite system.

Thinking Critically Why do you think it is important to track wildfire hazards in a national park?

What is a map projection?

INVESTIGATE

Making a Map Projection
HANDS-ON ACTIVITY

1. Look at a globe. With a felt-tip pen or permanent marker, roughly outline the continents on the surface of a grapefruit.

2. Carefully cut the grapefruit into quarters. Gently peel the skin off the grapefruit. Try not to tear the four pieces of peel into smaller pieces.

3. Lay the four pieces of peel flat on a table. Match up your pieces to form a flat map.

THINK ABOUT IT: What happens to the continents when you try to flatten the pieces? How can you adjust them to make them match better?

STEP 1

Objectives

Explain what a map projection is. Name three kinds of map projections.

Key Term

map projection (proh-JEHK-shuhn): drawing of Earth's surface, or part of it, on a flat surface

From Round to Flat A **map projection** is a flat map that represents all or part of Earth's curved surface. Imagine a clear plastic globe with a light inside. If paper is wrapped around the lighted globe, the outlines of the continents will be projected onto the paper. A mapmaker can trace these outlines to make a flat map. The result is called a map projection.

 DEFINE: What is a map projection?

Types of Map Projections There are several types of map projections. Although no type is completely accurate, each kind is useful.

Gerardus Mercator (1512–1594) was a Flemish cartographer, or mapmaker. He drew a huge world map in 1569 that used the system of projection now named for him. Mercator was one of the most respected geographers of his time.

Mercator projections are made by wrapping a sheet of paper into a tube around a globe. An example is shown in Figure 1-16. In a Mercator projection, the distances between land areas and the sizes of land areas near the poles are distorted.

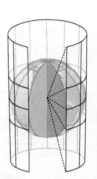

▲ **Figure 1-16** A Mercator projection

A polar projection, shown in Figure 1-17, is made by holding a flat sheet of paper on one pole of a globe. It shows little distortion near that pole. Farther from that pole, however, both direction and distance are distorted.

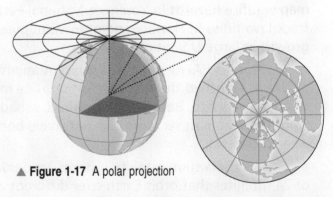

▲ **Figure 1-17** A polar projection

A conic (KAHN-ik) projection is shown in Figure 1-18. It is made by shaping a sheet of paper into a cone and placing it over a globe. When several conic projections are put together, the relative shapes and sizes of land areas on the map are almost the same as those on a globe.

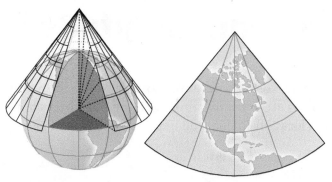

▲ **Figure 1-18** A conic projection

 INFER: Which kind of map projection would you use to explore Antarctica?

✓ CHECKING CONCEPTS

1. What is a flat map of a curved surface called?
2. How is a Mercator projection made?
3. How is a conic projection made?
4. How do mapmakers show Earth's surface on a flat map?
5. How is a polar projection made?

 THINKING CRITICALLY

6. **INFER:** Why do you think a conic projection and a polar projection are called by these names?

Web InfoSearch

Mercator Projections Mercator projections are very helpful to navigators at sea. They are widely used to create navigation charts. On Mercator projections, lines of latitude and longitude are straight, parallel lines. This allows a navigator to plot a straight course.

SEARCH: Use the Internet to find out more. How does a sailor use one to plot a course? What problems would occur if the sailor were heading for the poles? Start your search at www.conceptsandchallenges.com. Some key search words are **sailing projections** and **Mercator projections.**

 How Do They Know That?

LOCATING FEATURES ON EARTH'S SURFACE

When do you think the first maps were made? The earliest known maps are more than 4,000 years old. These early maps were carved on clay tablets. Maps during this time showed rivers, mountains, and human settlements. They may have been used to record property lines and help build roads, canals, and towns.

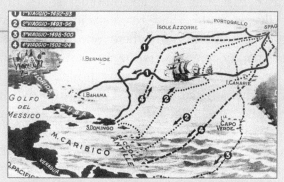

▲ **Figure 1-19** This early map shows the various routes Columbus took to reach and return from the New World.

The first people to show Earth as a sphere on maps were the Greeks. About A.D. 100, Ptolemy (TAHL-uh-mee), a Greek-born Egyptian astronomer, mathematician, and geographer, wrote a book based on Greek ideas called *Geography*. In this book, he described how to make maps and globes. Columbus may have used Ptolemy's maps when he set out on his voyage to the New World.

During the fifteenth and sixteenth centuries, the explorations of Columbus, Da Gama, and Magellan led to more accurate maps of Earth. The most famous mapmaker during this time was Mercator. Today, aerial photographs, satellites, and computers are all used to make detailed, accurate maps of Earth's surface.

Thinking Critically How has technology helped us make more accurate maps of Earth's surface?

1-6 What are latitude and longitude?

Objective

Explain how hemispheres, latitude, longitude, meridians, and parallels are all related.

Key Terms

parallel (PAR-uh-lehl): horizontal line on a map or globe that circles Earth from east to west at intervals starting at the equator

meridian (muh-RIHD-ee-uhn): line on a map or a globe running from the North Pole to the South Pole along Earth's surface

latitude (LAT-uh-tood): distance in degrees north or south of the equator

longitude (LAHN-juh-tood): measurement in degrees east or west of the prime meridian

Parallels and Meridians If you look at a globe or a map of the world, you will notice a series of lines drawn east and west and another series drawn north and south. These reference lines help people describe locations anywhere on Earth's surface. One handy reference is the equator. The equator is an imaginary line that runs around the middle of Earth's surface. It divides Earth into two half-spheres, or hemispheres — the Northern Hemisphere and the Southern Hemisphere. As shown in Figure 1-20, angles drawn from Earth's center to its surface are used to construct other east-west lines on Earth's surface. **Parallels** are lines on maps and globes that circle Earth east to west parallel to the equator.

Another set of lines on maps and globes, called meridians, run north and south across Earth's surface. A **meridian** is a half-circle that extends from the North Pole to the South Pole. Figure 1-21 shows how meridians are constructed.

▶ **COMPARE/CONTRAST:** How are parallels and meridians similar? How are they different?

Latitude Parallels and meridians are used to describe locations on Earth's surface. Parallels describe latitude. **Latitude** is the distance in degrees north and south of the equator. The latitude of the equator is 0°.

The North Pole is at 90° north latitude. The South Pole is at 90° south latitude. Figure 1-20 shows how the locations of latitude lines are determined.

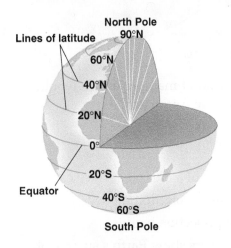

◀ **Figure 1-20**
Lines of latitude run horizontally around the globe.

▶ **MEASURE:** What is the latitude of the equator?

Longitude Meridians are used to describe longitude. **Longitude** is the distance in degrees east and west of the 0° meridian. Since there is no equator dividing Earth into north-south halves, scientists had to invent one. This 0° meridian, which runs through Greenwich, England, is called the prime meridian. On the other side of Earth from the prime meridian is the 180° meridian. Called the International Date Line, this is the place where the calendar day changes. Figure 1-21 shows how longitude lines are drawn.

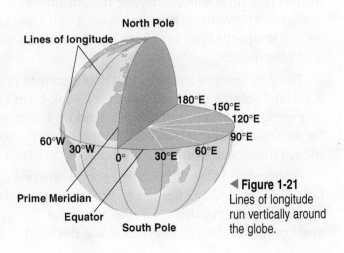

◀ **Figure 1-21**
Lines of longitude run vertically around the globe.

▶ **NAME:** What is the name of the meridian that passes through Greenwich, England?

Locating Places Every place on Earth has its own latitude and longitude. For example, Washington, D.C., is very close to the point where the parallel for 39° north meets the meridian for 77° west. So, Washington's location can be described as 39° north latitude and 77° west longitude. This number can be abbreviated as 39°N, 77°W.

 COMPARE: What describes the location of a place?

✓ CHECKING CONCEPTS

1. The parallel around the middle of Earth is the _____.

2. Each half of Earth's surface is called a _____.

3. Points on a sphere or angles in a circle are measured in units called _____.

4. Lines running horizontally on a map or globe are called _____.

5. Lines running from pole to pole on a map or globe are called _____.

THINKING CRITICALLY

6. **EXPLAIN:** How can you locate a particular city on a map of Earth's surface?

7. **NAME:** In what place on Earth's surface is there a latitude of 0° and a longitude of 0°?

8. **INFER:** What do you think the hemispheres formed by the prime meridian and the International Date Line are called?

9. **INFER:** What is the North Pole's latitude and longitude?

BUILDING SCIENCE SKILLS

Locating Use a globe or a map to identify the cities with the following latitudes and longitudes.

IDENTIFYING CITIES		
City	Latitude	Longitude
A	38° N	77° W
B	30° N	90° W
C	35° N	140°E

▲ **Figure 1-22**

Hands-On Activity

FINDING PLACES ON A MAP

1. Find the following cities on the map:
   New Orleans, LA
   Pittsburgh, PA
   San Antonio, TX
   Jacksonville, FL
   Springfield, IL
   Denver, CO

2. Write the latitude and longitude of each city. Estimate as closely as possible.

▲ **Figure 1-23** Latitudes and longitudes in the United States.

Practicing Your Skills

3. **EXPLAIN:** Why do you need to know both latitude and longitude to locate places on a map?

4. **IDENTIFY:** What is the approximate latitude and longitude of the city where you live?

How do you read a map?

Use the scale on a map. Interpret map symbols.

Key Terms

scale: feature that relates distances on a map to actual distances on Earth's surface

symbol: drawing on a map that represents a real object

legend (LEHJ-uhnd)**:** list of map symbols and their meanings

Showing Direction Most maps show directions. If you look at the map on this page, you will see an arrow marked N. This arrow shows the direction north. On most maps, north (N) is at the top of the map. From this you can infer that south (S) is at the bottom, east (E) is to your right, and west (W) is to your left.

Another way of showing direction on a map is using a compass rose. Most places on a map are not exactly north, south, east, or west. In Figure 1-24, you can see that Snake River flows both south and north and east and west. The direction between south and

west is called southwest (SW). The direction between north and east is called northeast (NE).

A compass rose is a circle divided into eighths. It shows the four directions and directions in between the four.

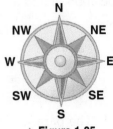

▲ Figure 1-25 Compass rose

1 OBSERVE: On a map, what shows the direction?

Scale A map's **scale** shows how the distance on a map compares with real distance on Earth's surface. Look at the scale in Figure 1-24. It shows that 1 cm on the map equals 5 km on Earth's surface. Measure the distance on the map from Point A to Point B. The distance is 4.4 cm. To find the actual distance between Point A and Point B, multiply 4.4 × 5, because each centimeter on the map represents 5 km on Earth. On Earth's surface, the actual distance from Point A to Point B is 22 km.

2 CALCULATE: The main street in a town is 10 km long. How many centimeters would the street be on a map that uses the scale 1 cm = 5 km?

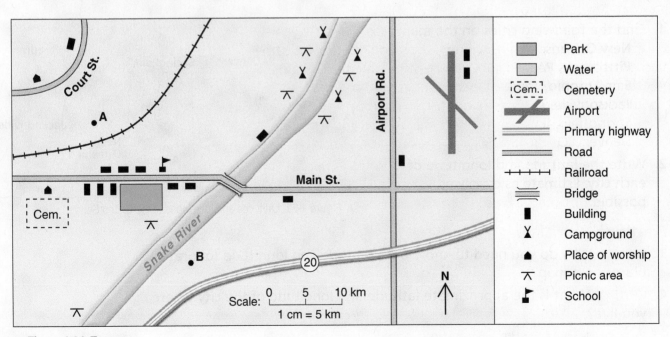

▲ Figure 1-24 Town map

Map Symbols Simple drawings on a map called **symbols** are used to show the location of real objects. Many different symbols are used on maps. These symbols are listed in a table called a **legend.** Different maps have different legends. The legend of each map explains the symbols used on that map. See the legend in Figure 1-24 for some common map symbols.

 ANALYZE: Why are symbols used on a map?

Color Color often has meaning on maps. Black is usually used for anything made by people. Symbols for buildings, railroads, and bridges are colored black. Blue is used to show bodies of water. Forests and parks are green.

4 ▶ **IDENTIFY:** What color would be used to show your school on a map?

✔ CHECKING CONCEPTS

1. The direction northwest would be shown on a map by the letters _____.
2. The _____ on a map shows distance.
3. Simple drawings on a map used to show real objects are called _____.

4. The symbols used on a map are listed in a _____.
5. A river would most likely be colored _____ on a map.

💡 THINKING CRITICALLY

6. CLASSIFY: What types of information do the scale and the legend on a map provide?
7. MODEL: Draw a simple map of the area around your school. Include a scale and a legend of all the symbols you think belong there.

INTERPRETING VISUALS

Use Figure 1-24 to answer the following questions.

8. OBSERVE: How many buildings are shown on the map?
9. OBSERVE: What kinds of buildings and roads are shown?
10. ANALYZE: What direction is to your left on the map?
11. ANALYZE: In what two directions does Main Street run?

 Real-Life Science

ORIENTEERING

Orienteering is a fun sport. The goal of the game is to find specific areas marked on a given course. As you move through the course, you race against other people looking for the same marked points as you. To win, you must be able to read a map quickly and use a compass. Classes in map and compass reading are offered at some orienteering meets.

Before an orienteering meet begins, the course is set up. Markers are left at different checkpoints along the course. Each orienteering participant is given a map that identifies each checkpoint. The first person to cross the finish line with each checkpoint marker wins.

You can participate in orienteering meets no matter where you live. Courses have been set up in cities as well as in wooded areas. You do not need any special equipment except a map and a compass.

Thinking Critically What checkpoints might there be along a city orienteering course?

▲ **Figure 1-26** Orienteering courses can be found in many places.

THE Big IDEA

How did maps help the United States grow?

Look at a modern map of the United States. You will see a vast stretch of land extending from the Atlantic Ocean to the Pacific Ocean and from Canada to the Gulf of Mexico. A map of what the United States looked like in 1800 would look very different. The country then was only about one-third of its current size. It consisted of lands that extended westward from the Atlantic Ocean to the Mississippi River.

President Thomas Jefferson dreamed of an America that would stretch from sea to sea. In 1803, he bought from France all of the lands between the Mississippi River and the Rocky Mountains. This so-called Louisiana Purchase doubled the size of the country. The United States paid only $15 million for this land.

No maps of the area existed. Jefferson decided to send explorers to map the region and report on local wildlife and climate. He asked his personal secretary, Meriwether Lewis, to lead the expedition. Lewis asked his friend, William Clark, to join him.

In 1804, the two men left St. Louis with 28 others. The group, known as the Corps of Discovery, arrived back home 2½ years later. The maps, charts, and journals they brought back opened the door to westward expansion.

Look at the illustrations that appear on these two pages. Then, follow the directions in the Science Log to learn more about "the big idea." ◆

Spring 1805

Lewis climbs to the top of a hill and views the Rocky Mountains for the first time.

Winter 1806

The expedition spends the harsh winter months at Fort Clatsop in present-day Oregon. Lewis and Clark make sketches of wildlife and of the Native Americans living in this previously unexplored area. This is a sample from their journal.

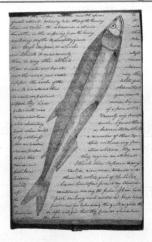

Ft. Clatsop

N

Pacific Ocean

WRITING ACTIVITY

Science Log

You are traveling with the Corps of Discovery. On your journey, you observe many strange new animals and eat new foods. You view the Rocky Mountains for the first time. Write down your observations. Draw a simple map with a legend of the place you are describing. Start your search at www.conceptsandchallenges.com.

Winter 1805

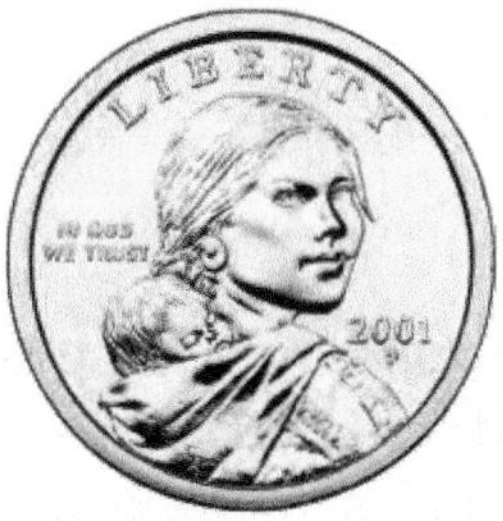
LIBERTY
IN GOD WE TRUST
2001

The Corps of Discovery sets up winter quarters near present-day Bismarck, North Dakota. During this time, Toussaint Charbonneau joins the group as an interpreter. His wife, a Shoshone named Sacagawea (sac-a-juh-WEE-ah), also joins the expedition as a guide. She is honored on the coin shown.

Fall 1804

The explorers leave the trail and meet the Arikara. Clark records information about this Plains group in his journal. He notes that the Arikara are farmers who live year round in earthen lodges.

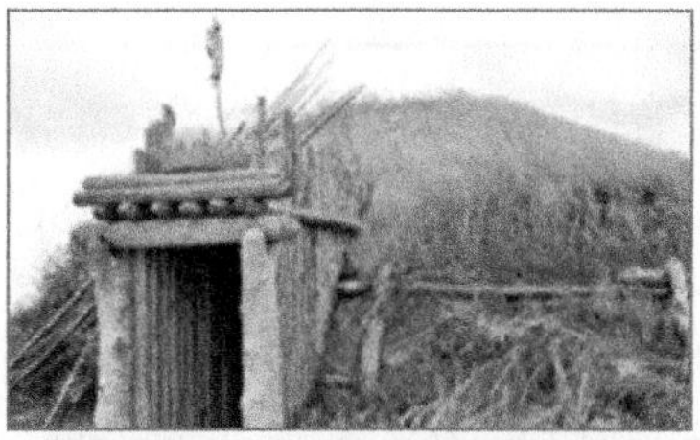

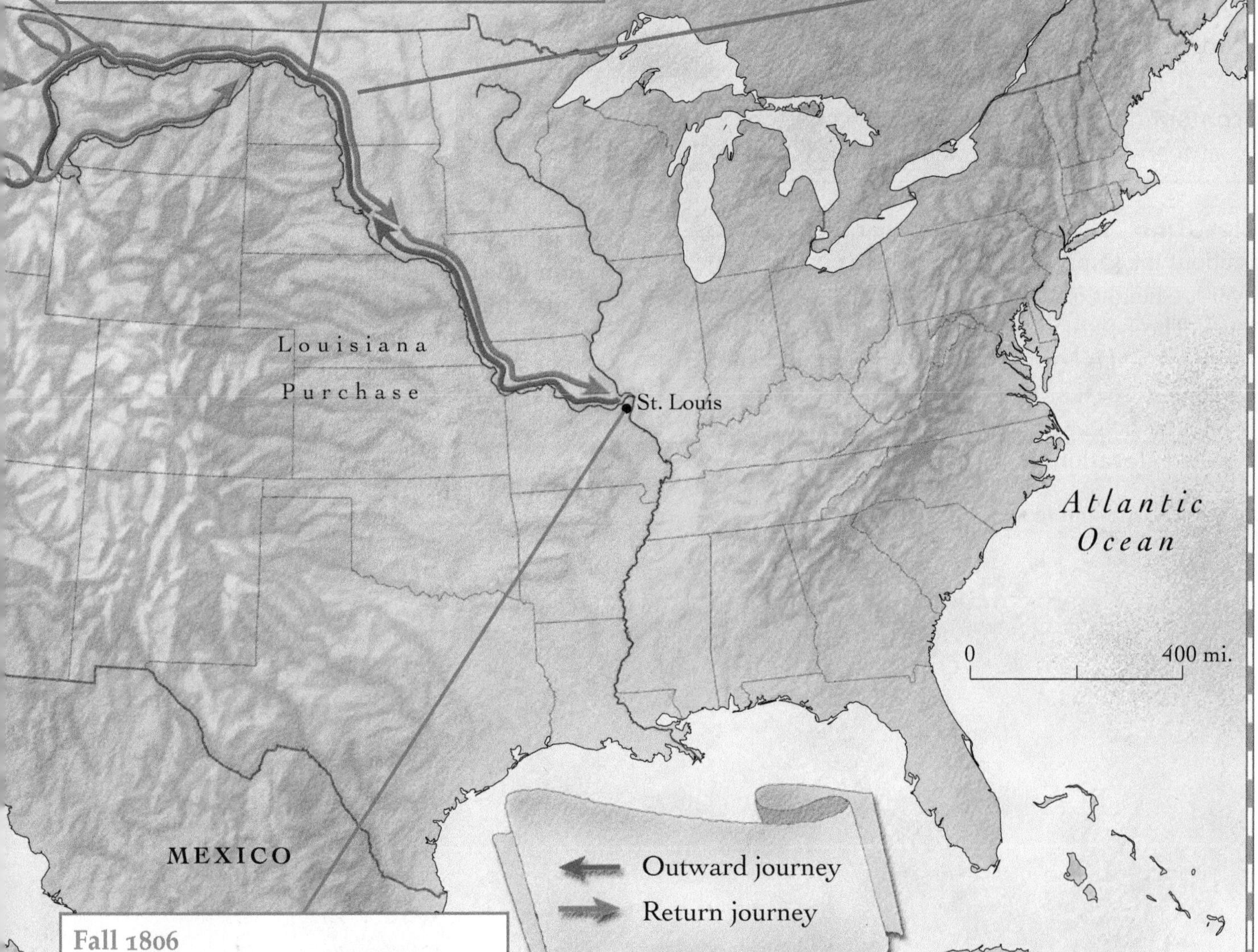
Louisiana
Purchase
St. Louis
Atlantic
Ocean
0
400 mi.
MEXICO
Outward journey
Return journey

Fall 1806

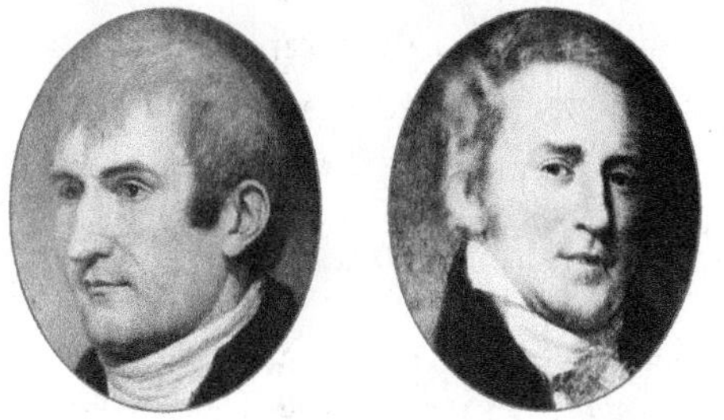

M. Lewis W. Clark

The explorers arrive back in St. Louis on September 23. The whole town turns out to give them a heroes' welcome.

▲ **Figure 1-27** This map of the early United States shows the travel route of Lewis and Clark. The maps Lewis and Clark created led to the expansion of the western United States.

1-8 What is a topographic map?

Objective

Describe what is shown on a topographic map.

Key Terms

elevation (ehl-uh-VAY-shuhn): height of a point on Earth above or below sea level

topography (tuh-PAHG-ruh-fee): general form and shape of the land on Earth's surface

contour (KAHN-toor) **line**: line drawn on a map that connects all points having the same elevation

Elevation The level of the water in the oceans is about the same height everywhere on Earth. The average height for water in the oceans is called sea level. The height of a place on land is measured from sea level. For example, the height of Mount McKinley, Alaska, is more than 6 km above sea level. The height of land above or below sea level is called **elevation.**

▶ **1** DEFINE: What is elevation?

Topography The general form and shape of the land on Earth's surface is called **topography.** Examples of topography on Earth's surface are mountains, valleys, plains, and plateaus. Mountains have high elevations and steep slopes. Valleys are low areas bordered by high ground. Plains are broad, flat areas that are usually only a little above sea level. Plateaus are broad, flat areas of land that have an elevation of at least 300 m above sea level.

▶ **2** IDENTIFY: What are three types of topography on Earth's surface?

Contour Lines The elevations of surface features can be shown on a map using contour lines. A **contour line** is a line that passes through all points on a map that have the same elevation. When you look at the contour lines on a map, you can identify the shape, or contour, of the land. Every point on a contour line has the same elevation.

▶ **3** DESCRIBE: What do contour lines on a map show?

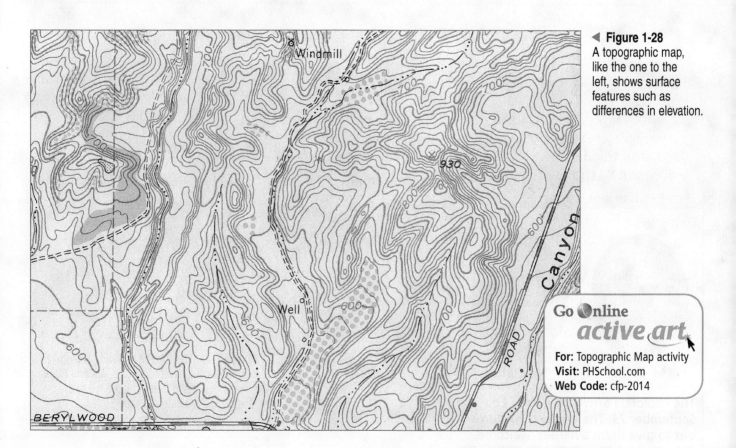

◀ **Figure 1-28**
A topographic map, like the one to the left, shows surface features such as differences in elevation.

Topographic Maps A map with contour lines shows the surface features, or topography, of the land. That is why these maps are called topographic maps. The contour lines found on a topographic map connect places on the map having the same elevation. Figure 1-28 is a topographic map of the Grand Canyon area in Arizona.

 EXPLAIN: What is a topographic map?

✓ CHECKING CONCEPTS

1. What is sea level?
2. What is topography?
3. What is a contour line?
4. What is the height of a point above or below sea level called?

💡 THINKING CRITICALLY

5. **CONTRAST:** What is the difference between sea level and elevation?
6. **EXPLAIN:** A contour line is marked 50 m. What does this mean?

7. **INFER:** Why are plateaus sometimes called "plains in the air"?
8. **RELATE:** Why is a map with contour lines called a topographic map?

Web InfoSearch

Contour Plowing Farmers planting on hilly ground are careful to plow their land in a special way. They plow along strips of land that are at the same elevation. In this way, all the furrows follow the slope of the hill. Water collects in the furrows and soaks into the soil. The furrows prevent the water from running down the hill and carrying away valuable topsoil. This kind of plowing is called contour plowing.

SEARCH: Use the Internet to find out more about contour plowing. In what countries is it used? Why? Start your search at www.conceptsandchallenges.com. Some key search words are **agriculture, farming, topsoil,** and **contour tilling.**

 People in Science

SURVEYOR

A surveyor measures land to find the exact location of certain physical features on Earth's surface. Engineers employ surveyors to measure the heights of objects, the slope of the land, and the distances between physical features. With this information, engineers design roads, bridges, and homes.

Ken Stigner began his surveying career in the military. He prepared maps for the construction of roads and bridges. He started as a member of a crew taking measurements ("chain man"). Then, he became an instrument operator. Later, he was made party chief. This meant he had his own crew.

▲ **Figure 1-29** Surveyors use many different tools, such as this transit, when working on building projects.

Surveyors come from all education levels. Some have little education and just want to work outdoors. Although on-the-job training is possible, it helps to have a background in mathematics. It requires many years of experience to obtain a surveying license. Some states now require a four-year degree in surveying to qualify.

Thinking Critically Why do you think the military may need to build roads and bridges?

1-9 How do you read a topographic map?

Objective
Explain how to read a topographic map.

Key Term
contour interval (KAHN-toor IHN-tuhr-vuhl): difference in elevation between one contour line and the next

Contour Intervals A topographic map shows the elevation of features on Earth's surface. Look at the topographic map shown in Figure 1-30. Every point on a contour line is at the same elevation.

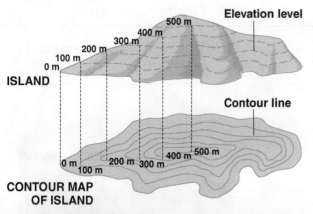

▲ **Figure 1-30** This drawing shows how an island's different elevations would look on a topographic map.

The places where contour lines are close together, the land has a steep slope. The places where the lines are far apart, the land has a gentle slope.

The difference in elevation between one contour line and the next is called a **contour interval.** If two contour lines near each other are marked 500 and 600 m, the contour interval between them is 100 m. Mapmakers use different contour intervals for different maps. A large contour interval is used for mountainous areas. A small contour interval is used for flat areas.

▶ 1 **OBSERVE:** What is the contour interval for the map in Figure 1-30?

Relief Map A map that uses color, shading, or contour lines to indicate the different heights of features is called a relief map. On a relief map, like the one in Figure 1-31, one color might be used to show high mountains. Another color might be used to show areas near sea level. Still other colors might be used to show elevations in between or for areas below sea level.

▶ 2 **EXPLAIN:** How is color sometimes used to show elevation on a relief map?

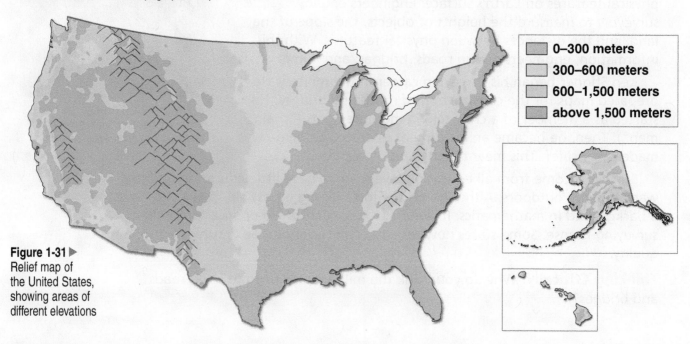

Figure 1-31 ▶
Relief map of
the United States,
showing areas of
different elevations

0–300 meters
300–600 meters
600–1,500 meters
above 1,500 meters

1. Where contour lines are close together, the land has a _____ slope.

2. The difference in elevation between two neighboring contour lines is called the _____.

3. A map of a flat area would usually have a _____ contour interval.

4. Instead of contour lines, some maps use _____ to show elevation.

THINKING CRITICALLY

Use Figures 1-30 and 1-31 to answer the following questions.

5. OBSERVE: What is the highest elevation shown in Figure 1-30?

6. ANALYZE: Is the land shown in Figure 1-30 flat or hilly? How do you know?

7. OBSERVE: What color is used in Figure 1-31 to show elevations from 0 to 300 m?

8. ANALYZE: What is the elevation of the land shown in dark green in Figure 1-31?

INTERPRETING VISUALS

Reading a Topographic Map The symbol X on a topographic map is called a benchmark. A benchmark is a mark on a map that shows a landmark with a known height. The landmark is used as a reference point in relation to the height of other things on the map. A depression is shown on a topographic map by using short, straight lines pointing toward the center of the depression. Look at Figure 1-32. Which point on the map is the benchmark? What is the elevation at the benchmark? Which point shows a depression?

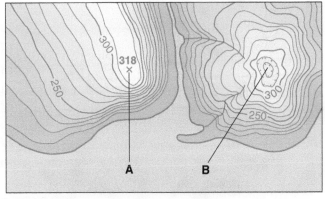

▲ **Figure 1-32** Elevation is shown in meters.

Hands-On Activity

INTERPRETING A TOPOGRAPHIC MAP

You will need a pencil, a sheet of paper, and a metric ruler. Examine the map in Figure 1-33. Then, answer the following questions.

Practicing Your Skills

1. IDENTIFY: What contour interval is used on the map in Figure 1-33?

2. CALCULATE: What are the elevations of Points *A, B,* and *C*?

3. CALCULATE: How many meters is the highest point on the map?

4. MEASURE: How long in meters is the river?

5. INFER: The hill shown on the map has three sides that are steep and one side that is gentle. How can you tell which are the steep sides and which is the gentle side? What is the compass direction of the gentle side of the hill?

6. ANALYZE: Which letter is in a depression? How do you know?

▲ **Figure 1-33** The contour lines on this map show several land features.

LAB ACTIVITY
Making a Topographic Map

Materials

Lab apron
Gloves (optional)
Modeling clay
Thread
(about 30 cm long)
Plain paper
Pencil
Metric ruler

BACKGROUND

Earth's surface is covered with mountains, valleys, plateaus, and broad plains. Topographic maps show these features. They contain contour lines. These lines show the look and shape of the land.

PURPOSE

In this activity, you will shape a clay model of a mountain. You will then construct a topographic map of your model.

PROCEDURE

1. Put on your lab apron.

2. Place a sheet of plain paper on your desk. Put a lump of clay in the middle of the paper. Shape the clay to form a mountain and a valley. Make the mountain 8 cm high.

3. Push a pencil through the top of your mountain all the way down to the paper to make a mark. Pull the pencil out. Make a second hole about 2 cm from the first hole. Make a mark on the paper. Pull out the pencil.

4. Stand a ruler beside your mountain. Mark your clay at a height of 7 cm.

5. Hold both ends of the thread tightly so it is parallel to the table. Slice the top of the mountain off at the 7 cm mark you just made. Remove it and set it aside.

6. Now, measure and mark a 6 cm height on the mountain. Using the thread again, slice the mountain off at the 6 cm mark. Set this piece aside.

▲ **STEP 2** Shape your clay to form a mountain.

▲ **STEP 3** Push a pencil down through the top of your mountain.

7. Repeat Steps 4 and 5 for heights of 5, 4, 3, 2, and 1 cm.

8. Use your pencil to trace a line around the bottom slice of the mountain. This is a contour line.

9. Remove the bottom slice from the paper. Place the slice that was on top of the bottom slice on the paper. Line up both holes in the slice with the pencil marks on the paper. Trace around this slice and remove it.

▲ **STEP 7** Slice off marked sections of the mountain.

10. Trace around each of the remaining four slices using the same paper. Be sure to line up both holes before you trace.

11. Rebuild your clay mountain by stacking all the pieces back together in order from largest to smallest. Compare your mountain to the topographic map you just drew.

▲ **STEP 10** Trace around your slices.

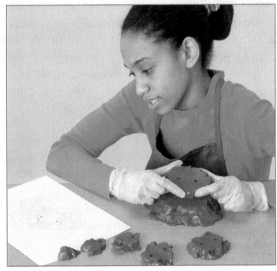

▲ **STEP 11** Rebuild your clay mountain.

CONCLUSIONS

1. ANALYZE: What do the contour lines on the topographic map show?
2. OBSERVE: What do widely spread contour lines tell you about the shape of the land?
3. OBSERVE: What do closely spaced contour lines tell you about the shape of the land?
4. INFER: How do you think geologists use topographic maps?

Chapter Summary

Lesson 1-1

- **Earth science** is the study of Earth and its history. The four branches of Earth science are geology, oceanography, meteorology, and astronomy.

Lesson 1-2

- A **sphere** is a round, three-dimensional object. The **lithosphere** is the solid part of Earth. The **hydrosphere** is made of liquid water or ice. The **atmosphere** is an envelope of gases surrounding Earth.

Lesson 1-3

- Earth has three layers. The **crust** is the outer layer. The **mantle** is below the crust. Its upper part is solid rock. The rock below this flows like a thick liquid. The **core** in the center has an outer liquid layer and an inner solid layer.

Lessons 1-4 and 1-5

- A **globe** is a spherical model of Earth. A **map** is a flat model of Earth. All maps have **distortions.**
- A **map projection** shows Earth's surface, or part of it, on a sheet of paper. Three examples of map projections are Mercator, polar, and conic.

Lessons 1-6 and 1-7

- The equator divides Earth's surface into northern and southern **hemispheres.** The distance a place is north or south of the equator is its **latitude.**
- **Meridians** are lines that run from pole to pole. The distance in degrees a place is east or west of the prime meridian is its **longitude.**
- A map's **scale** compares map distances with real distances. Map **symbols** represent real objects. The symbols are explained in a **legend.** Colors can be used to show different features.

Lesson 1-8

- Height above or below sea level is called **elevation.** The study of the form and shape of Earth's surface is called **topography.** Relief maps show elevation often using colors or shading.

Lesson 1-9

- Topographic maps use **contour lines** to show elevation. A **contour interval** is the difference in elevation between contour lines.

Key Term Challenges

atmosphere (p. 18)
contour interval (p. 34)
contour line (p. 32)
core (p. 20)
crust (p. 20)
distortion (p. 22)
Earth science (p. 16)
elevation (p. 32)
globe (p. 22)
hydrosphere (p. 18)
latitude (p. 26)
legend (p. 28)
lithosphere (p. 18)
longitude (p. 26)
mantle (p. 20)
map (p. 22)
map projection (p. 24)
meridian (p. 26)
parallel (p. 26)
scale (p. 28)
specialist (p. 16)
sphere (p. 18)
symbol (p. 28)
topography (p. 32)

MATCHING **Write the Key Term from above that best matches each description.**

1. layer of Earth below the crust
2. layer of gases surrounding Earth's surface
3. shows distance on a map
4. all the liquid water and ice on Earth
5. innermost region of Earth
6. flat drawing of part of Earth's surface
7. error in shape, distance, or size on a map

IDENTIFYING WORD RELATIONSHIPS **Explain how the words in each pair are related. Write your answers in complete sentences.**

8. contour line, elevation
9. map projection, globe
10. crust, lithosphere
11. contour interval, topography
12. latitude, parallel
13. longitude, meridian
14. symbol, legend
15. sphere, globe

Content Challenges TEST PREP

MULTIPLE CHOICE **Write the letter of the term or phrase that best completes each statement.**

1. The study of weather is called
   a. geology.
   b. oceanography.
   c. meteorology.
   d. specialist.

2. Earth's crust is part of the
   a. atmosphere.
   b. mantle.
   c. hydrosphere.
   d. lithosphere.

3. Rivers, lakes, and streams are part of Earth's
   a. core.
   b. mantle.
   c. hydrosphere.
   d. atmosphere.

4. The two main gases in the atmosphere are
   a. oxygen and nitrogen.
   b. oxygen and hydrogen.
   c. hydrogen and nitrogen.
   d. oxygen and helium.

5. The thickest layer of Earth is the
   a. crust.
   b. mantle.
   c. outer core.
   d. inner core.

6. Globes are
   a. two dimensional.
   b. one dimensional.
   c. three dimensional.
   d. flat.

7. A map projection made by holding a sheet of paper to one pole of a globe is called a
   a. Mercator projection.
   b. polar projection.
   c. conic projection.
   d. relief projection.

8. Lines on maps or globes that run from the North Pole to the South Pole are called
   a. meridians.
   b. latitudes.
   c. longitudes.
   d. contour lines.

9. The North Pole is at
   a. 0° latitude.
   b. 10° longitude.
   c. 90° north latitude.
   d. 90° north longitude.

10. The distance in degrees east or west of the prime meridian is a place's
    a. longitude.
    b. latitude.
    c. equator.
    d. parallel.

FILL IN **Write the term or phrase that best completes each statement.**

11. Elevation is the distance of a point above or below _____.

12. The symbols used on a map are listed in a _____.

13. Latitude and longitude are measured in _____.

14. The longest parallel on Earth's surface is the _____.

15. A narrow field of study within a larger field is called a _____.

16. Maps of _____ areas have the fewest distortions.

17. The layer of Earth between the core and the crust is the _____.

18. The hydrosphere is the part of Earth that is _____.

Concept Challenges TEST PREP

WRITTEN RESPONSE **Answer each of the following questions in complete sentences.**

1. **EXPLAIN:** What is the longitude of Greenwich, England? Why?

2. **INFER:** Why must both latitude and longitude be known to find the location of a place on a map?

3. **ANALYZE:** Why do two contour lines never cross each other?

4. **EXPLAIN:** Why does a polar projection have less distortion nearer the poles than it has farther from the poles?

5. **INFER:** Is the diameter of Earth larger when measured from pole to pole or when measured at the equator? Explain.

INTERPRETING VISUALS **Use Figure 1-34 to answer the following questions.**

6. **OBSERVE:** What color on the map is used to show bodies of water?

7. **CALCULATE:** What real distance on the map is shown by 2 cm?

8. **INTERPRET:** How many kilometers is it from Miami, Florida, to Austin, Texas? From Charlotte, North Carolina, to Louisville, Kentucky?

9. **INTERPRET:** In what direction is Chicago, Illinois, from San Diego, California?

10. **ANALYZE:** What is the latitude and longitude of Philadelphia, Pennsylvania?

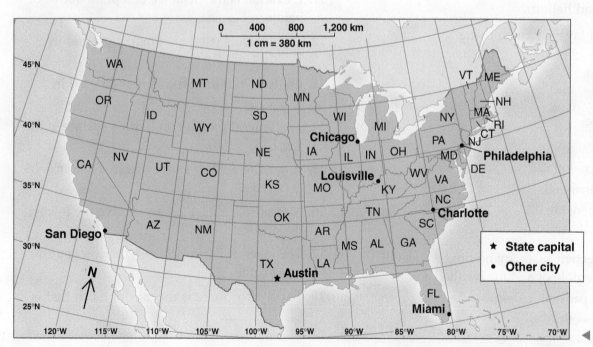

◀ Figure 1-34

Chapter 2 Minerals and Their Properties

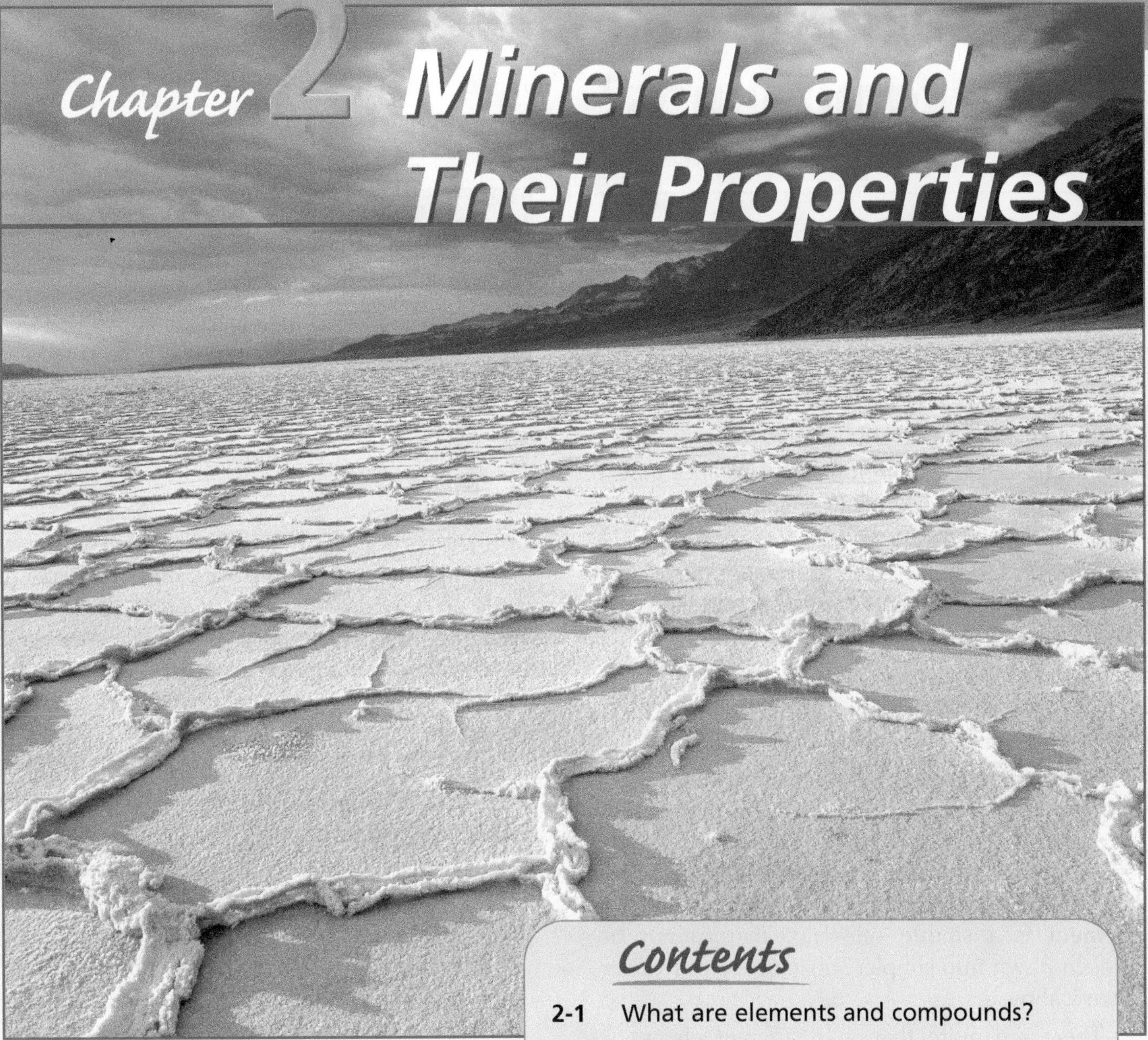

▲ **Figure 2-1** Death Valley, in southeastern California, has large salt flats.

Death Valley is a hot, dry place. Salt flats make up parts of the valley floor. Salt flats often form in pits. These pits sometimes fill with runoff from the mountain. Then, the water slowly seeps into the ground or evaporates forming salt flats. Death Valley attracts tourists and scientists because of its unusual properties.

▶Water carries dissolved minerals from the mountains to Death Valley below. What common substances do you think are left behind as the water evaporates?

Contents

2-1 What are elements and compounds?

Key Terms

atom: smallest part of an element that can be identified as that element

element (EHL-uh-muhnt): simple substance that cannot be broken down into simpler substances by ordinary chemical means

compound (KAHM-pownd): substance made up of two or more elements that are chemically combined

molecule (MAHL-ih-kyool): smallest part of a substance that has all the properties of that substance

Atoms and Elements All matter is made up of particles too small to be seen. These particles are called atoms. **Atoms** are the smallest parts of an element that can be identified as that element. An **element** is a simple substance that cannot be broken down into simpler substances by ordinary chemical means.

There are more than 100 different elements. Elements can be solids, liquids, or gases. Most elements are solids at room temperature. Only two elements, bromine and mercury, are liquid at room temperature. Oxygen, hydrogen, and nitrogen are gases. Figure 2-2 shows the states of some common elements at room temperature.

STATES OF COMMON ELEMENTS			
Element	Natural State	Element	Natural State
Carbon	Solid	Oxygen	Gas
Aluminum	Solid	Helium	Gas
Silver	Solid	Bromine	Liquid
Copper	Solid	Mercury	Liquid

▲ Figure 2-2

▲ **Figure 2-3** Mercury (left) and copper (right) in their natural states

 ANALYZE: How are atoms and elements related?

Compounds Many common substances are made up of combinations of elements. Water is made up of hydrogen and oxygen. Sugar is made up of hydrogen, oxygen, and carbon. Water and sugar are examples of compounds. A **compound** is a substance made up of two or more elements that are chemically combined.

Most compounds are made up of a string of atoms called **molecules.** A molecule is the smallest part of a substance that has all the chemical properties of that substance. The atoms in a molecule are chemically combined.

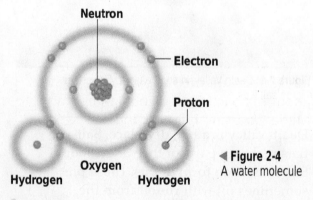

◀ Figure 2-4
A water molecule

ANALYZE: How are molecules and compounds related?

More Than Its Parts When two or more elements are combined chemically, a compound is formed. The elements in the compound are in definite proportion to each other. Most compounds have physical and chemical properties that are different from the physical and chemical properties of the elements that formed them.

Sodium is a soft metal that can be cut with a knife. Chlorine is a green gas. Both sodium and chlorine are poisonous elements. Combined, they form a solid compound that can be eaten. You know this compound, sodium chloride, as table salt.

▲ **Figure 2-5** Sodium (left) is part of the compound known as table salt (right).

 IDENTIFY: What elements make up table salt?

✔ CHECKING CONCEPTS

1. About how many elements are there?
2. What form are most elements found in at room temperature?
3. What is a compound?
4. What is a molecule?

5. EXPLAIN: The compound water is made from the gases oxygen and hydrogen. How is water different from the elements that make it up?
6. ANALYZE: How are atoms and molecules related?
7. IDENTIFY: What elements do the compounds sugar and water have in common?

Web InfoSearch

Alloys That Remember Alloys are metallic compounds or solutions made up of two or more elements. Some metal alloys can return to their original shape after being twisted, bent, or knotted. These are called shape memory alloys.

SEARCH: Use the Internet to find out more about alloys. What elements are they made from? What are they used for? Start your search at www.conceptsandchallenges.com. Some key search words are **shape memory alloys** and **intelligent materials.**

 ## How Do They Know That?

SOME ELEMENTS ARE RADIOACTIVE

A radioactive element gives off energy when particles inside its atoms break apart. Most of what is known today about radioactive elements can be traced to the work of Marie Curie and her husband, Pierre Curie.

The Curies worked with an ore called pitchblende. They observed that the pitchblende gave off unusual rays. The Curies soon discovered that these rays were being produced by two elements contained in the pitchblende. The Curies and another scientist, Henri Becquerel, shared the Nobel Prize in 1903 in physics for discovering these new elements. The elements were named polonium and radium. Polonium was named for Poland, the homeland of Marie Curie.

In 1906, Pierre Curie died in a tragic accident. However, Marie Curie continued her work with radium and polonium. In 1911, she received a second Nobel Prize, in chemistry.

Thinking Critically What do you think the energy inside an atom is used for?

▲ **Figure 2-6** Marie Curie (1867–1934) was born in Poland. However, she did her experiments in a laboratory in France.

2-2 What are chemical formulas?

Chemical Symbols

A **chemical symbol** is a shorthand way of writing the name of an element. Each element has its own chemical symbol. The chemical symbol is used to represent one atom of that element.

In 1813, a Swedish chemist named Jons Jakob Berzelius (buhr-ZEE-lee-uhs) suggested using the first letter of the Latin name of an element as its chemical symbol for classification. When more than one element has the same first letter, a second letter is added. That second letter is a lowercase letter.

CHEMICAL SYMBOLS			
Element	Symbol	Element	Symbol
Oxygen	O	Hydrogen	H
Nitrogen	N	Carbon	C
Aluminum	Al	Helium	He
Iron	Fe	Lead	Pb
Sodium	Na	Mercury	Hg

▲ Figure 2-7

Some elements do not use the first letters of their English names as their symbols. The symbols for these elements may come from the names of the elements in a different language.

Look at Figure 2-7 for some examples. The chemical symbol for sodium is Na. This comes from the Latin name for sodium, which is *natrium*.

1 ▶ IDENTIFY: Why do some elements have unusual letters for their symbols?

Chemical Formulas

We just learned that a chemical symbol is a shorthand way of writing the name of an element. Chemical symbols are most often used to write chemical formulas. A **chemical formula** shows the elements that make up a compound. Sodium chloride is the chemical name for table salt. The chemical formula for sodium chloride is NaCl. By looking at the formula, you can see that table salt is made up of sodium and chlorine. The chemical symbol for sodium is Na. For chlorine, it is Cl.

 ANALYZE: How are chemical symbols and chemical formulas related?

Subscripts

Hydrogen peroxide is a compound made from hydrogen (H) and oxygen (O). The chemical formula for hydrogen peroxide is H_2O_2.

The number 2 after the H and the O is called a **subscript.** Subscripts show how many of each atom are in a molecule of a compound. Subscripts are written slightly below the line.

The chemical formulas for some compounds are shown in Figure 2-8. The chemical formula for one compound of iron sulfide is FeS_2. This chemical formula shows that a molecule of this compound contains two atoms of sulfur (S) and one atom of iron (Fe). When there is no subscript, it means that there is only one atom of that element in the molecule.

CHEMICAL FORMULAS FOR COMMON COMPOUNDS	
Compound	Formula
Water	H_2O
Carbon monoxide	CO
Carbon dioxide	CO_2
Iron sulfide	FeS_2
Calcium carbonate	$CaCO_3$
Aluminum oxide	Al_2O_3
Ammonium hydroxide	NH_4OH
Silica	SiO_2
Sodium phosphate	$NaPO_4$
Hydrogen peroxide	H_2O_2

▲ Figure 2-8

▲ **Figure 2-9** The chemical compound iron sulfide (FeS_2), also known as pyrite, has two atoms of sulfur in each molecule.

 INTERPRET: What do subscripts show?

✔ CHECKING CONCEPTS

1. Chemical symbols are shorthand for

_____.

2. Subscripts are written slightly _____ the line.

3. A chemical symbol stands for one _____ of an element.

4. The first letter of a chemical symbol is always a _____ letter.

THINKING CRITICALLY

5. ANALYZE: Why do you think scientists need shorthand ways of writing elements and compounds?

INTERPRETING VISUALS

Use Figure 2-8 to answer the following questions.

6. CALCULATE: How many atoms make up one molecule of carbon dioxide?

7. ANALYZE: How does a molecule of carbon monoxide differ from a molecule of carbon dioxide?

8. IDENTIFY: How many different elements are in calcium carbonate?

Hands-On Activity

INTERPRETING CHEMICAL FORMULAS

1. Copy the table in Figure 2-10 onto a clean sheet of paper.

2. On your paper, fill in the information that is missing from the table. Use the tables from this lesson and Lesson 2-1 to help you identify the elements in each compound.

Practicing Your Skills

3. EXPLAIN: What information does a chemical formula contain?

4. COMPARE/CONTRAST: How does the chemical formula for aluminum oxide differ from the chemical formula for aluminum sulfide?

5. INFER: Why do scientists use chemical formulas?

CHEMICAL FORMULAS AND THEIR MEANINGS			
Chemical Formula	Name of Compound	Elements in Compound	Relative Numbers of Atoms in Compound
H_2O	Water	Hydrogen and oxygen	2 atoms of hydrogen for every 1 atom of oxygen
CO_2	Carbon dioxide	Carbon and oxygen	1 atom of carbon for every 2 atoms of oxygen
CO	Carbon monoxide		
NaCl	Sodium chloride		
Al_2O_3	Aluminum oxide		
Al_2S_3	Aluminum sulfide		
H_2SO_4	Sulfuric acid		

▲ **Figure 2-10**

2-3 What are minerals?

Objectives

Define mineral. Identify and describe some minerals found in Earth's crust.

Key Term

mineral (MIHN-uhr-uhl): naturally occurring, inorganic solid formed from elements or compounds and having a definite chemical makeup and regular atomic structure

Earth's Crust The crust is the outer layer of Earth. It is made up of large chunks of solid rock and smaller pieces of rock, sand particles, and soil. Sand and soil are rock that has been broken into small pieces. All materials in Earth's crust are made up of elements and compounds.

About 75 percent of Earth's crust is made up of the elements oxygen and silicon. When oxygen and silicon combine, silica is formed. Sand is composed mostly of silica in the form of quartz.

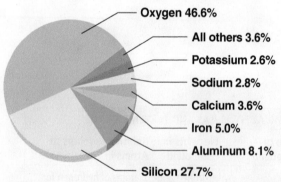

- Oxygen 46.6%
- All others 3.6%
- Potassium 2.6%
- Sodium 2.8%
- Calcium 3.6%
- Iron 5.0%
- Aluminum 8.1%
- Silicon 27.7%

▲ **Figure 2-11** Elements found in Earth's crust

Look at Figure 2-11 above. It shows the elements that make up most of Earth's crust. It also shows what percentage of Earth's crust is made up of each element. These elements are found combined into many different compounds.

▶ DESCRIBE: What does Earth's crust consist of?

Natural Solids A **mineral** is a naturally occurring solid. It is formed from elements or compounds in Earth's crust. All minerals are inorganic. This means that they are not formed from living things or from the remains of living things.

A mineral may be either an element or a compound. Each mineral has a definite chemical makeup. Gold and silver are examples of minerals that are made up of only one element. Mostly, however, minerals are combinations of elements. For example, the mineral quartz is a compound. Quartz is made up of silicon and oxygen. The chemical formulas for some commonly found minerals are shown in Figure 2-12.

SOME MINERALS AND THEIR CHEMICAL FORMULAS			
Mineral	**Formula**	**Mineral**	**Formula**
Gold	Au	Calcite	$CaCO_3$
Silver	Ag	Halite	NaCl
Copper	Cu	Galena	PbS
Quartz	SiO_2	Pyrite	FeS_2

▲ **Figure 2-12**

 INTERPRET: What are the elements that make up halite?

Rock-Forming Minerals The rocks that make up Earth's crust are made up of minerals. Scientists have identified more than 2,000 minerals. However, fewer than 20 of these minerals are commonly found in Earth's crust. These common minerals are called rock-forming minerals. Most rock-forming minerals are compounds.

▲ **Figure 2-13** Sand is made up mostly of silicon and oxygen. Silicon makes up a large part of Earth's crust.

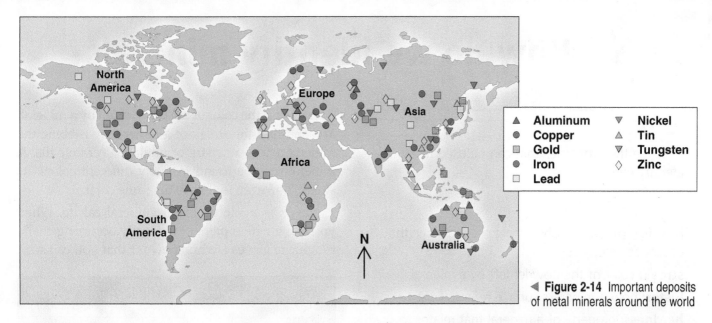

◀ **Figure 2-14** Important deposits of metal minerals around the world

In a rock, the minerals are usually found as mixtures. In a mixture, two or more substances come together. However, the substances do not chemically combine. They retain their original properties. In the case of rocks, each mineral retains its color, texture, and chemical makeup.

 EXPLAIN: Why are rocks called mixtures?

Metal Minerals Minerals that can be recovered for use are called mineral resources. Aluminum, iron, copper, and silver are some metal minerals. Metals are useful because they can be stretched into wire, flattened into sheets, and hammered or molded without breaking. Tools, machinery, and even the steel girders used in buildings were all made of materials found inside Earth's crust. Metals can be found in many places around the world. See Figure 2-14 for some examples.

 NAME: What are some metal minerals?

☑ CHECKING CONCEPTS

1. About three-fourths of Earth's crust is made up of oxygen and _____ .

2. Quartz is made up mostly of _____ .

3. Calcite has _____ atom of calcium for every three atoms of oxygen.

4. Gold is both an element and a _____ .

💡 THINKING CRITICALLY

Use Figure 2-11 to answer questions 5 through 8.

5. OBSERVE: Which element makes up almost half of Earth's crust?

6. IDENTIFY: What are two elements of Earth's crust that are found in only small amounts?

7. CALCULATE: What percentage of Earth's crust is made up of iron?

8. SEQUENCE: What five elements make up most of Earth's crust, from most common to least?

9. INTERPRET: What two ways does the map legend in Figure 2-14 use to show metal mineral resources?

10. INTERPRET: Based on Figure 2-14, what is the most abundant metal mineral found around the world?

BUILDING SCIENCE SKILLS

Organizing a Collection There are more than 2,000 different minerals. However, you are likely to find less than 100 of these. You can buy specimens from museums and rock and mineral shows. Or, you can look for your own minerals on mountains, in rock quarries, or at the beach. All you need is goggles, a hammer, chisel or a geologist's pick, and collecting sack. Record the date, location, and name of any mineral you find. Use a field guide to help you identify it. Put your samples in labeled boxes. ⚠ CAUTION: Do not trespass on private land. Also, be aware that some national parks and beaches do not permit the taking of minerals.

2-4 How do we identify minerals?

Objective

Describe the properties that can be used to identify minerals.

Key Terms

physical property: observable characteristic that describes an object

streak: color of the powder left by a mineral

luster: how a mineral's surface reflects light

hardness: property of a mineral that relates to how much the mineral resists being scratched

Physical Properties The characteristics of an object that can be observed or measured are its **physical properties.** The element iron is gray. Objects made out of iron are attracted to a magnet. These are two physical properties of iron. Physical properties can be used to help identify minerals. Some physical properties of minerals are color, streak, luster, and hardness.

▶ **1** **LIST:** What are some physical properties of minerals?

Color and Streak Color is an important property of minerals. However, most minerals cannot be identified by color alone. Many minerals are the same color. Gold and pyrite are both brassy yellow. Other minerals are found in more than one color. Quartz, for example, can be purple, yellow, pink, or colorless. It may also be brown, black, or white. Two minerals that are found only in a single color are malachite and azurite. Malachite is always green. Azurite is always blue.

▲ **Figure 2-15** Malachite is a green mineral.

Streak is the color of the powder left by a mineral. You can find the streak of a mineral by rubbing the mineral across a square of unglazed ceramic tile. A mineral may be found in many different colors. Its streak, however, is always the same color.

Chalk is made up of the mineral calcite. When you write with a piece of naturally occurring chalk, the calcite leaves a white powder that you can see.

▲ **Figure 2-16** Streaks of powder are made by scratching two forms of the mineral hematite on an unglazed ceramic tile.

▶ **2** **DESCRIBE:** What is the streak of calcite?

Luster The way a mineral's surface reflects light is called **luster.** A mineral can have either a metallic or a nonmetallic luster. Minerals with a metallic luster shine like new coins. Other minerals may look waxy, glassy, or dull. Quartz has a glassy luster. Calcite has a glassy or a dull luster.

▲ **Figure 2-17** Silver (left) is a metal valued for its high luster, among other properties. Fluorite has a dull, waxy, or glassy luster.

▶ **3** **IDENTIFY:** What are two kinds of luster?

Hardness The property of a mineral that relates to how much it resists being scratched is called **hardness.** In 1812, Friedrich Mohs, an Austrian mineralogist, worked out a scale of hardness for minerals.

Mohs' scale ranks ten minerals in hardness from 1 to 10. As the numbers increase, the hardness of the minerals also increases. A mineral with a high number can scratch any mineral that has a lower number. However, a mineral with a lower number cannot scratch a mineral that has a higher number.

MOHS' SCALE OF HARDNESS			
Mineral	Hardness	Mineral	Hardness
Talc	1	Orthoclase	6
Gypsum	2	Quartz	7
Calcite	3	Topaz	8
Fluorite	4	Corundum	9
Apatite	5	Diamond	10

▲ **Figure 2-18**

 ANALYZE: What mineral is the hardest on Mohs' scale?

 **CHECKING CONCEPTS**

1. What property allows one mineral to scratch another?
2. What is luster?
3. How is the streak of a mineral found?

 THINKING CRITICALLY

4. IDENTIFY: What are some physical properties of the mineral diamond?
5. INFER: Why is streak a better way to identify a mineral than color?

DESIGNING AN EXPERIMENT

Design an experiment to solve the following problem. Include a hypothesis, variables, a procedure with materials, and the type of data to study. Be sure to say how you will record your data.

PROBLEM: Joan had two blue minerals. One left a blue streak. The other left a white streak. What other tests could Joan do to identify the minerals?

 Hands-On Activity

PERFORMING HARDNESS TESTS

You will need a penny, a butter knife, a piece of glass, and an iron nail.

1. A field hardness scale, like the one in Figure 2-19, can help you determine a mineral's hardness. If a mineral scratches glass, it is harder than glass. If glass scratches the mineral, the mineral is softer than glass.

2. First, try to scratch the glass with your fingernail. ⚠ CAUTION: Do *not* scratch your fingernail with the glass.

FIELD HARDNESS SCALE	
Hardness	Test
1	Scratched easily with fingernail
2	Scratched by fingernail (2.5)
3	Scratched by a penny
4	Scratched easily by a butter knife; does not scratch glass
5	Hard to scratch with a butter knife; barely scratches glass (5.5)
6	Scratched by an iron nail (6.5); easily scratches glass
7	Scratches an iron nail and glass

▲ **Figure 2-19**

3. To find the hardest material, try scratching each material mentioned with the others. Look carefully where you scratched. Are there any marks?

Practicing Your Skills

4. SEQUENCE: List the objects in order from hardest to softest.
5. IDENTIFY: Which material will scratch all of the others?
6. CONCLUDE: How can you find the hardness of a mineral using the materials mentioned?

2-5 What are some other ways to identify minerals?

INVESTIGATE

Testing for Calcium Carbonate
HANDS-ON ACTIVITY

1. Obtain a sample of calcite or limestone and a sample of granite.
2. Put on goggles and a lab apron. Use an eyedropper to place a few drops of weak hydrochloric acid on each sample. Observe and record what happens to each.
   ⚠ CAUTION: Acids can cause serious burns.
3. Rinse both samples under warm running water and wash your hands.

THINK ABOUT IT: Coral has a similar chemical composition to limestone. How do you think it would react to the acid?

STEP 2

Objective
Explain how density, magnetism, and an acid test can be used to identify minerals.

Key Terms
density (DEHN-suh-tee): amount of matter in a given volume

magnetism (MAG-nuh-tihz-uhm): force of attraction or repulsion associated with magnets

acid test: test that helps identify minerals containing calcium carbonate

Density All matter has mass and volume. **Density** is the amount of matter in a given volume. You can calculate the density of an object by using the following formula:

$$Density = Mass \div Volume$$

As an example, suppose that you have a sample of the mineral talc. Your sample has a mass of 26 g and a volume of 10 cm³. If you divide 26 g by 10 cm³, you will get a density of 2.6 g/cm³.

▲ **Figure 2-20** Talc is a soft, light mineral.

Density is a property of minerals that never changes. For this reason, density can be used to help identify minerals. Density is measured in grams per cubic centimeter, or g/cm³. Most minerals have a density that measures between 2 and 3 g/cm³.

▶ 1 EXPLAIN: How can density be used to identify minerals?

Magnetism **Magnetism** is a force of attraction or repulsion shown by matter that is magnetic. Magnetism is displayed when objects made of iron, nickel, or cobalt are attracted to a magnet. Steel, which is an alloy of iron, also shows magnetism. Magnetite is a mineral that contains iron. If you held a small chunk of magnetite near a magnet, the magnetite would be attracted to the magnet. Magnetite can also sometimes act as a magnet itself. Magnetite shows the property of magnetism.

▲ **Figure 2-21** Magnetite is also called lodestone. This mineral attracts the steel in paper clips.

▶ 2 EXPLAIN: How could you use a magnet to determine if an unknown mineral is magnetite?

The Acid Test Some minerals contain calcium carbonate ($CaCO_3$). Knowing that a mineral contains this compound can help you identify the mineral. To test for calcium carbonate in a mineral, you place a drop of a weak acid on a small piece of the mineral, as you did in the activity at the start of this lesson. If the surface of the mineral fizzes, the mineral contains calcium carbonate. This is an **acid test.** Calcite and dolomite are two minerals that contain calcium carbonate.

 EXPLAIN: What is the acid test?

✓ CHECKING CONCEPTS

1. What is density?
2. Which common mineral is attracted to a magnet?
3. What kinds of minerals can be identified by the acid test?

 THINKING CRITICALLY

4. IDENTIFY: What two properties must be known to calculate the density of a mineral?
5. CALCULATE: What is the density of an object with a mass of 49 g and a volume of 7 cm^3?
6. ANALYZE: How can the property of magnetism be used to help you identify two gray minerals?

DESIGNING AN EXPERIMENT

Design an experiment to solve the following problem. Include a hypothesis, variables, a procedure, and the type of data to study. List the materials you need, and tell how you would record your data.

PROBLEM: How can the minerals quartz and calcite be identified?

 Integrating Physical Science

TOPICS: metallic elements, density

FINDING THE DENSITY OF GOLD

Pure gold scratches easily. It is often mixed with silver or copper to make it harder. Jewelers measure the purity of gold in karats, or parts per 24. Twenty-four-carat gold is pure gold. Fourteen-carat gold is 14/24 pure, or 58 percent gold.

Have you ever wondered whether a piece of yellow, shiny jewelry was really gold? Color and luster are important properties of minerals. However, other properties must be identified for gold to be considered genuine.

Legend has it that a king asked a goldsmith to make him a 1 kg crown of gold. The goldsmith replaced some of the gold with silver. The goldsmith then made the king a crown with a mass of 1 kg.

▲ **Figure 2-22**
Archimedes (above) may have tested a crown similar to the one shown here.

The king thought the goldsmith had stolen some of the gold but could not prove it. He asked Archimedes, a scientist and mathematician, for help. Archimedes calculated the density of the crown. He compared it with the density of gold. They were different. The crown was not pure gold. The goldsmith had stolen some of the king's gold.

Thinking Critically What are some properties of gold other than color and luster?

2-6 What are crystals, cleavage, and fracture?

Objectives
Define crystal and show how it is related to minerals. Distinguish between fracture and cleavage in minerals.

Key Terms

crystal (KRIHS-tuhl): solid substance with its atoms arranged in a regular, three-dimensional pattern

cleavage (KLEEV-ihj): tendency of some minerals to split along smooth, flat surfaces called planes

fracture (FRAK-chuhr): tendency of some minerals to break into pieces with uneven surfaces

Crystal Shapes All minerals are made up of crystals. A **crystal** is a solid material in which the atoms are arranged in a regular pattern. This pattern is repeated over and over in a regular internal structure. This structure determines the external shape of the crystal. The crystals that make up a given mineral always have the same shape, but they may differ in size.

Crystal shape is a property of minerals. There are six basic crystal systems that describe crystal structure. Scientists use X-rays to study the structures of crystals. They can use the structure of a crystal to help identify the mineral.

▶ 1 DEFINE: What is a crystal?

Cleavage Cleavage is a property of some minerals. **Cleavage** is the tendency of a mineral to split along smooth, flat surfaces called planes. Mica is a mineral that splits into flat sheets. Mica looks like layers of thin plastic.

Different minerals have different kinds of cleavage. However, the way the mineral splits, or shows cleavage, is always the same for that mineral. Mica cleaves into thin, flat sheets. Galena splits into small cubes. Feldspar shows what is called steplike cleavage.

▲ **Figure 2-24** Mica (top) and feldspar (bottom)

 2 DEFINE: What is cleavage in minerals?

Fracture A mineral shows **fracture** when it breaks into pieces with uneven surfaces. The fracture may be even, uneven, hackly, or concoidal. Hackly minerals have sharp, jagged surfaces. Copper shows a hackly structure. Concoidal minerals have ringed ridges or indentations like those of seashells. Obsidian shows concoidal

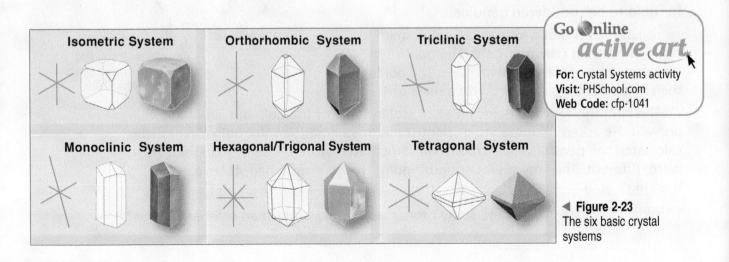

Isometric System   **Orthorhombic System**   **Triclinic System**

Monoclinic System   **Hexagonal/Trigonal System**   **Tetragonal System**

Go Online
active art

For: Crystal Systems activity
Visit: PHSchool.com
Web Code: cfp-1041

◀ **Figure 2-23**
The six basic crystal systems

fracture. Some minerals break into splinters or fibers. One example of this is asbestos.

HOW MINERALS BREAK APART			
Cleavage	Examples	Fracture	Examples
Pieces with smooth, flat surfaces	Mica, galena, feldspar	Pieces with rough, jagged, or uneven surfaces	Copper, obsidian, asbestos

 Figure 2-25

3 CONTRAST: How are fracture and cleavage different?

CHECKING CONCEPTS

1. How do scientists study crystal structure?
2. What kind of cleavage does mica show?
3. What is fracture?
4. What do the surfaces of a mineral with fracture look like?

💡 THINKING CRITICALLY

5. MODEL: Halite forms cubic crystals. Draw the crystal form of a piece of halite.
6. IDENTIFY: Steplike cleavage is a property of what mineral?
7. INFER: What property of minerals splits the mineral into pieces with uneven surfaces?
8. DESCRIBE: How does galena look when split?

BUILDING SCIENCE SKILLS

Classifying Minerals have either cleavage or fracture. Find out whether each mineral listed shows cleavage or fracture. Then, make a chart listing each mineral in the appropriate box.

pyroxene	quartz
anatase	corundum
periclase	calcite
amphibole	opal
brookite	hematite
thorianite	talc

 ## People in Science

GEMSTONE CUTTER

A gemstone cutter works with beautiful and valuable minerals called gems. The gem cutter may take the gemstone, such as a diamond, as it is found in nature and split it into two or three parts. Then, a grinding wheel and other tools are used to polish the dull stone. This creates flat surfaces called facets (FAS-ihts) that make the stone sparkle.

Most gem cutters cut gems for jewelry. Some create sculptures. Lawrence Stoller is a gem artist. He was taught gem-cutting by Glenn Lehrer. Stoller and Lehrer together developed many of the tools and technologies used to cut large stones.

Stoller has cut many of the world's largest gemstones. He is best known for his giant sculpted crystals. Some of these are in museums. Stoller also cuts tools for physicists and surgeons.

Gemstone cutting requires skill, focus, and patience. A mistake can destroy a costly stone. Most gem cutters learn their trade on the job.

Thinking Critically If you were to do gem cutting as a hobby, why would you use stones such as agate and quartz?

▲ **Figure 2-26** Gemstone cutters use grinding wheels to polish gemstones.

2-7 How are minerals formed?

INVESTIGATE

Forming Crystals Fast and Slow
HANDS-ON ACTIVITY

STEP 1

1. Put on safety goggles and gloves. Using tweezers or a spoon, put a small amount of baking soda on each of two microscope slides. Carefully place the slides on a hot plate set on low. ⚠ CAUTION: Be careful when using a hot plate.

2. When the baking soda melts, carefully move one slide aside with tweezers and put it on a paper towel to cool. Place the second slide on some ice cubes.

3. When the baking soda on both slides is hard, examine the slide using a hand lens or a microscope.

THINK ABOUT IT: How are the crystals on the two slides different?

Objective

Describe the main ways minerals are formed.

Key Terms

crystallization: formation of crystals caused by processes such as cooling and evaporation

evaporation (ee-vap-uh-RAY-shuhn)**:** process by which a liquid changes into a gas

solution: mixture in which the particles of one substance are evenly mixed with the particles of another substance

precipitation (pree-sihp-uh-TAY-shuhn)**:** process that occurs when elements and compounds leave a solution and crystallize out as solids

Minerals in the Crust Earth's crust is made up of rocks. Rocks, in turn, are made up of minerals. Most minerals are compounds in crystal form. In some rocks, the crystals are very large and easy to identify. In other rocks, the crystals are very tiny.

▷ **RELATE:** How are minerals and rocks related?

Magma Cooling Molten rock, or magma, is a very hot mixture of many different minerals. Magma is found in deep underground chambers. As long as the magma stays hot, it remains liquid. Eventually, though, the magma cools. If it cools slowly underground, large mineral crystals start forming. This is called **crystallization.** Eventually, the mineral crystals grow together to form rock.

Sometimes, cracks form in the rock above magma chambers. Pressure causes the magma to move up to the surface. When it comes out, the magma, now called lava, cools more quickly than it would have underground. Soon, the lava hardens into rock that contains small crystals.

▷ **CONTRAST:** How do crystals that cool very slowly differ from crystals that cool rapidly?

Evaporation The second way minerals form is by **evaporation.** In this process, water evaporates, or changes to a gas. The water in lakes and oceans contains dissolved minerals. As the water evaporates, only the mineral crystals remain. The crystals grow together to form rock.

▷ **IDENTIFY:** How do crystals form from evaporated water?

Precipitation Sometimes the elements in a mineral dissolve in water heated by magma. These dissolved minerals form solutions. A **solution** is a mixture in which the particles of one substance are evenly mixed with the particles of another substance. When the solution begins to cool, the elements and compounds leave the solution and crystallize out as solids. This process is **precipitation.**

Crystals can also form when water has more dissolved minerals than it can usually hold. For example, warm water can dissolve more halite (salt) than cold water can. The Great Salt Lake of Utah has very salty water. A very hot and dry climate causes evaporation and salt to crystallize out.

Many minerals form where there are cracks in the ocean floor. First, ocean water seeps down through the cracks. The water is heated by magma in the crust. The heated water dissolves the minerals in the crust. This hot solution is released through vents called chimneys, as shown in Figure 2-27. When the hot solution hits cold seawater, minerals crystallize out and then fall to the ocean floor.

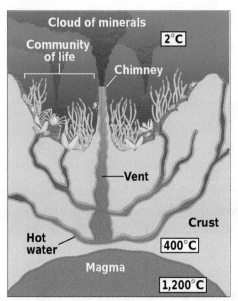

◄ Figure 2-27
A deep-sea vent is a crack in the ocean floor.

▶ **DESCRIBE:** What are chimneys?

☑ **CHECKING CONCEPTS**

1. What are minerals?
2. What causes big crystals to form?
3. What causes tiny crystals to form?
4. What happens as water containing dissolved minerals evaporates from lakes and oceans?

💡 **THINKING CRITICALLY**

5. INFER: What black, glassy mineral might you get if molten lava cooled so rapidly that crystals did not have time to form?
6. INFER: Sometimes rock has both large and small mineral crystals. How can you explain this?

BUILDING SCIENCE SKILLS

Classifying Find out what is meant by the following terms: *silicates, carbonates, sulfates, halides,* and *oxides*. Write a definition for each term. Then, find examples of two minerals that can be put into each group.

◈ *Integrating Life Science*

TOPICS: medicine, health

PROTEIN CRYSTALS

The human body contains more than 100,000 different proteins. Proteins perform many important functions. For example, they allow muscles to contract. They help bones grow and form the attachments for muscles. They also help fight diseases.

Proteins are made up of very complex molecules. These molecules are strung out like long, twisted ribbons. Scientists can crystallize the proteins and analyze the molecules. However, Earth's gravity distorts the crystals as they form.

In flight, the space shuttle acts as a gravity-free environment. Scientists have performed protein crystal experiments on the shuttle. This has allowed them to grow protein crystals that are not distorted by gravity. These crystals tend to be larger and have fewer optical defects.

▲ **Figure 2-28** A comparison of space-grown (left) and Earth-grown (right) insulin crystals

Thinking Critically The space shuttle can only remain in space for a few weeks. The International Space Station (ISS) will have a permanent orbiting laboratory. Would the ISS be better for growing crystals? Why or why not?

LAB ACTIVITY
Growing a Crystal Garden

Materials

Goggles, lab apron, sugar, salt, magnesium sulfate (Epsom salts), food coloring, hot water, plastic cups, plastic foam egg carton, scissors, tablespoon, ballpoint pen, magnifying glass

BACKGROUND

Most rocks contain minerals in crystal form. A crystal has a regular geometric shape, such as a cube. Some minerals form under water. Minerals dissolved in the water can crystallize out as the water evaporates or cools. Eventually, the crystals grow together and become minerals or rocks.

PURPOSE

In this activity, you will dissolve minerals in water to form solutions. As the solutions evaporate, the minerals will recrystallize.

PROCEDURE

1. Cut the egg carton so that you have three egg cups joined together. Leave a little of the carton lid above the hinge to write your name.
   ⚠ CAUTION: Be careful when using scissors.

2. Put on your safety goggles and lab apron.

3. Look at the crystal recipes listed in Figure 2-29. Place the right amount of salt for the first recipe in one of the plastic cups.

4. Add the right amount of hot water to the cup. Stir until all the chemicals dissolve.
   ⚠ CAUTION: Be careful when using hot water.

5. Add food coloring to the solution and stir.

6. Pour one tablespoon of your crystal solution into one egg cup. Share the rest of your solution with others doing the experiment.

▲ STEP 1 Cut the egg carton to form three cups.

▲ STEP 4 Stir until all chemicals are dissolved.

7. Mix and pour the other crystal solutions into the other cups. Do not touch the egg cups for one week unless instructed to do so by your teacher.

8. One week later, carefully pour any remaining crystal solutions in your egg cups into the sink. Let the crystals dry.

9. Examine the crystals with a magnifying glass. Record your observations in a notebook.

▲ **STEP 7** Pour one tablespoon of each crystal solution into an egg cup.

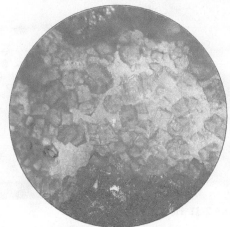

◀ **STEP 9** Examine the crystals with a magnifying glass.

Crystal Recipes

Halite (salt)	Sugar	Epsom salts
5 tbs salt	5 tbs sugar	5 tbs Epsom salts
6 tbs hot water	5 tbs hot water	5 tbs hot water
Green food coloring	Red food coloring	Blue food coloring

▲ **Figure 2-29** Use these recipes to make your crystal solutions.

CONCLUSIONS

1. OBSERVE: What do you see?

2. OBSERVE: What are the shapes of the crystals?

3. ANALYZE: Why are the crystals attached to each other?

4. INFER: How do your results resemble the way some kinds of rocks form at the bottom of the ocean?

How are minerals used?

Objective

State some common uses of minerals.

Key Terms

ore: mineral that is mined because it contains useful metals or nonmetals

gem: stone that has been cut and polished

Mineral Uses Many products are made from minerals. Diamond crystals are used to make jewelry. Because they are so hard, diamonds are also used to make cutting and drilling tools.

Gypsum is a mineral that is commonly used to make plaster. Many walls and ceilings are made of plaster. Some minerals and their uses are shown in Figure 2-30.

MINERALS AND THEIR USES	
Mineral	**Uses**
Quartz	Glass, sandpaper, telephone, radio
Feldspar	Porcelain, china, dishes
Mica	Insulators, toasters, irons, motors
Talc	Talcum powder, crayons, soap
Calcite	Building materials, medicine
Graphite	Pencil lead

▲ **Figure 2-30**

Tiny amounts of minerals are needed as part of your diet to keep your body healthy and working properly. Calcium and phosphorus are two examples of minerals needed by your body. These minerals are needed for strong bones and teeth. The body uses the mineral iron to make new red blood cells.

The minerals your body needs are found in food substances. Calcium, for example, is found in milk and other dairy products. Iron is found in red meat and some vegetables. The minerals that are used in dietary supplements are usually found in compounds.

▷ IDENTIFY: What are two minerals used by the human body?

Ores Minerals in the form of compounds contain useful metals and nonmetals. An **ore** is a rocky material that is mined because it contains useful metals or nonmetals that can be extracted from it.

Some examples of ores are hematite, bauxite, and halite. Hematite contains iron, which is used in the production of steel. Bauxite is mined to extract aluminum. Halite contains salt.

▲ **Figure 2-31** Hematite iron ore

▷ DEFINE: What is an ore?

Gemstones and Gems Some minerals are valued because they are beautiful and long lasting. These minerals are called gemstones. Rare and beautiful gemstones are called precious stones. Gemstones that are more common are called semiprecious stones. Because they are beautiful and long lasting, many precious and semiprecious stones are used to make jewelry.

▲ **Figure 2-32** Ruby (left) from corundum and emerald (right) from beryl are both precious stones used in making jewelry.

Gemstones that have been cut and polished are called **gems**. Diamonds, rubies, sapphires, and emeralds are precious stones that are often made into gems. Opal, amethyst, turquoise, topaz, garnet, aquamarine, and jade are some semiprecious stones that are made into gems.

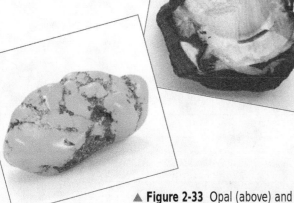

▲ **Figure 2-33** Opal (above) and turquoise (left) are both semiprecious stones used in making jewelry.

 IDENTIFY: What are three precious stones?

 CHECKING CONCEPTS

1. Calcium and _____ are both needed by the body for strong bones and teeth.
2. Bauxite is an _____ of aluminum.
3. Plaster is made from _____.
4. Very rare and beautiful minerals are called _____ stones.
5. Halite is an ore of _____.

THINKING CRITICALLY

6. LIST: What are four minerals that are commonly taken from ores?

INTERPRETING VISUALS

Use Figure 2-30 to answer the following questions.

7. LIST: Which minerals are used to make items found in the bathroom?
8. IDENTIFY: What is the most common use of graphite?
9. IDENTIFY: Which mineral do objects that require heat insulation usually contain?

Science and Technology

GEMS FROM THE LABORATORY

Precious stones are rare. They are prized for their color, luster, and hardness. Any combination of these properties makes a precious stone desirable and costly.

Many gems are now made in laboratories. For example, crystals of quartz are heated until they change color. They are then sold as topaz. Such stones are called treated gems. A three-piece sandwich of heat-treated aquamarine inside of green glass can be substituted for an emerald. This is an example of an assembled gem.

Corundum is the second hardest of all minerals. It can be specially treated to form synthetic rubies and sapphires. These look just like the naturally occurring gemstones.

Thinking Critically Manufactured gems are hard to tell from the real thing. Should they be as costly as the natural gems they resemble?

▲ **Figure 2-34** Synthetic gems, which are made in laboratories, can be very difficult to tell from natural gems. Above is a synthetic diamond.

THE Big IDEA

How can the element carbon form different substances?

How are a lump of coal, the point of a pencil, and a sparkling diamond alike? All three substances are made up mostly of carbon atoms. However, the carbon atoms are arranged in different ways.

Coal is a carbon-rich organic material. It took millions of years to form. Overgrown swamps once covered huge areas of land, and the climate was mild and rainy. As the plants died, they became buried. Pressure and heat caused the deep deposits of buried plants to change into coal.

Graphite is a mineral made up entirely of carbon. The atoms in graphite are arranged in sheets. They are held together by weak chemical bonds. When these bonds break, as they do under light pressure, some of the carbon atoms flake off. That is why graphite is often used in pencils. Pressing on the pencil leaves behind a trail of carbon. Graphite is also used to lubricate machines.

Diamond is also a mineral made up entirely of carbon atoms. However, the diamonds crystallize only under extreme pressure. In nature, they are created by geological processes deep within Earth. Other processes, such as the wearing away of surface rock, bring the diamonds to the surface.

The atoms that make up diamonds are tightly bonded together. Its internal crystal structure makes diamond the hardest natural substance known.

Look at the illustrations on these two pages. Then, follow the directions in the Science Log to learn more about "the big idea." ◆

Coal Swamp

Coal is not a mineral but an organic material. It is formed from the remains of living things, mostly plants. Most coal was formed in huge, overgrown swamps during the Carboniferous Period, 300 to 350 million years ago.

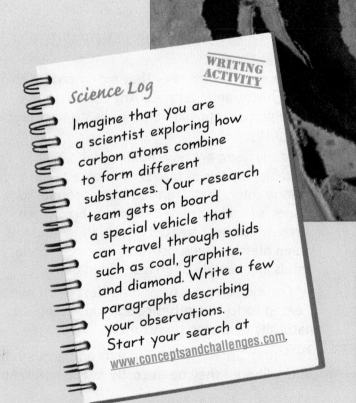

WRITING ACTIVITY

Science Log

Imagine that you are a scientist exploring how carbon atoms combine to form different substances. Your research team gets on board a special vehicle that can travel through solids such as coal, graphite, and diamond. Write a few paragraphs describing your observations. Start your search at www.conceptsandchallenges.com.

Anthracite

Bituminous

Lignite

Types of Coal

Coal forms from the remains of living things. It is not a mineral and does not have a regular atomic structure. Coal is classified according to the amount of carbon it contains. Anthracite (hard) coal is made up mostly of carbon. It is found in rocks that are more than 65 million years old. There is also bituminous coal and lignite, which are softer forms of coal and contain more impurities such as sulfer.

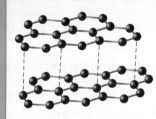

Graphite

Graphite is made up of layers of carbon. The layers are loosely bonded to each other. This internal crystal structure makes graphite a very soft substance.

Diamond

Diamond is made up of tightly packed carbon atoms. The Hope diamond is a world-famous deep blue gem that weighs more than 45 carats. You can see this magnificent combination of carbon atoms by visiting the Smithsonian Institution in Washington, D.C.

▲ **Figure 2-35** All of these forms of carbon can be mined from the earth. Diamonds come from a mine like this one in South Africa.

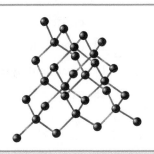

Chapter Summary

Lessons 2-1 and 2-2

- Matter is made up of **atoms.** An **element** has only one kind of atom. Elements can be solids, liquids, or gases.
- A **compound** is two or more elements chemically combined. A **molecule** is the smallest part of a compound showing the compound's properties.
- **Chemical symbols** stand for element names. **Chemical formulas** stand for compound names.

Lessons 2-3, 2-4, and 2-5

- **Minerals** are solids formed from elements or compounds. Most rock-forming minerals are made up of compounds. Sand contains the mineral quartz.
- **Physical properties** help identify minerals. Color alone cannot be used to identify a mineral. The color of the powder left by a mineral is called a **streak.**
- Minerals have a metallic or nonmetallic **luster.** The property of a mineral to resist being scratched is called **hardness.**
- **Density** is the amount of matter in a given volume. Every mineral has its own density. Some minerals show **magnetism.** An **acid test** can identify minerals that contain the compound calcium carbonate.

Lessons 2-6 and 2-7

- Minerals are made up of **crystals.** Crystals form in one of six basic crystal systems.
- **Cleavage** is the splitting of minerals into pieces with smooth, flat surfaces. There are different kinds of cleavage. **Fracture** is the splitting of minerals into jagged or uneven pieces.
- **Crystallization** and **evaporation** are some of the processes that form minerals.

Lesson 2-8

- Minerals have many uses. The human body uses minerals. A mineral that contains a useful metal or nonmetal is called an **ore.**
- Gemstones are rare, beautiful, and long-lasting minerals. Cut and polished **gems** are used in jewelry and art.

Key Term Challenges

acid test (p. 50)
atom (p. 42)
chemical formula (p. 44)
chemical symbol (p. 44)
cleavage (p. 52)
compound (p. 42)
crystal (p. 52)
crystallization (p. 54)
density (p. 50)
element (p. 42)
evaporation (p. 54)
fracture (p. 52)
gem (p. 58)
hardness (p. 48)
luster (p. 48)
magnetism (p. 50)
mineral (p. 46)
molecule (p. 42)
ore (p. 58)
physical property (p. 48)
precipitation (p. 54)
solution (p. 54)
streak (p. 48)
subscript (p. 44)

MATCHING **Write the Key Term from above that best matches each description.**

1. characteristic used to describe objects
2. solid material formed from elements and compounds in Earth's crust
3. the way a mineral reflects light
4. property of a mineral to resist being scratched
5. solid substance with a definite pattern in its atoms
6. amount of mass in a given volume
7. natural force that few minerals show
8. color of a mineral's powder

IDENTIFYING WORD RELATIONSHIPS **Explain how the words in each pair are related. Write your answers in complete sentences.**

9. gem, ore
10. streak, color
11. cleavage, fracture
12. compound, molecule
13. atom, element
14. chemical symbol, element
15. evaporation, crystallization

Content Challenges TEST PREP

MULTIPLE CHOICE **Write the letter of the term or phrase that best completes each statement.**

1. The smallest part of a compound that has all the properties of that substance is
   a. an atom.
   b. a molecule.
   c. an element.
   d. a formula.

2. CO_2 is
   a. an atom.
   b. a chemical symbol.
   c. a chemical formula.
   d. an element.

3. All materials in Earth's crust are made up of
   a. elements and compounds.
   b. elements and minerals.
   c. silicon and oxygen.
   d. crystals.

4. The softest mineral on Mohs' hardness scale is
   a. quartz.
   b. diamond.
   c. feldspar.
   d. talc.

5. The luster of pyrite can be described as
   a. metallic.
   b. glassy.
   c. dull.
   d. nonmetallic.

6. An acid test is used to test minerals for
   a. quartz.
   b. calcium carbonate.
   c. crystals.
   d. calcium sulfate.

7. The formula for density is
   a. Density = mass ÷ volume.
   b. Density = volume ÷ mass.
   c. Density = volume × mass.
   d. Density = mass × weight.

8. Scientists study the crystal structure of minerals using
   a. a hand lens.
   b. X-rays.
   c. the acid test.
   d. luster.

9. A mineral that breaks into thin, flat sheets is
   a. feldspar.
   b. mica.
   c. asbestos.
   d. quartz.

10. Bodies of water often contain minerals that are
    a. dissolved.
    b. precipitated.
    c. supercooled.
    d. solutions.

TRUE/FALSE **Write *true* if the statement is true. If the statement is false, change the underlined term to make the statement true.**

11. Most elements are <u>liquids</u> at room temperature.

12. A chemical <u>formula</u> stands for one atom of an element.

13. Mohs' scale is used to compare the <u>luster</u> of minerals.

14. There are <u>six</u> basic crystal systems.

15. A mineral with <u>cleavage</u> breaks into pieces with uneven edges.

16. A substance that is not formed from living things or the remains of living things is <u>inorganic</u>.

17. On Mohs' hardness scale, a mineral with a high number <u>cannot</u> scratch a mineral with a lower number.

18. One molecule of <u>CO_2</u> has one atom of carbon and two atoms of oxygen.

Concept Challenges TEST PREP

WRITTEN RESPONSE **Answer each of the following questions in complete sentences.**

1. ANALYZE: Why do you think it is important to test for more than one physical property of a mineral to identify it?

2. APPLY: If you were going to buy gold jewelry, what number carat of gold would you choose? Why?

3. INFER: Why would the acid test not be useful to identify a diamond?

4. IDENTIFY: Glass has a hardness of about 6. What minerals on Mohs' scale will scratch glass?

5. EXPLAIN: How would you test an unknown mineral to see if it was magnetite?

INTERPRETING VISUALS **Use Figure 2-36 to answer the following questions.**

6. Which minerals listed in the table are elements?

7. What element does pyrite have in common with magnetite?

8. Which minerals fracture?

9. Which minerals have a metallic luster?

10. What are the two hardest minerals listed?

11. What property would be most useful in distinguishing between black hematite and magnetite?

12. What are the minerals, in order, from softest to hardest?

13. Why might streak not be a useful property for telling apart quartz and diamond?

14. Which substance can scratch the other—corundum or hematite? Why?

15. Which minerals contain oxygen?

16. How does the chemical formula of magnetite differ from the chemical formula of hematite?

MINERAL PROPERTIES						
Mineral	Chemical Formula	Color	Streak	Luster	Hardness	Fracture or Cleavage
Pyrite	FeS_2	Yellow	Greenish, brownish black	Metallic	6–6.5	Fracture
Magnetite	Fe_3O_4	Black	Black	Metallic	5–6	Fracture
Hematite	Fe_2O_3	Reddish brown to black	Light to dark red	Metallic	5.5–6.5	Fracture
Gold	Au	Gold	Yellow	Metallic	2.5–3	Fracture
Silver	Ag	Silver white	Silver to light gray	Metallic	2.5	Fracture
Diamond	C	Colorless, pale yellow, black	Colorless	Nonmetallic	10	Cleavage
Quartz	SiO_2	Colorless, purple, yellow, pink	Colorless	Nonmetallic	7	Fracture
Corundum	Al_2O_3	Brown, red, blue	White	Nonmetallic	9	Fracture

▲ Figure 2-36

Chapter 3 Rocks and Their Origins

▲ **Figure 3-1** The Grand Canyon in northwestern Arizona

The Grand Canyon was cut into rock by the Colorado River. It is more than 1.6 km deep in places and from 6 to 29 km wide. The sides of the canyon are mostly layers of rock. The top has many tall peaks and other interesting landforms. As you can see, much of the canyon is red. However, each rock layer has slightly different coloring—beige and gray; green and pink; brown, silver-gray, and violet.

▶The rocks of the Grand Canyon show much about the history of the area. Why do you think the rock layers are different colors?

Contents

What are rocks?

INVESTIGATE

Observing Rocks
HANDS-ON ACTIVITY

STEP 3

1. Collect some samples of rocks. Draw pictures of them. Describe them in as much detail as you can.
2. Try to scratch all the rocks with a penny. What happens?
3. Use a ruler to measure the rocks and a triple-beam balance to find their mass.
4. Look for different materials within each rock.
5. Look at the rocks through a hand lens. Write down what you see.

THINK ABOUT IT: Do any of the rocks contain mixtures of materials? How do the rocks look different through the hand lens?

Objective
Identify and describe the three classes of rocks.

Key Terms
rock: mixture of minerals, generally cemented together

igneous (IHG-nee-uhs) **rock:** rock formed by the crystallization of hot melted rocks or minerals

sedimentary (sehd-uh-MEHN-tuh-ree) **rock:** rock formed from pieces of other rocks that are cemented together

metamorphic (meht-uh-MAWR-fihk) **rock:** rock formed when existing rocks are changed by heat and pressure

Rocks in Earth's Crust Earth's crust is made up of many kinds of rocks. **Rocks** are a mixture of minerals usually cemented together.

Small rocks found lying on the ground are fragments of larger rocks. Other rocks are so big that they are part of the landscape, as in Monument Valley in Arizona.

Petrologists (pet-RAH-low-jists) are Earth science specialists who study rocks and minerals and their origins. They also study rock composition and how rocks change. They can work in deserts, ocean or tropical environments, or arctic areas. They may do studies in areas affected by erosion, earthquakes, or volcanoes.

▲ **Figure 3-2** Monument Valley in northeastern Arizona

All rocks are made up of one or more minerals. There are more than 2,000 different minerals in Earth's crust. However, only a few of these minerals are found in most rocks.

▶ IDENTIFY: What are rocks made up of?

Classification of Rocks The grouping of objects that have certain features in common is called classification. Scientists often classify things to make them easier to study. Biologists classify things as living or nonliving. Chemists classify elements as metals or nonmetals. Petrologists classify rocks and minerals found in Earth's crust. They also classify the types of structures rocks form.

▶ DEFINE: What is classification?

Classes of Rocks Petrologists classify rocks by the way they form. Some rocks form from melted minerals that cool and harden. These rocks are classified as **igneous rocks.** Rocks that form when small pieces of minerals and rocks, or the remains of living things, become cemented or compacted together are classified as **sedimentary rocks.** Other rocks form from existing rocks, which are slowly changed by heat and pressure. These rocks are classified as **metamorphic rocks.**

 IDENTIFY: What are the three classes of rocks?

☑ CHECKING CONCEPTS

1. Rocks are made up of _____.
2. There are more than _____ different minerals in Earth's crust.
3. There are _____ classes of rocks.
4. Rocks are classified as igneous, _____, or metamorphic.
5. When melted minerals cool, _____ rocks form.
6. Scientists who study rocks and minerals are called _____.

THINKING CRITICALLY

7. INFER: How would you group rocks to make identifying them easier?
8. CONTRAST: How do sedimentary rocks differ from metamorphic rocks?

Web InfoSearch

Stone Monuments A monument is a structure built to honor a person or an event. Many monuments are made of stone, or rock. Different kinds of stone are used for different kinds of monuments. Often, the color, texture, and grain size influence the choice of stone.

SEARCH: Use the Internet to find out about famous stone monuments in the United States. What kinds of stone are they most often made of? Why did the builders choose those kinds of stone? Start your search at www.conceptsandchallenges.com. Some key search words are **national monument, landmarks,** and **statues.**

People in Science
GEOLOGIST

Geologists do many different kinds of work. Some help build roads, dams, and pipelines. Some search for fossil-fuel deposits. Others explore areas for valuable minerals. A petrologist is one type of geologist.

Dr. Michael W. Howell is a marine geologist. He studies deep-sea sediments to learn more about changes in the ocean over time. He analyzes how these changes affected past climates. Dr. Howell also teaches geology at the University of South Carolina. In 2001, he traveled to the Marion Plateau, off the coast of Australia. He was part of an ocean-drilling expedition run by the Ocean Drilling Program.

A geologist can work in industry, for the government, or as a college teacher. To become a geologist, you must complete at least four years of college. Some geologists also pursue postgraduate degrees or degrees from technical institutes.

Thinking Critically Why would a geologist want to drill into the ocean floor?

▲ **Figure 3-3** A marine geologist studies deep-sea sediments.

3-2 How are igneous rocks formed?

Objective
Identify two ways that igneous rocks are formed.

Key Terms

molten (MOHL-tuhn) **rock:** melted minerals

magma (MAG-muh)**:** molten rock inside Earth

pluton (PLOO-tahn)**:** large body of igneous rock that can form into different shapes when magma cools inside Earth's crust

lava (LAH-vuh)**:** magma that reaches Earth's surface

Heat Inside Earth If you dig about 300 m beneath Earth's surface, the temperature increases about 10°C. As you dig deeper, the temperature gets hotter. The deepest oil wells are drilled about 6 km into Earth's crust. Here, the temperature is more than 60°C. At about 60 km below Earth's surface, in the mantle, it is more than 1,000°C. At about 3,000 km, into the outer core, it is more than 2,200°C. The center of Earth may be as hot as 5,000°C.

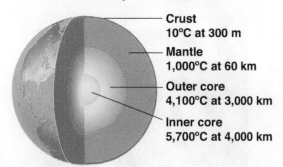

Crust
10°C at 300 m

Mantle
1,000°C at 60 km

Outer core
4,100°C at 3,000 km

Inner core
5,700°C at 4,000 km

▲ **Figure 3-4**
Temperatures inside Earth

The temperature of the upper mantle is hot enough to melt minerals and form **molten rock.** When the molten rock cools, it becomes solid, forming igneous rocks.

▲ **Figure 3-6** Basalt is from molten rock that cooled quickly.

1 INFER: Igneous means "formed by fire." Why are rocks formed from magma called igneous?

Magma and Igneous Rocks Molten rock inside Earth is called **magma.** There are large pools of magma inside Earth's upper mantle and lower crust. Sometimes, magma rises through cracks in rocks into the upper part of Earth's crust. Here, the temperature is cooler than the temperature inside the mantle. As magma rises through cracks in Earth's crust, it cools and crystallizes. As it hardens, igneous rock is formed. Igneous rock can take many thousands of years to form from magma.

▼ **Figure 3-5** Large bodies of igneous rock can form above or below ground.

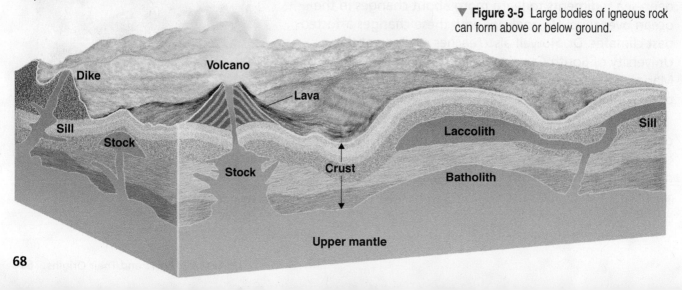

Dike

Volcano

Lava

Sill

Stock

Stock

Crust

Laccolith

Batholith

Sill

Upper mantle

Large bodies of igneous rock with different shapes are formed when magma cools inside Earth's crust. These bodies are called batholiths, stocks, laccoliths, dikes, and sills. A general name for all of these bodies of igneous rock is **pluton.** An example of each kind of pluton is shown in Figure 3-5.

 DEFINE: What is magma?

Lava and Igneous Rocks Sometimes magma rises through cracks in rocks and reaches Earth's surface. Magma that reaches Earth's surface is called **lava.** Lava cools upon contact with air or water. Cooling makes "red hot" lava harden into igneous rock. Igneous rocks form quickly from lava.

 DESCRIBE: How does lava rise to Earth's surface?

✓ CHECKING CONCEPTS

1. Igneous rocks formed from _____ form quickly.
2. Magma that reaches Earth's surface is called _____.

3. Melted minerals form _____ rock.
4. Large pools of _____ are found deep inside Earth.

💡 THINKING CRITICALLY

5. **PREDICT:** If you were to dig a hole 2 m deep into Earth's surface, would you be likely to find molten rock? Why or why not?
6. **GRAPH:** Make a bar graph comparing the temperatures of the crust, the mantle, the outer core, and the inner core.

Web InfoSearch

Plutons Plutons form inside Earth. However, you can see plutons on Earth's surface in some areas of the United States.

SEARCH: Use the Internet to find out more about plutons. Where can you see them on Earth's surface? How are they exposed? Start your search at www.conceptsandchallenges.com. Some key search words are **plutons, igneous rock,** and **volcano.**

 How Do They Know That?

THE ORIGIN OF ROCKS

James Hutton (1726–1797) was born in Edinburgh, Scotland. He was trained to be a doctor. However, after Hutton inherited a farm from his father, he became interested in the natural forces at work on Earth's surface. At the time, scientists thought that all rocks were sedimentary rocks. Hutton had a different idea. He said that many rocks, such as granite, were once molten, or melted, rock. Hutton also showed that mountains could be formed by the upward push of igneous rocks. Hutton published his ideas in a book called *Theory of the Earth* in 1795.

Based on his studies of Earth, Hutton proposed a theory about the history of Earth. Hutton's theory said that Earth was shaped in the past by the same forces, such as erosion and sedimentation, that were still at work. Hutton's theory was the beginning of the modern science of geology. Hutton is sometimes called the father of geology.

▲ **Figure 3-7** James Hutton, the father of geology

Thinking Critically Why do you think scientists once thought that all rocks were sedimentary?

3-3 How are igneous rocks classified?

Objective
Identify and describe igneous rocks by their minerals and textures.

Key Term

texture (TEHKS-chuhr): size of the crystals in an igneous rock

A Combination of Minerals Igneous rocks are made up of many different kinds of minerals. However, there are only six minerals that are commonly found in igneous rocks. These six common minerals are listed in Figure 3-8.

MINERALS IN IGNEOUS ROCKS		
Quartz	Mica	Amphibole
Feldspar	Olivine	Pyroxene

◀ **Figure 3-8**

Often, igneous rocks can be identified by their minerals. Granite is an igneous rock mostly made up of the minerals known as quartz, feldspar, and mica. Look at the photograph of granite in Figure 3-9. See if you can distinguish the different minerals that make up granite.

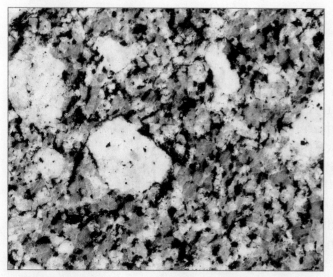

▲ **Figure 3-9** Granite is an igneous rock.

▶ OBSERVE: How do the quartz and feldspar crystals in granite differ?

Crystal Size Igneous rocks have mineral crystals of varying sizes. Crystal size depends on the amount of time it takes the molten rock to cool. The largest crystals form when the rock cools very slowly. Igneous rocks formed from magma have large mineral crystals.

Small crystals take less time to form. Most igneous rocks formed from lava have very small crystals.

Sometimes lava cools so quickly that there is no time for crystals to form. For this reason, a few igneous rocks do not have any crystals. Obsidian is an example of an igneous rock that does not have any crystals.

▲ **Figure 3-10** Obsidian looks like glass because it rarely contains crystals.

▶ INFER: How are cooling rate and crystal size related?

Texture The size of the crystals in an igneous rock is used to describe its **texture**. Texture can be used to identify different igneous rocks that are made up of the same minerals.

For example, you can tell if a rock is granite or rhyolite by looking at its texture. Granite has large crystals that you can see and feel. Rhyolite has very small crystals that are hard to see. Basalt is another commonly found rock with small crystals.

Igneous rocks are classified according to their textures. Igneous rocks with large crystals have a coarse texture. Igneous rocks with small crystals have a fine texture. Igneous rocks that do not have crystals have a glassy texture.

3 CLASSIFY: Classify granite, obsidian, basalt, and rhyolite according to their textures.

☑ CHECKING CONCEPTS

1. The six most common minerals in igneous rock are _____, feldspar, mica, olivine, amphibole, and pyroxene.

2. Granite is made up of the minerals quartz, _____, and mica.

3. An igneous rock that has very small mineral crystals most likely was formed from _____.

4. The texture of an igneous rock with no crystals is described as _____.

5. The texture of rhyolite would be described as _____.

💡 THINKING CRITICALLY

6. ANALYZE: A rock collector found five igneous rocks. The rocks had mineral crystals with the following sizes: Rock A = 2 mm; Rock B = 7 mm; Rock C = 4.5 mm; Rock D = 10 mm; Rock E = 0.5 mm.

   a. Which rock probably formed from lava?

   b. Which rocks could have formed from magma?

   c. Which rock probably took the longest time to cool?

BUILDING SCIENCE SKILLS

Classifying Scientists often classify igneous rocks according to where they were formed. Igneous rocks that were formed at Earth's surface are called extrusive igneous rocks. Igneous rocks that were formed inside of Earth are called intrusive igneous rocks. Research the roots and prefixes of the terms *intrusive* and *extrusive*. Then, using that information and the information in this lesson, classify granite, obsidian, basalt, and rhyolite as intrusive or extrusive igneous rocks.

Hands-On Activity

CLASSIFYING IGNEOUS ROCKS BY CRYSTAL SIZE

Classifying Igneous Rocks		
Rock	Crystal Size	Texture
Diorite		
Gabbro		
Basalt		

▲ **Figure 3-11**

You will need a hand lens; samples of the igneous rocks diorite, gabbro, and basalt; a sheet of paper; and a pencil.

1. Copy the table in Figure 3-11 onto a sheet of paper.

2. Carefully examine each of your rock samples with the hand lens.

3. Record your observations in your table.

Practicing Your Skills

4. INFER: Which of these igneous rocks formed deep inside Earth? Explain your answer.

5. INFER: Which of these rocks formed on Earth's surface? Explain your answer.

6. CLASSIFY: Using information from this lesson, add granite, obsidian, and rhyolite to your table.

▲ **STEP 2** Carefully examine the rock sample with a hand lens.

3-4 How are sedimentary rocks formed?

Forming Sedimentary Rock Layers
HANDS-ON ACTIVITY

1. Fill a 12-oz clear plastic jar with water.

2. Measure several spoonfuls each of sand, gravel, clay powder, and fine soil. Put them in the jar.

3. Stir them all together. Observe the color of the mixture.

4. Put a lid on the jar. Let the water sit for a while. Check it again to see the layers that have formed.

THINK ABOUT IT: Do you think the water will remain muddy? Why or why not? How can you tell which materials will end up at the bottom?

◀ **Figure 3-12** Observe the layers that form in your jar.

Objective

Describe two ways that sedimentary rocks are formed.

Key Term

sediment (SEHD-uh-muhnt): rock particles carried and deposited by water, wind, or ice

Sediments What happens when you mix soil and sand in a jar of water? The particles of soil turn to mud and, together with the sand, settle to the bottom of the jar in layers. The sand settles first because it is heavier than the mud. The mud settles on top of the sand. Mud and sand are sediments. **Sediments** are rock particles that are carried and deposited by wind, water, or ice.

 RESTATE: What are sediments?

Natural Cement Many sedimentary rocks form in much the same way as concrete. Concrete is made up of sand, gravel, and cement. Have you ever seen trucks pouring concrete for a building? Inside the trucks, sand, gravel, cement, and water are mixed. A chemical reaction then occurs that causes the sand, gravel, and cement to bind together into concrete. As the water evaporates, the concrete hardens.

How do sedimentary rocks form? Most sedimentary rocks are formed in water. These rocks form from sediments that settle to the bottom of lakes, rivers, or oceans. Over millions of years, the sediments pile up in layers. Some sedimentary rock forms from sediments deposited by wind or glaciers.

The layers of sediment may be hundreds of meters thick. As more sediment is added to the layers, the lower layers of sediment become tightly packed under the pressure and weight of the new layers. The older sediments become solid rock when water and air are squeezed out from between the sediment layers. The sediments may also become solid rock when dissolved minerals in the water cement the sediments together.

 DESCRIBE: When does sediment become solid rock?

Sedimentary Rock From Living Things Some types of sedimentary rocks form from the remains of living things. For example, the shells or skeletons of sea animals contain the compound calcium carbonate. When the organisms die, their remains are left on the bottom of the ocean. Over millions of years, the shells and skeletons build up on the ocean floor. Some of the calcium carbonate dissolves and comes out of solution to cement the minerals together. This forms solid rock.

Coquina limestone is a sedimentary rock formed from shells. Chalk limestone also forms from shells. However, you cannot see the shells in it because they were formed from microscopic organisms.

▲ **Figure 3-13** Coquina (left) and chalk (right)

 IDENTIFY: How can shells of marine animals form sedimentary rock?

✓ CHECKING CONCEPTS

1. Why does sand settle to the bottom of a jar faster than mud does?

2. What is sediment?

3. What sedimentary rock is made up of pieces of shells?

4. What are two types of sedimentary rock?

💡 THINKING CRITICALLY

5. IDENTIFY: What materials combine together to bind sedimentary rock?

6. EXPLAIN: Why does sedimentary rock form in layers?

7. EXPLAIN: Why must water evaporate or be pressed out for sedimentary rock to form?

8. COMPARE/CONTRAST: How are the rocks chalk and coquina alike and how are they different?

9. EXPLAIN: How does weight affect the way in which sediments form layers?

DESIGNING AN EXPERIMENT

Design an experiment to solve the following problem. Include a hypothesis, variables, a procedure, and a type of data to study. Also, tell how to record the data.

PROBLEM: How can you separate salt from sand?

Integrating Life Science

TOPICS: fossils, microorganisms

THE WHITE CLIFFS OF DOVER

The city of Dover is located along the southeastern coast of England. Dover is known for its beautiful white cliffs. These cliffs are composed of deposits of natural chalk and are more than 100 million years old.

How were the White Cliffs of Dover formed? The natural chalk comes from the fossil shells of microscopic animals called foraminifera (for-AM-ih-NIH-fer-ah). Close examination of the chalk deposits reveals the shells of the foraminifera that formed them.

The shells of foraminifera are made up of calcium carbonate ($CaCO_3$). When the foraminifera die, their shells sink to the ocean floor. These shells form fine sediments on the ocean floor. Gradually, the sediments build up until they are hundreds of meters thick. They are then compacted to form solid rock.

▲ **Figure 3-14** The White Cliffs of Dover

▲ **Figure 3-15** Foraminifera

Thinking Critically What compresses the shells of the foraminifera?

3-5 How are sedimentary rocks classified?

Identify and describe the two main groups of sedimentary rocks.

Key Terms

clastic (KLAS-tihk) **rock:** sedimentary rock made up of fragments of rock

nonclastic rock: sedimentary rock made up of dissolved minerals or the remains of living things

Groups of Sedimentary Rocks There are two groups of sedimentary rocks. One group is made up of fragments of rock that have been eroded, transported by water, wind, or ice, and deposited elsewhere. These sedimentary rocks are called **clastic rocks.** Another group of sedimentary rock is made up of dissolved minerals or the remains of plants and animals. These sedimentary rocks are **nonclastic rocks.**

▶ DEFINE: What are clastic rocks?

Particle Size Clastic rocks can be classified according to the sizes and shapes of the sediments that formed them. Conglomerates (kuhn-GLAHM-uhr-itz) are clastic rocks that are made up of rounded pebbles and gravel.

Sandstones are made of small grains of sand. Shales are clastic rocks made of silt and clay. Silt and clay are the smallest kinds of sediment.

 IDENTIFY: Name three groups of clastic rocks.

▲ **Figure 3-16** Sandstone (top) and shale (bottom)

Dissolved Minerals Most nonclastics form from dissolved minerals. Rocks formed in this way are chemical rocks. When water evaporates from salty lakes and shallow seas, the salts are left behind. These salts form a mineral called halite. Rock salt is a sedimentary rock made up of halite. Some kinds of limestone also form from dissolved minerals. One dissolved mineral that forms limestone is calcite.

Some caves have icicle-shaped deposits of limestone hanging from their ceilings. The cave shown in Figure 3-17 is an example. These deposits are called stalactites (stuh-LAK-tyts). The same cave may also have cone-shaped deposits of limestone rising from its floor. Deposits that rise from the floor are called stalagmites (stuh-LAG-myts).

▼ **Figure 3-17** Icicle-shaped deposits of limestone can be seen in this cave in Lincoln County, New Mexico.

Stalactites and stalagmites are formed from dripping water containing dissolved calcium carbonate. Sometimes, a stalactite and stalagmite may join to form a structure called a column.

 NAME: What mineral makes up rock salt?

Plants and Animals Some nonclastics form from the remains of plants and animals. Rocks formed from the remains of living things are organic rocks. Coals are nonclastic rocks formed from the remains of plants. Coal forms when the remains of plants are compacted for a long time. Coquina and chalk are both nonclastic limestones made up of seashells.

 DESCRIBE: How is coal formed?

☑ CHECKING CONCEPTS

1. Nonclastics are formed from the remains of _____ and _____.
2. Silt and _____ are two kinds of sediment in shale.
3. Caves often have structures called _____ hanging from their ceilings.
4. Coal is a _____ sedimentary rock.

THINKING CRITICALLY

5. CLASSIFY: Which group of nonclastic rock is most likely to form from plants buried for a long time?
6. CLASSIFY: Which group of clastic rock might form from the largest kinds of sediment?

Web InfoSearch

Spelunking Exploring caves is called spelunking. People who explore caves are called spelunkers. There are many caves in the United States to explore. If you go spelunking, follow all safety rules. For example, never go spelunking without an experienced spelunker.

SEARCH: Use the Internet to find out more about spelunking. List at least four safety rules you would need to know before entering a cave. Also, list the equipment you would need. Start your search at www.conceptsandchallenges.com. Some key search words are **spelunking, cave exploring,** and **stalactite.**

Hands-On Activity

FORMING CLASTIC ROCK

You will need safety goggles, three plastic foam cups, a tablespoon (tbsp), plaster of Paris, sand, pebbles, and water.

1. In one cup, stir together 2 tbsp each of sand and plaster of Paris. Add 1 tbsp of water. Stir.
2. In the second cup, stir together 1 tbsp each of pebbles, sand, and water. Add 2 tbsp of plaster of Paris and stir. Spoon this mixture on top of the mixture in the first cup.
3. In the third cup, prepare the same mixture as in Step 1. Spoon it on top of the other two layers in the first cup. Set the cup aside to harden.
4. The next day, peel away the cup from the clastic rock you created. Scrape away the surface from the side of the rock.

▲ **STEP 3** Spoon the mixture on top of the other layers.

Practicing Your Skills

5. DESCRIBE: What does the side of your rock look like?
6. OBSERVE: What kinds of particles does each layer have?

3-6 How are metamorphic rocks formed?

Objective
Describe two ways in which metamorphic rocks form.

Changed Rocks You can make bread from water, flour, salt, and yeast. First, you mix the ingredients. Then, you bake the mixture in an oven. After baking the mixture, you will not recognize any of the ingredients. The heat of the oven changes the water, flour, salt, and yeast.

The inside of Earth is like an oven. Heat and pressure inside Earth "bakes" rocks and changes the minerals in them. These chemically changed rocks are called metamorphic rocks.

 EXPLAIN: Why are metamorphic rocks called changed rocks?

Heat and Pressure Minerals in all types of rocks go through chemical changes when the rocks are heated. Minerals go through chemical changes at temperatures of between 200°C and 800°C. Minerals do not change chemically when the temperature is below 100°C. Above 800°C, the minerals melt into magma, or molten rock.

Rocks buried deep inside Earth's crust are also affected by forces. These forces cause pressure, which changes the form of minerals. Extreme pressure can flatten minerals into layers, as shown in Figure 3-18.

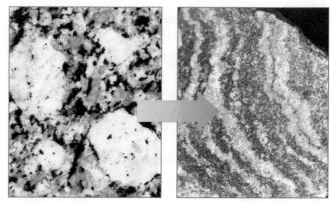

▲ **Figure 3-19** Pressure may cause minerals in rock to form into bands in metamorphic rock. Here granite (left), an igneous rock, becomes gneiss (right), a metamorphic rock.

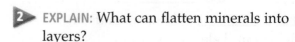 **EXPLAIN:** What can flatten minerals into layers?

Magma Metamorphic rocks are sometimes formed when existing rocks come into contact with or mix with magma. Magma can move into cracks in deeply buried sedimentary rocks. It may also flow between the layers of sedimentary rocks. The heat and chemical solutions in the magma cause the minerals inside the sedimentary rocks to change. The heat from magma can also change minerals in igneous rocks and turn one kind of metamorphic rock into a different kind of metamorphic rock.

3 **IDENTIFY:** What kinds of rocks are changed by coming into contact with magma?

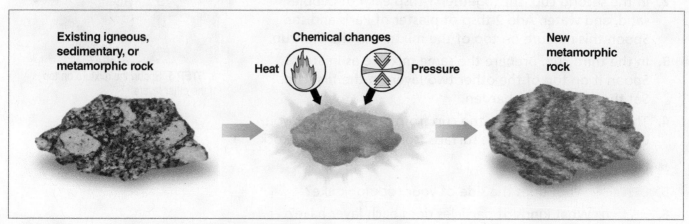

Existing igneous, sedimentary, or metamorphic rock

Chemical changes

Heat

Pressure

New metamorphic rock

▲ **Figure 3-18** Heat and pressure cause chemical changes in rock.

1. Igneous and sedimentary rocks can be changed into metamorphic rocks by _____ and _____.

2. Minerals in deeply buried rocks are flattened by great _____.

3. The minerals in rocks can be changed by the heat and chemical solutions in _____.

4. Pressure is caused by _____ that push against an object.

5. When rocks are heated to 200°C, the minerals in the rocks go through a _____ change.

 THINKING CRITICALLY

6. DESCRIBE: What happens to the minerals in rocks that are heated to a temperature of less than 100°C?

7. DESCRIBE: What happens to the minerals in rocks that are heated to a temperature of 950°C?

8. PREDICT: Would the minerals in a rock buried 2 m beneath Earth's surface be significantly affected by pressure? Explain.

Web InfoSearch

Stonemasonry In stonemasonry, stonemasons build structures using many types of stone from all around the world. Some of the most popular building stones are granite, marble, and slate. Stonemasons measure, cut, and carve stone to a specific shape or form. The stones are used in new and restored buildings. For restored buildings, the masons must often keep the new stonework as close as possible to the original stonework.

SEARCH: Use the Internet to find out more about stonemasonry. Are there different types of stonemasons? What training do you need to perform the job? What skills and interests should you have? After finishing your research, write a help wanted ad for a stonemason to restore old stone fireplaces. Start your search at www.conceptsandchallenges.com. Some key search words are **stonemasonry, fireplace restoration,** and **masonry.**

Integrating Physical Science

TOPICS: force, pressure

CALCULATING PRESSURE

The definition of pressure is force per unit of area. Pressure changes rocks and affects the atmosphere and oceans. The amount of pressure applied to an object can be calculated using the following formula:

Pressure = force ÷ area

In this formula, force is measured in units called newtons (N). A 1 kg weight exerts a downward force of 9.8 N. Area is measured in square units.

You can calculate pressure using the formula above. Suppose a person exerts a force of 120 N while pressing down on something with the heel of his or her shoe. The heel of the shoe has an area of 60 cm². What would the pressure be? Of course, in the real world, the entire weight of a person may not be concentrated on his or her heel.

▲ **Figure 3-20** Footprints in sand show the force of pressure.

Thinking Critically When would you not put all your weight into stepping down?

3-7 How are metamorphic rocks classified?

Objective
Explain the difference between foliated and nonfoliated metamorphic rocks.

Key Terms
foliated (FOH-lee-ay-tuhd): texture of a metamorphic rock that has mineral crystals arranged in bands

nonfoliated: texture of a metamorphic rock that does not have mineral crystals arranged in bands

Classifying Metamorphic Rocks Petrologists classify metamorphic rocks based on the texture of the rock. Metamorphic rocks have two kinds of textures, foliated and nonfoliated. The texture of a metamorphic rock is determined by the arrangement of its mineral crystals.

CLASSIFICATION OF METAMORPHIC ROCKS		
Original Rock	**Metamorphic Rock**	**Texture**
Granite, shale	Gneiss	Foliated
Granite, shale, basalt	Schist	Foliated
Shale	Slate	Foliated
Sandstone	Quartzite	Nonfoliated
Limestone	Marble	Nonfoliated

▲ **Figure 3-21**

 CLASSIFY: How are metamorphic rocks grouped?

Banded Metamorphic Rocks The mineral crystals in some metamorphic rocks are arranged in bands. The texture of a metamorphic rock with minerals arranged in bands is called **foliated.** Foliated rocks tend to break along their mineral crystal bands.

Foliated metamorphic rocks are formed when existing rocks are placed under great heat and pressure. Under this great heat and pressure, the minerals in the rocks melt and recrystallize into minerals that form bands.

Gneiss (NICE) is a foliated metamorphic rock. Gneiss is formed when granite is put under great heat and pressure.

Schist is another rock that has bands of recrystallized minerals. Schist is formed from shale, basalt, or granite. Slate is also formed from shale.

▲ **Figure 3-22** Shale (left) becomes slate (right).

 COMPARE: How are gneiss and schist similar?

Metamorphic Rocks Without Bands The texture of a metamorphic rock that does not have its minerals arranged in bands is **nonfoliated.** Nonfoliated metamorphic rocks do not break in layers.

Marble and quartzite are nonfoliated metamorphic rocks. Marble is formed from limestone. Marble contains large mineral crystals of calcite.

Quartzite is formed from sandstone put under great heat and pressure. Quartzite has large crystals of quartz.

▲ **Figure 3-23** Limestone (left) becomes marble (right).

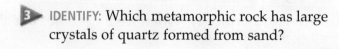 IDENTIFY: Which metamorphic rock has large crystals of quartz formed from sand?

☑ CHECKING CONCEPTS

1. What are the two textures of metamorphic rock?
2. What causes banding in metamorphic rock?
3. How do foliated rocks break?
4. A metamorphic rock without banding has what kind of texture?

💡 THINKING CRITICALLY

Use Figure 3-21 to answer the following questions.

5. INTERPRET: Which metamorphic rocks are formed when granite is subjected to high heat and pressure?
6. INTERPRET: Which metamorphic rock is formed from limestone?
7. INTERPRET: Which metamorphic rocks can be formed from shale?
8. INTERPRET: From which sedimentary rock is quartzite formed?
9. CLASSIFY: Is slate a foliated or a nonfoliated metamorphic rock? Why?

BUILDING SCIENCE SKILLS

Researching Metamorphic rocks, such as marble and slate, are economically important. Use the Internet or reference books to find out where in the United States deposits of marble and slate can be found. Determine how these varieties of rock are different from those found elsewhere, such as in Italy. Also, find out how the impurities in the rocks give them their special colors. Finally, list some ways in which marble and slate are important to business and industry.

▲ **Figure 3-24** India's Taj Mahal is made of white marble from India.

 Real-Life Science

MARBLE IN ART AND ARCHITECTURE

Marble is often used in architecture and sculpture because it is beautiful to look at and lasts a long time. The Lincoln Memorial was built to honor our sixteenth president, Abraham Lincoln. Construction began in 1914. It was not completed until 1922.

The Piccirilli brothers, both well-known marble sculptors, were chosen to carve the statue. It is 5.8 m tall and contains 28 blocks of white Georgia marble. The statue itself took four years to complete. The outside of the memorial contains marble from Colorado and Tennessee. The ceiling looks clear. The marble used in it was soaked in a waxy, whitish mixture known as paraffin to make it shine.

▲ **Figure 3-25** The Lincoln Memorial in Washington, D.C.

Another famous memorial made of marble is the Taj Mahal in India. It was built by an emperor in the 1600s to honor his wife.

Are there buildings or statues in your town that contain marble? Take a walk around your community and see if you can find some.

Thinking Critically What kind of rock is marble?

3-8 What is the rock cycle?

Objective

Explain the rock cycle.

Key Terms

cycle: series of events that happen over and over again

rock cycle: series of natural processes by which rocks are slowly changed from one kind of rock to another kind of rock

Nature's Cycles A series of events that happen over and over again for a certain length of time is called a **cycle.** In nature, there are many different cycles. If you look around you, you will probably find many different examples of nature's cycles.

The rise and fall of the ocean tides is a natural cycle that occurs twice each day. The movement of Earth around the Sun is a natural cycle that takes a year to complete. The Moon going through its phases is another cycle.

▶ **1** DEFINE: What is a cycle?

The Rock Cycle Rocks on Earth change over time. Some of the changes in rocks take place inside Earth. There, tremendous heat and pressure can slowly change rocks from one kind of rock into another. Other changes in rocks take place at the surface. On Earth's surface, rocks may be changed by rain, ice, wind, or the action of chemicals in air or water. The series of natural processes by which rocks are slowly changed from one kind of rock to another kind of rock is called the **rock cycle.** Look at the diagram of the rock cycle in Figure 3-26. It shows the ways that rocks are changed from one rock type to another.

▶ **2** INFER: How do you think ice, rain, and wind can change rocks?

A Closer Look at the Rock Cycle Look again at the diagram of the rock cycle. Notice that all three classes of rock eventually lead to sedimentary rock. The three classes of rocks can also be changed into metamorphic rocks or back into magma. However, only igneous rocks form directly from magma.

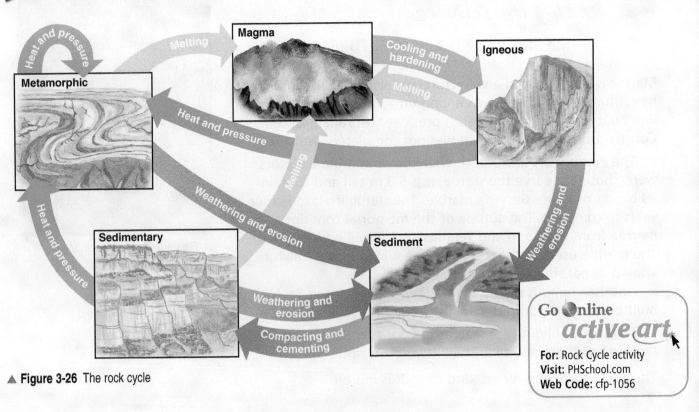

▲ **Figure 3-26** The rock cycle

Go **Online**
active art

For: Rock Cycle activity
Visit: PHSchool.com
Web Code: cfp-1056

At Earth's surface, rocks are broken apart by the forces of nature—moving water, ice, plant action, and wind. The particles of rock may then settle in lakes or oceans to form sediment that eventually makes up sedimentary rock.

Deeply buried igneous and sedimentary rocks can change into metamorphic rock or melt back into magma. Intense heat and pressure can change any rock into metamorphic rock. High temperatures can change any rock back into magma.

 OBSERVE: How does magma become igneous rock?

CHECKING CONCEPTS

1. What changes rock inside Earth?

2. What can all rocks be broken down into?

3. What kind of rock does magma cool and harden into?

4. What two conditions slowly change one type of rock into another?

THINKING CRITICALLY

5. COMPARE: How is the rock cycle like other natural cycles on Earth?

6. INFER: Why can only igneous rocks be formed directly from magma?

7. APPLY: Look around your neighborhood. What examples can you find of the rock cycle in action? What do you think caused the rocks to change?

INTERPRETING VISUALS

Use Figure 3-26 to answer the following questions.

8. EXPLAIN: How can igneous or metamorphic rock eventually become sedimentary rock?

9. IDENTIFY: What processes change sedimentary rock into metamorphic rock?

10. NAME: What processes or forces change metamorphic rock into igneous rock?

Hands-On Activity

CLASSIFYING ROCKS BY TYPE

You will need 10 different rocks, a hand lens, stickers, paper, pencil, and (optional) a field guide to rocks or other reference books.

1. Collect 10 different rocks from around your town. Label each rock with a numbered sticker.

2. Look at each rock with a hand lens. Record your observations on a sheet of paper.

3. Using your notes, classify each rock as sedimentary, igneous, or metamorphic.

4. Using reference materials, identify as many of your rock samples as you can. Write the name of each rock in your notes.

▲ **STEP 2** Use a hand lens to study each rock.

Practicing Your Skills

5. CLASSIFY: How many rocks did you classify as igneous? How many rocks did you classify as sedimentary? How many rocks did you classify as metamorphic? Explain your choices.

6. EXPLAIN: How many rocks were you not able to identify? Why weren't you able to identify these?

LAB ACTIVITY
Modeling What Lies Beneath Earth's Surface

Materials

Lab apron, three different colors of modeling clay, plastic picnic knife, plain paper, wax paper, colored pencils or markers, metric ruler, clear plastic straws, scissors.

BACKGROUND

Beneath Earth's surface lies a complex structure of rock layers. These layers provide clues as to how Earth's crust formed. Geologists drill deep into these layers of rock. The drills are like apple corers. They bring up rock cores for study.

PURPOSE

In this activity, you will work with a group to create a model of a hill made up of several rock layers. You will then trade your model for the model created by another group. Using clear plastic straws, you will determine what lies beneath the surface and make a profile graph.

PROCEDURE

1. Put on your lab apron.

2. Each color of clay should represent a different type of rock. For example, yellow could be sedimentary rock; blue, metamorphic rock; and red, igneous rock. Place a lump of modeling clay on a sheet of wax paper. Shape the clay to form a gentle hill.

3. Add additional layers to the hill using colored clay. Create a gentle hill 4 cm high and 20 cm wide. The top layer should cover all the layers below.

4. Exchange your model with one made by another group.

5. Use the ruler and a pencil to make a light line straight across the model at its widest point (20 cm). This is your profile line.

▲ **STEP 3** Add layers to your hill using different colors of clay.

▲ **STEP 5** Make a line straight across your model.

6. Draw a straight line 20 cm long on a sheet of paper.

7. Place the end of a straw along the profile line on one end of the hill. Twirl the straw and slowly push it through the clay to the tabletop. Remove the straw. It will have a core sample inside. Cut the straw a short distance above the clay core sample.
⚠ CAUTION: Be careful when using scissors.

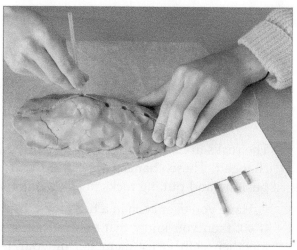

▲ **STEP 7** Slowly push the straw through the clay to the tabletop.

8. Place the lower edge of the core sample on the 20 cm line that you drew. The core should be in the same place on the line as it was on the model.

9. Using the remainder of the straw, take other core samples a few centimeters apart along the profile line until you have sampled the length of the hill.

10. Use colored pencils or markers to fill in the spaces on the paper between your core samples. This will complete the profile diagram.

11. Slice the clay model in half along the profile line. Compare the clay model to the profile diagram.

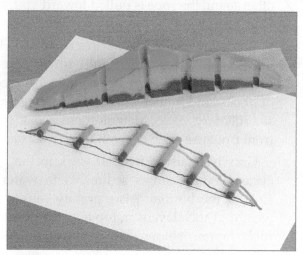

▲ **STEP 11** Compare your model to the diagram you made.

CONCLUSIONS

1. OBSERVE: How close was the profile graph you drew to the model?

2. OBSERVE: How many core samples did you take? Could you have used fewer cores?

3. INFER: How do profile graphs help geologists determine the history of a region on Earth?

Integrating Physical Science

THE Big IDEA

What drives the rock cycle?

The rocks in Earth's crust are constantly being changed. These changes are caused by forces pushing and pulling rocks in all directions.

Have you ever been in a tug-of-war contest? If so, then you know that you pull on a rope together with other members of your team. Your team exerts a force on the rope. If that force is greater than the force exerted by the other team, the rope is pulled toward you, and your team wins the contest!

Forces are exerted on Earth's rocks, too. The effects of these push-pull forces create pressure. This pressure causes bits and pieces of rocks and minerals to join together into sedimentary rock. Metamorphic rocks form from pressure deep beneath Earth's surface.

Gravity is also a force at work in the rock cycle. Gravity causes sediments in water to sink to the bottom. Also, gravity causes the weight of rock layers on top to press down on rock layers below. This, in turn, causes compaction.

Heat is a form of energy. Heat can change rock. When the minerals in rocks are under great heat and pressure, they may melt and combine chemically to form metamorphic rock.

Removing heat from a substance also causes changes in rocks. When a substance cools, it loses heat energy. Its molecules slow down and move closer together. The substance hardens to form a solid. Igneous rocks form this way. As the molten rock moves towards Earth's surface, it cools. Molecules in the molten rock slow down, and minerals crystallize to form igneous rock.

Look at the illustrations on these two pages. Then, follow the instructions in the Science Log to learn more about "the big idea." ✦

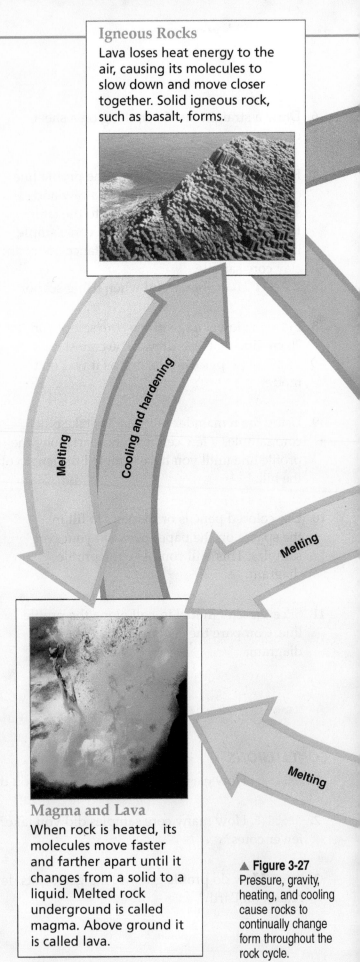

Igneous Rocks
Lava loses heat energy to the air, causing its molecules to slow down and move closer together. Solid igneous rock, such as basalt, forms.

Melting

Cooling and hardening

Melting

Melting

Magma and Lava
When rock is heated, its molecules move faster and farther apart until it changes from a solid to a liquid. Melted rock underground is called magma. Above ground it is called lava.

▲ **Figure 3-27**
Pressure, gravity, heating, and cooling cause rocks to continually change form throughout the rock cycle.

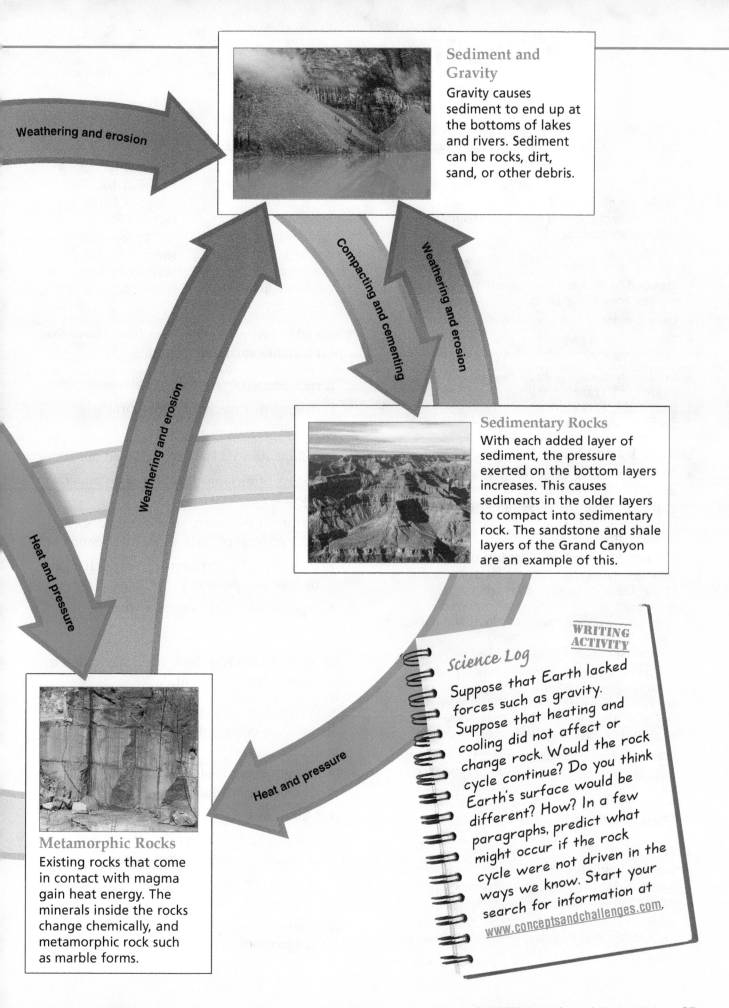

Sediment and Gravity

Gravity causes sediment to end up at the bottoms of lakes and rivers. Sediment can be rocks, dirt, sand, or other debris.

Weathering and erosion

Compacting and cementing

Weathering and erosion

Weathering and erosion

Heat and pressure

Sedimentary Rocks

With each added layer of sediment, the pressure exerted on the bottom layers increases. This causes sediments in the older layers to compact into sedimentary rock. The sandstone and shale layers of the Grand Canyon are an example of this.

Heat and pressure

Metamorphic Rocks

Existing rocks that come in contact with magma gain heat energy. The minerals inside the rocks change chemically, and metamorphic rock such as marble forms.

WRITING ACTIVITY

Science Log

Suppose that Earth lacked forces such as gravity. Suppose that heating and cooling did not affect or change rock. Would the rock cycle continue? Do you think Earth's surface would be different? How? In a few paragraphs, predict what might occur if the rock cycle were not driven in the ways we know. Start your search for information at www.conceptsandchallenges.com.

Chapter Summary

Lesson 3-1

- **Rocks** are made up of one or more minerals. The three types of rock are **igneous, sedimentary,** and **metamorphic.**

Lessons 3-2 and 3-3

- **Igneous rocks** form from **magma.** Magma is **molten rock** inside Earth.
- **Lava** is magma that has reached Earth's surface.
- The minerals in an igneous rock can be used to identify the rock.
- Crystal size is influenced by the rate at which molten rock cools. Crystal size in igneous rock determines its **texture.** Igneous rocks can be classified according to their textures.

Lessons 3-4 and 3-5

- **Sediment** is small pieces of rocks and minerals and the remains of living things that settle to the bottom of water. **Sedimentary rock** is formed when sediments are cemented together by dissolved minerals.
- **Clastics** and **nonclastics** are two groups of sedimentary rock. Clastics are classified according to the size and shape of their sediments. Nonclastics form from minerals dissolved in water or from the remains of plants and animals.

Lessons 3-6 and 3-7

- **Metamorphic rock** is formed when great heat and pressure inside Earth chemically change the minerals in rocks. The heat and chemical solutions in magma can also change the minerals in rocks.
- Metamorphic rocks have two kinds of textures. The mineral crystals in **foliated** metamorphic rocks are arranged in bands. The texture of a metamorphic rock that does not have bands is called **nonfoliated.**

Lesson 3-8

- The **rock cycle** is a series of natural processes by which rocks slowly change from one kind of rock to another kind of rock.
- All rocks can change into another type of rock or back to magma. Heat and pressure can change any rock into metamorphic rock.

Key Term Challenges

clastic rock (p. 74)
cycle (p. 80)
foliated (p. 78)
igneous rock (p. 66)
lava (p. 68)
magma (p. 68)
metamorphic rock (p. 66)
molten rock (p. 68)

nonclastic rock (p. 74)
nonfoliated (p. 78)
pluton (p. 68)
rock (p. 66)
rock cycle (p. 80)
sediment (p. 72)
sedimentary rock (p. 66)
texture (p. 70)

MATCHING Write the Key Term from above that best matches each description.

1. rock formed from molten material

2. magma that reaches Earth's surface

3. size of crystals in a rock

4. sedimentary rocks from dissolved minerals

5. texture of metamorphic rock with mineral crystals arranged in bands

6. texture of metamorphic rock that does not have mineral crystals arranged in bands

7. rock formed when another rock is changed by heat and pressure

8. process that occurs over and over

FILL IN Write the Key Term from above that best completes each statement.

9. A rock that forms when rocks and minerals are cemented together is classified as a _____.

10. Conglomerates belong to a group of sedimentary rocks called _____.

11. Molten rock inside Earth is called _____.

12. The process by which rocks slowly change from one kind of rock to another is the _____.

13. Rock materials that settle in water are called _____.

14. A large body of igneous rock formed by magma cooling is called a _____.

Content Challenges TEST PREP

MULTIPLE CHOICE **Write the letter of the term or phrase that best completes each statement.**

1. All rocks are made up of one or more
   a. sediments.
   b. minerals.
   c. magmas.
   d. metals.

2. A scientist who studies and classifies rocks is a
   a. chemist.
   b. geographer.
   c. biologist.
   d. petrologist.

3. The kind of rock formed when melted minerals cool and harden is
   a. molten rock.
   b. sedimentary rock.
   c. igneous rock.
   d. metamorphic rock.

4. A rock formed when an existing rock is changed by heat and pressure is
   a. molten rock.
   b. sedimentary rock.
   c. igneous rock.
   d. metamorphic rock.

5. Rocks formed from once-living things are usually classified as
   a. molten rocks.
   b. igneous rocks.
   c. sedimentary rocks.
   d. metamorphic rocks.

6. Magma that reaches Earth's surface cools and hardens into
   a. igneous rock.
   b. sedimentary rock.
   c. molten rock.
   d. metamorphic rock.

7. The only kind of rock that can form directly from magma is
   a. sedimentary rock.
   b. molten rock.
   c. igneous rock.
   d. metamorphic rock.

8. Crystal size in an igneous rock is determined by the rate at which the magma in the rock
   a. cools.
   b. melts.
   c. reaches Earth's surface.
   d. freezes.

9. Silt and sand are examples of
   a. molten rock.
   b. magma.
   c. lava.
   d. sediments.

TRUE/FALSE **Write *true* if the statement is true. If the statement is false, change the underlined term to make the statement true.**

10. Most nonclastic sedimentary rocks are made up of <u>mud</u>.

11. Magma that reaches Earth's surface is called <u>lava</u>.

12. <u>Metamorphic</u> rocks are formed when existing rocks are changed by heat and pressure.

13. The texture of a <u>sedimentary</u> rock that does not have minerals arranged in bands is described as nonfoliated.

14. Limestone is formed from dissolved <u>halite</u>.

15. <u>Igneous</u> rocks can be identified by their minerals.

16. Igneous rocks formed from lava usually have <u>large</u> crystals.

17. Marble is an <u>igneous</u> rock formed when limestone is heated.

18. Slate is a <u>foliated</u> metamorphic rock.

Concept Challenges TEST PREP

WRITTEN RESPONSE **Answer each of the following questions in complete sentences.**

1. EXPLAIN: The law of conservation of matter states that matter cannot be created or destroyed. However, matter can be changed from one form to another. Explain how the rock cycle supports the law of conservation of matter.

2. CLASSIFY: Pumice is a kind of rock often formed from volcanic lava. In what class of rocks should pumice be classified?

3. EXPLAIN: What is the difference between magma and lava?

4. CONTRAST: How do igneous rocks formed from lava differ from igneous rocks formed from magma?

5. CLASSIFY: Slate is a metamorphic rock that breaks into sheets along its crystal bands. Is slate foliated or nonfoliated metamorphic rock? Explain your answer.

INTERPRETING VISUALS **Use Figure 3-28 below to answer the following questions.**

6. What are the three types of rock?

7. How does magma form igneous rock?

8. What processes break down igneous rocks into sediments?

9. What happens when the minerals in igneous, sedimentary, and metamorphic rocks melt?

10. How do igneous rocks change into metamorphic rocks?

11. What are two kinds of rock that can form sedimentary rock?

12. What is the only kind of rock that can form directly from magma?

13. What kinds of rocks can form metamorphic rocks?

14. When does the rock cycle end? Explain.

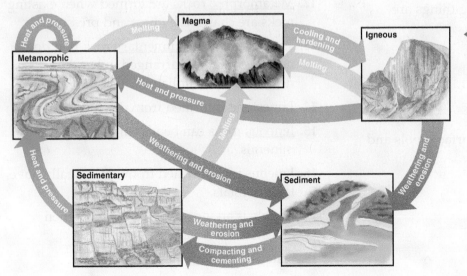

◀ **Figure 3-28** The rock cycle

chapter 4 The Rock Record

▲ **Figure 4-1** A plant fossil imprint in sedimentary rock

Fossils are important tools for reconstructing the distant, or geologic, past. They give us clues as to what life was like on Earth millions of years ago, when the environment was different. Knowing the different species that existed at different times can help us guess what the climate and land were like at those times. Fossils can also help scientists match rocks of similar ages from different locations.

►How might the land during earlier ages have been different from today?

Contents

4-1 How are organisms preserved?

INVESTIGATE

Making a Time Capsule
HANDS-ON ACTIVITY

1. A time capsule is one way to preserve objects and information for people of the future. To make your own time capsule, get a very large plastic container with a lid.

2. Put an object in the container. Have five of your classmates each place an object in it.

3. Write something down about each of the objects in the container. Put the note inside.

4. Close the lid.

5. Find an appropriate place to bury the container in the ground.

THINK ABOUT IT: Why did you include the objects you did in your time capsule? Why did you bury the time capsule where you did?

Objectives
Define fossil. Describe how organisms are preserved in rock and elsewhere.

Key Terms
fossil (FAHS-uhl): remains or traces of an organism that lived long ago

mold: imprint or hollow in rock that is shaped like and made by an organism

cast: mold filled with hardened sediments

amber: hardened tree sap

What Are Fossils? The remains or traces of organisms that lived long ago are called **fossils.** A fossil can be a bone, a whole skeleton, an imprint, a shell, or even the body of an ancient species.

▲ **Figure 4-2** *Tyrannosaurus rex* was a very large, carnivorous dinosaur that lived more than 65 million years ago.

Many species that lived long ago are extinct. That means they are no longer found alive on Earth. Dinosaurs are extinct. However, their remains have been found in many places.

 DEFINE: What are fossils?

Fossils in Rock Most fossils are found in sedimentary rock that was once under water. It takes millions of years for fossils to form. A fossil begins to form when an organism dies and is buried quickly by sediment. The soft parts of the organism decay. Usually, only the hard parts, such as shells and bones, are left. Through chemical processes, the sediments slowly harden into rock.

Sometimes, as the organism decays, it leaves a hollow opening in a rock. This hollow opening is called a **mold.** Later, the mold may fill up with sand or mud that later hardens. This material forms a **cast.**

Some fossils are only imprints, or marks, of the organisms in the rock. For example, footprints are made when an animal steps into soft mud. The mud hardens

▲ **Figure 4-3** Some fish imprints show the bones of the fish.

into rock, preserving the footprint. Scientists have also found many fish and leaf imprints.

 NAME: What kind of rock contains the most fossils?

Fossils in Ice and Tar Freezing helps preserve things by preventing decay. The bodies of about 50 elephantlike extinct animals called mammoths have been found frozen in Siberian and Alaskan soil and ice. Woolly rhinoceroses have also been found.

▲ **Figure 4-4** Museum model of a woolly mammoth

Animal remains have also been found in ancient pits of thick, sticky tar. These tar pits often become covered by water. Animals that went to them to drink were trapped in the tar. Other animals that tried to eat the trapped animals also became trapped. The animals sank into the tar and were preserved. In southern California, the bones of extinct animals such as saber-toothed cats and dire wolves have been found in the LaBrea tar pits. Parts of extinct camels, mastodons, vultures, and bison have also been found there. Tarlike oil deposits in Poland contained entire specimens of woolly rhinoceroses.

▲ **Figure 4-5** The skeleton of a saber-toothed cat

3 IDENTIFY: How are animals trapped in tar pits?

Fossils in Amber
A clear, sticky sap flows from some kinds of trees. This hardened tree sap is called **amber.** Millions of years ago, many insects and leaf fragments became trapped in the sticky sap. More sap covered these organisms. The sap hardened, and the organisms were perfectly preserved inside.

▲ **Figure 4-6** Insects are often found perfectly preserved in amber.

4 DEFINE: What is amber made from?

☑ CHECKING CONCEPTS

1. What four substances help preserve the remains of organisms?
2. What animal parts are most often preserved?
3. Which extinct animals were preserved in ice?
4. What else besides plants are usually preserved in amber?

💡 THINKING CRITICALLY

5. INFER: How do we know that dinosaurs existed?
6. HYPOTHESIZE: Why are fossils rarely found in igneous rocks?
7. PREDICT: Which of the following would most likely be found as a fossil: a clam shell, a flower petal, or an ancient worm? Why?

Web InfoSearch

Petrified Fossils Sometimes fossils are preserved by a process called petrification. To *petrify* means to "turn to stone."

SEARCH: Use the Internet to find out more about petrification. How does the process work, and exactly what does it do to the organism? Start your search at www.conceptsandchallenges.com. Some key search words are **fossils, petrified forest,** and **petrification.**

LAB ACTIVITY
Modeling a Fossil Formation

Materials

Safety goggles, lab apron, modeling clay, sugar cubes, small jar or disposable plastic food tub, wax paper (15 cm square), small seashells or snail shells, plaster of Paris, water, mixing tub, large spoon, toothpicks

BACKGROUND

Many sedimentary rocks contain the remains of ancient animal and plant life. These remains are called fossils. A seashell, bone, or leaf is buried in sediment. Its remains may leave an impression in the sediment. Fossil impressions are called molds. Later, more sediment fills in the mold and hardens. These fossils are called casts.

PURPOSE

In this activity, you will experiment with creating fossil molds and casts.

PROCEDURE

1. Put on your lab apron and goggles.

2. Place the square of wax paper on your table and spread a small lump of clay on it. Press a sugar cube into the clay.

3. Remove the clay with the sugar cube from the wax paper and place them in a container with cold water. Set it aside and leave it overnight.

4. Place a larger lump of clay on the wax paper. Flatten it out. Pinch up the edges to form a shallow dish.

5. Press a small seashell or snail shell into the clay to make an impression. Gently remove the shell. You can make more impressions with different shells if there is extra clay.

▲ **STEP 2** Press a sugar cube into the clay.

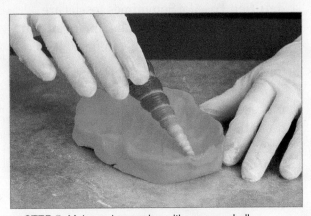

▲ **STEP 5** Make an impression with your seashell.

6. Mix the plaster of Paris with just enough water to make it easy to pour.

7. Gently spoon plaster into your dish to fill it. You must leave the plaster to set overnight. Place a small name tag next to your clay dish to identify it.

8. After a full day has passed, examine your sugar cube experiment and answer the questions below. Then, gently remove the clay from the outside of your plaster fossil. If any bits stick to the model, you can clean them off with toothpicks. Compare your fossil to the shell that made it. Copy the chart in Figure 4-7 and record your observations.

▲ **STEP 7** Spoon enough plaster of Paris into the clay dish to fill it.

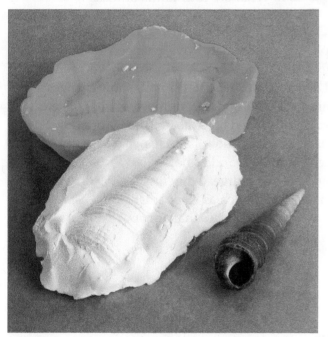

▲ **STEP 8** Compare your plaster fossil shell with the shell from which it was made.

Fossil Observations	
Sugar cube	Shell

▲ **Figure 4-7** Use a copy of this chart to record your observations.

CONCLUSIONS

1. OBSERVE: What happened to the sugar cube?

2. ANALYZE: Why did the change take place?

3. APPLY: How are fossils of life forms made in rocks?

4. IDENTIFY: What two kinds of fossils did you make?

4-2 Why do scientists study fossils?

Objective

Explain how fossils are clues to Earth's history.

Key Terms

coprolite (KAHP-roh-lyt)**:** fossilized dung or the stomach contents of ancient animals

gastrolith (GAS-troh-lihth)**:** stone used to grind food

The History of Life on Earth Fossils show that many kinds of organisms lived at different times in Earth's history. Many species are now extinct. Dinosaurs lived between 65 million and 220 million years ago. There were hundreds of species of dinosaurs. Not one dinosaur lives on Earth today. Saber-toothed cats, giant sloths, giant deer, and tiny shelled animals called trilobites are also examples of extinct animals.

▲ **Figure 4-8** Giant giraffes with antlers once roamed Earth.

Animal bones, shells, and teeth give us clues to past life. So do animal tracks. Another type of fossil that helps us to understand life in the past are animal burrows. These holes or tubes were made by animals in sediment, wood, or rock. They were later filled with sediment and became preserved. Some of the oldest known fossils of this type are worm burrows.

Coprolites are fossilized dung or the stomach contents of ancient animals. Coprolites can tell us what the organisms ate. Some ancient reptiles, including dinosaurs, may have swallowed stones that were used during digestion to grind food. These fossilized stones, which are highly polished, are called **gastroliths.**

▶ **LIST:** What are four kinds of fossils?

Changes in Living Things Fossils show that plants and animals have changed over time. For example, many fossils of horses have been found. Look at Figure 4-9. These fossils show changes in the animal's size and the number of toes. There was once a four-toed horse about the size of a dog. Fossils of horses also show that changes occurred in their teeth and legs. Today, horses have hooves, not toes, and are fairly large. Other fossils show that modern-day animals such as elephants, giraffes, and camels are related to species that are now extinct.

▶ **EXPLAIN:** How has the horse changed over millions of years?

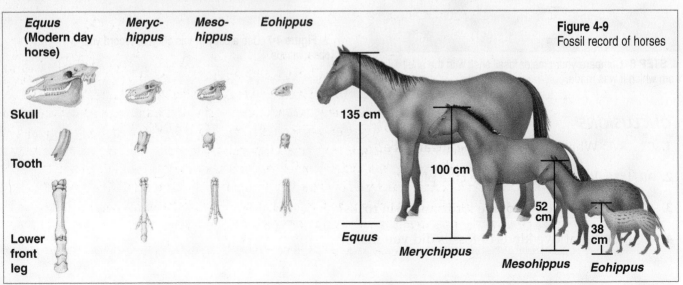

Equus (Modern day horse)	Meryc- hippus	Meso- hippus	Eohippus	
Skull				**Figure 4-9** Fossil record of horses
Tooth				
Lower front leg				135 cm — Equus; 100 cm — Merychippus; 52 cm — Mesohippus; 38 cm — Eohippus

Past Climates and Topography Fossils show that Earth's climate and surface have changed over time. Fossils of alligator-like animals have been found in Canada. Alligators usually live in warm climates. The fossils show that Canada once had a warmer climate than it has today.

Fossils of ferns have been found in Antarctica. These indicate that Antarctica was once very warm. Today, Antarctica is covered with ice and snow. Fossils of coral have been found in Arctic ice.

Fossils of ocean animals have been found in the Andes Mountains in South America. The Andes are 4,000 m above sea level. Scientists believe that the Andes were once under the ocean.

 INFER: How do we know that climates change through the ages?

☑ CHECKING CONCEPTS

Write an E for each extinct organism. Write an N for each living organism.

1. Mammoth
2. Saber-toothed cat
3. Horse
4. Alligator
5. Trilobite
6. Elephant

💡 THINKING CRITICALLY

7. ANALYZE: What do fossils tell us about Earth's surface and climate?
8. ANALYZE: What do fossils tell us about living things?

INTERPRETING VISUALS

Use Figure 4-9 to answer the following questions.

9. OBSERVE: How many toes did the earliest horses have?
10. OBSERVE: Which horse has the largest skull?
11. ANALYZE: How has the size of the horse changed over time?

 How Do They Know That?

ANCIENT HUMANLIKE SPECIES

Imagine finding a humanlike skull that is millions of years old. In the late 1950s, the Leakeys did just that. The Leakeys were a family of anthropologists. Anthropologists are scientists who study the history and development of humans and humanlike species.

▲ **Figure 4-10** Mary and Louis Leakey

Mary Leakey and her husband Louis studied fossils for more than 50 years. Much of their work involved looking for fossils of early humans or humanlike species. The Leakeys looked mostly in Tanzania, in the Olduvai Gorge.

In 1959, Mary Leakey found part of a humanlike skull that was more than 1.75 million years old. Over the years, Mary, Louis, and their son, Richard, found other humanlike fossils. Because he found stone tools at one site, Richard Leakey called the humanlike species he found nearby "Handyman."

Louis died in 1972. Mary died in 1996. Richard continues to study fossils.

Thinking Critically What did the Leakeys infer when they found ancient stone tools near the humanlike fossils?

4-3 How do fossils help us date rocks?

Objective

Describe how the relative ages of fossils and rock layers can be determined.

Key Terms

law of superposition: states that each undisturbed sedimentary rock layer is older than the layer above it

relative age: age of an object compared to the age of another object

index fossil: fossil used to help determine the relative age of rock layers

Reading Rock Layers Rock sediments are carried from one place and deposited in another by water and wind. These sediments pile up layer upon layer. The bottom layer is deposited first. Each layer is deposited on top of other layers. The sediments are pressed together and harden into sedimentary rock layers that form beds of rock.

The **law of superposition** states that each undisturbed rock layer is older than the layer above it. This law is used by scientists to read rock layers.

Where would you expect to find the oldest layer? Usually, the bottom layer is the oldest layer. The youngest layer is the top layer.

A
B
C

▲ **Figure 4-11** Rock formed in layers will usually follow the law of superposition.

▶ **OBSERVE:** Which rock layer is the youngest in the rock bed illustrated in Figure 4-11?

Relative Age Using the law of superposition, scientists can tell the **relative age** of a rock layer. Relative age is the age of an object compared to the age of another object. Relative age does not tell the exact age of a rock layer.

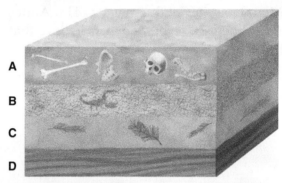

A
B
C
D

▲ **Figure 4-12** The relative age of a rock layer tells scientists only that one rock layer is older or younger than another rock layer.

 INFER: What is the relative age of rock layer C in Figure 4-12?

Index Fossils Fossils that can be used to help determine the relative age of rock layers are called **index fossils.** To be an index fossil, a species must have existed for only a short time in Earth's history. Many fossils of this short-lived species need to be recovered from rock layers. These fossils must have a wide geographic range. The fossil organisms must also be unique.

Many kinds of trilobites and graptolites are used as index fossils. Trilobites appeared about 590 million years ago and lived until 250 million years ago. They were small, shelled animals that lived in the ocean. There were many different species of trilobites.

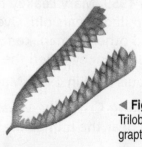

◀ **Figure 4-13** Trilobite and graptolite

Trilobite   **Graptolite**

Trilobites had three body parts. They also had a skeleton made of chitin (KY-tihn). Chitin is what your fingernails are made of. If a sedimentary rock contains trilobite fossils, it must have formed between 590 and 250 million years ago, when trilobites were still living. Graptolites appeared about 500 million years ago and lived until 335 million years ago.

Index fossils can also be used to date rock layers from two different parts of the world. Suppose rock layers found in different places contain fossils of the same species of trilobite. Scientists can infer that the layers are about the same age.

 EXPLAIN: What are index fossils used for?

CHECKING CONCEPTS

1. The youngest rock layer is usually the _____ layer.
2. Trilobites are examples of _____ fossils.
3. If one rock layer is older than another, you know the _____ ages of the rock layers.

THINKING CRITICALLY

4. **DESCRIBE:** What four qualities make up an index fossil?
5. **MODEL:** Draw a rock bed with four layers. In one layer, there are 25 trilobite fossils. In another, there are 37 graptolite fossils. The oldest layer is about 600 million years old. Label the oldest and youngest layers and the trilobite and graptolite layers.

BUILDING SCIENCE SKILLS

Modeling Two igneous rock formations can be used to find relative age. These formations are called extrusions and intrusions. They are always younger than the sedimentary rock beds in which they are found. You learned earlier what an extrusion and an intrusion are. Draw a model of a rock bed that has an intrusion and an extrusion. Color the oldest layer in your drawing red. Color the youngest layer yellow.

Hands-On Activity

MODELING HOW SEDIMENTS ARE DEPOSITED

You will need several different colors of clay, a bowl, and a cheese slicer or plastic knife.

1. Make a stack of different colored layers of clay. Each layer should be about the diameter and thickness of a pancake.
2. Turn the stack into a dome by pressing it over a small rounded object, such as a bowl.
3. With the cheese slicer or plastic knife, carefully slice down from the top and across through the dome so you can see a cross section of the stack. Examine the layers exposed.
4. Push your rock layers close together and then press them down.

▲ **STEP 3** Examine the layers you have exposed.

Practicing Your Skills

5. **IDENTIFY:** Which layer was deposited first?
6. **IDENTIFY:** Which layer is the oldest?
7. **APPLY:** How does this model show how sediments are usually deposited?
8. **APPLY:** Is the oldest layer on the top or the bottom now?

4-4 How is a rock's absolute age determined?

Objectives
Define absolute age in rocks and fossils. Describe ways used to measure it.

Key Terms
absolute age: true age of a rock or fossil

half-life: length of time it takes for one-half the amount of a radioactive element to change into a stable element

Absolute Age To measure your age, you count the number of years from the time you were born. This number is your age. The true age of a rock layer is called its **absolute age.** Absolute age tells scientists the approximate number of years ago a rock layer formed.

▶ 1 DESCRIBE: What is meant by absolute age?

Natural Clocks The process of a radioactive element changing into another element is called radioactive decay. Radioactive elements were first discovered in 1896. They are elements that emit, or give off, particles and energy. As a radioactive element gives off particles and energy, it decays. This causes new elements to form that may or may not be radioactive.

The rate at which radioactive decay happens can be measured. Each radioactive element decays at a regular, steady rate. Radioactive elements are like natural clocks.

▶ 2 EXPLAIN: What is radioactive decay?

Half-life The **half-life** of a radioactive element is the time it takes for one-half of the mass of a sample of a radioactive element to decay. Each radioactive element has a different half-life.

Uranium is a radioactive element. One form of it, called U-238, slowly decays into lead. If you begin with 6 kg of U-238, 3 kg will decay into lead after 4.5 billion years. After another 4.5 billion years, only 1.5 kg of U-238 would be left. By comparing the amount of the radioactive element in a rock to its decay element, scientists can find the absolute age of a rock.

▶ 3 INFER: If a rock has equal amounts of lead and U-238 in it, how old would the rock be?

Carbon-14 Carbon-14 is used to date the remains of living things. As long as living things are alive, they take in carbon-14. Carbon-14 is a radioactive form of carbon. It decays into nitrogen gas. The half-life of carbon-14 is about 5,800 years.

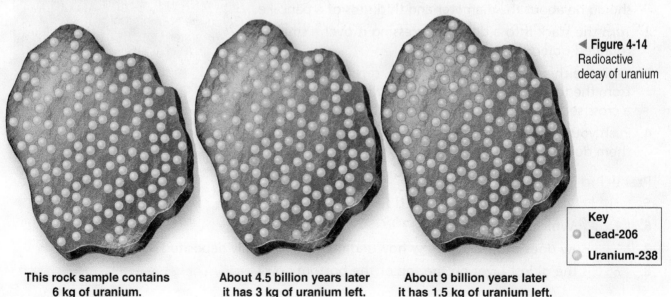

◀ **Figure 4-14**
Radioactive decay of uranium

Key
- Lead-206
- Uranium-238

This rock sample contains 6 kg of uranium.

About 4.5 billion years later it has 3 kg of uranium left.

About 9 billion years later it has 1.5 kg of uranium left.

Carbon-14 is used to find out the absolute ages of wood, bones, and so on. It is also used to date "young" samples of fossils. If a sample is more than 50,000 years old, this process cannot be used, since almost all of the carbon-14 has already decayed into nitrogen-14.

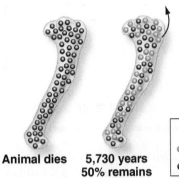

◄ Figure 4-15 In the animal bone, the amount of carbon-14 decreases as the carbon-14 decays into the gas nitrogen-14. This gas disperses into the air.

Animal dies

**5,730 years
50% remains**

Key
- **Nitrogen-14**
- **Carbon-14**

 DESCRIBE: What is carbon-14 used for?

✓ CHECKING CONCEPTS

1. The decay element of U-238 is _____.
2. Radioactive uranium gives off particles and _____.

3. If you read that a fossil is 350-400 billion years old, you are reading its_____ age.
4. The radioactive element _____ is used to find out the absolute age of once-living things.

💡 THINKING CRITICALLY

5. **INFER:** A radioactive element has a half-life of 70 million years. How much of a 10 g sample will be unchanged after 140 million years?
6. **INFER:** Would you use carbon-14 or uranium to find the age of a tooth you think is 20,000 years old? Why?

HEALTH AND SAFETY TIP

Radioactive elements emit radiation. Large amounts of radiation are harmful to living things. Radiation harms cells. Find out what the universal symbol for radiation danger looks like. Draw it on a sheet of paper. What two colors are used in the symbol?

 Science and Technology

LASER DATING OF SEDIMENTS

A laser is a very strong, focused beam of light. The light has only one wavelength, or color. You may have several appliances in your house that use laser beams. CD and DVD players use laser beams to read the stored sounds and images on the discs. In Earth science, lasers are used to estimate the age of sediments.

How can lasers be used to estimate the age of sediments? Scientists bombard sediment layers with lasers. The lasers free electrons from the sediments. Electrons are negatively charged particles that can be trapped in sediments. When the electrons are freed, they give off light. Scientists measure how much light is given off. Older sediments give off more electrons than younger sediments do. Laser dating is used to determine the ages of sediments that are up to 700,000 years old. It can also be used to determine the age of river sediments and glacial deposits.

▲ Figure 4-16 Scientists use lasers to date sediments.

Thinking Critically Why might scientists want to find out the age of glaciers?

4-5 What is the geologic time scale?

INVESTIGATE

Making a Time Line of Your Life
HANDS-ON ACTIVITY

1. List important events that have occurred in your life.
2. Draw a long line across a sheet of paper to represent your life. Break it up into years. You can use a scale of 2 cm for every year.
3. Write each event in the correct year along the time line.

4. Now, divide the time line into parts that describe major periods in your life, such as preschool years, elementary school years, and middle school years.

THINK ABOUT IT: If you had to break up your time line into different groupings or divisions, what might they be?

Objective
Read and interpret the geologic time scale.

Key Term
geologic (jee-uh-LAHJ-ihk) **time scale:** outline of the major divisions in Earth's history

Age of Earth The oldest rocks found on Earth are about 4 billion years old. Moon rocks are older.

Scientists think that Earth and the Moon were formed at about the same time. However, because of the rock cycle, Earth's earliest rocks are gone.

Based on the age of Moon and Earth rocks, scientists think that Earth may be about 4.6 billion years old.

▶ **DESCRIBE:** About how old is Earth?

Outlining Earth's History By studying rocks and fossils, geologists have developed a geologic time scale. The **geologic time scale** outlines the major divisions in Earth's history. It also outlines the kinds of organisms that lived on Earth in the past. The geologic time scale begins when Earth was formed. It continues until the present day.

▶ **DESCRIBE:** What is the geologic time scale?

GEOLOGIC TIME SCALE				
Era	**Period**	**Epoch**	**Approximate Start Date** (millions of years ago)	**Organisms First Appeared**
Cenozoic	Quaternary	Recent	0.025	Modern humans
		Pleistocene	1.75	Mammoths
	Tertiary	Pliocene	14	Large carnivores
		Miocene	26	Many land mammals
		Oligocene	40	Primitive apes
		Eocene	55	Early horses
		Paleocene	65	Primates
Mesozoic	Cretaceous		130	Flowering plants
	Jurassic		180	Dinosaurs
	Triassic		225	Conifers
Paleozoic	Permian		275	Seed plants
	Carboniferous		345	Reptiles
	Devonian		405	Insects, amphibians
	Silurian		435	Fishes
	Ordovician		480	Algae, fungi
	Cambrian		600	Invertebrates
Precambrian			4,600	Bacteria, blue-green bacteria

◀ **Figure 4-17**

Divisions of Geologic Time A year is divided into units called months, weeks, and days. Geologic time is also divided into units. The major unit is an era. Each era in geologic history lasted for millions of years. There are four eras. The eras are divided into periods. The more recent periods are divided into epochs.

The divisions of geologic time are based on important changes that occurred on Earth at these times. Some examples are the extinction of an important group of organisms and afterward the appearance of new categories of animals.

 NAME: What are the divisions of geologic time?

✓ CHECKING CONCEPTS

1. How many eras make up the geologic time scale?
2. How old are the oldest Earth rocks ever found?
3. What does the geologic time scale model?
4. What is the largest unit of geologic time?
5. What is the most recent period of geologic time?

THINKING CRITICALLY

6. INFER: Why are only the most recent periods divided into epochs?
7. HYPOTHESIZE: If the oldest Earth rocks are only 4 billion years old, why do scientists think that Earth is 4.6 billion years old?

BUILDING SCIENCE SKILLS

Modeling Use adding machine tape to make your own time line. Have each centimeter equal 10 million years. Calculate the length of each era in centimeters. Draw lines on the tape to mark each era. Mark each of the events listed below. Add five other events to your time line using Figure 4-17.

- First fossils appeared 3.4 billion years ago.
- First fish appeared 450 million years ago.
- First reptiles appeared 290 million years ago.
- Age of dinosaurs began 200 million years ago.
- First mammals appeared 200 million years ago.
- First birds appeared 150 million years ago.
- First humanlike animals appeared 2 million years ago.
- Last major ice age ended 10,000 years ago.

 Integrating Life Science

TOPICS: extinction, biodiversity

THE DIVERSITY OF LIFE

Earth is teeming with life. However, scientists estimate that for every species existing today, at least 100 others are now extinct.

Earth has changed greatly over its history. Mountains have been built up. Volcanoes have formed. There have been ice ages. The Sun's output has varied over time. Each time a great change has occurred, species that could not adapt died out. Others replaced them. Today, Earth may have up to 100 million species.

▲ **Figure 4-18** An asteroid striking Earth is believed to have led to the extinction of the dinosaurs.

Scientists call this vast variety of organisms biodiversity. Together, the various species keep natural cycles, such as the water and nitrogen cycles, running smoothly. Each species helps balance the ecosystem of which it is a part. For example, some species break down wastes. Others add oxygen to the air. The loss of even a few species can result in the destruction of an ecosystem.

Thinking Critically How do pollution and the spread of civilization threaten biodiversity?

4-6 What are fossil fuels?

Objective
Describe how coal, oil, and natural gas were formed.

Key Term
fossil fuel (FYOO-uhl): natural fuel that was formed from the remains of living things

Fossils as Fuel A fuel is a substance that gives off energy when it is burned. A fuel may be a solid, a liquid, or a gas. **Fossil fuels** are fuels that were formed from fossils.

Coal and natural gas are fossil fuels. The liquid fuel known as petroleum is also a fossil fuel. Most of the energy that heats our homes and runs our appliances comes from fossil fuels.

1 DEFINE: What are the fossil fuels?

▲ **Figure 4-19** During the coal-forming age, much of Earth was covered by huge swamps.

Hydrocarbons Fossil fuels are made up mostly of hydrocarbons. Hydrocarbons are compounds made up of the elements hydrogen and carbon. Hydrocarbons store energy. This energy comes from the sunlight absorbed by plants and microorganisms that lived millions of years ago. When hydrocarbons are burned, they give off this energy as light and heat.

2 IDENTIFY: What two forms of energy are given off when hydrocarbons are burned?

The Formation of Coal Coal is formed in swamps. Swamps are areas of shallow water with a lot of plant life. When the plants in the swamps die, they are covered by water and by sediments such as mud. Bacteria, pressure, and heat slowly cause chemical changes to take place in the plants. After many millions of years, the decaying plant material changes to peat. Peat is the first stage in coal formation. After another long period of time, peat changes into soft coal. Pressure changes soft coal into hard coal. Soft and hard coal are mostly carbon. They give off a lot of heat when they burn.

3 NAME: What are the three basic stages of coal formation?

The Formation of Oil and Natural Gas Geologists think that petroleum, or crude oil, and natural gas were formed from decaying microorganisms. When these microorganisms died, they were covered with sediments that became sedimentary rock.

Like coal, petroleum and natural gas were formed by the actions of bacteria, heat, and pressure. Petroleum moved with water through the cracks and pores in rock. When it reached a rock layer it could not pass through, the mixture of petroleum and water began to collect. Petroleum is usually found in pools that collect in layers of shale or sandstone. The petroleum floats on top of the water.

If natural gas is also present, it is on top of the oil. To get to the oil and natural gas, it is necessary to drill into Earth's crust.

 4 ▶ NAME: What types of ancient organisms formed oil and natural gas?

☑ CHECKING CONCEPTS

1. What compounds are found in fossil fuels?
2. What are three fossil fuels?
3. What three things act on decaying organisms to help form fossil fuels?
4. In what kind of rock layers would you most likely find petroleum and natural gas?

THINKING CRITICALLY

5. INFER: Why are coal, petroleum, and natural gas called fossil fuels?
6. IDENTIFY: What is the source of the energy stored in hydrocarbons?
7. INFER: Why is natural gas found above petroleum in an oil deposit?

INTERPRETING VISUALS

A pictograph is a graph that uses a picturelike symbol to show an idea. Use the pictograph below to do the following exercises.

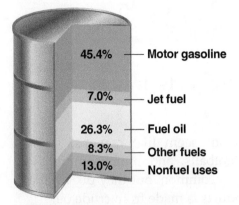

45.4% —— Motor gasoline

7.0% —— Jet fuel

26.3% —— Fuel oil

8.3% —— Other fuels

13.0% —— Nonfuel uses

▲ **Figure 4-20** Uses of Petroleum

8. Place the uses of petroleum in order from greatest use to least use.
9. Give the percentage of petroleum that is used to make all fuels.
10. What total percentage of petroleum fuel goes toward transportation needs?

People in Science

OIL-RIG OPERATOR

An oil-rig operator often works at sea. The drilling structure is a tall steel frame called a jacket. It is built onshore and carried out to sea on a barge. Then, it is anchored to the seafloor. The machines used to extract the oil are on a platform on top of the jacket. The construction crew sets the derrick, which holds the drilling equipment, over the spot where the well is to be drilled.

The workers live on the platform. They may be away from home for up to three weeks at a time. They run the drill, pumps, the power plant, and the control room. The drilling crew changes bits that are dull or cannot penetrate the rock. Most drilling crews have one driller, one or more derrickmen, and several other workers. Many oil-rig workers start out as roustabouts. Roustabouts do the heavy, unskilled labor. Many companies train roustabouts to do more skilled work.

Oil-rig workers must be physically fit. They must also usually take what is called the Basic Offshore Survival and Firefighting training course.

Thinking Critically What kind of labor might roustabouts do?

▲ **Figure 4-21** An oil rig in operation off the coast of California

THE Big IDEA

What products are made from oil?

It might not seem like crayons, guitar strings, footballs, and bubble gum have anything in common, but they do. Each of these products is made from crude oil.

Ancient peoples recognized the value of this natural resource. The Chinese used oil to waterproof their homes. Egyptians wrapped their dead in rags saturated with oil to preserve them. Native Americans added a drop or two of oil to medicines, and ancient Romans applied oil to cuts and wounds. Thanks to technology, today there are more than 500,000 different uses for this natural resource.

The first step in creating these products is separating crude oil into its different parts. This is called fractional distillation and takes place in an oil refinery. Pipes carry raw crude oil from oil wells to the refinery. The crude oil is heated to about 430°C. This causes the liquid to turn into vapor. The vapor is then pumped into a tall tower divided into different levels. Each of these levels is kept at a certain temperature.

As the evaporated crude oil moves through the tower, its substances condense at different temperatures. The heaviest parts condense in the warmer, lower levels of the tower. The lightest parts condense in the cooler, higher levels of the tower. The separated substances are drawn from each level and sent to other locations, where they are used to make many products.

Look at the illustrations on these two pages. Then, follow the directions in the Science Log to learn more about "the big idea." ✦

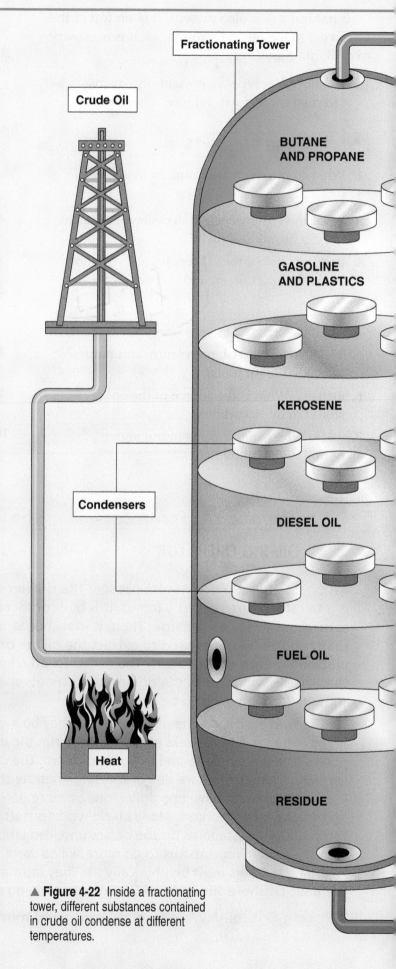

▲ **Figure 4-22** Inside a fractionating tower, different substances contained in crude oil condense at different temperatures.

Butane and Propane

The lightest parts of evaporated crude oil condense in the coolest level of the tower. Butane used in lighters and propane used in barbecue grills are collected here.

Gasoline and Plastics

The gasoline that cars run on comes from substances that condense in this level. Chemicals and plastics used to make clothing, sporting equipment, and telephones start at this level.

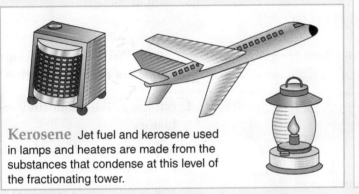

Kerosene Jet fuel and kerosene used in lamps and heaters are made from the substances that condense at this level of the fractionating tower.

Diesel Oil Trucks and trains run on diesel fuel made from substances that condense at this level.

Fuel Oil Heating oil is used to keep many homes warm. Certain fuels power ships and factories. All are made from substances that condense at this level.

Residue Lubricants, paraffin, and asphalt are made from the residues that condense in the lowest level of the tower.

WRITING ACTIVITY

Science Log

List all of the crude oil products that you have used this week. Name at least five. Then, write several paragraphs entitled "A Day Without Oil Products." Describe in these paragraphs what your day would be like without these items. Start your search for information using www.conceptsandchallenges.com.

Chapter Summary

Lesson 4-1

- **Fossils** are the remains or traces of organisms that lived many years ago.
- Fossils form in sedimentary rock. Members of some extinct species have been preserved in frozen soil or ice.
- The bones of many animals trapped in tar pits were preserved.
- Some insects and plant parts have been perfectly preserved in **amber.**

Lesson 4-2

- Fossils show that many kinds of organisms lived at different times in Earth's history. They show that some living things have changed over millions of years. They also show that Earth's climate and surface have changed over million of years.

Lesson 4-3

- Scientists use the **law of superposition** to tell the **relative age** of a rock layer.
- **Index fossils** can be used to help find the relative age of rock layers in the same area or from two different parts of the world.

Lesson 4-4

- The specific age of a rock or a fossil is called its **absolute age.**
- Radioactive elements are like natural clocks. The **half-life** of radioactive elements can be used to find the absolute age of a rock or fossil.
- Carbon-14 is used to find the absolute age of the remains of living things.

Lesson 4-5

- Some scientists estimate that Earth is more than 4.6 billion years old.
- The **geologic time scale** is a record of the major divisions in Earth's history.
- The major divisions of geologic time are eras, periods, and epochs.

Lesson 4-6

- Petroleum, coal, and natural gas are **fossil fuels.**
- When hydrocarbons are burned, they give off energy as light and heat.

Key Term Challenges

absolute age (p. 98)
amber (p. 90)
cast (p. 90)
coprolite (p. 94)
fossil (p. 90)
fossil fuel (p. 102)
gastrolith (p. 94)

geologic time scale (p. 100)
half-life (p. 98)
index fossil (p. 96)
law of superposition (p. 96)
mold (p. 90)
relative age (p. 96)

MATCHING **Write the Key Term from above that best matches each description.**

1. outline of the major divisions in Earth's history

2. imprint in a rock that has the shape of an extinct organism

3. age of an object compared to the age of another object

4. specific age of a rock or fossil

5. length of time it takes for one-half the amount of a radioactive element to change into another element

FILL IN **Write the Key Term from above that best completes each statement.**

6. Oil, coal, and natural gas are three kinds of _____.

7. A mold that has been filled with sediments forms a _____.

8. The bodies of entire insects have been found preserved in hardened tree sap called _____.

9. The traces or remains of living things that lived long ago are called _____.

10. A trilobite can be used as an _____.

11. A _____ was a stone some ancient animals swallowed to help grind up their food.

12. Scientists use the _____ to tell the relative age of rocks and fossils.

Content Challenges TEST PREP

MULTIPLE CHOICE Write the letter of the term or phrase that best completes each statement.

1. A species that once lived on Earth but is no longer found alive is called
   a. a fossil.
   b. an imprint.
   c. a cast.
   d. extinct.

2. Most fossils are found in
   a. metamorphic rock.
   b. sedimentary rock.
   c. mud.
   d. igneous rock.

3. Footprints are a kind of fossil called
   a. a mold.
   b. a cast.
   c. an imprint.
   d. amber.

4. The bodies of woolly mammoths and woolly rhinoceroses have been found preserved in
   a. amber.
   b. sedimentary rocks.
   c. ice.
   d. petrified forests.

5. Three ways in which the entire bodies of organisms are preserved are
   a. ice, tar, and amber.
   b. ice, molds, and casts.
   c. tar, molds, and casts.
   d. molds, petrified wood, and amber.

6. Graptolites and trilobites are two kinds of
   a. radioactive elements.
   b. molds.
   c. casts.
   d. index fossils.

7. Peat is the first stage in the formation of
   a. natural gas.
   b. tar.
   c. coal.
   d. petroleum.

8. The law of superposition states that each undisturbed rock layer is older than the one
   a. beside it.
   b. above it.
   c. below it.
   d. to its left.

9. Fossils show how Earth's climate and topography have
   a. changed over time.
   b. stayed about the same over time.
   c. improved over time.
   d. worsened over time.

TRUE/FALSE Write *true* if the statement is true. If the statement is false, change the underlined term to make the statement true.

10. Shells and <u>nails</u> are often the only parts of organisms that are preserved.

11. Elephantlike animals called <u>saber-toothed cats</u> have been discovered preserved in ice.

12. The LaBrea tar pits are located in southern <u>California</u>.

13. The bodies of entire insects have been found preserved in <u>amber</u>.

14. When fossil fuels are burned, they give off energy in the forms of heat and <u>electricity</u>.

15. Fossil fuels are formed when <u>bacteria</u>, heat, and pressure act on decaying plants and animals.

16. Fossils of alligatorlike animals found in Canada indicate that the climate of Canada was <u>always cold</u>.

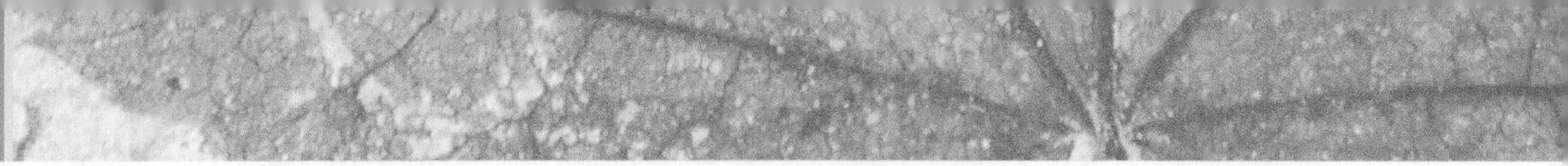

Concept Challenges TEST PREP

WRITTEN RESPONSE **Answer each of the following questions in complete sentences.**

1. INFER: Suppose you find fossils of clams in rock high on a mountain. What can you infer about the mountain?

2. DESCRIBE: How is U-238 used for the specific dating of rocks?

3. DESCRIBE: What is the geologic time scale? Give examples in your explanation.

4. EXPLAIN: Why is carbon-14 not useful for dating rocks that are more than 50,000 years old?

5. ANALYZE: What method would you use to date a sedimentary rock that you think is about 1 million years old? Why?

INTERPRETING VISUALS **Use Figure 4-23 to answer the following questions.**

6. What is the name of the most recent era in geologic time?

7. How long ago did dinosaurs roam Earth's surface?

8. During which period did conifers such as pine trees first appear?

9. During which period did snakes first appear?

10. Which era lasted the longest?

GEOLOGIC TIME SCALE				
Era	**Period**	**Epoch**	**Approximate Start Date** (millions of years ago)	**Organisms First Appeared**
Cenozoic	Quaternary	Recent	0.025	Modern humans
		Pleistocene	1.75	Mammoths
	Tertiary	Pliocene	14	Large carnivores
		Miocene	26	Many land mammals
		Oligocene	40	Primitive apes
		Eocene	55	Early horses
		Paleocene	65	Primates
Mesozoic	Cretaceous		130	Flowering plants
	Jurassic		180	Dinosaurs
	Triassic		225	Conifers
Paleozoic	Permian		275	Seed plants
	Carboniferous		345	Reptiles
	Devonian		405	Insects, amphibians
	Silurian		435	Fishes
	Ordovician	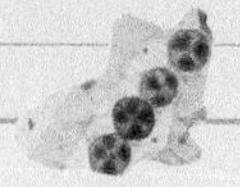	480	Algae, fungi
	Cambrian		600	Invertebrates
Precambrian			4,600	Bacteria, blue-green bacteria

▲ Figure 4-23

Chapter 5 The Changing Landscape

▲ **Figure 5-1** Mount Fuji in Japan

According to legend, the volcano on Mount Fuji was formed in 286 B.C. by an earthquake. It appears to be a single volcano. However, it is actually made up of three separate volcanoes: Komitake, Ko Fuji, and Shin Fuji. The most recent is Shin Fuji ("New Fuji"). Shin Fuji first became active about 10,000 years ago. It still smolders and erupts from time to time.

▶Mount Fuji is called a volcanic cone. Why do you think it is called this?

Contents

5-1 What processes change Earth's crust?

Objective

Compare and contrast the processes of folding and faulting in Earth's crust.

Key Terms

anticline (AN-tih-klyn): upward fold

syncline (SIHN-klyn): downward fold

fracture (FRAK-chuhr): break in a rock

fault: break in Earth's crust along which movement occurs

Folding Earth's surface is always changing. Some changes occur very suddenly. Others take hundreds or thousands of years, or even longer. Over millions of years, pressure in Earth's crust can cause rock layers to bend, curve, and wrinkle. This is called folding. Folding occurs when rock layers are squeezed from the sides. The rocks may crack under the pressure. However, the layers stay together.

Folds in rock look like waves. An upward fold is called an **anticline.** A downward fold is called a **syncline.** Some folds are small enough to be seen in a single rock. Others are very large. You often see anticlines and synclines along roads cut through rock.

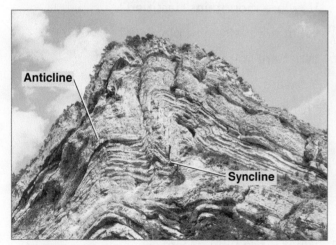

▲ **Figure 5-2** Rock layers can fold upward or downward.

▶ DEFINE: What is a fold?

Faulting Pressure deep inside Earth can also break rocks. A break in a rock is called a **fracture.** When movement of rock takes place along a fracture, it is called a **fault.** Four common kinds of faults are shown in Figure 5-3.

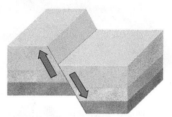

NORMAL FAULT
A normal fault is a fault along which the movement is vertical.

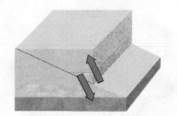

REVERSE FAULT
A reverse fault is a fault in which the crust above the fault plane rises in relation to the crust below.

STRIKE-SLIP FAULT
A strike-slip fault is a fault along which the movement is horizontal.

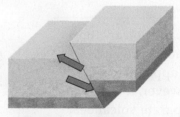

THRUST FAULT
A thrust fault is a low-angle reverse fault.

▲ **Figure 5-3** Common types of faults

Faulting causes rocks to move up and down or side to side a tiny distance. Each time movement occurs along a fault, the pressure between rock layers along the fault eases. Then, the pressure builds up again. Movement occurs again when this pressure is released.

 DESCRIBE: What is a strike-slip fault?

110

San Andreas Fault There is a huge strike-slip fault that runs through a large part of California. This fault is called the San Andreas Fault. The San Andreas Fault extends from the Gulf of California through San Francisco Bay. The fault reaches more than 30 km down into Earth's crust.

▲ **Figure 5-4** The San Andreas Fault is a strike-slip fault.

Movement along this fault caused the great San Francisco Earthquake of 1906. In 1989, another earthquake hit Santa Cruz and the Bay area. In 1994, an earthquake in the Northridge area put further stress on the San Andreas Fault and other faults nearby. Areas with networks of faults, such as southern California, have many earthquakes.

3 INFER: Why would a network of faults have many earthquakes?

 **CHECKING CONCEPTS**

1. What is a fracture?
2. Which way does a syncline fold?
3. What do rock layers that change shape but do not break form?
4. What do rock layers that break but do not move form?
5. What do rock layers that break and move form?

 THINKING CRITICALLY

6. INFER: What slowly changes Earth's crust?
7. INFER: What suddenly changes Earth's crust?

INTERPRETING VISUALS

Use Figure 5-3 to answer the following questions.

8. IDENTIFY: Along which fault is the movement horizontal?
9. COMPARE/CONTRAST: How is the movement along a reverse fault similar to and different from that along a normal fault?
10. INFER: Why do you think the thrust fault was given its name?

 Hands-On Activity

MODELING THE FOLDING OF ROCK LAYERS

You will need 4 different colors of modeling clay, a plastic knife, a metric ruler, and a sheet of wax paper 30 cm long.

1. Flatten each color of clay into a strip about 9 cm wide and 24 cm long. Each strip should be about 1 cm thick.
2. Using the plastic knife, trim the clay strips so that they form a rectangle 8 cm × 23 cm.
3. Stack the four strips of clay on the sheet of wax paper.
4. Push both ends of the stacked clay layers toward the center.
5. Sketch the folded layers. Label the layers by color.
6. Label the anticlines and synclines on your drawing.

▲ **STEP 4** Push both ends of the clay together.

Practicing Your Skills

7. MODEL: What do the clay layers represent?
8. ANALYZE: What caused the clay layers to fold?
9. OBSERVE: Did any cracks appear in the clay layers? If so, what are they called?

5-2 What are mountains?

Objective

Identify the world's major mountain systems.

Key Terms

landform: physical feature on Earth's solid surface

elevation (el-uh-VAY-shuhn): height of a point on Earth above or below sea level

summit: highest point on a mountaintop

Defining Mountains A mountain is a landform that reaches a high elevation. A **landform** is any physical feature on Earth's solid surface. **Elevation** is the height of a point on Earth above or below sea level. For a hill or a mound of land to be classified as a mountain, its **summit**, or highest point, must be more than a few hundred meters above the land around it.

 DEFINE: What is a mountain?

Mountain Systems Most mountains do not stand alone. They are part of a group of mountains. A group of mountains with the same general shape and structure is called a mountain range. For example, Mount St. Helens in Washington State is part of the Cascade mountain range. Groups of mountain ranges form into what are called mountain systems.

In the eastern part of the United States is the Appalachian mountain system. The Blue Ridge and Great Smoky mountain ranges are part of the Appalachian system.

▲ **Figure 5-5** The Blue Ridge Mountains are in the Appalachian mountain system.

Some scientists break up mountain systems into two major groups, called belts. These belts, shown in Figure 5-6, are called the Eurasian-Melanesian belt and the Circum-Pacific belt.

 OBSERVE: Where are the major mountain belts?

Mountain Development Over millions of years, mountains change and take on different forms. Mountains change as the crust is either built up or worn away by various processes. This process is called mountain development.

Some mountains have steep slopes. The peaks are sharp and jagged. The valleys are narrow. These mountains are often called "young" because they are formed from new crust.

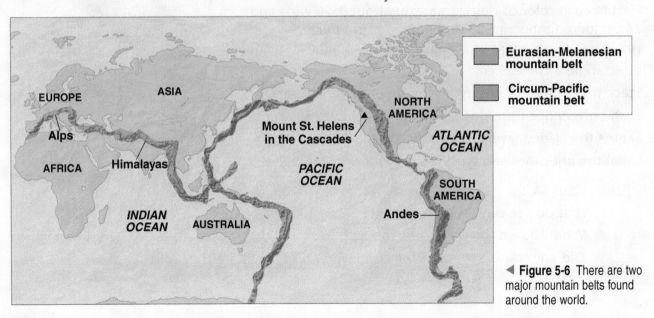

Eurasian-Melanesian mountain belt

Circum-Pacific mountain belt

EUROPE
ASIA
Alps
AFRICA
Himalayas
Mount St. Helens in the Cascades
NORTH AMERICA
ATLANTIC OCEAN
PACIFIC OCEAN
INDIAN OCEAN
AUSTRALIA
SOUTH AMERICA
Andes

◀ **Figure 5-6** There are two major mountain belts found around the world.

As time passes, a mountain's peak is worn down by weather conditions. These make the peak more rounded. The slopes become less steep. Mountains like these are sometimes called "mature" mountains.

Some mountains continue to be worn away for a very long time. No buildup occurs. These "old" mountains are almost flat and have no jagged peaks. They have many rolling hills, and the valleys between these mountains are wide.

 CLASSIFY: The Appalachians have very rounded peaks. Do you think they are young or old?

✔ CHECKING CONCEPTS

1. The highest point of a mountain is its _____.

2. There are narrow valleys between _____ mountains.

3. Mountain systems make up mountain _____.

4. If a mountain contains many rolling hills, the mountain is _____.

5. A mountain's stage depends on the _____ of the mountain.

 ## THINKING CRITICALLY

6. **SEQUENCE:** Place the following terms in order, from smallest to largest: mountain belt, single mountain, mountain range, mountain summit, mountain system.

7. **CLASSIFY:** A mountain has high jagged peaks and steep slopes. Its valleys are narrow. Is the mountain a young mountain or an old mountain? Explain your answer.

8. **INTERPRET A VISUAL:** What are two mountain ranges found in the Eurasian-Melanesian Belt shown in Figure 5-6?

BUILDING SCIENCE SKILLS

Researching and Organizing Mount McKinley, Mount Whitney, Mount Everest, Mont Blanc, Mount Nebo, and Mount Logan are some famous mountains. Find out the height in meters or kilometers of each mountain. Identify the country in which the mountain is located. Also, find out the name of the mountain range in which each mountain is located. Organize the information into a table.

 People in Science

MOUNTAIN EXPLORERS

On May 29, 1953, two mountain climbers reached the top of Mount Everest. They had climbed to 8,848 meters above sea level. Edmund Hillary from New Zealand and Tenzing Norgay, a Sherpa tribesman from Nepal, were the first mountain climbers to reach the summit of Mount Everest. Mount Everest is the highest mountain in the world. Many people had tried before them, but no one had succeeded in climbing to the top. Heavy snow, strong winds, and thin air make climbing the cliffs of Mount Everest very difficult. Sir Edmund's book, *High Adventure*, describes his experiences during the 1953 climb.

▲ **Figure 5-7** Edmund Hillary (left) and Tenzing Norgay pose for pictures right after climbing to the top of Mount Everest.

In 1957, Hillary set forth on an expedition to the South Pole. On January 4, 1958, he reached the South Pole by tractor. In 1977, he led the first jet boat expedition up the Ganges River to find its source. When the boat could go no farther, Hillary climbed the Himalayas to reach the source of the river.

Thinking Critically Why do you think Hillary wanted to climb Mount Everest?

5-3 How are mountains classified?

Objectives
Identify three types of mountains. Describe how they are formed.

Key Terms
folded mountain: mountain formed by the folding of rock layers

dome mountain: mountain formed when upfolds in rocks create a rounded structure that looks like a bowl turned upside down

fault-block mountain: mountain formed when normal faults uplift a block of rock

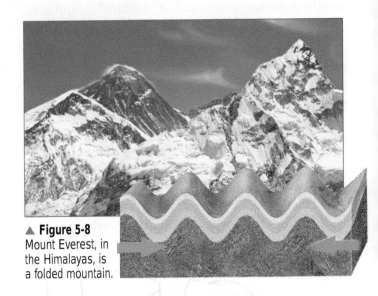

▲ **Figure 5-8**
Mount Everest, in the Himalayas, is a folded mountain.

Classifying Mountains Mountains are classified based on how they are formed. There are three main types of mountains. These are volcanic, folded, and fault-block mountains.

Volcanic mountains are formed from lava or debris, such as ash or rocks, thrown out of a volcano. Mount Fuji, shown in the photo at the beginning of this chapter, is a volcanic mountain. Volcanic mountains are built up from eruptions that occur over thousands or even millions of years. They will be discussed in more detail in Lesson 5-6.

1 EXPLAIN: How are mountains classified?

Folded Mountains When rock layers are subject to certain forces, they can become bent in a process called folding. Mountains formed by the folding of rock layers are called **folded mountains.**

Earth's continents move slowly on top of the upper mantle. Most folded mountains form when the continents collide.

The movements of the continents squeeze rock layers together. Over millions of years, pressure builds up. The rock layers of the crust buckle and fold.

Large upfolds, or anticlines, form folded mountains. The Himalayas in south central Asia and the Urals in Russia are folded mountains. The Appalachian Mountains in the United States are also folded mountains.

When some mountains fold upward they produce a shape that looks like a bowl that has been turned upside down. These mountains are called **dome mountains.**

The rock layers in a dome mountain dip down and out in all directions from a center point. As the top layers of unfolded sedimentary rock are worn away, older igneous or metamorphic rock beneath is exposed. The Black Hills of South Dakota are an example. The upper rock layers of these dome mountains have been worn away unevenly. This has resulted in many separate peaks being formed.

▲ **Figure 5-9**
The Black Hills of South Dakota are dome mountains.

Dome

Magma

2 DESCRIBE: How are folded mountains formed?

Fault-Block Mountains Fractures can form in Earth's crust. These fractures may break the crust into large blocks. Sometimes faulting lifts these large blocks. One side of the fault slips past the crust on the other side. If the blocks are pushed up enough, a mountain is formed. Mountains formed in this way are called **fault-block mountains.**

The Grand Tetons in Wyoming are fault-block mountains. The Sierra Nevada in California are also fault-block mountains.

▲ Figure 5-10
The Sierra Nevada are fault-block mountains.

 LIST: Name two fault-block mountain ranges in the United States.

☑ **CHECKING CONCEPTS**

1. Which type of mountain is usually formed by colliding continents?
2. Which type of mountain is formed by vertical pressure?
3. Which type of mountain is formed by upward thrusts of Earth's crust?

💡 **THINKING CRITICALLY**

4. CLASSIFY: Classify each mountain range listed as dome, folded, or fault-block. Explain your choices.
   a. Appalachian Mountains
   b. Grand Tetons
   c. Himalayas

BUILDING SCIENCE SKILLS

Modeling On a sheet of paper, make a series of drawings to show the formation of a dome mountain. Use arrows to show the movement of magma and pressure. Color your drawings. Use a key to show what the colors mean.

 Real-Life Science

MOUNTAIN CLIMBING

Mountain climbing, or mountaineering, is a sport enjoyed around the world. It can range from simple trail hiking to more difficult rock and ice climbing. Professional climbers prefer folded mountains. These are some of the world's tallest mountains. They feature very rugged and challenging terrains. The Himalayas are folded mountains. They contain all but one of the 14 tallest mountains on Earth.

Fault-block mountains often have high cliffs. This provides climbers with special challenges. Dome and volcanic mountains tend to be easier to climb. However, they attract climbers of all skill levels because of their unique terrains and beautiful scenery.

As with all sports, one must follow some basic safety rules. Climbing gear such as helmets and ropes must be suitable for the climber. A person should never climb alone. A qualified rock climbing instructor should train and supervise all climbing activities.

Thinking Critically Why would dome mountains be easier to climb than other mountains?

▲ Figure 5-11 Special gear is needed for climbing snow-covered mountains.

5-4 What are plains and plateaus?

Objectives
Compare and contrast plains and plateaus. Describe how they form.

Key Terms
plain: large, flat area just above sea level
plateau: large, flat area at a high elevation

Plains Large, flat areas that are just above sea level are called **plains.** There are coastal plains and interior plains. Coastal plains are located in coastal areas. Interior plains are located inland. All plains slope gently over great distances.

▲ Figure 5-12 The Great Plains of the United States are interior plains.

Plains are formed in several ways. One way is for land of uneven elevation to be worn down by weather conditions. The Great Plains of the United States were formed this way.

Another way for plains to form is for material to be deposited in a large body of water. Then, something causes the water level to drop or the land to rise. A flat, dry area of land remains.

▶ NAME: What are the two kinds of plains?

Plateaus **Plateaus** have much higher elevations than plains. Yet, plateaus are also large, flat areas, like plains. Most plateaus are located inland. Plateaus that are near oceans have cliffs that face the ocean.

Many plateaus have canyons. A canyon is a steep-sided valley formed by a river. The Colorado Plateau has many canyons carved out by the Colorado River. This same river also formed the Grand Canyon.

▲ Figure 5-13 The Colorado Plateau was carved out by the Colorado River.

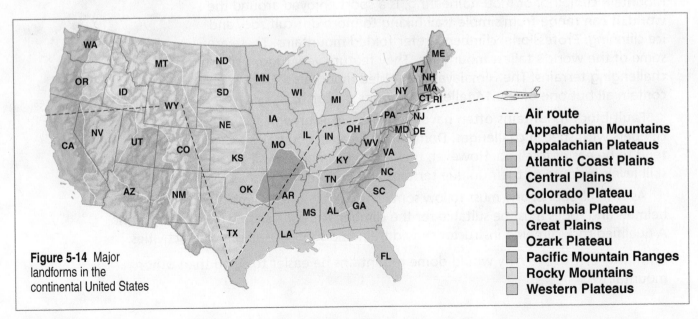

Figure 5-14 Major landforms in the continental United States

--- Air route
Appalachian Mountains
Appalachian Plateaus
Atlantic Coast Plains
Central Plains
Colorado Plateau
Columbia Plateau
Great Plains
Ozark Plateau
Pacific Mountain Ranges
Rocky Mountains
Western Plateaus

The same forces that build mountains form plateaus. Large areas of the crust are pushed upward. Some plateaus are formed by lava pouring out of a volcano or a chain of volcanoes. The lava cools and hardens. This forms a large, raised, flat area. The Columbia Plateau in Washington State was formed in this way.

 DESCRIBE: What is a plateau?

Landform Regions Mountains, plains, and plateaus are the three main kinds of landforms. Landforms make up the regions of the world. Figure 5-14 shows the different landform regions of the United States.

 OBSERVE: In what landform region do you live?

✓ CHECKING CONCEPTS

1. What are the three main kinds of landforms?
2. Which landform has the lowest elevation?
3. What lava plateau is found in the United States?
4. What river formed the Grand Canyon?

THINKING CRITICALLY

Use Figure 5-14 to answer the following questions.

5. COMPARE/CONTRAST: How are plains and plateaus alike and how are they different?
6. SEQUENCE: You are taking an airplane flight across the United States, going from east to west. Your plane will follow the air route shown in the illustration. List the landform regions of the United States in the order that you will pass over them as you make the trip.
7. CLASSIFY: Choose five states. In which landform region or regions is each state located?

BUILDING READING SKILLS

Vocabulary There are many landforms other than the ones talked about so far. Find out where the names of the following landforms come from. Then, tell if and how their names relate to how they are formed: *butte, peneplain, monadnock, mesa.*

 Integrating Life Science

TOPICS: agriculture, biomes

AMERICA'S BREADBASKET

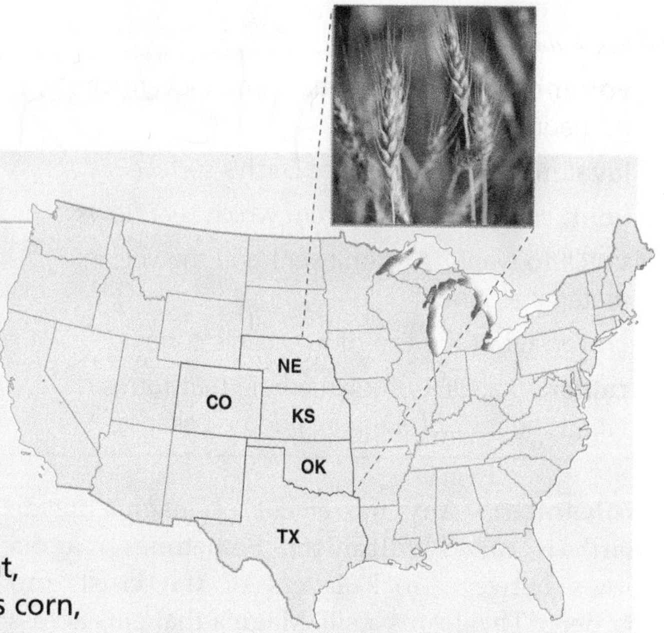

Most of the Great Plains, shown in light green on Figure 5-14, are flat. There are few hills or mountains. The states in the Great Plains have rich soil that is good for growing crops, especially Colorado, Kansas, Nebraska, Oklahoma, and Texas. Many grains used to make bread, such as oat, wheat, and rye, are grown there. Other food crops such as corn, potatoes, soybeans, and alfalfa are also grown there. Beef cattle and sheep graze on the grasslands. Hogs are raised on farms. In the northern part of the breadbasket, dairy farms are more common.

▲ **Figure 5-15**
The five breadbasket states, outlined, grow crops such as wheat (inset).

The Great Plains are grasslands, also known as prairies. Grasslands are usually found in the centers of continents, where rainfall is relatively low. These regions generally have hot summers and very cold winters. Tallgrass prairies have grasses more than a meter high. Many of the grains grown in the Great Plains are tallgrasses.

Thinking Critically Why are plains good grazing areas?

5-5 What are volcanoes?

INVESTIGATE

Modeling a Volcano
HANDS-ON ACTIVITY

1. Take a handful of sand and make a fist over an aluminum pie plate. Dribble a little of it out at a time onto the plate. Do not touch the sand or move the plate.
2. Take another handful of sand and make a fist. Again, dribble the sand out onto the pie plate over the first pile. Keep taking handfuls of sand until you have a good-sized pile in the plate.
3. Note the shape the sand takes as it builds up on the plate.

THINK ABOUT IT: What does the sand represent? How is the shape like that of a typical volcano?

STEP 2

Objective
Describe volcanism.

Key Terms

volcanism (VAHL-kuh-nihz-uhm): movement of magma inside Earth

lava: magma that reaches Earth's surface

vent: volcano opening from which lava flows

volcano (vahl-KAY-noh): vent and the volcanic material around it

crater: pit at the top of a volcanic cone

caldera (kal-DER-uh): large hole that forms when the roof of a magma dome collapses

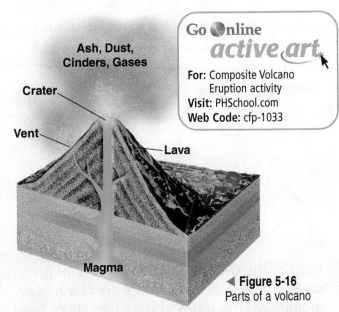

Ash, Dust, Cinders, Gases

Crater

Vent

Lava

Magma

◀ **Figure 5-16**
Parts of a volcano

Go Online
active art

For: Composite Volcano Eruption activity
Visit: PHSchool.com
Web Code: cfp-1033

Volcanism Any movement of magma inside Earth is called **volcanism.** Sometimes magma flows between rock layers of the crust and hardens. This forms a sill. Magma that cuts across rock layers and hardens forms a dike.

Sometimes magma breaks through the crust and flows onto Earth's surface. Then, it is called **lava.** The opening that lava flows through is called a **vent.** Dust, ash, and rock particles are often thrown out of the vent.

The word **volcano** really refers to the volcanic mountain, or cone, that forms from the materials that collect around the vent. It also refers to the vent itself.

1 DEFINE: What is lava?

Craters and Calderas At the top of a volcanic cone there may be a deep pit. This pit, called a **crater,** forms as material is blown out of the volcano's vent.

The top of a volcano may also explode, emptying the vent. This can turn the mountain into a huge, hollow shell. The walls of the crater may fall back into the vent. This partly filled gaping hole is called a **caldera.**

Some calderas fill with water from rain or snow. They form large lakes such as Crater Lake in Oregon. Crater Lake is 9.6 km long and 8 km wide. It is about 600 m deep.

▲ **Figure 5-17** Crater Lake in Oregon is a caldera that filled with water.

 CONTRAST: What is the difference between a crater and a caldera?

The Story of Parícutin In 1943, a farmer in Mexico saw a mountain form! First, the ground started shaking. A few weeks later, cracks, called fissures, appeared and widened. Hot gases came out of the fissures. Soon, lava began to seep out. After several months, a volcanic cone about 400 m high and 5 km wide had formed. The volcano was called Parícutin (pah-ree-koo-TEEN).

 DESCRIBE: What signs were there that a volcano was forming at Parícutin?

 CHECKING CONCEPTS

Explain the differences in each word pair.

1. magma, lava
2. caldera, crater
3. vent, volcano
4. mountain, volcanic cone

THINKING CRITICALLY

5. **INFER:** How are volcanoes like windows to the inside of Earth?

Web InfoSearch

Krakatoa Krakatoa (krah-kah-TOH-uh) is a volcano found near Indonesia. In August 1883, it erupted in a huge volcanic explosion that was heard in Australia, thousands of kilometers away.

SEARCH: Use the Internet to find out more about Krakatoa. How did it change the surrounding islands? Start your search at www.conceptsandchallenges.com. Some key search words are **Krakatoa**, **Krakatoa island**, and **Krakatoa Volcano**.

 ## *Science and Technology*

PREDICTING VOLCANIC ERUPTIONS

On May 18, 1980, Mount St. Helens in Washington State blew its top! The force of the blast destroyed much of the area around the mountain. Scientists knew years before that the volcano in the Cascade Mountains might erupt. However, they could not predict when.

New technologies have now made such predictions possible. Seismometers alert scientists when a volcano rumbles. Tiltmeters and geodimeters measure the tiniest swelling of a volcano, caused by movement of magma. Correlation spectrometers (COSPECS) measure gases such as sulfur and carbon dioxide. These gases are released in increasing amounts before an eruption.

Earth-observation satellites also help in predicting volcanic eruptions. Instruments on the satellites monitor Earth's surface temperature. This data can alert scientists to any volcanic changes that may signal trouble.

Thinking Critically Why is it important to predict volcanic eruptions?

▲ **Figure 5-18** Mount St. Helens erupted in 1980.

5-6 How are volcanoes classified?

Objective
Identify and describe the three kinds of volcanic cones.

Key Terms
shield cone: volcanic cone made up of layers of hardened lava

cinder cone: volcanic cone made up of rock particles, dust, and ash

composite (kuhm-PAHZ-iht) **cone:** volcanic cone made up of alternating layers of lava and rock particles

Classifying by Eruption Volcanic eruptions may be classified as quiet or explosive. During a quiet eruption, lava flows freely through a vent or a fissure. Explosive eruptions shoot rocks, lava, gases, ash, and dust high into the air. Different kinds of volcanic eruptions form different types of volcanic cones. Volcanic mountains are really just large volcanic cones.

1 NAME: What are the two basic kinds of volcanic eruptions?

Shield Cones A **shield cone** is a type of volcano, or volcanic cone. It is made up of layers of hardened lava. A shield cone forms from quiet eruptions. Lava flows over a large area and hardens.

Layers of lava build up to form the cone. The cone has a wide base. The sides of the cone have gentle slopes.

Mauna Loa in the Hawaiian Islands is one of the largest shield cone volcanoes in the world. It is more than 4 km above sea level.

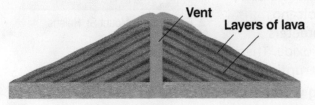
▲ **Figure 5-19** Shield cone volcano

2 DESCRIBE: How does a shield cone form?

Cinder Cones Explosive eruptions form **cinder cones.** Dust, ash, and rock particles are thrown out of the vent and settle to form the cone. Cinder cone volcanoes have steep sides and narrow bases. The rock particles are loose and roll down the slope. Parícutin is a cinder cone volcano.

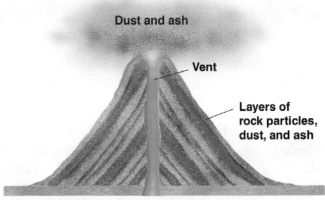
▲ **Figure 5-20** Cinder cone volcano

3 DESCRIBE: How does a cinder cone form?

Composite Cones A **composite cone** is made up of layers of lava and rock particles. It is formed from a series of quiet and explosive eruptions. A quiet eruption results in the lava forming a wide base. An explosive eruption adds a layer of dust, ash, and rock particles. Then, another quiet eruption adds more lava. Eventually, a very high, wide volcanic cone with steep sides is formed. Mount St. Helens and Mount Hood, in Oregon, are composite cones.

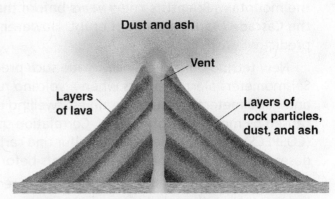
▲ **Figure 5-21** Composite cone volcano

4 INFER: How could you tell what kind of eruption formed a layer of a composite cone?

Volcanoes in Space Io is a bright red and yellow moon of Jupiter. Scientists think Io's color is caused by volcanic action. Io is the first moon or body other than Earth on which scientists have seen active volcanoes. The volcanoes on Io are very powerful. They shoot out many metric tons of material high into Io's atmosphere each month.

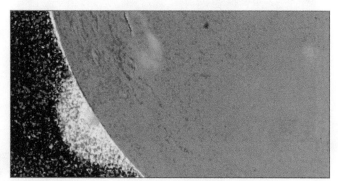

▲ **Figure 5-22** Red-hot gases shoot out from this volcanic eruption on Io.

 INFER: What types of cones do you think Io's volcanoes are forming?

✓ CHECKING CONCEPTS

1. Cinder cones are formed by _____ eruptions.
2. There are _____ kinds of volcanic cones.
3. Volcanic cones with gentle slopes and wide bases are _____ cones.
4. Shield cones are formed by _____ eruptions.

💡 THINKING CRITICALLY

5. **SEQUENCE:** Place these volcanic cones in order from steepest to flattest: shield, cinder, and composite.
6. **PREDICT:** What type of eruption do you think each of these volcanoes might have in the future: Mauna Loa, Mount Hood, and Parícutin?

Web InfoSearch

Volcanoes of the World Both active and inactive volcanoes can be found in many places around the world.

SEARCH: Use the Internet to make a list of five volcanoes and find out about each of them. Are they active or inactive? Have they erupted in recent years? Start your search at www.conceptsandchallenges.com. Some key search words are **volcano, Ring of Fire,** and **volcano observatory.**

 Hands-On Activity

MODELING VOLCANIC CONES

You will need a lab apron, goggles, crushed cereal flakes, 2 paper plates, a metric ruler, plaster of Paris, a measuring cup, and a teaspoon.

1. In the measuring cup, mix 3 teaspoons of plaster of Paris with about 75 mL of water. Be sure the mixture is not too runny.
2. Hold the measuring cup about 15 cm over a paper plate. Pour the plaster of Paris slowly onto the plate. Let it harden.
3. Clean the cup. Fill it halfway with crushed cereal flakes. Hold it about 15 cm above the second paper plate. Slowly pour the cereal onto the plate.

▲ **STEP 3** Slowly pour the cereal onto the plate.

Practicing Your Skills

4. **INFER: a.** What does the plaster of Paris represent? **b.** What does the cereal represent?
5. **MEASURE:** What is the width of each base?
6. **ANALYZE:** Which kind of volcanic cone does each model represent? Explain.

THE Big IDEA

How do volcanic eruptions affect ecosystems?

Ecosystems are made up of living and nonliving things in balance with each other. A volcanic eruption may disrupt that balance. Gases with temperatures of more than 1,000°C shoot into the air. Ash released by the eruption forms thick clouds that can block out sunlight. Huge chunks of rock are hurled onto the surrounding land. Many plants and animals are killed. Even the soil and water can be damaged. Hundreds of years may pass before the ecosystem returns to its former state.

On May 18, 1980, Mount St. Helens in Washington State erupted. Nearly 7,000 land animals were killed in the blast. Millions of fish died when the ash and dust settled in streams and lakes. The number of trees blown down by the eruption would have provided enough wood to build 300,000 homes.

By 1982, life had begun returning to the area. Ecological succession had started. Succession is the often predictable series of changes an environment undergoes over time. Pioneer plants such as mosses and lichens began growing on bare rocks. Wind and birds deposited seeds that soon sprouted. A few years later, larger plants began to grow. Animals began returning to the area. Ecologists studied the changes. From them, we have learned more about how ecosystems and volcanoes interact with each other.

Look at the illustrations that appear on these two pages. Then, follow the directions in the Science Log to learn more about "the big idea."◆

Ecosystem Thrives

In early 1980, Mount St. Helens is a thriving ecosystem. The volcano has been dormant since 1857. However, later that year, it shows signs of erupting. Magma begins pushing up inside the mountain. This causes the north face of the mountain to bulge out.

Volcano Erupts

On May 18, 1980, an earthquake causes a landslide on Mount St. Helens. This triggers the eruption. Ash and steam rush out of the volcano at speeds of up to 1,000 km/h. The blast kills 57 people.

Ecosystem Destroyed

For at least a month after the explosion, the ecosystem is stripped of most of its life forms. The blast damages the land and kills wildlife for about 200 sq km around. A larger area is covered by dust and ash. The height of the mountain is decreased by about 400 m.

WRITING ACTIVITY

Science Log

Find out about the current conditions at Mount St. Helens, Mount Pinatubo, or another volcano of your choice. Write a brief news article about it. Compare conditions today to what conditions were like just after an eruption. You can start your search for information about volcanoes at www.conceptsandchallenges.com.

Ecosystem Thrives Again

By the summer of 1987, much of the area near Mount St. Helens is coming back to life. A new ecosystem is developing. It is similar to but also different from the one that was there before. Here, we see Indian paintbrush and purple wildflowers blooming on recovering slopes near the mountain.

▲ **Figure 5-23**
Mount St. Helens erupting

Life Returns

By fall of 1982, life starts returning to the area in the form of pioneering plants, such as moss. Pioneer plants are also called bryophytes. Their root-like rhizoids help break down rocks to form soil. As the plants die and decay, they add nutrients to the soil. This helps other plants to grow.

5-7 What are earthquakes?

Objectives

Explain what causes earthquakes. Describe what happens during an earthquake.

Key Terms

earthquake: sudden, strong movement of Earth's crust

focus (FOH-kuhs)**:** point beneath Earth's surface where an earthquake starts

epicenter (EHP-ih-sehnt-uhr)**:** place on Earth's surface directly above the focus

seismic (SYZ-mihk) **wave:** earthquake wave

seismograph (SYZ-muh-graf)**:** instrument that detects and measures earthquakes

Tremors and Shakes Earth's crust is always moving. However, most of the movements are so small that you do not even feel them. Movements of the crust that you may or may not feel are called tremors. There may be more than six million tremors each year. Sudden, strong, shaking movements of Earth's crust are called **earthquakes.** Earthquakes can cause a lot of damage.

▶ DEFINE: What is an earthquake?

Focus and Epicenter Earthquakes begin deep inside Earth's crust. The point beneath Earth's surface where an earthquake starts is called the **focus.** The place on Earth's surface that is directly above the focus is called the **epicenter.** The surface of Earth shakes the hardest at the epicenter.

▶ DEFINE: What is the focus of an earthquake?

Cause of Earthquakes Earthquakes are associated with faulting. Usually, the rocks on both sides of a fault are squeezed together very tightly. However, they have no place to go. Geologists say that the fault is "locked." The pressure on the rocks increases. Eventually, the rocks break at their weakest point. Rocks first slip and move near the focus. As the rocks slip, they release energy in the form of waves, or vibrations. These vibrations are called **seismic waves,** or earthquake waves.

Seismic waves travel out from the focus in all directions. Imagine throwing a pebble into a pond. At the point where the pebble hits the water, waves move outward in all directions. Earthquake waves move out from the focus in the same way.

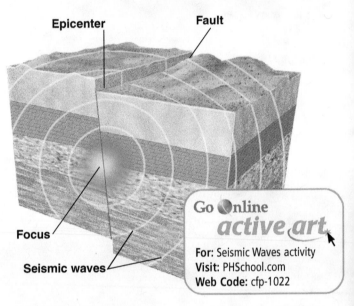

Epicenter

Fault

Focus

Seismic waves

Go **Online**
active.art

For: Seismic Waves activity
Visit: PHSchool.com
Web Code: cfp-1022

▲ **Figure 5-24** Seismic waves travel from the focus in all directions.

▶ NAME: What is the main cause of earthquakes?

Measuring Earthquakes A **seismograph** is an instrument that detects and measures earthquakes. A seismograph can even measure very small tremors that most people cannot feel. It records the movements in Earth's crust on a sheet of paper. This record is called a seismogram. The seismogram has wavy lines. The higher the wavy lines are on the seismogram, the stronger the earthquake.

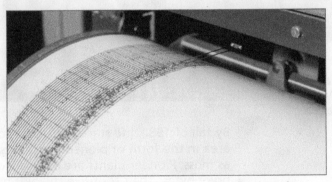

▲ **Figure 5-25** A seismograph records earthquake strength.

▶ DESCRIBE: What is a seismograph?

1. What are small, often unfelt shifts of Earth's crust called?

2. What are strong, shaking movements of Earth's crust called?

3. Where does the ground shake the hardest during an earthquake?

4. How do the vibrations known as seismic waves travel?

5. What internal process causes most earthquakes?

THINKING CRITICALLY

Explain the difference between the words in each of the following pairs.

6. focus, epicenter

7. earthquake, tremor

8. seismograph, seismogram

INTERPRETING VISUALS

Use Figure 5-26 below to answer the following questions.

9. IDENTIFY: What are diagrams A and B called?

10. ANALYZE: Which shows the stronger earthquake?

A

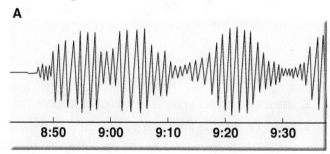

B

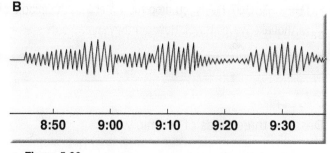

▲ Figure 5-26

People in Science

SEISMOLOGIST

The study of earthquakes is a specialty in the field of Earth science. This specialty is called seismology. Earthquake scientists are known as seismologists.

Seismologists study areas of Earth's surface where earthquakes tend to occur. After an earthquake, seismologists will study the ground along the faults. When an earthquake occurred near San Francisco, California, in 1989, seismologists studied the San Andreas Fault. They wanted to learn more about how Earth's crust moves along the fault.

▲ **Figure 5-27** A seismologist checks a seismogram.

Seismologists collect a lot of data about earthquakes. They take measurements and examine the damage caused by earthquakes. They analyze seismograms, which are records of the movement of Earth during an earthquake. Using the data, seismologists can try to predict where earthquakes will most likely happen. They may even someday be able to find ways to prevent earthquakes.

Thinking Critically What can seismologists learn from studying the damage caused by an earthquake?

5-8 What are the different kinds of seismic waves?

Modeling How Seismic Waves Move
HANDS-ON ACTIVITY

1. Fill a shallow pan or pie plate with water. You may also use a white plastic tub or a plastic foam bowl that has a rim.
2. Use an eyedropper to add a few drops of water to the center of the pan.
3. Watch carefully for the waves on the bottom of the plate. You will more easily see the shadows of the waves on the bottom than the waves themselves.

STEP 2

THINK ABOUT IT: If you drop the water into the middle of the pan, the waves will spread out the way certain earthquake waves travel. How did they spread out?

Objective
Describe three kinds of seismic waves.

Key Terms
P-wave: fastest earthquake wave

S-wave: second earthquake wave to be recorded at a seismograph station

L-wave: surface wave

Primary Waves The fastest-moving seismic waves are primary waves, or **P-waves.** P-waves are push-pull waves. They cause the particles in materials to move back and forth in place. The wave itself moves out from the focus. The particles move together and apart along the direction of the wave. P-waves move through solids, liquids, and gases.

▶ 1 DESCRIBE: What are P-waves like?

Secondary Waves The second waves that are recorded by a seismograph are called secondary waves, or **S-waves.** S-waves move more slowly than P-waves. S-waves travel through solids only. S-waves cause the particles in materials to move from side to side. The particles move at right angles to the direction in which the waves are traveling.

▶ 2 COMPARE: Which move faster, P-waves or S-waves?

Surface Waves Surface waves are also called long waves, or **L-waves.** L-waves are the slowest-moving waves. They are the last waves to be recorded. L-waves can travel through solids, causing Earth's surface to rise and fall like ocean waves. They cause great damage by bending and twisting Earth's surface.

▶ 3 NAME: What is another name for L-waves?

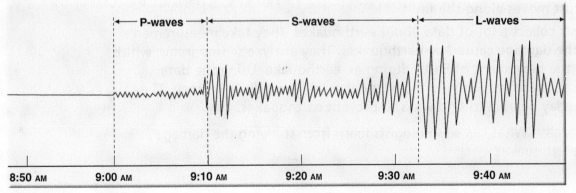

◀ **Figure 5-28**
The different types of earthquake waves are recorded on a seismogram.

Studying Earthquake Waves A seismogram tells scientists a great deal about earthquakes. For example, it can indicate how far away the epicenter of an earthquake is and the force of the earthquake.

Look at the seismogram in Figure 5-28. When did the first P-wave arrive? The time shows 9:00 AM When did the first S-wave arrive? It arrived at 9:10 AM There was a 10-minute difference between the arrival times of the P-waves and the S-waves. Using this time difference, called an S-P interval, scientists can tell how far the epicenter is from the seismograph. Figure 5-29 shows how these intervals change depending on distance.

S-P INTERVALS AND DISTANCE	
S-P Interval	Distance From Epicenter
1 min	700 km
2 min	1,200 km
3 min	1,800 km
4 min	2,500 km
5 min	3,400 km

▲ **Figure 5-29**

 DESCRIBE: What two things can a seismogram indicate?

Finding the Epicenter To find the epicenter, seismograms from three stations are needed. Look at Figure 5-30. A red circle has been drawn on the map around each station.

Each station is at the center of its circle. The diameter of the circle is based on the travel time measured. There is only one point where all three circles cross. The epicenter is near this point.

 OBSERVE: Where is the epicenter of the earthquake shown on the map?

✔ **CHECKING CONCEPTS**

1. There are _____ kinds of seismic waves.
2. The slowest-moving waves are _____.

💡 **THINKING CRITICALLY**

3. DESCRIBE: Why are P-waves called push-pull waves?
4. ANALYZE: Why do you think surface waves are also called long waves?

INTERPRETING VISUALS

Use Figure 5-29 to answer the following question.

5. ANALYZE: If the difference in travel time of P-waves and S-waves is 4 minutes, how far from the epicenter is the seismograph station that recorded it?

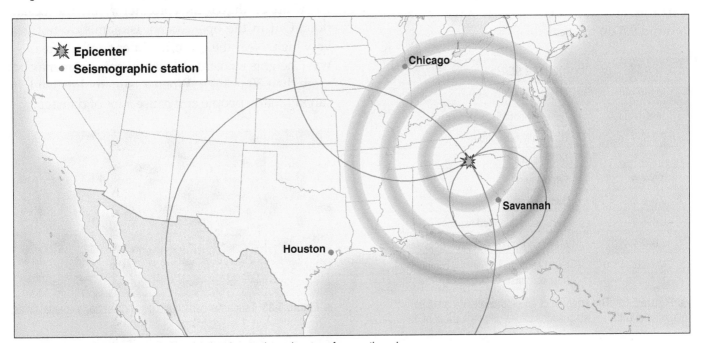

▲ **Figure 5-30** Seismograms help scientists locate the epicenter of an earthquake.

How do earthquakes cause damage?

Objective

Recognize the power of earthquakes and the damage they can cause.

Key Terms

Richter (RIHK-tuhr) **scale:** scale that measures the energy released by an earthquake

tsunami (tsoo-NAH-mee): large ocean wave caused by an earthquake

The Richter Scale In 1935, a geologist named Charles Richter developed a scale to measure the energy released by earthquakes. The **Richter scale** shows an earthquake's relative strength, or magnitude. On the Richter scale, an earthquake is given a number, usually between 1 and 9. The stronger the earthquake, the higher the number. For each increase in number, the earthquake is said to release ten times more energy.

An earthquake measuring 7 or more on the Richter scale can cause a great deal of damage. Earthquakes that measure 2.5 or less on the Richter scale are usually not felt by people. The largest earthquakes recorded so far have measured around 9.5 on the scale.

RICHTER SCALE	
Magnitude	**Effects Near Epicenter**
Less than 2.0	Generally not felt but recorded
2.0–2.9	Potentially perceptible
3.0–3.9	Felt by some
4.0–4.9	Felt by most
5.0–5.9	Damaging shocks
6.0–6.9	Destructive in settled regions
7.0–7.9	Major earthquakes; inflict serious damage
More than 8.0	Great earthquakes; destroy communities near epicenter

▲ **Figure 5-31** The strength of an earthquake is called its magnitude. Different magnitudes cause different levels of damage.

▶ **EXPLAIN:** What is the Richter scale?

Earthquake Damage Many new buildings are built to be "earthquake-proof." This means they are not likely to collapse during an earthquake. Older buildings, however, may be destroyed completely. Tall buildings might sway or even topple over. Earthquakes can also damage electrical lines, telephone lines, and water pipes. Explosions and fires are caused by broken electric and gas lines.

▲ **Figure 5-32** Earthquakes can destroy homes and buckle roads.

▶ **EXPLAIN:** What is meant by "earthquake-proof"?

Tsunamis A large ocean wave that is caused by an earthquake is called a **tsunami.** A tsunami forms when an earthquake's epicenter is on the ocean floor. Out in the open ocean, tsunamis do not get very high. Near the shore, as water depth decreases, wave heights increase. A tsunami near shore may be more than 30 m high. When a tsunami hits land, it can kill many people and cause a lot of damage.

▲ **Figure 5-33** Tsunamis can cause great damage to coastal cities.

▶ **DESCRIBE:** What is a tsunami?

Predicting Earthquakes Scientists use past earthquakes to help predict future earthquakes. Small movements in Earth's crust are a signal that an earthquake may soon occur. Scientists look at the ground in the area to see if it has moved up or down. Laser field stations record the smallest movements along faults. Lasers are very strong, focused light beams. The laser beam is aimed at a reflector. By measuring the time it takes the beam to hit the reflector and come back, scientists can find out if there has been any movement along a fault. Using past earthquake information, scientists have developed a seismic risk map. The map shows where earthquakes may occur and the kind of damage they may cause.

 INFER: Why is it helpful to be able to predict an earthquake?

CHECKING CONCEPTS

1. A strong earthquake on the Richter scale measures _____ or more.

2. Earthquakes less than _____ on the Richter scale are usually not felt.

3. Buildings built to stand during an earthquake are called _____.

4. A map that shows where an earthquake may happen is called a _____ map.

THINKING CRITICALLY

5. SEQUENCE: Place the following earthquakes in order from weakest to strongest on the Richter scale.

   a. San Francisco, California, 1906, 8.3
   b. Santa Cruz, California, 1989, 7.0
   c. Mexico City, Mexico, 1985, 8.1
   d. New York, New York, 1984, 5.0
   e. Tokyo, Japan, 1923, 8.3
   f. Sumatra, Indonesia, 1994, 7.2

BUILDING SCIENCE SKILLS

Researching The Mercalli scale is also used to measure earthquakes. Find out about the Mercalli scale. Make a poster that shows the Mercalli scale. How does this scale measure earthquakes? How is it different from the Richter scale?

 Real-Life Science

EARTHQUAKE SAFETY

☑ **Earthquake Checklist**

BEFORE: Be prepared
☐ 1. Always have a supply of ready-to-eat canned food and bottled water on hand.
☐ 2. Have a portable radio and extra batteries also on hand.
☐ 3. Learn how to turn off the electricity, gas, and water in your house.

DURING: Stay calm
☐ 1. If you are indoors, stay indoors. Protect yourself from falling materials by standing in a doorway or taking cover under a desk or large table.
☐ 2. Stay away from glass, especially windows.
☐ 3. If you are outdoors, move away from buildings and overhead electrical and telephone wires.
☐ 4. If you are in a car, stop as long as you are away from buildings, bridges, tunnels, and so on. Stay in the car until the shaking stops. Get out of a tunnel or off a bridge if you can.

AFTER: Be careful
☐ 1. Check the gas, water, and electricity. Look for fires or fire hazards. If you smell gas, open windows, and turn off the gas. Leave the building. Contact the gas company or police. Do not go back into the building. If water pipes are broken, turn off the main water valve. If there are electrical shorts, turn off the electricity at the main fuse box or circuit breaker.
☐ 2. Do not use the telephone except for emergencies.
☐ 3. Turn on a radio to get emergency information. Use the television if you can.
☐ 4. Do not enter badly damaged buildings.
☐ 5. Do not go sightseeing.

Thinking Critically Why is it important to be prepared before an earthquake happens?

5-10 What is the Ring of Fire?

Objective
Identify the three major volcanic and earthquake zones on Earth.

Key Term
Ring of Fire: major earthquake and volcanic zone that almost forms a circle around the Pacific Ocean

Zones of Activity Most big earthquakes and volcanic eruptions on Earth occur in three areas, or zones. These zones are called the Ring of Fire, the Mid-Atlantic Ridge, and the Eurasian Belt. A lot of movement and activity happen in these places. There are many active volcanoes. Volcanoes that have erupted at least once within recorded history are called active volcanoes. There are more than 500 active volcanoes on land. There are many more under the oceans.

▶ STATE: How many major volcanic and earthquake zones are there?

Ring of Fire One major volcanic and earthquake zone is the **Ring of Fire.** The Ring of Fire almost forms a circle or ring around the Pacific Ocean. This is how it got its name. Most of the active volcanoes on landmasses are located in the Ring of Fire. Many earthquakes also occur in this area. The western coasts of North and South America are part of the Ring of Fire.

▶ IDENTIFY: What is the name of the earthquake and volcanic zone around the edge of the Pacific Ocean?

Mid-Atlantic Ridge A second major volcanic and earthquake zone is located in the Atlantic Ocean. This zone is called the Mid-Atlantic Ridge. The Mid-Atlantic Ridge is a long underwater chain of volcanic mountains. In this zone, earthquakes and volcanoes are caused by the formation of new parts of Earth's crust. Iceland is part of this zone. Iceland is a volcanic island.

▶ DESCRIBE: What is the most important feature of the Mid-Atlantic Ridge?

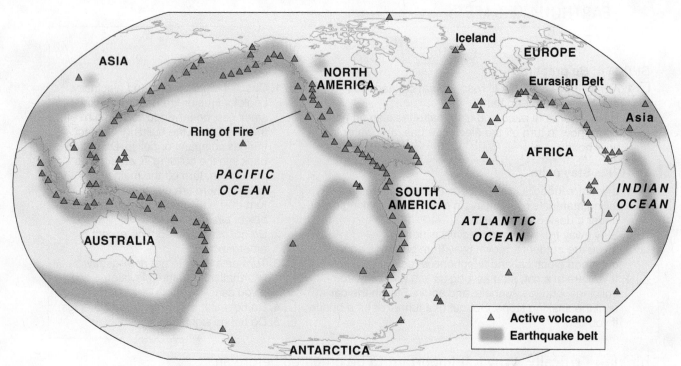

▲ **Figure 5-34** There are three major areas worldwide where earthquakes and volcanic eruptions are common.

Eurasian Belt Many countries in Europe have had big earthquakes. Many also have active volcanoes. These countries are in the third zone, called the Eurasian Belt. The mountains along this belt were formed when parts of Earth's crust collided.

 DESCRIBE: What formed the Eurasian-Melanesian Belt?

✓ CHECKING CONCEPTS

1. The Ring of Fire nearly surrounds the _____ Ocean.

2. The second major earthquake and volcanic zone is located in the middle of the _____ Ocean.

3. The third major volcanic and earthquake zone is the _____.

💡 THINKING CRITICALLY

4. **INTERPRET:** Use Figure 5-34 and a map of the United States to name two states that are part of the Ring of Fire.

Web InfoSearch

New Madrid Between 1811 and 1812, a series of major earthquakes hit New Madrid, Missouri. They caused flooding. They even changed the course of the Mississippi River. Scientists did not know why the earthquakes happened in New Madrid. Then, in the 1970s, they discovered three faults in the area. The faults were buried deep beneath Earth's surface. Scientists think that movement along these faults caused the earthquakes.

SEARCH: Use the Internet to find out more about this event. What did the earthquakes measure on the Richter scale? How were the New Madrid earthquakes different from earthquakes in the western United States? Start your search at **www.conceptsandchallenges.com**. Some key search words are **earthquake, New Madrid 1811**, and **New Madrid seismic zone**.

How Do They Know That?

THE STORY OF POMPEII

Mount Vesuvius (vuh-SOO-vee-uhs) is one of the few active explosive volcanoes in Europe. In A.D. 79, Vesuvius erupted in a giant explosion. It rained hot, wet ashes and cinders on the city of Pompeii (pahm-PAY). The entire city was completely covered. Some of the people of Pompeii escaped. However, many others died from the hot ash and poisonous fumes in the air.

▲ **Figure 5-35** The restored city of Pompeii

In the 1500s, people were digging a tunnel when they came across some of the remains of Pompeii. The ash and cinders had preserved the city. Today, more than half of Pompeii has been uncovered and restored.

Mount Vesuvius has not erupted since 1944. However, the longer the volcano is quiet, the more explosive the next eruption may be. Hundreds of thousands of people live on or near the fertile slopes of Vesuvius. Scientists constantly monitor the volcano. They measure escaping gases and slight ground movements. Scientists hope to predict an eruption two or three weeks ahead of time. This would give people time to leave the area.

Thinking Critically Why would people want to live on the slope of the volcano?

LAB ACTIVITY
Making an Earthquake-Proof Structure

Materials

Uncooked spaghetti, small gumdrops, a metric ruler, paper, a pencil, a piece of cardboard, cellophane tape, a stopwatch or timer, an earthquake simulator (constructed by your teacher or done as a class project)

BACKGROUND

An earthquake can last from a few seconds to a few minutes. If you have ever felt an earthquake, you will know that it is a terrifying experience. The solid land beneath your feet begins to shake. In small earthquakes, dishes in cupboards and pictures on walls fall to the floor. Brick chimneys crack. Trees and light poles sway. In large earthquakes, entire buildings and bridges may break apart. However, not all buildings are destroyed. Some survive with little damage because of their designs.

PURPOSE

In this activity, you and your engineering team will design and construct a model of a tower. This tower is planned for an earthquake-prone area. You will test the tower to see how well it withstands a simulated earthquake.

PROCEDURE

1. Draw sketches of the kinds of towers you might want to build using spaghetti and gumdrops. Your tower should be at least 60 cm tall.

▲ **STEP 2** Construct your tower.

2. Construct your tower according to your plan. Use only the supplies listed. Handle the spaghetti carefully. The strands break easily. To insert the spaghetti strands into the gumdrops, hold the spaghetti near the end. If you need to shorten it, grip the spaghetti strand on each side of where you want it to break. Then bend it gently until it breaks.

3. After you have finished the base for your tower, lightly tape it to the cardboard.

▲ **STEP 3** Tape your tower to the cardboard.

4. When the tower is completed, draw a picture of it. Label the height and width of the tower on your drawing. Then take it for testing to the earthquake simulator.

5. Time how long your building remains standing at different "strengths" of shaking. Copy the chart in Figure 5-36. Record your observations and times on it.

▲ **STEP 4** Test your tower with the simulator.

	P-Wave Test	S-Wave Test	L-Wave Test
Did your tower survive the test?			
Where did the tower shake the most?			

▲ **Figure 5-36** Use a copy of this chart to record your observations.

CONCLUSIONS

1. OBSERVE: What happened to your tower when it was tested? Where did it vibrate? Did it break or survive the test?

2. OBSERVE: Did any towers from other groups perform better than yours? Compare their height and other features.

3. INFER: How could you build a stronger tower?

Chapter Summary

Lesson 5-1

• Folds form when rock bends. A **fracture** is a break in a rock. Faulting causes rocks to move.

Lessons 5-2 and 5-3

• Mountains can form by rock layers folding, large blocks of crust being lifted during faulting, and by molten rock pushing up crust. Most mountains are part of ranges, systems, or belts.

Lesson 5-4

• The three main landforms are **plains, plateaus,** and mountains. Plateaus are large, flat plains with high elevations. The same forces that build mountains also form plateaus.

Lesson 5-5

• **Volcanism** is magma moving inside Earth. A **volcano** is a **vent** with **lava,** dust, ash, and rocks.

• A **crater** is a pit on top of a volcanic cone. A **caldera** forms when crater walls fall back into a vent or when a volcano explodes.

Lesson 5-6

• Volcanoes form different volcanic cones. These include **shield, cinder,** and **composite cones.**

Lesson 5-7

• An **earthquake** is a sudden, strong movement of Earth's crust. It starts at a **focus. Seismic waves** travel from there in all directions. Most earthquakes are associated with faulting. A **seismograph** detects and measures earthquakes.

Lessons 5-8 and 5-9

• **P-waves** are the fastest waves. **S-waves** are second. **L-waves** are the slowest waves.

• **Seismographs** help locate **epicenters** and record an earthquake's force. The **Richter scale** indicates the energy released by an earthquake.

• A **tsunami** is a giant wave caused by an earthquake on or under the ocean floor.

Lesson 5-10

• The three major volcanic and earthquake zones are the **Ring of Fire,** the Mid-Atlantic Ridge, and the Eurasian Belt.

Key Term Challenges

anticline (p. 110)
caldera (p.118)
cinder cone (p. 120)
composite cone (p. 120)
crater (p. 118)
dome mountain (p. 114)
earthquake (p. 124)
elevation (p. 112)
epicenter (p. 124)
fault (p. 110)
fault-block mountain (p. 114)
focus (p. 124)
folded mountain (p. 114)
fracture (p. 110)
L-wave (p. 126)
landform (p. 112)

lava (p. 118)
P-wave (p. 126)
plain (p. 116)
plateau (p. 116)
Richter scale (p. 128)
Ring of Fire (p. 130)
S-wave (p. 126)
seismic wave (p. 124)
seismograph (p. 124)
shield cone (p. 120)
summit (p. 112)
syncline (p. 110)
tsunami (p. 128)
vent (p. 118)
volcanism (p. 118)
volcano (p. 118)

MATCHING **Write the Key Term from above that best matches each description.**

1. earthquake wave

2. second earthquake wave to be recorded at a seismograph station

3. height above or below sea level

4. ocean wave caused by an earthquake

5. major earthquake and volcanic zone around the Pacific Ocean

6. opening from which lava flows

7. instrument that records earthquake activity

8. type of mountain formed when rock layers fold upward due to vertical pressure

APPLYING DEFINITIONS **Explain the difference between the words in each pair. Write your answers in complete sentences.**

9. anticline, syncline

10. epicenter, focus

11. crater, caldera

12. fracture, fault

13. composite cone, shield cone

14. folded mountain, fault-block mountain

Content Challenges

MULTIPLE CHOICE Write the letter of the term or phrase that best completes each statement.

1. Folding and faulting are caused by
   a. heat.
   b. earthquakes.
   c. volcanoes.
   d. pressure.

2. The peaks of a young mountain are
   a. sharp and jagged.
   b. worn.
   c. rounded.
   d. flat.

3. A group of mountains with the same general shape and structure make up a mountain
   a. range.
   b. system.
   c. cascade.
   d. belt.

4. Magma that reaches Earth's surface is called
   a. crater.
   b. lava.
   c. magma.
   d. volcanic ash.

5. Magma that flows between rock layers and hardens forms a
   a. dike.
   b. composite cone.
   c. sill.
   d. cinder cone.

6. A volcanic cone made up of rock particles, dust, and ash is a
   a. fault-block cone.
   b. composite cone.
   c. shield cone.
   d. cinder cone.

7. An instrument that detects and measures earthquakes is a
   a. seismogram.
   b. focus.
   c. seismic map.
   d. seismograph.

8. Earthquake waves that travel along Earth's surface are
   a. P-waves.
   b. S-waves.
   c. L-waves.
   d. N-waves.

9. One example of a landform on Earth's surface is
   a. the Pacific Ocean.
   b. the San Andreas Fault.
   c. the Colorado Plateau.
   d. the continent of North America.

TRUE/FALSE Write *true* if the statement is true. If the statement is false, change the underlined term to make the statement true.

10. The second seismic waves to be recorded by a seismograph are <u>P-waves</u>.

11. Parícutin in Mexico is an example of a <u>cinder cone</u>.

12. A volcanic cone with layers of lava and rock particles is a <u>shield cone</u>.

13. A funnel-shaped pit at the top of a volcanic cone is called a <u>crater</u>.

14. A large, flat landform with a high elevation is a <u>plateau</u>.

15. Mountains, plateaus, and <u>sills</u> are the three main landforms of Earth's crust.

16. The Great Plains of the United States are <u>coastal</u> plains.

Concept Challenges TEST PREP

Answer each of the following questions in complete sentences.

1. EXPLAIN: How could you use observations to distinguish between a cinder cone and a shield cone?

2. CONTRAST: How does a mountain differ from a plateau?

3. CONTRAST: How does a dike differ from a sill?

4. ANALYZE: Which is likely to do more damage, an earthquake that occurs on land or an earthquake that occurs beneath the ocean? Explain.

5. PREDICT: What kind of damage is likely to be caused by a tsunami?

INTERPRETING VISUALS **Use Figures 5-37 to 5-40 to complete the following.**

6. Identify each of the lettered parts in Figure 5-37.

7. What kind of volcanic cone is shown in Figure 5-38?

8. What kind of volcanic cone is shown in Figure 5-39?

9. What kind of volcanic cone is shown in Figure 5-40?

10. How does the makeup of the volcanic cone in Figure 5-38 differ from that of the volcanic cone in Figure 5-39?

▲ Figure 5-38

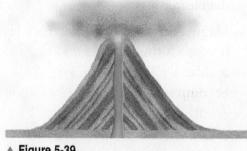

▲ Figure 5-39

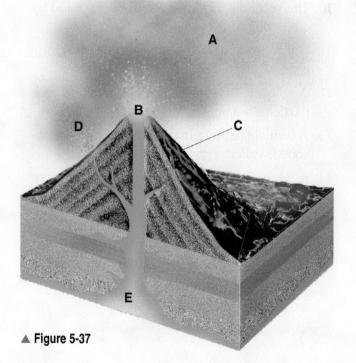

▲ Figure 5-37

▲ Figure 5-40

Chapter 6 Plate Tectonics

▲ **Figure 6-1** This power plant uses steam to generate electricity.

Earth's core heats the mantle. This contributes to the process known as plate tectonics. Rocks deep in the crust above the mantle also become hot in some spots. The power plant you see in the background has drilled into this hot rock. When cold water from the lagoon is pumped down into the hot rock, steam forms. The steam is then brought to the surface to power electrical generators. The warm waste water of this plant is released into the Blue Lagoon.

▶During the summer, Iceland is very cold. Why are people still able to swim in the lagoon?

Contents

6-1 What is continental drift?

Objective

Explain the theory of continental drift and the evidence that supports it.

Key Terms

continental (kahnt-ihn-EHNT-uhl) **drift:** theory that the continents were at one or more times a single landmass that broke apart and eventually moved into the positions they are in today

Pangaea (pan-JEE-uh)**:** single, giant landmass, or continent, that later broke apart

Continental Drift Most scientists think that millions of years ago, Earth was very different from the way it is today. There was only one supercontinent that had water all around it. Over time, the continent began to break apart. Pieces of it slowly drifted apart and then came together again. Eventually, those pieces became today's seven continents.

The theory that the seven modern continents split apart one or more times from a single landmass was suggested by German scientist Alfred Wegener in 1915. Wegener called his theory **continental drift.** He named the giant landmass **Pangaea,** meaning "all lands." Others added to Wegener's theory. One scientist suggested that Pangaea had separated into two landmasses: Laurasia (law-RAY-zhuh) in the north and Gondwanaland (gahnd-WAH-nuh-land) in the south. The Tethys (TEE-thihs) Sea was in the middle. Laurasia later broke apart to form North America, Europe, and Asia. Gondwanaland became South America, Africa, Australia, India, and Antarctica.

1 IDENTIFY: Who first stated the modern theory of continental drift?

A Giant Jigsaw Puzzle To support his theory, Wegener showed how the continents could fit together. Look at the shapes of the coastlines of South America and Africa in Figure 6-5. They seem to fit together like jigsaw puzzle pieces. Other places can be found that might once have fit together as well.

2 DESCRIBE: In what ways do the continents seem to fit together?

Fossil Evidence Coastline shapes were only one of many clues Wegener used to support his theory of continental drift. Fossils of once-living organisms also provided support for Wegener's theory.

Wegener studied the fossils of *Mesosaurus* (meh-soh-SAWR-uhs). *Mesosaurus* fossils were found in both Africa and South America. *Mesosaurus* was an animal that lived in fresh water. How could it have swum across the salty Atlantic Ocean? Wegener believed that it had not. Instead, he believed that it had lived at a time when there was only one large landmass. Later, that landmass broke apart, and some of the fossils remained on each part.

3 EXPLAIN: How did Wegener use *Mesosaurus* fossils to help explain his continental drift theory?

More Evidence Today, most scientists support the theory of continental drift. Here is some other evidence scientists have uncovered.

- Some mountain ranges on different continents seem to match. A mountain range along the eastern United States and Canada is similar to ranges in Greenland and northwestern Europe. Figure 6-5 shows where the mountains match.

Go **Online**
active art
For: Continental Drift activity
Visit: PHSchool.com
Web Code: cfp-1015

▲ **Figure 6-2** Alfred Wegener

▲ **Figure 6-3** Pangaea, 225 million years ago

▲ **Figure 6-4** Gondwanaland and Laurasia, 180–200 million years ago

- The ages and kinds of rocks along the edge of one continent match those of rocks along the edge of another continent. Even the sizes of the diamonds found in Brazilian and West African mines are the same.

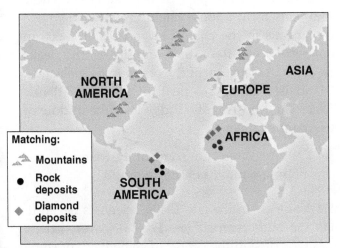

Matching:
- **Mountains**
- **Rock deposits**
- **Diamond deposits**

▲ **Figure 6-5** Evidence from matching mountains, rocks, and diamonds supports Wegener's theory.

4 EXPLAIN: How do similarities among certain mountain ranges support the theory of continental drift?

✓ CHECKING CONCEPTS

1. What is the theory of continental drift?
2. Which continents seem to fit together?
3. What are three things that scientists use to support the theory of continental drift?
4. How do the shapes of coastlines today support the theory of continental drift?

💡 THINKING CRITICALLY

5. RELATE: How does the idea of Pangaea support the theory of continental drift?
6. INFER: Fossils of the plant *Glossopteris* (glaw-SAWP-tuh-rihs) have been found on four continents. The continents are Africa, Asia, Australia, and South America. *Glossopteris* dates back more than 245 million years. It was a fern plant that may have produced spores, which are seedlike structures similar to those of a flowering plant. What might *Glossopteris* fossils tell scientists about these continents?

Hands-On Activity

MODELING PANGAEA

You will need a sheet of tracing paper, scissors, glue, and two sheets of construction paper.

1. Trace and label the continents shown on the map.
2. Glue the tracing paper onto a sheet of construction paper.
3. Carefully cut out the continents and Greenland. Do not cut Europe and Asia apart. Keep them as one continent.
   ⚠ CAUTION: Be careful when using scissors.
4. Arrange the pieces to form Pangaea. Glue the model of Pangaea onto another sheet of construction paper.

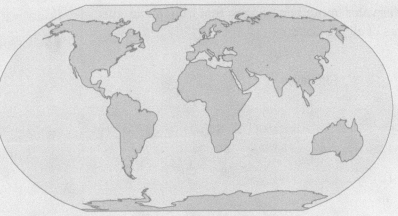

▲ **Figure 6-6** Earth's current landmasses are divided into seven continents.

Practicing Your Skills

5. EXPLAIN: Which continents seem to fit together?
6. IDENTIFY: Label your model. Then write a caption for it.
7. COMPARE: How is the reconstructed Pangaea like a jigsaw puzzle?

Objective

Relate seafloor spreading to the forming of new oceanic crust.

Key Terms

mid-ocean ridge: ocean-floor feature resembling a mountain ridge on land

rift valley: flat area between two ridges that is formed by spreading plates

seafloor spreading: process that forms new seafloor

Two Kinds of Crust There are two kinds of crust on Earth. One kind is continental crust. This crust makes up Earth's continents. The other kind is called oceanic (oh-shee-AN-ihk) crust. Oceanic crust, which makes up the ocean floor, is denser than continental crust.

▶ **NAME:** What are the two kinds of crust?

Mid-Ocean Ridges The most obvious features of the crust that makes up the ocean floor are the **mid-ocean ridges.** These ridges are part of a series of underwater mountain ranges that run along the floors of all the oceans.

Some of the longest mountain ranges and tallest peaks on Earth are part of oceanic crust. These mountains form a loose chain around the world. Some peaks in the chain rise more than 3,000 m above the ocean floor. In a few places, the peaks rise above the surface of the ocean to form islands. Iceland is a mountain peak of the Mid-Atlantic Ridge. The Mid-Atlantic Ridge is in the middle of the Atlantic Ocean.

▶ **IDENTIFY:** Where are some of the longest mountain ranges on Earth found?

Rift Valleys In the late 1940s, scientists began to map the mid-ocean ridges. They discovered deep cracks, or rifts, in the center of some parts of some ridges. Magma pouring out of the rift had hardened and formed broad underwater valleys with steep sides. These valleys are called **rift valleys.** There are many earthquakes and volcanoes in rift valleys.

On land, spreading plates form steep, wide valleys in the continental crust, as shown in Figure 6-7. The East African Rift System extends for 6,400 km, from Jordan in southwestern Asia through eastern Africa to Mozambique. The valley averages 48 km to 64 km in width. Other rift valley floors are below sea level and form deep lakes.

▶ **DEFINE:** What is a rift valley?

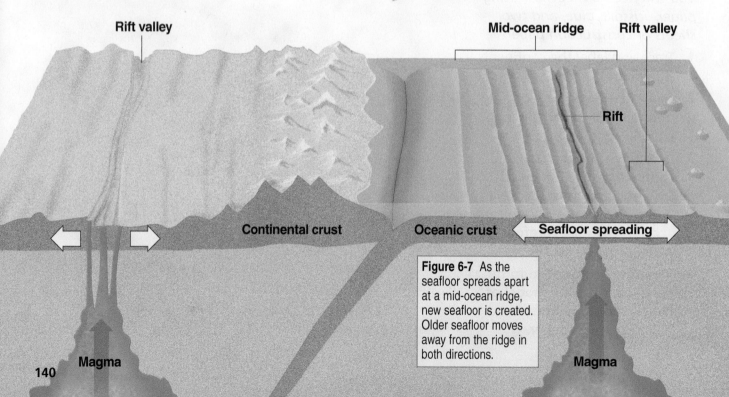

Rift valley · Mid-ocean ridge · Rift valley · Rift · Continental crust · Oceanic crust · Seafloor spreading · Magma · Magma

Figure 6-7 As the seafloor spreads apart at a mid-ocean ridge, new seafloor is created. Older seafloor moves away from the ridge in both directions.

Formation of New Seafloor Deep-sea drills have been used to bring up samples of oceanic crust. Most of these samples turn out to be younger than samples of continental crust. In addition, the oceanic crust near the mid-ocean ridges is younger than oceanic crust farther from the center of the ridge. The youngest oceanic crust is found in the center of the ridge.

Below the mid-ocean ridges, magma rises through the crust. As the magma cools, it forms new crust on both sides of a rift. The new crust pushes the seafloor apart at the ridges. Scientists called the process **seafloor spreading.** Seafloor spreading is partly what drives the movements of the continents, or continental drift.

 DESCRIBE: What happens as magma rises through the crust of the mid-ocean ridges?

✓ CHECKING CONCEPTS

1. Which kind of crust is made up of heavy, dense material?
2. What is the Mid-Atlantic Ridge?
3. How does magma come out of a chamber to form a ridge and valley?
4. Where did scientists find the youngest crust on the ocean floor?

 THINKING CRITICALLY

5. **MODEL:** Draw a diagram that illustrates seafloor spreading. Label your diagram.
6. **CONCLUDE:** How do you think seafloor spreading helps explain the theory of continental drift?

BUILDING SCIENCE SKILLS

Modeling To make a model of seafloor spreading, do the following:

STEP 1 Tape two sheets of red construction paper together along their short ends. Then push two desks together.

STEP 2 Fold the sheets of construction paper together along the tape.

STEP 3 Push the open ends of the construction paper up through the crack between the desks until some paper falls on each side. Keep pushing the paper up.

7. **CONCLUDE:** What does the crack between the desks represent? What does the construction paper represent? How could you make your model more accurate?

 Real-Life Science

THE SUMATRA-ANDAMAN EARTHQUAKE

On December 26, 2004, an undersea earthquake rocked the Indian Ocean off the coast of Sumatra. The magnitude of the quake registered at 9.1 on the Richter scale. It was the 3rd largest earthquake since 1900. It literally shook the planet.

During the earthquake, an underwater landslide displaced a large volume of water. This triggered a series of giant waves, called tsunamis, that devastated the coasts of the Indian Ocean. These waves were over 100 meters high. Nearly 230,000 people were killed or missing. This incident is now known as the Asian Tsunami.

▲ **Figure 6-8** A giant tsunami hits the shore.

Thinking Critically What effects might an undersea earthquake have on the ocean floor?

6-3 What evidence supports seafloor spreading?

INVESTIGATE

Modeling Seafloor Spreading
HANDS-ON ACTIVITY

1. Three students stand in a row. The student in the middle holds a sheet of paper with "Mid-Ocean Ridge" written on it.

2. After one minute, the other two students write "1 minute" on their sheets of paper.

3. Two students join the row on either side of the person in the middle. They are the "lava" that forms the "new crust."

4. After another minute, everyone records how long they have been standing.

5. Repeat this process until all students are standing in the row.

THINK ABOUT IT: Compare the numbers on the sheets of paper. How does your model show seafloor spreading? What part of the new seafloor will be the youngest part?

Objective
Describe some evidence of seafloor spreading.

Key Terms
trench: deep canyon

subduction (suhb-DUHK-shuhn) **zone:** place where old oceanic crust is forced back down into an ocean trench

Trenches On the ocean floor, there are deep canyons called **trenches**. Trenches are the deepest parts of the oceans. They may be more than 10,000 m deep. Most trenches are found in the Pacific Ocean along the coasts of continents.

Some trenches are found near chains of islands. The volcanic region known as the Ring of Fire in the Pacific Ocean contains many examples of these.

 DEFINE: What is a trench?

Disappearing Crust The oldest rocks found on the ocean floor are only about 160 million years old. Yet, Earth is about 4.6 billion years old. How is this possible? As new crust is made in one place, old crust is destroyed someplace else. If crust were not being destroyed, our planet would keep growing. Old crust on the ocean floor ends up deep down in ocean trenches. There, it melts and becomes magma again.

 STATE: What happens to older crust?

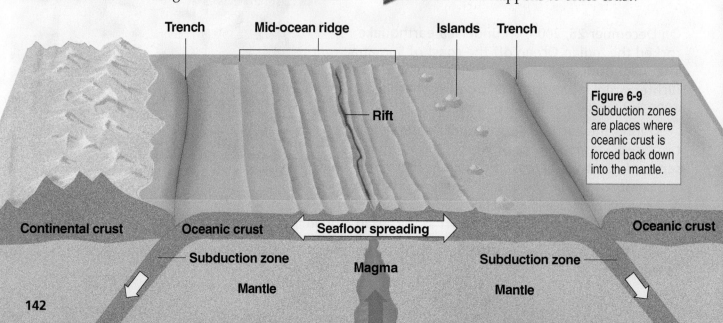

Figure 6-9
Subduction zones are places where oceanic crust is forced back down into the mantle.

142

Subduction Zones The areas in which oceanic crust is forced back down into ocean trenches are called **subduction zones,** shown in Figure 6-9. A lot of volcanic activity and many earthquakes occur near subduction zones. The Ring of Fire has many subduction zones. In these, the older oceanic crust is forced back down into the mantle. It is in these areas that trenches are formed.

▶ **3** DEFINE: What are subduction zones?

Ages of Fossils In 1968, the crew of the research ship *Glomar Challenger* made an important discovery. They drilled holes at various sites along the Mid-Atlantic Ridge and brought up samples of crust. Scientists studied the fossils in the samples. They discovered that the rock samples closest to the rift valley held the youngest fossils. The fossils farthest from the rift valley were older. The fossil evidence supports the idea that new oceanic crust is forming along the ridge. It also supports the theory of continental drift.

▶ **4** IDENTIFY: Where were the oldest fossils found?

Magnetic Fields There is another important piece of evidence that supports the theory of seafloor spreading. It was found in rocks near the Mid-Atlantic Ridge.

Earth has a magnetic field. If you have ever used a compass, you know that a compass needle always points toward Earth's magnetic north pole. Some minerals are magnetic. When magnetic minerals form, their particles, like the compass needle, line up with Earth's magnetic field.

Earth's magnetic poles have switched places many times. If the poles were to switch again, your compass would point south instead of north. When rocks with magnetic minerals are formed, their minerals point to where Earth's magnetic north pole was when the minerals formed. Scientists found bands of rock in the Mid-Atlantic Ridge with minerals pointing toward present-day north. These alternated with bands of rock pointing toward present-day south. Both sides of the ridge showed the same pattern.

You cannot see the magnetic bands on the ocean floor. They can only be detected with scientific instruments. However, this pattern is evidence that new ocean floor is being created and that the seafloor is spreading in places.

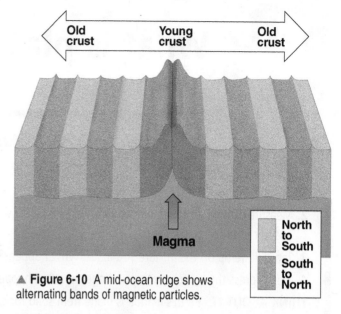

▲ **Figure 6-10** A mid-ocean ridge shows alternating bands of magnetic particles.

▶ **5** PROVE: What evidence shows that Earth's magnetic field has changed?

✓ CHECKING CONCEPTS

1. The deepest parts of the ocean are _____.
2. The oldest rocks found on the ocean floor are only _____ million years old.
3. A compass needle always points _____.

💡 THINKING CRITICALLY

4. INFER: Why is there a lot of volcanic and earthquake activity at subduction zones?
5. CALCULATE: Seafloor spreading adds about 2.5 cm of new material to Iceland each year. How much wider could Iceland be in 150 years?

Web InfoSearch

Challenger Deep The deepest place on Earth is Challenger Deep. Challenger Deep is a trench 11,033 m deep. It is part of the Mariana Trench in the Pacific Ocean. If Mount Everest were put into it, its top would be covered by 1,600 m of water.

SEARCH: Use the Internet to find out more about Challenger Deep. What else do we know about it? Start your search at www.conceptsandchallenges.com. Some key search words are **Mariana Trench, Mount Everest,** and **Ring of Fire.**

INVESTIGATE

Modeling Earth's Mantle
HANDS-ON ACTIVITY

STEP 4

1. Begin by measuring 250 mL of cornstarch. Pour it into a container.

2. Measure 100 mL of room-temperature water. Pour it over the cornstarch, and stir until blended smoothly.

3. Tap a fingertip on the mixture you made. What happens?

4. Slowly press the mixture with your fingertip. What happens?

THINK ABOUT IT: Earth's mantle is made from solid rock. Like your mixture, the mantle rock can also flow like a very thick liquid. How do you think this property affects the crust on top of the mantle?

Objectives
Name some crustal plates. Describe the theory of plate tectonics.

Key Terms
tectonic plate: large, solid piece of Earth's surface

theory of plate tectonics (tehk-TAHN-ihks): theory that Earth's crust is broken into plates that float on the upper part of the mantle

Tectonic Plates Earth's lithosphere is made up of crust and the solid, uppermost part of the mantle. The mantle is the layer of rock below the crust. The lithosphere is broken up into large pieces called **tectonic plates.**

There are 7 large tectonic plates and about 14 smaller ones. The largest plate is the Pacific plate. Figure 6-11 below shows some of the tectonic plates.

▶ **1 IDENTIFY:** About how many tectonic plates have been identified?

Floating Plates Part of the mantle contains rock that flows like a thick liquid. This part, called the athenosphere, is just below the more solid rock of the uppermost mantle. Tectonic plates float on the athenosphere like rafts floating on a lake. The continents and oceans are carried along on the plates like passengers on a raft.

▶ **2 NAME:** On which part of Earth do the tectonic plates float?

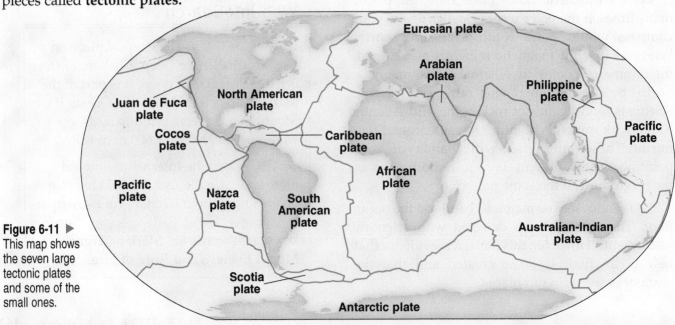

Figure 6-11 ▶
This map shows the seven large tectonic plates and some of the small ones.

Eurasian plate

Arabian plate

Philippine plate

Juan de Fuca plate

North American plate

Pacific plate

Cocos plate

Caribbean plate

African plate

Pacific plate

Nazca plate

South American plate

Australian-Indian plate

Scotia plate

Antarctic plate

Theory of Plate Tectonics Using information that supports seafloor spreading and continental drift, scientists have developed the **theory of plate tectonics.** The theory of plate tectonics combines the theories of continental drift and seafloor spreading. The theory of plate tectonics explains how and why the continents move. It states that Earth's lithosphere is broken into plates that float on the upper mantle. The continents move because they are carried along on the moving plates.

 NAME: What two theories does plate tectonics combine?

✓ CHECKING CONCEPTS

1. Which layer of Earth is below the crust?
2. How many large tectonic plates are there?
3. What is the uppermost mantle rock like?
4. What is the theory of plate tectonics?

THINKING CRITICALLY

5. MODEL: Draw a picture of a raft on a lake with people on the raft. Using the lake, the people, and the raft, label your picture with the following terms: tectonic plate, athenosphere, continents.

INTERPRETING VISUALS

Use Figure 6-11 to answer the following.

6. On which plate is Australia?
7. Name one plate that the United States is on.
8. What are three large plates and two of the smaller plates?
9. Do you think the present number, sizes, and shapes of tectonic plates will remain the same as they are today? Explain your answer.

How Do They Know That?

PREDICTING PANGAEA ULTIMA

Many geologists study how Earth's continents were formed. They can use that information to answer questions such as whether we can predict volcanic eruptions and earthquakes. Geologists use many techniques for studying Earth's movements. One way is to bounce laser beams from stations on Earth off satellites. The time it takes for the beams to return tell them how far the crust has moved since previous measurements.

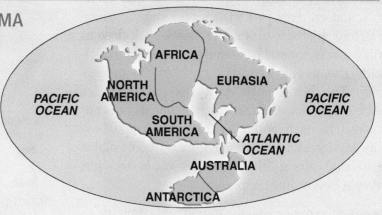
▲ **Figure 6-12** Pangaea Ultima

Dr. Christopher Scotese is a geologist at the University of Texas in Arlington, Texas. Dr. Scotese creates maps of Earth's continents and oceans from computer and satellite data. He uses the data to help him predict what the continents might look like in the future. According to Dr. Scotese, most of today's continents could rejoin as one giant continent in about 250 million years. The Pacific Ocean will become much larger. The Atlantic Ocean will become a small landlocked sea. Dr. Scotese has named his future world Pangaea Ultima.

Thinking Critically How might Africa's new position affect the wildlife there?

What causes plate tectonics?

Objective
Describe the causes of plate tectonics.

Key Terms
convection current: movement of a gas or a liquid caused by changes in temperature

plate boundary: place where two plates meet

Convection Currents A **convection current** is the movement of a gas or a liquid caused by differences in temperature and density. For example, warm air rises and cool air sinks. When a pan of water boils on a stove, the water near the bottom of the pan heats first. The less dense hot water rises. The cooler and denser water near the top of the pan sinks.

▶ DEFINE: What is a convection current?

Inside the Mantle Scientists think that giant convection currents in Earth's upper mantle cause the tectonic plates to move. The mantle rock close to Earth's core is hot and has some properties of a thick liquid. The mantle rock farther from the core is cooler. The hot mantle rock rises. The cooler mantle rock sinks. As the cooler rock moves closer to the core, it heats up and rises. This process repeats in an endless cycle, as shown in Figure 6-13. The plates are carried along like packages on a moving conveyor belt or like people on a raft.

▶ STATE: What causes the movement of plates?

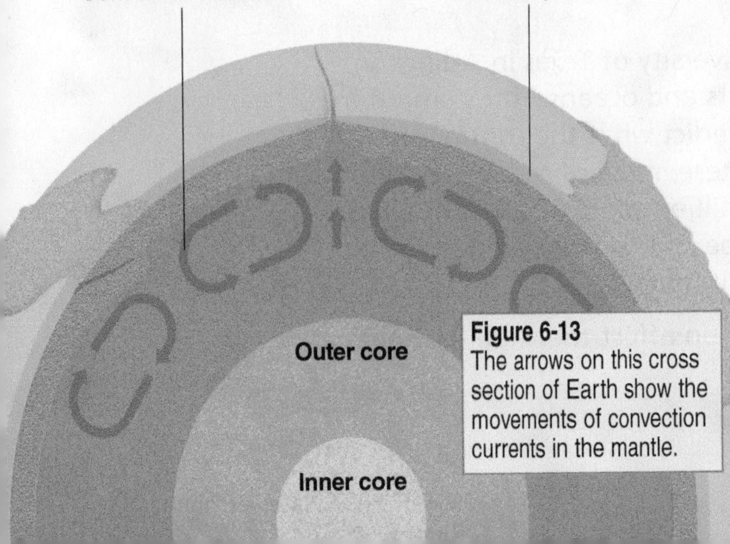

Convection current   Crustal plate

Figure 6-13
The arrows on this cross section of Earth show the movements of convection currents in the mantle.

Outer core

Inner core

Plate Boundaries and Movements The place where two plates meet is called a **plate boundary.** Scientists have identified three different kinds of plate boundaries: transform, convergent, and divergent.

At transform boundaries, two plates slide past each other. The movement is not smooth. This sliding movement causes earthquakes, as shown in Figure 6-20 on page 150.

At a convergent boundary, the plates move toward each other. When oceanic crust meets continental crust, the denser oceanic crust slides under the continental crust. This downward movement of the oceanic crust produces a subduction zone, as shown in Figure 6-14.

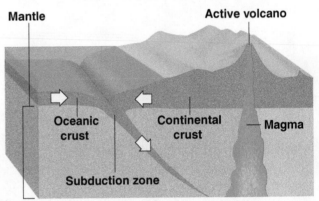

Mantle   Active volcano

Oceanic crust   Continental crust   Magma

Subduction zone

▲ **Figure 6-14** When oceanic crust meets continental crust at a convergent boundary, a subduction zone forms. This is often an area of volcanic activity.

If two continental plates meet, the crust crumples upward. This kind of movement is shown in Figure 6-15.

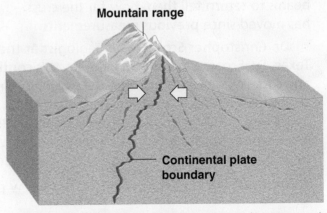

Mountain range

Continental plate boundary

▲ **Figure 6-15** When two continental crusts meet at a convergent boundary, they crumple upward. Mountains may be formed.

At a divergent boundary, the plates move apart. These plates sometimes form rift valleys, as shown in Figure 6-16.

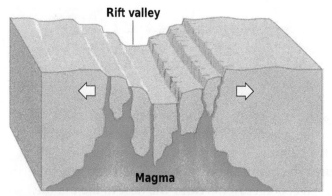

Rift valley

Magma

▲ **Figure 6-16** A rift valley may form at a divergent boundary.

 LIST: What are three ways plates move?

CHECKING CONCEPTS

1. What causes the movement of plates?
2. How is crustal rock heated inside the mantle?

3. At which type of boundary do plates move apart?
4. What happens when two plates move toward each other?

THINKING CRITICALLY

5. INFER: What land feature may be formed when two continental plates meet?

DESIGNING AN EXPERIMENT

Design an experiment to solve the following problem. Include a hypothesis, variables, a procedure with materials, and a type of data to study. Also say how you would record your data.

PROBLEM: Scientists believe that rift valleys are created by the movement of continental plates away from each other. As the plates pull apart, a valley forms between them. Design a small-scale experiment to show how a rift valley forms.

People in Science
VOLCANOLOGIST

Volcanologists are scientists who study volcanoes. They collect data and samples, and observe volcanoes. A volcanologist must know geology, physics, chemistry, and math.

Volcanologists have very dangerous jobs because they walk on active volcanoes! Often called lava hunters, they travel the world to observe volcanoes in action.

Two famous French lava hunters were Maurice and Katia Krafft. Their goal was to educate people on the dangers of volcanic eruptions.

In many parts of the world, warnings about possible eruptions are often ignored by local people. For example, mudflows from the 1985 Nevado del Ruiz eruption in Colombia killed 25,000 people. The Kraffts produced videos about how to survive an eruption.

▲ **Figure 6-17** Lava hunters must wear protective gear when near an active volcano.

Together, the Kraffts observed and filmed more active volcanoes than any other volcanologists. Sadly, they were killed by an explosion of hot ash and gases from an eruption of Mount Unzen in Japan on June 3, 1991.

Thinking Critically Why do you think people often ignore warnings of possible volcanic eruptions?

LAB ACTIVITY
Modeling Convection Currents

▲ **STEP 6** Carefully place the cup of hot water under the plastic box.

▲ **STEP 7** Add the food coloring to the bottom of the box.

BACKGROUND

Earth's continents are moving on tectonic plates that float on the mantle. The part of the mantle they float on flows like a thick liquid. It is very hot and is under great pressure. The mantle's heat comes from deep inside Earth's core. Convection currents carry the heat to the mantle.

PURPOSE

In this activity, you will observe convection currents forming in water as a model of how convection currents are formed in Earth's mantle.

PROCEDURE

1. Put on your safety goggles and lab apron.

2. Place four plastic cups upside down on a table top to make pillars that will support the food storage box at its corners.

3. Fill the food storage box about half full with cold water from a faucet, and place it on the pillars.

4. Wait five minutes for the water to stop moving completely. Try not to bump the table.

5. While waiting for the water to settle, copy the chart in Figure 6-19 onto your paper. Make six rows on your chart. Title the chart *Observing Convection Currents.*

6. Fill the last cup with very hot water from a faucet and gently slide this cup under the middle of the box. Do not bump the box or the pillars.
   ⚠ CAUTION: Be extremely careful when handling the hot water.

7. Gently place four to five drops of the food coloring in the water near the center and bottom of the box.

8. Begin timing the experiment. Once each minute for five minutes, observe and record what you see on your chart. Write your observations in the third column. In the last column, draw pictures of what you see. Draw in arrows to show any motions you observe.

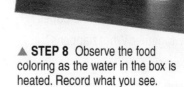

▲ **STEP 8** Observe the food coloring as the water in the box is heated. Record what you see.

◄ **Figure 6-18** The food coloring shows a convection current forming.

Observing Convection Currents

Observation	Time	Written Description	Diagram
1	0 min.		
2	1 min.		

▲ **Figure 6-19** Make a chart like this one with six rows. Leave enough room to write and draw in each row.

CONCLUSIONS

1. OBSERVE: What happened in the experiment?
2. MODEL: What does the cold water in the experiment represent?
3. MODEL: What does the hot water in the experiment represent?
4. INFER: How might this modeling experiment help to explain why the continents are moving?
5. ANALYZE: How are convection currents within Earth similar to the ones you created in your model?

6-6 What are some effects of plate tectonics?

INVESTIGATE

Modeling Mountain Formation
HANDS-ON ACTIVITY

1. Flatten two different pieces of clay into two squares or rectangles.
2. Place each piece of clay on a different sheet of construction paper. Line the short edge of the clay along the short edge of the paper.
3. Push the pieces of clay gently together. What happens?
4. Repeat Steps 1 to 3 several times.

THINK ABOUT IT: Based on your clay model, how do you think some mountains are formed?

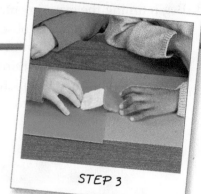

STEP 3

Objective

Explain how plate tectonics causes changes on Earth's surface.

Key Terms

magma chamber: underground pocket of molten rock

hot spot: place where magma reaches the surface of a tectonic plate

Earthquakes In some areas, two tectonic plates slide past each other at a transform boundary. The San Andreas Fault, in California, is one example. Many earthquakes are caused by the movement of plates at a fault.

The San Francisco earthquakes of 1906 and 1989 were caused by the movement of tectonic plates at the San Andreas Fault. This movement is shown in Figure 6-20.

 DESCRIBE: What can happen when two plates slide past each other at a fault?

Mountain Building When two plates collide, the force of the collision may push oceanic crust under continental crust. Such a collision causes the continental crust to crumple. It may even be pushed upward to form new mountains. Mountains along the western coasts of North and South America were formed in this way. They are young mountains that are still being pushed upward.

Two plates carrying continents may collide without one plate being pushed down under the other. The Himalayas were formed in this way. The plate carrying India collided with the Eurasian plate. The edges of the two plates buckled upward, forming the Himalayas.

 IDENTIFY: What mountain range was formed by the collision of two continental plates?

Volcanoes At subduction zones, oceanic plates dip back down into the hot mantle. The heat from the mantle melts the rocks in the subducting plate, forming magma. The magma collects in underground pockets called **magma chambers.** Hotter than the surrounding rock, the magma melts the solid rock around it and rises to the surface.

San Andreas Fault

North American plate

Pacific plate

San Francisco Bay

Crust

Mantle

▲ **Figure 6-20** Plates slide past each other at a transform boundary.

Magma also moves through cracks in rock. When it reaches the surface, a volcano forms. Mount St. Helens, in Washington State, formed in this way.

 DESCRIBE: How does magma reach the surface?

Islands Some islands are formed by plate tectonics. The Hawaiian Islands are a chain of volcanic islands in the Pacific Ocean. The islands formed one after the other as the Pacific plate drifted over a hot spot. A **hot spot** is a place where magma works its way to the surface within a plate. As the plate moves over the hot spot, new layers of volcanic mountains are built up.

The islands that are farthest northwest are the oldest. Kauai (koo-EYE) is the oldest of the large islands. Five million years ago, it was the only Hawaiian island. The islands to the southeast are the youngest. The big island of Hawaii is now over the hot spot. It is still being formed.

 DESCRIBE: How were the Hawaiian Islands formed?

 **CHECKING CONCEPTS**

1. What is a hot spot?
2. What is a magma chamber?
3. How were the Himalayas formed?
4. In what direction is the oceanic crust beneath the Hawaiian Islands moving?

 THINKING CRITICALLY

5. INFER: What are some of the possible surface features along the San Andreas Fault?
6. INFER: If railroad tracks were built over the boundary of two plates, such as in Figure 6-20, what would happen to the railroad tracks as the plates moved?
7. INFER: How can the chain of islands that make up Hawaii be used to show the direction the plate beneath them is moving?

 Integrating Physical Science

TOPICS: alternate energy sources, heat

GEOTHERMAL ENERGY

The opening page of this chapter shows Iceland's Blue Lagoon. The Blue Lagoon is heated by geothermal energy.

Geothermal energy is energy stored by heated rock deep inside Earth's crust. The heat from Earth's liquid core causes the movement of rock below Earth's surface. Iceland is a hot spot in the Mid-Atlantic Ridge. Deep pockets of water below the Blue Lagoon are heated by hot rocks. Steam forms and is pumped to the surface. The power plant uses the steam to turn a turbine, which generates electricity. Heated water is also pumped directly into homes to provide heat. Most commercial energy used in Iceland today also comes from geothermal energy.

▲ **Figure 6-21** The Blue Lagoon in Iceland is heated by geothermal energy.

The movement of rock below Earth's surface is part of plate tectonics. Iceland is affected by plate tectonics in many different ways. It has about 200 volcanoes. Only 70 have erupted in the last 10,000 years. Islands off the coast of Iceland were created by volcanoes. Iceland has many hot springs and geysers. Also, earthquakes are common in Iceland.

Thinking Critically How are islands created by volcanoes?

THE Big IDEA

How does plate tectonics affect countries around the world?

Like Earth science, geography is the study of Earth's surface. The word *geography* comes from two Greek words. *Geo* means "Earth," and *graphia* means "writing." Geography, then, means writing about, or describing, Earth. However, a geographer looks at Earth's surface differently from the way an Earth scientist does. Most geographers are not usually concerned about how the features were formed.

Geography has two main branches. One branch, called physical geography, describes the physical features of Earth's surface, such as mountains, valleys, plains, oceans, and rivers. It is this branch that is most closely related to Earth science. The other branch, called human geography, describes the people who live in or near those places and the cultures of the people who live there.

Iceland is not the only country affected by plate tectonics. Countries all over the world have many interesting land features that were formed by plate tectonics. Geographers are as interested in those features as Earth scientists are. The callouts that appear on these two pages point out some places on Earth where plate tectonics have left a mark on the geography of a region.

Look at the illustration that appears on these two pages. Then, follow the directions in the Science Log to find out more about "the big idea." ✦

Western North America
All along the San Andreas Fault, which runs through California, earthquakes are common.

Galápagos Rift
Along the Galápagos Rift, deep-sea vents and strange sea life have been discovered.

Baños, Ecuador
In December 1999, the Tungurahua volcano, also known as the Black Giant, erupted. It killed people and ruined farmland.

Iceland

Iceland is a land of fire and ice. It is home to many glaciers as well as the Blue Lagoon, hot springs, earthquakes, geysers, and active volcanoes. All of these features are caused by plate tectonics.

The Alps

This chain of mountains, formed millions of years ago, crosses Europe. It is one of the most popular skiing and hiking locations on Earth.

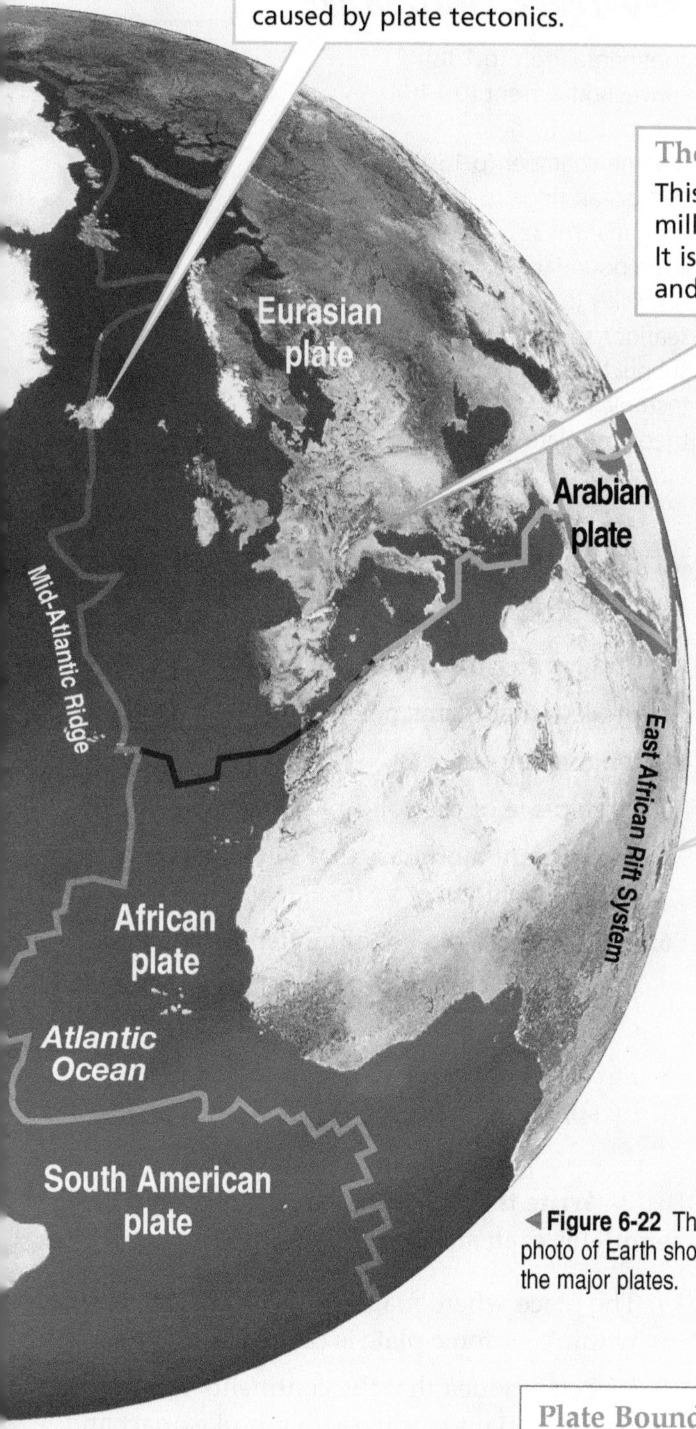

East African Rift System

This long system of cliffs and valleys in eastern Africa is due to the rifting apart of the African plate, which will someday become two plates. The Rift System can be clearly seen from as far away as the Moon!

Eurasian plate

Arabian plate

Mid-Atlantic Ridge

East African Rift System

African plate

Atlantic Ocean

South American plate

◀ **Figure 6-22** This satellite photo of Earth shows some of the major plates.

Plate Boundaries

—— Transform
—— Convergent
—— Divergent

WRITING ACTIVITY

Science Log

What place on this map would you like to visit? Do some research, and write a report describing why you would like to go there. Then, explain what effect plate tectonics has on the area and what you would expect to see because of it. Start your search at www.conceptsandchallenges.com.

Chapter Summary

Lesson 6-1

- Most scientists think that millions of years ago there was one giant continent called **Pangaea.**
- The theory of **continental drift** states that Pangaea split apart to eventually form today's continents.

Lesson 6-2

- Magma rising through the crust forms new crust on each side of the **mid-ocean ridges.** This process, which also creates **rift valleys,** is called **seafloor spreading.**

Lesson 6-3

- The direction in which the magnetic particles in rocks point is evidence that the ocean floor is spreading out from both sides of the Mid-Atlantic Ridge.
- Old oceanic crust is forced into ocean **trenches,** where it is changed to magma. **Subduction zones** are places where old oceanic crust is forced back down into an oceanic trench.

Lesson 6-4

- The crust of Earth and the upper, solid part of the mantle are broken into **tectonic plates** that float on the athenosphere, the part of the mantle that can flow. This theory is called **plate tectonics.**

Lesson 6-5

- Scientists think that **convection currents** in Earth's mantle cause the movement of tectonic plates.
- The tectonic plates move toward or away from each other at **plate boundaries.** They may also slide past each other.

Lesson 6-6

- Earthquakes often occur where two plates slide past each other. When two plates collide, sometimes the crust crumples up to form mountains.
- Volcanoes often form near subduction zones. This is because of the melting that occurs as the plate subducts into the hotter mantle.
- Some islands are formed when plates move over **hot spots.**

Key Term Challenges

continental drift (p.138)
convection current (p.146)
hot spot (p.150)
magma chamber (p.150)
mid-ocean ridge (p.140)
Pangaea (p.138)
plate boundary (p.146)
rift valley (p.140)
seafloor spreading (p.140)
subduction zone (p.142)
tectonic plate (p.144)
theory of plate tectonics (p.144)
trench (p.142)

MATCHING **Write the Key Term from above that best matches each description.**

1. underwater mountain chain

2. process that forms new seafloor

3. long valley

4. large piece of the solid part of Earth's surface

5. single giant landmass that scientists think existed millions of years ago

6. underground pocket of molten rock

7. movement of a gas or a liquid caused by changes in temperature

8. flat area between two ridges that is formed by spreading plates

FILL IN **Write the Key Term from above that best completes each statement.**

9. The place where magma reaches the surface within a tectonic plate is called a _____.

10. Wegener's idea that the continents were once part of a giant landmass that broke apart and moved into the positions they are in today is called _____.

11. The place where old crust is forced into a trench is a _____.

12. The idea that Earth's crust is broken into pieces that float on the mantle is the _____.

Content Challenges TEST PREP

MULTIPLE CHOICE **Write the letter of the term or phrase that best completes each statement.**

1. Wegener called the giant landmass that later formed the seven continents
   a. *Mesosaurus.*
   b. Pangaea.
   c. Gondwanaland.
   d. Tethys.

2. The oldest rocks found on the ocean floor are about
   a. 160 million years old.
   b. 160 billion years old.
   c. 4.6 million years old.
   d. 4.6 billion years old.

3. Scientists estimate that the age of Earth is
   a. 160 million years.
   b. 160 billion years.
   c. 4.6 million years.
   d. 4.6 billion years.

4. The deepest parts of the ocean floor are
   a. rift valleys.
   b. trenches.
   c. mid-ocean ridges.
   d. subduction zones.

5. When continental crust is pushed upward,
   a. a trench forms.
   b. a mountain forms.
   c. a rift valley forms.
   d. an island forms.

6. Tectonic plates sliding past each other are most likely to cause
   a. an earthquake.
   b. a mountain to form.
   c. a volcano to form.
   d. an island to form.

7. An animal fossil that is used to support the theory of continental drift is
   a. Tethys.
   b. Gondwana.
   c. *Mesosaurus.*
   d. Panthalassa Laurasia.

8. In a model of Pangaea, the coastline of South America seems to fit together with the coastline of
   a. Australia.
   b. northern Asia.
   c. North America.
   d. Africa.

9. Plates are made up of continental crust and
   a. islands.
   b. oceanic crust.
   c. magma.
   d. convection currents.

TRUE/FALSE **Write *true* if the statement is true. If the statement is false, change the underlined term to make the statement true.**

10. Peaks of mid-ocean ridges that rise above the surface of the ocean form <u>continents</u>.

11. Earthquakes and volcanic activity often take place along <u>mid-ocean ridges</u>.

12. The <u>oldest</u> crust on the ocean floor is found in the center of mid-ocean ridges.

13. Continental crust is <u>younger</u> than oceanic crust.

14. The theory that Earth's crust is broken into plates that float on the mantle is called <u>continental drift</u>.

15. The movement of tectonic plates is caused by <u>convection currents</u>.

Concept Challenges TEST PREP

WRITTEN RESPONSE **Answer each of the following questions in complete sentences.**

1. APPLY: How is the San Andreas Fault explained by the theory of plate tectonics?

2. EXPLAIN: How does the activity at subduction zones balance the activity at mid-ocean ridges?

3. INFER: How could mineral deposits formed along mid-ocean ridges become magma?

4. EXPLAIN: How does the theory of plate tectonics combine the idea of continental drift and seafloor spreading?

5. ANALYZE: Why doesn't Earth get bigger as a result of seafloor spreading?

6. CALCULATE: The oldest rocks found on the ocean floor are only about 160 million years old. For how many years of Earth's history are we missing ocean floor samples?

INTERPRETING VISUALS **Use Figure 6-23 to answer the following questions.**

7. Which two continents have similar mountain ranges?

8. What evidence on the continents of South America and Africa supports continental drift?

9. How does the evidence shown in the map support the idea of continental drift?

10. How do the shapes of the coastlines of South America and Africa support the idea of continental drift?

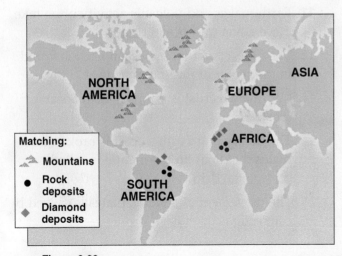

Matching:
- ⛰ Mountains
- ● Rock deposits
- ◆ Diamond deposits

▲ Figure 6-23

Chapter 7 Weathering and Soil

▲ **Figure 7-1** The Great Sphinx at Giza in Egypt

Ancient peoples carved stone statues to honor their gods and heroes. They believed the statues would last forever. Today, we know that rocks, statues, and even whole mountains do break down over time. They are worn away in a process known as weathering.

►The sphinx is a mythical creature. It has a lion's body and a human head. What signs of weathering show on this limestone carving of the Great Sphinx?

Contents

7-1 What is mechanical weathering?

INVESTIGATE

Modeling Weathering
HANDS-ON ACTIVITY

1. Pour 1 cup (250 mL) of tap water into each of two jars.

2. Add 1 piece of hard candy to each jar and close the lids.

3. Put one jar where it will not be disturbed.

4. Shake the other jar until the candy dissolves.

THINK ABOUT IT: What happened to the candy in the jar you shook? How is it different from the other candy? What do you think will eventually happen to the candy in the other jar?

Objective

Explain the ways that Earth's surface is worn away by mechanical weathering.

Key Terms

weathering: breaking down of rocks and other materials on Earth's surface

chemical (KEHM-ih-kuhl) **weathering:** weathering that changes the chemical makeup of rocks

mechanical (muh-KAN-ih-kuhl) **weathering:** weathering in which the chemical makeup of rocks does not change

ice wedging: mechanical weathering caused by the freezing and melting of water

Weathering The breaking down of rocks and other materials on Earth's surface is called **weathering.** Newly made bricks are bright red. They have sharp corners and edges. Old bricks are darker red. They have rounded corners and edges. What changes the bricks' color and shape? The process of weathering.

▼ **Figure 7-2** Over long periods of time, weathering changes the shape of mountains.

There are two kinds of weathering. **Chemical weathering** occurs when the chemical makeup of the rocks changes. The sizes and shapes of the rocks may also change.

Mechanical weathering involves only physical changes, such as size and shape. The chemical makeup of the rocks does not change. Mechanical weathering occurs as a result of temperature changes, ice wedging, and root action.

1 NAME: What are the two different types of weathering?

Temperature Changes Rocks may be broken apart by changes in temperature. Heat makes things expand, or become larger. Cooling makes things contract, or become smaller. During the day, heat can cause the outside of a rock to expand. The inside of the rock stays cool. At night, the outside of the rock cools and contracts. The repeated heating and cooling of the rock's surface each day may cause pieces of it to flake or peel off.

2 CLASSIFY: What kind of weathering do changes in temperature cause?

Ice Wedging The repeated freezing and melting of water causes **ice wedging.** Water enters cracks in rocks. When the temperature drops below freezing (0°C), water freezes and expands. The expanding water is like a wedge, making the crack wider. After the repeated freezing and melting of water, the rock breaks apart. Potholes in streets are caused by ice wedging.

3 IDENTIFY: What property of water causes it to act like a wedge when it freezes in cracks?

Root Action Plant roots in search of minerals and water can grow into cracks in rocks. Look at the sidewalk near a tree. Is the sidewalk cracked or raised? Tree roots may have caused the cracks by lifting up the sidewalk. The pressure of the growing root can make the cracks in rocks larger. As the roots grow, they can break the rocks apart.

▲ **Figure 7-3** Growing plant roots can lift up sidewalks.

 CLASSIFY: Does root action cause mechanical or chemical weathering?

 CHECKING CONCEPTS

1. Is breaking a rock into pieces chemical or mechanical weathering? Explain your choice.
2. What kind of weathering causes potholes?
3. What causes ice wedging?

 THINKING CRITICALLY

4. HYPOTHESIZE: Why should trees not be planted near underground water pipes?
5. ANALYZE: The breaking apart of rocks by growing roots is sometimes called root-pry. Is this is a good name? Explain.
6. PREDICT: Would you find potholes caused by weathering in tropical regions? Why or why not?

BUILDING SCIENCE SKILLS

Classifying Use the definitions of chemical change and mechanical change to classify each of the following.

a. A rock breaks into many pieces.
b. A match burns.
c. A sidewalk is cracked by a tree root.

 Real-Life Science

THE STATUES OF EASTER ISLAND

Easter Island is in the South Pacific Ocean. Its name comes from the fact that a Dutch explorer landed there on Easter Day in 1722. Tourists visit Easter Island to see its most famous attraction—the statues. The statues are carved in the form of humans. A typical statue might stand 4 m tall and weigh more than 12 metric tons. The statues were carved from hardened volcanic ash. This material was probably taken from the volcanic cone Rano Raraku, on the southern coast of the island.

▲ **Figure 7-4** The statues of Easter Island show the effects of weathering.

There are about 800 to 1,000 of these statues on Easter Island. Several other Pacific island cultures have statues like these. It is believed that all of these statues were carved for religious purposes.

Perhaps one-third of the statues on Easter Island are still standing. Weathering has caused the stone to slowly crumble away. Efforts are being made to preserve the statues.

Thinking Critically How do you think these statues could be preserved?

7-2 What is chemical weathering?

Objective

Explain how Earth's surface is worn away by chemical weathering.

Key Terms

oxidation (ahk-sih-DAY-shuhn): chemical change that occurs when oxygen reacts with another substance

hydrolysis (hy-DRAHL-uh-sihs): chemical reaction that occurs when minerals with little water content react with water

carbonation (kahr-buh-NAY-shuhn): chemical reaction that occurs when carbonic acid reacts with certain minerals

Kinds of Chemical Weathering In chemical weathering, substances in water cause substances in rocks to dissolve. This action weakens the structure of the rocks.

Chemical changes occur when minerals in rocks are broken down into other substances. They also occur when minerals are added to or removed from rocks. Chemical weathering is usually caused by reactions with oxygen, water, or acids.

▲ **Figure 7-5** The Statue of Liberty contains a large amount of copper. Its thin copper skin reacts with oxygen in the air to form a green coating.

1 NAME: What substances cause most chemical weathering?

Oxidation One kind of chemical weathering is **oxidation.** Oxidation occurs when oxygen combines with another substance. New substances called oxides are formed. Rust is an iron oxide (Fe_2O_3). Many rocks, such as pyrite and magnetite, have minerals that contain iron. When these rocks are exposed to the air, the iron undergoes oxidation. The rocks weaken and may crumble.

▲ **Figure 7-6** Like copper statues, rocks can be oxidized. Oxidized rocks change color. Here, the iron in the rock has reacted with oxygen in the air. The red streaks are oxidized iron, or rust.

2 DEFINE: What is oxidation?

Water Most chemical weathering is caused by water. Water reacting chemically with a mineral that has little water content is called **hydrolysis.** Many minerals in rocks undergo hydrolysis. For example, feldspar may combine chemically with water and change to clay. When heated or dried even a little, minerals formed by hydrolysis may fall apart.

3 EXPLAIN: What does hydrolysis do?

Acids Carbon dioxide can dissolve in rain to form weak carbonic acid. When this acid comes into contact with certain minerals, a chemical change called **carbonation** occurs. The mineral calcite is changed by this process. Limestone and marble are made of calcite. Buildings made of these materials are often weathered by carbonation.

▲ **Figure 7-7** Many buildings and building decorations are made of limestone. Limestone can be damaged by carbonation.

Some green plants produce weak acids. Mosses, which grow on rocks, are an example. The acids can wear away a rock's surface. As acid seeps into cracks in a rock, it can break the rock apart. Decaying organisms also produce acids, which contribute to chemical weathering. Chemical weathering changes the chemical composition of materials. This can weaken the material's internal structure.

 IDENTIFY: What acid forms from carbon dioxide and water?

1. How are minerals in a rock oxidized?
2. What does carbonation do to minerals?
3. How can plants cause chemical weathering?
4. What process will most likely chemically weather an iron-rich rock?

 THINKING CRITICALLY

5. INFER: Why do you think structures containing iron are painted?
6. CLASSIFY: Identify the kind of chemical weathering described in each case.
   a. A marble statue's nose can no longer be seen.
   b. A bicycle fender rusts.

BUILDING SCIENCE SKILLS

Experimenting Place one piece of steel wool outside your home. Make sure it is exposed to the weather. Place another piece in your room. Wait two weeks. Check the pieces often. What changes did you observe? Are there any differences in the two pieces of steel wool? If so, why?

 Science and Technology

PREVENTING CORROSION

Corrosion is the chemical weathering of materials such as metals. One common kind of corrosion is rust. Rust damages iron and steel. It weakens these metals and changes their color. Rusting affects highways and bridges, underground pipes and tanks, and building pipes.

▲ **Figure 7-8** Rusting made this bridge unsafe.

One of the best ways to slow rusting is to paint metals. Paint stops water from corroding the metals. Building steel is often coated with the metal zinc to protect it. Zinc resists corrosion. Steel coated with zinc is called galvanized steel.

Rust is also a big problem in cars and trucks. Rust destroys more cars each year than accidents do. New cars come with some corrosion protection. A wax-based spray can be applied to a car to give it added protection. A car can also be sprayed each year with an oil-based product that contains antirust agents. These methods help keep out the moisture that can cause corrosion.

Thinking Critically What might happen if water pipes in a building rusted?

LAB ACTIVITY
Modeling the Weathering of Sedimentary Rocks

Materials
- Safety goggles
- Lab apron
- 30 Sugar cubes
- 4 Craft sticks
- Beaker
- Dropper bottle
- Water
- Red or blue food coloring

BACKGROUND

If you ever walk through an old cemetery, you will see that many markers are hard to read. Walk along an old sidewalk, and you will see many cracks. Stone steps leading to an old building will be thinner in the middle than at the edges. Old stone statues look worn and cracked. Weathering has caused these changes. Weathering also changes rocks that make up the surface of Earth.

PURPOSE

In this activity, you will create a model of a small section of Earth's crust out of sugar cubes. Sugar cubes are made of small crystals joined together.

PROCEDURE

1. Copy the chart in Figure 7-9. In it, describe the appearance of a sugar cube.

2. Place the four craft sticks side by side across the rim of the beaker. ⚠ CAUTION: Be careful when working with glass.

3. Carefully place two side-by-side rows of five sugar cubes each on the sticks. The rows should touch each other.

4. Gently stack two more rows of cubes on top of the first rows.

5. Put on your safety goggles and a lab apron. Fill the dropper bottle with water mixed with one drop of food coloring.

▲ **STEP 3** Stack the sugar cubes in two rows.

▲ **STEP 6** Squeeze drops of water on the sugar cubes.

▲ **STEP 8** Observe what happens each time you add more water to your sugar cube structure.

6. Moving up and down the rows, squeeze single drops of water on the center of each cube. Repeat this step four times until each cube has received five drops.

7. Observe what happens to the sugar cubes. Write your observations in the chart.

8. Repeat Step 6 and 7 at least five times. Describe the results each time.

Number of water drops/cube	Total number of water drops/cube	Observations	Sugar cube appearance

▲ Figure 7-9

CONCLUSIONS

1. OBSERVE: What happened to the cubes?

2. OBSERVE: Which of the sugar cubes changed first?

3. INFER: What caused the sugar cubes to change?

4. INFER: Why did the walls between the rows of sugar cubes start dissolving?

5. HYPOTHESIZE: Are you modeling mechanical or chemical weathering?

7-3 What factors affect the rate of weathering?

Objective
Identify three factors that affect the rate of weathering.

Key Term
acid rain: rain containing acids produced by water chemically combining with certain gases

Climate The amount of water in the air and the temperature of an area are both part of an area's climate. Moisture speeds up chemical weathering. The more water there is in the air, the faster something weathers. Weathering occurs fastest in hot, wet climates. It occurs very slowly in hot, dry climates. Without liquid water, most chemical weathering cannot occur. Without temperature changes, ice wedging cannot occur. In very cold, dry areas, there is little weathering.

▶ 1 IDENTIFY: What two climate factors affect the rate of weathering?

Surface Area Most weathering occurs on exposed surfaces of rocks and minerals. Picture a large block of granite. It has six exposed surfaces. If the block is cut in half, two more surfaces are exposed. If each half is cut in half, four more surfaces are exposed. The more surface area a rock has, the more quickly it will weather. So, the smaller pieces of granite will weather faster than the large block of granite.

| 6 sides | 12 sides | 24 sides |

▲ **Figure 7-10** A block has more surface area when it is cut into smaller pieces.

▶ 2 DESCRIBE: How does surface area affect the weathering of rocks?

Rock Composition Some minerals that hold rocks together weather more quickly than others. Quartz, for example, resists weathering. Feldspar weathers quite easily. So, rocks rich in quartz will weather slowly, and rocks rich in feldspar will weather much faster. Some rocks, such as limestone, have large amounts of calcite in them. These rocks weather very quickly, often by carbonation. Rocks with iron generally weather faster than rocks without iron.

▶ 3 ANALYZE: What substances in rocks cause them to weather at different rates?

Chemical Reaction Carbon dioxide in the air becomes dissolved in rainwater. This forms carbonic acid, which is a weak acid. As the rainwater moves through soil, the carbonic acid dissolves calcite, a mineral found in marble and limestone. Limestone caves show the effects of this kind of weathering.

◀ **Figure 7-11** Formations in limestone caves show the effects of chemical weathering. The calcite solution drips into the cave, forming stalagtites, such as those shown here, and stalagmites. This formation is in Luray Caverns in Virginia's Shenandoah Valley.

Weathering is usually a slow process. However, pollution tends to speed it up. Factories and cars release carbon dioxide and other gases such as sulfur and nitrogen into the air. These become dissolved in the rainwater. Rain containing acids is called **acid rain.** Acid rain, which contains droplets of nitric and sulfuric acid, causes rocks and minerals to weather faster. The effects of acid rain can be seen on buildings and statues.

▶ 4 LIST: What acids are often present in acid rain?

✓ CHECKING CONCEPTS

Choose the word *increase* or *decrease* for each question.

1. The rate of weathering will _____ with moisture.

2. A rock that contains more quartz than feldspar will _____ the rate of weathering.

3. As a rock is broken into smaller pieces, the rate of weathering will _____.

4. In very polluted air, the weathering of a statue will probably _____.

THINKING CRITICALLY

5. LIST: What factors affect the rate of weathering?

6. PREDICT: Which would most likely have more weathered building stones: a city, a farm, or a desert? Explain.

Web InfoSearch

Cleopatra's Needle In 1881, a large stone monument called Cleopatra's Needle was moved from Egypt to New York City. It had stood for more than 3,000 years in Egypt. Writings carved on its surface had changed very little. Since its move to New York City, most of the writing has worn away.

▲ **Figure 7-12**
Cleopatra's Needle

SEARCH: Use the Internet to find out more about Cleopatra's Needle. What happened in New York City? Why? Start your search at **www.conceptsandchallenges.com**. Some key search words are **Cleopatra's Needle** and **Cleopatra's New York.**

Hands-On Activity

OBSERVING THE EFFECTS OF WEATHERING ON SURFACE AREA

You will need 2 plastic cups, a hammer, 2 pieces of chalk, a paper towel, vinegar, safety goggles, and a lab apron.

1. Break a piece of chalk in half. Place one half of the chalk into a plastic cup.

2. Wrap the other piece of chalk inside of a paper towel. Break it into small pieces with a hammer. Place these pieces into the second cup.
   ⚠ CAUTION: Wear your safety goggles and apron.

3. Pour enough vinegar into each cup to cover the chalk. Observe what happens.

▲ **STEP 3** Cover the chalk with vinegar.

Practicing Your Skills

4. COMPARE: Of the two pieces of chalk, which has the greater surface area?

5. IDENTIFY: What kind of weathering takes place when the pieces of chalk are placed in vinegar?

6. INFER: How is the rate of weathering affected by breaking up the chalk?

7-4 How does soil form?

Objective
Explain how soil is a product of weathering and organic processes.

Key Terms
bedrock: solid rock that lies beneath the soil

humus (HYOO-muhs)**:** decaying remains of plants and animals

soil: mixture that includes silt, sand, and clay

Formation of Soil If you dig a hole through the soil, sooner or later you will hit a layer of solid rock that is called **bedrock.** Bedrock is the parent material of soil.

In some areas, bedrock is at Earth's surface. Soil formation begins when bedrock is broken down by weathering. Weathering breaks the parent material into smaller and smaller pieces. Over time, the weathered rock is broken down into soil particles.

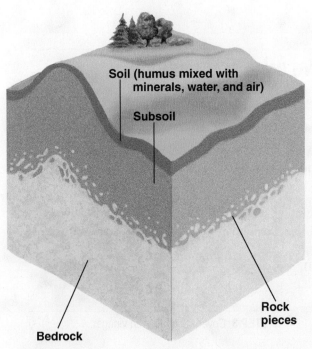

Soil (humus mixed with minerals, water, and air)

Subsoil

Rock pieces

Bedrock

▲ **Figure 7-13** Bedrock is the parent material of soil.

▶ IDENTIFY: From what parent material does soil form?

Living Things and Soil Many different kinds of organisms live in or on the soil. Living things also help to form soil. Some, such as mosses and lichens, form acids that help break down rocks. Bacteria in the soil cause dead plants and animals to decay. Fungi, such as mushrooms, also help break down dead animals and plants. Acids formed by decay speed up soil formation. The decayed remains of plants and animals form humus. **Humus** is the organic material in soil.

Animals that live in the soil help to form it. Earthworms, ants, prairie dogs, and moles burrow through the ground. As they do, they help break apart large pieces of soil. The burrowing also lets more water and air into the soil. The water helps speed up the breakdown of rock.

▲ **Figure 7-14** Prairie dogs live in burrows in the ground. In digging out their tunnels, they help form soil.

▶ DESCRIBE: What is humus?

Soil Silt, sand, and clay help make up the mixture known as **soil.** Weathered pieces of rocks, minerals, and humus are also in soil. Humus has a lot of minerals in it, especially quartz. These mixtures, which lie above bedrock, are important to plants. Soil that is rich in humus is very dark in color. Air and water are also in soil. They fill the spaces between soil particles.

▶ LIST: What things make up soil?

The Importance of Soil Soil is important to plants. It supplies plants with water and support. Most plants need the nutrients, or chemical elements, in soil to grow properly. Important nutrients such as potassium, phosphorus, and nitrogen are part of soil.

Soil is also important to people. Houses, cities, and roads are built on soil. Food crops are grown in soil. Many animals eat plants and could not survive without them. Other animals hunt and kill plant-eating animals for food. Without soil, few organisms could live on Earth.

 NAME: What are three important nutrients needed by plants?

CHECKING CONCEPTS

1. The parent material of soil is _____.
2. The organic material in soil is _____.
3. Air and _____ fill the spaces between soil particles.
4. The chemical elements in soil that are needed by plants are called _____.
5. The process that forms soil is _____.

THINKING CRITICALLY

6. **INFER:** Why is bedrock called the parent material of soil?
7. **ANALYZE:** How do ants help to speed up the formation of soil?
8. **DESCRIBE:** Explain how soil meets the needs of plants for support, water, and nutrients.

Web InfoSearch

Lichens Not many organisms can live on bare rock. Rocks hold little water and are battered by heat and wind. Lichens, however, can live and grow on bare rocks. Lichens are fungi that form a permanent partnership with certain algae, bacteria, or both. Each organism is helped by the partnership. This is called mutualism.

SEARCH: Use the Internet to find out why lichens are important. How do they help to form soil? Start your search at www.conceptsandchallenges.com. Some key search words are **lichens, lichen soil,** and **lichen uses.**

Integrating Life Science

TOPICS: food chain, ecology

LIFE IN THE SOIL

The soil is teeming with living things. Some organisms mix the soil and make room in it for air and water. Others make humus.

Fallen, decaying leaves form a loose layer in the soil called litter. Humus forms during decomposition. Decomposers break down the litter and the remains of dead organisms and return their nutrients to the soil. Mushrooms, protists, insects, bacteria, and worms are the main soil decomposers. Earthworms carry humus down to the subsoil. Mice, moles, prairie dogs, and gophers break up hard soil. Animal waste also adds nitrogen to the soil.

Thinking Critically What is mixed into the soil when prairie dogs break it up?

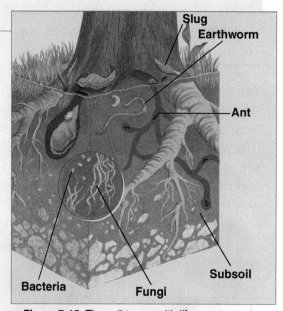

▲ **Figure 7-15** The soil teems with life.

How do soils differ?

Examining Soil Composition
HANDS-ON ACTIVITY

1. Obtain soil from the ground, and buy a peat-based soil and one with fertilizers added. Keep the packaging that shows the composition of the soil from the store.
2. Put the three different soils on paper plates.
3. Using your eyes alone, examine the soils.
4. Using a magnifying glass, examine the soils again.

THINK ABOUT IT: How are the various soils different? What was added to the soil you bought from the store? Why were these added?

STEP 4

Objective

Describe differences in soils in terms of texture, mineral content, and where the soil was formed.

Key Terms

texture (TEHKS-chuhr): size of soil particles

transported (trans-POR-tihd) **soil:** soil moved away from the bedrock from which it was formed

residual (rih-ZIJ-oo-uhl) **soil:** soil remaining on top of the bedrock from which it formed

leaching (LEECH-ing): removing or washing away of the minerals in soil

Texture Soils have different textures. **Texture** describes the size of the soil particles. Sandy soils have a coarse texture. Sand particles are between 0.06 mm and 2 mm in diameter. Some soils contain silt. Silt particles are only between about 0.008 mm and 0.016 mm in diameter. Silty soils are finer than sandy soils.

▲ **Figure 7-16** Soil comes in three basic textures: fine, medium, and coarse.

The smallest particles in soil are clay. Clay particles are 0.004 mm or smaller. Soils with a lot of clay have a fine texture. When these soils are wet, they feel sticky or muddy.

▶ **1 DESCRIBE:** What is meant by soil texture?

Bedrock and Soil Sometimes soil is carried away from the place in which it is formed. Soil can be moved by running water, glaciers, wind, or waves. The soil is then deposited in a new place. This soil is called **transported soil.**

Transported soil may differ from the bedrock, or parent material, that is beneath it. The process that moves the soil from one place to another may also act to change it chemically.

Many soils stay on top of the bedrock from which they were formed. These are called **residual soils.** Residual soils have a chemical makeup similar to that of their parent material.

▶ **2 CONTRAST:** How do transported and residual soils differ?

Minerals in Soil Weathering rates depend on the mineral makeup of the soil. The kinds and amounts of minerals in soil vary. It all depends on the parent material. For example, the minerals in the rock granite are different from those in limestone. Weathered granite produces one kind of soil. Weathered limestone produces a different kind of soil.

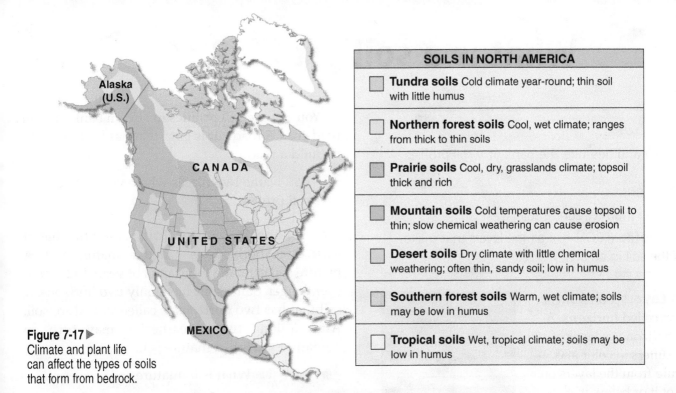

SOILS IN NORTH AMERICA	
☐ **Tundra soils**	Cold climate year-round; thin soil with little humus
☐ **Northern forest soils**	Cool, wet climate; ranges from thick to thin soils
☐ **Prairie soils**	Cool, dry, grasslands climate; topsoil thick and rich
☐ **Mountain soils**	Cold temperatures cause topsoil to thin; slow chemical weathering can cause erosion
☐ **Desert soils**	Dry climate with little chemical weathering; often thin, sandy soil; low in humus
☐ **Southern forest soils**	Warm, wet climate; soils may be low in humus
☐ **Tropical soils**	Wet, tropical climate; soils may be low in humus

Figure 7-17 ▶
Climate and plant life can affect the types of soils that form from bedrock.

Chemical weathering also affects the minerals in soil. Minerals are removed from soils by plants and by leaching. **Leaching** is the removing or washing away of minerals by water. The minerals in the soil are dissolved and washed deeper into the soil or are washed away completely.

On farmland, these minerals need to be replaced. Crops need minerals to grow properly. Farmers add fertilizers to the soil to replace minerals used up by plants or washed away by leaching.

3 ▶ DESCRIBE: How are minerals removed from soil?

Climate and Soil An area's climate helps to determine the type of soil formed from bedrock. Scientists classify different types of soil into groups based partly on a region's climate. Look at Figure 7-17 above to see where each of the major soil types is found in North America.

4 ▶ IDENTIFY: Which soil type is found on your part of the continent?

☑ CHECKING CONCEPTS

1. The size of particles in soil describes the _____ of the soil.

2. If a soil is very different from the bedrock beneath it, the soil is probably a _____ soil.

3. A soil with a fine texture probably has a lot of _____ in it.

4. The movement of minerals by water deeper into the soil is called _____.

💡 THINKING CRITICALLY

5. INFER: Which types of soil described in Figure 7-17 would you expect to form most slowly?

6. HYPOTHESIZE: How might chemical weathering affect the minerals in soil that is forming?

Web InfoSearch

Soil Conservation One job of the federal government's Natural Resources Conservation Service (NRCS) is to help protect natural resources. NRCS soil conservationists work with farmers and ranchers to prevent soil erosion, protect wildlife, and keep water supplies clean.

SEARCH: Use the Internet to find out how you can work for the NRCS. Start your search at www.conceptsandchallenges.com. Some key search words are **National Resources Conservation Service, NRCS, and NRCS jobs.**

7-6 What is a soil profile?

Objective
Identify and describe the parts of a soil profile.

Key Terms
horizon (huh-RY-zuhn): soil layer
soil profile (PROH-fyl): all the layers that make up the soil in an area

Soil Layers Soil forms in layers called **horizons**. A soil horizon is a layer of soil that differs in color and texture from the layers on top of it or below it.

▲ **Figure 7-18** The layers of soil are easy to see here.

Most soils have at least three horizons. Each one is named with a capital letter. The A horizon is the top layer of soil. However, this layer is actually covered with a thin coating of organic material called the O horizon. The O horizon is made up mostly of plant litter, such as loose and decaying leaves. It is also teeming with microscopic life and the remains of plants and animals.

The A and O horizon together make up the top layer of soil. The B horizon is beneath the A horizon. The C horizon is the bottom layer. All the soil layers together are called a **soil profile.**

You can see soil profiles in stream banks and in road cuts. A road cut is land that has been dug out to build a road.

1 LIST: Name two places where you might see a soil profile.

Mature and Immature Soils A soil that has at least three horizons is called a mature soil. A mature soil can take thousands of years to form or even longer. Some soils have only two horizons. A soil that has two horizons is called immature soil. After a long time, weathering may turn an immature soil into a mature soil.

2 DESCRIBE: What is immature soil?

The A Horizon The A horizon is found below the O horizon, the thin layer of organic material. The A horizon is usually the topsoil, a mixture of humus and rock particles. Humus gives topsoil its dark color.

Topsoil is rich in nutrients. Most organisms that live in the soil are found in the A horizon. Plants grow best in topsoil.

3 IDENTIFY: What is topsoil made up of?

The B Horizon The B horizon, called subsoil, is found beneath the A horizon. Subsoil is mostly clay, small pieces of weathered rock, and minerals. Leaching moves minerals from the A into the B horizon. Because the subsoil has a lot of clay in it, it is much firmer than the topsoil. For this reason, only the roots of very large plants grow into the B horizon.

4 COMPARE: Why is the B horizon firmer than the A horizon?

Go Online
active art

For: Soil Layers activity
Visit: PHSchool.com
Web Code: cfp-2022

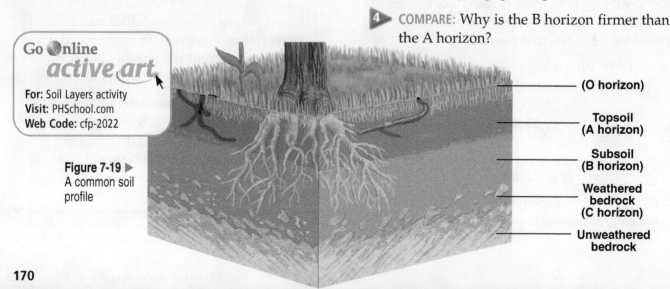

Figure 7-19 ▶
A common soil profile

(O horizon)

Topsoil
(A horizon)

Subsoil
(B horizon)

Weathered bedrock
(C horizon)

Unweathered bedrock

The C Horizon The C horizon is the bottom layer of a soil profile. The C horizon is made up of large pieces of rock. Weathering of these large pieces of rock is the first step in forming soil. At the bottom of the C horizon is solid bedrock. The large pieces of rock in the C horizon come from the weathering of bedrock.

 DESCRIBE: Where is the C horizon located in a soil profile?

✓ CHECKING CONCEPTS

1. Soil forms in layers called _____.
2. The B horizon is the _____.
3. The number of horizons in immature soil is _____.
4. The A horizon is made up of a dark-colored soil called _____.
5. If a soil has at least three horizons, it is a _____ soil.
6. In the C horizon, the large pieces of rock are weathered _____.

THINKING CRITICALLY

7. **RELATE:** What is the relationship between soil horizons and a soil profile?
8. **CONTRAST:** What is the difference between mature and immature soils?

BUILDING READING SKILLS

Prefixes Find out the meaning of the prefix *sub-*. Then, use it to help you define the words in the list below. Write a definition for each word. Circle the word or words in the definition that relate to the meaning of the prefix *sub-*.

- subheading
- submarine
- submerge
- subsoil
- substance
- subway

Hands-On Activity

MODELING A SOIL PROFILE

You will need a clear plastic cup, modeling clay, sand, gravel, soil, and a marking pen.

1. In a clear plastic cup, arrange layers of modeling clay, sand, gravel, and soil to make a model of a soil profile. Let the modeling clay represent the bedrock.
2. Use a marking pen to identify each layer of your soil profile. Label the A, B, and C horizons, and the bedrock.
3. Draw a diagram of your soil profile. Compare your drawing with the soil profile in Figure 7-20.

Practicing Your Skills

4. **IDENTIFY:** Which material did you use to represent the A horizon? The B horizon? The C horizon?
5. **CLASSIFY:** Does your soil profile show a mature soil or an immature soil? Explain.
6. **IDENTIFY: a.** Which horizon of a soil profile is the topsoil?
   b. Which horizon is the subsoil?

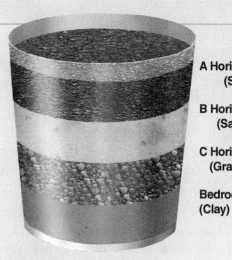

A Horizon (Soil)

B Horizon (Sand)

C Horizon (Gravel)

Bedrock (Clay)

▲ **Figure 7-20** Be sure to label each layer of your soil profile.

THE Big IDEA

How does the chemistry of soil affect plant growth?

To carry out life processes, plants must obtain certain nutrients. Plants get these essential nutrients from the soil. But not all soil is alike. The chemical makeup of soil differs from place to place. This difference affects how easily nutrients can be absorbed by a plant.

For example, some soils are more acidic than others. Chemists measure acid content using the **pH scale**. The pH scale consists of numbers between 0.0 and 14.0. A pH of 7 means that the substance is neutral. A pH above 7 means that the substance is basic, or alkaline. A pH below 7 means that the substance is acidic. Neutral solutions are neither basic nor acidic.

Most plants grow well in slightly acidic soil, with a pH of between 6 and 7. Soils with pH levels between 4 and 5 often have high amounts of aluminum, iron, and manganese, which harm plants. Soils with pH levels between 7 and 8 often contain a lot of calcium, potassium, magnesium, and sodium. Few plants will grow in soils with a pH below 4 or above 8.

The acidity of soil can be checked with a pH meter. It can also be tested using an **indicator kit**. Indicators change color in acidic and basic solutions. After testing, the soil pH can be adjusted by adding certain materials. To raise the pH, the soil can be "sweetened" with lime. Lime is finely ground limestone. To lower the pH, peat moss or sulfur can be added.

Look at the illustrations on these two pages. Then, follow the directions in the Science Log to learn more about "the big idea." ✦

Growing Plants in Acidic Soil
Rhododendrons grow well in acidic soil with a pH between 4.0 and 6.0.

Growing Plants in Alkaline Soil
Cabbage grows well in slightly alkaline soil with a pH of about 7.5.

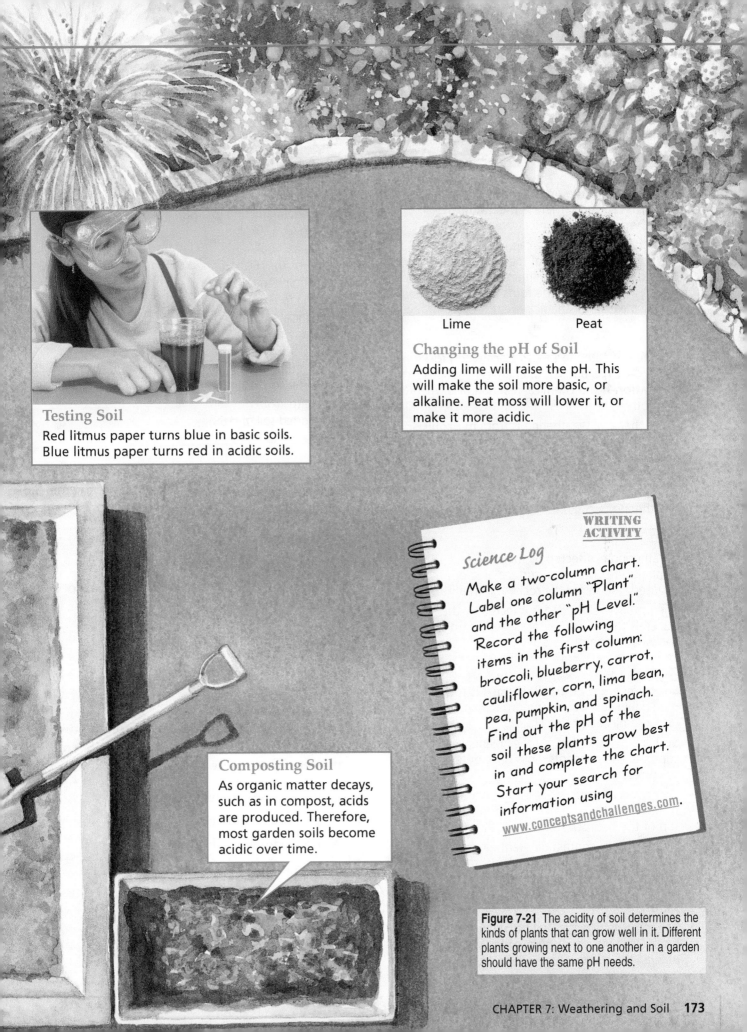

Testing Soil

Red litmus paper turns blue in basic soils. Blue litmus paper turns red in acidic soils.

Lime   **Peat**

Changing the pH of Soil

Adding lime will raise the pH. This will make the soil more basic, or alkaline. Peat moss will lower it, or make it more acidic.

WRITING ACTIVITY

Science Log

Make a two-column chart. Label one column "Plant" and the other "pH Level." Record the following items in the first column: broccoli, blueberry, carrot, cauliflower, corn, lima bean, pea, pumpkin, and spinach. Find out the pH of the soil these plants grow best in and complete the chart. Start your search for information using www.conceptsandchallenges.com.

Composting Soil

As organic matter decays, such as in compost, acids are produced. Therefore, most garden soils become acidic over time.

Figure 7-21 The acidity of soil determines the kinds of plants that can grow well in it. Different plants growing next to one another in a garden should have the same pH needs.

Chapter Summary

Lesson 7-1

- **Weathering** is the breaking down of materials on Earth's surface. There is **mechanical weathering** and **chemical weathering.**
- Changes in temperature can break rocks apart. **Ice wedging** is a kind of mechanical weathering caused by the repeated freezing and melting of water. Pressure from the roots of growing trees can also cause mechanical weathering.

Lesson 7-2

- Chemical weathering takes place when rocks break down as a result of chemical changes. **Oxidation** is the chemical reaction of oxygen with other substances.
- Most chemical weathering is from **hydrolysis,** which is water reacting with water-poor substances.
- **Carbonation** breaks down minerals in rocks. Plants also produce acids that cause chemical weathering.

Lesson 7-3

- Weathering is affected by moisture and temperature. The more surface area of rocks exposed, the faster the rocks will weather.
- The rate of weathering is affected by the minerals that make up rocks. **Acid rain** speeds the weathering process.

Lessons 7-4 and 7-5

- Soil forms from **bedrock. Humus** is the organic material in soil. Burrowing organisms help break up large pieces of soil.
- **Soil** is a mixture that supplies plants with water, support, and nutrients. Soils have different **textures.**
- **Transported soils** are soils that were moved from where they formed. **Residual soils** stay on top of the bedrock from which they formed.
- Different soils contain different kinds and amounts of minerals. Minerals are removed from soils by plants and by **leaching.**

Lesson 7-6

- Soil forms in layers called **horizons.** These horizons make up a **soil profile.** Mature soil has at least three horizons: A, B, and C.

Key Term Challenges

acid rain (p. 164)
bedrock (p. 166)
carbonation (p. 160)
chemical weathering (p. 158)
horizon (p. 170)
humus (p. 166)
hydrolysis (p. 160)
ice wedging (p. 158)
leaching (p. 168)
mechanical weathering (p. 158)
oxidation (p. 160)
residual soil (p. 168)
soil (p. 166)
soil profile (p. 170)
texture (p. 168)
transported soil (p. 168)
weathering (p. 158)

MATCHING **Write the Key Term from above that best matches each description.**

1. layer of rock beneath soil
2. size of soil particles
3. breaking down of rocks and materials of Earth's surface
4. rain containing harmful acids
5. washing away of minerals in soil
6. soil layer

IDENTIFYING WORD RELATIONSHIPS **Explain how the words in each pair are related. Write your answers in complete sentences.**

7. residual soil, transported soil
8. chemical weathering, mechanical weathering
9. ice wedging, hydrolysis
10. oxidation, carbonation
11. horizon, soil profile
12. humus, soil
13. acid rain, weathering
14. leaching, chemical weathering

Content Challenges TEST PREP

MULTIPLE CHOICE **Write the letter of the term or phrase that best completes each statement.**

1. Hydrolysis, carbonation, and oxidation are kinds of
   a. leaching.
   b. mechanical weathering.
   c. chemical weathering.
   d. acid rain.

2. Subsoil is located in
   a. the O horizon.
   b. the A horizon.
   c. the B horizon.
   d. the C horizon.

3. A soil that has only two horizons is classified as
   a. a sweet soil.
   b. a sour soil.
   c. a mature soil.
   d. an immature soil.

4. Topsoil is located in
   a. no horizon.
   b. the A horizon.
   c. the B horizon.
   d. the C horizon.

5. Most chemical weathering is caused by the process called
   a. acid rain.
   b. carbonation.
   c. oxidation.
   d. hydrolysis.

6. Chemical weathering occurs the fastest in
   a. hot, dry climates.
   b. cold, dry climates.
   c. cold, wet climates.
   d. hot, wet climates.

7. Soil carried away from where it was formed is called
   a. residual soil.
   b. mature soil.
   c. transported soil.
   d. immature soil.

8. The smallest particles in soil are
   a. silt.
   b. sand.
   c. clay.
   d. weathered rock.

FILL IN **Write the term or phrase that best completes each statement.**

9. Mechanical weathering does not change the _____ of rocks.

10. Potholes in streets are caused by _____.

11. Root action and ice wedging are kinds of _____ weathering.

12. Oxidation forms new substances called _____.

13. Carbon dioxide can dissolve in rain to form _____.

14. A rock containing quartz weathers _____ than a rock containing calcite.

15. Bedrock is the _____ material of soil.

16. The organic material found in soil is called _____.

17. Most plants need the _____ found in soil to grow properly.

18. Sandy soils have a _____ texture.

19. Farmers add _____ to the soil to replace minerals washed away by leaching or used by plants.

20. An area's _____ helps to determine what kind of soil is formed from bedrock.

Concept Challenges TEST PREP

WRITTEN RESPONSE **Answer each of the following questions in complete sentences.**

1. EXPLAIN: Why is weathering slow in a cold, dry climate?
2. PREDICT: What kind of chemical weathering is most likely to affect a rock containing calcite? Why?
3. EXPLAIN: How do living things help to form soil?
4. INFER: How does leaching affect plant life?

INTERPRETING VISUALS **Use Figure 7-22 below to answer the following questions.**

5. What is shown in the diagram?
6. What is each layer of soil called?
7. What is the name of the layer indicated by the letter *K*?
8. What is the name of the layer indicated by the letter *L*?
9. What kind of soil makes up the layer labeled *L*?
10. What is the soil that makes up layer *M* called?
11. What material makes up the layer labeled *N*?
12. Is this mature or immature soil? Explain your answer.

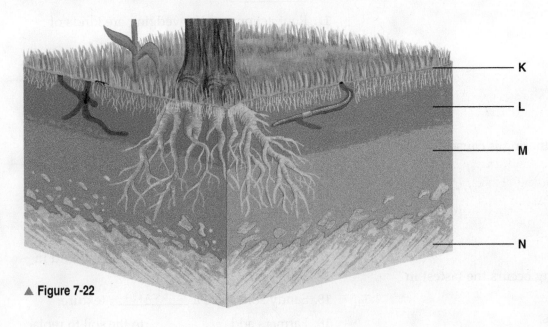

▲ **Figure 7-22**

Chapter 8 Erosion

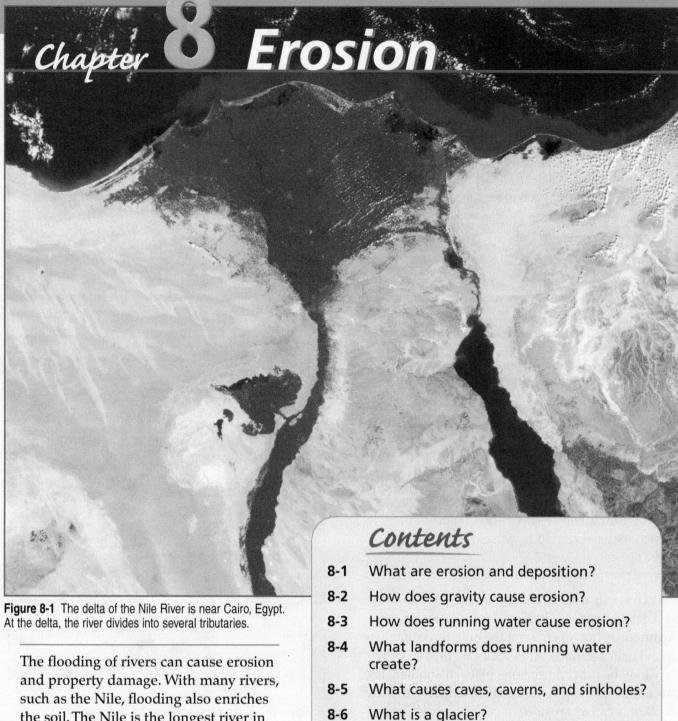

Figure 8-1 The delta of the Nile River is near Cairo, Egypt. At the delta, the river divides into several tributaries.

The flooding of rivers can cause erosion and property damage. With many rivers, such as the Nile, flooding also enriches the soil. The Nile is the longest river in the world. About 5,000 years ago, the first great African civilization developed in the Nile Valley, where Egypt is today. As an agricultural state, Egypt relied on the yearly flooding of the Nile. The rich soil around the Nile made Egypt a very successful civilization. Egypt ruled much of northeastern Africa for thousands of years.

▶What benefits did the yearly flooding of the Nile bring to Egypt?

Contents

Preventing Erosion
HANDS-ON ACTIVITY

1. Fill a pie plate with a pile of sand or soil.

2. See if you can find a way to keep the soil from washing away when water is poured over it. You can try using small wooden sticks, strips of paper, pebbles— anything you can think of.

THINK ABOUT IT: Do any of the methods prevent the soil from washing away? If so, how?

STEP 2

Objectives

Define erosion and deposition. List five agents of erosion.

Key Terms

erosion (ee-ROH-zhuhn)**:** process by which weathered material is removed and carried from a place

deposition (dehp-uh-ZIHSH-uhn)**:** process by which material carried by erosion is dropped in new places

Weathering and Erosion The rocks that make up Earth's crust are broken down by weathering. Weathering, however, is not the only force that acts upon Earth's surface. After rocks are broken down, they may be moved from one place to another. The process of moving weathered material from place to place is called **erosion.**

 DEFINE: What is erosion?

Agents of Erosion Through erosion, parts of Earth's surface are worn away. One example is the Grand Canyon in Arizona. The Grand Canyon is a gash in Earth's surface almost 2 km deep. At the bottom of the Grand Canyon is the Colorado River. As the river flows, it carries away small pieces of weathered rock. Over millions of years, enough rock bits were carried away to carve out the Grand Canyon.

▲ **Figure 8-2** Rivers carry debris such as weathered rocks to new places.

Running water, glaciers, wind, waves, and gravity are five common agents of erosion. Running water and glaciers carry with them large amounts of rock and soil. Waves move sand onto and off a beach. Wind picks up sand and moves dirt and dust. Gravity causes soil and rocks to move down a slope.

 LIST: What are five common agents of erosion?

Deposition Materials removed by erosion are laid down in new places. The process by which weathered materials are carried by agents of erosion and dropped in new places is called **deposition.** Deposition builds landforms on Earth.

▲ **Figure 8-3** This sandbar was built by deposition.

3 DEFINE: What is deposition?

☑ CHECKING CONCEPTS

1. The Grand Canyon was formed by the process of _____.

2. There are _____ common agents of erosion.

3. Running water, wind, _____, gravity, and glaciers are agents of erosion.

4. The dropping of rocks carried by a glacier is an example of _____.

💡 THINKING CRITICALLY

5. CONTRAST: What is the difference between erosion and deposition?

6. INFER: A roadside sign on a mountain road says, "Beware of Falling Rocks." Which agent of erosion is probably at work in the area?

7. ANALYZE: Are shells on the beach an example of erosion or deposition? How do you think the shells were carried there?

BUILDING SCIENCE SKILLS

Researching and Writing The federal government spends millions of dollars each year repairing damage caused by erosion. Research the types of damage that are caused by erosion in your area. Explain what is being done to stop the damage and whether you think the effort is worth the money spent.

Real-Life Science

RECLAIMING THE LAND

Coal was formed millions of years ago from buried plants and other organisms. Today, more than half of our country's electric power comes from burning coal.

In the method of mining coal called strip mining, plants and topsoil are removed to reach the coal inside the rock. The exposed coal is called a coal seam. This process leaves a gash in Earth's surface. The newly exposed broken rock is now subject to weathering and begins to erode.

▲ **Figure 8-4** A coal seam is exposed in this strip mine.

Until the 1970s, there were no federal laws about abandoned mines. Many were simply left behind by the companies that had dug them. However, the Surface Mining and Reclamation Act of 1977 changed that. Today, mining companies must put down new layers of topsoil. They must replant former crops or grass. Dry ground must be irrigated. Finally, the site is studied for many years. This is to help make sure that the land weakened by mining returns to its original state.

Thinking Critically Why is it necessary to put down new topsoil?

8-2 How does gravity cause erosion?

Objective
Describe how erosion can be caused by gravity.

Key Terms
mass erosion: downhill movement of weathered materials caused by gravity

talus: pile of rocks and rock particles that collects at the base of a slope

The Effects of Gravity On Earth, the force of gravity pulls all things toward Earth's center. This downward pull of gravity can cause materials to move from areas of high elevation to areas of low elevation.

Most erosion begins with the force of gravity pulling materials toward the center of Earth. For example, the force of gravity can cause rocks and glaciers to move down mountain slopes. Gravity also causes rivers to flow toward the oceans.

▶ **1** EXPLAIN: How does gravity cause erosion?

Mass Movement The downhill movement of weathered materials caused by gravity is called **mass erosion.** Mass erosion can occur quickly or slowly. Materials moved by gravity come to rest in piles at the base of a slope. A pile of these materials is called **talus.** The talus may be carried away by running water or other agents of erosion.

▲ **Figure 8-5** Talus that was moved down the mountain by gravity

▶ **2** DEFINE: What is mass erosion?

Landslides and Mudflows The sudden mass erosion of rocks down a hill is called a landslide. Rocks on a hill can be loosened by earthquakes, volcanic eruptions, or even heavy rains. The force of gravity may suddenly pull the loosened rocks down the slope of the hill. The moving rocks in a landslide can seriously damage anything that gets in their path.

A mudflow is the rapid mass erosion of mud down a hillside. Mudflows usually happen in dry, mountainous regions after a heavy rainfall.

Like landslides, mudflows can damage property. In the United States, mudflows commonly occur in the hillside communities of southern California.

▲ **Figure 8-6** Mudflow caused this property damage.

▶ **3** CONTRAST: How do mudflows differ from landslides?

Earthflow and Creep Earthflow and creep are both slower forms of mass erosion. Earthflow is the slow movement of soil, rocks, and plant life down a slope. Loose earth and extra moisture help cause it. Earthflow can cause part of a hillside to look like it is sliding away.

Creep is even slower. It is caused by gravity pulling soil and rocks down a gentle slope. Creep can be very hard to see. However, bent trees or bent telephone poles are important clues that it is happening.

▲ **Figure 8-7** Creep is hard to see happening. However, its effects, such as bent trees, are obvious.

4 ▸ IDENTIFY: What are two examples of slow mass erosion?

✔ CHECKING CONCEPTS

1. The force of gravity can cause rocks and _____ to move down mountain slopes.
2. Gravity causes rivers to flow toward the _____.
3. The sudden movement of rocks down a hillside is called a _____.
4. Weathered material that collects at the base of a slope is called _____.

 THINKING CRITICALLY

5. CLASSIFY: Identify each description as evidence of a landslide, mudflow, earthflow, or creep. **a.** A hillside slowly slides down toward the bottom. **b.** A car driving on a mountain road must swerve to avoid falling rocks. **c.** Mud from a heavy rain blocks a road at the base of a mountain. **d.** The fenceposts on a slope are tilting slightly.

Web InfoSearch

Nevado del Ruiz November 13, 1985: The Nevado del Ruiz volcano in Colombia, South America, erupts. The explosion sends lahars rushing down nearby valleys. Lahars are mixtures of water, rock, sand, and mud. The lahars rip huge boulders, trees, and houses from the ground and carry them away. Over 23,000 people are killed.

SEARCH: Use the Internet to find out more about landslides. How do they cause erosion? How do lahars form? Start your search at www.conceptsandchallenges.com. Some key search words are **landslide, lahars,** and **Nevado del Ruiz.**

 Hands-On Activity

MODELING GRAVITY ON A SLOPE

Friction is a force that opposes motion. Friction affects how easily material that has been eroded travels down a slope. For this activity, you will need a board, a block of wood, a marble, and sandpaper.

1. Place a board flat on your desk. Place a marble on the board and slowly tip the board up. Observe what happens.
2. Place a block of wood on the board. Slowly lift up one end of the board.
3. Now, cover the wood block with sandpaper. Use tape to hold the sandpaper in place. Repeat Step 2.

Practicing Your Skills

4. EXPLAIN: What do you think caused the differences in your observations?
5. RELATE: Which type of gravity erosion does each of the setups model?

▲ **STEP 3** Repeat Step 2 using the wood block covered with sandpaper.

Go Online
active art
For: Mass Movement activity
Visit: PHSchool.com
Web Code: cfp-2031

How does running water cause erosion?

STEP 3

INVESTIGATE

Modeling Erosion by Water
HANDS-ON ACTIVITY

1. Turn on a faucet and let water slowly drip from it.

2. Place a bar of soap in a dry place. Place another bar of the exact same soap under the dripping faucet. Let the faucet drip for 10 minutes.

3. Turn off the faucet and compare the two bars of soap.

THINK ABOUT IT: What did you think would happen to the soap when you placed it under the faucet? Why? What do you think it would look like if you left it there longer? How can you speed up or slow down the process?

Objective

Describe how running water causes erosion.

Key Terms

runoff: water from rain or snow that flows into streams and rivers from surface areas

tributary (TRIHB-yoo-tehr-ee): smaller stream that flows into the main stream of a river system

Running Water Running water changes more of Earth's surface than any other agent of erosion. Rivers, streams, and runoff are forms of running water. **Runoff** is water from rain or snow that flows over Earth's surface. Runoff empties into streams and standing bodies of water such as lakes and ponds.

▶ **LIST:** What are three forms of running water?

Runoff and Erosion As runoff flows over Earth's surface, the running water carries away soil particles. The faster the water moves, the more soil the water may carry away. For example, gullies in a hillside are formed by erosion from runoff.

The amount of rainfall, plant growth, and shape of the land affect the amount of runoff in an area. During heavy rains, there is a lot of runoff. However, plants help to stop erosion from runoff.

The roots of plants take in some water and hold soil particles in place. For this reason, areas with a lot of plant growth have less runoff than areas with little plant growth. Areas with steep slopes have the most runoff. The greater the amount of runoff, the more erosion there will be.

▶ **PREDICT:** Would there be more erosion from runoff on a hillside or on flat land? Explain.

River Systems A river is made up of a main stream and all the smaller streams that flow into the main stream. The smaller streams that flow into the main stream of a river system are called **tributaries,** or branches. The Mississippi River is the main stream of a large river system.

▲ **Figure 8-8** The Mississippi River has many tributaries.

The Mississippi River has many tributaries. One of them, the Missouri River, is almost as long as the Mississippi River itself. Runoff from the surrounding land feeds the many tributaries of a river system.

 IDENTIFY: What are two rivers in the Mississippi River system?

Formation of a River A river system usually forms in mountains or in hills. The place where a river starts is called its source. When water cannot soak into the ground, runoff flows down the slope of the hill or mountain. The running water erodes the soil and cuts gullies into the slope. A small channel forms. Channels are the paths the streams follow. The small stream may join other small streams to form a larger stream. Larger streams may flow together to form the tributaries of the main stream, or river, of a river system.

 EXPLAIN: How do channels form?

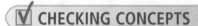 **CHECKING CONCEPTS**

1. How does runoff cause erosion?
2. What causes gullies in a hillside?

3. What is a tributary?
4. What is a river system?
5. Where do river systems usually form?

 THINKING CRITICALLY

6. **PREDICT:** Can planting trees on a hillside help to prevent running water from eroding the land? Explain.
7. **SEQUENCE:** Place the following terms in the correct order to show how rivers can form: channel, small stream, river, large stream, and tributary.
8. **INFER:** How does snow help to form rivers?

BUILDING SCIENCE SKILLS

Modeling and Researching Draw and label a diagram comparing a river and its tributaries to a tree and its branches. Indicate what part of a tree is like the main stream of a river. Then, do research to find out the names of at least one tributary of each of the following rivers: the Nile, the Colorado, the Thames, and the Amazon. Tell where each river is located.

 Integrating Environmental Science

TOPICS: pollution, agriculture

PESTICIDE RUNOFF

Pesticides are poisons used to kill insects and other pests. Farmers use them to protect their crops. Sometimes, though, the pesticides are washed away by water, such as during heavy rainstorms. The pesticides can then travel long distances, polluting streams and water in the ground. This can be dangerous for fish and other organisms. In some areas, pesticides are starting to reach poisonous levels.

One solution to this problem is farming without chemical fertilizers and pesticides. More and more farmers are combining programs of soil conservation with methods of natural pest control. One pest-control technique is to release natural predators into the farm fields.

Thinking Critically Who might be harmed by poisoned groundwater?

8-4 What landforms does running water create?

Valleys The bed, or bottom, of a river is often solid rock. Small pieces of rock bounce along the bed of a fast-moving river. **Abrasion** is the wearing away of rock particles by scraping. Abrasion occurs as pieces of rock scrape and then settle into the riverbed. Over time, the bed is cut deeper into the rock, and a valley is formed. A valley is a landform that can be created by running water. Fast-moving rivers can cut very deep V-shaped valleys.

▲ **Figure 8-10** Fast-moving rivers can cut deep valleys.

▶ IDENTIFY: What is a valley?

Delta A triangular-shaped deposit of muddy land called a **delta** often forms at the mouth, or end, of a river. The word *delta* is a Greek letter. The Greek letter delta looks like a triangle.

How does a delta form? When a fast-moving river empties into a larger body of water, it slows down. Pieces of rock and soil carried by the now slow-moving water are deposited. The particles of soil and rock that settle to the bottom, or bed, of a river are called **sediments.** Sediments in the water are deposited at the mouth of the river. This forms the triangle of land known as the delta.

▲ **Figure 8-11** Sediment deposits in the Mississippi River delta as seen from a satellite.

▶ LOCATE: Where does a delta form?

Floodplains During periods of heavy rain, some rivers overflow their banks, or sides. When a river floods its banks, fertile soil carried along by the river is deposited on the sides of the river. The fertile soil is deposited in low-lying flat areas called **floodplains.**

The soil deposited in floodplains is sometimes carried to the river by tributaries that feed the river. Other times, the soil is picked up by the river itself as it flows along.

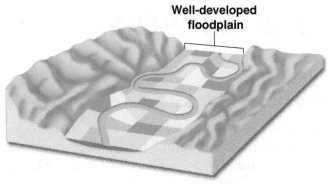

Figure 8-12 Water spills onto the floodplain.

Well-developed floodplain

 DEFINE: What are floodplains?

✓ CHECKING CONCEPTS

1. What is the bed of a river made of?
2. What happens when pieces of rock bounce along the bed of a river?
3. What is sediment?
4. How is a delta formed?
5. Where does the fertile soil in a floodplain come from?

THINKING CRITICALLY

6. INFER: Why is the triangle of sediments deposited at the mouth of a river called a delta?
7. INFER: Why does a river usually flow more slowly at its mouth than at its source?
8. INFER: Why are floodplains valued for planting crops?

INTERPRETING VISUALS

Use Figure 8-12 to answer the following questions.

9. COMPARE: How does the level of the floodplain compare to the rest of the area?
10. HYPOTHESIZE: What would Figure 8-12 look like after a heavy rain?
11. INFER: What would happen to the farms and houses in the floodplain after a heavy rain?
12. HYPOTHESIZE: How could flooding possibly be prevented here?

Hands-On Activity

MODELING LANDFORMS CREATED BY WATER EROSION

You will need sand or soil, a baking pan, several ice cream sticks, leaves and grass clippings, a straw, and a watering can.

1. Make a mountain of sand or soil at one end of a shallow baking pan.
2. Tilt the pan on one side.
3. Mark off centimeters on the edges of several ice cream sticks. Place the sticks around the mountain, burying them at least 3 cm.
4. Cover the right side of the mountain with leaves and grass clippings.
5. Using a straw, try blowing away the sides of the mountain.
6. Now, use a watering can to make it rain on the mountain.

▲ **STEP 6** Use a watering can to make it rain on the mountain.

Practicing Your Skills

7. OBSERVE: Judging from the marks on your sticks, which side is eroding faster?
8. ANALYZE: How do the leaves and grass clippings help prevent erosion? If these plants had roots, would it help to prevent erosion even more? Why?

What causes caves, caverns, and sinkholes?

Objective

Name and describe some features of karst topography.

Key Terms

karst topography: land that has sinkholes, caverns, and underground rivers

cave system: series of connected underground caves

sinkhole: large hole in the ground formed when the roof of a cavern collapses

Karst Topography In some places in the world, the topography, or general shape and look of the land, is irregular. The land is bare and rocky. There is little or no plant growth. There are no lakes or streams on the surface. Instead, there are underground pools of water, caves, and large holes in the ground. This kind of topography is called **karst topography.**

Karst topography gets its name from a region in Yugoslavia where these kinds of features are common. Karst topography can be seen in some areas of the United States, including parts of Florida and Kentucky.

▶ IDENTIFY: What features are typical of karst topography?

Chemical Weathering of Limestone Karst topography results from the action of water in the ground on limestone. In many areas of the world, layers of limestone rock are found under a thin layer of other rocks.

As water in the ground seeps through the layers of rock, the water mixes with carbon dioxide in the rocks. This forms carbonic acid. When carbonic acid reaches the limestone layers, carbonation takes place. The acid reacts with the limestone. The limestone is chemically weathered, or broken down, by the acid.

▶ EXPLAIN: How does carbonic acid affect limestone?

Caverns As carbonic acid seeps into small cracks and holes in underground limestone deposits, it reacts with the limestone. Over the years, the holes increase in size and form caves. A series of connected caves forms a **cave system.** Underground water often pools in these caverns.

▲ **Figure 8-13** Many caverns have underground pools of water.

▶ DEFINE: What is a cave system?

Natural Bridges When water empties out of a cavern, part of the roof of the cavern may collapse. The remaining section of the roof may form a natural bridge. Natural bridges can also be formed by erosion.

◀ **Figure 8-14** Natural Bridge, near Lexington, Virginia, is over 100 million years old. Made of limestone, this natural wonder is about 66 m tall and between 15 m and 45 m wide.

A natural bridge can also form when a surface stream runs through a crack that is beneath the surface. It then flows back onto the surface. The weathering and erosion is a continuing process that causes rock to wear away. The stream wears away the rock, and the crack gets bigger. Scientists think that Natural Bridge in Virginia formed as a result of a stream wearing away rock.

 PREDICT: What can happen when part of a cavern roof collapses?

Sinkholes Sometimes the whole cavern roof may collapse. When that happens **sinkholes,** or sinks, are formed. A sinkhole may serve as an entrance to a cavern. Tourists enter sinks to visit places such as Carlsbad Caverns in New Mexico and Howe Caverns in New York. If a sinkhole fills with water, a sinkhole lake results.

 DEFINE: What are sinkholes?

✓ CHECKING CONCEPTS

1. The reaction of carbonic acid on limestone is a form of _____.

2. Karst topography gets its name from a region in _____.

3. A _____ is a series of underground connected caves.

4. A large opening from the surface into a cavern is a _____.

💡 THINKING CRITICALLY

5. EXPLAIN: Why does karst topography develop where the underground rock is limestone?

6. HYPOTHESIZE: Why would karst topography not develop in a desert?

7. INFER: Why would you find few surface streams in a karst topography region?

BUILDING GEOGRAPHY SKILLS

Mapping Trace an outline of a map of the United States on a sheet of paper. Look up the locations of the following caverns: Carlsbad Caverns, New Mexico; Howe Caverns, New York; Mammoth Cave, Kentucky; Luray Caverns, Virginia; and Wind Cave, South Dakota. Plot the location of each cavern on your outline map. Have you ever visited any of them? If so, describe what the caverns looked like.

▲ **Figure 8-15** Bats leave their caves at dusk.

 Integrating Life Science

TOPICS: mammals, habitats

BAT CAVE IN CARLSBAD CAVERNS

In Carlsbad, New Mexico, the skies sometimes fill with dark clouds just before sunset. These clouds are not made of smoke or dust but of huge numbers of bats. The bats live inside Carlsbad Caverns, clinging to cave walls. Carlsbad is one of the world's largest natural caverns. It provides a perfect habitat for bats.

The most common bat species found in the cave is the Mexican free-tailed bat. Mostly females, the Mexican free-tailed bats that live in the caverns stay there about half the year. Young bats, called pups, are born there. The darkness protects them from predators. At sunset, the bats leave the caverns to hunt insects for food. Clouds of departing bats may have led to the discovery of the caves in the 1800s.

The caverns became a national monument in 1923. Tourists are not allowed into Bat Cave. Some bat species hibernate there in cold weather.

Thinking Critically Why do you think some bats hibernate?

8-6 What is a glacier?

Objectives

Explain how a glacier is formed. Name two kinds of glaciers.

Key Terms

glacier (GLAY-shuhr)**:** moving river of ice and snow

ice cap: large sheet of ice found near Earth's poles

iceberg: large piece of a glacier that enters the ocean

Ice Rivers A **glacier** is a moving river of ice and snow. Glaciers form where the temperature is close to or below freezing most of the year. In these places, the snow does not melt after heavy snowfalls. More snow falls on top of snow that is already on the ground. The snow gets deeper and deeper. Ice forms at the bottom of this deep layer of snow.

Gravity and the weight of the snow on top of the ice cause the ice to move forward. When more snow melts than falls, the glacier begins to recede.

▲ **Figure 8-16** Glaciers look like what they are—rivers of ice.

 DEFINE: What is a glacier?

Kinds of Glaciers There are two kinds of glaciers. Glaciers that form in mountains and move slowly downhill are called valley glaciers or alpine glaciers.

Other glaciers form near Earth's poles. These glaciers form from very large sheets of ice called **ice caps.** Another name for these glaciers is continental glaciers.

 NAME: What are two kinds of glaciers?

Icebergs When a glacier reaches the ocean, a large piece of it may break off and float away. This is called an **iceberg.** Large amounts of sediment may be frozen into an iceberg. As the iceberg melts, these sediments sink to the ocean bottom.

Most of an iceberg is below the surface of the water. Only a small part of the iceberg is visible above the water's surface.

Many ships have crashed into icebergs. To protect ships, the U.S. Coast Guard keeps track of where icebergs are and the direction in which they are heading. Sometimes icebreakers are used to break up icebergs and clear the way for ships.

▲ **Figure 8-17** Iceberg in the ocean near Antarctica

 EXPLAIN: How do icebergs threaten ships?

Ice Ages An ice age is a period of very cold temperatures. Glaciers grow and spread during ice ages. There have been many ice ages in Earth's history. The last one ended about 8,000 to 15,000 years ago.

During the last ice age, the sheet of ice around the North Pole grew larger. The expanding ice cap eventually covered much of North America.

 IDENTIFY: What is an ice age?

1. Another name for a moving river of ice and snow is a _____.

2. A glacier that forms in mountains is a _____ glacier.

3. A glacier that forms near Earth's poles is a _____ glacier.

4. An _____ is a period during which glaciers spread over Earth's surface.

5. The last ice age ended about _____ years ago.

 THINKING CRITICALLY

6. INFER: How are glaciers "rivers of ice"?

7. PREDICT: Even a small increase in average temperatures around the world could cause the ice caps to melt. This melting would raise the sea level. How would this affect coastal cities?

8. INFER: What happens to sea level during an ice age? Explain your answer.

Web InfoSearch

Titanic The British steamer *Titanic* was the largest ship in the world when it was built. It was thought to be unsinkable. In April 1912, the *Titanic* set sail on its first voyage. As it sailed toward New York, it struck an iceberg and sank. Of the more than 2,200 people on board, only 705 were rescued.

SEARCH: Use the Internet to find out more about the *Titanic*. Why did it sink? Why didn't the crew see the iceberg in time? Start your search for information at www.conceptsandchallenges.com. Some key search words are *Titanic*, **RMS Titanic,** and **titanic—movie.**

▲ **Figure 8-18** *Titanic*

How Do They Know That?

GLACIERS GROW AND SHRINK

Jean Louis Agassiz (AG-uh-see) (1807–1873) was a Swiss naturalist, geologist, and teacher. Agassiz earned degrees in philosophy and medicine. His early research was on fossil fishes. In 1836, Agassiz began to study glaciers. He built a shack on top of a glacier to study the glacier's movement. Agassiz was the first person to discover that the center of a glacier moves faster than the sides.

Agassiz observed that as glaciers moved, rocks carried by the glacier carved scratches into other rocks the glacier passed over. Using these observations, Agassiz showed that sheets of ice had once covered large areas of land. From his research, Agassiz also concluded that Earth had gone through several ice ages.

In 1846, Agassiz moved to the United States. He taught at Harvard University and founded Harvard's Museum of Natural History. At his death, a boulder carried by a glacier was placed near his grave as a memorial.

▲ **Figure 8-19** Jean Louis Agassiz giving a lecture

Thinking Critically What might have led Agassiz to conclude that there had been several ice ages?

8-7 How do glaciers cause erosion?

Objectives

Explain how a glacier causes erosion. Describe two results of glacial deposition.

Key Terms

hanging valley: small glacial valley above a main valley

till: rock material deposited by a glacier

erratic (ih-RAT-ihk)**:** boulder left behind by a retreating glacier

Erosion by Abrasion Gravel and pieces of rock are frozen into the ice at the bottom and along the sides of a glacier. As the glacier moves over bedrock, small pieces of the bedrock are scraped and carved away by the rocks set into the glacier. This rock abrades the valley as the glacier moves forward.

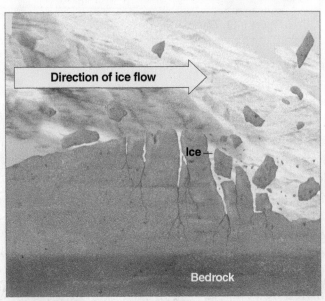

▲ **Figure 8-20** Glaciers abrade, or scrape away, pieces of bedrock as they flow over it.

▶ EXPLAIN: How does a glacier cause abrasion?

U-shaped Valleys As a glacier scrapes away the floor and sides of a valley, the valley becomes U-shaped. Sometimes small side glaciers flow into the main glacier. When the side glaciers melt, they leave small glacier valleys. These valleys are called **hanging valleys.**

▲ **Figure 8-21** This hanging valley is located in New Zealand.

2 EXPLAIN: What causes a U-shaped valley to form?

Glacial Deposition Frozen into a glacier are large rocks and sediments. As the glacier moves, these materials are carried to new places. If a glacier moves into a warmer area, the ice around the edges begins to melt. The glacier appears to be shrinking. Rocks and sediments that were frozen in the ice are left behind. This loose material deposited by the glacier is called **till.**

3 DESCRIBE: What happens to sediments as a glacier melts?

Erratics A boulder left behind by a retreating glacier is called an **erratic.** Central Park in New York City has many erratics. These boulders are not like the bedrock beneath the surface. The bedrock they came from is located many kilometers away.

▲ **Figure 8-22** Erratics in Central Park, New York City

The boulders are too large and too heavy to have been moved by running water. How did they get to Central Park? They were carried there by a glacier. The boulders were frozen into the ice and left behind when the glacier melted.

 EXPLAIN: How are erratics moved?

✓ CHECKING CONCEPTS

1. What is frozen into the ice at the bottom and sides of a glacier?
2. What happens to the shape of a valley as a result of glacial erosion?
3. What happens when small side glaciers melt and disappear?
4. What happens when a glacier moves into a warmer area?
5. What is the loose material deposited by a glacier called?

💡 THINKING CRITICALLY

6. **HYPOTHESIZE:** How can you tell if a valley was formed by a glacier?
7. **EXPLAIN:** Why is the main valley of a glacier lower than a hanging valley left behind by a side glacier?
8. **COMPARE:** How is erosion caused by a glacier similar to erosion caused by a river?

DESIGNING AN EXPERIMENT

Design an experiment to solve the following problem. Include a hypothesis, variables, a procedure with materials, and a type of data to study. Also tell how you would record your data.

PROBLEM: Using a board, sand, and a liquid, how can you demonstrate that glaciers change the shape of the land?

 Hands-On Activity

OBSERVING ABRASION CAUSED BY GLACIERS

You will need safety goggles, sand, water, a bar of soap, a plastic container, and paper towels.

1. Put some sand into a plastic container.
2. Fill the container with water.
3. Place the container in a freezer until the water turns to ice.
4. Remove the ice from the container.
5. Hold the piece of ice with paper towels. Move the ice, sand side facing it, over the bar of soap.
6. Press some sand into the soap. Repeat Step 5.

Practicing Your Skills

7. **OBSERVE:** What happened to the soap when you moved the ice and sand over it?
8. **OBSERVE:** Did the sand in the soap mix with the sand in the ice?
9. **OBSERVE:** What marks, if any, were left in the soap by the sand?
10. **MODEL:** How does this activity show how a glacier can erode the land?

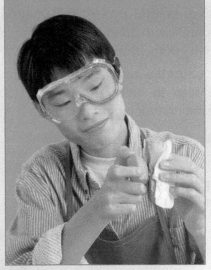
▲ **STEP 5** Rub the soap against the sand-coated ice.

8-8 What landforms do glaciers create?

Objective
Describe two landforms created by glaciers.

Key Terms
moraine (muh-RAYN): ridge of till deposited by a melting glacier

drumlin: oval-shaped mound of till

kettle lake: lake formed by a retreating glacier

Moraines Glaciers are enormous and well-insulated blocks of ice. It takes a very long time for them to melt. When a glacier melts, it deposits till. The till builds up a long, low ridge. This ridge of till is called a **moraine.** When till is deposited at the front edge of a glacier, a terminal moraine is formed. When till is deposited along the sides of a glacier, a lateral moraine is formed.

▶ **NAME:** What are two kinds of moraines?

Drumlins Sometimes when a glacier moves, it leaves behind oval-shaped mounds of till. These mounds are called **drumlins.** The tip of a drumlin points in the direction the glacier was moving.

Drumlins often form in groups. Drumlins can be seen in New York and in the farmlands of Vermont, among other places.

▶ **DEFINE:** What is a drumlin?

Glacial Lakes During the last ice age, glaciers formed in many river valleys. These glaciers weathered and eroded the valleys and made them deeper. As the glaciers moved, till carried by them was left behind. Then the glaciers melted. The water of a melting glacier is called meltwater. Meltwater filled the valleys with water and formed lakes. Glacial lakes are usually narrow, long, and deep. Ocean water can also fill glacial valleys to form long, narrow inlets called fjords.

▲ **Figure 8-24** View from a fjord in Glacier Bay National Park

Sometimes, a moving glacier leaves behind huge masses of ice. These ice masses can become covered with sediments. When the ice melts, it leaves a large hole in the ground. The sediments in the meltwater fall to the bottom. The hole fills with meltwater, and a lake is formed. A lake formed in this way is called a **kettle lake.** Lake Ronkonkoma in New York is a kettle lake.

▶ **DEFINE:** What is a kettle lake?

▼ **Figure 8-23**
Many different landforms are carved by glaciers.

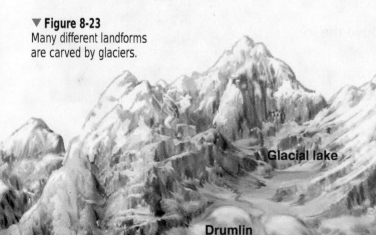

Glacial lake

Drumlin

Kettle lake

U-shaped valley

Lateral moraine

1. A ridge formed by a glacier is a _____.
2. The material deposited at the front edge of a glacier forms a _____ moraine.
3. Glacial lakes are usually long and _____.
4. A lake formed when a block of ice from a glacier melts is called a _____ lake.
5. Melting glaciers deposit _____.

THINKING CRITICALLY

6. INFER: What can a scientist learn about a glacier by studying moraines?
7. ANALYZE: Why was the name *kettle* given to this kind of glacial lake?
8. ANALYZE: The tip of a drumlin points south. In what direction was the glacier that formed the drumlin moving?
9. INFER: Why do you think glacial lakes are usually narrow, long, and deep?

Web InfoSearch

The Ross Ice Shelf More than 65 percent of the fresh water on Earth is locked up in ice. One of the world's largest bodies of floating ice is the Ross Ice Shelf in Antarctica. In 2001, a huge iceberg, about 160 km long and 35 km wide, was found in the sea of Antarctica. It had broken off from the Ross Ice Shelf. Scientists placed tracking devices and other scientific instruments on the iceberg. They are concerned that it could block shipping lanes in the area.

SEARCH: Use the Internet to find out the size of the piece that broke off the Ross Ice Shelf. Where did the Ross Ice Shelf get its name? Start your search at www.conceptsandchallenges.com. Some key search words are **Ross Ice Shelf, ice shelf, Ross Sea, icebergs,** and **Antarctic icebergs.**

People in Science

PALEOCLIMATOLOGIST

Paleoclimatologists (pale-ee-oh-KLEYE-muh-TAHL-uh-jihsts) are scientists who study past climates. They do not use thermometers or barometers. They look for clues to past climates in ocean sediment, coral, glaciers, ice caps, and tree rings.

Lonnie Thompson, a paleoclimatologist who teaches at Ohio State University, led an expedition to Nevado Sajama in the late 1990s. This is Bolivia's highest mountain. Drilling equipment, scientists, technicians, and a hot-air balloon crew were all taken to the top. During the expedition, frozen ice cores were removed from the summit glacier. They were taken away, still frozen, by the hot-air balloon crew. The cores would be studied to learn more about the climate 14,000 years ago.

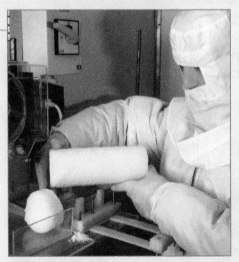

▲ **Figure 8-25** A paleoclimatologist saws off a section of an ice core for further study.

To be a paleoclimatologist, you need a background in mathematics and science. For fieldwork, you must be in good physical shape. Also, paleoclimatologists are often gone from home for a long time.

Thinking Critically Why are the usual weather tools useless to a paleoclimatologist?

8-9 How do ocean waves cause erosion?

Wave Erosion A **wave** is an up-and-down movement of water. Ocean waves are formed when wind blows over the water. Tides, storms, and earthquakes also cause waves.

The force of ocean waves striking a shoreline can break rocks into small pieces. The rock pieces grind against one another. This grinding motion causes abrasion. Abrasion wears down the rock particles until they become sand. The sand is then carried away by the waves.

▲ **Figure 8-26** Waves crash against a shoreline in Oregon.

Waves also cause chemical weathering of the rocks along a shoreline. As waves meet the shoreline, salt water is forced into cracks in rocks.

The chemical action of salt water causes the rocks to break down and makes the cracks larger. Broken pieces of rock are then carried away by the waves.

1 ▷ DESCRIBE: How do waves cause shoreline erosion?

Sea Cliffs, Caves, and Terraces Waves pound into the rocks on a rocky shoreline. The rocks are broken down into small pieces. The broken rock is carried away by the waves. A sea cliff is formed. A sea cliff is a steep rock face caused by wave erosion. Soft rock is eroded more quickly than hard rock. When waves hollow out the soft rock in a sea cliff, a sea cave is formed.

Over time, the bottom of a sea cliff may be slowly worn away. A flat section of rock may remain below the surface of the water. This flat platform is called a **wave-cut terrace.**

2 ▷ DEFINE: What is a sea cliff?

Sea Arches and Sea Stacks When waves cut completely through a section of rock, a **sea arch** is formed. The sea arch looks like a natural bridge. In time, the top of the sea arch may fall into the water. The remaining columns of rock are called **sea stacks.** Sea stacks were once the sides of an arch.

▲ **Figure 8-27** A sea arch in Quebec, Canada

3 ▷ IDENTIFY: What is left when the top of a sea arch falls into the water?

☑ CHECKING CONCEPTS

1. What are two causes of ocean waves?
2. What are two ways waves break down rocks?
3. What is the term for a steep rock face caused by erosion along a rocky shoreline?
4. What is formed when part of a sea cliff is hollowed out?
5. What is the shoreline feature that looks like a natural bridge called?

💡 THINKING CRITICALLY

6. ANALYZE: What processes or events other than wave erosion might change the shape of a shoreline?
7. HYPOTHESIZE: The shoreline of Cape Cod, Massachusetts, is made up of loose glacial deposits. Would you expect this shoreline to erode quickly or slowly? Explain.

BUILDING MATH SKILLS

8. CALCULATE: Barrier island beaches are easily eroded by storm waves. An entire shoreline can be reshaped in a day. If a shoreline erodes at 1.5 m per year, how much erosion would occur over 25 years?

HEALTH AND SAFETY TIP

Hurricanes are the most powerful storms on Earth. They erode coastlines, damage homes, and cause injury. If a hurricane watch is issued, be sure you have canned goods, gasoline for the car, and first-aid kits on hand. Put fresh batteries in flashlights and portable radios. Tape your windows or close your shutters to avoid flying glass. If a hurricane warning is issued, leave the area if you live near the shore. If you stay, don't go out in the storm. Fill your bathtub with water. Tie down anything that can be blown away. After the storm, watch out for downed power lines and broken gas mains.

Real-Life Science
COASTAL EROSION AND STORMS

Hurricanes batter the U.S. Atlantic coastline each year. During the 1990s, there were more than 150 hurricanes reported. Twenty of those hurricanes were major storms. In 2005, the southern coast of the United States was hit by Hurricane Katrina and Hurricane Rita. These storms caused millions of dollars of damage and forced millions of people from their homes. Hurricane Katrina caused over 200 billion dollars of damage and killed 1,500 people. It stands as the most destructive storm in U.S. history.

▲ **Figure 8-28** Hurricane damage in New Orleans, Louisiana.

Large storms cause rapid changes along a coastline. However, slow changes are always occurring in coastal areas. Beaches are moved, sand grain by sand grain, by wind and waves. A beach washed away in one place may build up in another place. Sand dunes are slowly moved by the wind. Houses built on sand dunes or hills near a shore may be washed away.

People have tried to protect shorelines by building breakwaters and jetties. However, these only slow down coastal erosion. They cannot prevent it.

Thinking Critically Artificial structures can reduce erosion. However, shoreline changes are natural, and some people believe that shorefront development should be limited. What do you think?

8-10 What landforms do ocean waves create?

Objective

Describe three shoreline features created by wave deposition.

Key Terms

longshore current: movement of water parallel to a shoreline

spit: long, narrow deposit of sand connected at one end to the shore

sand bar: long, offshore underwater deposit of sand

Beaches A beach is an offshore stretch of land covered by sediment, sand, or pebbles. Waves carry rock particles and other material away from a shoreline. A beach is formed when sand and rock particles are deposited on a shoreline by waves.

Materials that form beaches may vary in size and color. Pebble beaches are found along some shorelines. Along the east and west coasts of the United States, weathered quartz forms white sand beaches. Weathered volcanic rock forms black sand. Hawaii has some black sand beaches. Some Florida beaches are made up of broken shells.

▲ **Figure 8-29** This black sand beach in Hawaii is made of weathered volcanic rock.

 EXPLAIN: How is a beach formed?

Longshore Currents Waves do not usually move in a straight line to the shore. They come in to shore at an angle. A **longshore current** is a current formed as waves approach a beach at an angle. The current itself runs parallel to the shoreline. Longshore currents can carry sand away from the beach.

 DEFINE: What is a longshore current?

Spits A curved or hooked deposit of sand on a shoreline is called a **spit.** One end of a spit is always connected to the shore.

How is a spit formed? A longshore current in the ocean carries sand in a direction parallel to the beach. The sand keeps moving in a straight line until the shoreline of the beach changes direction. Then, the sand is deposited at the spot where the beach curves, forming a spit. Sandy Hook in New Jersey and Cape Cod in Massachusetts are both examples of spits.

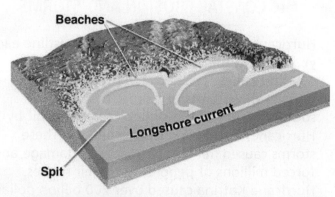

▲ **Figure 8-30** One end of a spit is always connected to the shore.

B DESCRIBE: How is a spit formed?

Sand Bars Waves can carry a lot of sand away from an ocean shoreline. Most of the sand is dropped offshore. This deposit of sand builds up parallel to the shoreline.

A long, offshore underwater deposit of sand is called a **sand bar.** Sometimes, a sand bar completely crosses a bay, sealing it off from the open ocean. This type of sand bar is called a bay mouth bar.

If a sand bar reaches above the water, a barrier beach or an island is formed. Miami Beach, Florida, and Padre Island in Texas are both built on barrier islands.

▲ **Figure 8-31** Padre Island is a barrier beach.

 DESCRIBE: What is a barrier beach?

☑ CHECKING CONCEPTS

1. A beach is formed when _____ and rock particles are deposited on a shoreline.
2. The material forming a beach may vary in size and _____.

3. Weathered _____ forms black sand.
4. A longshore current is formed when waves approach a beach at an _____.
5. A curved sand deposit that is connected to land is called a _____.

THINKING CRITICALLY

6. **EXPLAIN:** Why do some beaches appear different from other beaches?
7. **DESCRIBE:** How is a sand bar formed?

INTERPRETING VISUALS

Use Figure 8-30 to complete the following.

8. **MODEL:** Draw and label a diagram that shows the direction a longshore current is moving after it has formed near the shoreline.
9. **MODEL:** Draw and label a diagram that shows the relationship of a sand bar to a beach.

Integrating Physical Science

TOPICS: energy, waves

THE ENERGY OF WAVES
Energy is the ability to do work. Work is done when a force moves an object. The forces of wind and tide cause waves to form. These waves contain energy that can make objects move. Sand and pebbles are moved each time a wave breaks along the shoreline. The energy in waves does work.

▲ **Figure 8-32** Energy in waves

The waves in water move up and down to form crests and troughs. Half of the difference in height between the crest and the trough is called the amplitude. The greater a wave's amplitude, the greater the energy carried by it. A wavelength is the distance between two consecutive crests.

You can feel the energy in waves if you stand in the water when the surf comes in. This energy may have traveled across the ocean. The water itself does not travel all that distance. Only the pattern of motion in the wave makes the entire trip. When the waves reach shore, they pass most of their energy onto the land at the water's edge.

Thinking Critically What happens to the rocks on the shoreline when they are hit by the energy in waves?

8-11 How does wind cause erosion?

Objective
Describe two kinds of wind erosion and deposition.

Key Terms
deflation (dee-FLAY-shuhn)**:** removal of loose material from Earth's surface by wind

loess (LOH-ehs)**:** thick deposits of wind-blown dust

Deflation Wind has energy. Wind can move a sailboat across a lake and turn the blades of windmills. Wind can also move loose materials, such as sand and dust particles. The removal of loose materials from Earth's surface by the wind is called **deflation.** Deflation most often occurs in deserts, in plowed fields, and on beaches.

▶ **1** EXPLAIN: How can wind be an agent of erosion?

Abrasion Sand particles blown about by the wind can wear away rocks. Have you ever rubbed sandpaper against a piece of wood? The sand on the sandpaper wears away the surface of the wood.

The same thing happens when sand and rock particles are blown over exposed rock or soil. Sand particles carried by the wind are bounced along close to the ground. As the sand particles hit rocks and exposed soil, some of the surface of the rock and soil is worn away or abraded.

▶ **2** EXPLAIN: How is blowing sand like sandpaper?

Sand Dunes Particles in fast-moving wind have kinetic energy. When a rock or other barrier blocks the wind, the wind slows down. As the wind slows down, it drops the sand it carries the same way moving rivers drop their sediment. The sand builds up and forms a mound called a sand dune. Sand dunes are found in deserts and on beaches.

A sand dune has two sides. The side facing the wind is the windward side. The windward side has a gentle slope. Sand is blown up the windward side and over the top, or crest, to the other side. The side away from the wind is called the slipface. The slipface has a steep slope.

▶ **3** INFER: The north side of a sand dune has a gentle slope. From which direction is the wind blowing?

▲ **Figure 8-33** Sand dunes form from sand deposited by slow-moving wind.

Loess Wind carries silt and clay higher and farther than it carries sand. Thick deposits of wind-blown dust, called **loess,** may build up many kilometers away. Loess deposits are found in parts of the Mississippi River valley, Washington State, and Oregon.

▲ **Figure 8-34** A loess plateau in Inner Mongolia, China

 DEFINE: What is loess?

✔ CHECKING CONCEPTS

1. The removal of loose materials from Earth's surface by the wind is called _____.
2. Wind erosion is common in deserts and _____ fields.
3. The _____ of a sand dune has a steep slope.
4. Deposits of wind-blown _____ are called loess.

THINKING CRITICALLY

5. **INFER:** Why are rocks placed around the bottom of telephone poles in the desert?
6. **CLASSIFY:** Is abrasion an example of chemical or mechanical weathering? Explain.

INTERPRETING VISUALS

7. Label the parts of the sand dune in Figure 8-35 below.

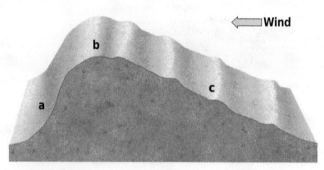

▲ **Figure 8-35**

Science and Technology

WIND EROSION LAB

Wind erosion is worst in very dry regions such as northern Africa. In North America, it is a serious problem for the Great Plains states.

During the 1930s, a very long, dry spell led to dust storms and widespread soil destruction in the Great Plains. The damage caused by the wind led the U.S. Department of Agriculture to set up a research program on wind erosion with Kansas State University (KSU). Today, the KSU laboratory is officially known as the Wind

▲ **Figure 8-36** An approaching dust storm

Erosion Research Unit (WERU). Researchers there use wind tunnels to perform tests. Scientists conduct field studies on the mechanics of wind erosion. They also predict wind erosion and the environmental impacts of erosion.

Thinking Critically What are some possible environmental impacts of wind erosion?

LAB ACTIVITY
Modeling the Effects of Wind on Sand

Materials

Safety goggles, 4 large cardboard boxes, duct tape, scissors, clear plastic wrap, electric hair dryer, sand, small rocks, metric ruler

BACKGROUND

On a windy day, you will occasionally get a small particle of dust or sand in your eye. The wind picked up the particle and transported it perhaps great distances before your eye got in the way. Wind is a powerful agent of erosion. A strong wind can pick up sand and dust particles and toss them great distances. It can also wear away rocks. When flying sand and dust strike a rock cliff, tiny chips are broken off. When the wind stops, the particles fall and pile up in layers as sediment.

PURPOSE

In this activity, you will study the force of wind as an agent of erosion.

PROCEDURE

1. First, you will construct a wind tunnel. Remove the bottoms of four large boxes. Tape the boxes together with duct tape to form a long tunnel.

2. Stand the tunnel on its short side. Use tape to keep the boxes from sagging if necessary.

3. Cut two 25 cm square viewing windows on opposite sides of the last box. Cover the windows with clear plastic wrap and hold them in place with tape.
   ⚠ CAUTION: Be careful when working with scissors.

4. Copy the chart in Figure 8-37. Put on your goggles.

5. Place a small sand pile inside the wind tunnel. Measure the height of the sand pile and record this number in your chart.

6. Hold a hair dryer at the end of the tunnel nearest the windows. Direct its stream of air into the tunnel. The dryer should be powerful and have adjustable speeds.

▲ **STEP 1** Tape the boxes together with duct tape.

▲ **STEP 3** Cover the windows with clear plastic wrap and tape them down.

▲ STEP 5 Create a small pile of sand inside the tunnel.

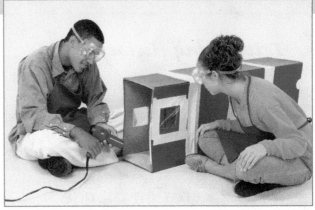

▲ STEP 6 Direct the stream of air into the tunnel.

7. Turn on the hair dryer for 1 minute and observe what happens. Try different dryer speeds for the best effect. Measure how high the pile is now. Record this number.

8. Return the sand to a pile. Push the top of the pile down to form a crater. Turn on the hair dryer for 1 minute and observes what happens. Record your observations.

9. Spread a thin layer of sand across the tunnel. Place several small rocks in different places on the sand. Turn on the hair dryer for 1 minute and observe what happens. Record your observations.

Wind and Sand

Test Performed	Data or Observations	Explanation
1.		
2.		
3.		

▲ Figure 8-37 Use a copy of this chart to record your data.

CONCLUSIONS

1. OBSERVE: What happened to the sand when the wind began blowing?

2. OBSERVE: What happened to the crater in your second experiment?

3. OBSERVE: What happened to the sand in front of and behind the small rocks in your third experiment?

4. ANALYZE: What does this tell you about how wind erodes land?

THE Big IDEA

How did erosion change American history?

In 1917, the United States entered World War I. Americans throughout the country were called to help their country. While some served as soldiers, others back home produced items for the troops. Farmers in the Midwest set to work growing increased amounts of wheat that could be made into food for the soldiers. They cleared millions of acres of grassland. When the war ended, the farmers continued growing wheat. The soil's thick mass of tough roots kept the soil in place and held the moisture.

However, the practice of planting the same crop over and over again was hard on the soil. The nutrients in the once fertile soil disappeared. The soil began to lose its ability to hold water, and the topsoil quickly dried out.

In 1931, a severe drought hit the region. The lack of rain caused the already dry soil to turn to dust. Strong winds blew the dusty topsoil away in huge black clouds. The area became known as the Dust Bowl.

As the drought continued, more dust storms occurred. Crops were destroyed. Livestock caught in the storms became sick from inhaling the soil-filled air. Homes and farm machinery were damaged.

Many farmers left the area. They traveled westward to California in the hope of starting new, successful farms. They believed the state's mild climate and long growing season would guarantee success. By 1940, the number of people who had moved out of the Great Plains states grew to a record number of 2.5 million. No other event in American history has led to a greater migration of people from one part of the country to another.

Look at the illustrations that appear on this page and the next. Then, follow the directions in the Science Log to learn about "the big idea."✦

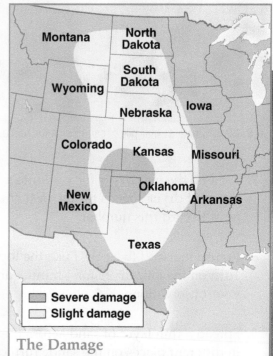

Severe damage
Slight damage

The Damage
About 50 million acres of land in the Midwest states were damaged by the dust storms of the 1930s.

The People
This famous photograph was taken by Dorothea Lange. Lange traveled around the Midwest during the 1930s. She is known for her striking photographs of poverty and hopelessness. Both were results of the drought and the Great Depression.

The Migration

Dust-covered farms were abandoned by one out of every four farmers in the Midwest. More than 200,000 farmers moved to California.

WRITING ACTIVITY

Science Log

On April 14, 1935, one of the most severe storms of the Dust Bowl struck the Midwest. Afterwards, people referred to the day as "Black Sunday." Find firsthand accounts of that day. Then, write a brief description of it as if you had been there yourself. Also, find out how farmers in the old Dust Bowl states are doing now. Begin your search for information by going to www.conceptsandchallenges.com.

▲ **Figure 8-38** Daytime skies would darken, as huge black clouds swept over farmland.

The Soil Conservation Service

Government agencies, such as the Soil Conservation Service, helped farmers practice soil conservation methods.

Chapter Summary

Lessons 8-1 and 8-2

- **Erosion** removes material from a place. **Deposition** drops material in new places.
- **Mass erosion** is the downhill movement of weathered materials due to gravity. Landslides, mudflows, and creep are mass movements.

Lesson 8-3

- **Runoff** causes erosion. The amount of rainfall, plant growth, and topography all affect erosion.
- A river system has a main stream and **tributaries.**

Lessons 8-4 and 8-5

- Rock and sand carried by wind or water weathers rocks and soil. This is **abrasion.**
- A **delta** forms when sediments are deposited by slow-moving water at the mouth of a river. **Floodplains** deposit fertile soil on both sides.
- Caves, underground rivers, and **sinkholes** are features typical of **karst topography.** They are formed by the chemical weathering of limestone.
- **Cave systems** are made up of several connected caves.

Lessons 8-6 and 8-7

- A **glacier** is a moving river of ice and snow. An **iceberg** breaks off of continental glaciers.
- A **hanging valley** forms when a small side glacier melts. **Till** is loose material left by a glacier. **Erratics** are boulders left by glaciers.

Lessons 8-8 and 8-9

- Till left by a glacier forms terminal or lateral **moraines. Drumlins** are oval mounds of till.
- Glacial lakes form when valley glaciers melt. **Kettle lakes** form when ice is buried, then melts.
- Waves can break up rocks on shore. An eroded rocky shoreline may have sea cliffs, sea caves, **sea arches, sea stacks,** or **wave-cut terraces.**

Lessons 8-10 and 8-11

- A **longshore current** is formed when waves approach a beach at an angle. Longshore currents create **spits** and **sand bars.**
- **Deflation** removes loose material from Earth's surface. Sand dunes form when wind is blocked. Wind-blown dust forms **loess** deposits.

Key Term Challenges

abrasion (p. 184)	loess (p. 198)
cave system (p. 186)	longshore current (p. 196)
deflation (p. 198)	mass erosion (p. 180)
delta (p. 184)	moraine (p. 192)
deposition (p. 178)	runoff (p. 182)
drumlin (p. 192)	sand bar (p. 196)
erosion (p. 178)	sea arch (p. 194)
erratic (p. 190)	sea stack (p. 194)
floodplain (p. 184)	sediment (p. 184)
glacier (p. 188)	sinkhole (p. 186)
hanging valley (p. 190)	spit (p. 196)
iceberg (p. 188)	talus (p. 180)
ice cap (p. 188)	till (p. 190)
karst topography (p. 186)	tributary (p. 182)
kettle lake (p. 192)	wave-cut terrace (p. 194)

MATCHING **Write the Key Term from above that best matches each description.**

1. water from rain or snow that flows on Earth's surface

2. land that has sinkholes, caverns, and underground pools of water

3. smaller stream that flows into the main stream of a river system

4. flat section of rock formed by the erosion of a sea cliff

5. moving river of ice and snow

6. boulder left behind by a retreating glacier

7. small glacial valley above a main valley

8. underwater deposit of sand

9. downhill movement of weathered materials caused by gravity

APPLYING DEFINITIONS **Explain the difference between the words in each pair. Write your answers in complete sentences.**

10. talus, till

11. sea arch, sea stack

12. deflation, deposition

13. erosion, weathering

14. loess, sediment

15. floodplain, delta

Content Challenges TEST PREP

MULTIPLE CHOICE Write the letter of the term or phrase that best completes each statement.

1. Mudflows, creep, landslides, and earthflow are caused by
   a. wind.
   b. waves.
   c. running water.
   d. gravity.

2. Weathered material is removed from a place by
   a. abrasion.
   b. deposition.
   c. erosion.
   d. moraines.

3. The sudden movement of rocks down a hillside is
   a. an earthflow.
   b. a mudflow.
   c. creep.
   d. a landslide.

4. Tilted telephone or fence poles on a hillside is evidence of
   a. creep.
   b. earthflow.
   c. runoff.
   d. glaciers.

5. Gullies in a hillside are caused by
   a. creep.
   b. talus.
   c. runoff.
   d. glaciers.

6. Sediments that are carried by a glacier are called
   a. till.
   b. talus.
   c. moraines.
   d. drumlins.

7. The Great Lakes and New York's Finger Lakes are
   a. kettle lakes.
   b. drumlins.
   c. oxbow lakes.
   d. glacial lakes.

8. Sea cliffs, sea stacks, and sea arches are caused by
   a. glaciers.
   b. wind.
   c. waves.
   d. gravity.

9. A piece of glacier that breaks off and goes into the ocean is
   a. a spit.
   b. an iceberg.
   c. a drumlin.
   d. a valley glacier.

10. Glaciers that form in mountains are
    a. valley glaciers.
    b. ice caps.
    c. continental glaciers.
    d. moraines.

FILL IN Write the term or phrase that best completes each statement.

11. The rocks that make up Earth's crust are removed and then carried away to new places by _____.

12. Deposition builds _____ on Earth's surface.

13. A piece of ice that has broken off from a glacier is called an _____.

14. Landslides and _____ are forms of rapid mass erosion.

15. A delta usually forms at the _____, or end, of a river.

Concept Challenges TEST PREP

WRITTEN RESPONSE **Answer each of the following questions in complete sentences.**

1. ANALYZE: If the tip of a drumlin points north, in which direction was the glacier that formed the drumlin moving? Explain how you know.

2. PREDICT: What would happen to the sea level if Earth's temperature rose and caused glaciers to melt?

3. INFER: Why does deflation occur mostly in deserts, in plowed fields, and on beaches?

4. INFER: Why can wind carry dust farther than it can carry sand?

5. INFER: Why do most mudflows occur in dry mountainous regions after a heavy rainfall?

6. PREDICT: How would runoff in a forest area change if all the trees were cut down?

7. ANALYZE: You find a large boulder that is unlike the bedrock in that area. It is too heavy to have been carried by running water. How did the boulder get there?

8. INFER: Why does the windward side of a sand dune have a gentle slope while the slipface has a steep slope?

9. EXPLAIN: Why do fast-moving rivers cut deep valleys?

10. DESCRIBE: In what ways does a glacier change a landscape?

INTERPRETING VISUALS **Use Figures 8-39 and 8-40 below to answer the following questions.**

11. What is shown in Figure 8-39?

12. Which agent of erosion causes what is shown in Figure 8-39?

13. What is the name of the landform shown in Figure 8-40?

14. What natural force created the landform shown in Figure 8-40?

15. Was the landform shown in Figure 8-40 caused by erosion, deposition, or both? Explain your answer.

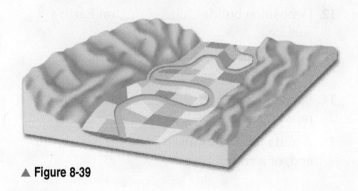

▲ Figure 8-39

▲ Figure 8-40

Chapter 9 Inland Waters

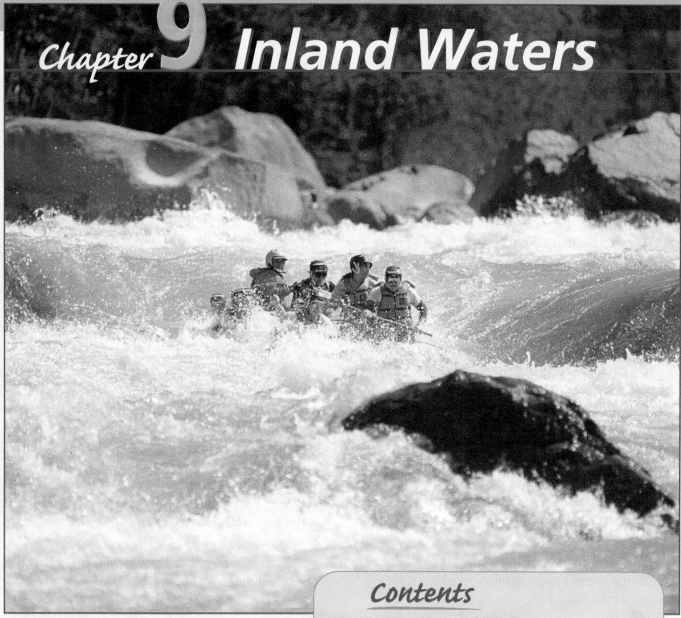

▲ **Figure 9-1** Riding the rapids is one way to explore rivers. It is also a fun pastime for many people.

Running water is important to people. It helps shape the land on which we live. We depend on rivers for transportation, farming, energy, and food. We also use rivers for recreational activities, such as boating and rafting. Many people enjoy riding the rapids. A rapid forms where a streambed has a steep slope.

▶How is running water important in transportation?

Contents

9-1 What is the water cycle?

Objective
Trace the steps in the water cycle.

Key Terms

evaporation (ee-vap-uh-RAY-shuhn): changing of a liquid to a gas

condensation (kahn-duhn-SAY-shuhn): changing of a gas to a liquid

precipitation (pree-sihp-uh-TAY-shuhn): water that falls to Earth's surface from the atmosphere

water cycle: repeated pattern of water movement between Earth and the atmosphere

Evaporation and Condensation Liquids change to gases by a process called **evaporation.** Most of Earth's surface is covered with water. When liquid water absorbs enough heat energy from the Sun, it changes into the gas water vapor. Air always contains some water vapor through evaporation. We become more aware of water vapor when the air is humid.

The changing of a gas to a liquid is called **condensation.** When air containing water vapor is cooled, the water vapor loses heat. If enough heat is lost, the water vapor changes to a liquid.

Water vapor condenses into tiny water droplets. These water droplets join to form clouds. If the temperature reaches freezing, ice forms. A cloud is a collection of water droplets or ice crystals.

 DESCRIBE: What is a cloud?

Precipitation Water that falls to Earth from the atmosphere is called **precipitation.** Rain and snow are two forms of precipitation. As the water droplets in a cloud grow bigger, they become too heavy to stay in the air. Gravity pulls them toward Earth. The water falls as rain. If the rain passes through very cold air, the water may turn to a solid and fall to Earth as snow, hail, or sleet.

 LIST: What are two forms of precipitation?

The Water Cycle Water is always changing state. As water evaporates from Earth's surface, it changes from a liquid to water vapor. In the atmosphere, the water vapor condenses to a liquid. This forms clouds. Finally, the water falls to Earth as precipitation. The repeated movement of water between Earth and the atmosphere is called the **water cycle.** The water cycle is also known as the hydrologic cycle.

About 97 percent of Earth's water is salt water. The rest is fresh water.

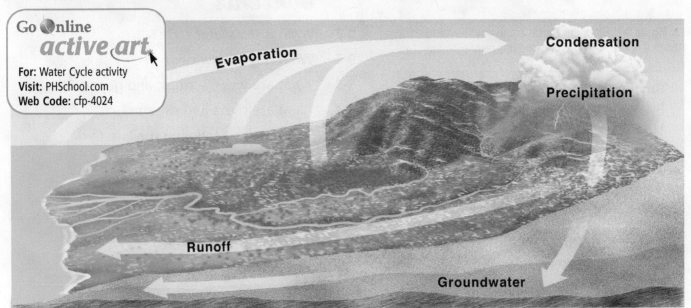

Go Online
active art

For: Water Cycle activity
Visit: PHSchool.com
Web Code: cfp-4024

Evaporation
Condensation
Precipitation
Runoff
Groundwater

▲ **Figure 9-2** In the water cycle, water continually moves between the atmosphere and Earth.

About 76 percent of fresh water is frozen into ice caps near the North and South poles. A tiny amount is in the air in the form of water vapor. Only about 23 percent of Earth's fresh water is readily available for use by living things. That water is found in lakes, rivers, and streams, and below Earth's surface.

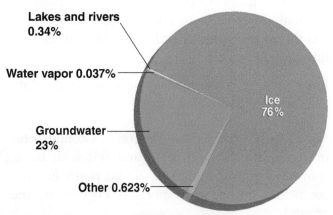

Lakes and rivers 0.34%

Water vapor 0.037%

Groundwater 23%

Ice 76%

Other 0.623%

▲ **Figure 9-3** Fresh water distribution on Earth

 STATE: What is the water cycle?

☑ CHECKING CONCEPTS

1. What happens when water absorbs enough heat?
2. During condensation, what happens to gas?
3. What makes up a cloud?
4. What processes make up the water cycle?

💡 THINKING CRITICALLY

5. HYPOTHESIZE: How might the water cycle be affected when dust in the air blocks sunlight?
6. INTERPRET: Based on Figure 9-3, what would you say is the largest source of fresh water available for use by living things?

BUILDING SCIENCE SKILLS

Classifying Write *Solid*, *Liquid*, and *Gas* across the top of a sheet of paper. Put each of the following terms under its correct state in your chart: rain, snow, water vapor, ocean, river, ice cap, and glacier.

Hands-On Activity

OBSERVING THE STATES OF WATER

You will need safety goggles, a glass, plastic wrap, a rubber band, hot water, and ice cubes.

1. Fill a glass halfway with hot tap water. Put a piece of plastic wrap tightly over the top of the glass. Use a rubber band to secure it. ⚠ CAUTION: Be careful not to burn yourself with the hot water.
2. Place 5 or 6 ice cubes on the plastic wrap as shown in Figure 9-4.
3. Allow the glass to stand for about 5 minutes. Observe what happens.
4. Pick up the plastic wrap. Feel the side that was closest to the hot water.

▲ **Figure 9-4** Set up your experiment as shown.

Practicing Your Skills

5. IDENTIFY: In what state was the hot water? The ice cubes? What state could not be seen?
6. ANALYZE: What happened to the ice? What caused this?
7. ANALYZE: What is on the underside of the plastic wrap? How did it get there?
8. INFER: Which state of matter are glaciers?

9-2   What is groundwater?

Objective

Explain how groundwater collects in soil.

Key Terms

pore: tiny hole or space

groundwater: water that collects in pores in soil and sinks into the ground

water table: upper layer of saturated rock and soil

Pores and Groundwater Some of the rain or snow that falls to Earth soaks into the soil. The water collects in the spaces, or **pores,** between bits of rock and soil. Water that collects between the bits of rock and soil and sinks into the ground is called **groundwater.** About 23 percent of Earth's freshwater supply is stored as groundwater.

 DEFINE: What is groundwater?

Properties Affecting Groundwater Different kinds of rock and soil can hold different amounts of groundwater. Loosely packed rock or soil has many pores. It can hold a lot of groundwater.

Tightly packed rock or soil does not have many pores. It holds very little groundwater. Rock and soil containing particles that are all the same size can hold a lot of water. Suppose the soil particles are of all different sizes. Then, the smaller particles can fill up the pores. This kind of rock or soil has little room for water.

 DESCRIBE: When can rocks and soil hold a lot of groundwater?

Movement of Groundwater Groundwater moves easily through rocks and soil with large, connected pores. However, if the pores are not connected, the water cannot sink deeper into the ground.

 DESCRIBE: How does groundwater travel?

The Water Table Groundwater eventually reaches bedrock, where it almost stops moving. The pores in the rock above begin to fill up. When the pores are completely filled, the rock or soil is saturated (SACH-uh-rayt-ihd). The underground water level rises. The upper layer of saturated soil and rock is called the **water table.**

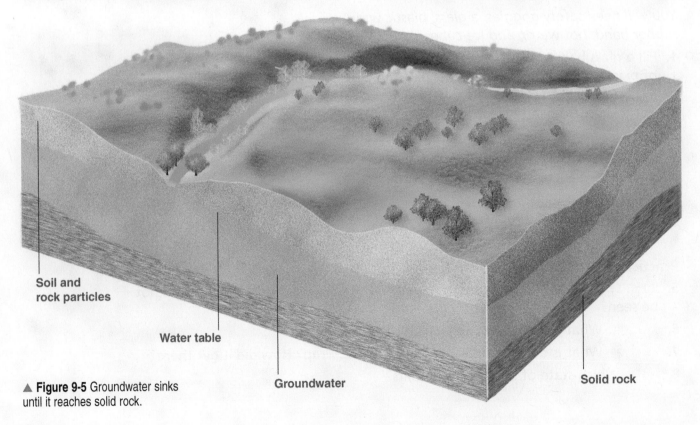

Soil and
rock particles

Water table

Groundwater

Solid rock

▲ **Figure 9-5** Groundwater sinks until it reaches solid rock.

Because of the differences in soil density, not all of the water in the ground sinks down to the water table. Some of it stays near the surface, in the topsoil. Plant roots need this water because the roots of most plants do not reach the water table.

▶ **DEFINE:** What is the water table?

✓ CHECKING CONCEPTS

1. Groundwater collects in _____ between soil particles.
2. About _____ percent of fresh water is stored as groundwater.
3. Loosely packed soil holds a lot of _____.
4. The upper layer of saturated rock forms the _____.

💡 THINKING CRITICALLY

5. **INFER:** Describe two ways in which your life would change if supplies of fresh water ran low.

INTERPRETING VISUALS

Use Figure 9-6 to answer the following question.

6. **ANALYZE:** Which soil sample can hold more groundwater, *A* or *B*? Why?

A
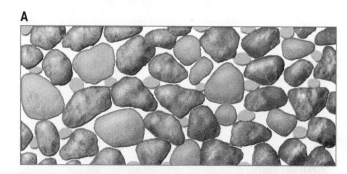

B
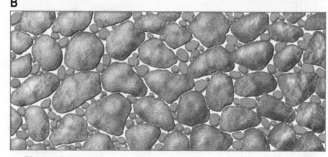

▲ **Figure 9-6**

People in Science
HYDROLOGIST

All living things need water to live. Water is also used for cooking, cleaning, bathing, and recreational activities. Industry and farming are dependent on water supplies.

Scientists who study Earth's water supplies are called hydrologists. Hydrologists work to keep us supplied with the fresh water we need. They may help select the best place to dig a well. They may draw up plans on how to route water from its source to a city. They help farmers irrigate their land by showing them how to use artificial canals or sprinkler systems. A hydrologist may also do research on how to keep water supplies clean. Many hydrologists work outdoors. A hydrologist must have a college degree and a background in geology, physics, chemistry, and mathematics.

▲ **Figure 9-7** A hydrologist searches in rock openings for groundwater sources.

Thinking Critically A developer is planning to build new homes with private wells. How could a hydrologist help this builder?

What are wells, springs, and geysers?

Objective

Describe how groundwater reaches Earth's surface.

Key Terms

well: hole dug below the water table that fills with groundwater

spring: natural flow of groundwater to Earth's surface

geyser (GY-zuhr)**:** heated groundwater that erupts onto Earth's surface

Wells In many places, people get their fresh water from wells. A **well** is a hole dug into the soil to reach below the water table. Water enters an opening in a pipe placed in the well. The water can then be pumped to the surface.

The level of the water table changes from season to season. When there is little rain, the level of the water table drops. The pipe for a well must be set much deeper than the water table line. This will ensure that the well will not run dry during dry weather.

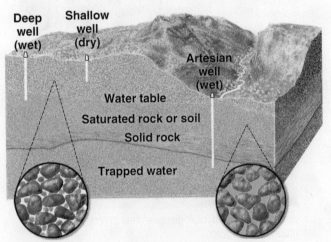

▲ **Figure 9-8** A well must reach below the water table.

 DEFINE: What is a well?

Artesian Wells A pump is not necessary to get water out of artesian (ahr-TEE-zhen) wells. Water rises freely from them.

The water level in an artesian well can rise higher than ground level. The water source, called a trapped aquifer, is under pressure. The pressure makes the water rise. An artesian well may be located far from its original water source.

 EXPLAIN: What makes water rise in an artesian well?

Springs A **spring** is a natural flow of groundwater that reaches Earth's surface. The side of a steep hill may dip below the water table. Water can then flow out of cracks in the rocks. This is why springs are usually found on hillsides. Spring water is often sold in stores as high-quality drinking water. Most spring water is cold. But when it is near an underground heat source, hot springs may form.

 IDENTIFY: Where are most springs found?

Geysers Sometimes steam and boiling water shoot into the air, forming a geyser. A **geyser** is heated groundwater that erupts onto Earth's surface. Water in a deep hot spring may be heated above the boiling point of water. If the water is trapped and pressure is generated, the water becomes superheated. This superheated water turns to steam. The pressure of the steam forces the water above it out into the air. Geothermal areas containing geysers are found in Wyoming, New Zealand, and Iceland, among other places.

▲ **Figure 9-9** This geyser, called Old Faithful, is found in Yellowstone National Park in Wyoming.

 EXPLAIN: What force causes geysers to erupt?

CHECKING CONCEPTS

1. A well must be dug _____ than the water table.

2. Wells with no need for pumps are called _____ wells.

3. The temperature of spring water is usually _____.

4. Hot water erupting onto Earth's surface forms a _____.

5. Water heated above the boiling point is called _____ water.

 THINKING CRITICALLY

6. INFER: What states of water are found in geysers?

7. HYPOTHESIZE: Why does the temperature of spring water stay the same all year?

8. INFER: How is the hot water and steam found in hot springs and geysers used to generate electricity from geothermal energy?

Web InfoSearch

Oases An oasis is a very rich piece of land in the middle of a desert. Oases vary in size from less than 1 square kilometer to several square kilometers. The land for hundreds of kilometers around is dry and barren. However, an oasis has plenty of plant life and a natural spring. Many people live in oases.

SEARCH: Use the Internet to find out more about oases. Why do they have water? What is it like to live there? You can start your search at www.conceptsandchallenges.com.

Some key search words are **desert oasis** and **geology**.

◀ **Figure 9-10**
Oasis in an Egyptian desert

Hands-On Activity

MODELING GROUNDWATER USE

You will need gravel or aquarium stones, one aquarium tank, one small plastic tub, sandy soil, a watering can, and clean spray pumps from bottles.

1. Put a 7.5 cm layer of gravel or stones in the aquarium. Cover with a layer of sandy soil.

2. Using the watering can, let it rain on your aquarium until you have at least 5 cm of groundwater.

3. Insert the spray pump into the gravel. Start pumping into the plastic container. Record your observations. Note that if the soil is too sandy, it will clog your pump.

4. Add a few drops of food coloring to the watering can and water again. Repeat Step 3 and record your observations.

▲ **STEP 3** Pump the water into the plastic container.

Practicing Your Skills

5. OBSERVE: What happens to the water level as you pump?

6. INFER: How would adding food coloring to one water source affect the other?

Objective

Describe the three stages in the life cycle of a river or stream.

Key Terms

rapids: part of a river where the current is swift

waterfall: steep fall of water, as of a stream, from a height

meander (mee-AN-duhr): loop in a mature river

oxbow lake: curved lake formed when a bend in a river is cut off at both ends

What Is a River? A river is a large, natural channel containing flowing water. River water flows downhill because of the force of gravity. The main sources of the water in the river are runoff from rainwater, streams that flow into the river, groundwater from springs, and melting snow.

▶ **1 DEFINE:** What is a river?

The Stages of a River Rivers go through three stages in their development. The three stages can be described as youthful, mature, or old. However, the stage of a river is not really determined by the age of a river in years. It depends on how fast the water in the river flows and how steep the slope is that it is on.

▶ **2 IDENTIFY:** What are the three stages in the development of a river?

Youthful Rivers A youthful river has a steep slope and fast-moving water. The Yellowstone River and the Niagara River are examples of youthful rivers. The fast-moving water erodes the riverbed, or bottom, and forms a narrow, V-shaped valley. The river fills almost the whole valley from side to side.

Two features of a youthful river are **rapids** and **waterfalls.** As the moving water rushes over steep slopes and rocks, rapids are formed. Sometimes the slope drops straight down. Then, a waterfall is formed.

▲ **Figure 9-11** Niagara Falls is a waterfall on the Niagara River.

▶ **3 INFER:** What evidence indicates that the Niagara River is a young river?

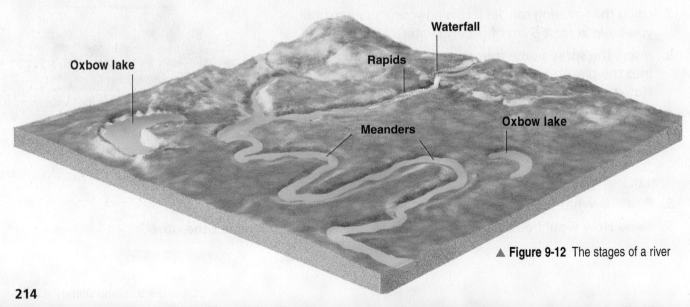

▲ **Figure 9-12** The stages of a river

Mature Rivers The waters of a mature river move more slowly than the waters of a youthful river. A mature river is on a shallower slope. It does not have rapids and waterfalls. Erosion widens the river and the valley floor. This creates gentle slopes. The bottom is flatter. The sides are smoother and rounder. The river winds back and forth in loops called **meanders.** The Missouri River and the Ohio River are mature rivers.

 DEFINE: What are meanders?

Old Rivers Water moves very slowly in an old river. The Mississippi River is an old river. An old river has a nearly flat slope. Because of this, it floods easily. The slow river cannot get rid of the extra water, so it overflows.

▲ **Figure 9-13** A river floods its banks.

Flooding causes erosion and deposition along the meanders. Meanders do not extend to the valley walls. Over long periods of time, they change position. A meander may be cut off from the rest of the river. This forms a C-shaped lake called an **oxbow lake,** as shown in Figure 9-12.

 INFER: Why does an old river flow very slowly?

Endangered Rivers Rivers can be endangered. How? Mostly it is the pollution that results from developing new energy sources that endangers rivers. This includes building dams for power, draining acid from coal mines, and drilling for oil and natural gas resources. Since 1986, a report has been issued each year listing America's most endangered rivers. In 2007, the most endangered river on the list was the Santa Fe. Figure 9-14 lists endangered rivers from earlier years.

ENDANGERED RIVERS		
Year	River	Threat
2007	Santa Fe River	Dams
2005	Susquehanna River	Raw Sewage
2004	Colorado River	Dams
2003	Big Sunflower River	Flood control projects
2002	Missouri River	Dams
2000	Snake River	Dams

▲ **Figure 9-14**

 EXPLAIN: What activities endanger a river?

☑ CHECKING CONCEPTS

1. Use the terms *youthful, mature,* or *old* to identify the stage of each river described:
   a. has a steep slope; **b.** has a nearly flat slope; **c.** forms oxbow lakes; **d.** has many rapids; **e.** has meanders.

💡 THINKING CRITICALLY

2. EXPLAIN: Why is a river with meanders sometimes said to "snake along"?

3. PREDICT: How can we tell if a lake near a river was once part of the river?

Web InfoSearch

The Nile River In the mid-1860s, the Royal Geographical Society sent the Scottish explorer Dr. David Livingstone to look for the source of the Nile River. Livingstone believed the source was Lake Tanganyika. He was gone a long time. No one heard from him. It was feared he was missing. A New York newspaper assigned Henry Morton Stanley, a journalist, to find him.

SEARCH: Use the Internet to find out more about this. What is the source of the Nile? Did Livingstone find it? What happened when Stanley finally met up with Livingstone? Start your search at www.conceptsandchallenges.com. Some key search words are **Nile River, Dr. David Livingstone,** and **H. M. Stanley.**

LAB ACTIVITY
Modeling the Life Cycle of a Stream

Materials

Safety goggles, lab apron, large plastic under-the-bed storage box, 2-liter soft drink bottle, two pieces of narrow aquarium hose (about 60 cm each), drill, waterproof cement, bucket, water, sand, funnel

BACKGROUND

Water in mountain streams moves very fast. It carries with it boulders, pebbles, and sand. These cause erosion. Downstream, water moves slower and has only enough force to carry silt. As streams erode the land, they become more winding and move more slowly. This is the typical life cycle of a stream.

PURPOSE

In this activity, you will study the development of a stream as it flows over sand.

PROCEDURE

1. Have your teacher drill a small hole in one end of the plastic box, near the bottom. This hole should be just large enough to put one piece of your aquarium tubing into it. Seal the hose around the hole with waterproof cement. This is your stream table.

2. Fill the tray evenly with sand about 6 cm deep. Shape the sand into a mound near the upper end. The other end should be almost free of sand.

3. Set the plastic box on a table. The end with the hole should be near the end of the table so that the hose can hang down. Put the catch bucket directly below the hose end. Raise the upper end of the box about 5 cm, using two or three textbooks.

4. Fill the plastic bottle almost full with water. Raise it about 12 cm by resting it on top of another large box or several large books. Put one end of the second piece of hose into the bottle.

5. Push the hose almost entirely under the water in the bottle so that the tube fills. Now, pinch off the free end of the hose.

▲ **STEP 3** Raise the upper end of the box about 5 cm.

▲ **STEP 4** Insert the second hose into the bottle.

6. Let go of the pinched end, and the water will start flowing. Make sure this end is lower than the water level in the bottle. Aim the water into the sand at the upper end of the stream table. Remember to keep the other end of the tube in the water.

▲ **STEP 6** Aim the water into the sand at the upper end of the stream table.

7. Keep adding water to the sand until it is saturated. You will know it is saturated when water begins to flow over the surface. Watch what happens to the water and sand as you let the water continue to flow for 15 minutes. Use the funnel to add water to the bottle as needed.

8. Copy the chart in Figure 9-15. In your chart, describe the appearance of the stream after 10 minutes. Also sketch the shape of the valley.

◀ **STEP 7** Watch what happens as water continues to flow over the sand.

Life Cycle of a Stream

	Appearance of stream	Valley sketches
Upper end		
Middle		
Lower end		

▲ **Figure 9-15** Use a copy of this chart to record your observations and draw your sketches.

CONCLUSIONS

1. OBSERVE: What happened to the sand when the water began flowing over it?
2. OBSERVE: What happened to the sand as it entered the "lake" at the lower end of the stream table?
3. ANALYZE: How does the stream change the land?
4. INFER: What will happen to the sand that ends up in a lake or an ocean?

9-5 What are lakes and ponds?

Objective

Describe how lakes and ponds form and how they change.

Key Terms

lake: low spot in Earth's surface filled with still water

pond: body of water similar to a lake but usually smaller and shallower

kettle lake: lake formed by a retreating glacier

reservoir: artificial lake

Still Waters Surface water that collects in hollows and low spots on Earth's continents forms **lakes** and **ponds.** Unlike the running waters of rivers and streams, lakes and ponds contain relatively still water. Ponds are similar to lakes but are usually smaller and shallower.

Over 98 percent of the surface water on the continents is found in lakes. Most lakes contain fresh water. However, some of the largest lakes in the world are salty.

Like oceans, lakes have shorelines that erode. Many lakes are small enough to see across. Some lakes are so big that you cannot see the other side. Most of the water collected in lakes and ponds originally came from rain, snow, or melting ice.

 DEFINE: What is a lake?

Formation of Lakes Low spots on Earth's surface are created in many ways, including erosion. Also, when glaciers receded from North America, big chunks of ice were left behind. These became covered by soil and slowly melted. The soil on top fell in, and large kettle-shaped depressions were formed. Water filled the kettles, making **kettle lakes.**

Land that shifts during earthquakes sometimes forms low spots that become lakes. Large rocks from space, called meteorites, have also caused holes that have later become lakes.

 DESCRIBE: How do lakes form?

Reservoirs Not all lakes are made by nature. People create lakes by building dams across rivers. A dam blocks the water until it reaches the top. The lake that is formed behind the dam is called a **reservoir.** As more water flows down the river, it is directed through a gate near the dam's top. The force of the running water can be used to power electric generators.

 DEFINE: What are reservoirs?

Growing Old Lakes and ponds change over long periods of time. Look at Figure 9-16 as an example. At their peak, ponds are clear pools of water. In time, sand, silt, and dead leaves and branches may fill in the bottom. The water near the shore can become very shallow, and many plants may start growing there. Eventually, the shoreline may become a marsh.

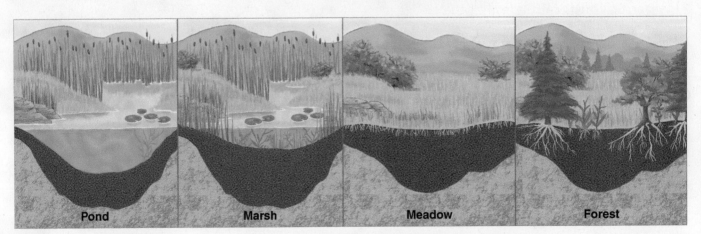

| Pond | Marsh | Meadow | Forest |

▲ **Figure 9-16** Life cycle of a pond

▲ **Figure 9-17** Lake George in New York State is fed by mountain streams and underground springs. It is a clear, deep lake with many fish and other wildlife.

When a pond is completely filled in, a meadow or a forest may grow on top. Only a slight dip in the land will show that a pond was once there. As old lakes and ponds fill in, new ones are being created elsewhere.

 DESCRIBE: How do lakes change over time?

☑ CHECKING CONCEPTS

1. Where does the water in lakes and ponds come from?
2. What can happen to a lake as it grows old?
3. How can people create artificial lakes?

💡 THINKING CRITICALLY

4. **INFER:** What happens to wildlife when a lake grows old?

DESIGNING AN EXPERIMENT

Design an experiment to solve the following problem. Include a hypothesis, variables, a procedure with materials, and a type of data to study. Also include a way to record the data.

PROBLEM: A river is bringing sediment from upstream into a dam. The engineers need to prevent the reservoir from filling with sediment. How can they stop the sediment from filling the dam's reservoir?

Real-Life Science

FINDING FRESH WATER

You can see the Great Lakes in pictures of Earth taken from as far away as the Moon. The Great Lakes consist of five connected lakes along the border of the United States and Canada. The lakes are Superior, Michigan, Huron, Erie, and Ontario. Together, they contain a very large supply of fresh water. Scientists calculate that the five lakes combined hold 23,000,000,000,000,000 liters of fresh water. This is equal to about 20 percent of the world's total supply of fresh water. If this water were spread evenly over the United States, the country would be covered with almost 3 m of water.

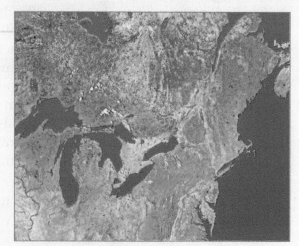

▲ **Figure 9-18** Satellite image of the Great Lakes

The deepest Great Lake is Lake Superior. It averages 150 m deep. The shallowest is Lake Erie. It averages only 19 m deep. Water from the Great Lakes flows to the Atlantic Ocean. Niagara Falls connects Lake Ontario to Lake Erie.

Thinking Critically Cities around the country want to build pipelines to move Great Lake water to their growing communities. Do you think this is a good idea? Why or why not?

THE Big IDEA

Why are wetlands important to the environment?

How are swamps, bogs, and marshes alike? All are types of wetlands, or areas covered with shallow water.

For years, people thought that wetlands were simply a waste of good property. They drained the water and put down dry soil. Homes, roads, even shopping malls were then built on the newly landscaped areas. Almost half the original wetlands in the continental United States may have been destroyed in this way.

The destruction of wetlands has several harmful consequences. The chances for flooding increase. This is because wetlands act like giant sponges, soaking up runoff, groundwater, and precipitation. Another harmful result of wetland destruction is an increase in shoreline erosion. The roots of cordgrass and other saltwater plants commonly found in coastal wetlands anchor the soil. Without these natural anchors, bits of shoreline are broken off and carried away by waves.

Perhaps more importantly, filling in wetlands destroys the natural habitats of many plant and animal species. Inland wetlands are home to muskrats, beavers, and wood ducks. Coastal wetlands contain flounder, sea trout, and striped bass. They are also nurseries for many kinds of fish and crustaceans. Shrimp and crab populations are harmed every time a wetland is destroyed. Without wetlands, many of these animals could not survive.

Look at the illustrations on these two pages. Then, complete the Science Log to find out more about "the big idea." ◆

Mammals

Many mammals visit the wetlands regularly. Raccoons are mammals found throughout the United States, southern Canada, and Central and South America. Some types of raccoons live mainly on crabs they obtain from wetland areas.

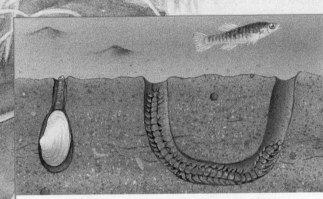

Invertebrates

Crabs, worms, and clams are invertebrates that live in wetlands. They burrow in mud and are exposed as the water recedes during low tide. Invertebrates are animals that have no backbones. Because of their widespread diversity and abundance, invertebrates are an important part of many food webs.

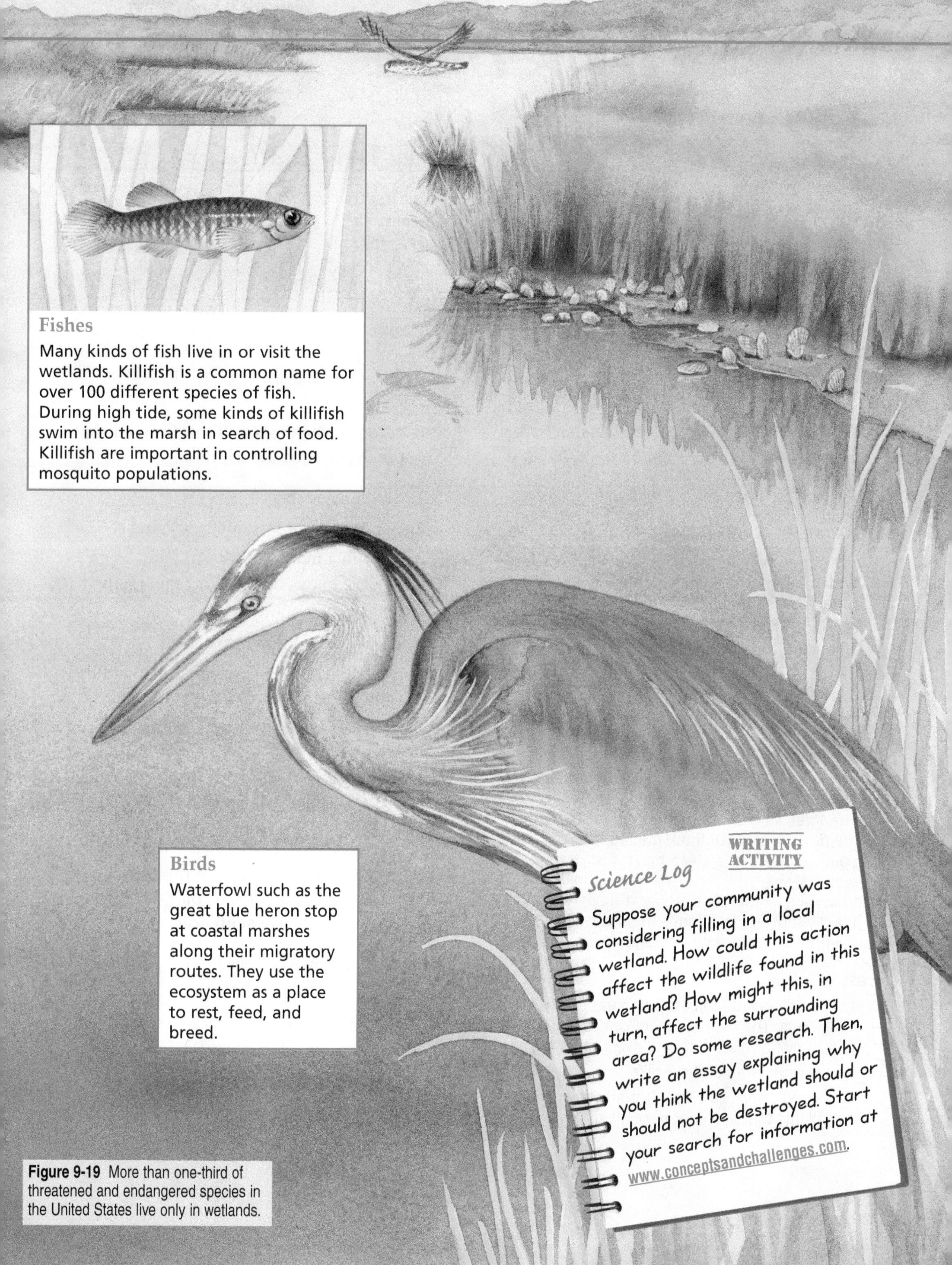

Fishes

Many kinds of fish live in or visit the wetlands. Killifish is a common name for over 100 different species of fish. During high tide, some kinds of killifish swim into the marsh in search of food. Killifish are important in controlling mosquito populations.

Birds

Waterfowl such as the great blue heron stop at coastal marshes along their migratory routes. They use the ecosystem as a place to rest, feed, and breed.

Figure 9-19 More than one-third of threatened and endangered species in the United States live only in wetlands.

WRITING ACTIVITY

Science Log

Suppose your community was considering filling in a local wetland. How could this action affect the wildlife found in this wetland? How might this, in turn, affect the surrounding area? Do some research. Then, write an essay explaining why you think the wetland should or should not be destroyed. Start your search for information at www.conceptsandchallenges.com.

Chapter Summary

Lesson 9-1

- When liquid water takes in enough heat energy, it **evaporates,** or changes to a gas called water vapor. When water vapor loses enough heat, it **condenses,** or changes to a liquid.
- **Precipitation** is any form of water that falls from the atmosphere to Earth.
- The **water cycle** is the repeated movement of water between Earth and the atmosphere.

Lessons 9-2 and 9-3

- **Groundwater** collects in **pores** in soil. Soil with the same size particles can hold more groundwater than can soil with different-sized particles. Groundwater can move easily through soil with large, interconnected pores.
- The upper level of a layer of saturated rock is the **water table.** Some water remains near the surface of the soil.
- Groundwater can reach Earth's surface by means of a **well.** The level of the water table changes from season to season. Water rises freely out of an artesian well, so a pump is not needed.
- A **spring** is a natural flow of groundwater that reaches Earth's surface. Superheated groundwater breaks through to the surface as a **geyser.**

Lesson 9-4

- The three stages in the development of a river are described as youthful, mature, and old. A youthful river has a steep slope, fast-moving water, V-shaped valleys, and many rapids and waterfalls. A mature river has a shallower slope, is slow-moving, and forms **meanders.** An old river has a nearly flat slope and floods easily.

Lesson 9-5

- **Lakes** and **ponds** form in low areas of Earth's continents. The water in them comes mostly from rain, snow, or glacial ice and rivers and streams.
- A **reservoir** is an artificial lake.
- Lakes and ponds can age. This affects animals and plants that live in or near them.

Key Term Challenges

condensation (p. 208)
evaporation (p. 208)
geyser (p. 212)
groundwater (p. 210)
kettle lake (p. 218)
lake (p. 218)
meander (p. 214)
oxbow lake (p. 214)
pond (p. 218)

pore (p. 210)
precipitation (p. 208)
rapids (p. 214)
reservoir (p. 218)
spring (p. 212)
water cycle (p. 208)
waterfall (p. 214)
water table (p. 210)
well (p. 212)

MATCHING **Write the Key Term from above that best matches each description.**

1. tiny hole or space
2. upper layer of saturated rock and soil
3. bend in a mature river
4. low spot in Earth's surface filled with water from rain or snow
5. changing of a liquid to a gas
6. hole dug below the water table that fills with groundwater
7. heated groundwater that erupts onto Earth's surface
8. repeated pattern of water movement between Earth and the atmosphere

APPLYING DEFINITIONS **Explain the difference between the words in each pair. Write your answers in complete sentences.**

9. evaporation, condensation
10. precipitation, water cycle
11. spring, geyser
12. groundwater, well
13. lake, pond
14. kettle lake, oxbow lake
15. waterfalls, rapids

Content Challenges *TEST PREP*

MULTIPLE CHOICE **Write the letter of the term or phrase that best completes each statement.**

1. The process by which a gas changes to a liquid is called
   a. precipitation.
   b. evaporation.
   c. sublimation.
   d. condensation.

2. The main forms of precipitation are
   a. rain and sleet.
   b. sleet and hail.
   c. rain and hail.
   d. rain and snow.

3. About 23 percent of Earth's fresh water supply is stored
   a. as groundwater.
   b. in wells.
   c. in the oceans.
   d. in geysers.

4. In dry weather, the level of the water table in an area
   a. rises.
   b. drops.
   c. stays the same.
   d. increases, then decreases.

5. Old Faithful is
   a. a warm spring.
   b. an artesian well.
   c. a geyser.
   d. a hot spring.

6. The valley of a mature river is
   a. V-shaped with steep banks.
   b. V-shaped with gentle banks.
   c. narrow.
   d. steep.

7. The main threat to rivers is
   a. human recreation.
   b. overfishing.
   c. pollution.
   d. age.

8. A pump is usually used to get water from a
   a. geyser.
   b. spring.
   c. well.
   d. pond.

9. Artificial lakes are called
   a. reservoirs.
   b. oxbow lakes.
   c. kettle lakes.
   d. ponds.

10. Most of the fresh water that is found on Earth is found
    a. in groundwater.
    b. in lakes.
    c. in oceans.
    d. frozen in the polar ice caps.

FILL IN **Write the term or phrase that best completes each sentence.**

11. Water that evaporates from Earth and is changed to a gas is called _____.

12. A cloud is a collection of _____.

13. The pipe for a well should be _____ than the lowest level of the water table.

14. The temperature of spring water is usually _____.

15. A reservoir is a _____ created by a dam.

16. Like oceans, lakes have shorelines that _____.

17. The Yellowstone and Niagara Rivers are _____ rivers.

18. Ponds are similar to lakes but are usually _____.

19. Glaciers help to form _____ lakes.

20. In 2007, the most endangered river in the United States was the _____ River.

Concept Challenges TEST PREP

WRITTEN RESPONSE Answer each of the following questions in complete sentences.

1. CALCULATE: If the level of a water table is 10 m below Earth's surface during the wet season and 15 m below the surface during the dry season, at what depth should a pipe for a well be placed? Why?

2. CONTRAST: How does a hot spring differ from a geyser?

3. EXPLAIN: How does a lake change over time?

4. ANALYZE: How can you tell the stage of a river by observing the shape of the river's valley?

5. EXPLAIN: How can a meander turn into an oxbow lake?

6. ANALYZE: How do plants get water if their roots do not go deep enough into the soil to reach the groundwater?

7. HYPOTHESIZE: How can people help rivers get off the endangered rivers list?

8. HYPOTHESIZE: What would happen to Earth's water supply if water did not evaporate?

INTERPRETING VISUALS Use Figure 9-20 below to answer the following questions.

9. What letter on the diagram shows evaporation taking place?

10. What is evaporation?

11. Which letter on the diagram shows groundwater?

12. Where does groundwater come from?

13. Which letter in the diagram shows precipitation?

14. What are three other forms of precipitation?

15. Where does condensation take place?

16. What is condensation?

▲ Figure 9-20

Chapter 10 The Oceans

▲ **Figure 10-1** Coral reefs are home to a wide variety of life forms.

The oceans form the largest living environment on Earth. As on land, there are many smaller environments within the larger ocean environment. Coral reefs are an example. In addition to living things, the oceans contain valuable nonliving resources. They are great storehouses of dissolved minerals. For example, if all the water evaporated from the oceans, a layer of salt about 50 m thick would cover the ocean floor.

▶ Coral reefs are often described as underwater rain forests. Why?

Contents

10-1 What is the world ocean?

Objectives

Describe the world ocean. Explain what is meant by oceanography.

Key Terms

world ocean: body of salt water covering much of Earth's surface

oceanography (oh-shuh-NAHG-ruh-fee): study of Earth's oceans

The Water Planet About 70 percent of Earth's surface is covered with water. Most of this is salt water. This large body of salt water is known as the **world ocean.** Earth is the only planet in the solar system that has a covering of liquid water.

1 CALCULATE: About what percentage of Earth's surface is dry land?

Divisions of the World Ocean The world ocean is divided into three major bodies of salt water, also called oceans. These are the Atlantic Ocean, the Pacific Ocean, and the Indian Ocean. Geographers often mention two more oceans, the Arctic and the Antarctic. However, these are regarded by Earth scientists as parts of the Atlantic and Pacific oceans.

The word *sea* is sometimes used as another name for ocean. It also refers to a smaller body of water connected to or near an ocean.

Some inland bodies of water are also called seas. Most seas, though, are at least partly connected to an ocean. A gulf is a large area of ocean, larger than a bay, reaching into land.

▲ **Figure 10-2** Because of its great amounts of liquid water, Earth is often known as the blue planet.

2 IDENTIFY: What are the three major oceans?

Size and Depth The Pacific Ocean is the largest of the world's oceans. More than half of Earth's ocean water is in the Pacific Ocean. The Pacific is also Earth's deepest ocean. Its average depth is 4.3 km.

The Atlantic Ocean is the second largest ocean. Several seas and gulfs are part of the Atlantic Ocean. Its average depth is 3.3 km.

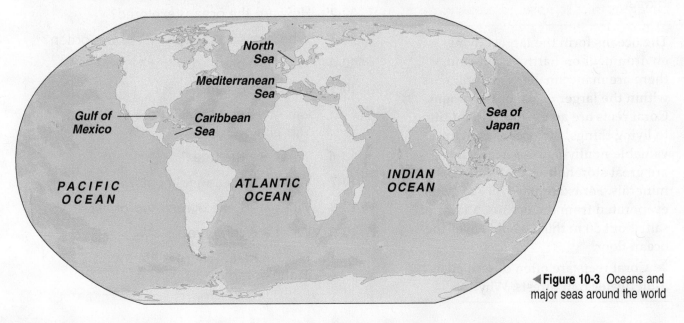

North Sea

Mediterranean Sea

Gulf of Mexico

Caribbean Sea

Sea of Japan

PACIFIC OCEAN

ATLANTIC OCEAN

INDIAN OCEAN

◀ **Figure 10-3** Oceans and major seas around the world

The Indian Ocean is the smallest ocean. It is deeper than the Atlantic Ocean, but not as deep as the Pacific. The average depth of the Indian Ocean is 3.8 km.

 OBSERVE: Use Figure 10-3 to name two seas and a gulf that are part of the Atlantic Ocean.

Oceanography The study of Earth's oceans is called **oceanography.** Scientists who study the oceans and ocean life are called oceanographers. An oceanographer might specialize in the study of the oceans' depths, coral reefs, or the geography of the ocean floor.

 DEFINE: What is oceanography?

✓ CHECKING CONCEPTS

1. About how much of Earth's surface is covered with water?

2. How many oceans do geographers often name?

3. Which of Earth's oceans is the deepest?

4. About what fraction of Earth's ocean water is in the Pacific Ocean?

5. Why are Earth's oceans collectively called "the world ocean"?

💡 THINKING CRITICALLY

6. INFER: Why is Earth often called the blue planet?

7. HYPOTHESIZE: Why would an oceanographer need to specialize?

8. SEQUENCE: List the three major oceans in order, from the smallest to the largest: Atlantic, Indian, Pacific.

BUILDING SCIENCE SKILLS

Graphing Create a bar graph that compares the relative depths of the three oceans.

People in Science

MARINE BIOLOGIST

Marine biologists are oceanographers who study life in the ocean. They work in laboratories, aboard research ships at sea, or in coastal areas. If they work in the ocean, they must be in good physical shape. For example, they may dive into the deep ocean to observe the interactions of living things with the environment.

Research is a large part of marine biology. Some marine biologists take samples of ocean water to test the amount of pollution in it. They may investigate how the pollution affects sea life.

Research work is often done in special laboratories near the seacoasts. Among these laboratories are the Scripps Institution of Oceanography in California and

▲ **Figure 10-4** This marine biologist is studying hammerhead sharks.

the Marine Biological Laboratory of the Woods Hole Oceanographic Institute in Massachusetts. Marine biologists must know biology, physics, chemistry, and math.

Some of the most exciting discoveries in marine biology have been made on the ocean floor. Deep-sea, or hydrothermal, vents are cracks in the ocean floor that leak hot, acidic water. The discovery of them gave marine biologists whole new communities of organisms to study.

Thinking Critically What tool would a marine biologist use to study ocean bacteria?

10-2 How are the oceans explored?

INVESTIGATE

Modeling Buoyancy in the Ocean
HANDS-ON ACTIVITY

You will need a drinking cup, soda water, and grapes.

1. Fill the cup almost full with the soda water.

2. Immediately add five grapes to the cup, one at a time.

3. Wait and watch.

STEP 3

THINK ABOUT IT: What physical force makes the grapes rise to the surface?
What happens when the bubbles are knocked off the surface of the grapes? Why? How might this effect help underwater submersibles explore the deep ocean?

Objective
Describe three ways scientists explore the oceans.

Key Terms
sonar: echo-sounding system that bounces sound waves off the ocean floor

submersible (suhb-MUHR-suh-buhl): underwater research vessel

Deep-Sea Drilling Samples of rock from the ocean floor can be obtained by drilling. Studying these samples allows scientists to learn more about the ocean floor. The Deep Sea Drilling Project (DSDP) was an important ocean research program that ended in 1983. The research ship *Glomar Challenger* was specially built for the DSDP. It could drill 1 km into the crust beneath the ocean. The DSDP was replaced in 1985 by another program called the Ocean Drilling Program (ODP). A new ship, called the *JOIDES Resolution,* took over for the retired *Glomar Challenger.*

▶ **EXPLAIN:** How do we get rock samples from the ocean floor?

Sonar Scientists can map the ocean floor by using sonar. The word *sonar* comes from the letters in <u>so</u>und <u>na</u>vigation and <u>r</u>anging. **Sonar** is an echo-sounding system. Sound waves travel through water at about 1,500 m/s. A transmitter bounces a sound wave off the ocean floor. The

returning sound wave, or echo, is picked up by a receiver. Scientists can measure the time it takes for the sound wave to return. This number can be used to calculate the depth of the ocean floor.

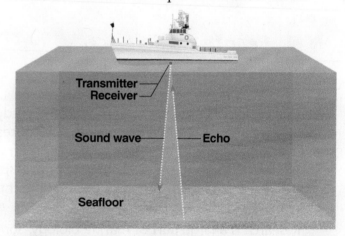

▲ **Figure 10-5** Sonar uses echoes of sound waves.

Suppose a sound wave makes a round trip in 10 seconds. The sound wave takes 5 seconds to reach the ocean floor. It takes another 5 seconds to bounce back to the ship. The depth of the ocean at that point is 1,500 m/s × 5 s = 7,500 m.

▶ **DESCRIBE:** What is sonar used for?

Submersibles Scientists also study the oceans by traveling in underwater research vessels called **submersibles.** One of the first submersibles to be developed was a bathysphere (BATH-ih-sfeer). The bathysphere remained attached to the research ship. Therefore, its movements were limited.

Another kind of submersible is called a bathyscaph (BATH-ih-skayf). A bathyscaph is not attached to anything. It can hold one pilot and two scientists. Scientists in the bathyscaph *Alvin* discovered many unusual forms of life in deep-sea vents. Robot submersibles equipped with underwater cameras can reach great depths and stay there for long periods of time.

▲ **Figure 10-6** This deep-diving minisub is a bathyscaph.

 EXPLAIN: How are robot submersibles better for deep-ocean research than other submersibles are?

✔ CHECKING CONCEPTS

1. What was the Deep Sea Drilling Project?
2. What does the word *sonar* stand for?
3. What is a submersible?

 THINKING CRITICALLY

4. **CONTRAST:** How are a bathysphere and a bathyscaph different?
5. **CALCULATE:** A sonar signal sent out returns in 55 seconds. How deep is the ocean floor in that spot?

Web InfoSearch

Robot Submersibles Many submersibles have robots aboard. These can both explore and take pictures of the ocean floor. In 1985, Dr. Robert D. Ballard used the robot submersible *Argo* to find the remains of the sunken *Titanic*. On board was a robotic camera called Jason, Jr.

SEARCH: Use the Internet to find out more about these amazing vehicles. What else have they found in exploring the ocean floor? Start your search at www.conceptsandchallenges.com. Some key search words are **submersibles, underwater exploration,** *Titanic*, and **Robert Ballard.**

 ## *How Do They Know That?*

PEOPLE CAN BREATHE IN THE OCEAN

People were not designed to breathe underwater. Yet, different devices have been invented to help us do just that.

In 1939, the self-contained underwater breathing apparatus, or scuba, was designed for use by the U.S. military. In 1943, two Frenchmen, Jacques Cousteau and Emile Gagnan, invented the Aqua-lung. This device allowed a diver both to breathe and to move about freely underwater. A tank filled with compressed air was strapped to a diver's back. A hose carried air from the tank to the diver's mouth. A valve controlled air flow. Cousteau tested the Aqua-lung in more than 500 dives. Aqua-lungs are still used today. In the 1950s, Cousteau built an underwater diving station at the edge of the continental shelf. Divers lived and worked there. Cousteau himself traveled all over the world exploring the oceans. He died in 1997. His granddaughter Alexandra continues his work.

Thinking Critically How did the Aqua-lung help in the study of the oceans?

▲ **Figure 10-7** A scuba diver can breathe underwater by using tanks filled with air.

10-3 What are some properties of the ocean?

INVESTIGATE

Testing the Density of Ocean Water
HANDS-ON ACTIVITY

1. Fill two 250 ml beakers or jars with 200 ml of tap water.

2. Add 3 tsp of salt to one beaker. Stir until the salt dissolves.

3. Place a whole, uncooked egg in each jar. Handle the eggs carefully to avoid breaking them. ⚠ CAUTION: Wash your hands when you are finished with this activity.

THINK ABOUT IT: What happened to the two eggs? What does this tell you about the difference between saltwater and freshwater?

STEP 3

Objective

Explain why ocean temperatures and salinity in the oceans vary.

Key Terms

salinity (suh-LIHN-uh-tee): amount of dissolved salts in ocean water

thermocline (THUHR-muh-klyn): layer of ocean water in which the temperature drops sharply with depth

The Salty Sea The water in Earth's oceans is saltwater. Saltwater contains more dissolved salts and other minerals than freshwater does.

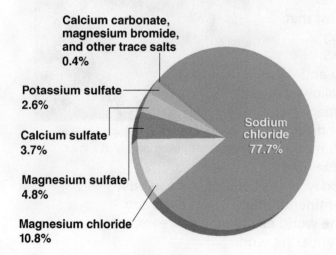

Calcium carbonate, magnesium bromide, and other trace salts 0.4%

Potassium sulfate 2.6%

Calcium sulfate 3.7%

Magnesium sulfate 4.8%

Magnesium chloride 10.8%

Sodium chloride 77.7%

▲ **Figure 10-8** Minerals in saltwater

The amount of dissolved salts in ocean water is called **salinity.** Ocean water contains from 33 to 37 g of dissolved salt in every 1,000 g of water.

 DEFINE: What is salinity?

Levels of Salinity The salinity of ocean water differs slightly from place to place. Freshwater from rivers, precipitation, and melting glaciers lowers ocean salinity.

During the day, water evaporates from the surface of the ocean. Evaporation leaves behind dissolved salts. This raises salinity. Salinity varies more at the surface than in deep ocean water.

 INFER: Would rain increase or decrease the salinity in ocean water? Explain.

Temperature Layers Oceanographers recognize three "layers" of the ocean based on temperature. These layers are surface, thermocline, and deep.

Heat from the Sun warms ocean water. The water is warmest at the surface and coldest near the ocean floor. The surface layer is from 100 to 300 m deep. Constant winds and waves keep the water in the surface layer well mixed. As a result, the temperatures vary slightly in the ocean's surface layer.

Below the surface layer is the **thermocline.** In this layer, temperatures drop sharply with depth. The ocean below the thermocline, the deep layer, is even colder. Here the temperatures are usually below 5°C.

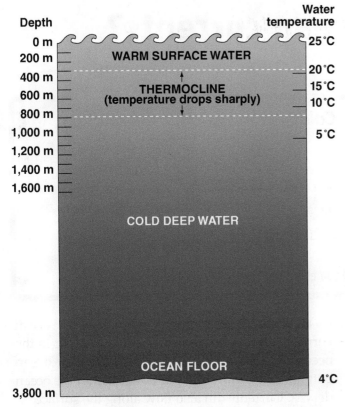

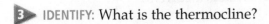

▲ **Figure 10-9** Ocean temperature decreases as depth increases.

▶ IDENTIFY: What is the thermocline?

Desalination Only a small part of Earth's freshwater is **potable** (POHT-uh-buhl), or fit to drink. Fresh water is a valuable natural resource that is in short supply.

As the population of the world increases, more freshwater is needed. Most supplies of freshwater depend on precipitation. During dry periods, those supplies are reduced.

Scientists have discovered a way to use ocean water to meet the increasing need for water. Before people can use the supply of water available in the ocean, minerals and salts in the ocean water must be removed.

In many places, desalination (dee-sal-uh-NAY-shuhn) plants have been built to remove the salts from ocean water. These plants use several different methods to remove salts. The most common is to heat the water until it evaporates, leaving the salts behind. The water vapor is then condensed to recover fresh water. Another method is to freeze ocean water. When ocean water is frozen, the ice formed is free of salts. The ice is then cleaned and melted to provide freshwater. Currently, Saudi Arabia, Israel, Malta, and some U.S. states operate desalination plants.

▲ **Figure 10-10** A desalination plant changes saltwater into drinking water.

 DESCRIBE: What happens when you desalinate water?

☑ CHECKING CONCEPTS

1. The amount of dissolved salts in ocean water is called _____.
2. Adding freshwater to saltwater _____ the salinity of the water.
3. Ocean water is warmest at the _____.
4. There are _____ different temperature layers in the ocean.
5. Salinity varies more at the _____ than in deep ocean water.

💡 THINKING CRITICALLY

6. SEQUENCE: Use Figure 10-8 to list the minerals found in oceans, from the greatest percentage to the least.
7. PREDICT: The Mediterranean Sea has a high rate of evaporation. Would it have a high or low salinity? Explain.

BUILDING READING SKILLS

Vocabulary Write the definitions of the following words that contain the prefix *thermo*, meaning "heat": thermocline, thermoelectric, thermograph, thermomagnetic, and thermometer. Circle the part of the definition that relates to the prefix.

10-4 What are ocean currents?

INVESTIGATE

Comparing Densities of Cold and Warm Water
HANDS-ON ACTIVITY

STEP 3

1. Fill a plastic container half full with warm water. Wait for the water to stop moving.
2. Add several drops of food coloring to a cup of ice water and stir.
3. Using an eyedropper, gently dribble the colored water down the inside of the plastic container.

THINK ABOUT IT: What happened? Why? What does this tell you about the density of cold and warm water?

Objectives

Define current. Describe how surface currents and density currents are formed.

Key Terms

current: stream of water flowing in the oceans

density current: stream of water that moves up and down in ocean depths

Coriolis effect: bending of Earth's winds and ocean currents by Earth's rotation

On the Move The water in Earth's oceans is always moving. Have you ever heard of someone throwing a bottle containing a message into the ocean? Sometime later, the bottle is found far away.

How did it get there? It was carried by ocean currents. These **currents** are streams of water in the oceans. Some currents move along the ocean bottom. Some move up and down within the ocean depths. Currents can also flow along the surface.

▶ 1 **DEFINE:** What is a current?

Density Currents Differences in density can cause currents to move up and down in the ocean depths. This movement of water causes **density currents.**

Ocean currents can be warm or cold. Currents flowing from areas near the equator are warm. They bring warm water into cooler regions. These warm currents tend to warm the air over nearby land areas.

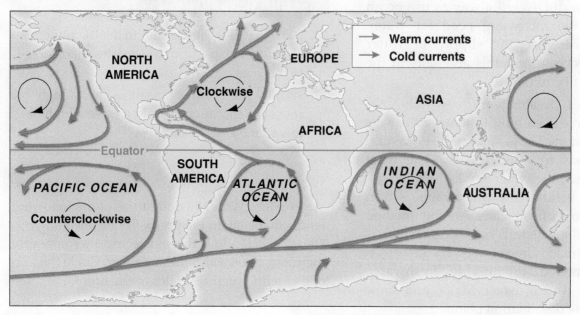

◀ **Figure 10-11**
Different densities in ocean water cause density currents.

Currents coming from areas near the poles are cold. They bring cold water into warmer regions and cool these areas. Cold water is denser than warm water. Cold water around the poles sinks to the ocean bottom. Water around the equator is warm. Warm water rises up toward the ocean surface.

Different amounts of salt in ocean water also cause density currents. Water with a lot of salt is denser than water with only a little salt. Dense, salty water sinks. Less salty water rises.

 DESCRIBE: What conditions cause density currents in the ocean?

Surface Currents Winds cause most surface currents. Winds near the equator blow mainly from east to west. In the Northern Hemisphere, these winds blow from the northeast. In the Southern Hemisphere, these winds blow from the southeast. Earth's rotation causes the winds in the Northern Hemisphere to curve toward the west and the winds in the Southern Hemisphere to curve toward the east. This is called the **Coriolis effect.** Continents and large islands also influence ocean currents. As a result, surface currents move in huge circles. They move clockwise in the Northern Hemisphere and counterclockwise in the Southern Hemisphere.

 STATE: What causes most surface currents?

CHECKING CONCEPTS

1. Ocean currents are streams of _____ in the oceans.

2. Most surface currents are caused by _____.

3. Surface currents from the _____ are cold currents.

4. Surface currents from the _____ are warm currents.

THINKING CRITICALLY

5. HYPOTHESIZE: Why do large land areas cause surface currents to change direction?

6. COMPARE: Which is probably denser, the water in the Arctic Ocean or the water in the Caribbean Sea? Explain your answer.

HEALTH AND SAFETY TIP

An undertow is a current that moves beneath and in a different direction from the surface current. Undertows can be very dangerous. This is one reason you should never swim alone. Interview a lifeguard to find out about other safety guidelines for swimming. Make a chart that outlines some of these guidelines.

Real-Life Science
TRAVELING ON CURRENTS

Knowing the direction and the strength of ocean currents is important to the shipping industry. Any good sailor knows that traveling with a current saves time.

In 1768, King George III asked Benjamin Franklin why it took mail ships longer to go from England to the colonies than to return to England. Franklin asked the captain of a whaling ship. He was told of a strong current of warm, salty water that flowed along the eastern coast of North America, then across the North Atlantic. Whaling ships rode the current going out but stayed outside of it when returning home. That ocean current is the Gulf Stream.

Thinking Critically How do you think ships today shorten their trips to Europe?

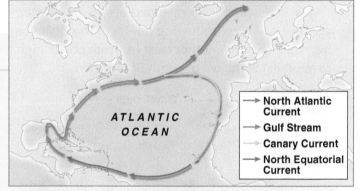

▲ **Figure 10-12** Currents can help ships cross the Atlantic Ocean faster.

10-5 What are ocean waves?

Objective

Identify the properties of an ocean wave.

Key Terms

wave: regular up-and-down movement of water

crest: highest point of a wave

trough (TRAWF)**:** lowest point of a wave

How Waves Form When a wind blows across the water, waves are formed. A **wave** is a regular up-and-down movement of water. On a windy day at the beach, the ocean water gets rough. The waves are high when the wind is strong. On a calm day, the waves are not as high.

1 DEFINE: What is a wave?

Wave Shape A wave has a high point and a low point. The highest point, or top of a wave, is the **crest.** The lowest point of a wave is the **trough.** The height of a wave is the distance from crest to trough. Waves can reach heights of more than 15 m. However, eventually a wave reaches a point when it becomes too high and topples over. A white cap is then formed.

As you watch waves move across the water, you see one crest following another. The distance from one crest to another crest (or from one trough to another) is the wavelength of the wave.

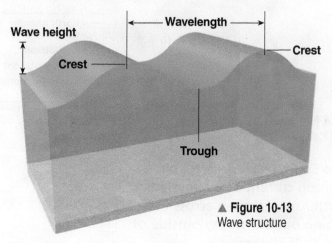

▲ Figure 10-13
Wave structure

2 EXPLAIN: How is wave height measured?

Water Movement in Waves In deep water, the water in a wave does not move forward as the wave moves. Only the energy in the wave moves forward.

You can see the movement of water by watching a floating object. As a wave moves by, the object moves slightly forward. As the wave passes, the object falls back about the same distance. The object appears to be moving up and down in the same place.

As a wave moves across the ocean, water particles in the wave move in circles. At the surface, the size of the circles is the same as the height of the waves.

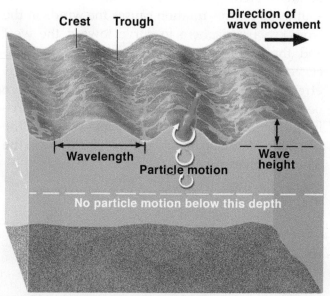

▲ Figure 10-14 Particle motions in waves

3 DESCRIBE: How do water particles move in a wave?

Breaking Waves As waves move through deep water, they are not affected much by the depth of the water. However, the shallow waters of the shoreline drag on the wave and cause it to slow down.

As a wave slows down, its height rises until a certain critical height is reached. At this critical point, the wave breaks. The energy contained in the wave up until then changes form. The wave no longer moves in an up-and-down motion. It advances up the shore as a sheet of water.

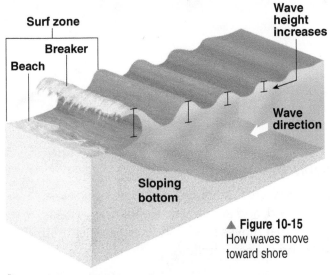

Surf zone

Breaker

Beach

Wave height increases

Wave direction

Sloping bottom

▲ **Figure 10-15**
How waves move toward shore

4 EXPLAIN: Why does a wave slow up in shallow water?

✓ CHECKING CONCEPTS

1. Most waves are caused by _____.
2. The top of a wave is the _____.
3. The distance between crests is the _____.
4. Only the _____ of a wave moves forward.

💡 THINKING CRITICALLY

5. MODEL: Draw a wave and label it.
6. INFER: Early in the day, the water at the beach is fairly calm. Later in the day, the water begins to get rough. What do you think might be causing this?

Web InfoSearch

Tsunamis A tsunami (soo-NAH-mee) is an ocean wave. However, unlike other ocean waves, tsunamis are not caused by wind. Tsunamis carry a great deal of energy. They can be very destructive.

SEARCH: Use the Internet to find out more about tsunamis. What causes them? What happens as they approach the shore? To find out, start your search at www.conceptsandchallenges.com. Some key search words are **tsunamis, how tsunamis form**, and **underwater earthquakes**.

Hands-On Activity

MODELING WAVE MOTION

You will need an aquarium tank, metal washers, and four or five corks.

1. Fill the aquarium tank about 3/4 full of water.
2. Tie enough metal washers to a cork so that it floats about 3 cm from the tank bottom.
3. Repeat Step 2 with more corks so that they float 9 cm from the bottom, 15 cm from the bottom, and so on, until the last cork floats on the surface.
4. Make small, steady waves in the tank by moving your hand up and down in the water. Note what happens to each cork.
5. Repeat Step 4, but increase the height of the waves by moving your hand faster.

▲ **STEP 4** Make small, steady waves in the tank.

Go Online
active art

For: Water Motion activity
Visit: PHSchool.com
Web Code: cfp-3031

Practicing Your Skills

6. ANALYZE: How does increasing the wave height affect the motion of each cork?
7. OBSERVE: What features of a wave did you observe in this activity?

LAB ACTIVITY
Modeling the Shapes of Shorelines

BACKGROUND

Large waves carry great amounts of energy. Waves toss around rocks, sand, and swimmers. Gentle waves also contain energy that moves sand and finer particles around. Waves erode and shape shorelines.

PURPOSE

In this activity, you will study the development of a shoreline as it is struck by waves.

PROCEDURE FOR WATER-ONLY SHORELINE TABLE

1. Use the plastic storage box for the shoreline table. Set the shoreline table on a flat working surface. Raise one end of the box about 5 cm. Fill the box part way with water.

2. Create a wave generator by gluing together two paint sticks in a T-shape. Move the sticks back and forth in the water for a minute to create gentle waves.

3. Observe what happens to the waves as they approach shallower water. How do they change shape? Copy the first column only of the chart in Figure 10-16 and draw a picture of what you observe. Be sure to label your drawing.

4. Create more powerful waves and again observe what happens to the shoreline.

PROCEDURE FOR WATER AND SAND SHORELINE TABLE

5. Use the same plastic storage box for the next shoreline table. Set the shoreline table on a flat working surface. Raise one end of the box about 5 cm.

6. Fill the raised end of the shoreline table with sand that is 6 cm deep. Then, fill the box part way with water.

▲ **STEP 1** Raise one end of the storage box about 5 cm.

▲ **STEP 2** Move your wave generator around in the water.

7. Again, move the wooden paint sticks back and forth in the water to act as wave generators. Create gentle waves in your shoreline table.

8. Observe what happens to the sand on the shoreline as waves strike it. Copy the whole chart below and draw pictures of what you observe. Be sure to label your drawings.

9. Scoop out sand to make a small bay. Create waves for one minute and observe what happens to the bay. Draw what you see.

▲ **STEP 9** Create waves and draw how the bay looks now.

10. Place a small pile of sand in the middle of the shoreline to make a small peninsula. A peninsula is a land area that projects out into water.

11. Create waves for one minute and observe what happens to the peninsula. Draw what you see.

Waves and Shorelines		
Diagram of how waves change as they enter shallow water	Diagram of how waves changed the bay	Diagram of how waves changed the peninsula

▲ **Figure 10-16** Use a copy of this table on which to draw your diagrams.

CONCLUSIONS

1. OBSERVE: How did the waves change as they reached shallower water in the water-only shoreline table?

2. OBSERVE: What happened to the sand as waves broke on the shore of the water and sand shoreline table?

3. ANALYZE: How do waves change the shoreline?

4. INFER: What might happen to a shoreline that has both a bay and a peninsula?

What are the tides?

Objective

Describe what causes and affects the tides.

Key Terms

tide: regular change in the level of Earth's oceans

flood tide: incoming, or rising, tide

ebb tide: outgoing, or falling, tide

Ocean Water Levels The water level of the ocean rises and falls throughout the day. Early in the day, ocean water rises and covers part of the beach. Later in the day, the ocean level falls. The beach is exposed. These regular changes in ocean water levels are called **tides.** A low water level is called low tide. A high water level is called high tide.

▲ **Figure 10-17** Low tide (above) and an incoming tide (below) in the same location

▶ **DEFINE:** What are tides?

Causes of Tides You probably know that Earth's gravitational pull on the Moon keeps the Moon in orbit around us. But did you know that the Moon also pulls back on Earth and causes the tides? The Sun's gravitational pull also affects Earth's tides, but because it is so far away from us, not as strongly.

Earth's continents are slightly stretched by the pull of the Moon. Earth's oceans, which move more freely, are stretched even more. This stretching effect creates two bulges of water on Earth, one facing the Moon, the other directly opposite it. These bulges are the high tides. The bulging water also causes two areas with low tides between the high tides. As the Earth turns on its axis, the tide levels rise and fall.

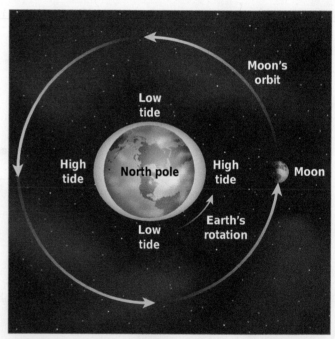

▲ **Figure 10-18** The Moon, along with the Sun, causes the tides. Whether it is high tide or low tide depends mostly on where you are on Earth relative to the Moon.

▶ **IDENTIFY:** What mainly causes tides on Earth?

Changing Tides Some newspapers print tide tables. A tide table tells the times at which high tide and low tide will occur. If you look at a tide table, you will notice that it often shows two high tides and two low tides each day. The tides change about every 6 hours and 15 minutes.

TIDE TABLE

Sunday	Monday	Tuesday	Wednesday
1 Low 4:45a	2 Low 5:38a	3 Low 6:27a	4 Low 7:11a
High 11:31a	High 12:32p	High 1:25p	High 2:10p
Low 4:30p	Low 5:24p	Low 6:15p	Low 7:02p
High 10:24p	High 11:10p	High 11:55p	
8 Low 2:47a	9 Low 3:31a	10 Low 4:18a	11 Low 5:10a
High 9:40a	High 10:13a	High 10:48a	High 11:23a
Low 4:26p	Low 4:58p	Low 5:30p	Low 6:05p
High 9:58p	High 10:46p	High 11:36p	

▲ **Figure 10-19** A newspaper gives the times for high and low tide.

Each quarter rotation of Earth causes a major change in tides. Water slowly floods the beach until high tide is reached. The incoming tide is called a **flood tide.** As Earth rotates another quarter turn, the water begins to leave the beach until low tide is reached. This outgoing tide is called an **ebb tide.**

3 INFER: How often each day do flood tides occur?

CHECKING CONCEPTS

1. What is the outgoing tide called?
2. What causes tides?
3. What is a flood tide?
4. How many times do the tides change each day?

THINKING CRITICALLY

5. INFER: Who would use a tide table? Why?
6. PREDICT: If low tide occurs at 6:30 AM, when will the next low tide probably occur?
7. HYPOTHESIZE: Suppose you docked a boat where the tides rise and fall about 1 m. How would this affect the use of the boat?

INTERPRETING VISUALS

Use Figure 10-19 to answer the following question.

8. INFER: Fishing is best on mornings with high tides. Which day should you go?

Real-Life Science

TIDES AND FISHING

Grunions are small silver fish that live in the Pacific Ocean off the coast of California. Grunions spawn and lay their eggs on sandy beaches from late February to early September, but only on nights of the highest tides. During this time, thousands of grunions cover the beaches. Many people gather on the beaches and catch the fish by hand. Some newspapers announce the nights the fish are expected to be on the beach.

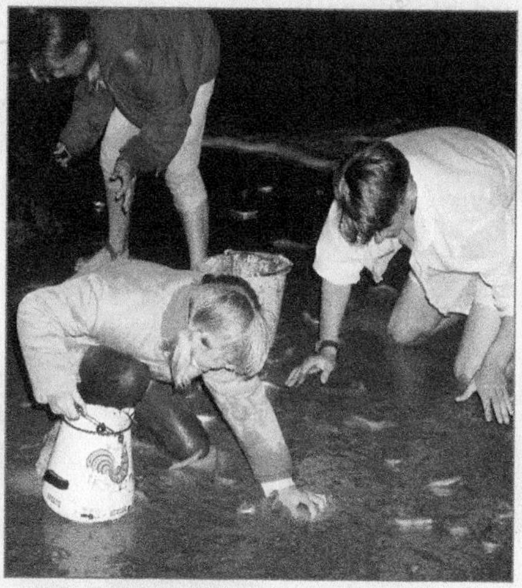

▲ **Figure 10-20** Catching grunions on the beach is a common event in California.

Much of the fishing industry depends on an understanding of tides. Tides involve the movements of huge volumes of water. The water carries fresh oxygen. It also carries microorganisms, which serve as food for fish. Fish carried in with high tides can be easily trapped in nets later in the day.

The Bay of Fundy, between Nova Scotia and New Brunswick, Canada, is known worldwide for its tides. The difference between high and low tides can be over 10 m. This region is famous for its fishing industry.

Thinking Critically Why do you think the fish carried in with the high tides are easily trapped in the nets?

10-7 What are ocean sediments?

Objective

Describe different kinds of ocean sediments.

Key Terms

nodule (NAHJ-ool): mineral lump found on the ocean floor

ooze: ocean sediment that contains the remains of many ocean organisms

Sediment Formation Ocean sediments are formed by materials that collect on the ocean floor. Some sediments come from eroded land rocks. Others contain the remains of living things. Dust and ash from volcanoes sink to the ocean floor. Dust from space also falls and sinks to the ocean floor.

 LIST: What makes up ocean sediments?

Eroded Rock Sediments Most of the sediments near the shore are eroded rock particles. Rivers carry rocks of all sizes to the ocean. Waves and wind also weather the rocks along the shoreline. These rock particles become ocean sediments. The sediments gradually spread out over the ocean floor. Large particles settle close to shore. Smaller particles settle farther from shore.

▲ **Figure 10-21** An arch can be formed by wind and waves eroding rock.

 EXPLAIN: What weathers rock to form sediment?

Nodules Lumps of minerals called **nodules** are found on the ocean floor. Nodules form very slowly by a chemical process. Nodules are made up mostly of compounds of manganese, nickel, and iron. Small amounts of copper, lead, zinc, and silver are also found in ocean sediments. Most of the nodules lie thousands of meters deep in the ocean. Suction devices similar to huge vacuum cleaners have been used to collect them.

▲ **Figure 10-22** Nodules are lumps of minerals.

 DEFINE: What are nodules?

Ooze Much of the ocean floor is made up of fine, soft sediments called **ooze.** At least 30 percent of ooze is the remains of ocean organisms. When ocean organisms die, their shells and skeletons sink to the ocean floor. These remains eventually fall apart or decompose. This material mixes with volcanic dust, clay, and water to form ooze.

▲ **Figure 10-23** Ooze may contain the decomposing skeletons of organisms such as these diatoms.

Much of the ooze on the ocean floor comes from tiny plants and animals such as the diatoms shown in Figure 10-23. Larger animals, such as clams and corals, also add to ooze.

 DEFINE: What is ooze?

Underwater Canyons Beyond the shoreline of the ocean, the land gradually slopes downward. Ocean sediments collect near the edges of these slopes. From time to time, the sediments slide down the slope, pushing water ahead of them. Gradually, this underwater landslide erodes the slope in places and forms canyons.

 IDENTIFY: What causes underwater landslides?

✓ CHECKING CONCEPTS

1. Fallen materials on the ocean floor form _____.

2. The largest rock particles settle _____ to shore.

3. Nodules are made up mostly of manganese, nickel, and _____.

4. Ooze is formed from _____.

5. Rocks are carried to the ocean by _____.

💡 THINKING CRITICALLY

6. **INFER:** Why do small rock particles settle farther from shore than larger rock particles?

7. **INFER:** How do sediments from a volcano on land get into the ocean?

8. **EXPLAIN:** A large rock is located in a river. Outline the steps that might lead to this rock eventually breaking apart and being deposited as sediment on the ocean floor.

BUILDING SCIENCE SKILLS

Researching Find out about other kinds of ocean sediment. Then, make a chart listing them all. Add those discussed here. Say where they come from and what structures they form.

 Hands-On Activity

OBSERVING THE SETTLING OF OCEAN SEDIMENTS

You will need safety goggles, a plastic container with a lid, small pebbles, sand, soil, and water.

1. Place a small amount of pebbles, sand, and soil into a plastic container. Fill the container halfway with water. Then, put on the lid.

2. Shake the container gently for about 10 seconds.

3. Leave the particles undisturbed for several hours. Then, observe how the particles settled.

Practicing Your Skills

4. **OBSERVE:** Which particles settled on the bottom of the container? Which particles settled on top?

5. **ANALYZE:** Why did the particles settle out the way they did?

6. **COMPARE:** How is this like sediments settling out on the ocean floor?

▲ **STEP 2** Shake the container for 10 seconds.

10-8 What are some ocean landforms?

Objective
Describe the ocean floor.

Key Terms

continental shelf: part of a continent that slopes gently away from the shoreline

continental slope: part of a continent between the continental shelf and the ocean floor

trench: deep canyon on the ocean floor

seamount: volcanic mountain on the ocean floor

guyot (GEE-oh)**:** flat-topped, underwater seamount

Continental Margin The continental margin divides a continent from the ocean floor. The edges of the continent extend into the oceans. At first, the continent slopes gently down under the ocean. This area is called the **continental shelf.** In some places, the continental shelf is very narrow. In other places, it extends for more than 150 km from the edge of the continent. Beyond the continental shelf is the **continental slope.** The continental slope is steeper than the continental shelf. It ends at the ocean floor.

 COMPARE: Which is steeper, the continental shelf or the continental slope?

The Ocean Floor Like Earth's surface, the ocean floor has different landforms. The flat parts are plains. Plains cover about half of the ocean floor. High mountain ranges run along the middle of the oceans. These ranges are the mid-ocean ridges. In some places, mid-ocean ridges rise above the ocean surface to form islands.

 IDENTIFY: What two landforms are on the ocean floor?

Trenches The ocean floor has deep **trenches,** or underwater canyons. The deepest of these is the Mariana Trench in the Pacific Ocean. This trench is more than 11,000 m deep. Mount Everest, the tallest mountain on land, is about 8,900 m high. Mount Everest could fit into the Mariana Trench and still be more than 2,000 m below the ocean's surface.

 COMPARE: How does the depth of the Mariana Trench compare with the height of Mount Everest?

Seamounts and Guyots There are many mountains scattered around the ocean floor. These are called **seamounts.** Seamounts were once active underwater volcanoes. The ones that reach above the ocean surface form volcanic islands. The Hawaiian Islands are the peaks of underwater volcanoes.

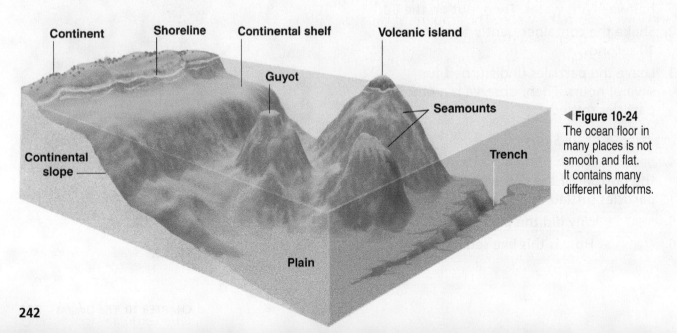

◀ **Figure 10-24**
The ocean floor in many places is not smooth and flat. It contains many different landforms.

Some underwater seamounts have flattened tops. These seamounts are called **guyots**.

 4 DEFINE: What is a guyot?

✔ CHECKING CONCEPTS

1. Two parts of the continental margin are the continental shelf and the continental _____.

2. Three landforms on the ocean floor are _____, mountains, and trenches.

3. Mountains on the ocean floor are called _____.

4. A _____ is an underwater seamount with a flat top.

💡 THINKING CRITICALLY

5. PREDICT: What would happen to the continental shelf if the sea level dropped sharply?

6. HYPOTHESIZE: On the ocean floor, mountains are higher and plains are flatter than they are on Earth's surface. Why do you think this is so?

Web InfoSearch

Fishing on the Grand Banks The most productive fishing grounds in the world are found on continental shelves. The Grand Banks off the east coast of Canada is an example. Fishing boats from Canada, the United States, Japan, and Europe catch tons of fish off the Grand Banks every year.

SEARCH: Use the Internet to find out more about the Grand Banks. What kinds of fish are found there? Start your search at www.conceptsandchallenges.com. Some key search words are **fishing, Grand Banks,** and **continental shelves.**

◀ **Figure 10-25** Fishing on the Grand Banks

 ## How Do They Know That?

MAPPING THE OCEAN FLOOR

Much of the ocean floor cannot be seen from the surface. Until the twentieth century, the best method to map it was to tie a heavy object to a piece of rope and lower it into the water. The amount of rope used showed how deep the bottom was.

Certain technologies have made the ocean floor more visible to us. These technologies allow us to map it in great detail. The main advance in mapping occurred when sonar was developed in the 1920s. Modern sonar systems produce very detailed images.

Another advance was the camera sled. This device takes photographs of the ocean floor while it is being towed across it. For the mapping of small areas, submersibles are used. Also, satellites provide very precise measurements of seafloor features.

Thinking Critically What seafloor features does sonar map?

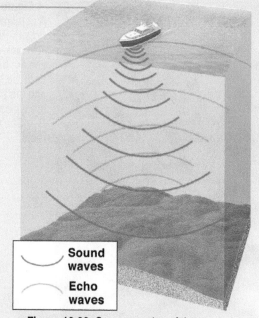

Sound waves

Echo waves

▲ **Figure 10-26** Sonar mapping of the ocean floor

10-9 What are coral reefs?

Objective
Describe three kinds of coral reefs.

Key Terms

coral: small animals found in warm, shallow ocean waters

fringing reef: coral reef that is directly attached to a shore

barrier reef: coral reef that forms around a sunken volcanic island

lagoon: shallow body of water between a reef and the mainland

atoll (A-tawl): ring-shaped coral reef around a lagoon

Building the Reefs Tiny animals called **coral** live in warm, shallow ocean waters. Corals absorb calcium from the water. They use it to make hard skeletons of limestone, or calcium carbonate, around their bodies. Corals often attach themselves to other coral, forming a colony. New corals grow on top of dead ones. In time, a coral reef is formed.

◀ **Figure 10-27** A coral reef in Egypt's Red Sea. The pink-orange fish are basslets. Both the basslets and the soft coral are typical of Red Sea coral reefs.

▶ DESCRIBE: What is a coral reef made of?

Fringing Reefs and Barrier Reefs Two kinds of coral reefs are fringing reefs and barrier reefs. A **fringing reef** is a coral reef that is directly attached to a shore. It borders the coastline closely or is separated from it by only a narrow stretch of water. Fringing reefs are located along the east coast of Florida, among other places.

▲ **Figure 10-28** This fringing reef surrounds the South Pacific island of Bora Bora.

Barrier reefs form around sunken volcanic islands. The reef once extended out from the shore. As the island sank, the reef became separated from the mainland by a body of water. This body of water is a **lagoon.**

The Great Barrier Reef off the northeast coast of Australia is the world's largest barrier reef. It is more than 2,000 km long. In some places, it is almost 200 km wide. The Great Barrier Reef has been described by some as the largest structure ever built by living creatures. It actually consists of about 2,100 individual reefs and about 800 fringing reefs.

▶ IDENTIFY: Where do barrier reefs form?

Atolls A ring-shaped coral reef around a lagoon is called an **atoll.** An atoll forms around a sunken volcanic island. Only the circular coral reef remains above the ocean's surface. In the center of the atoll is the lagoon. Ships are sometimes able to enter the lagoons through channels that connect the ocean and the lagoon. Most atolls are in the Pacific Ocean.

▲ **Figure 10-29** Aerial view of Kayangel Atoll in the western Pacific Ocean

 DEFINE: What is an atoll?

✓ CHECKING CONCEPTS

1. Where do the tiny animals known as corals live?
2. What do corals absorb from water to build reefs?

3. What is a reef colony?
4. What is found in the center of an atoll?
5. What are three kinds of coral reefs?

💡 THINKING CRITICALLY

6. COMPARE/CONTRAST: How are fringing reefs and barrier reefs alike and different?
7. INFER: Why is the sand on a coral island white?
8. HYPOTHESIZE: Fossil coral reefs have been found beneath farmland far from the ocean. What might this discovery mean?

DESIGNING AN EXPERIMENT

Design an experiment to solve the following problem. Include a hypothesis, variables, a procedure with materials, and a type of data to study. Also include a way to record that data.

PROBLEM: Do the skeletons of coral contain calcium carbonate?

Integrating Environmental Science

TOPIC: ecosystems

ARTIFICIAL REEFS

Natural coral reefs support ecosystems. However, natural reefs take a long time to form. To help increase the fish population in the ocean, especially of those species used for food, people are building artificial reefs. These reefs also reduce beach erosion by blocking waves before they reach shore. The Japanese have been building artificial reefs for more than 300 years. The first artificial reef in the United States was built in 1830 off the coast of South Carolina.

Old oil rigs, old tires, sunken ships, concrete blocks, even old subway cars can serve as artificial reefs. Battle tanks and armored vehicles are part of a large artificial reef off the coast of Long Island in New York. Near Miami Beach, Florida, a 727 airliner was sunk to serve as a reef. Sea creatures such as coral, sea anemones (ah-NEM-oh-neez), mussels, barnacles, and sponges cling to or grow on the metal surfaces.

Thinking Critically How do reefs help increase the fish population?

▲ **Figure 10-30** Artificial reefs can be built of almost anything, such as this cargo container.

THE Big IDEA

Where is life found in the ocean?

Many different kinds of organisms live in the ocean. Living things in the ocean are found in two main zones. The waters lying above the ocean bottom are called the pelagic zone. The waters next to the ocean floor are called the benthic zone.

Plankton are organisms that float along the surface of the pelagic zone. The motion of wind, waves, and currents moves these microscopic organisms. Some rise and fall in response to the day/night cycle.

There are two kinds of plankton. Phytoplankton (fyt-oh-PLANK-tuhn) are floating, plant-like protists. These organisms use sunlight to make food from carbon dioxide and water. Phytoplankton are a source of food for floating animal-like protists called zooplankton.

Nekton are free-swimming ocean animals that move throughout the pelagic zone in search of food. Fishes, whales, dolphins, seals, and squids are nekton. Some nekton eat plankton. Others eat animals that have eaten plankton.

Organisms that live in the benthic zone are called benthos. Benthos are found in shallow waters along a coast and in the deepest parts of the ocean. Some benthos attach themselves to the ocean floor. They stay in that spot until they die. Mussels, barnacles, and some seaweeds are benthos that remain attached to the ocean floor. Some benthos bury themselves in sand or mud. Others, such as sea stars and crabs, move around on the ocean bottom.

Look at the illustrations on these two pages. Then, complete the Science Log to learn more about "the big idea."✦

Diatoms

Diatoms are one type of phytoplankton. When these single-celled organisms die, their glasslike shells sink to the ocean bottom, forming sediment.

Go Online
active art

For: Ocean Food Web activity
Visit: PHSchool.com
Web Code: cfp-3042

Whales

Like all other mammals, whales have lungs and must come to the water surface to take in air. However, some whales, such as sperm whales, can dive to depths of 1,000 m in the pelagic zone.

Lantern Fish and Angler Fish

Organs that give off light are located along the bodies of the lantern fish (shown in photo below). This adaptation helps the animal survive the cold, dark benthic zone. Female angler fish, which live on or near the ocean floor, have structures that look like fishing rods or lures on top of their heads to attract prey. The illustration shows two types of angler fish.

Dolphins

Just like other members of the whale family, dolphins are warm-blooded animals. Their body temperature stays about the same regardless of water temperature. Dolphins are strong swimmers and can dive to depths of 300 m.

Sea Stars

Sea stars, also known as starfish, can grow a new arm if they lose one. They have tiny tube feet on their arms that help them move about the ocean floor. These organisms live in the shallow part of the benthic zone.

Mackerel

The streamlined body of a mackerel is adapted to swimming throughout the pelagic zone. Mackerel generally live and travel in large groups called shoals.

Figure 10-31 Sunlight and water temperature decrease as you move from the pelagic zone down to the benthic zone of the ocean. This affects the kinds of ocean life that live there.

WRITING ACTIVITY

Science Log

Available sunlight, water depth, temperature, salinity, and seafloor sediments all influence how an ocean organism adapts to its environment. Choose a marine organism. Research how its environment relates to how it lives. Write a report to be sent to an agency that monitors the environment, such as the Environmental Protection Agency (EPA). Start your search at www.conceptsandchallenges.com.

Chapter Summary

Lessons 10-1 and 10-2

- The world ocean is divided into three major oceans. The Pacific is the largest. The Atlantic is the second largest. The Indian is the smallest.
- Oceanographers use small **submersibles, sonar,** and ocean cores from drilling to study the oceans.

Lesson 10-3

- Saltwater contains many more dissolved salts and other minerals than freshwater does.
- The ocean has three different temperature layers. In the **thermocline,** the temperature drops sharply.

Lessons 10-4, 10-5, and 10-6

- **Currents** of water move through the oceans. Most surface currents are caused by wind. They move in different directions in each hemisphere. Ocean currents can be warm or cold. **Density currents** move up and down in the ocean depths.
- Waves are formed by wind. They have **crests** and **troughs.**
- Only the energy, not the water, in a wave moves forward. Waves form breakers near the shore.
- High and low tides change the ocean's surface level. They are caused mostly by the Moon's gravity. **Flood tides** and **ebb tides** are caused by the rotation of Earth.

Lesson 10-7

- Eroded rock particles form most of the sediments close to shore. Minerals also help form ocean sediments.
- Much of the ocean floor is made up of **ooze.**

Lessons 10-8 and 10-9

- The **continental shelf** and **continental slope** lead into the ocean floor. Deep canyons, or **trenches,** are found on the floor. The flat parts of the ocean floor are called plains.
- **Seamounts** are underwater volcanoes and mountains. A **guyot** is a flattened seamount.
- A coral reef is made up of the skeletons of living and dead **coral. Fringing reefs** are attached to a coastline. **Barrier reefs** form around partially sunken volcanic islands. **Atolls** are ring-shaped coral reefs around **lagoons.**

Key Term Challenges

atoll (p. 244)
barrier reef (p. 244)
continental shelf (p. 242)
continental slope (p. 242)
coral (p. 244)
Coriolis effect (p. 232)
crest (p. 234)
current (p. 232)
density current (p. 232)
ebb tide (p. 238)
flood tide (p. 238)
fringing reef (p. 244)
guyot (p. 242)
lagoon (p. 244)

nodule (p. 240)
oceanography (p. 226)
ooze (p. 240)
salinity (p. 230)
seamount (p. 242)
sonar (p. 228)
submersible (p. 228)
thermocline (p. 230)
tide (p. 238)
trench (p. 242)
trough (p. 234)
wave (p. 234)
world ocean (p. 226)

MATCHING Write the Key Term from above that best matches each description.

1. study of Earth's oceans

2. underwater research vessel

3. amount of dissolved salts and minerals in ocean water

4. layer of ocean water in which temperature drops sharply

5. stream of water flowing in the ocean

6. regular up-and-down movement of water at the surface

7. stream of water that moves up and down in the ocean's depths

8. mineral lump found on the ocean floor

9. kind of ocean sediment

10. deep canyon on the ocean floor

APPLYING DEFINITIONS Explain the difference between the words in each pair. Write your answers in complete sentences.

11. crest, trough

12. continental shelf, continental slope

13. seamount, guyot

14. coral, atoll

15. lagoon, sea

16. barrier reef, fringing reef

Content Challenges TEST PREP

MULTIPLE CHOICE **Write the letter of the term or phrase that best completes each statement.**

1. The three major oceans are the
   a. Indian, Atlantic, Pacific.
   b. Pacific, Antarctic, Indian.
   c. Arctic, Pacific, Indian.
   d. Atlantic, Pacific, Caribbean.

2. The study of the world's oceans is called
   a. hydrology.
   b. geography.
   c. oceanography.
   d. technology.

3. To find the depth of the ocean, scientists use
   a. hydrology.
   b. sonar.
   c. bathyspheres.
   d. bathyscaphs.

4. Ocean water is warmest
   a. at the surface.
   b. in the thermocline.
   c. in the deep ocean.
   d. at the continental margin.

5. Warm ocean currents come from areas near the
   a. North Pole.
   b. South Pole.
   c. prime meridian.
   d. equator.

6. The distance between crests is the
   a. trough.
   b. wavelength.
   c. wave height.
   d. density.

7. Nodules are mostly nickel, iron, and
   a. manganese.
   b. chlorine.
   c. sodium.
   d. volcanic dust.

8. The process by which a gas changes to a liquid is called
   a. precipitation.
   b. evaporation.
   c. sublimation.
   d. condensation.

9. Just beyond the shoreline of a continent you would find a
   a. continental slope.
   b. continental shelf.
   c. deep sea trench.
   d. guyot.

10. Salinity of ocean water can rise when
    a. glaciers melt.
    b. it rains.
    c. water evaporates.
    d. runoff from rivers increases.

FILL IN **Write the term or phrase that best completes each sentence.**

11. Most of the water on Earth's surface is _____ water.

12. Oceanographers are specialists who study the _____.

13. Underwater research vessels are called _____.

14. Heat from the _____ warms ocean water.

15. Tides are caused mainly by the _____.

16. The time of low water level is _____ tide.

17. A ring-shaped coral reef around a lagoon is called an _____.

18. A guyot is an underwater, flat-topped _____.

Concept Challenges TEST PREP

WRITTEN RESPONSE **Answer each of the following questions in complete sentences.**

1. CALCULATE: If a sonar signal sent from a ship returns 8 seconds later, how deep is the ocean floor in that spot?

2. EXPLAIN: Why was a bathysphere considered an advancement in ocean exploration technology?

3. PREDICT: How would the salinity of the oceans be affected if increased temperatures caused the polar ice caps to melt into the oceans?

4. COMPARE: How can you tell the difference between a barrier reef and a fringing reef?

5. DESCRIBE: What are some specialties within the field of oceanography?

6. COMPARE/CONTRAST: How are oceans and seas alike and different?

7. DESCRIBE: What is the purpose of deep-sea drilling?

8. ANALYZE: What kinds of weathering and erosion change the shoreline?

INTERPRETING VISUALS **Use Figure 10-32 below to answer the following questions.**

9. How do you think the seafloor feature labeled *C* got its name?

10. What is the name of the landform labeled *D*?

11. How would the size of the shoreline change if sea levels rose due to global warming?

12. What parts of the continent, labeled *B*, *C*, and *G* on the diagram, extend into the ocean?

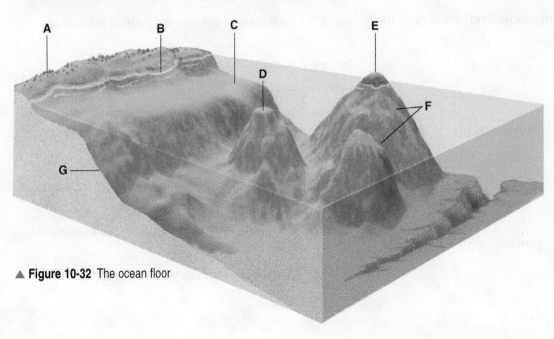

▲ **Figure 10-32** The ocean floor

Chapter 11 Air

▲ **Figure 11-1** Colorful balloons dot the sky as they gracefully rise in the atmosphere.

Heating air causes it to rise. This is how the balloons in the picture can rise and float. The heating and rising of air is how air currents are formed. Air currents affect the water cycle and weather patterns. Air thins out the higher you go in the atmosphere. Therefore, hot-air balloons cannot go too high.

▶What do you think would happen if you tried to take a balloon where there is very little air?

Contents

11-1 What is air?

Objectives

Describe air as matter. Identify and describe the main gases in air.

Key Terms

matter: anything that has mass and volume

atmosphere (AT-muh-sfeer)**:** envelope of gases surrounding Earth

cellular respiration (rehs-puh-RAY-shuhn)**:** process by which a cell releases energy from food molecules

A Mixture of Gases Air is a colorless, tasteless, odorless mixture of gases. Air is matter. **Matter** is anything that has mass and takes up space, or has volume.

◀ **Figure 11-2**
Air has mass and volume.

The **atmosphere,** or air, is the envelope of gases surrounding Earth. Air is made up mostly of nitrogen and oxygen. Air is also made up of other gases. Figure 11-3 shows the approximate percentages of the gases that make up air.

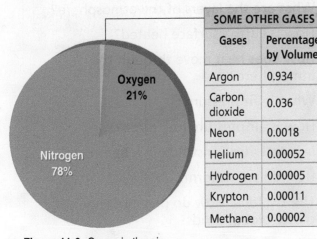

SOME OTHER GASES	
Gases	Percentage by Volume
Argon	0.934
Carbon dioxide	0.036
Neon	0.0018
Helium	0.00052
Hydrogen	0.00005
Krypton	0.00011
Methane	0.00002

▲ **Figure 11-3** Gases in the air

1 ANALYZE: What percentage of air is made up of helium, neon, and krypton?

Nitrogen About 78 percent of the atmosphere is nitrogen. All organisms need nitrogen. However, most living things cannot use nitrogen gas from the air.

Bacteria are microscopic organisms that live in soil, in water, and in the air. Some bacteria can change the nitrogen gas in the air into nitrogen compounds. Plants get the nitrogen they need by absorbing the nitrogen compounds made by these bacteria. Animals get the nitrogen they need by eating plants.

2 DEFINE: What are bacteria?

Oxygen About 21 percent of air is oxygen. Living things need oxygen to carry on cellular respiration. **Cellular respiration** is the process by which a cell releases energy from food molecules. The energy comes from the food made, eaten, or absorbed by an organism. Plants make their own food. Most animals must eat food. Some other organisms absorb food from their environment. Most living things get the oxygen they need from air.

3 INFER: How do people get the oxygen they need to carry on respiration?

Carbon Dioxide About 0.04 percent of air is made up of carbon dioxide. Carbon dioxide is released when things burn. Respiration produces carbon dioxide as a by-product. You get rid of carbon dioxide when you breathe out. Plants need carbon dioxide to make their own food.

4 STATE: How does carbon dioxide get into air?

Other Components in Air Most of the time, air looks and feels dry to us. However, it is never really completely dry. In addition to the gases mentioned above, air contains water vapor. Water vapor is water in the form of a gas. Steam is heated water vapor. Sometimes steam contains tiny droplets of water, which is what you see. The water vapor itself is invisible. The amount of water vapor in the air varies greatly from place to place and over time. In rain forests, up to 5 percent of the air may be water vapor.

Water vapor plays an important role in weather. Clouds form as water vapor condenses out of air that has cooled. It forms tiny drops of liquid water or crystals of ice. If these drops or crystals grow large enough, they can fall as rain or snow.

In addition to the gases that make it up, air contains tiny particles of dust, smoke, salt, and other chemicals. You can see some of these particles. They are not part of the air itself. They float in the air, and sometimes they make the air unhealthy to breathe.

 LIST: What is in air besides the gases?

✓ CHECKING CONCEPTS

1. What two main gases make up air?
2. What is matter?

3. Why do living things need oxygen?
4. How does water vapor affect the weather?
5. What are two nongaseous particles in air?

💡 THINKING CRITICALLY

6. **CONTRAST:** How is water vapor different from other gases that make up air?

INTERPRETING VISUALS

Use Figure 11-3 to answer the following questions.

7. **ESTIMATE:** What gas makes up most of air?
8. **CALCULATE:** What percentage of air is made up of methane, krypton, and hydrogen?
9. **IDENTIFY:** What gases make up the 1 percent of air not composed of nitrogen and oxygen?

 Real-Life Science

BRONCHIAL ASTHMA

We all need air to live. For people who suffer from bronchial asthma, getting that air into their lungs can be a struggle. There are more than 14 million asthma sufferers in the United States alone.

An asthma attack usually starts with a swelling in the passages that carry air into our lungs when we breathe. One of the most common signs of an asthma attack is wheezing. Wheezing is the high-pitched noise caused by air moving through a narrowed air passage.

What causes an asthma attack? Usually, the air passages become irritated by tiny particles floating in the air. Often, these particles are things that a person with asthma is allergic to, such as pollen or animal dander. Household cleaners and cigarette smoke can also cause asthma attacks. The body's immune system releases a substance called histamine to fight the invaders. It is the histamine that causes the swelling.

Asthma cannot be cured. Its symptoms can be controlled, though, with treatment.

Thinking Critically How can the condition of asthma be triggered by particles suspended in air?

▲ **Figure 11-4** Pollen grains from a plant in the genus *Lavatera*

11-2 What are the layers of the atmosphere?

Objective

Name and describe the layers of the atmosphere.

Key Terms

troposphere (TROH-puh-sfeer): lowest layer of the atmosphere

stratosphere (STRAT-uh-sfeer): second layer of the atmosphere

mesosphere (MEHZ-uh-sfeer): third layer of the atmosphere

thermosphere (THER-muh-sfeer): upper layer of the atmosphere

Parts of the Atmosphere The atmosphere begins at Earth's surface and goes more than 700 km up. Not all parts of the atmosphere are the same. The atmosphere is made up of four main layers. These layers are the troposphere, the stratosphere, the mesosphere, and the thermosphere.

 LIST: What are the four main layers of the atmosphere?

The Troposphere The **troposphere** is the layer of the atmosphere closest to Earth. The air you breathe into your lungs is part of the troposphere. Most of the water vapor found in the atmosphere is in the troposphere. This water vapor forms clouds. Weather takes place in the troposphere.

The higher you go in the troposphere, the colder it gets. Near the top of the troposphere, the temperature stops getting colder. The boundary between the troposphere and the layer above is called the tropopause.

 DEFINE: What is the tropopause?

The Stratosphere The **stratosphere** is the second layer of the atmosphere. The temperature of the air remains almost constant here. There is no weather in the stratosphere. Airplanes travel in this layer.

The upper stratosphere contains a layer of ozone. Ozone is a form of oxygen. Ozone prevents most of the ultraviolet light given off by the Sun from reaching Earth. Large amounts of ozone, however, are harmful to breathe and can irritate the lungs.

 PREDICT: What might happen if the ozone layer of the stratosphere were destroyed?

The Mesosphere and Thermosphere Above the stratosphere is the third layer of the atmosphere, the **mesosphere,** which means "middle layer." In the mesosphere, temperatures begin to fall again. Above the mesosphere is the fourth region, the **thermosphere.** Here temperatures actually rise with height. Beyond the thermosphere is mostly empty space. This region is called the exosphere.

From the mesosphere up to the top of the thermosphere is a broad region of space that contains many charged particles called ions. Radio waves sent from Earth are reflected or bounced off of these ions. Because of ions, radio signals can be sent between distant parts of Earth. The area where the ions are most concentrated is called the ionosphere.

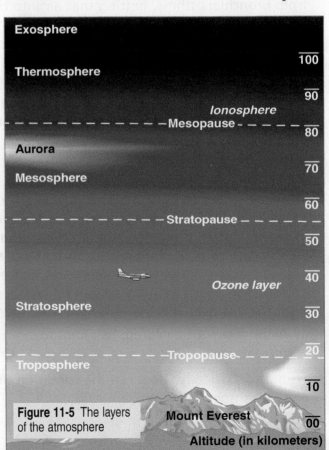

Figure 11-5 The layers of the atmosphere

Exosphere

Thermosphere

Ionosphere
—Mesopause— — —

Aurora

Mesosphere

— — — — — — —Stratopause — — — —

Ozone layer

Stratosphere

—Tropopause— — — —

Troposphere

Mount Everest

Altitude (in kilometers)

100
90
80
70
60
50
40
30
20
10
00

Sometimes, in the night sky near the poles, you can see glowing colored light, usually green. These glowing lights, called auroras, are caused by charged particles from the Sun. The particles are interacting with matter in Earth's upper atmosphere. In the northern polar region, these events are known as the aurora borealis, or the northern lights. In the Southern Hemisphere, they are known as aurora australis.

▲ **Figure 11-6** The aurora borealis lights up the northern sky at night.

 DESCRIBE: How is the ionosphere used in communications?

CHECKING CONCEPTS

1. The atmosphere is made up of _____ main layers.

2. The upper boundary of the troposphere is the _____.

3. Ozone is a form of _____.

THINKING CRITICALLY

4. INFER: Why do most airplanes travel in the stratosphere?

5. COMPARE: How do air temperatures differ in the troposphere and stratosphere?

INTERPRETING VISUALS

Use Figure 11-5 to answer the following questions.

6. INFER: In which layer of the atmosphere do we fly kites? Why?

7. CALCULATE: About how thick is the stratosphere?

8. CALCULATE: About how thick is the troposphere?

Integrating Physical Science

TOPICS: air pressure, force

GETTING A LIFT INTO THE AIR

Daniel Bernoulli (bur-NOO-lee) was a Swiss scientist known for his work with fluids. Bernoulli found that the faster a fluid moves, the less pressure it exerts. Pressure is the amount of force acting on a surface. Bernoulli further stated that the pressure of a moving stream of fluid or gas is lower than the pressure of any fluid or gas around it. This explains how air moving around a wing can produce a force called lift, allowing an airplane to fly.

Objects can be designed so air moves at different speeds around them. If the air moves faster above the object, pressure pushes the object upward.

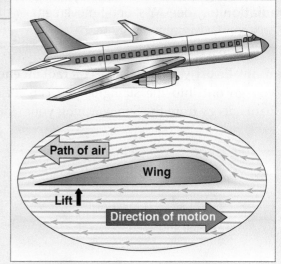
▲ **Figure 11-7** Airplane wings are curved on top, like bird wings.

Like a bird's wing, the top of an airplane wing is curved. Air that moves over the top of the wing must travel farther than air that moves along the bottom. The air moving over the top moves faster so its pressure is lower than the air pressure on the bottom. This difference in pressure creates the lift.

Thinking Critically Why are airplane wings curved on top?

11-3 How is Earth's surface heated?

Modeling the Absorption of Light
HANDS-ON ACTIVITY

1. Place an aluminum plate under a lamp whose light is directed downward.
2. Fill half the plate with dry, dark soil and half with dry sand.
3. Insert a thermometer into each side. Record the temperatures.
4. Turn on the lamp and let the plate stand for a while. Compare the new temperatures with the starting ones.

THINK ABOUT IT: How do the temperatures change? Why is one higher than the other?

STEP 4

Objective

Describe how energy from the Sun warms Earth's surface.

Key Terms

radiant (RAY-dee-uhnt) **energy:** energy given off by the Sun that can travel through empty space

radiation (ray-dee-AY-shuhn)**:** movement of the Sun's energy through empty space

Radiant Energy The Sun gives off **radiant energy.** If you go out into the sunlight, you can feel the radiant energy from the Sun warming your skin.

Light is a form of radiant energy. Radiant energy can travel across millions of kilometers of empty space. The movement of this energy through empty space is called **radiation.** Most of Earth's energy comes from the radiation given off by the Sun.

1 NAME: What kind of energy is sunlight?

Absorption of Energy Dark surfaces absorb light. When light is absorbed, or taken in, it is usually changed into heat.

Suppose you wrap two ice cubes with cloth. You wrap one ice cube in a dark-colored cloth and the other in light-colored cloth. You place both ice cubes in sunlight. Which one would melt first?

100% Sun's energy

20% absorbed by gases, clouds, and dust

30% reflected by clouds, dust, air, and Earth's surface

Dust particles

Figure 11-8 Radiant energy is absorbed or reflected, depending on what it comes into contact with in the atmosphere.

50% absorbed by Earth's surface

The ice cube wrapped in the dark cloth would melt faster. Surfaces that reflect light, such as white surfaces, remain cooler than surfaces that absorb light, such as dark surfaces.

 DESCRIBE: What happens when light is absorbed by a surface?

Energy from the Sun Only a small part of the Sun's energy reaches Earth. Some of the Sun's energy is absorbed by the atmosphere. Clouds, dust particles, and water droplets in the atmosphere also absorb or reflect some of the Sun's energy. The energy that is reflected goes back into space. Some of the energy that passes through the atmosphere is absorbed by Earth's surface. This energy is changed into heat. As a result, Earth becomes warmer. The entire process is shown in Figure 11-10 on page 258.

 STATE: What happens when the Sun's energy is absorbed by Earth's surface?

☑ CHECKING CONCEPTS

1. Light is a type of _____.
2. The Sun's energy reaches Earth by _____.

3. When light is _____, it is changed into heat.
4. Clouds, _____, and water droplets can absorb or reflect the Sun's energy.

💡 THINKING CRITICALLY

5. **PREDICT:** If there was no wind, would it be cooler on a cloudy or on a clear day? Why?

Web InfoSearch

Electromagnetic Radiation Electromagnetic radiation is energy in the form of waves of different frequencies. *Frequency* refers to how often the wave occurs in a given amount of time. Light is only one type of electromagnetic radiation.

SEARCH: Use the Internet to find out more about this topic. What are other types of electromagnetic radiation? In what technologies are they used? Start your search at www.conceptsandchallenges.com. Some key search words are **electromagnetic radiation, light waves,** and **X-rays.**

 Science and Technology

SOLAR ENERGY

The Sun is a potentially huge source of energy. It could be used to meet all of the world's energy needs. Scientists are working to develop efficient ways to use solar energy.

At one power plant in California's Mojave Desert, rings of huge mirrors capture sunlight and reflect it to a central tower. A liquid runs through pipes in the tower. The liquid becomes hot. The hot liquid is then used to boil water to make steam. The steam turns a turbine and a generator. In this way, solar energy can be converted to produce electricity when people need it, even after sunset.

▲ **Figure 11-9** On this artist's drawing of a communications satellite, the large blue panels contain the solar cells.

Solar cells can also be used to turn solar energy directly into electricity. Solar cells are also called photovoltaic, or PV, cells. In the 1950s, PV cells were developed for use on U.S. spacecraft. Panels of solar cells power satellites in space. You might have a calculator or a watch that uses a solar cell. Some small, experimental cars are powered by solar cells.

Thinking Critically Why is it important to develop solar energy for heating homes?

11-4 How does heat move through the atmosphere?

Objective
Explain how the atmosphere is heated.

Key Terms
conduction (kuhn-DUHK-shuhn): transfer of heat through matter by direct contact

convection (kuhn-VEK-shuhn): transfer of heat within a liquid or a gas

Conduction Heat moves through Earth's atmosphere in three main ways. These ways are conduction, radiation, and convection.

The troposphere, or lower layer of the atmosphere, is heated by a process that moves heat through matter. A metal pan placed over a flame will get hot. The metal molecules directly over the flame begin to move faster. They bump into the slower-moving molecules surrounding them and make them move faster. This is how heat moves through the metal pan.

Heat generally moves from an area of higher temperature to an area of lower temperature. This kind of movement of heat through matter is called **conduction.**

Sunlight absorbed by Earth's surface is changed into heat. This warms the surface. Air touches the warmed surface and is heated by conduction.

 NAME: How does heat move through matter?

Radiation The atmosphere is also heated by the process of radiation. Radiant energy travels from the Sun through space in waves.

Most of the Sun's energy is short-wave radiation. This radiation passes easily through the atmosphere and strikes Earth's surface, where it is mostly absorbed and changed into heat energy. Heat energy is long-wave radiation. Earth's surface warms up and radiates most of the heat energy back into the atmosphere. There it is absorbed by gases. This warms the atmosphere.

 DESCRIBE: What happens to the energy radiated by Earth?

Convection The transfer of heat within a liquid or a gas is called **convection.** When air is heated, it expands. As the warm air expands, it becomes lighter, because it becomes less dense. Warm air is lighter than cool air. Warm air rises. The cooler, denser air sinks.

 DEFINE: What is convection?

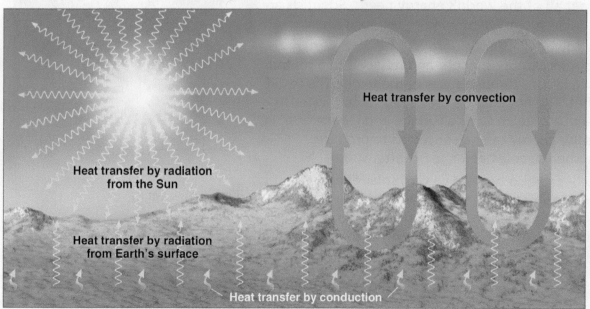

Heat transfer by convection

Heat transfer by radiation from the Sun

Heat transfer by radiation from Earth's surface

Heat transfer by conduction

◀ **Figure 11-10** There are three types of heat transfer: conduction, radiation, and convection.

☑ CHECKING CONCEPTS

1. When a solid is heated, its _____ move faster.
2. Solids are heated by _____.
3. Earth's radiant energy is _____ -wave radiation.
4. Energy traveling in waves from the Sun is called _____ energy.
5. Heat moves through air by_____.

THINKING CRITICALLY

6. IDENTIFY: Which of the following is conduction, which is radiation, and which is convection?

   a. The water in a fish tank becomes warmer after the heater in it is turned on.

   b. The Sun warms your skin on a summer day.

   c. A glass bowl is warmed by the steaming rice it contains.

   d. A burning log in a fireplace causes the temperature in a room to go up.

INTERPRETING VISUALS

Use Figure 11-11 to answer the following questions.

7. EXPLAIN: Why do the balloons rise?
8. INFER: What does the flame do?

▲ **Figure 11-11** Hot-air balloons

HEALTH AND SAFETY TIP

Never grab the handle of a hot pot with your bare hands. Use a pot holder. Metal is a good conductor of heat. The pot holder is not. It keeps most of the heat from passing through to your hands.

Hands-On Activity

DETERMINING THE EFFECT OF TEMPERATURE ON AIR MOVEMENT

You will need scissors, a ruler, tissue paper, thread, cellophane tape, a desk lamp, and a partner.

1. Cut a 6-cm-long spiral from the tissue paper.
2. Cut a piece of thread 15 cm long.
3. Tape one end of the thread to the center of the paper spiral.
4. Turn on the desk lamp. Point the light up.
5. Have your partner hold the end of the thread. Position the paper spiral about 10 cm above the light. ⚠ CAUTION: Do not allow the paper to touch the light bulb.

▲ **STEP 5** Be sure the spiral does not touch the light bulb.

Practicing Your Skills

6. DESCRIBE: What happens to the spiral?
7. INFER: How do temperature differences affect what happens?
8. CONCLUDE: How is this an example of convection?

 11-5 What is air pressure?

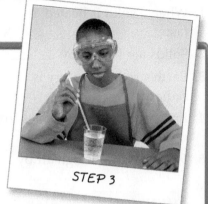

INVESTIGATE

Observing Air Pressure
HANDS-ON ACTIVITY

1. Place a drinking straw in a cup of water.

2. Put your finger over the top end of the straw.

3. Take the straw out of the water. Observe the water inside the straw.

4. Hold the straw over the cup and remove your finger. Observe what happens.

STEP 3

THINK ABOUT IT: What happened when you removed the straw from the water with your finger on top of it? What holds the water in the straw? Why does the water fall out when you take your finger away? How is this activity related to air pressure?

Objective

Explain air pressure and describe what affects it.

Key Terms

newton: metric unit of force

pressure: amount of force per unit of area

Weight and Pressure Weight is a force. If you hold a book in the palm of your hand, you feel the weight of the book pressing down. This force is measured in units called **newtons (N).** A 1-kg mass has a force of about 10 N.

The amount of force per unit of area is called **pressure.** When you hold the book in the palm of your hand, the book's weight is spread over your hand. Suppose the book's force is 10 N, and your hand has an area of 100 square cm, or 100 cm². The force on each square centimeter is then 10 N divided by 100 cm², or 0.1 N/cm². The pressure of the book on your hand is 0.1 N/cm².

$$\frac{\text{Force}}{\text{Area}} = \text{Pressure}$$

$$\frac{10 \text{ N}}{100 \text{ cm}^2} = 0.1 \text{ N/cm}^2$$

A force exerted over a small area causes more pressure than the same force applied over a large area. See Figure 11-12 for an example of this.

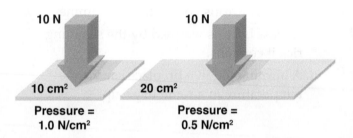

10 N	10 N
10 cm²	20 cm²
Pressure = 1.0 N/cm²	Pressure = 0.5 N/cm²

▲ **Figure 11-12** The same force exerted over a smaller area causes more pressure.

Air has weight. One liter of air weighs about 0.01 N at sea level. This is about the weight of a paper clip. The surface of Earth is at the bottom of the atmosphere. Air molecules are in constant motion and are pulled toward Earth's center by gravity. The force of all these moving molecules causes air pressure. Most of the air in the atmosphere is concentrated near Earth's surface. So air pressure is greatest near Earth's surface and decreases as altitude increases.

1 EXPLAIN: Why does air exert pressure on Earth's surface?

Elevation Air pressure changes with elevation, or height above sea level. The atmosphere is over 100 kilometers thick. The weight of all this air causes more pressure near the ground. This pushes the air molecules closer together. Near the top of the atmosphere, the air molecules remain farther apart. There is very little weight of air pressing down. Therefore, the air pressure is lower. The higher the elevation, the lower the air pressure.

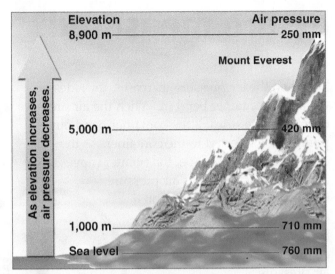

▲ **Figure 11-13** Elevation affects air pressure, which is measured in millimeters of mercury.

Air pressure decreases as distance above the surface increases. The air pressure on top of a mountain is less than the air pressure at sea level.

2 DESCRIBE: How does elevation affect air pressure?

Water Vapor The more water vapor in the air, the lower the air pressure. Water evaporates from lakes, rivers, and oceans. Living things give off water vapor. All of this water vapor goes into the air. The lighter molecules of water vapor replace some of the other gas molecules in air. Air with a lot of water vapor weighs less than dry air with less water vapor. Thus, moist air exerts less pressure. Air pressure goes down as the amount of water vapor in the air goes up.

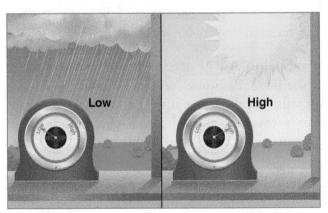

▲ **Figure 11-14** The weather conditions outside influence the air pressure.

3 DESCRIBE: How does water vapor affect air pressure?

Temperature Under ordinary conditions, the higher the temperature, the lower the air pressure. Heat makes air molecules move faster. As the molecules move faster, they spread apart. This makes the air less dense.

So warm air is less dense than cool air. In summer, when temperatures are higher, the air pressure is usually lower.

4 RELATE: How is temperature related to air pressure?

✓ CHECKING CONCEPTS

1. Pressure is the amount of _____ on a unit of area.
2. Air pressure at sea level is _____ than air pressure on top of a mountain.
3. Air pressure _____ as elevation increases.
4. Warm air weighs _____ than cool air.

💡 THINKING CRITICALLY

5. CALCULATE: A 5-N force pushes down on an area that is 10 cm^2. How much pressure does the force have?
6. HYPOTHESIZE: Why do ears "pop" in an airplane?

Web InfoSearch

The Magdeburg Hemispheres In 1654, Otto von Guericke, the mayor of a small German town called Magdeburg, did an experiment. He made a hollow metal sphere with two halves, or hemispheres, fitted tightly together. Air was pumped out of the sphere through a valve. This lowered the air pressure inside. The higher outside air pressure held the sphere together.

SEARCH: Use the Internet to find out more about this experiment. Why couldn't horses pull the two hemispheres apart? Start your search at www.conceptsandchallenges.com. Some key search words are **air pressure, von Guericke,** and **Magdeburg.**

11-6 How is air pressure measured?

Objective

Explain how a barometer measures air pressure.

Key Term

barometer (buh-RAHM-uht-uhr)**:** instrument used to measure air pressure

Mercury Barometer Air pressure is measured with an instrument called a **barometer.** A mercury barometer is a glass tube filled with mercury. It is open at one end. The space at the closed end of the tube forms a vacuum. The open end of the tube sits in a container of mercury. Air pressure pushes down on the surface of the mercury in the container. The mercury is pushed up the vacuum. At sea level, air pressure can raise a column of mercury to a height of 760 mm. As the air pressure changes, the level of mercury in the tube rises or falls.

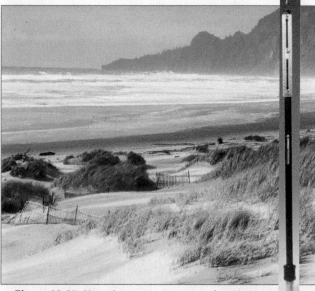

▲ **Figure 11-15** Near the ocean, a mercury barometer (on right) shows a reading of 760 mm.

1 DEFINE: What does a barometer do?

Aneroid Barometer Another kind of barometer is called an aneroid barometer. The word *aneroid* means "without liquid." An aneroid barometer is made of an airtight metal container. The sides of the container are very thin. They can bend in or out.

When the air pressure increases, the sides of the metal container bend in. When the air pressure decreases, the sides of the container bend out. A pointer is connected to the container. As the container changes shape, the pointer moves along a scale. The scale shows air pressure in millimeters of mercury. Some aneroid barometers, called barographs, keep a continuous record of air pressure.

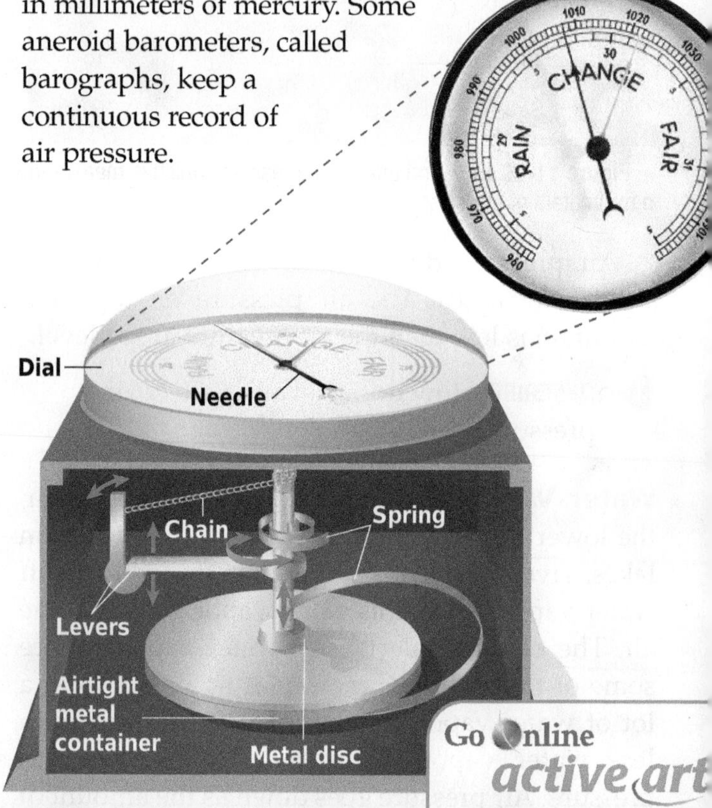

CHANGE
RAIN
FAIR
Dial
Needle
Chain
Spring
Levers
Airtight metal container
Metal disc

▲ **Figure 11-16** Aneroid barometer

Go Online *active art*
For: Measuring Air Pressure activity
Visit: PHSchool.com
Web Code: cfp-4012

2 DESCRIBE: How does an aneroid barometer work?

Measuring Air Pressure Standard air pressure at sea level measures 760 mm of mercury. This is sometimes called one atmosphere. Air pressure is also measured in millibars (mb). Standard air pressure is equal to 1,013.20 mb.

3 ANALYZE: How many millimeters of mercury equal 1,013.20 mb?

Measuring Altitude An altimeter is a device used to measure altitude. Pilots, scientists, surveyors, and mountain climbers all use altimeters.

At sea level, air pressure will raise a column of mercury 760 mm. As you go higher, air pressure decreases. The mercury column drops.

Mount Everest is about 8,900 m high. It is the highest point on Earth. The mercury column here is only about 250 mm high.

Skydivers and parachuters wear devices that contain altimeters. These let them see how high they are as they descend. This type of altimeter is actually an aneroid barometer.

▲ **Figure 11-17** Parachuters wear devices that contain altimeters.

 INFER: Why do parachuters wear altimeters?

✓ CHECKING CONCEPTS

1. Air pressure is measured with a _____.
2. Two kinds of barometers are mercury barometers and _____ barometers.
3. The mercury column in a mercury barometer rises or falls with changes in _____.
4. Air pressure is measured in _____.

 ## THINKING CRITICALLY

5. **CALCULATE:** Mercury is 13.6 times more dense than water. If a container of water can hold 20 g of water, how much more massive would an equal volume of mercury be?

6. **CALCULATE:** The density of mercury is 13.6 g/cm³. If air pressure at sea level supports a 760-mm column of mercury, how high a column of water can air pressure support at sea level?

BUILDING MATH SKILLS

Graphing At sea level, normal air pressure is 760 mm of mercury. It drops about 10 mm for every 123-m rise in elevation. First, calculate normal air pressure for the following places, which are above sea level: Denver, CO (1,600 m); Kansas City, MO (230 m); Mount Whitney, CA (4,400 m); Mount St. Helens, WA (2,950 m); Mount Washington, NH (1,916 m); the Empire State Building in New York City (380 m). Then, calculate air pressure in Death Valley, CA (85 m below sea level). Make a bar graph showing the air pressure for each location.

 ## How Do They Know That?

MEASURING AIR PRESSURE

Evangelista Torricelli (eh-vahn-jeh-LEES-tah tawr-uh-CHEL-ee) (1608–1647) was an Italian scientist. During his lifetime, he made important improvements both in the microscope and in the telescope. His greatest accomplishment, however, was inventing the mercury barometer in 1643.

Torricelli filled a long glass tube with mercury. He placed his finger over one open end. (⚠ CAUTION: Mercury is poisonous to the touch. Do not attempt to repeat this experiment.) Then, he turned the tube upside down and placed it straight up in a container filled with mercury. When the mouth of the glass tube was under the surface of the mercury, Torricelli took his finger off the opening. The mercury in the tube dropped. It stopped at about 750 mm. At the top of the tube was a vacuum. Torricelli hypothesized that it was air pressure keeping the mercury in place.

Thinking Critically What was the air pressure in the city where Torricelli did his experiment?

▲ **Figure 11-18** Torricelli and his barometer

LAB ACTIVITY
Constructing a Barometer

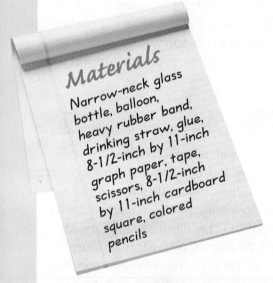

Materials

Narrow-neck glass bottle, balloon, heavy rubber band, drinking straw, glue, 8-1/2-inch by 11-inch graph paper, tape, scissors, 8-1/2-inch by 11-inch cardboard square, colored pencils

BACKGROUND

Some days, the weather is clear and warm. Other times, it is stormy and cold. Weather forecasters try to predict changes in the weather. One of the tools they use is a barometer.

PURPOSE

In this activity, you will construct a barometer and use it to forecast the weather.

PROCEDURE

1. Tightly cover the mouth of the glass bottle with the rubber balloon. Cut the opening of the balloon as needed to fit over the mouth. Stretch the balloon so that it doesn't have any wrinkles. Use a rubber band to hold the balloon in place around the bottle's neck. ⚠ CAUTION: Be careful when using scissors.

2. Cut the tip of the drinking straw to make a pointer.

3. Put a small dab of glue on the other end of the straw and stick it to the balloon, as shown in photo. Hold the straw up until the glue sets.

4. Tape or glue the graph paper to the cardboard for support.

5. Using a pencil, darken one of the vertical lines in the center of the graph. This will become the barometer's scale.

6. When the glue holding the straw sets, begin calibrating the barometer. Put graph paper glued to the cardboard behind the barometer. Mark where the point of the straw is each day. You may want to mark the top of the barometer on graph paper also. You can use this as a reference point.

▲ **STEP 1** Hold the balloon in place with a rubber band.

▲ **STEP 3** Glue the straw to the balloon.

7. Hold the graph paper behind the pointer end of the straw so that it is next to the line you drew. Mark the spot where the pointer is pointing. Ask your teacher to tell you what the actual pressure is. Write this next to the spot.

▲ **STEP 7** On your graph paper, mark where the straw is pointing.

8. Copy the chart in Figure 11-19. For the next two weeks, use your barometer to measure the air pressure each day. Mark where the barometer is pointing and the correct pressure. Use the chart to record what the weather outside is like each day.

9. Using your barometer, predict what the future weather will be like.

◄ **STEP 8** Using different colored pencils, mark where your barometer is pointing each day for two weeks.

Air Pressure and Weather

Date	Barometric Pressure	Weather for the Day

▲ **Figure 11-19** Use a copy of this chart to record your observations.

CONCLUSIONS

1. **OBSERVE:** What happened to the barometer pointer when the pressure became greater?

2. **OBSERVE:** What happened to the barometer pointer when the pressure decreased?

3. **ANALYZE:** What caused the pointer to move?

4. **INFER:** What do air pressure changes tell us about the coming weather?

Objective
Explain how winds form.

Key Terms
wind: horizontal movement of air
air current: up-and-down movement of air

Winds and Air Pressure Earth's atmosphere is nearly always in motion. Some air movements are weak and end quickly. Others are strong and last a long time.

Air is free to move in any direction. Its actual movements are determined by many factors. The horizontal movement of air along Earth's surface is called **wind.** Wind has often been described as "air in a hurry."

Air can also move vertically. Instead of being called wind, small vertical movements are usually called updrafts or downdrafts. Vertical movements are also important in the atmosphere. However, a much greater volume of air moves horizontally.

Winds form as cool, heavy air moves toward warm, light air. Cool air moves in under warm air. The cool air moves along the surface of Earth toward warmer air.

Winds are caused by differences in air pressure. Regions of cold, heavy air have high air pressure. These regions are called highs. Regions of warm, light air have low air pressure. These regions are called lows.

Air moves from regions of high pressure to regions of low pressure. Winds form when air moves. The speed of the wind depends on the differences in air pressure.

▲ **Figure 11-20** The winds that move these sailboards are produced by differences in air pressure.

1 ▶ PREDICT: Will the speed of a wind be greater if the difference in air pressure is large or small?

Air Currents Up-and-down movements of air are called **air currents.** Air currents are formed because the Sun does not heat all parts of Earth equally. Some areas of Earth are warmed more than other areas. As air over the warmer regions is heated, it expands and becomes less dense. As air over cooler regions is cooled, it becomes heavier, or denser. The cool air moves in under the warm air. It pushes the warm air upward. As the warm air mixes with the cool air, it becomes heavier and moves downward.

2 ▶ DEFINE: What is an air current?

▼ **Figure 11-21** How winds form

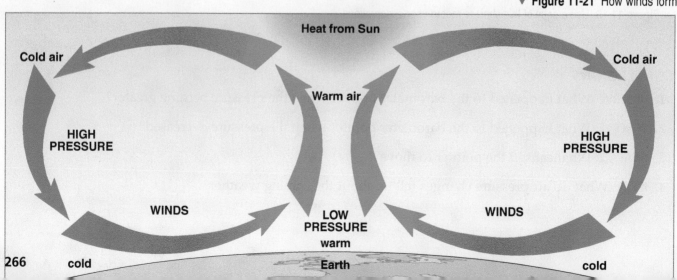

Heat from Sun

Cold air

Warm air

Cold air

HIGH
PRESSURE

HIGH
PRESSURE

WINDS

LOW
PRESSURE
warm

WINDS

cold

Earth

cold

1. An air current is an _____ movement of air.

2. Cool air is more _____ than warm air.

3. As cool air moves in under warm air, it pushes the warm air _____.

4. Wind is the _____ movement of air along Earth's surface.

5. Wind speed depends on differences in _____.

THINKING CRITICALLY

6. INFER: The Sun does not heat the surface of Earth equally. What effect does this have on weather patterns?

7. CONTRAST: What are the differences between highs and lows?

8. EXPLAIN: Why does cold air push warm air upward?

9. INFER: **a.** Where on Earth would you expect to find the warmest and least dense air? Why? **b.** Where would you expect to find the coldest and densest air? Why?

Web InfoSearch

El Niño Changes in the temperatures of surface ocean water may be responsible for some global weather patterns. Such changes have been linked to El Niño events. El Niño is a warm ocean current that appears off the coast of Peru in December each year and may spread south. El Niño affects Earth's wind patterns and can cause extreme weather far from where it occurs.

SEARCH: Use the Internet to find out more about this. What happens during an El Niño event? Start your search at www.conceptsandchallenges.com. Some key search words are **El Niño, trade winds,** and **climate change.**

Hands-On Activity

OBSERVING AIR PRESSURE

You will need safety goggles, an oven mitt, a plastic foam cup, hot water, a funnel, and a small plastic bottle with a screw-on cap.

1. Your teacher will provide you with some hot water in a plastic foam cup. Carefully pour the water into the plastic bottle using a funnel.
⚠ CAUTION: Use an oven mitt to hold the bottle. Also, be careful when handling the cup of hot water.

2. Quickly pour the hot water out of the plastic bottle back into the plastic foam cup.

3. Immediately screw the cap on the plastic bottle.

Practicing Your Skills

4. OBSERVE: What happened to the plastic bottle after you screwed on the cap?

5. INFER: What can you say about the pressure of the warm air compared to the pressure of the cold air?

▲ **STEP 2** Pour the hot water quickly into the cup.

6. CONCLUDE: Based on your observations, should wind move from cold areas to warm or from warm areas to cold?

7. RELATE: How does this activity relate to the way winds form?

Integrating Physical Science

THE Big IDEA

How do pressure changes create global winds?

We know that there is energy in winds. We use this energy to move a sailboat and turn a wind turbine. A cool breeze from the wind on a hot day is a pleasure. On a cold, windy day, we do not think it is a pleasure when we feel the wind's force on our bodies.

Because cool air is denser than warm air, it exerts greater pressure, or force, on a surface. That is why a pocket of cold air is called an area of high pressure. A pocket of less dense, warmer air is called an area of low pressure.

Winds blow from regions of high pressure to regions of low pressure. Warm air over the equator forms a region of low pressure. Bands of high pressure are found north and south of the equator. The cold air over the poles forms regions of high pressure. These differences in air pressure produce patterns of global winds. Global winds are large wind systems that circle Earth. At the equator, warm air rises and moves toward the poles. At the poles, cool air sinks and moves toward the equator.

Because Earth rotates, or spins like a top, winds curve as they move from high- to low-pressure regions. The winds moving toward the equator curve to the west in the Northern Hemisphere. The winds moving toward the poles curve to the east. In the Southern Hemisphere, the directions in which the wind curves are reversed. This is called the Coriolis effect.

Look at Figure 11-22 and the information on these two pages. Then, follow the directions in the Science Log to learn more about "the big idea."✦

Trade Winds

Some of the sinking cool air from the horse latitudes moves back toward the equator. It replaces the warm air rising in the doldrums. Earth's rotation causes this pocket of cool air to blow from east to west. These so-called trade winds are very reliable in terms of both speed and direction. Their name, trade winds, actually means "winds of commerce." European sailors and merchants in the sixteenth century realized that sailing with the trade winds was the quickest and safest route from Europe to America.

Doldrums

Warm air near the equator rises to form an area of low pressure. Because the region has little wind, sailors who traveled on tall ships named these winds the doldrums, which means "dull."

Prevailing Westerlies

Some of the sinking cool air from the horse latitudes moves toward Earth's poles. Because they are moving in a direction opposite to the trade winds, the prevailing westerlies are also called the antitrade winds.

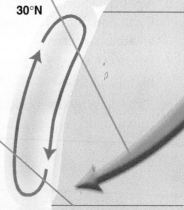

Figure 11-22 Global winds are large wind systems that travel around the world.

268

90°N (North Pole)

Polar Easterlies

Air surrounding Earth's poles is very cold and dense. These high pressure areas slowly move toward the equator. If they meet a mass of warm air moving upward from the equator, a weather condition known as a polar front forms.

Go Online
active art

For: Global Winds activity
Visit: PHSchool.com
Web Code: cfp-4023

Horse latitude

Horse Latitudes

Air moving away from the equator cools off. The dense, cool air sinks back to Earth, forming high-pressure areas called the horse latitudes. These latitudes may have been named by the crews of sailing ships. The sailors would sometimes throw horses overboard to save water when their ships were stranded in the high-pressure areas.

Doldrums

PACIFIC OCEAN

Horse latitude

WRITING ACTIVITY

science Log

In the 1940s, high-speed bands of global winds called jet streams were discovered. The jet streams weave through the atmosphere, moving from west to east. Airplanes flying eastward in a jet stream gain speed. Research and then write a news article on current jet stream conditions in your area. Start your search for information at www.conceptsandchallenges.com.

90°S (South Pole)

11-8 What causes local winds?

Objective
Describe patterns of local winds.

Key Term
monsoon: wind that changes direction with the seasons

Sea and Land Breezes All winds are produced by temperature differences caused by unequal heating of Earth's surface. Local winds are simply small-scale winds produced by local changes in air pressure.

A breeze coming from the sea toward the land is a sea breeze. A breeze going from the land toward the sea is a land breeze. Land and sea breezes are local winds.

The Sun heats land faster than it does water. As a result, during the day, air over the land is warmer and lighter than air over the water. The cooler, heavier air over the ocean moves in toward the land. The warmer, lighter air over the land rises. The result is a sea breeze.

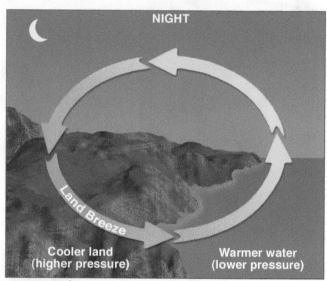
▲ **Figure 11-24** Land breeze

1 COMPARE: Which cools faster, land or water?

Mountain and Valley Breezes Mountain regions also have local winds. During the day, the air on a mountain slope is warmer than the air in the valleys. Warm air has low pressure. Air in the valley is cooler and has high pressure. Air moves from the high pressure of the valley to the low pressure of the mountain slope. This is a valley breeze. At night, the valleys are warmer than the mountaintops. The heavier mountain air moves downhill toward the valley. This is a mountain breeze.

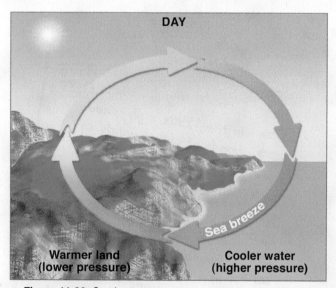
▲ **Figure 11-23** Sea breeze

At night, the land cools faster than the water. The air over the land becomes cooler than the air over the water. The heavier air over the land moves toward the water. The warmer, lighter air over the water rises. The result is a land breeze.

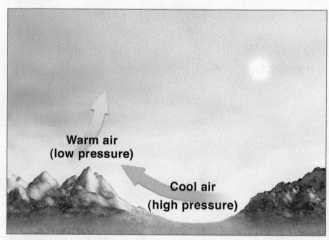
▲ **Figure 11-25** Valley breeze

2 DESCRIBE: In which direction do valley breezes move?

Monsoons Parts of some continents have winds that change direction with the seasons. These winds are called **monsoons.**

In the summer, when the land is warmer than the water, winds move from the ocean toward the land. In the winter, when the land is colder than the water, the winds move from the land toward the ocean. Winds blow toward the ocean all winter. India is famous for its monsoons. The summer monsoon brings warm, moist air with heavy rains. The winter monsoon carries dry air. There is little rain in winter.

 DEFINE: What are monsoons?

✓ CHECKING CONCEPTS

1. A sea breeze blows toward the _____ from the ocean.
2. Land is heated _____ than water.
3. Movement of air from the land toward the ocean is called a _____ breeze.
4. A _____ breeze moves downhill toward a valley.
5. Winds that change direction with the seasons are _____ .

THINKING CRITICALLY

6. ANALYZE: During part of the year, monsoons bring heavy rains and warm temperatures to many countries. Do these rainy seasons occur in the summer or winter? Explain.
7. MODEL: Draw and label a diagram of a mountain breeze. Use Figure 11-25 to help you.

BUILDING READING SKILLS

Vocabulary Mistral, foehn (FUHN), and chinook are the names of three local winds. Use a dictionary or other references to look up each of these winds. Write a brief description of each wind on a sheet of paper. Where does each wind occur?

 Science and Technology
WIND ENERGY

For years, farmers have used windmills to pump water. Today, many communities are using the wind to produce electricity. Modern materials and engineering could combine to make wind energy an important source of power for the future. Wind energy is a promising source of power because the wind is free and no pollution is produced. However, the speed and direction of the winds are unpredictable.

In some places, large windmill farms provide power for electric generators. Windmill farms may include hundreds or even thousands of windmills. Over 6,000 wind generators located at Altamont Pass, east of San Francisco, California, are already in operation and producing electricity. One of the largest windmills was in Medicine Bow, Wyoming. This one windmill provided enough electricity for 1,200 homes. It was torn down in 2002.

Modern windmills do not look much like the windmills used to pump water on farms. Some of the newer windmills look more like airplane propellers or eggbeaters. Instead of wood, they are made of new, lightweight materials.

▲ **Figure 11-26** A large windmill farm near Palm Springs, California

Thinking Critically Why are fields with many windmills called wind farms?

11-9 How is wind measured?

Objective

Explain how weather instruments are used to describe wind.

Key Terms

wind vane: instrument that indicates wind direction

anemometer (an-uh-MAHM-uht-uhr): instrument that measures wind speed

Showing Wind Direction Both wind speed and wind direction are significant to weather watchers. A wind is named for the direction from which it comes. If a wind comes from the north, it is a north wind. If it comes from the east, it is an east wind.

The direction of a wind is determined with a wind vane. A **wind vane** shows the direction a wind is coming from. Many wind vanes are shaped like arrows. When the wind blows, the arrow turns and points into the wind. Often the direction of the wind is shown on a dial connected to the wind vane. The dial may indicate wind direction by points on a compass (E, W, N, S) or by degrees on a scale.

▲ **Figure 11-27** A wind vane indicates wind direction.

▶ NAME: What is a wind that blows from the northeast named?

Measuring Wind Speed An **anemometer** is an instrument used to measure wind speed. It is often made of cups turned on their sides. These cups are attached to rods. Wind blowing against the cups causes the anemometer to turn. The faster and stronger the wind, the faster the anemometer turns. Anemometers usually have a meter attached to them that measures how fast the wind is blowing. It does this by measuring how fast the cups turn.

▲ **Figure 11-28** An anemometer measures wind speed.

▶ DESCRIBE: How does an anemometer work?

Weather Balloons Scientists sometimes use weather balloons to determine wind speed and direction. A weather balloon is filled with the gas helium. Helium gas is lighter than air. As a result, balloons filled with helium gas rise into the air.

▲ **Figure 11-29** Weather balloons often carry instrument packages called radiosondes. These contain temperature, pressure, and humidity sensors.

Winds high in the troposphere move a weather balloon along. Scientists can measure the speed of the wind by measuring the speed at which the balloon moves along. The direction it moves shows wind direction.

 IDENTIFY: What do weather balloons measure?

CHECKING CONCEPTS

1. Winds are named based upon the _____ from which they come.
2. Wind direction is shown with a _____ .
3. Wind speed is measured with an _____.
4. Weather balloons are filled with _____.
5. Helium gas is _____ than air.

THINKING CRITICALLY

6. **INFER:** A weather vane points to the north. From which direction is the wind blowing?
7. **HYPOTHESIZE:** If carbon dioxide is heavier than air, can it be used in a weather balloon? Explain.

8. **INFER:** Why is it important for weather forecasters to know the speed and direction of the wind?
9. **INFER:** What happens to the cups on an anemometer when the wind gusts?

BUILDING SCIENCE SKILLS

Classifying Winds are classified by their speed or strength. They are also classified by the damage they do to homes and property. Place each wind below in order from calmest to strongest.

a. Hurricane: great damage is done to buildings
b. Strong breeze: hard to walk against the wind and open umbrellas
c. Calm: smoke goes straight up
d. Gale: branches are broken from trees; store windows break; TV antennas break
e. Moderate to fresh breeze: small trees sway; papers are blown around
f. Strong gale: trees are uprooted

Hands-On Activity

MAKING A WIND VANE

You will need cardboard, glue, a ballpoint pen cover, a compass, a pencil, and scissors.

1. Cut out two cardboard arrows about the same size. ⚠ CAUTION: Be careful when using scissors.
2. Clip a ballpoint pen cover in the middle between the two arrows. Then, glue the two arrows together.
3. Place the pen cover on the point of a pencil. Move the cover back and forth between the arrows until the arrow balances.
4. Go outside and hold up your vane where the wind will not be blocked by buildings or trees. Use a compass to see where the arrow points.

▲ **STEP 4** Hold your wind vane where the wind can blow it freely.

Practicing Your Skills

5. **INFER:** In what direction does your wind vane point?
6. **ANALYZE:** A strong wind would blow your cardboard vane away. What could you use to make a more sturdy wind vane?

Chapter 11 Challenges

Chapter Summary

Lesson 11-1

- The **atmosphere** is an envelope of gases that surrounds Earth. About 78% of air is nitrogen, 21% is oxygen, and 0.04% is carbon dioxide.

Lesson 11-2

- The atmosphere is made up of four basic layers. The **troposphere** is the lowest layer. The **stratosphere** is the second layer. The ozone layer here protects us from harmful rays from the Sun. The third layer is the **mesosphere.** The fourth is the **thermosphere.** Within the mesosphere and thermosphere are concentrations of ions useful in radio communications.

Lessons 11-3 and 11-4

- The Sun gives off **radiant energy** that travels through space by **radiation.** When light energy is absorbed, it is changed into heat energy. Earth's surface changes light energy into heat energy.
- Heat moves through matter and the troposphere by **conduction.** It moves through the entire atmosphere by **convection.**

Lessons 11-5 and 11-6

- **Pressure** is the amount of force per unit of area. The weight of the air in the atmosphere exerts pressure on Earth's surface.
- Air pressure is affected by altitude, temperature, and water vapor.
- A **barometer** measures air pressure. Barometers can be mercury or aneroid.
- Air pressure is measured in millimeters of mercury or in millibars.

Lessons 11-7, 11-8, and 11-9

- **Air currents** are caused by the unequal heating of air. **Wind** is air moving horizontally along Earth's surface. Winds are caused by air pressure differences.
- Land breezes and sea breezes are local winds. Mountain regions have local winds called mountain breezes and valley breezes. A **monsoon** is a wind that changes direction with the seasons.
- A **wind vane** measures wind direction. An **anemometer** measures wind speed. Weather balloons measure wind speed and direction.

Key Term Challenges

air current (p. 266)
anemometer (p. 272)
atmosphere (p. 252)
barometer (p. 262)
cellular respiration (p. 252)
conduction (p. 258)
convection (p. 258)
matter (p. 252)
mesosphere (p. 254)
monsoon (p. 270)
newton (p. 260)
pressure (p. 260)
radiant energy (p. 256)
radiation (p. 256)
stratosphere (p. 254)
thermosphere (p. 254)
troposphere (p. 254)
wind (p. 266)
wind vane (p. 272)

MATCHING **Write the Key Term from above that best matches each description.**

1. anything with mass and volume
2. envelope of gases that surrounds Earth
3. process by which a cell releases energy from food molecules
4. upper layer of the atmosphere
5. movement of heat through matter
6. wind that changes direction with the seasons
7. lowest layer of the atmosphere
8. horizontal movement of air

IDENTIFYING WORD RELATIONSHIPS **Explain how the words in each pair are related. Write your answers in complete sentences.**

9. radiant energy, radiation
10. newton, pressure
11. wind, anemometer
12. convection, air current
13. breeze, local wind
14. wind, wind vane
15. stratosphere, troposphere

Content Challenges TEST PREP

MULTIPLE CHOICE **Write the letter of the term or phrase that best completes each statement.**

1. An altimeter measures
   a. wind speed.
   b. wind direction.
   c. altitude.
   d. rainfall.

2. Seventy-eight percent of the air is made up of
   a. nitrogen.
   b. oxygen.
   c. helium.
   d. carbon dioxide.

3. The layer of atmosphere closest to Earth is
   a. the tropopause.
   b. the stratosphere.
   c. the ionosphere.
   d. the troposphere.

4. The region of the atmosphere that reflects radio signals is the
   a. tropopause.
   b. stratosphere.
   c. ionosphere.
   d. troposphere.

5. Heat travels through empty space by
   a. convection.
   b. conduction.
   c. evaporation.
   d. radiation.

6. Earth's surface is heated by
   a. ozone.
   b. conduction.
   c. ions.
   d. radiation.

7. Air pressure is measured with
   a. a barometer.
   b. an altimeter.
   c. a wind vane.
   d. an anemometer.

8. Regions of cold, heavy air are called
   a. highs.
   b. lows.
   c. convections.
   d. monsoons.

9. A wind that blows from the southwest is a
   a. southwest wind.
   b. monsoon.
   c. local wind.
   d. northeast wind.

10. Sea breezes and land breezes are two kinds of
    a. local winds.
    b. monsoons.
    c. jet streams.
    d. global winds.

FILL IN **Write the term or phrase that best completes each sentence.**

11. Heat moves through _____ by conduction.

12. Heat moves through liquids and _____ by convection.

13. During respiration, living things give off _____ and water vapor as by-products.

14. Air is a _____ of gases.

15. Oxygen, argon, and _____ are the three main gases in air.

16. Beyond the atmosphere is the region known as the _____.

17. The ozone layer of the stratosphere protects Earth from _____ light from the Sun.

18. Ozone is a form of _____.

19. When air is heated, it _____.

20. Cool air is heavier and more _____ than warm air.

Concept Challenges TEST PREP

WRITTEN RESPONSE **Answer each of the following questions in complete sentences.**

1. ANALYZE: As elevation increases, what happens to air pressure? Explain why it does this.

2. EXPLAIN: How does a wind vane indicate wind direction?

3. PREDICT: Would air pressure on top of a mountain be greater in the summer or in the winter? Explain.

4. EXPLAIN: Why do you think mercury is used in barometers instead of water?

5. INFER: How do mountain and valley breezes get their names?

6. CONTRAST: How is a wind vane different from an anemometer?

7. HYPOTHESIZE: Why would dark-colored clothing be warmer in the winter than light-colored clothing?

8. INFER: Why are most wind vanes shaped like arrows?

INTERPRETING VISUALS **Use Figure 11-30 to answer the following questions.**

9. What is shown in the diagram?

10. In what layer of the atmosphere do auroras occur?

11. What are the names of the layers of the atmosphere?

12. What is the name of the upper part of the atmosphere?

13. How far does the troposphere extend?

14. Where is the ozone layer located?

15. What is the name of the layer of the atmosphere in which most weather takes place?

16. What kinds of particles make up most of the upper atmosphere?

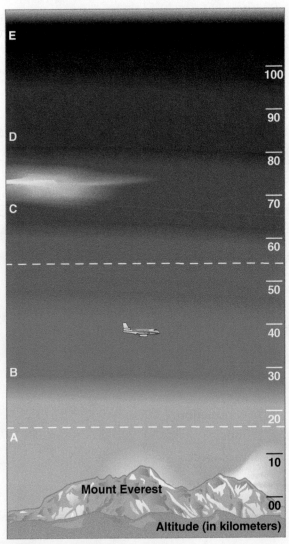

▲ Figure 11-30

Chapter 12 Weather

▲ **Figure 12-1** Severe thunderstorms produce lightning and sometimes even tornadoes.

Every day, about 40,000 thunderstorms occur around the world. Most of these develop in the regions near the equator. The power of a thunderstorm can be enormous. Bright bolts of lightning flash across the sky. This is followed by the ear-splitting roar of thunder. Many thunderstorms bring heavy rains or strong winds. Sometimes there is even hail or tornadoes.

▶What evidence of a storm is there in this picture?

Contents

12-1 Where does water in the atmosphere come from?

Objective

Explain how water gets into the atmosphere.

Key Terms

evaporation (ee-vap-uh-RAY-shuhn): changing of a liquid to a gas

transpiration (tran-spuh-RAY-shuhn): process by which plants give off water vapor into the air

Water Vapor

On a warm day, droplets of water may form on the outside of a window. The window surface is cooler than the outside air. The water comes from the air. Water in air is in the form of a gas called water vapor. Water vapor is an odorless,

▲ **Figure 12-2** Up to 5 percent of the water in the rain forests may be in the form of water vapor.

colorless gas. It mixes freely with other gases in the atmosphere. Most other gases change state only under extreme conditions. Water changes state at ordinary temperatures and pressures. It is because of these changes of state at ordinary temperatures that water leaves the oceans as a gas and returns again as a liquid. Water is also found in the atmosphere as clouds and fog. These are made up of tiny droplets of water or ice.

The amount of water vapor in the air varies from place to place and over time. However, it has been estimated that there are a total of about 14 million tons of water vapor in the atmosphere.

▷ NAME: What is water called when it is a gas?

Evaporation Water vapor enters the air through the process of evaporation. **Evaporation** is the changing of a liquid to a gas. Most of the water in the air evaporates from the oceans.

Every day, millions of tons of water evaporate from the surface of the oceans. Water also evaporates from lakes, rivers, puddles, and wet soil. Winds carry the water vapor in the air all over Earth's surface.

▷ ② IDENTIFY: Where does most of the water in the air come from?

Heat and Evaporation Molecules in a liquid are always moving. Some are moving faster than others. Some of the fast-moving molecules near the surface escape from the liquid. They enter and become part of the air. This is evaporation.

When a liquid is heated, its molecules move faster. More of the molecules can escape from the surface. Evaporation occurs more rapidly in warm liquids. Water in a pan over a heater evaporates faster than does water in a pan on a table. Evaporation from the oceans occurs most rapidly around the equator, where the water is heated by the more direct rays of the Sun.

▲ **Figure 12-3** Near the equator, evaporation occurs rapidly.

▷ ③ DESCRIBE: What causes a liquid to evaporate faster?

Living Things and Water Vapor If you blow on a cold mirror, moisture forms on it. When it is cold outside, you can see your breath. This is water vapor changing back into liquid water droplets. Breathing adds moisture to air. Plants also give off water vapor through a process called **transpiration.** Transpiration occurs in the leaves of plants through tiny openings called stomata.

◀ **Figure 12-4**
Stomata, or tiny openings, on a leaf release water vapor.

 NAME: How do plants give off water vapor?

☑ CHECKING CONCEPTS

1. About how much water vapor is in the air?
2. How do animals add water to the air?

3. What happens to the molecules in a liquid when they are heated?
4. What part of a plant gives off water vapor through openings called stomata?
5. What is the gaseous form of water called?

💡 THINKING CRITICALLY

6. IDENTIFY: Where does most of the moisture in the air come from?
7. HYPOTHESIZE: If you wipe a damp cloth across a tabletop, the table is wet. What will probably happen to the water in a few minutes? Why?

DESIGNING AN EXPERIMENT

Design an experiment to solve the following problem. Include a hypothesis, materials needed, variables, a procedure, and a type of data to study. Also tell how you would record your data.

PROBLEM: How can you show that heated water evaporates faster than unheated water?

 Hands-On Activity

OBSERVING TRANSPIRATION

You will need a small potted houseplant, a twist tie, a clear plastic bag, and a graduated cylinder.

1. Carefully cover the plant with the plastic bag. Use a twist tie to secure the bag near the bottom of the plant stem. ⚠ CAUTION: Plastic bags can be dangerous when placed over a person's head.

2. Set the plant in a place where it will get plenty of sunlight. Water the plant. Observe the inside of the plastic bag for five days. Record your observations each day.

3. On the fifth day, carefully remove the plastic bag. Measure the amount of water in the bag using the graduated cylinder. Record the amount of water that was collected in five days.

▲ **STEP 1** Cover the plant with a plastic bag.

Practicing Your Skills

4. OBSERVE: On which day did you first see water in the bag?
5. COMPARE: What happened to the amount of water in the plastic bag each day?
6. INFER: How much water did the plant give off in five days? Where did the water come from?

12-2 What is humidity?

Objective

Explain how we measure the amount of water vapor in the air.

Key Terms

humidity amount of water vapor in the air

capacity (kuh-PAS-ih-tee): amount of material something can hold

saturated (SACH-uh-rayt-ihd): filled to capacity

specific humidity (hyoo-MIHD-uh-tee): actual amount of water in the air

Humidity The amount of water vapor in a particular parcel of air is its **humidity**. High humidity means the air in that location contains a large amount of water vapor. Low humidity means that there is just a small amount of water vapor in

▲ **Figure 12-5** Water is always moving into or out of air.

the air in that location.

▶ DEFINE: What is humidity?

Capacity How much water can a 100-mL glass hold? If the glass is filled to the top, its capacity is 100 mL. **Capacity** is the amount of matter something can hold. The capacity of a 100-mL glass is always the same.

Air has a capacity for holding water vapor. Air's capacity for holding water vapor changes with the air temperature. As the temperature of the air goes down, air's capacity to hold water vapor goes down.

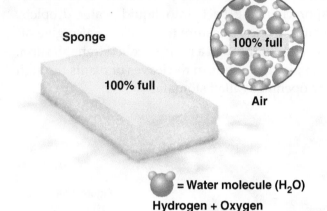

Sponge

100% full

100% full

Air

= Water molecule (H_2O)

Hydrogen + Oxygen

▲ **Figure 12-6** Air can be filled to capacity, just like this sponge.

▶ STATE: What affects the capacity of air to hold water?

Saturated Air If you place a sponge in a pan of water, the sponge soaks up the water. Soon the sponge is filled with water. It cannot hold any more water. It is **saturated.** Air can be saturated, too. When air is saturated, it holds all the water vapor it can at a certain temperature. As the temperature goes up, the capacity of air for holding water goes up.

SATURATION OF AIR		
Temperature		**Grams of Water Vapor per Kilogram of Air**
(°C)	**(°F)**	
−40	−40	0.1
−30	−22	0.3
−20	−4	0.75
−10	14	2
0	32	3.5
5	41	5
10	50	7
15	59	10
20	68	14
25	77	20
30	86	26.5
35	95	35
40	104	47

▲ **Figure 12-7**

▶ INFER: At which temperature will air hold more water vapor, 5°C or 25°C?

Specific Humidity The actual amount of water vapor that is in air is called **specific humidity**. Meteorologists express specific humidity as the number of grams of water vapor in 1 kg of air. Because specific humidity is measured by units of mass, it does not change with temperature or pressure. Only adding more water vapor to the air can change the specific humidity.

 NAME: How is specific humidity expressed?

☑ CHECKING CONCEPTS

1. The amount of _____ in the air is its humidity.
2. The amount of water vapor the air can hold is its _____.
3. The actual amount of water vapor in the air is called _____.
4. When air is _____, it holds all the water vapor it can at a given temperature.
5. The amount of water vapor that air can hold changes with _____.

💡 THINKING CRITICALLY

6. INFER: The air temperature in Boise, Idaho, is 25°C. The air temperature in Austin, Texas, is 35°C. Which city's air could hold more water vapor? Why?
7. COMPARE: How is a sponge similar to air in terms of capacity?

BUILDING SCIENCE SKILLS

Experimenting Obtain three different brands of paper towels. Take one sheet from each. Put water in a measuring cup, graduated cylinder, or marked beaker. Slowly saturate each towel with water and check to see how much water each towel holds by how much is left in the cup. Which brand has the greatest capacity for holding water? Is it the most expensive brand? Compare how much water each towel can hold to the price for each towel.

 People in Science

METEOROLOGIST

During an airplane flight, a pilot radios to the tower to find out weather conditions. The pilot needs to know wind speed and direction, visibility, and cloud conditions. The pilot depends on weather information gathered by meteorologists.

Meteorologists are scientists who study the atmosphere and try to forecast the weather. They gather information about the atmosphere from hundreds of different places and at many altitudes. Weather satellites and computers also help meteorologists gather and analyze data.

▲ **Figure 12-8** A meteorologist checks all kinds of weather data.

Meteorologists work for the National Weather Service, airports, news bureaus, and farming organizations. Some work as weather broadcasters for TV or radio stations.

To be a meteorologist, you need a college education and a background in mathematics and science. The military services also offer special training programs in meteorology.

Thinking Critically What kinds of data do weather satellites gather?

How is relative humidity measured?

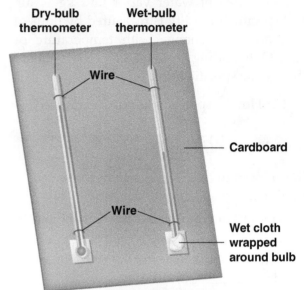

▲ **Figure 12-9** A simple psychrometer

Objective

Explain relative humidity and how it is measured.

Key Terms

relative humidity: amount of water vapor in the air compared with the amount of water vapor the air can hold at capacity

psychrometer (sy-KRAHM-uht-uhr)**:** instrument used to find relative humidity

Relative Humidity The amount of water vapor in air compared with its capacity is **relative humidity.** The relative humidity of air that is saturated, or filled to its capacity, is 100 percent. Air is usually not filled to capacity. It may be filled to half its capacity. The relative humidity is then 50 percent.

The relative humidity of air changes as water vapor leaves the air and returns to the ocean or falls as precipitation. It also changes when water evaporates and goes into the air. If the amount of water vapor stays the same and the temperature drops, the relative humidity goes down. Relative humidity goes up if the temperature goes up.

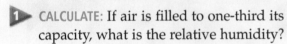 **CALCULATE:** If air is filled to one-third its capacity, what is the relative humidity?

Measuring Relative Humidity A **psychrometer** is sometimes used to find relative humidity. Figure 12-9 shows a simple psychrometer made up of two thermometers. The bulb of one thermometer is covered with a damp piece of cloth. The other bulb is dry. Air is then passed over the psychrometer. This causes water on the cloth to evaporate. The dry thermometer measures air temperature. Water evaporating from the cloth cools the wet thermometer. The wet thermometer is cooled more when the relative humidity is low than when it is high. Relative humidity can be found by using the difference in temperature between dry- and wet-bulb thermometers and a chart such as the one shown in Figure 12-10.

Suppose the dry-bulb thermometer reads 25°C and the wet one reads 18°C. The difference is 7°C. Find 25°C along the top of Figure 12-10. Find 7°C down the left side. Where the two rows meet, you see the number 50. This means the relative humidity is 50 percent.

		Temperature of Air from Dry-Bulb Thermometer (°C)								
		−5	0	5	10	15	20	25	30	35
Difference Between Dry-Bulb and Wet-Bulb Thermometer (°C)	1	75	81	86	88	90	91	92	93	94
	2	52	64	72	77	80	83	85	86	87
	3	29	46	58	66	70	74	77	79	81
	4	6	29	46	55	62	66	70	73	75
	5		13	32	44	53	59	63	67	70
	6			20	34	44	51	57	61	70
	7			0	24	36	44	50	55	59
	8				15	28	37	45	50	54

Relative Humidity (%)

▲ **Figure 12-10**

Another type of psychrometer is the sling psychrometer. This instrument can measure both relative humidity and dew point. The thermometers on this instrument are spun around until the temperature of the wet-bulb thermometer stops dropping.

 DEFINE: What is a psychrometer?

Humidity and Comfort As we perspire, moisture evaporates from our skin. The moisture evaporating from our bodies cools us. The faster the moisture evaporates, the cooler we feel. When the humidity is low, the rate of evaporation is faster. This makes us feel cooler. People living in a hot, dry climate may feel more comfortable than those in a cooler, moister climate. High relative humidity makes people feel uncomfortable. A temperature of 35°C with very low relative humidity may be quite comfortable. However, a temperature of 25°C with high relative humidity can be uncomfortable.

TEMPERATURE AND HUMIDITY IN THREE CITIES		
City	Temperature	Humidity
A	35°C	17%
B	35°C	62%
C	25°C	44%

▲ **Figure 12-11**

 INFER: What do you think an air conditioner does to the air temperature and humidity in a room?

 CHECKING CONCEPTS

1. The relative humidity of air filled to capacity at a given temperature is _____ percent.
2. The relative humidity goes up if the air temperature _____.
3. A _____ has two thermometers and is used to find relative humidity.
4. The relative humidity of air changes as _____ leaves the air.

THINKING CRITICALLY

5. CALCULATE: Use Figure 12-10 to find the relative humidity when the psychrometer readings are as follows: **a.** wet bulb, 12°C; dry bulb, 20°C; **b.** wet bulb, 33°C; dry bulb, 35°C; and **c.** wet bulb, 22°C; dry bulb, 30°C.

INTERPRETING VISUALS

Use Figure 12-11 to answer the following question.

6. INFER: In which city would people be the most comfortable? The least comfortable?

 Hands-On Activity

EVAPORATION AND COOLING

You will need safety goggles, isopropyl (rubbing) alcohol, water, an index card, a stopwatch, and two cotton balls.

1. Gather your materials and put on the goggles. Fan your arm with an index card. Describe how it feels.
2. Dip a small cotton ball into some water and rub it on your arm. Fan the spot for 25 seconds. Describe how it feels.
3. Dip another cotton ball into some alcohol and rub this on your other arm. Fan this spot for 25 seconds. Describe how it feels.

▲ **STEP 1** Gather your materials.

Practicing Your Skills

4. OBSERVE: What happens to the water and to the alcohol when you fan your arm?
5. EXPLAIN: Why do evaporating liquids make your arm feel cooler?
6. INFER: Why do you feel cooler after you swim on a hot day?
7. COMPARE: Which evaporates faster, water or alcohol?
8. INFER: Why does sweating help to cool you down?
9. HYPOTHESIZE: Why do you feel warmer on a humid day?

12-4 What is the dew point?

Objective

Explain what happens when air temperature goes above or below the dew point.

Key Terms

condensation (kahn-duhn-SAY-shuhn): changing of a gas to a liquid

dew point: temperature to which air must be cooled to reach saturation

frost: ice formed from condensation below the freezing point of water

Condensation Air always contains some water vapor. As the temperature of air drops, water vapor in the air changes from a gas to a liquid. The process of changing a gas to a liquid is called **condensation.**

Have you ever seen water form on the outside of a cold can or bottle? The water forms when water vapor in the air condenses into liquid water on the cold metal or glass.

▶ **DESCRIBE:** What happens during the process known as condensation?

Dew Point The temperature of air at which condensation takes place is called the **dew point** of air. Condensation takes place when saturated air is cooled.

Warm air can hold more water vapor than cold air can. As the air cools, it can hold less and less water vapor. If the temperature of the air drops enough, the air becomes saturated. Its relative humidity reaches 100 percent.

If saturated air continues to be cooled, some of the water vapor in the air condenses. The water vapor changes to liquid water.

At night, the ground cools faster than the air. Air near the ground is then cooled by the ground. The temperature of the air may drop to or below its dew point. When this happens, condensation takes place. Drops of water called dew begin to form on grass and bushes. Dew may also form on the windows of cars.

▲ **Figure 12-12** Dew forms on leaves when condensation occurs.

▶ **DEFINE:** What is dew?

Frost The freezing point of water is 0°C. At this temperature, water changes from a liquid to a solid. When the humidity is low, the dew point of the air may be lower than the freezing point of water. If the air temperature drops below the dew point, water vapor will come out of the air. However, the water vapor will change directly to ice instead of water. Ice that forms this way is called **frost.**

▲ **Figure 12-13** Frost forms if the air temperature drops below the freezing point and the dew point.

▶ **HYPOTHESIZE:** Why doesn't frost form at temperatures above 0°C?

☑ CHECKING CONCEPTS

1. What is the process of condensation?
2. When does the process of condensation take place?
3. What is the dew point?
4. What happens to the relative humidity when the air becomes saturated?
5. What is the freezing point of water in the Celsius temperature scale?

💡 THINKING CRITICALLY

6. APPLY: Suppose condensation begins to form on the window of a car at 8°C. What is the dew point?
7. EXPLAIN: Why is the relative humidity of saturated air 100 percent?
8. CONTRAST: How do evaporation and condensation differ?
9. HYPOTHESIZE: How could you show that dew found on grass that is in direct sunlight evaporates quicker than dew found on grass that grows in the shade?

Web InfoSearch

Aircraft Deicing
One of the most dangerous things that can happen to an airplane is icing. Icing is caused by the freezing of so-called supercooled water droplets. Icing usually occurs on the wings and upper body of an airplane. The extra weight of the ice can reduce the ability of the airplane to fly. Airports usually deice airplanes, or melt the ice, during dangerous weather conditions.

▲ **Figure 12-14**
Plane being deiced

SEARCH: Use the Internet to find out how ice affects airplanes. Also, how do airports deice an airplane? Start your search at www.conceptsandchallenges.com. Some key search words are **airplane deicing, airplane safety**, and **airplane disasters**.

Hands-On Activity

MEASURING DEW POINT

You will need an empty can, water, a cup of ice cubes, and a thermometer.

1. Fill a can about two-thirds full of water.
2. Place a thermometer into the water. Do not let the bulb of the thermometer touch the bottom or sides of the can.
3. Add the ice cubes to the water. Observe the outside of the can. Record the temperature on the thermometer as soon as condensation appears on the outside of the can.

▲ **STEP 3** Observe the condensation on the outside of the can.

Practicing Your Skills

4. MEASURE: At what temperature did condensation appear on the can?
5. IDENTIFY: What are the water droplets that formed on the outside of the can called?
6. IDENTIFY: What is the name for the temperature at which condensation took place?
7. APPLY: What is the room's dew point?

How do clouds form?

Objectives
Describe how clouds form. Identify kinds of clouds.

Key Terms
cirrus (SIR-uhs) **cloud:** light, feathery cloud

cumulus (KYOO-myuh-luhs) **cloud:** big, puffy cloud

stratus (STRAY-tuhs) **cloud:** sheetlike cloud that forms layers across the sky

Cloud Formation From space, Earth sometimes seems to be covered with clouds. Clouds form from condensation in the atmosphere. Water droplets and ice form around dust and other particles in the air. Many billions of tiny water droplets and ice crystals form clouds. A cloud's shape is determined by how it formed.

 NAME: What process forms clouds?

Kinds of Clouds There are three basic kinds of clouds. Light, feathery clouds are called **cirrus clouds.** They are made up of ice crystals. They sometimes form at heights above 10,000 m.

Big, puffy clouds are called **cumulus clouds.** They form from rising currents of warm air that build to great heights. The base is usually flat.

Sometimes the sky is covered with a layer of sheetlike clouds. These are **stratus clouds.** Stratus clouds form layer upon layer, usually at low altitudes.

 LIST: What are the three basic kinds of clouds?

Fog A cloud that forms near the ground is fog. Fog forms from condensation. At night, the ground cools quickly. It cools the layer of air that lies above it. The air may be cooled to the dew point. If it is, the water vapor condenses and forms fog.

▲ **Figure 12-16** Fog rolls in off the ocean.

Thick blankets of fog can cover valleys or other low areas. Sometimes fog forms over rivers and lakes. This happens when cool air moves in over warm water.

 DESCRIBE: What is fog?

◀ **Figure 12-15**
Clouds come in three basic types: cirrus, cumulus, and stratus.

Cumulonimbus Clouds

▲ **Figure 12-17** Cumulonimbus clouds are associated with thunderstorms.

Cumulonimbus clouds are cumulus clouds that are often associated with thunderstorms. Updrafts can raise a cumulonimbus cloud to heights taller than Mount Everest. As the clouds rise, their tops become flattened against the tropopause, the top of the troposphere. This large, flat top resembles a blacksmith's anvil. An anvil is a good indication that a thunderstorm is coming.

 COMPARE: How is a cumulonimbus cloud like a cumulus cloud?

✔ CHECKING CONCEPTS

1. What are clouds made of?
2. What are light, feathery clouds called?
3. What are sheetlike, layered clouds called?
4. What are three places you might see fog?
5. What kinds of clouds are large and puffy?

THINKING CRITICALLY

6. **DESCRIBE:** Look outside at the sky. Are there clouds? What kind are they?
7. **MODEL:** Use cotton balls or wads of cotton to make models of the three kinds of clouds. Mount the clouds on a sheet of blue construction paper. Label the clouds.

Web InfoSearch

Thunderheads Another name for a cumulonimbus cloud is thunderhead. The sudden appearance of a thunderhead can mean that strong winds and heavy rains are on the way.

SEARCH: Use the Internet to find out more about thunderheads. How do they develop? How do meteorologists use them to learn more about the atmosphere? Start your search at www.conceptsandchallenges.com. Some key search words are **cumulus**, **cumulonimbus**, and **meteorology**.

Science and Technology

CLOUD SEEDING

Imagine being able to make it rain on very hot days. How about making it snow so that you could go sledding or skiing? There is a way to do this. Cloud seeding can sometimes make it rain or snow.

In cloud seeding, crystals of carbon dioxide or silver iodide are dropped on clouds from high-flying airplanes. Ice crystals form around these crystals. The ice crystals grow until they become heavy and fall from the clouds. Whether it rains or snows depends on the air temperature.

▲ **Figure 12-18** Cloud seeding can sometimes make it rain or snow.

Cloud seeding can help prevent severe storms by causing it to rain before a storm grows too large. It can also help during droughts. However, cloud seeding does not work all of the time. Better technologies need to be developed to improve its success rate.

Thinking Critically Some people think that cloud seeding is like stealing. Farmers in one area that have the clouds seeded may be taking water from farmers in another area. What do you think?

LAB ACTIVITY
Making Cloud Models

Materials
Safety goggles
2-Liter soft drink bottle
Bicycle hand pump
Paper match
Water
Thermometer

BACKGROUND

Clouds are made from billions of tiny water droplets. The droplets form around nearly invisible particles of dust, volcanic ash, and pollution.

PURPOSE

In this activity, you will investigate what is needed to make a cloud in a bottle.

PROCEDURE

1. Put on your goggles. Copy the chart in Figure 12-19 onto a clean sheet of paper.

2. For the first experiment, carefully slide the thermometer into the bottle. Screw on the cap with the thermometer still inside.

3. Have your teacher make a small hole in the bottle top. The hole should be just big enough for the hose of the bicycle hand pump to fit. Attach the hose of the bicycle pump to the cap of the cloud bottle. Make sure you have no air leaking out once you have the hose inserted into the bottle. Pump 10 to 20 times. Record the temperature.

4. Remove the hose. Observe what happens when you unscrew the cap and let the air out. Record the temperature again.

5. For the second experiment, add about a teaspoon of water to the bottle. Cap the bottle and shake it for about a minute with your thumb over the hole. Record the temperature.

▲ **STEP 3** Pump air into the bottle.

▲ **STEP 5** Add a teaspoon of water to the bottle.

6. Attach the bicycle pump and pump the same number of times as in Step 3. Observe what happens when you unscrew the cap. Some water will still be in the bottle. Record the temperature.

7. For the third experiment, ask your teacher to light a paper match and blow it out. Your teacher should immediately drop the used match into the bottle to capture its smoke inside. Cap the bottle. Record the temperature.

8. Once again, attach the bicycle pump and pump the bottle as before. Observe what happens when you unscrew the cap. Record the temperature.

▲ **STEP 8** Attach the bicycle pump and pump the bottle again.

Making Clouds			
Experiment	Temperature Before	Temperature After	What Happened?
Air Only			
Water and Air			
Water, Smoke, and Air			

▲ **Figure 12-19** Use a copy of this chart for recording your observations.

CONCLUSIONS

1. OBSERVE: What happened to the temperature when you pumped air into the bottle? What happened when you released the pressure?

2. OBSERVE: In which experiment did you create the best cloud?

3. INFER: What are the parts of a cloud?

4. ANALYZE: How does air temperature affect cloud formation?

12-6 What is precipitation?

Objective
Identify and describe forms of precipitation.

Key Terms
precipitation (pree-sihp-uh-TAY-shuhn): water that falls to Earth from the atmosphere

rain gauge (GAYJ): device used to measure rainfall

Precipitation Conditions of the atmosphere vary greatly from place to place and season to season. This results in several different types of precipitation. **Precipitation** is water that falls to Earth from clouds. Precipitation may be a liquid or a solid. There are four major kinds of precipitation: rain, snow, sleet, and hail. All precipitation begins when water condenses in cool air.

▶ LIST: What are the four kinds of precipitation?

Rain, Snow, and Sleet Droplets of water and crystals of ice that make up clouds are very small. They are kept up in the air by air currents. The droplets of water are always moving. They hit into each other. When they hit, they join together. When they become too heavy, they fall as rain. Snow falls when ice crystals grow too heavy.

A very heavy snowstorm with strong winds and low temperatures is called a blizzard. During a blizzard, it is difficult to see. The heavy falling snow can block highways, airports, and railroad tracks.

Sometimes rain falls through cold layers of air. Sleet is rain that freezes as it falls through a layer of cold air near the ground.

Occasionally, the freezing of the rain doesn't occur until the rain strikes a surface near the ground. In this event, the rain forms a thick sheet of ice. When these conditions occur, it is called an ice storm.

▶ CONTRAST: How are rain and snow different?

Hail Hail is made up of lumps of ice. These lumps form as winds toss ice crystals up and down in a rain cloud. Each time the crystals move up, water freezes around them. These heavy lumps of ice eventually fall to the ground, often damaging property and crops. Hail usually occurs during strong thunderstorms.

▶ OBSERVE: What does a hailstone look like?

Measuring Precipitation A **rain gauge** is a device used to measure rainfall. Rain gauges collect water in one spot. The amount of rain that falls is usually measured in millimeters.

Rain

Sleet

Wet snow

Hail

▲ **Figure 12-20** Precipitation can take many different forms.

Snow can also be measured with a rain gauge. The snow is collected, melted, and then measured. Snow depth is measured with a meter stick.

 4 DEFINE: What is a rain gauge?

✓ CHECKING CONCEPTS

1. Precipitation may be a _____ or a solid.
2. There are _____ kinds of precipitation.
3. A liquid form of precipitation is _____.
4. Rain that freezes as it falls to Earth is called _____.
5. Snow depth is usually measured with a _____.

💡 THINKING CRITICALLY

6. CLASSIFY: What state of matter—liquid or solid—is each kind of precipitation?
7. CONTRAST: What is the difference between sleet and freezing rain?
8. INFER: What effect do you think an ice storm might have on tree branches?

Web InfoSearch

Cloud Forests
On the tops of mountains in Central America, hidden by mist, are the cloud forests. Trees in cloud forests are much shorter

▲ **Figure 12-21** A cloud forest in Central America

than lowland tropical trees. Their branches are usually covered with thick carpets of mosses, lichens, and ferns. Plants and animals in these high-elevation forests are like those in milder climates.

SEARCH: Use the Internet to find out more about cloud forests. How are they alike and different from rain forests? What species are found in there? Start your search at www.conceptsandchallenges.com. Some key search words are **cloud forests, mountains,** and **Central America.**

Hands-On Activity

MAKING A RAIN GAUGE

You will need safety goggles, a wide-mouthed jar, tape, and a ruler with both metric and inch markings.

1. Stand a ruler inside a wide-mouthed jar. Tape the ruler to the side of the jar.
2. Place the jar in an open area outdoors.
3. After it rains, measure the water in the jar. If it snows, allow the snow to melt. Measure in both inches and millimeters, then write down the numbers.
4. Compare your results with those listed in your local newspaper.

▲ **STEP 3** Write down your measurements in both inches and millimeters.

Practicing Your Skills

5. INFER: Why should a rain gauge be placed in an open area?
6. **a.** COMPARE: How did your readings compare with those listed in the newspaper?
   b. EXPLAIN: Were your readings and the newspaper readings of the weather different? Explain.
7. INFER: Why should you allow snow to melt before measuring it?

12-7 What are air masses?

Objective

Describe different kinds of air masses.

Key Terms

air mass: large volume of air with about the same temperature and amount of moisture throughout

polar air mass: air mass that forms over cold regions

tropical (TRAHP-ih-kuhl) **air mass:** air mass that forms over warm regions

Air Masses One day, it may be rainy. The next, it may be cloudy or sunny. To understand why weather changes, you need to know about air masses. An **air mass** is a large volume of air with about the same temperature and amount of moisture throughout. Air masses form when air stays over an area for a while or moves slowly over an area more than 1,000 km across.

An air mass is affected by the region it covers. Air masses that form over land are dry. Air masses that form over water are moist. Air masses that form over warm regions are warm. Those that form over cold regions are cold.

▶ **1** INFER: What is an air mass formed over the ocean in a cold region like?

Polar Air Masses Cold air masses that form over cold regions are called **polar air masses.** There are two kinds of polar air masses. The United States is affected by continental polar (cP) air masses that form over Canada. These are called continental polar air masses because the air mass forms over land. Continental polar air masses that form over Canada in the winter are very cold and dry.

Air masses that form over oceans in cold regions are moist. These air masses are called maritime polar (mP) air masses. The United States is affected by maritime polar air masses that form over the northern Pacific and Atlantic oceans.

▶ **2** NAME: What is a cold, dry air mass called?

Tropical Air Masses Warm air masses that form near the tropics are called **tropical air masses.** There are two kinds of tropical air masses. If they form over water, they are moist and warm. These are called maritime tropical (mT) air masses. The United States is affected by maritime tropical air masses that form over the oceans, the Caribbean Sea, and the Gulf of Mexico. Continental tropical (cT) air masses are warm and dry. They form over tropical land areas such as northern Mexico.

▶ **3** NAME: Where do warm, moist air masses in the United States form?

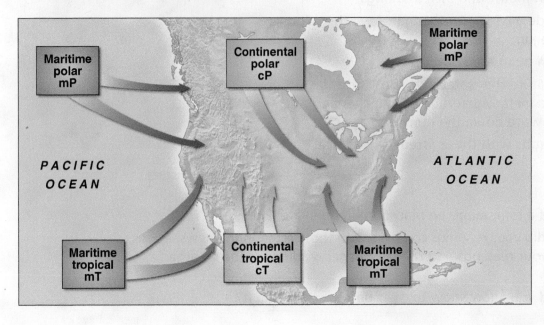

◀ **Figure 12-22**
Air masses over the United States

CHECKING CONCEPTS

1. What is an air mass?
2. What are the four main kinds of air masses?
3. What is a warm, dry air mass called?
4. Does a continental polar air mass form over land or water?
5. What is a cold, moist air mass called?

THINKING CRITICALLY

Use Figure 12-22 to answer the following questions. Abbreviations are used to show the four kinds of air masses.

6. APPLY: Which type of air mass would be represented by mT?
7. APPLY: Which type of air mass is represented by cP?
8. INFER: What do you think the letters for a maritime polar air mass would be?

INTERPRETING VISUALS

Use Figure 12-23 below to do the following exercise.

9. INFER: Seven air masses affect the weather of North America. Four are tropical and three are polar. The air masses are listed below. Match them to the letters on the map.

   Polar Pacific; polar Atlantic; tropical Pacific; tropical gulf; polar Canadian; tropical continental

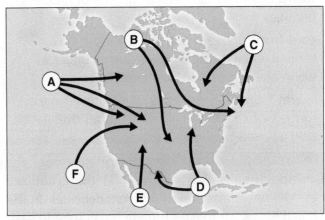

▲ Figure 12-23

How Do They Know That?

RIVERS OF AIR

Jet streams are rivers of fast-moving air. They can travel more than 300 km/h in a west-to-east direction. American pilots discovered the jet streams during World War II. Before then, planes were not equipped to reach the altitudes where jet streams occur. The World War II pilots were able to take advantage of the jet streams' high speeds to save fuel and time when traveling east. However, airplanes flying at high altitudes were slowed down when traveling west against the jet stream winds.

▲ Figure 12-24
Clouds in a jet stream

Jet streams form because of temperature and pressure differences. During winter, when there are greater variations in temperature, the jet streams are stronger.

Meteorologists often study jet streams with weather balloons. It appears that jet streams can strengthen and even change the movements of some weather systems. This affects the climate in some places. In India, for example, the jet stream is linked to the heavy monsoon rains.

Thinking Critically Why are jet streams weaker in the summer?

12-8 What is a front?

Objective

Describe the different kinds of fronts and the weather they cause.

Key Terms

front: boundary between air masses of different densities

cold front: forward edge of a cold air mass, formed when a cold air mass pushes under a warm air mass

warm front: forward edge of a warm air mass, formed when a warm air mass pushes over a cold air mass

Boundaries in Air A **front** is the boundary between two air masses of different densities. In the United States, air masses usually travel west to east. As they move, they meet up with other air masses.

Individual air masses do not usually mix. Instead, a front forms between them. A front can be hundreds of kilometers long. Fronts bring changes in the weather.

▲ **Figure 12-25** Fronts can be detected in satellite photos or sometimes by just looking up at the sky.

▶ EXPLAIN: What do fronts bring?

Cold Fronts A **cold front** is the forward edge of a cold air mass. A cold front is formed when a cold air mass pushes its way underneath a warm air mass.

Cold air is denser than warm air. As a cold front moves through an area, the warm air over a region is pushed upward. Gusty winds are formed because of differences in air pressure. Cold fronts usually bring rain and cloudy skies. Once the cold front passes, the cold air mass moves in.

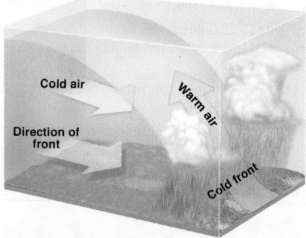

▲ **Figure 12-26** A cold front forms when cold air pushes warm air upward.

▶ DESCRIBE: What kind of weather does a cold front bring?

Warm Fronts What happens when a warm front moves into an area? A **warm front** is the forward edge of a warm air mass. A warm front forms when a warm air mass pushes over a cooler air mass.

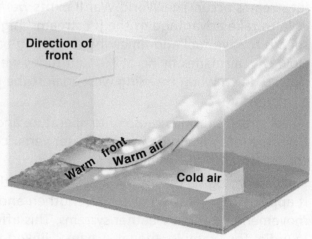

▲ **Figure 12-27** A warm front forms when a warm air mass pushes over cold air.

Warm air moves more slowly than cold air. Warm air rises above cold air. The rising warm air forms a gentle slope. The warm air slowly moves up and over the cold air. As the warm air rises, it cools. Cirrus clouds form high up, and precipitation may follow. Slow clearing and warmer temperatures show that a warm front has passed and the warm air mass has moved in.

 DEFINE: What is a warm front?

Stationary Fronts Sometimes cold and warm air masses stay put for a while. They do not move. They remain stationary. This forms a stationary front. A stationary front brings very little change in the weather.

▲ **Figure 12-28** A stationary front brings little change in weather conditions.

 DEFINE: What is a stationary front?

Occluded Fronts The most complex weather situation occurs with occluded fronts. In an occluded front, a warm air mass is between two cooler air masses.

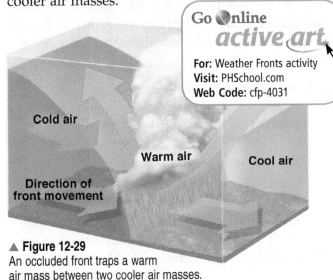

Go Online
active art

For: Weather Fronts activity
Visit: PHSchool.com
Web Code: cfp-4031

▲ **Figure 12-29**
An occluded front traps a warm air mass between two cooler air masses.

In an occluded front, the cooler air masses move beneath the warm air mass and push it up. They then come together in the middle and may mix. This makes the temperature near the ground cooler. The warm air mass is cut off, or occluded, from the ground. As the warm air cools and its water vapor condenses, the weather often turns cloudy, rainy, or snowy.

5 **DESCRIBE:** What happens to the weather with an occluded front?

✓ CHECKING CONCEPTS

1. What are four kinds of fronts?
2. How does a cold front form?
3. What kinds of clouds form when a warm front approaches?
4. Which kind of front causes very little change in weather?
5. What kind of weather is common with an occluded front?

💡 THINKING CRITICALLY

6. **INFER:** A city gets a day of rain and on the next day skies clear. The temperature rises. Which kind of front has passed?
7. **INFER:** If a city has clear skies and warm temperatures for three days, which kind of front might be keeping the weather the same?

Web InfoSearch

Tracking the Weather Go to the Internet to find out the weather report for three days. Keep a record of the fronts that are coming to your area. Write down the weather conditions that are forecast. Using that information, forecast the weather for the next two days. Check your forecast with current weather reports.

SEARCH: Start your search at www.conceptsandchallenges.com. Some key search words are **weather** and **fronts**.

What causes severe storms?

Making a Boom
HANDS-ON ACTIVITY

1. Take a paper lunch bag and blow into it.

2. Close the open end of the bag with your hand, keeping the air inside.

3. With force, quickly hit the bag with your other hand.

THINK ABOUT IT: What happens when you hit the bag? What part of a storm does this noise remind you of? How do you think air was involved in making the sound?

STEP 3

Objective

Identify three kinds of severe storms.

Key Terms

thunderstorm: storm with thunder, lightning, and often heavy rain and strong winds

tornado (tawr-NAY-doh)**:** small, very violent, funnel-shaped cloud that spins

hurricane (HUR-ih-kayn)**:** tropical storm with very strong winds

Thunderstorms A **thunderstorm** is a storm with thunder, lightning, and often heavy rain and strong winds. Thunderstorms usually occur in summer, when a cold front forces warm, moist air to rise rapidly. Cumulus clouds build up to form cumulonimbus clouds. From these, heavy rain or hail falls.

▲ **Figure 12-30** A tornado acts like a giant vacuum when it touches the ground.

Lightning occurs when a cloud discharges electricity. The current causes the air to heat and expand explosively. It creates a wave of compressed air. The wave produces the boom you hear as thunder. You see lightning flash before you hear thunder because light travels faster than sound does.

 DESCRIBE: What is a thunderstorm like?

Tornadoes A **tornado** is a funnel-shaped cloud that spins. Tornadoes cause very small, but very violent, storms. They frequently occur with severe thunderstorms. Tornadoes that form over water are called waterspouts.

Most tornadoes form during the spring or in early summer. Scientists are not sure how they form. They do know that a storm cloud may develop a small, spinning funnel that reaches down to the ground.

The funnel has very low air pressure. When it touches the ground, it acts like a giant vacuum cleaner, sucking everything up. As the funnel zigzags along, nearly all objects in its path are destroyed.

 DESCRIBE: What is a tornado?

Hurricanes A **hurricane** is a tropical storm with strong winds. These winds spiral toward the center. The winds may be stronger than 300 km/h.

People who study hurricanes may fly over or even into them to gather information. Most are scientists who work for the National Weather Service (NWS) or the National Oceanic and Atmospheric Administration (NOAA).

From an airplane, the hurricane looks like bands of spinning clouds. The rain is heavy. The wind grows stronger and more destructive the closer you get to the eye of the storm. The eye is the calm, clear center of the storm. After the eye passes, the winds change direction.

▲ **Figure 12-31** Satellite photo of a hurricane

3 DESCRIBE: What is the eye of a hurricane like?

✓ CHECKING CONCEPTS

1. When do thunderstorms usually happen?
2. What causes thunder?
3. What is the air pressure like in a tornado?
4. In what seasons do tornadoes usually form?

 THINKING CRITICALLY

5. INFER: Not all the houses on a block may be damaged by a tornado. How can this be?
6. CLASSIFY: Which type of severe storm has each of these features? **a.** thunder and lightning **b.** funnel-shaped cloud **c.** giant cumulus clouds **d.** calm eye **e.** low air pressure

Web InfoSearch

Storms in History Many storms have changed history. Columbus and later the passengers on the *Mayflower* met with severe storms. During World War II, one storm sank three U.S. naval destroyers and many smaller boats.

SEARCH: Use the Internet to find out more about this. How did storms affect Columbus's journey, World War II, and the *Mayflower* voyage? Start your search at **www.conceptsandchallenges.com**. Some key search words are **hurricanes, World War II,** and **voyages of Columbus.**

 Real-Life Science

TORNADO ALLEY

More tornadoes occur in the United States than anywhere else on Earth. During some years, more than 800 tornadoes are counted in the United States. Most of these tornadoes form in the Great Plains and the southwestern United States. Oklahoma and Kansas have more tornadoes than most other states. This area of the United States is called the Tornado Belt or Tornado Alley.

In Tornado Alley, tornadoes occur most often in April, May, and June. Usually, they strike during the middle or late afternoon.

▲ **Figure 12-32** Tornadoes cause a great deal of destruction where they touch down.

The National Weather Service warns communities when dangerous thunderstorms are approaching. During a tornado, the best place to go is a basement or the lowest floor of a building. Crouch under a table or another heavy piece of furniture. Stay away from windows and doors. After the tornado passes, watch out for dangerous debris and damaged structures.

Thinking Critically Why do most thunderstorms form in late afternoon?

Integrating Physical Science

THE Big IDEA

How do electrical charges cause lightning?

Every atom of matter is made up of smaller particles of matter. Some of these particles called protons have a positive electrical charge. Other particles called electrons have a negative electrical charge.

If the number of protons and electrons is equal, the atom is neutral. This means that the atom lacks any electrical charge.

Rubbing an atom can cause it to lose some of its electrons. An example is when you drag your feet across a rug on a dry day. As your feet rub against the rug, they pick up electrons. As a result, your body has more electrons than protons. It carries an electrical charge. If you touch a metal object, the extra electrons travel through your fingers to the metal. The shock you feel is actually the movement of electrons.

Clouds that float above Earth's surface are made of water and ice. Temperature differences caused by the freezing of water droplets result in electrons being transferred between atoms. The clouds build up an electrical charge that is released as lightning.

Lightning can travel within a single cloud, between two clouds, or from a cloud to the ground. It can even travel from the ground to a cloud. When the electricity travels through the air, it causes the air to warm and expand quickly. The rapid expansion and then contraction of air molecules is heard as thunder.

Look at the illustrations on these two pages. Then, follow the directions in the Science Log to find out more about "the big idea." ✦

Saint Elmo's fire
The sparks of light called Saint Elmo's fire occur during a storm when not enough charges have built up to form a lightning bolt. Instead, a mass of sparks appears above the ground. This phenomenon was first noted above ships' mast, and so was named for the patron saint of sailors.

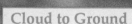

Cloud to Ground
In cloud-to-ground lightning, electrical charges flow from a cloud to Earth's surface. Some violent storms produce as many as 100 electrical charges per second. The air around lightning can become as hot as 30,000°C.

Cloud to Cloud

Lightning always travels along the path of least resistance. Usually, that means moving from one cloud to another.

Lightning Strokes

A lightning stroke begins when a leader stroke moves downward in a series of short jumps. Thin branches of lightning move outward from the leader stroke and fizzle. As the leader stroke strikes Earth's surface, a return stroke moves upward from Earth to the cloud.

Ground to Cloud

Sometimes, electrical charges can flow from the ground up to a cloud. This happens when a postively charged cloud passes over a tall object on the ground that is negatively charged.

WRITING ACTIVITY

Science Log

A single lightning bolt can release as much as 100 million volts of electricity. Unfortunately, hundreds of people are struck by these powerful charges each year. Find out how to keep safe in a lightning storm. Start your search at www.conceptsandchallenges.com. Make a list of five safety rules.

Figure 12-33 Lightning is a very large electrical current flowing through the air. Its energy produces a bright flash of light and often a loud clap of thunder.

What is a station model?

Objective
Understand how to read a station model.

Key Terms
station model: record of weather information at a weather station

millibar (MIHL-ih-bahr): unit of measurement for air pressure

Station Models A **station model** shows the weather conditions at a particular weather station. Station models such as the one in Figure 12-34 are used to depict weather conditions on a weather map. A station model uses symbols instead of words to describe weather. Each weather factor has a different symbol. Meteorologists, or weather scientists, use these symbols to make a station model.

Reading Station Models Each station model has a circle, which represents cloud cover. The amount of shading in the circle tells how much cloudiness there is. It is given in percentages. Figure 12-35 shows these percentages and their symbols. Symbols are also used for rain, snow, and other conditions.

Wind speed and direction are indicated on a station model with an arrow shaft leading to the station circle and small "feathers" sticking out at the end of this shaft. Look at Figure 12-34 for an example. The shaft is slanted in the direction from which the wind is coming. In the illustration, this is northeast. The length and number of feathers represent wind speed. Wind direction symbols are also given.

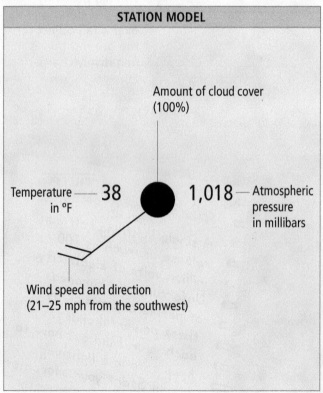

STATION MODEL

Amount of cloud cover (100%)

Temperature in °F — 38

1,018 — Atmospheric pressure in millibars

Wind speed and direction (21–25 mph from the southwest)

▲ Figure 12-34

STATION MODEL SYMBOLS			
Wind Speed (mph)	Symbol	Cloud Cover (%)	Symbol
1–2		0	
3–8		10	
9–14		20–30	
15–20		40	
21–25		50	
26–31		60	
32–37		70–80	
38–43		90	
44–49		100	
50–54			
55–60			
61–66			
67–71			
72–77			

▲ Figure 12-35

1 DEFINE: What is a station model?

2 OBSERVE: What is the wind speed on the station model shown in Figure 12-34?

Air Pressure In the United States, air pressure is measured in **millibars** (mb). A bar is a unit of pressure. It is based on the pressure created by a column of mercury that rises 750 mm at a temperature of 0°C. A millibar (mb) is a thousandth of a bar. Air pressure at the ground, or standard atmospheric pressure, is 1,013 mb.

Normal air pressure at ground level can range from 980 to 1,040 mb. The air pressure during a storm is usually lower than normal. From the outer edge of a hurricane to its center, air pressure can drop from over 950 mb to less than 800 mb. The lowest pressures ever recorded in the Western Hemisphere are associated with these storms. The steep drop in pressure creates the rapid, inward-spiraling winds of a hurricane. High pressure, on the other hand, usually brings with it clear, sunny skies.

 ANALYZE: What is the air pressure shown on the station model in Figure 12-34?

✓ CHECKING CONCEPTS

1. What does a station model show?
2. How can you tell how cloudy it is by looking at a station model?
3. How is wind direction shown on a station model?
4. How is the pressure measured?

 THINKING CRITICALLY

5. MODEL: Cut out a weather map from your local newspaper. Gather other weather information about your local area. Using the weather map and the information you are able to gather, draw a station model of your local area for that day.

INTERPRETING VISUALS

Use the station model shown in Figure 12-34 to answer the following questions.

6. INTERPRET: From which direction is the wind blowing?
7. INTERPRET: How would you describe the cloud cover?
8. INTERPRET: What is the wind speed?

DESIGNING AN EXPERIMENT

Design an experiment to solve the following problem. Include a hypothesis, variables, a procedure with materials, and a type of data to study. Also tell how you would record the data.

PROBLEM: Suzie wants to collect data on the percentage of cloud cover in her neighborhood over a week's time. She will use the following materials to do so: a crayon, a ruler, and a large mirror. How can Suzie collect data using these materials?

 Hands-On Activity

READING A STATION MODEL

Examine the station models shown. Then answer the questions.

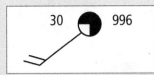

A

Practicing Your Skills

1. DESCRIBE: What is the sky condition for *A*?
2. MEASURE: What is the air pressure for *A* and *B*?
3. OBSERVE: What is the temperature for each?
4. **a.** OBSERVE: How fast is the wind blowing in each?
   b. IDENTIFY: From which direction is the wind blowing in each?
5. INFER: What kind of precipitation might be falling in *B*?
6. MODEL: Draw a station model that shows the conditions listed: **a.** air pressure, 1,018.8 mb; **b.** no cloud cover; **c.** temperature, 64°F; **d.** wind direction, from the southwest; **e.** wind speed, 35 mph.

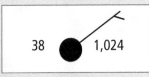

B

12-11 How do you read a weather map?

Objective
Read and interpret a weather map.

Key Terms
isobar (EYE-soh-bahr): line on a weather map that connects points of equal air pressure

isotherm: line on a weather map that joins places that have the same temperatures

Weather Maps A weather map shows weather conditions for many places at one time. You can find the temperature, cloud cover, wind speed, and so on for many different locations. Data from more than 300 weather stations all over the country are assembled by the National Weather Service into weather maps each day. These maps are then used by newspapers and TV stations to prepare weather maps for their area.

1 DEFINE: What do weather maps show?

Reading a Weather Map Different weather maps can show different things. A key on a weather map helps you to read it. The pink lines that you see on the map in Figure 12-36 are called **isobars.** They connect points of equal air pressure. The pink numbers tell the pressure in millibars. Areas of high pressure are usually called highs. They are shown with an "H." Areas of low pressure are called lows. They are shown with an "L." On a different map, the pink lines might show isotherms. **Isotherms** are lines joining places that have nearly the same temperatures. Other symbols show fronts. Precipitation is shown as shading or with symbols like those in Figure 12-36.

2 OBSERVE: What was the temperature in Atlanta on the day this map was made?

Highs and Lows High-pressure regions have different weather from low-pressure regions. Highs usually bring clear skies. Lows usually bring cloudy skies and possibly precipitation.

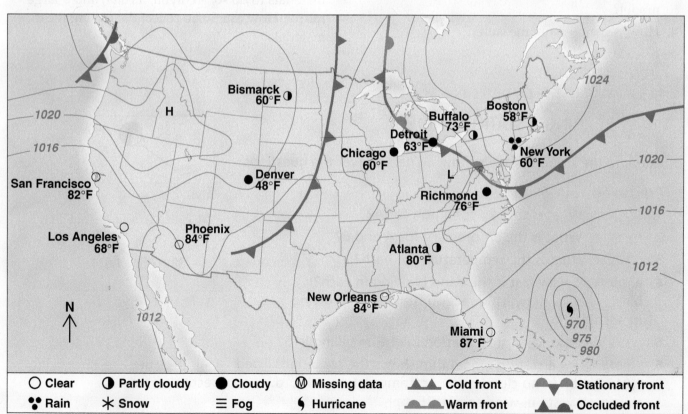

| ○ Clear | ◑ Partly cloudy | ● Cloudy | Ⓜ Missing data | ▲▲ Cold front | ⌒⌒ Stationary front |
| •• Rain | ✳ Snow | ≡ Fog | ⟆ Hurricane | ⌒⌒ Warm front | ▲⌒ Occluded front |

▲ **Figure 12-36** Weather map

Highs and lows usually move from west to east across the United States. As they pass through a region, they bring changes in the weather.

3 DESCRIBE: What type of weather does a low bring?

✓ CHECKING CONCEPTS

1. What are three weather conditions that you might find indicated on a weather map?
2. What do isobars show?
3. What are two ways to show precipitation on a weather map?
4. What do meteorologists usually call areas of low pressure?
5. What is the symbol weather maps use to indicate high pressure?
6. What do isotherms do?

💡 THINKING CRITICALLY

Use Figure 12-36 to do the following exercise.

7. IDENTIFY: Find a city that has each of the following weather conditions.

    a. clear skies   **e.** lowest temperature

    b. cloudy   **f.** low air pressure

    c. partly cloudy   **g.** inside a high

    d. highest temperature

BUILDING SCIENCE SKILLS

Researching Many different symbols are used on weather maps. Do some research to find out some other weather symbols or different weather symbols for the same weather conditions. Draw and label the symbols on 3- × 5-inch index cards. What new symbols did you find? Make a list.

Real-Life Science

THE WEATHER PAGE IN A NEWSPAPER

Everyone is interested in the weather. Is it going to be sunny or stormy? Can we have our picnic? Will the ballgame be canceled? Weather has a big effect on our daily lives.

To find out the forecast, people often look in the newspaper. In it, you might find a four- to five-day local forecast, weather maps, a national forecast, and temperature graphs. Some newspapers contain a weather map for the local area. Others have a map of the country. Most newspapers have expected temperatures, in Fahrenheit. They also show fronts, precipitation data, and severe weather zones.

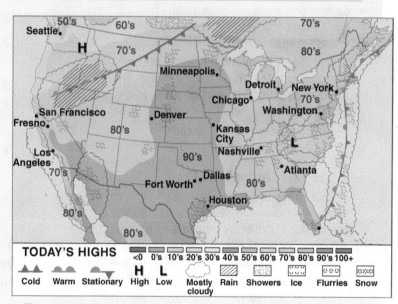

▲ **Figure 12-37** A typical newspaper weather map of the United States

Temperature zones may be shaded in different colors. High- and low-pressure areas are indicated. Symbols for the fronts, steady rain, showers, flurries, and snow are shown. Some papers give average temperatures for that month. Others have the temperatures for different cities around the world.

Thinking Critically Why do newspapers have so much weather data?

Chapter 12 Challenges

Chapter Summary

Lessons 12-1, 12-2, and 12-3

- The gaseous form of water is water vapor. Most of the water vapor in the air evaporates from the oceans. Living things also add water to air. Humidity is the amount of water in the air.
- Air is **saturated,** or filled to **capacity,** when it holds all the water vapor it can at a given temperature.
- **Specific humidity** is the actual amount of water vapor in air. **Relative humidity** is the amount of water vapor in the air compared with what air can hold at full capacity. Temperature changes cause the relative humidity to change. A **psychrometer** is used to find relative humidity.

Lessons 12-4, 12-5, and 12-6

- When saturated air is cooled, **condensation** takes place. Water vapor condenses at the **dew point.**
- Saturated air cooled close to the ground forms dew. **Frost** forms when the dew point is below water's freezing point.
- Clouds form from condensation in the atmosphere. The three basic kinds of clouds are **cirrus, cumulus,** and **stratus.** Fog is a cloud that forms near the ground.
- Types of **precipitation** are rain, snow, sleet, and hail. Precipitation is measured with a **rain gauge.**

Lessons 12-7 through 12-11

- An **air mass** is a large volume of air with about the same temperature and moisture level throughout. **Polar air masses** form over cold regions. **Tropical air masses** form near the equator. Either can form over land or water.
- A **front** is where two air masses meet. Moving fronts cause weather changes. A **cold front** is the forward edge of a cold air mass. A **warm front** is the forward edge of a warm air mass.
- **Thunderstorms** include lightning, thunder, strong winds, heavy rains, and sometimes tornadoes. **Tornadoes** have funnel-shaped clouds that touch down on Earth's surface. A **hurricane** is a tropical storm with strong, spiraling winds.
- **Station models** describe local weather conditions. **Millibars** are units of air pressure.
- Weather maps show the weather for an area.

Key Term Challenges

air mass (p. 292)
capacity (p. 280)
cirrus cloud (p. 286)
cold front (p. 294)
condensation (p. 284)
cumulus cloud (p. 286)
dew point (p. 284)
evaporation (p. 278)
front (p. 294)
frost (p. 284)
hurricane (p. 296)
isobar (p. 302)
isotherm (p. 302)
millibar (p. 300)

polar air mass (p. 292)
precipitation (p. 290)
psychrometer (p. 282)
rain gauge (p. 290)
relative humidity (p. 282)
saturated (p. 280)
specific humidity (p. 280)
station model (p. 300)
stratus cloud (p. 286)
thunderstorm (p. 296)
tornado (p. 296)
transpiration (p. 278)
tropical air mass (p. 292)
warm front (p. 294)

MATCHING **Write the Key Term from above that best matches each description.**

1. process in which plants give off water
2. filled to capacity
3. line on a weather map that connects points of equal air pressure
4. funnel-shaped cloud
5. temperature to which air must be cooled to reach saturation
6. amount of matter something can hold
7. unit of measurement for air pressure
8. record of weather data at a weather station

APPLYING DEFINITIONS **Explain the difference between the words in each pair. Write your answers in complete sentences.**

9. evaporation, condensation
10. cirrus cloud, stratus cloud
11. air mass, front
12. thunderstorm, hurricane
13. humidity, specific humidity
14. cold front, warm front
15. frost, precipitation
16. isobar, isotherm

Content Challenges TEST PREP

MULTIPLE CHOICE **Write the letter of the term or phrase that best completes each statement.**

1. Light, feathery clouds are called
   a. cirrus clouds.
   b. cumulus clouds.
   c. stratus clouds.
   d. nimbus clouds.

2. Each station model is marked by a
   a. word.
   b. circle.
   c. square.
   d. triangle.

3. In the United States, air pressure is measured in
   a. millibars.
   b. meters.
   c. milliliters.
   d. kilograms.

4. If air is filled to half its capacity, the relative humidity is
   a. 100 percent.
   b. 75 percent.
   c. 50 percent.
   d. 25 percent.

5. Fog forms over rivers and lakes when cool air moves in over
   a. cold water.
   b. warm water.
   c. warm air.
   d. cirrus clouds.

6. Air masses do not usually
   a. form fronts.
   b. move.
   c. mix.
   d. meet.

7. Tornadoes usually form during
   a. early winter.
   b. late fall.
   c. early summer.
   d. late winter.

8. Most of the water in the air evaporates from
   a. the oceans.
   b. the soil.
   c. puddles.
   d. lakes and rivers.

FILL IN **Write the term or phrase that best completes each statement.**

9. As temperature drops, the capacity of air for holding water goes _____.

10. Molecules in a liquid are always _____.

11. Air masses that form over oceans are _____.

12. Standard air pressure is about _____ millibars.

13. As the temperature of the air reaches the dew point, water vapor changes from a gas to a _____.

14. Lightning is caused when giant storm clouds discharge _____.

15. The way a cloud forms gives it its _____.

16. A front brings changes in the _____.

17. Relative humidity goes _____ if the temperature drops.

18. There is no wind or rain in the _____ of a hurricane.

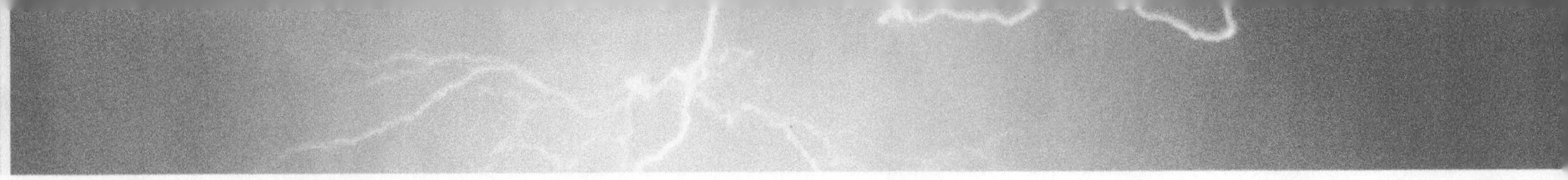

Concept Challenges TEST PREP

WRITTEN RESPONSE **Answer each of the following questions in complete sentences.**

1. RELATE: How are specific humidity and relative humidity related?

2. CONTRAST: What is the difference between sleet and hail?

3. EXPLAIN: Why does a cold air mass push under a warm air mass?

4. EXPLAIN: Why is the wet thermometer of a psychrometer cooled more when the relative humidity is low than when it is high?

5. APPLY: How do different air masses affect the weather in the United States?

6. RELATE: How does the process of changing a liquid to a gas relate to different forms of weather?

7. EXPLAIN: How is specific humidity measured?

8. EXPLAIN: How are each of the four kinds of precipitation formed?

9. INFER: The grass outside in the morning is wet, and it has not rained. What process probably took place to cause the dew?

INTERPRETING VISUALS **Use Figure 12-38 below to answer the following questions.**

10. What is the relative humidity when the dry-bulb thermometer reads 5°C and the wet-bulb thermometer reads 0°C?

11. What is the relative humidity when the dry-bulb thermometer reads 20°C and the wet-bulb thermometer reads 13°C?

12. If the relative humidity is 50 percent and the dry-bulb thermometer reads 30°C, what does the wet-bulb thermometer read?

		Temperature of Air from Dry-Bulb Thermometer (°C)								
		−5	0	5	10	15	20	25	30	35
	1	75	81	86	88	90	91	92	93	94
	2	52	64	72	77	80	83	85	86	87
	3	29	46	58	66	70	74	77	79	81
Difference Between Dry-Bulb and Wet-Bulb Thermometer (°C)	4	6	29	46	55	62	66	70	73	75
	5		13	32	44	53	59	63	67	70
	6			20	34	44	51	57	61	70
	7			0	24	36	44	50	55	59
	8				15	28	37	45	50	54

Relative Humidity (%)

▲ Figure 12-38

Chapter 13 Climate

▲ **Figure 13-1** Tree trunks reveal changes in climate over the years. This cross section is from a giant redwood.

Look at a cross section of a tree trunk. You should see a series of bands or rings. Starting in spring, the trunks of trees grow by producing bands of new material just beneath the bark. The bands produced in late summer look darker. This forms a pattern of rings. One combined ring represents one year of a tree's life. Rings provide a clue to climate. In good weather, there is more growth. That means the darker bands will be wider.

▶About how old was the tree that produced the trunk in this picture?

Contents

13-1 What is climate?

Objectives
Explain how weather and climate are related.
Identify the factors that determine climate.

Key Terms
weather: day-to-day conditions of the atmosphere
climate (KLY-muht): average weather conditions of an area over many years

Weather and Climate Air temperature, the appearance of the sky, winds, and the amount of moisture in the air all are part of weather. **Weather** is the day-to-day conditions of the atmosphere. The average weather conditions of an area from year to year is its **climate.** Climate describes the weather patterns of an area over time.

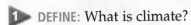 **DEFINE:** What is climate?

Average Temperatures Average monthly and yearly temperatures can be used to describe climate. The monthly average is found by adding together the daily average temperature for each day of the month and dividing by the number of days in the month. The yearly average temperature is a total of the twelve monthly averages divided by twelve.

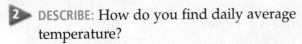 **DESCRIBE:** How do you find daily average temperature?

Temperature Range How much the temperature changes during the year is also important in describing climate. This is temperature range. To find the temperature range, subtract the lowest monthly average temperature from the highest. In Eureka, California, for example, the average monthly temperature for July is 14°C. In January it is 9°C. In New York City, the average monthly temperature goes from 25°C in July to about −0°C in January. New York City has a greater temperature range than Eureka does. The temperature range for Eureka is 5°C. New York City has a temperature range of 31°C. Eureka and New York City have different climates partly because they have different temperature ranges.

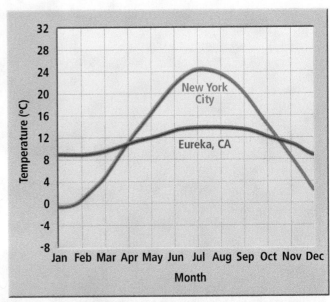

▲ **Figure 13-2** Average monthly temperatures for New York City and Eureka, California

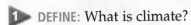 **INFER:** Does New York City or Eureka have a colder climate?

Average Precipitation Average monthly precipitation is also used to describe climate. Precipitation is rain, snow, sleet, or hail. Average monthly precipitation is the average amount of water from rain, snow, sleet, or hail that falls in an area in a month. It is measured in centimeters or inches.

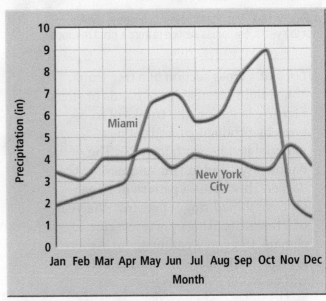

▲ **Figure 13-3** Average monthly precipitation for New York City and Miami, Florida, over a thirty-year period.

However, average precipitation is not enough to describe climate. Both Miami, Florida, and New York City get moderate amounts of precipitation yearly. However, Figure 13-3 shows that in New York City, precipitation falls steadily throughout the year. New York City gets rain, snow, sleet, and hail. In Miami, the most rain falls during a rainy season. The rainy season is May through October. Miami usually does not get snow or sleet. New York City and Miami have very different climates.

 INFER: Which probably has a colder climate, Miami or New York City? Explain.

✓ CHECKING CONCEPTS

1. The condition of the atmosphere today is the _____.

2. The _____ of an area describes the average weather conditions from year to year.

3. Temperature _____ describes the yearly change in temperature.

4. Rain and snow are two different kinds of _____.

 THINKING CRITICALLY

5. **CALCULATE: a.** The high temperature in Chicago was 12°C. The low was 8°C. What was the temperature range that day? **b.** The high temperature in Houston was 25°C. The low was 21°C. What was the average temperature in Houston that day?

6. **INFER:** What two factors have the greatest effect on climate?

BUILDING SCIENCE SKILLS

Comparing and Contrasting In warm, dry climates, people usually wear loose-fitting, lightcolored, lightweight clothing. In cooler climates, they wear snug-fitting clothing and dark colors. Find out about the kinds of clothing that are appropriate to each kind of climate. What fabrics are best? How do the clothing styles of different cultures relate to their climates? Write a brief report on the relationship between clothing and climate.

 ## *How Do They Know That?*
THE LOST COLONY OF GREENLAND

In A.D. 986, during a warm period, Erik the Red led an expedition to Greenland from Iceland. As a result, two small Norse settlements were established on the western coast. By the early twelfth century, there were about 10,000 people living there. They had cattle, sheep, and goats. There was plenty of wildlife. The colonists received supplies from Iceland and Scandinavia regularly.

▲ **Figure 13-4** Traces of the lost settlements of Greenland are still found there today.

Later that century, the weather in Greenland cooled sharply. This cooling of temperature was ahead of any climate change in Europe. The following century was even colder. These changes caused more frequent storms. More pack ice grew around the island. Visits from Icelanders decreased. By the late 1400s, both settlements had died out completely. One possible cause was malnutrition. This is the only recorded example of an established European society being completely wiped out.

Thinking Critically How did the change in climate cause the settlements to disappear?

13-2 What factors determine climate?

Objective
Identify and describe the conditions that determine climate.

Key Terms
latitude (LAT-uh-tood)**:** distance in degrees north or south of the equator in degrees

altitude (AL-tuh-tood)**:** height above sea level

Latitude The climate of an area is affected by its latitude. **Latitude** is the distance in degrees north or south of the equator. Latitude determines how much heat energy an area gets from the Sun. At the equator, the Sun's rays fall almost directly on Earth. The closer an area is to the equator, the warmer is its climate. At higher latitudes, the Sun's rays strike Earth at more of an angle. The heat energy from the Sun is spread out, and the climate is colder. Global wind patterns at different latitudes also alter the number and kinds of storms in an area.

 RELATE: How does latitude affect climate?

Altitude The height above sea level is called **altitude.** Air is warmer at sea level than it is at higher altitudes. The average air temperature drops about 1°C for every 100-m rise in altitude. Even near the equator, mountaintops are snow-covered all year.

▲ **Figure 13-5** This picture shows the kinds of vegetation that can be found at different altitudes, from mountaintop to sea level.

 DEFINE: What is altitude?

Ocean Currents Ocean currents have an effect on the climate of areas along the seacoast. An ocean current is like a river of water within the ocean. Some ocean currents are warm. Other ocean currents are cold. Winds passing over ocean currents are either warmed or cooled by them. When these winds reach nearby land areas, they heat or cool the land.

3 DESCRIBE: How do ocean currents affect land temperatures?

Mountains When air passes over a mountain range, the air rises and cools. The side on which the air rises is called the windward side. Moisture condenses from the cooled air, causing it to either rain or snow.

As the air moves down the other side of the mountain, the leeward side, it is warmed and most of the moisture is removed. It rarely rains on the leeward side of a mountain. Many deserts, such as Death Valley, are found on the leeward sides of mountains. These areas are sometimes called rain shadow deserts.

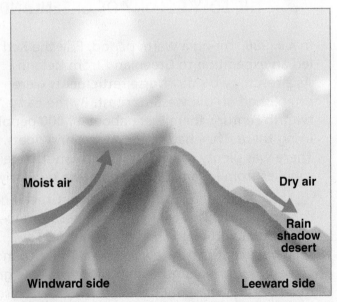

▲ **Figure 13-6** Different sides of a mountain often have different weather patterns.

4 OBSERVE: What side of a mountain faces the wind?

☑ CHECKING CONCEPTS

1. The closer an area is to the equator, the _____ its climate.

2. At _____ latitudes, the Sun's rays strike Earth at more of an angle.

3. Air at sea level is _____ than air at higher altitudes.

4. Land areas near cold-water currents usually have _____ temperatures.

💡 THINKING CRITICALLY

5. CALCULATE: How much lower will the temperature be on top of a 1,500-m mountain than at sea level?

6. INFER: Miami, Florida, is at a lower latitude than San Francisco, California. Which city probably has a warmer climate? Explain.

Web InfoSearch

The Butterfly Effect Many factors influence the weather. A change in any one can affect the others in unpredictable ways. This is chaos theory. Weather patterns do repeat over the years. This is climate. However, past patterns are never repeated exactly. This is partly the result of the butterfly effect, which is the idea that a butterfly's wings stirring the air in one place can lead to large storms a month later far away.

SEARCH: Use the Internet to find out more about chaos theory. What besides the weather does it affect? Start your search at www.conceptsandchallenges.com. Some key search words are **chaos theory, climate change,** and **weather patterns.**

Real-Life Science

THE RAINIEST PLACES ON EARTH

You might think that the rain forests are the rainiest places on Earth. They do get more than 150 cm of rain per year. Some get up to 1,000 cm each year. Where could it rain more than that?

Actually, some of the rainiest places on Earth are found on windward mountain slopes. Mount Waialeale (wy-ahl-ay-AHL-ay) in Hawaii gets 1,150 cm per year, the highest average annual rainfall in the world. Cherrapunji (cher-uh-PUN-jee), India, is second, with about 1,125 cm a year. Cherrapunji holds the record for the most rainfall in one year, at 2,605 cm. Most of this rain fell in one month, July. Compare this with Seattle, Washington, which is known for its rainy weather. The average rainfall there is about 80 cm per year.

▲ **Figure 13-7** Mount Waialeale in Hawaii has the highest annual rainfall in the world.

Mountain areas get a lot of rain and snow. Runoff from mountains such as the Rockies can be a source of water for dry areas in the southwestern United States. Reservoirs in mountain areas can store spring runoff. This water can then be delivered to Los Angeles and other cities by a network of canals.

Thinking Critically Based on the climate, what do you think you would see on a hike up Mount Waialeale?

13-3 What are climate zones?

INVESTIGATE

Reading a Climograph
HANDS-ON ACTIVITY

1. Climographs allow scientists to compare different weather conditions to see if they are related. For example, scientists might compare hours of daylight and temperatures. Look at the climograph in Figure 13-8. In it, total rainfall and average monthly temperatures are compared.

2. Observe which month is warmest.

3. Observe which month has the most rainfall.

THINK ABOUT IT: Are precipitation and temperature related in Kansas City, Missouri? How can you tell?

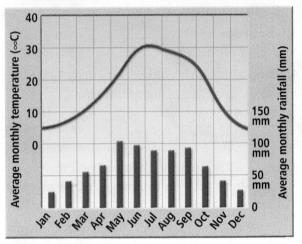

▲ **Figure 13-8** Climograph of Kansas City, Missouri

Objective
Identify and describe the three main climate zones.

Key Terms
tropical (TRAHP-ih-kuhl) **zone:** warm region near the equator

polar zone: cold region above 60°N and below 60°S latitude

middle-latitude zone: region between 30° and 60°N and S latitude

Latitudes and Climate Zones A climate zone is an area of Earth that has a certain temperature range and similar weather conditions. Figure 13-9 on the next page shows the three main climate zones. The warm zone near the equator is the **tropical zone.** It is between 30°N and 30°S latitude. The average monthly temperature is 18°C or higher. The coldest climate zones are the **polar zones.** These are above 60°N and below 60°S latitude. Temperatures do not go above 10°C. Between 30° and 60°N and S latitude are the **middle-latitude zones.** The temperature in the coldest months in these places averages no less than 10°C. The warmest month averages no colder than 18°C.

▶ DEFINE: What is a climate zone?

Solar Energy and Climate Zones The biggest influence on climate and weather is energy from the Sun. The amount of solar energy received at a particular spot is determined by the tilt of Earth on its axis. This tilt influences the angle at which sunlight strikes Earth.

Climate conditions and weather are affected by how directly the Sun's rays strike an area. The Sun's rays are most direct and have the greatest effect at the equator. The places on Earth closest to the equator have the warmest climates.

Because Earth's poles get the least amount of sunlight, they are the coldest places on Earth. In between, it depends on the seasons. Other factors that can affect the climate of a region include topography, location of lakes and oceans, availability of moisture, global wind patterns, ocean currents, and location of air masses.

▶ INFER: What is a state in the United States that has long, cold winters and short, warm summers?

Rainfall and Climate Zones In each climate zone, there are many smaller climate zones based on rainfall. In the tropics, climates may be very arid, or dry. They can also be very humid, or wet. In the polar zones, the climate is always cold and never humid. The middle-latitude zones have many different climates.

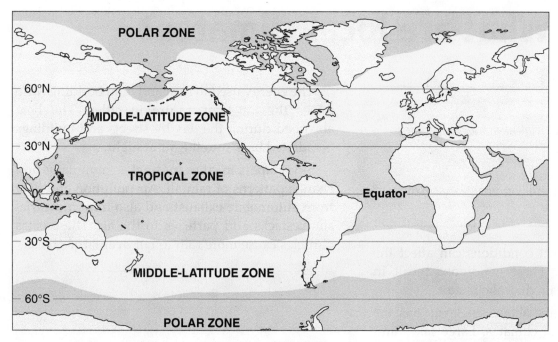

Figure 13-9 The three main climate zones are the tropical, middle-latitude, and polar zones.

The importance of climate cannot be overestimated. In addition to its effects on human life, climate determines the type of soil and vegetation found in a given area. This, in turn, determines how the land supports living things.

 ANALYZE: What creates smaller climate zones within the larger ones?

✓ CHECKING CONCEPTS

1. Earth is divided into _____ climate zones.

2. Places with the coldest temperatures are located in the _____ zone.

3. Places with the warmest temperatures are located in the _____ zone.

4. The middle-latitude zone has many different combinations of _____ and amounts of rainfall.

5. The middle-latitude zone is located between _____ N and S latitude.

💡 THINKING CRITICALLY

6. **IDENTIFY:** Using Figure 13-9, indicate the lines of latitude that separate the tropical zone from the middle-latitude zones.

INTERPRETING VISUALS

Copy the table in Figure 13-10 onto a sheet of paper. Look at the three cities listed and their locations. Use the terms warm, moderate, *and* cold *to fill in the column titled "Type of Climate." Study the list of temperatures. Match each city with its temperature. Write the numbers in the table. Then, answer the questions.*

LATITUDE AND CLIMATE				
City	Location (Latitude)	Type of Climate	Average Temperature	
			January	July
Singapore	1°N			
Point Barrow, AK	71°N			
Boston, MA	42°N			

▲ Figure 13-10

Coldest Month	**Warmest Month**
January average: 78°F	July average: 79°F
January average: 30°F	July average: 73°F
January average: −11°F	July average: 44°F

7. **EXPLAIN:** Why are regions closer to the equator (0° latitude) warmer than those farther from the equator?

8. **CALCULATE:** What is the yearly temperature range for each city listed in your table?

CHAPTER 13: Climate **313**

13-4 What are local climates?

Objective

Describe some factors that affect local climates.

Key Term

microclimate (MY-kroh-kly-muht): very small climate zone

Local Climate Local conditions can affect the climate of any area. These conditions result in small climate zones called local climates.

Altitude, or distance above sea level, has the greatest effect on local climates. Large lakes and forests also affect local climates. Like oceans, large lakes can warm or cool the temperature of the air. Forests are another factor. They slow down winds and add water vapor to the air. This increases humidity.

▲ **Figure 13-11** Large lakes can cool or warm the air temperature of nearby regions.

▶ IDENTIFY: What are three factors that can affect local climates?

Microclimates Local climates can be broken down into even smaller climate zones. These very small climate zones are called **microclimates.** A microclimate can be as small as a schoolyard.

All cities have microclimates. The average temperature in a city is higher by several degrees than it is in surrounding areas. Heavy traffic in cities warms the air and raises average temperatures.

The energy used to heat and light buildings also raises the air temperature in cities. The heat absorbed during the day by streets and buildings is radiated back into the air at night.

Skyscrapers in cities may act as mountains and change patterns of rainfall. Air pollution and dust from automobile exhaust and also from industrial smokestacks add particles to the air. These extra particles cause more rain to fall over large cities.

▲ **Figure 13-12** Tall buildings, such as skyscrapers in New York City, create city microclimates.

▶ EXPLAIN: How do skyscrapers affect the microclimate in cities?

Global Warming Climate has changed many times during Earth's history. These changes were mostly due to natural causes. Today, human activities may be changing Earth's climate. Increased air pollution may cause temperatures around the world to increase. This pattern of increased temperature is called global warming.

Global warming could cause the polar ice caps to melt. Sea levels might rise as much as 60 m. New York City would be almost covered with water. Only the tops of very tall buildings would be above the water.

 PREDICT: What would New York City look like if the ice caps melted?

✓ CHECKING CONCEPTS

1. What factor affects local climates the most?

2. Is the average temperature in a city lower or higher than that of surrounding areas? Why?

3. Can air pollution affect the amount of rainfall in an area? Explain.

4. What is global warming?

💡 THINKING CRITICALLY

5. HYPOTHESIZE: Chicago is located in the north central United States. It is on one of the Great Lakes. How does this location affect the local climate?

6. INFER: Would you expect a city or its suburbs to get more snow? Explain.

Web InfoSearch

The Greenhouse Effect Earth's surface is surrounded by gases. Some of these gases trap heat from the Sun. Without these so-called greenhouse gases, Earth would be much colder. The warming that occurs is known as the greenhouse effect.

In the last few centuries, people have been burning wood, coal, oil, and gasoline for fuel. This has released huge amounts of carbon dioxide into the atmosphere. Carbon dioxide is a greenhouse gas. The burning of wood and fossil fuels is thought to be a major cause of global warming.

SEARCH: Use the Internet to find out more about the greenhouse effect. Will Earth continue to warm up? If so, what changes could occur? Start your search at www.conceptsandchallenges.com. Some key search words are **greenhouse effect, carbon dioxide, greenhouse gases,** and **global warming.**

 How Do They Know That?

LONG-TERM CLIMATE TRENDS

Changes in the surface temperatures of ocean water can cause long-term changes in climate. These changes could explain sudden climate shifts, such as the Little Ice Age. The Little Ice Age was a cold period from about 1450 to 1850 that included many harsh winters in Europe.

Climate changes may occur because ocean water is always on the move. Scientists see the ocean as a kind of giant conveyor belt that moves and mixes water in a never-ending cycle around the globe.

Cold, salty water sinks into the deep ocean in the North Atlantic. The water flows south and then east around southern Africa. There, the water rises again to the surface. This water is then warmed in the Indian and Pacific oceans. Surface currents carry the warmed water back through the Pacific and South Atlantic oceans. The round trip takes between 500 and 2,000 years.

Thinking Critically How can ocean currents affect climate?

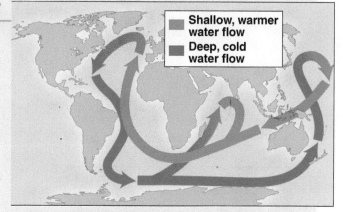

▲ **Figure 13-13** Ocean water makes a never-ending round-trip journey around the world.

LAB ACTIVITY
Investigating How Land Surface Affects Air Temperature

Materials

Safety goggles
Lab apron, gloves.
3 Paper or foam plates
3 Thermometers
Aluminum foil
Dark rock or pieces of asphalt
Grass sod
Light-colored sand

BACKGROUND

Year round, cities are warmer than suburbs and rural areas. When land is cleared of trees to make way for roads, buildings, and parking lots, the local climate is changed.

PURPOSE

In this activity, you will investigate the relationship between air temperature and land surface.

PROCEDURE

1. Put on goggles. Prepare three plates for your experiment. Cover one plate with grass sod. Cover another plate with dark-colored rock or asphalt. Cover the last plate with light-colored sand.

2. Copy the chart in Figure 13-14.

3. Cover the end, or bulb, of each thermometer with aluminum foil. Take the plates outside and place them in the sunlight. Hold your thermometer 2.5 cm above the middle of each plate. In your chart record the temperatures.

4. Measure and record the temperatures again 5 minutes later.

5. Measure and record the temperatures after 10 minutes.

▲ **STEP 1** Pour sand into one plate.

▲ **STEP 3** Use foil to cover your thermometer bulbs.

6. Measure and record the temperatures after 15 minutes.

7. Take your plates out of the sunlight, so that they can start to cool. In your chart, below the first group of numbers, record the temperatures after 5, 10, and 15 minutes for each plate.

STEP 7 ▶
Take the temperatures above the three plates as they cool.

Air Temperature and Land Surfaces			
Time Outdoors	Temperature above dark surface	Temperature above grassy surface	Temperature above light surface
0 minutes			
5 minutes			
10 minutes			
15 minutes			
Cooling Times			
0 minutes			
5 minutes			
10 minutes			
15 minutes			

▲ **Figure 13-14** Use a copy of this chart to record the temperatures.

CONCLUSIONS

1. OBSERVE: Which plate had the highest temperature?

2. OBSERVE: Which plate had the lowest temperature? Which cooled fastest? Which stayed warmer the longest?

3. INFER: Why was there a difference?

4. ANALYZE: How could cities be changed to make them cooler?

How does climate affect living things?

Biomes A large region with a characteristic climate and certain kinds of living things is called a **biome.** Scientists identify a biome mainly by the major types of plants growing in the area. Because many animals eat only certain kinds of plants, each biome also has a particular group of animals and other organisms living there.

▶ **IDENTIFY:** How do scientists identify a biome?

Climate and Vegetation Climate affects the vegetation in an area. **Vegetation** refers to the plants in an area. Rainfall and temperature are the climate factors that most affect vegetation.

Some kinds of plants need a lot of water. For example, many species of trees grow only in tropical rainy climates. Some plants grow where there is very little water. Cacti are an example. They grow in desert climates.

Many plants cannot survive very cold temperatures. Live oak trees, for example, may be killed by frost. Orange trees need both rainfall and warm temperatures to grow well.

▶ **DEFINE:** What is vegetation?

Climate and Animals

Animals that eat certain plants can live only in climates where those plants grow. For example, eucalyptus leaves are the main food of koalas. Koalas live only in areas where eucalyptus trees can grow.

▲ **Figure 13-16** Koalas eat mainly eucalyptus leaves.

Figure 13-15 ▶
Major land biomes found on Earth

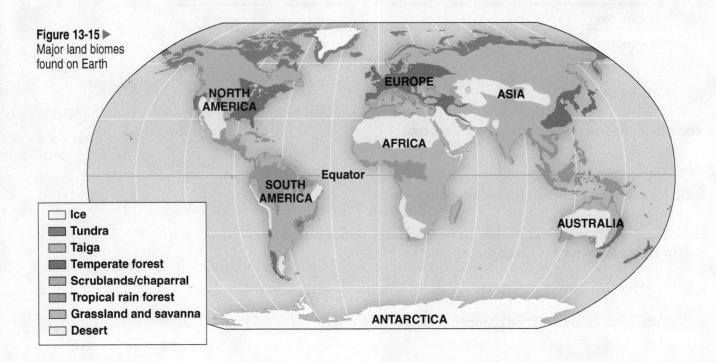

- ☐ Ice
- ☐ Tundra
- ☐ Taiga
- ☐ Temperate forest
- ☐ Scrublands/chaparral
- ☐ Tropical rain forest
- ☐ Grassland and savanna
- ☐ Desert

NORTH AMERICA
EUROPE
ASIA
AFRICA
Equator
SOUTH AMERICA
AUSTRALIA
ANTARCTICA

Other animals are directly affected by temperature. The body temperature of cold-blooded animals is about the same as the air temperature. The animals would die if the air temperature were too low. Most snakes, for example, live in warm climates. They could not survive in a cold climate.

 NAME: What are two ways animals are affected by climate?

✓ CHECKING CONCEPTS

1. What is a biome?
2. How are scientists able to identify different biomes?
3. What are all the plants in a biome called?
4. What are two climate factors that can affect vegetation?
5. What kind of climate do most species of snakes live in?

 THINKING CRITICALLY

6. **INFER:** Giant pandas are bearlike animals. They eat only bamboo shoots. Bamboo grows only in China and Tibet. Where do you think giant pandas live? Explain.
7. **HYPOTHESIZE:** There is a forest biome in the northern United States that is called the spruce-moose belt. How might this area have received this name?

INTERPRETING VISUALS

Use Figure 13-15 to answer the following questions.

8. **IDENTIFY:** Which type of biome covers the most land area?
9. **ANALYZE:** Which type of biome has hot and wet weather?
10. **INFER:** Which type of biome has hot and dry weather?

 Integrating Environmental Science

TOPICS: natural resources, ecosystems

TROPICAL RAIN FORESTS

Tropical rain forests are very dense areas of vegetation. They have hot, humid climates. Many different kinds of animals and plants live in rain forests. Scientists estimate that in 10 square km, there may be more than 750 different species of trees and more than 1,000 different species of animals.

Many rain-forest plants are natural resources for medicines and other products. Some rain-forest animals are found nowhere else. Scientists are concerned because the rain forests are being cut down, burned, and used for farming and development. Once the nutrients in the soil are gone, farmers move to a new area. Many countries are trying to stop the destruction of the rain forests. They also hope to save some species that are in danger of extinction.

▲ **Figure 13-17** Tropical orchids produce the flavoring of vanilla from vanilla beans. The beans (right) are found in rain forests from Florida to South America.

Thinking Critically What are some ways governments can help stop the rain forests from being destroyed?

THE Big IDEA

How do organisms adapt to climate?

In nature, you would never see a palm tree and a cactus plant growing in the same location. Each type of plant is suited to a particular climate. A palm tree grows best in a warm, moist, tropical climate. A cactus grows best in a hot, dry, desert climate. A palm tree could not survive in the Arctic. A cactus could not survive in a tropical location.

Most living things have adaptations that help them survive in their climate zone. Adaptations are features that let an organism live and reproduce in its environment.

Look at the map and photographs that appear on these two pages. Then, follow the directions in the Science Log to learn more about "the big idea."✦

Bighorn Sheep
Bighorns are wild sheep found only in North America. Their feet are adapted to gripping slippery surfaces. This helps them leap across mountain ledges.

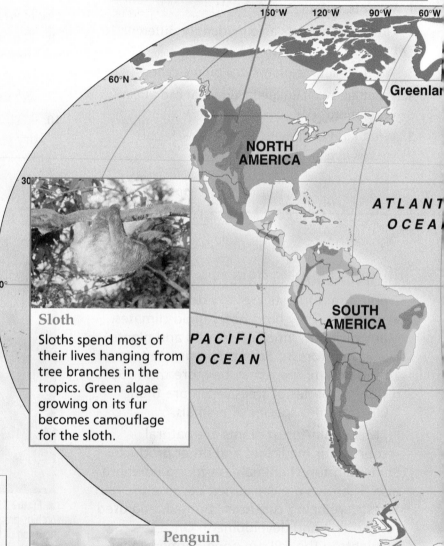

Greenla

NORTH AMERICA

ATLANT OCEA

Sloth
Sloths spend most of their lives hanging from tree branches in the tropics. Green algae growing on its fur becomes camouflage for the sloth.

PACIFIC OCEAN

SOUTH AMERICA

TROPICAL RAINY	TEMPERATE CONTINENTAL
▢ Tropical wet	▢ Humid continental
▢ Tropical wet-and-dry	▢ Subarctic
DRY	**POLAR**
▢ Semiarid	▢ Tundra
▢ Arid	▢ Ice cap
TEMPERATE MARINE	**HIGHLANDS**
▢ Mediterranean	▢ Highlands
▢ Humid subtropical	
▢ Marine west coast	

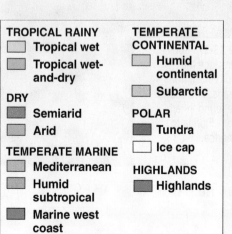

Penguin
Unlike other birds, penguins cannot fly. Their winglike flippers are well suited to their watery life. Thick layers of body fat help them survive in the cold polar regions.

▲ **Figure 13-18**
Each type of living thing has adaptations suited for life in its particular climate zone.

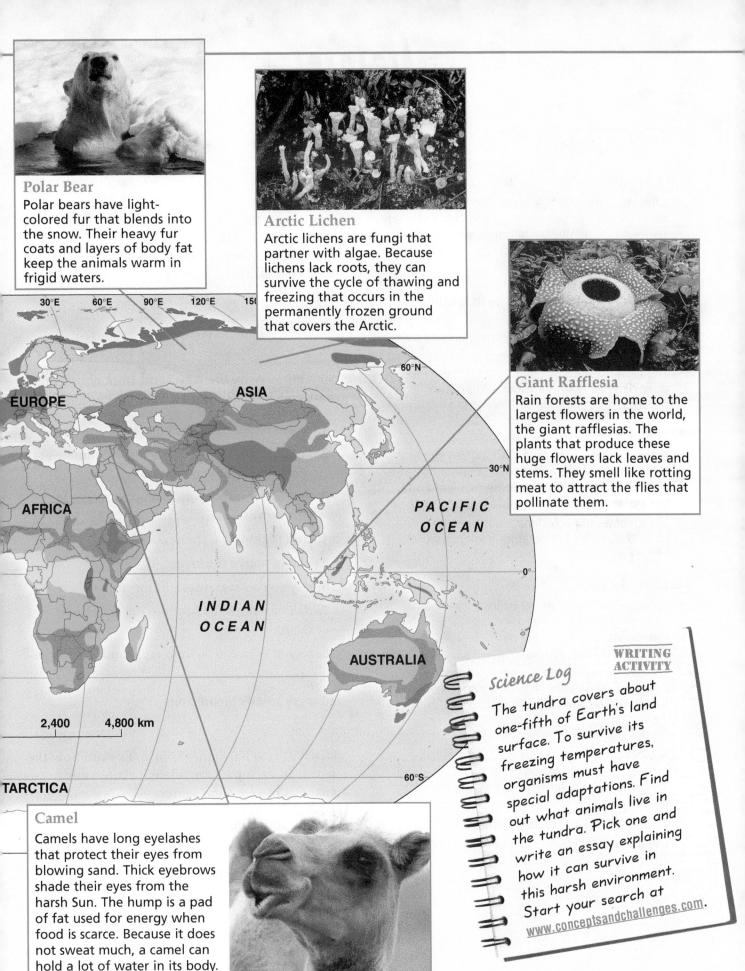

Polar Bear
Polar bears have light-colored fur that blends into the snow. Their heavy fur coats and layers of body fat keep the animals warm in frigid waters.

Arctic Lichen
Arctic lichens are fungi that partner with algae. Because lichens lack roots, they can survive the cycle of thawing and freezing that occurs in the permanently frozen ground that covers the Arctic.

Giant Rafflesia
Rain forests are home to the largest flowers in the world, the giant rafflesias. The plants that produce these huge flowers lack leaves and stems. They smell like rotting meat to attract the flies that pollinate them.

Camel
Camels have long eyelashes that protect their eyes from blowing sand. Thick eyebrows shade their eyes from the harsh Sun. The hump is a pad of fat used for energy when food is scarce. Because it does not sweat much, a camel can hold a lot of water in its body.

EUROPE
ASIA
AFRICA
PACIFIC OCEAN
INDIAN OCEAN
AUSTRALIA
TARCTICA

30°E 60°E 90°E 120°E 150°
60°N
30°N
0°
60°S

2,400 4,800 km

WRITING ACTIVITY

Science Log
The tundra covers about one-fifth of Earth's land surface. To survive its freezing temperatures, organisms must have special adaptations. Find out what animals live in the tundra. Pick one and write an essay explaining how it can survive in this harsh environment. Start your search at www.conceptsandchallenges.com.

Chapter 13 Challenges

Chapter Summary

Lesson 13-1

- **Climate** is the average weather conditions in an area from year to year. Average monthly and yearly temperature, temperature range, and average precipitation are used to describe climate.

Lesson 13-2

- An area's climate is affected by its **latitude** and **altitude.**
- Ocean currents affect the temperatures of areas along coasts.
- The leeward sides of mountains have warmer, drier climates than the windward sides of mountains do.

Lesson 13-3

- A climate zone is an area with a given yearly temperature range and regular weather patterns. The three climate zones are the **tropical zone,** the **polar zone,** and the **middle-latitude zone.**
- The climates in each climate zone can be characterized by temperature and amount of rainfall.

Lesson 13-4

- Local climates are formed by local conditions. Very small climate zones are called **microclimates.** Cities are microclimates.
- Human activities and skyscrapers can affect the climate in an area. Global warming due to increased air pollution could cause temperatures to rise around the world.

Lesson 13-5

- A **biome** is a large region of Earth that has a characteristic climate and certain kinds of living things. It is characterized by the plant life found there.
- Climate affects the **vegetation** in an area.
- The animals and other organisms in an area are affected by climate.

Key Term Challenges

altitude (p. 310)
biome (p. 318)
climate (p. 308)
latitude (p. 310)
microclimate (p. 314)
middle-latitude zone (p. 312)
polar zone (p. 312)
tropical zone (p. 312)
vegetation (p. 318)
weather (p. 308)

MATCHING **Write the Key Term from above that best matches each description.**

1. warm region near the equator
2. large region with a characteristic climate and plant and animal communities
3. average weather conditions in an area from year to year
4. cold region near the poles
5. height above sea level
6. day-to-day conditions of the atmosphere
7. distance north or south of the equator in degrees
8. region between 30° and 60°N and S latitudes
9. plants
10. very small climate zone

IDENTIFYING WORD RELATIONSHIPS **Explain how the words in each pair are related. Write your answers in complete sentences.**

11. altitude, latitude
12. biome, vegetation
13. climate, weather
14. microclimate, local climate
15. tropical zone, middle-latitude zone

Content Challenges TEST PREP

FILL IN Write the term or phrase that best completes each statement.

1. To find average temperature, you add two or more temperatures and divide the sum by the number of _____.

2. The amount of temperature change in an area is its temperature _____.

3. Rain, snow, sleet, and hail are forms of _____.

4. At higher latitudes, the Sun's rays strike Earth _____.

5. Areas at low latitudes have a _____ climate than areas at higher latitudes do.

6. Air is _____ at sea level than it is at higher altitudes.

7. Land areas near cold-water currents have _____ temperatures than land areas near warm-water currents do.

8. When air passes over a mountain range, it rises and _____.

9. It hardly ever rains on the _____ side of a mountain.

10. The leeward side of a mountain is the side of the mountain that faces _____ the wind.

11. The tropical zone is located between _____ north and south latitude.

12. Some scientists think that _____ will lead to global warming.

13. Energy from the _____ is the biggest factor influencing weather and climate.

14. Biomes are identified mainly by the type of _____ found in the area.

15. The type of vegetation found in an area depends on the area's _____.

TRUE/FALSE Write *true* if the statement is true. If the statement is false, change the underlined term to make the statement true.

16. The day-to-day condition of the atmosphere is called the <u>climate</u>.

17. The leeward side of a mountain gets <u>more</u> rain than the windward side.

18. <u>Dry</u> climates are also described as arid.

19. Antarctica is located in the <u>tropical</u> zone.

20. A city is an example of a <u>microclimate</u>.

21. Latitude, ocean currents, and mountains affect an area's <u>climate</u>.

22. Climate has <u>never</u> changed during Earth's history.

23. Each <u>biome</u> has certain kinds of plants and animals.

24. Most snakes live in <u>cool</u> climates.

25. Cacti grow best in <u>tundra</u> climates.

26. Average <u>daily</u> temperature and temperature range are both used to describe the climate of an area.

27. The temperature gets <u>colder</u> as you climb a mountain.

28. Global warming might cause sea levels to <u>fall</u>.

29. A rain shadow desert is sometimes found on the <u>windward</u> side of a mountain.

30. The <u>tilt</u> of Earth directly influences climate and weather.

Concept Challenges

WRITTEN RESPONSE **Answer the following questions in complete sentences.**

1. PREDICT: What kind of climate would a coastal town located near a cold-water current have?

2. INFER: Why are many deserts located on the leeward sides of mountains?

3. INFER: If Earth had no tilt, how would this affect the world's climates?

4. EXPLAIN: How do the types of objects found in a city help to create a microclimate?

5. INFER: Why would vegetation affect the types of animals that can live in a biome?

6. INFER: Why is having a stem that stores water an important adaptation for a cactus?

INTERPRETING VISUALS **Use Figure 13-19 below to answer the following questions.**

7. Which biome is found most often along the equator?

8. Which biome covers most of Australia?

9. What are the biomes found in North America?

10. Where is polar ice found? Why?

11. Which continent has the most biomes? What are they?

12. Which biome do you live in? What are some common plants and animals that are found in this biome?

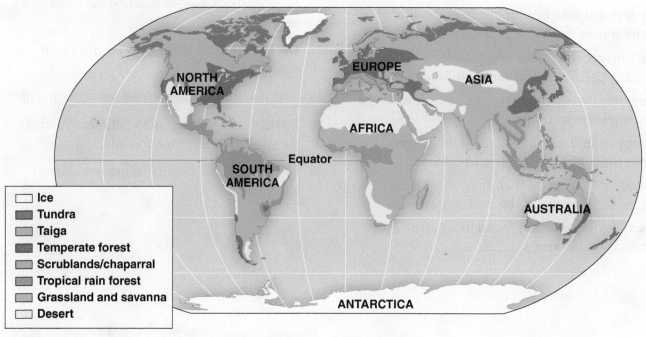

▲ Figure 13-19

Chapter 14 The Motions of Earth, the Sun, and the Moon

▲ **Figure 14-1** Sunsets are enjoyed for their many colors.

The passing of a single day can be seen by watching the Sun in the sky. The Sun appears each morning in the east. This is sunrise. During the daytime, the Sun appears to move westward across the sky. Finally, at sunset, it disappears below the western horizon. This is what we call a day. A few hours later, the Sun seems to rise again in the east to begin a new day. However, the Sun never actually rises or sets. It is just an illusion.

▶ How do you think the motions of Earth makes it seem as if the Sun is moving across the sky?

Contents

14-1 What are the motions of Earth?

INVESTIGATE

Modeling Day and Night
HANDS-ON ACTIVITY

STEP 3

1. Push a wooden stick through a plastic foam ball. Mark a line of dots around the ball.
2. Place the stick upright in modeling clay. Tilt it at about a third of the distance to the desk. Turn on a flashlight or desk lamp and darken the room.
3. Point the angled stick toward the light source. Rotate it and observe.
4. Move the ball so the stick points away from the light source and observe.

THINK ABOUT IT: What happens to the light when it hits the ball? What do you observe when you rotate the ball on its stick?

Objective
Explain Earth's motions.

Key Terms
revolution (rehv-uh-LOO-shuhn): movement of a planet or other body orbiting another body

axis (AK-sihs): imaginary line through the center of a planet or other body around which that body spins

rotation (roh-TAY-shuhn): spinning of a planet or other body on its axis

Revolution Although you cannot feel it, Earth is always moving. It moves in an orbit around the Sun. This movement is called **revolution.** One complete revolution around the Sun takes 365¼ days, or one year. Earth's path as it goes around the Sun is called its orbit. As Earth travels around the Sun, Earth's orbit forms a slightly flattened circle, or oval, shape.

▶ DESCRIBE: What is the motion of Earth around the Sun called?

Rotation Besides revolving, Earth also spins on its axis. An **axis** is an imaginary line through the center of a planet or other body around which that body spins. Earth's axis is tilted at an angle of 23½ degrees relative to an imaginary line drawn perpendicular to its orbit. The North Pole of Earth always points toward Polaris, the North Star.

The spinning of a planet or other body on its axis is called **rotation.** Our planet rotates once every 24 hours. This gives us a daily cycle of daylight and darkness, or day and night. The side of Earth's surface that faces the Sun has daylight. The side that faces away from the Sun has darkness. At any moment, half of Earth is experiencing daylight. The other half is experiencing darkness.

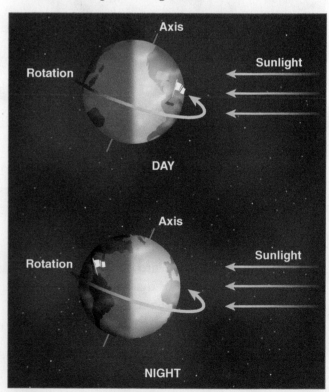

▲ **Figure 14-2** Earth rotating on its axis causes day and night.

▶ IDENTIFY: What is the motion of Earth on its axis called?

Sunrise and Sunset When viewed from above the North Pole, Earth rotates on its axis from west to east. This makes the Sun appear to rise in the east and set in the west. As Earth rotates, the Sun seems to move across the sky from east to west. This is called the Sun's apparent motion.

 RELATE: In which direction does Earth rotate?

 CHECKING CONCEPTS

1. How long does Earth take to make one complete revolution around the Sun?
2. What causes the change from day to night?
3. Why does the Sun appear to rise in the east?
4. At what angle is Earth's axis tilted?

THINKING CRITICALLY

5. **CONTRAST:** How is rotation different from revolution?
6. **DESCRIBE:** What is the shape of Earth's orbit?

7. **PREDICT:** What would happen if Earth did not rotate?
8. **INFER:** Like the Sun, the Moon seems to rise in the east and set in the west. Why?

Web InfoSearch

The 24-Hour Day Since ancient times, people have had an interest in measuring and recording the passage of time. The ancient Egyptians were the first to use a 24-hour day. Their system was based on observing a series of 36 stars called decan stars. The decan stars rise and set in the sky every 40 to 60 minutes.

SEARCH: Use the Internet to find out more about decan stars. What are they? How did they lead the Egyptians to create the 24-hour day? Start your search at **www.conceptsandchallenges.com**. Some key search words are **decan stars**, **Egyptian astronomy**, and **ancient calendars**.

 How Do They Know That?

EARTH ROTATES ON ITS AXIS

A pendulum is a weight that swings freely back and forth. It can be used to show that Earth rotates.

French physicist Jean Bernard Leon Foucault (1819–1868) provided proof of Earth's rotation with a pendulum. Using an early camera, he photographed the Sun. The camera took pictures on a light-sensitive plate. Leaving the camera focused on the Sun for some time, Foucault showed that the Sun's position relative to Earth changed. He invented a pendulum-driven device to keep the camera in line with the Sun. However, he noticed that his pendulum tended to swing in the direction from which it was first released. If he tried to turn it, it always returned to its original path. From this experiment, he concluded that Earth was rotating.

▲ **Figure 14-3** Foucault's pendulum

Foucault set up a demonstration to prove his conclusion. He released a giant ball over a pile of sand. The ball scratched a straight line in the sand. Over the course of the day, that line shifted again and again to the right. Eventually, it came full circle.

Thinking Critically What did it mean that the pendulum was not changing course?

14-2 What are time zones?

Objectives

Use standard time zones to compare times around the world. Identify eight U.S. time zones.

Key Terms

solar noon: time of day when the Sun is highest in the sky

standard time: system whereby all places within a time zone all have the same time

International Date Line: boundary formed where the first and 24th time zones meet

Solar Time The Sun can be used to tell time. Using the Sun to measure time is called solar time. When the Sun is highest in the sky, the time is **solar noon.** Because Earth rotates, different places have solar noon at different times. For example, when it is solar noon in Philadelphia, it is 4 minutes after solar noon in New York and 17 minutes after solar noon in Boston.

> **1** HYPOTHESIZE: What problem is likely to arise using solar time?

Standard Time Even though clocks allowed people to keep track of time, there was still a problem. Each region set its own time, and there was no way to coordinate among regions. This problem grew when railroads were built and people traveled more. A system was needed on which to base a train schedule. This system would also help travelers schedule meetings in other towns.

In 1884, an international agreement was reached that divided Earth's surface into 24 time zones. Each of these time zones was to be 15 degrees of longitude wide. All places within a time zone would have the same time. This time was called **standard time.**

> **2** DESCRIBE: What is standard time?

U.S. Time Zones The United States has eight time zones. These are Eastern Standard, Central Standard, Mountain Standard, Pacific Standard, Alaska Standard, Hawaiian Standard, Samoa Standard, and Atlantic Standard.

As you move west, the time in each zone is one hour earlier than in the previous time zone. As a result, when it is noon in New York, it is 11:00 A.M. in Chicago.

Look at Figure 14-4. Notice that time zones do not have straight boundaries. The boundaries were drawn this way to keep whole states or large neighboring cities in the same time zone.

> **3** CALCULATE: If it is 12:00 noon in California, what time is it in Virginia?

World Time Zones There are 24 standard time zones and 24 hours in a day. The first time zone is on one side of the boundary called the **International Date Line.** The twenty-fourth time zone is on the other side. As you cross over the International Date Line, you either gain or lose 24 hours. If you were to travel west, you would have to move your calendar ahead one full day when you crossed the International Date Line.

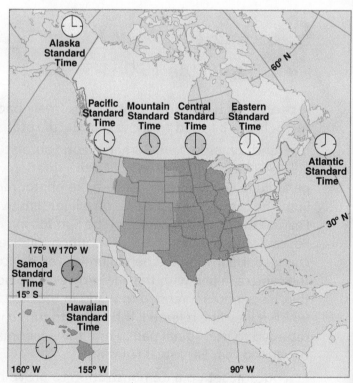

▲ **Figure 14-4** Time zones of the United States

> **4** INFER: What happens to the date if you cross the International Date Line going east?

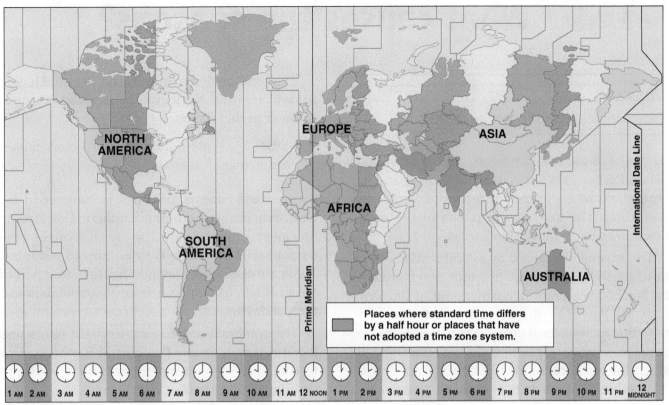

▲ **Figure 14-5** Time zones around the world

✔ CHECKING CONCEPTS

1. There are _____ time zones in the world.

2. Using the Sun to measure time is _____.

3. The 48 states in the continental United States have _____ time zones.

4. If you cross the International Date Line going east, you would _____ 24 hours.

5. As you travel west, you move the clock _____ one hour for each time zone.

💡 THINKING CRITICALLY

Use Figures 14-4, 14-5, and Appendix B in this book to help you answer the following questions.

6. IDENTIFY: In which time zone is Texas located?

7. ANALYZE: If it is 3:00 P.M. in Florida, what time is it in Oregon?

8. CALCULATE: Suppose you leave California at 12:00 noon Pacific Standard Time and take a six-hour plane trip to Boston. When you land in Boston, what would the time be there?

9. IDENTIFY: In which time zone do you live?

10. ANALYZE: Earth rotates from west to east. Would a town to your west have solar noon before or after you? Explain.

Web InfoSearch

Jet Lag *Jet lag* is a term given to the tired feeling people get when they travel across three or more time zones. Jet lag occurs because your body is adjusted to the time zone where you live and not adjusted to the time zone to which you have just traveled. It is easier for your body to adjust to a longer day traveling west than to a shorter day traveling east. For this reason, jet lag usually affects people who are flying east more than it affects people who are flying west.

SEARCH: Use the Internet to find out more about jet lag. How does it affect choice of flying times? What methods are there for overcoming the effects of jet lag? Start your search at www.conceptsandchallenges.com. Some key search words are **time zone, jet lag,** and **avoiding jet lag.**

What causes the seasons?

Objective

Explain what causes the change of seasons.

Why the Seasons Change As you learned earlier, Earth's axis is tilted at 23 1/2 degrees. The North Pole of Earth points toward Polaris, the North Star. The axis always points in the same direction as Earth moves in its orbit.

The seasons are caused by a combination of the tilt of Earth's axis and Earth's movement around the Sun. At one point in Earth's orbit of the Sun, the North Pole of Earth is tilted toward the Sun. Six months later, the North Pole is tilted away from the Sun. This change in position changes the angle at which the Sun's rays strike Earth's surface and is responsible for the change of seasons.

When the North Pole is tilted toward the Sun, the Northern Hemisphere receives the Sun's rays almost directly. The more direct the rays are, the better that part of Earth's surface is heated.

The tilt of Earth's axis also causes the total number of daylight hours to change. When the North Pole is tilted toward the Sun, the Northern Hemisphere has more hours of daylight than it does of darkness.

The combination of more direct rays and longer days warms the Northern Hemisphere. It causes summer in that region.

▶ **DESCRIBE:** What combination of factors causes the change of seasons?

Opposite Seasons When it is summer in the Northern Hemisphere, the Southern Hemisphere tilts away from the Sun. The rays it receives from the Sun are less direct. They are spread out more. There are also fewer daylight hours in that part of the world. In fact, there are more hours of darkness than of daylight.

The combination of fewer daylight hours and less direct rays causes that part of Earth's surface to cool. The lower temperatures cause winter in that part of the world.

The Northern and Southern hemispheres have opposite seasons. Look at Figure 14-6. Notice that when the Northern Hemisphere is tilted away from the Sun, it has winter.

At the same time it is winter in the Northern Hemisphere, the Southern Hemisphere is tilted toward the Sun and has summer. When summer comes to the Northern Hemisphere, it is winter in the Southern Hemisphere.

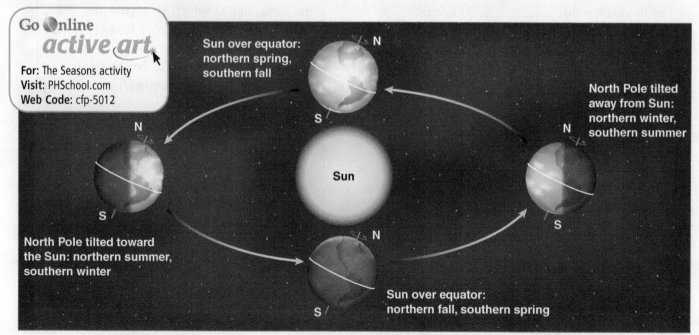

Go **Online**
active art

For: The Seasons activity
Visit: PHSchool.com
Web Code: cfp-5012

Sun over equator: northern spring, southern fall

North Pole tilted away from Sun: northern winter, southern summer

Sun

North Pole tilted toward the Sun: northern summer, southern winter

Sun over equator: northern fall, southern spring

▲ **Figure 14-6** The seasons are caused by Earth's tilt and its revolution around the Sun.

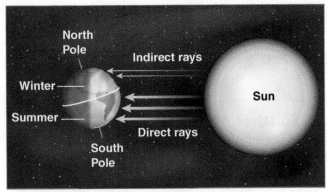

▲ **Figure 14-7** December in New York City

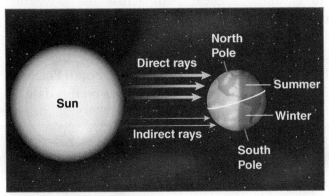

▲ **Figure 14-8** June in Australia

 IDENTIFY: If it is summer in the Northern Hemisphere, what season is it in the Southern Hemisphere?

☑ CHECKING CONCEPTS

1. The North Pole points _____ the Sun during the summer in the Northern Hemisphere.
2. Seasons are caused by the _____ of Earth's axis.

💡 THINKING CRITICALLY

3. **ANALYZE:** If it is summer at the North Pole, what season is it at the South Pole?
4. **INFER:** Why do you think direct sunlight produces more heat than indirect sunlight?

BUILDING MATH SKILLS

Measuring Light from the Sun strikes Earth's surface at different angles. Angles are measured in degrees. A full circle has 360 degrees. When the Sun is directly overhead, near the equator, it is at an angle of 90 degrees to Earth's surface. A 90 degree angle is called a right angle. It is one-fourth of a circle. When the Sun is near the horizon, it is at an angle of 0 degrees to Earth's surface. Earth's axis is tilted at an angle of 23½ degrees. About what fraction of a right angle is this?

🌍 *Hands-On Activity*

MODELING DIRECT AND INDIRECT RAYS

You will need a flashlight and graph paper.

1. Hold a flashlight about 20 cm above a sheet of graph paper. Shine the flashlight straight down. On the paper, trace around the outer edge of light. Count how many boxes are inside the circle you made. Record the number.
2. Tilt the flashlight, making sure you keep it at the same height. Again, trace around the edge of the light. Count the number of boxes inside this. Record the number.

▲ **STEP 2** Again trace around the outline of light made by the flashlight.

Practicing Your Skills

3. **OBSERVE: a.** Which light rays were spread out over a larger area, the direct rays or the slanted rays? **b.** Which rays were brighter, the direct rays or the slanted rays?
4. **HYPOTHESIZE:** Which rays do you think heat better, direct rays or slanted rays?
5. **CONCLUDE:** When do you think Earth's surface in the Northern Hemisphere gets the more direct rays of the Sun, in the summer or in the winter? Explain.

14-4 What are the solstices and equinoxes?

Objective
Define solstice and equinox.

Key Terms
perihelion (per-uh-HEE-lee-uhn)**:** point in a planet's orbit at which it is closest to the Sun

aphelion (uh-FEE-lee-uhn)**:** point in a planet's orbit at which it is farthest from the Sun

solstice (SAHL-stihs)**:** day of the year the Sun reaches its highest or lowest point in the sky

equinox (EE-kwih-nahks)**:** day the Sun shines directly on the equator

Near and Far During the year, the distance between Earth and the Sun changes. Earth is at **perihelion,** or closest to the Sun, in early January. Earth and the Sun are then about 147 million km apart. The Northern Hemisphere has winter. In early July, Earth is at **aphelion,** or its farthest point from the Sun. This distance is about 152 million km. Yet, this is summer in the Northern Hemisphere. The seasons do not depend on how far Earth is from the Sun.

▶ **1 NAME:** During which season is the Northern Hemisphere closest to the Sun?

The Solstices The beginning of the summer and winter seasons is marked by a day called a solstice. The word **solstice** means "Sun stop."

In the Northern Hemisphere, the first day of summer is on or about June 21. The Sun seems to travel in its highest path across the sky. This day is called the summer solstice. On this day, Earth is very close to aphelion. The North Pole has 24 hours of daylight. At the same time, the South Pole points away from the Sun. The South Pole has 24 hours of darkness. Winter begins on this date in the Southern Hemisphere.

▲ **Figure 14-10** The period of daylight reaches a full 24 hours at the polar zones in summer. This phenomenon is known as the midnight Sun.

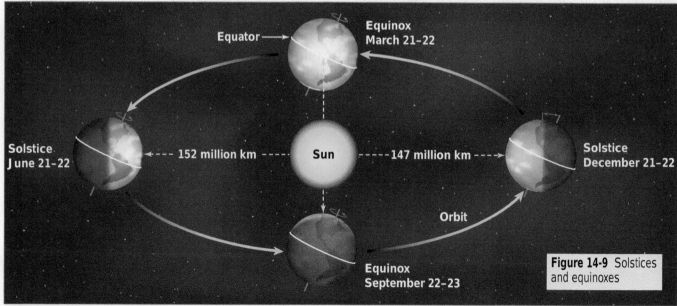

Equator →

Equinox
March 21-22

Solstice
June 21-22

←--- 152 million km ---- **Sun** ----147 million km ---→

Solstice
December 21-22

Orbit

Equinox
September 22-23

Figure 14-9 Solstices and equinoxes

The first day of winter in the Northern Hemisphere is on or about December 21. This day is called the winter solstice. On the winter solstice, Earth is very close to perihelion. The North Pole points away from the Sun. The Sun seems to follow its lowest path across the sky. On this day, the South Pole has 24 hours of daylight.

 IDENTIFY: What day marks the first day of winter in the Southern Hemisphere?

The Equinoxes Because of the tilt of Earth's axis, the Sun's position relative to Earth's equator is constantly changing. Most of the time, the Sun is north or south of the equator at solar noon. Two times during the year, the Sun is directly over the equator at solar noon. These are the **equinoxes.** The equinoxes mark the beginning of the spring and fall seasons. The spring, or vernal, equinox occurs around March 21. The fall, or autumnal, equinox occurs around September 21. During an equinox, there are 12 hours of darkness and 12 hours of daylight everywhere on Earth.

 NAME: On which days of the year does the North Pole have 12 hours of daylight and 12 hours of night?

✓ **CHECKING CONCEPTS**

1. What is a day with 12 hours of daylight and 12 hours of darkness called?

2. What date marks the beginning of winter in the Northern Hemisphere?

3. Are the days longer or shorter in the Northern Hemisphere right after the autumnal equinox?

4. *Equinox* means "equal night." How many hours of daylight and darkness are there during the fall and spring equinoxes?

THINKING CRITICALLY

5. DESCRIBE: What is winter like in your area? Explain why.

6. HYPOTHESIZE: On the winter solstice, the North Pole has 24 hours of darkness. How might this affect your life that day if you lived there?

BUILDING READING SKILLS

Using Prefixes The prefix *equi-* means "equal." Find five words in the dictionary that contain this prefix. Write down these words and their definitions on a sheet of paper. Circle the part of the definition that relates to the prefix.

How Do They Know That?

PREDICTING THE CHANGE OF SEASONS

Ancient peoples made calendars based on astronomical events that occurred the same time each year. Some of these calendars were monuments. One such monument is called Stonehenge.

▲ **Figure 14-11** Stonehenge is a giant calendar that predicts solstices and equinoxes.

Stonehenge stands on a plain in Salisbury, England. It was built around 1848 B.C. The monument is made of huge blocks of sandstone about 8 m high. They form a circle 30 m across. Inside the circle, there are two horseshoe-shaped sets of stones. A flat block of sandstone 5 m long rests inside the inner horseshoe. About 73 m away from the flat sandstone block is a stone marker.

Stonehenge is a giant calendar that can predict the change of seasons. It can also predict the solstices and equinoxes. A shadow is cast by the stone marker onto the flat sandstone block. This marks the direction in which the Sun rises and sets on the longest day of the year, the summer solstice.

Thinking Critically What might ancient peoples have needed calendars for?

THE Big IDEA

How does the change of seasons affect animal behavior?

Does the weather in your town change with the seasons? If so, you probably respond to this by wearing different clothing and participating in different activities. Animals respond to environmental changes, too. Some shed thick coats to prepare for warm summer weather. Others store food to prepare for the time cold weather makes food scarce. Animals that migrate take more drastic actions. They leave their homes and travel thousands of miles in search of better living conditions for the season. Many breed in their winter homes.

California gray whales are migratory animals. During the summer and early fall, the whales live in the cold waters of the Chukchi and Bering seas. In late fall, they migrate southward. They travel more than 8,000 km to the calm, warm waters of Baja California, in Mexico. In the shallow waters of their winter home, the whales breed and produce young. In the late spring, they return to their Arctic summer home.

Monarch butterflies migrate in the same general direction as California gray whales. The butterflies spend the summer in the northern United States. In the fall, they migrate to the California coast, Mexico, and Florida.

Of all migrating animals, Arctic terns travel the greatest distance. These birds spend the summer breeding in northern Canada. In the fall, they travel more than 17,600 km southward to their Antarctic winter home. The arrival of spring triggers a return trip northward.

Look at the illustrations and photos that appear on these two pages. Then, follow the directions in the Science Log to find out more about "the big idea." ◆

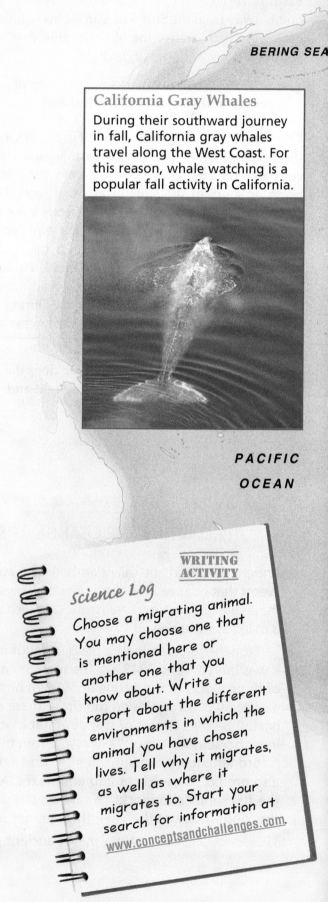

BERING SEA

California Gray Whales
During their southward journey in fall, California gray whales travel along the West Coast. For this reason, whale watching is a popular fall activity in California.

PACIFIC OCEAN

WRITING ACTIVITY

Science Log

Choose a migrating animal. You may choose one that is mentioned here or another one that you know about. Write a report about the different environments in which the animal you have chosen lives. Tell why it migrates, as well as where it migrates to. Start your search for information at www.conceptsandchallenges.com.

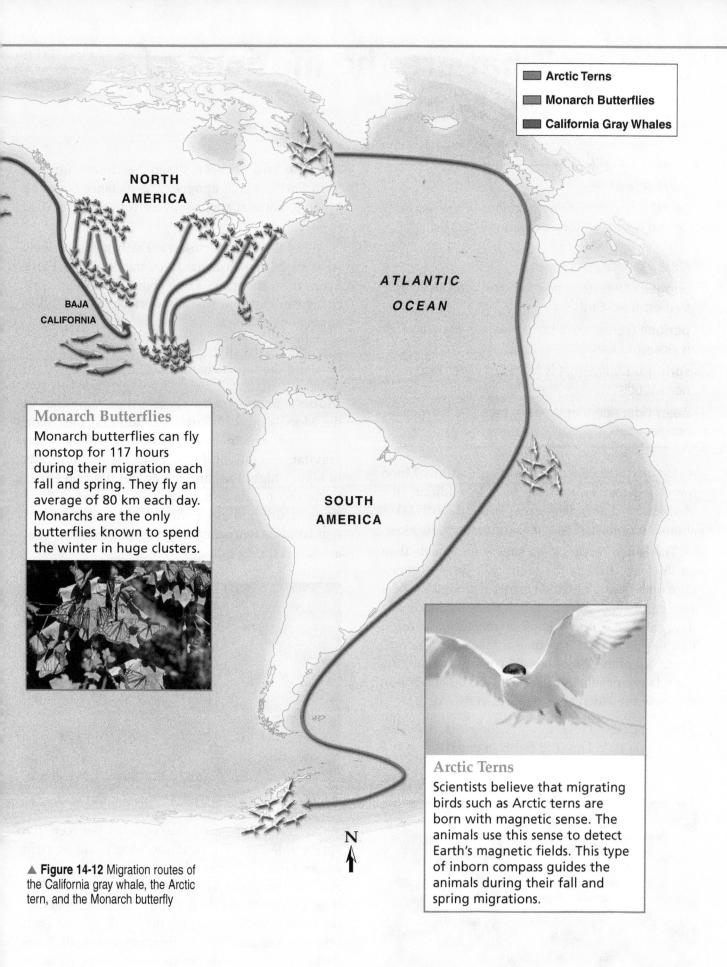

Arctic Terns

Monarch Butterflies

California Gray Whales

NORTH AMERICA

BAJA CALIFORNIA

ATLANTIC OCEAN

SOUTH AMERICA

Monarch Butterflies

Monarch butterflies can fly nonstop for 117 hours during their migration each fall and spring. They fly an average of 80 km each day. Monarchs are the only butterflies known to spend the winter in huge clusters.

Arctic Terns

Scientists believe that migrating birds such as Arctic terns are born with magnetic sense. The animals use this sense to detect Earth's magnetic fields. This type of inborn compass guides the animals during their fall and spring migrations.

N

▲ **Figure 14-12** Migration routes of the California gray whale, the Arctic tern, and the Monarch butterfly

14-5 What are the motions of the Moon?

Objectives
Describe and identify two motions of the Moon. Explain how the Moon's motions affect the tides.

Key Terms
apogee (AP-uh-jee): point at which the Moon is farthest from Earth

perigee (PER-uh-jee): point at which the Moon is closest to Earth

spring tide: tide that is higher or lower than a normal tide

neap tide: tide that is not as high or as low as a normal tide

Rotation and Revolution Earth and its Moon travel together around the Sun. In addition, the Moon orbits Earth. Its journey around Earth takes about a month. The Moon also rotates on its axis.

The Moon rotates more slowly on its axis than Earth does. It takes the Moon 27⅓ days to rotate once on its axis. The Moon revolves around Earth at a speed of about 3,500 km/h. It takes the Moon 27⅓ days to make one complete revolution around Earth. This is the same time it takes the Moon to rotate. All of these motions are constantly changing the relative positions of the Sun, Earth, and Moon and how the Moon appears to us in the sky.

 CALCULATE: How many kilometers does the Moon travel around Earth in one day?

▼ **Figure 14-13** The revolution and rotation of the Moon

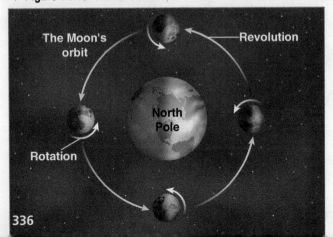

Apogee and Perigee When the Moon is farthest from Earth, it is at **apogee**. The distance from the Moon to Earth at apogee varies from about 404,000 to 407,000 km.

When the Moon is closest to Earth, it is at **perigee**. At perigee, the distance from the Moon to Earth varies from about 350,000 to about 370,000 km. This change in distance has an effect on Earth's tides, among other things.

 INFER: Why do the distances between Earth and the Moon change?

Moon's Gravity and Tides At certain times in the Moon's orbit of Earth, the Sun and the Moon are lined up in their orbits. The combined gravitational pull of the Sun and the Moon results in higher high tides and lower low tides on Earth. Therefore, the daily tidal range is greatest at these times. During these periods, which occur in a regular cycle twice a month, the tides become what are called **spring tides.**

▲ **Figure 14-14** Spring tides

At certain times of the year, in between the spring tides, the Sun and the Moon pull at right angles to each other in relation to Earth. Because the Sun and the Moon pull at right angles to each other, their gravity forces do not combine or act together on Earth's oceans. Instead, they pull against each other. As a result, the daily tidal range is small. Tides that occur during this time are called **neap tides.**

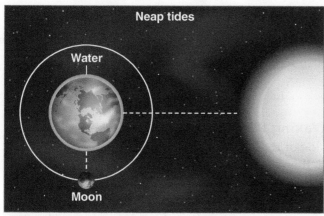
▲ Figure 14-15 Neap tides

1. How long does it take the Moon to make one complete revolution around Earth?

2. What causes the tides?

3. Why does the Moon not always rise at the same time?

 INFER: How often do spring and neap tides occur?

THINKING CRITICALLY

4. EXPLAIN: Why does the Moon appear to rise in the east and set in the west?

5. ANALYZE: How many times does the Moon rotate during one revolution around Earth?

6. CALCULATE: If the Moon rose at 6:45 P.M. on Tuesday, at about what time would it rise on Thursday?

Moonrise Like the Sun, the Moon appears to rise in the east and set in the west. As the Moon revolves around Earth, Earth must go through more than one rotation to "catch up" with the Moon. Earth must rotate 24 hours and 50 minutes to bring the Moon back into view. As a result, the Moon comes into view at moonrise about 50 minutes later each day.

BUILDING READING SKILLS

Using Prefixes The prefix *peri-* means "around," "surrounding," or "close." Perigee is when the Moon is closest to Earth. Using a dictionary, find five other words that contain this prefix. Explain how the prefix relates to the meaning of each word.

 EXPLAIN: Why does the Moon rise about 50 minutes later each day?

 People in Science

ASTRONAUT

The first person to travel in space was a Soviet air force pilot named Yuri Gagarin. His one orbit around Earth in April 1961 took less than two hours. American astronauts first flew in space in the *Mercury* and *Gemini* missions. However, it was the dramatic landing of American *Apollo* astronauts on the Moon in July 1969 that really marked the beginning of a human presence in space.

▲ Figure 14-16 An astronaut collects lunar samples from the Moon's surface.

An astronaut travels and works in space. The word *astronaut* usually refers to a person involved in the American space program. Astronauts help design and test spacecraft and other space equipment. While in space, they operate their spacecraft and analyze any problems that arise. They also carry out experiments in space. Astronauts work for the National Aeronautics and Space Administration, or NASA. Many are also military officers. To be an astronaut, you need a background in mathematics and science. Most astronauts have advanced degrees. Astronauts who are pilots also have many hours of flight experience.

Thinking Critically Which Earth science specialists might want to be astronauts?

14-6 What are the phases of the Moon?

Objective

Identify the different phases of the Moon.

Key Terms

phases (FAYZ-uhz): changing shapes of the Moon

crescent (KREHS-uhnt) **phase:** phase when less than half the Moon is visible

gibbous (GIHB-uhs) **phase:** phase when more than half the Moon is visible

Phases of the Moon From Earth, the Moon sometimes looks round. Other times, it looks like a thin sliver. The Moon appears to change shape because of the way it reflects light from the Sun. The changing shapes of the Moon are called **phases.** These phases depend on the positions of the Sun, the Moon, and Earth.

▶ 1 IDENTIFY: Why does the Moon appear to change shape?

Waxing Phases Look at Figure 14-17. When the side of the Moon facing Earth is dark, it appears as if there is no Moon at all. This is called a new Moon. As the Moon revolves around Earth, a small part of it becomes visible. As the visible part of it increases, the Moon is said to be waxing. The first phase is called the waxing **crescent phase.** During the crescent phase, less than half of the Moon is visible. When the Moon has moved one-quarter of the way around Earth, it enters the first quarter phase. This means that half of the side of the Moon facing Earth is visible.

As the Moon continues in its orbit, more and more of the side facing Earth becomes visible. This is called the waxing **gibbous phase.** During the gibbous phase, more than half of the Moon is visible. Finally, the Moon completes half of its trip around Earth. The whole side facing Earth is visible. This is the full Moon.

▶ 2 DEFINE: What is the Moon's gibbous phase?

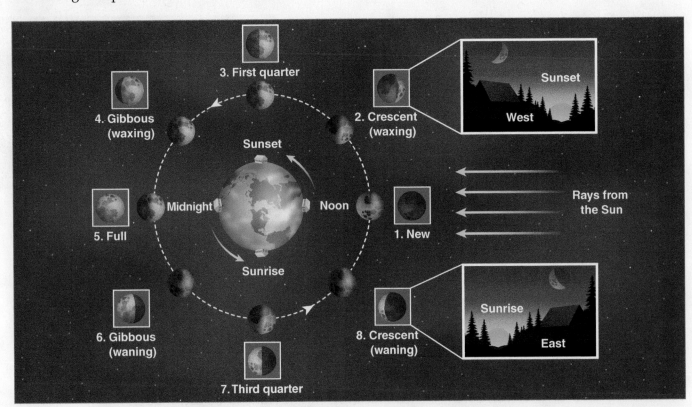

3. First quarter

4. Gibbous (waxing)

2. Crescent (waxing)

Sunset

West

Sunset

Midnight

Noon

Sunrise

Rays from the Sun

5. Full

1. New

6. Gibbous (waning)

8. Crescent (waning)

Sunrise

East

7. Third quarter

▲ **Figure 14-17** The phases of the Moon

Waning Phases As the Moon continues to move around Earth, less and less of the surface becomes visible. The Moon is waning. After the full Moon, the Moon enters the waning gibbous phase. At the last quarter phase, only half of the Moon's surface facing Earth is visible. The last phase of the Moon is the waning crescent phase.

The Moon takes 29½ days to go through all of its phases. This is a little longer than the time for one revolution of the Moon around Earth. The reason for this is that as the Moon orbits Earth, the two bodies are also moving around the Sun. The Moon must travel a little farther to get directly between Earth and the Sun.

 COMPARE: When do the waxing and waning crescent phases of the Moon take place?

☑ CHECKING CONCEPTS

1. The Moon reflects light from the _____.
2. The phases of the Moon depend on the positions of Earth, _____, and the Sun.
3. During the _____ phase of the Moon, half of the side of the Moon facing Earth is visible.

4. When the Moon has finished half of its revolution around Earth, the Moon is called a _____ Moon.
5. The Moon goes through all of its phases in _____ days.

💡 THINKING CRITICALLY

6. **CONTRAST:** How do the crescent phase and the quarter phase of the Moon differ?
7. **PREDICT:** What would the Moon look like if it did not reflect light from the Sun?
8. **SEQUENCE:** List the eight phases of the Moon in order, beginning with the new Moon.

BUILDING SCIENCE SKILLS

Comparing The time period between one full Moon and the next is called a lunar month. On a calendar, identify each of the Moon's phases for the next two months. How does the length of the lunar month compare to the length of the calendar month?

 Integrating Physical Science

TOPICS: radiation, light

HOW THE MOON IS LIT

Light travels in a straight line. Usually, it cannot go through an object. When light strikes an object, it may be totally absorbed, in which case it appears black. If the light is totally or partially reflected, then the object can appear white. Different colors of light might also be partially absorbed, with only some of them being reflected. The object will then appear in the reflected color.

We see the Moon because some of the light from the Sun is reflected off of the Moon rather than absorbed. The Moon appears white in the sky. Unlike stars, the Moon makes no light of its own. If it were not for the Sun, we would not be able to see the Moon. As the Moon revolves around Earth, the Sun's light strikes the Moon at different angles. This makes the Moon appear to change shape as viewed from Earth. We call this feature of the Moon "going through phases."

▲ **Figure 14-18** The crescent phase of the Moon

Thinking Critically Could we see the Moon if it absorbed all of the light instead of reflecting some of it?

LAB ACTIVITY
Modeling the Phases of the Moon

BACKGROUND

Moonshine is actually light from the Sun reflecting off the Moon's surface. When viewed from Earth on different nights throughout the month, the Moon appears to have different shapes. These shapes are called phases.

PURPOSE

In this activity, you will investigate why the Moon has phases.

PROCEDURE

1. Work with a partner in a darkened room. Place the lamp on a shelf or bookcase so that the bulb is about 120 cm above the floor. The bulb represents the Sun, the ball is the Moon, and your head is Earth.

2. Sit facing the lamp and hold the ball level with the bulb, between you and the lamp. Have your partner stand behind you and draw three circles to represent the Sun, Moon, and Earth in this setup.

3. Now have your partner shade in the part of the Moon that is not lighted by the Sun. Label this drawing Position 1.

4. Turn your body and the Moon about 45 degrees to the left. With the Moon in this position, have your partner draw the shape of the lighted part of the Moon that can be seen from Earth. Label this drawing Position 2.

▲ **STEP 2** The ball should be held level with the bulb, between you and the lamp.

▲ **STEP 4** Turn your body and the Moon about 45 degrees to the left.

▲ **STEP 5** Turn your body and the Moon another 45 degrees.

5. Turn your body and the Moon to the left another 45 degrees and repeat Step 4. Label this drawing Position 3.

6. Continue turning the ball in the same direction, 45 degrees at a time, until you come back to your original position. Have your partner draw and label the Moon shape at each position.

7. Copy the chart in Figure 14-19. Using the information from your partner's diagrams, draw each phase of the Moon in its appropriate section in the chart.

Moon's Phases			
New	First quarter	First half	Three-quarters
Full	Three-quarters	Last half	Last quarter

▲ **Figure 14-19** Use a copy of this chart to organize your diagrams.

CONCLUSIONS

1. OBSERVE: In what position is the Moon when it is in its first quarter phase?

2. OBSERVE: What position of the Moon is opposite its new Moon phase?

3. ANALYZE: Why does the Moon have phases?

4. INFER: What happens when the Moon is directly between Earth and the Sun?

14-7 What causes an eclipse of the Moon?

Objectives

Describe a lunar eclipse. Distinguish between a total and a partial lunar eclipse.

Key Terms

umbra (UHM-bruh)**:** center or dark part of a shadow

penumbra (pih-NUHM-bruh)**:** light part of a shadow

lunar eclipse (ih-KLIHPS)**:** passing of the Moon through Earth's shadow

Casting Shadows When you walk outside on a sunny day, you can see your shadow. A shadow is formed when an object blocks a light source. A shadow has two parts. The center of a shadow is very dark. The dark part of a shadow is called the **umbra.** Around the outside of a shadow, you will see a lighter part. The light part of a shadow is called the **penumbra.**

People and objects are not the only things that can cast shadows. Earth, the Moon, and other bodies in space also cast shadows.

▶ IDENTIFY: What are the two parts of a shadow?

Eclipse of the Moon As the Moon revolves around Earth, it usually passes above or below Earth's shadow. Sometimes the Moon passes directly through Earth's shadow. As a result, sunlight is blocked from reaching the Moon. When the sunlight is blocked from the Moon, a **lunar eclipse** occurs. A lunar eclipse can occur only during the full-Moon phase.

▶ DEFINE: What is a lunar eclipse?

Total or Partial Eclipses Sometimes the Moon moves entirely into Earth's umbra. When this happens, all of the Sun's light is blocked. The entire face of the Moon darkens. This is called a total lunar eclipse.

Sometimes, only part of the Moon moves into Earth's umbra. Sunlight can still reach the Moon. As a result, only part of the Moon darkens. This is called a partial lunar eclipse.

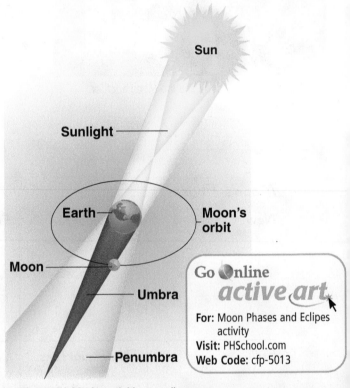

Go Online
active art
For: Moon Phases and Eclipes activity
Visit: PHSchool.com
Web Code: cfp-5013

▲ **Figure 14-20** A partial lunar eclipse

Total lunar eclipses are rare. Also, they do not occur at regular intervals. They may occur as often as six months apart or as much as 2½ years apart.

▲ **Figure 14-21** A partial lunar eclipse

▶ DESCRIBE: How does the Moon look during a total lunar eclipse?

☑ CHECKING CONCEPTS

1. The dark part of a shadow is the _____.

2. A lunar eclipse occurs when Earth is between the _____ and the Moon.

3. A _____ lunar eclipse occurs when part of the Moon is in Earth's umbra.

4. During a _____ lunar eclipse, all of the Moon is dark.

💡 THINKING CRITICALLY

5. HYPOTHESIZE: When would a partial lunar eclipse be difficult to see?

6. INFER: Can a lunar eclipse occur during the quarter-Moon phase? Why or why not?

7. INFER: Can Earth's shadow have only an umbra and not a penumbra? Explain your answer.

INTERPRETING VISUALS

Use Figure 14-22 to answer the following questions.

8. EXPLAIN: The Moon in Figure 14-22 is in a total eclipse. What would happen if the Moon were to move into the penumbra?

9. HYPOTHESIZE: If Earth and the Moon were closer to the Sun, how would the size of the umbra change?

10. EXPLAIN: Why can a lunar eclipse occur only during a full Moon?

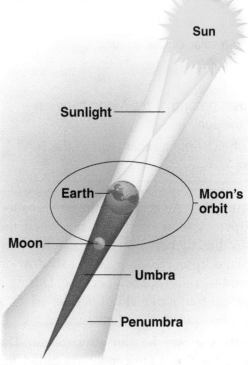

▲ **Figure 14-22** A total lunar eclipse

Hands-On Activity

MODELING LUNAR ECLIPSES

You will need tracing paper, a ruler, and a pencil.

1. Figure 14-23 shows the Moon in three different positions as it revolves around Earth. Copy the diagram onto a sheet of paper.

2. Indicate on your diagram which position represents a total eclipse, which represents a partial eclipse, and which represents no eclipse of the Moon.

Practicing Your Skill

3. ANALYZE: Does Position 1 represent a total eclipse, a partial eclipse, or no eclipse of the Moon? Explain.

4. ANALYZE: Does Position 2 represent a total eclipse, a partial eclipse, or no eclipse of the Moon? Explain.

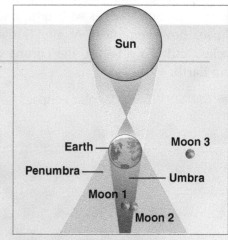

▲ **Figure 14-23** The Moon revolving around Earth

5. ANALYZE: Does Position 3 represent a total eclipse, a partial eclipse, or no eclipse of the Moon? Explain.

6. MODEL: Draw a model of a total eclipse of the Moon.

What causes an eclipse of the Sun?

Objective

Explain how a solar eclipse occurs.

Key Terms

solar eclipse: passing of the Moon between Earth and the Sun

corona (kuh-ROH-nuh)**:** outer layer of the Sun's atmosphere

Casting Shadows An eclipse of the Sun is called a **solar eclipse.** A solar eclipse occurs when the Moon passes directly between Earth and the Sun. During a solar eclipse, the Moon casts a shadow on Earth. Figure 14-24 shows a solar eclipse. During a solar eclipse the Sun looks like it is covered by a black circle. This circle is the Moon.

Like Earth, the Sun has an atmosphere. The outer layer of the Sun's atmosphere is called the **corona.** The corona is like a halo around the Sun. Usually, the corona cannot be seen from Earth because the Sun itself is so bright. During a solar eclipse, however, most of the Sun's surface is blacked out. As a result, the corona can be seen from Earth.

▶ DEFINE: What is a solar eclipse?

Kinds of Solar Eclipses Like lunar eclipses, solar eclipses can either be total or partial. A total solar eclipse occurs when the entire face of the Sun is blocked by the Moon. Only the outer atmosphere of the Sun still shows. A partial solar eclipse happens when only part of the Sun's face is blocked.

▲ Figure 14-24 A total solar eclipse

▶ DESCRIBE: What causes a total solar eclipse?

Viewing Solar Eclipses Look at Figure 14-25 below. When the Moon's umbra touches Earth, people within it see a total solar eclipse.

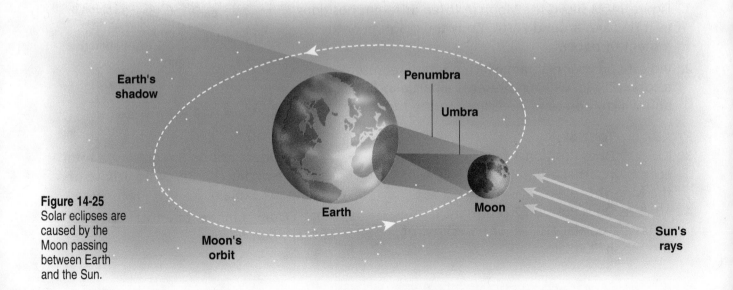

Earth's shadow

Penumbra

Umbra

Figure 14-25
Solar eclipses are caused by the Moon passing between Earth and the Sun.

Moon's orbit

Earth

Moon

Sun's rays

The umbra of the Moon is very small. Therefore, a total solar eclipse is visible from only a small area of Earth. People who are in the Moon's penumbra see a partial solar eclipse.

The penumbra of the Moon's shadow is much larger than the umbra. As a result, a partial solar eclipse can be seen over a larger area of Earth than a total solar eclipse can. Partial solar eclipses are seen more often than total solar eclipses.

 IDENTIFY: Which kind of solar eclipse is seen more often, a total or a partial solar eclipse?

☑ CHECKING CONCEPTS

1. When does a solar eclipse occur?
2. What is a partial eclipse of the Sun?
3. What happens when the Moon's umbra touches Earth?
4. Which part of the Moon's shadow is the largest?

THINKING CRITICALLY

Use Figure 14-25 to answer the following questions.

5. ANALYZE: What part of the Moon's shadow are you in if you see a total solar eclipse?
6. EXPLAIN: What can people outside the area of a total solar eclipse see?
7. COMPARE: How are total eclipses of the Moon and the Sun similar?
8. INFER: Why is a partial solar eclipse seen more often than a total solar eclipse?

HEALTH AND SAFETY TIP

Never look directly at the Sun, especially during a total solar eclipse. Doing this can cause permanent eye damage. Some people use a special filter to view the Sun. However, poorly made filters can also cause eye damage. The best way to watch a solar eclipse is with a pinhole box. Go online to learn how to make one. Use the key search words **pinhole box.**

 How Do They Know That?

PREDICTING SOLAR ECLIPSES

People have always been fascinated by solar eclipses. In some cultures, solar eclipses were connected with superstition, mystery, and fear. Some ancient cultures thought the darkened sky caused by a solar eclipse was a sign of the displeasure of certain spirits. The ancient Chinese thought that solar eclipses happened when a dragon in the sky tried to swallow the Sun.

Descriptions of solar eclipses have been found dating back many centuries. In Babylon, a record of solar eclipses was kept from 747 B.C. on. In China, 36 solar eclipses were recorded between 720 B.C. and 495 B.C. Scientists have calculated the exact dates of many past solar eclipses. The records of eclipses in ancient writings have been used to pinpoint the dates of historical events.

▲ **Figure 14-26** This moment during a solar eclipse is known as the diamond ring effect. Can you see why?

Today, scientists can accurately predict solar eclipses. This is important in the study of the Sun and the Moon.

Thinking Critically Why do you think solar eclipses were once feared?

Chapter Summary

Lessons 14-1 and 14-2

- **Revolution** and **rotation** are movements of Earth. Earth's rotation causes day and night. The number of daylight hours changes because Earth's **axis** is tilted.
- The Sun appears to rise in the east and set in the west because of Earth's rotation. When the Sun is highest in the sky, the time is **solar noon.**
- Earth is divided into 24 time zones. There are eight **standard time** zones in the United States. As you cross the **International Date Line,** you either gain or lose one full day.

Lesson 14-3

- The seasons are caused by Earth's tilt and orbit around the Sun. The Northern and Southern hemispheres have opposite seasons.

Lesson 14-4

- During the year, the distance between Earth and the Sun varies.
- **Solstices** and **equinoxes** mark the changes in seasons. The North Pole tilts toward the Sun on the summer solstice. The North Pole tilts away from the Sun on the winter solstice. The Sun shines directly on the equator during the vernal and autumnal equinoxes.

Lesson 14-5

- The Moon revolves around Earth in the same way Earth revolves around the Sun. The Moon rotates once every 27⅓ days.
- **Apogee** and **perigee** describe the Moon's position in relation to Earth.
- The motions of the Moon cause changes in tides. Two kinds of tides are **spring tides** and **neap tides.**

Lesson 14-6

- The Moon has waxing and waning **phases.**

Lessons 14-7 and 14-8

- The **umbra** and the **penumbra** are the two parts of a shadow.
- A **lunar eclipse** occurs when the Moon passes through Earth's shadow. A **solar eclipse** occurs when the Moon passes between Earth and the Sun. Eclipses can be partial or total.

Key Term Challenges

aphelion (p. 332)
apogee (p. 336)
axis (p. 326)
corona (p. 344)
crescent phase (p. 338)
equinox (p. 332)
gibbous phase (p. 338)
International Date Line (p. 328)
lunar eclipse (p. 342)
neap tide (p. 336)
penumbra (p. 342)
perigee (p. 336)
perihelion (p. 332)
phases (p. 338)
revolution (p. 326)
rotation (p. 326)
solar eclipse (p. 344)
solar noon (p. 328)
solstice (p. 332)
spring tide (p.336)
standard time (p. 328)
umbra (p. 342)

MATCHING **Write the Key Term from above that best matches each description.**

1. time when the Sun is highest in the sky
2. changing shapes of the Moon
3. daily tidal range is the largest
4. imaginary line through the center of a planet or other body on which that body spins
5. passing of the Moon through Earth's shadow
6. movement of Earth on its axis
7. movement of Earth in its orbit
8. point in its orbit when Earth is farthest from the Sun

IDENTIFYING WORD RELATIONSHIPS **Explain how the words in each pair are related. Write your answers in complete sentences.**

9. rotation, revolution
10. International Date Line, meridian
11. equinox, solstice
12. apogee, perigee
13. penumbra, umbra
14. crescent phase, gibbous phase
15. solar eclipse, lunar eclipse

Content Challenges TEST PREP

FILL IN Write the term or phrase that best completes each statement.

1. When viewed from above the North Pole, Earth rotates on its axis from _____.

2. Earth's axis is tilted at an angle of _____.

3. Because of Earth's tilted axis, the North Pole of Earth always points toward _____.

4. In the Northern Hemisphere, the summer solstice occurs on _____.

5. During an equinox, the number of daylight hours and nighttime hours are _____.

6. The 48 states of the continental United States have _____ standard time zones.

7. The Moon takes _____ days to make one complete revolution around Earth.

8. The Moon takes _____ days to make one complete rotation on its axis.

9. As the visible part of the Moon decreases, the Moon is _____.

10. The waxing crescent phase of the Moon occurs _____ the full Moon.

11. When the daily tide range is largest, this is called a _____ tide.

12. When the daily tide range is smallest, this is called a _____ tide.

13. Because Earth rotates, the Sun appears to set in the _____.

14. Earth is closest to the Sun during the month of _____.

15. The darkest center part of a shadow is called the _____.

TRUE/FALSE Write *true* if the statement is true. If the statement is false, change the underlined term or phrase to make the statement true.

16. The change from day to night is caused by Earth's <u>revolution</u>.

17. The number of daylight hours is not equal all year because of Earth's <u>tilted axis</u>.

18. The change in seasons is caused by Earth's <u>rotation</u>.

19. In the Southern Hemisphere, the first day of summer is <u>June 21</u>.

20. The vernal equinox marks the first day of <u>spring</u>.

21. Earth is divided into <u>24</u> time zones, each 15 degrees of longitude wide.

22. As you move <u>east</u>, each time zone is one hour earlier than the previous time zone.

23. When the Moon is <u>closest</u> to Earth, it is at apogee.

24. The Moon rises 50 minutes <u>earlier</u> each day.

25. As the part of the Moon that is visible increases, the Moon is <u>waxing</u>.

26. The Moon appears to <u>change shape</u> because of the way it reflects light from the Sun.

27. During a total lunar eclipse, the entire face of the <u>Moon</u> is darkened.

28. When the Moon moves entirely into Earth's umbra, people within see a <u>solar</u> eclipse.

29. The difference between high tide and low tide is greatest during <u>spring</u> tides.

30. The Sun is farthest from Earth at <u>perihelion</u>.

Concept Challenges TEST PREP

WRITTEN RESPONSE **Answer each of the following questions in complete sentences.**

1. CALCULATE: If the Moon rises at 6:30 P.M. on Thursday, what time will it rise on Friday? Explain your answer.

2. COMPARE: How does the number of days between one full Moon and the next compare to how long it takes the Moon to revolve once around Earth?

3. HYPOTHESIZE: Gravitational attraction decreases with distance. Is the Moon's gravitational attraction to Earth stronger at apogee or perigee? Explain.

4. COMPARE: How does the number of time zones on Earth compare with the number of hours in a day?

5. CONTRAST: How do the position of the Sun, the Moon, and Earth during a solar eclipse differ from their positions during a lunar eclipse?

6. INFER: How do the tides on Earth change during the Moon's apogee and perigee?

INTERPRETING VISUALS **Use Figure 14-27 below to answer the following questions.**

7. Which phase of the Moon does the picture labeled *A* represent?

8. Which phase of the Moon does the picture labeled *C* represent?

9. Which phase of the Moon does the picture labeled *F* represent?

10. Which phase of the Moon is not shown?

11. Why is the phase of the Moon labeled *E* called a waning phase?

12. Which phase of the Moon follows a full Moon?

13. How long does it take the Moon to go from one new Moon phase to the next new Moon phase?

14. Name the phases of the Moon in the correct order, beginning with the one labeled *A*.

15. What causes the Moon to change phases?

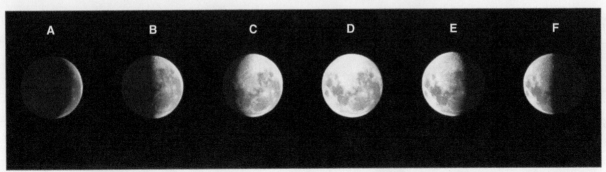

▲ **Figure 14-27** Phases of the Moon

Chapter 15 The Human Impact on the Environment

▲ **Figure 15-1** Cutting down trees threatened the northern spotted owl.

The northern spotted owl is a small bird found mostly in the old-growth forests of the Pacific Northwest. Because of its limited range, the population of spotted owls has always been a small one. However, the species is becoming even rarer and is now on the endangered species list. To help save the birds, the U.S. Forest Service banned the cutting down of trees on government land in the area. This angered the timber industry.

►How have humans had an impact on the spotted owl's environment?

Contents

15-1 What is the environment?

Objectives

Describe the cycles in nature. Define pollution.

Key Terms

environment (ehn-VY-ruhn-muhnt)**:** everything that surrounds a living thing

pollution (puh-LOO-shuhn)**:** anything that harms the environment

pollutant (puh-LOOT-uhnt)**:** harmful substance in the environment

A Support System for Life Living things get everything they need from their environment. The **environment** is everything that surrounds a living thing. The atmosphere, the hydrosphere, and the lithosphere are parts of the environment. For example, the atmosphere supplies living things with important gases. The hydrosphere provides water. The lithosphere provides important materials such as minerals and soil.

Some of these resources pass through cycles. For example, the water cycle allows Earth's water to be used again and again. Carbon dioxide, oxygen, and nitrogen also cycle through the environment.

 DESCRIBE: What is the environment?

Pollution Anything that harms the environment is called **pollution**. Pollution occurs when harmful substances, or **pollutants,** are released into the environment. Pollutants harm Earth's air, water, and land. They upset nature's cycles.

An example of how humans upset nature's cycles is thermal pollution. Thermal pollution raises water temperatures in aquatic systems. The problems result mostly from industry using water to cool equipment or materials during various processes. The electric power industry, steel mills, oil refineries, and paper mills all use huge amounts of water for cooling. After the equipment has cooled, the "waste" water is often returned to where it came from. However, its temperature is higher than it was before. This temperature change can upset nature's cycles and the balance of the environment.

Farming also causes pollution through pesticide use. Pesticides are meant to protect food supplies from pests such as insects, rodents, weeds, molds, and bacteria. However, pesticides can kill birds and fish, as well as pests. They can also poison the foods people eat.

 EXPLAIN: How does pollution upset nature's cycles and the balance of the environment?

The Nitrogen Cycle One important cycle in the environment is the nitrogen cycle. In the nitrogen cycle, bacteria take nitrogen gas from the air and make it into compounds. Both plants and animals use these compounds. Bacteria that make these compounds are called nitrogen-fixing bacteria.

Nitrogen-fixing bacteria live in the soil and in the roots of plants such as legumes. Farmers who grow crops often plant legumes in their fields to add nitrogen compounds to the soil.

When plants and animals die, the nitrogen compounds are broken down by different bacteria.

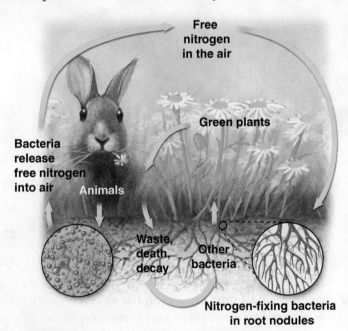

Free nitrogen in the air

Green plants

Bacteria release free nitrogen into air

Animals

Waste, death, decay

Other bacteria

Nitrogen-fixing bacteria in root nodules

▲ **Figure 15-2** The nitrogen cycle

Nitrogen is then released back into the air or soil.

 DESCRIBE: What happens in the nitrogen cycle?

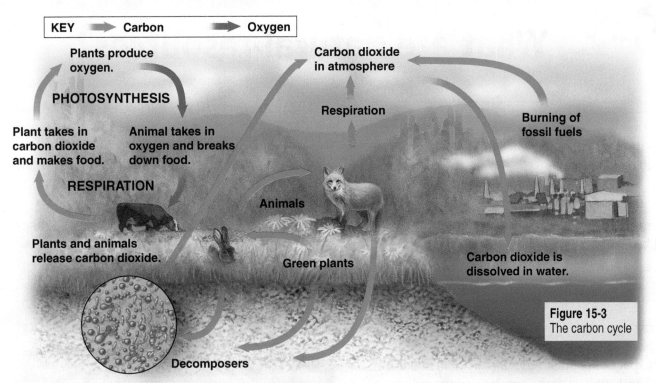

KEY ➡ Carbon ➡ Oxygen

Plants produce oxygen.

PHOTOSYNTHESIS

Plant takes in carbon dioxide and makes food.

Animal takes in oxygen and breaks down food.

RESPIRATION

Plants and animals release carbon dioxide.

Decomposers

Animals

Green plants

Carbon dioxide in atmosphere

Respiration

Burning of fossil fuels

Carbon dioxide is dissolved in water.

Figure 15-3
The carbon cycle

The Carbon Cycle Living things are made up of organic compounds. These contain carbon. Carbon is found in the atmosphere in the form of the gas carbon dioxide. The process by which carbon is recycled is called the carbon cycle. It is the repeated movement of carbon between Earth's atmosphere and living things. Green plants are producers. They use carbon dioxide to make food in photosynthesis. Some carbon dioxide is returned to the atmosphere when the food is used for energy during cellular respiration. The rest is stored as sugar. Animals are consumers. They eat producers or other consumers and use the food for energy. Some stored carbon dioxide is released when they breathe out.

All organisms eventually die. Their bodies are broken down by decomposers. Decomposers also release carbon dioxide into the atmosphere.

Fossil fuels are formed from the remains of ancient organisms. When fossil fuels are burned to release energy, more carbon dioxide is released into the atmosphere. This affects the carbon cycle.

4 ▶ IDENTIFY: What gas do animals release when they breathe out?

✓ CHECKING CONCEPTS

1. What resources cycle through the environment?

2. What part of the environment supplies water?

3. What gas do animals that have lungs take in from the air when they breathe in?

4. What happens to the nitrogen compounds used by plants and animals when they die?

5. When does pollution occur?

💡 THINKING CRITICALLY

Use Figure 15-2 to answer the following questions.

6. ANALYZE: How do animals get nitrogen compounds?

7. OBSERVE: What living things make nitrogen compounds?

Web InfoSearch

Rachel Carson Rachel Louise Carson (1907–1964) worked for the U.S. Fish and Wildlife Service. She was a marine biologist and science writer. Carson wrote about the ocean and pollution. Her most famous book, *Silent Spring*, was published in 1962. In this book, Carson warned that pesticides were harmful to the environment.

SEARCH: Use the Internet to find out more about Rachel Carson. What pesticide was banned because of her book? Are pesticides still used widely today? Start your search at www.conceptsandchallenges.com. Some key search words are **Rachel Carson** and **banned pesticides**.

What are natural resources?

Objective

Distinguish between renewable and nonrenewable natural resources.

Key Terms

natural resource: material from the earth that is used by living things

conservation (kahn-suhr-VAY-shuhn): wise use of natural resources

Natural Resources When a spaceship travels into space, it carries everything its crew needs to live. A spaceship must have a supply of food, air, water, and fuel. Earth can be compared to a spaceship. Earth has everything living things need to survive. Materials from the earth that are used by living things are called **natural resources.**

① DEFINE: What is a natural resource?

Renewable Resources Natural resources that can be reused or replaced are called renewable resources. Air, water, soil, and living things are renewable resources.

The water cycle allows Earth's water to be used over and over. New soil is formed to replace soil that has been carried away by wind and water. New plants grow to replace those that die. Animals are born to replace animals that die.

▲ **Figure 15-5** Freshly cut timber, considered a renewable resource, is often floated down a river to reach factories in distant locations.

② LIST: What are four renewable resources?

Nonrenewable Resources Oil, coal, and natural gas are fossil fuels. They were formed from plants and animals that lived long ago.

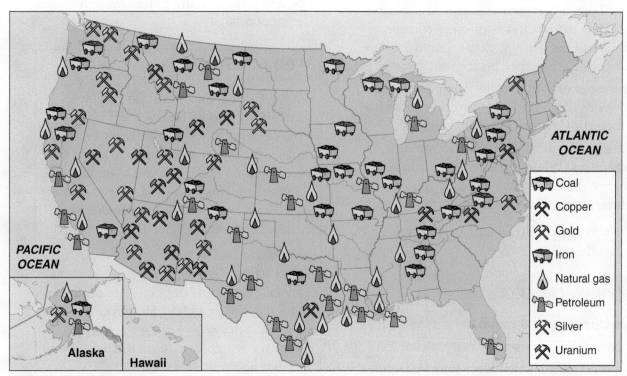

PACIFIC OCEAN

ATLANTIC OCEAN

Alaska

Hawaii

Legend:
- Coal
- Copper
- Gold
- Iron
- Natural gas
- Petroleum
- Silver
- Uranium

▲ **Figure 15-4** Natural resources in the United States

Fossil fuels and minerals are called **nonrenewable resources.** Nonrenewable resources are natural resources that are not easily replaced by nature or by human effort. Nonrenewable resources can take millions of years to form. Once nonrenewable resources are used up, they are basically gone forever.

 DEFINE: What is a nonrenewable resource?

Conservation The wise use of a natural resource is called **conservation.** As the number of people on Earth gets larger, the need for natural resources increases. People must learn how to use natural resources wisely to help them last longer.

 ANALYZE: What happens to the need for natural resources as Earth's population grows?

✓ CHECKING CONCEPTS

1. Water, soil, and air are _____ natural resources.
2. Oil is a _____ natural resource.
3. Natural resources come from _____.
4. Fossil fuels _____ be reused or replaced.
5. The wise use of natural resources is called _____.

💡 THINKING CRITICALLY

6. **CLASSIFY:** Classify each of the following as a renewable or a nonrenewable resource: trees, coal, nitrogen, people, diamonds, water, natural gas, soil, oil, and iron.

7. **CONCLUDE:** Why is it important to conserve even renewable resources?

Web InfoSearch

National Parks The U.S. National Park Service protects natural scenery, wildlife, and historic sites for the public to enjoy. Yellowstone National Park was the first national park in the world.

SEARCH: Use the Internet to find out more about the U.S. national park system. What parks are part of the system? Also, how are national parks a resource? Start your search at www.conceptsandchallenges.com. Some key search words are **Yellowstone Park, National Park System,** and **National Park Service.**

 Integrating Life Science

TOPICS: endangered species, predation

THE WHALING AGREEMENT

In nature, whales have very few natural enemies. However, they have been preyed upon by people for centuries. People have invented ways, such as better harpoons and faster ships, to make the hunting and killing of many whales at once easier.

By 1946, many whale populations had been listed as endangered. In response, the International Whaling Commission (IWC) was formed. It set limits on the killing of whales. However, whale populations kept decreasing. So in 1986, the IWC asked countries to voluntarily stop killing whales altogether. Japan, Norway, and Iceland refused and still hunt whales. So do Alaska Natives.

Thinking Critically What human actions have endangered the whales?

▲ **Figure 15-6** Whales were almost driven to extinction because people viewed them as a renewable resource. However, the whales could not breed fast enough to replace lost individuals.

What are our main energy sources?

Observing Coal
HANDS-ON ACTIVITY

1. Observe a lump of hard coal (anthracite) or soft coal (lignite). Look at its color, texture, and shape. Record your observations in detail.

2. Use a hand lens to examine the coal more closely. Look for fossils or imprints of plant or animal remains.

THINK ABOUT IT: What more did you notice about the coal when you used the hand lens? What does this tell you about what coal is made of?

STEP 2

Objective

Name and describe the main sources of energy.

Key Terms

hydroelectric (HY-droh-ee-LEHK-trihk) **power:** electrical energy produced from moving water

nuclear (NOO-klee-uhr) **energy:** energy produced by splitting or combining atoms

Fossil Fuels Fossil fuels are the world's main energy sources. Oil, coal, and natural gas are fossil fuels. Fossil fuels can generate electricity and heat. They can also run car engines and other types of machinery.

Go Online
active art

For: Hydroelectric Power activity
Visit: PHSchool.com
Web Code: cfp-3025

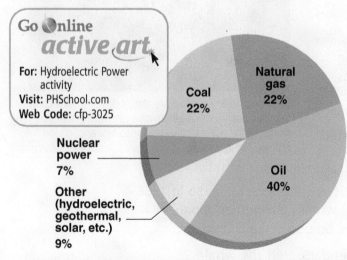

- Nuclear power 7%
- Other (hydroelectric, geothermal, solar, etc.) 9%
- Coal 22%
- Natural gas 22%
- Oil 40%

▲ **Figure 15-7** Current energy sources in the United States

However, most of our current energy sources have problems associated with them. Fossil fuels are rapidly being used up. Their use can also harm the environment.

People need to find ways to cut down on the use of fossil fuels. Some ways to do this include using energy-efficient cars, carpooling, lowering the heat, and turning off unneeded lights.

▶ **NAME:** What are three fossil fuels?

Hydroelectric Power
Water stored behind a dam has potential energy. When this water flows downhill, its stored potential energy changes to the energy of motion, which is called kinetic energy. The electrical energy power plants produce from running water is called **hydroelectric power.** At hydroelectric power plants, the moving water turns the blades of a machine called a turbine. The turbine drives an electric generator that produces electricity.

▲ **Figure 15-8** Hydroelectric plant on the Tocantins River in Brazil

Today, falling water is used to produce about 20 percent of the world's electricity. Hydroelectric power does not pollute the air. Also, its energy source, moving water, is renewable. However, dams can affect the wildlife living on or near a river by changing the environment. Dams can also alter the natural flow of rivers.

 DESCRIBE: What are two advantages of hydroelectric power plants?

Nuclear Energy Energy produced by splitting atoms is **nuclear energy.** The heat given off when atoms are split can be used to produce steam. The steam powers generators to make electricity. Uranium is commonly used as fuel.

There are drawbacks to using nuclear energy. Deadly radiation is produced in nuclear reactors. An accident could release this radiation. Also, a way must be found to safely store the wastes, which remain deadly for thousands of years.

Energy can also be released by combining atoms. However, this kind of nuclear energy is very difficult and costly to produce.

 IDENTIFY: What are some problems with using nuclear energy?

 CHECKING CONCEPTS

1. What is the most commonly used fossil fuel?
2. How can people produce electricity from moving water?
3. What kind of energy does a dam store?
4. How is nuclear energy produced commercially?

THINKING CRITICALLY

5. **HYPOTHESIZE:** How might building a dam affect the living things in an area? Give an example.
6. **CLASSIFY:** Classify each of the following items as having potential or kinetic energy: **a.** a book on a shelf; **b.** milk in a bottle; **c.** a book falling to the floor; **d.** a parked car; **e.** juice being poured; **f.** a moving car.

BUILDING MATH SKILLS

Researching and Graphing Find out how energy sources are used in the United States. Then, create a pie graph comparing the different uses.

 Science and Technology

CLEANING UP OIL SPILLS

Every year, there are thousands of crude oil spills. These spills harm aquatic life and seashores. Within hours, oil slicks—large bodies of oil floating on the surface of the water—are formed. The oil is spread quickly by waves and sea animals moving through the water. Swift action must be taken to prevent serious damage to the environment.

▲ **Figure 15-9** The damage from some oil spills can be limited by using special equipment.

Scientists have developed some technologies for cleaning up oil spills. None is perfect. Special nets called containment booms keep the oil in an enclosed area, where it can be pumped out later. Controlled burning of oil slicks is another method. Some chemicals can break up the grease. These allow the oil to rise above the water. The oil can then be moved away from the spill site. Certain bacteria can also be brought in to break down the complex chemicals in oil. Fertilizers and minerals can also encourage other bacteria already in the water to break down the oil.

Thinking Critically How do sea animals spread the oil?

What are some alternative energy sources?

Objective
Describe five alternative energy sources.

Key Terms
solar energy: energy from the Sun

solar cell: device that converts sunlight into electricity

geothermal (jee-oh-THUHR-muhl) **energy:** energy produced from heat inside Earth

Solar Energy Alternative energy refers to energy not produced by burning fossil fuels or wood. Like fossil fuels, all alternative energy sources have problems related to their use.

Energy from sunlight, or **solar energy**, is one alternative energy resource. Solar energy is already used to heat some homes. It can also be used to produce electricity. Solar collectors collect the Sun's energy, and devices called **solar cells** on the collector convert the sunlight into electricity.

Solar energy is a renewable resource. It does not pollute. However, solar energy is only a good source of energy in places that receive above-average amounts of sunlight all year.

▶ DEFINE: What are solar cells?

Geothermal Energy Heat produced deep inside Earth is called **geothermal energy.** This heat melts rocks and warms groundwater. In some places, steam is produced and can generate electricity for heating homes. In other places, the heated water is piped directly into homes. In Iceland, about 80 percent of the homes get their hot water and heat from geothermal energy.

▶ IDENTIFY: Where is geothermal energy produced?

Wind Energy The energy from moving air, or wind energy, is another renewable resource. Windmills have been used for many years to pump water and produce electricity. In California, big windmill farms are used to make electricity in some areas. Windmills do not pollute the air. However, there are few places on Earth where the wind blows steadily enough for windmills to be efficient sources of energy.

▶ EXPLAIN: What are windmills mostly used for?

Energy from the Tides Tidal energy is the energy of rising and falling tides. Tidal energy can be used to produce electricity. However, it can be used only near a shoreline where the tides vary from very high to very low.

Figure 15-10 ▶
Shown are two different kinds of solar heating systems. On the left, panels of solar cells are used to generate electricity. On the right, a solar collector heats water on the roof. It then pumps the heated water down through a heat exchanger. A fan circulates the warm air around the house.

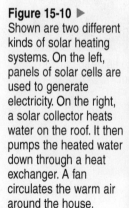

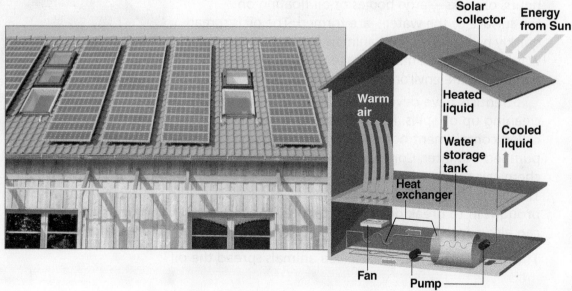

Solar collector

Energy from Sun

Warm air

Heated liquid

Cooled liquid

Water storage tank

Heat exchanger

Fan

Pump

▲ **Figure 15-11** A tidal energy plant in Nova Scotia, Canada

 APPLY: Where in the United States could tidal energy be produced?

CHECKING CONCEPTS

1. What devices change sunlight into electricity?
2. What is geothermal energy?
3. Why can we not rely on windmills for energy?

 THINKING CRITICALLY

4. **ANALYZE:** Which alternative energy source do you think is best? Why?
5. **INFER:** If you were building a house, where would you put your solar collectors? Why?
6. **EXPLAIN:** How does a pinwheel or a kite show that wind has energy?

Web InfoSearch

Biomass Fuels Material from living things is called biomass. Biomass can be a fuel source. Wood and solid animal waste are biomass fuels. Methane gas from sewage is also a biomass fuel. Ethanol from sugarcane is already used heavily in Brazil.

SEARCH: Use the Internet to find out more about biomass fuels. How are they produced? What are they used for? Start your search at www.conceptsandchallenges.com. Some key search words are **biomass fuels, biomass fuel uses,** and **biomass alternative energy.**

Hands-On Activity

MEASURING SOLAR ENERGY ABSORPTION

You will need black construction paper, white construction paper, and two thermometers.

1. Place two thermometers in a sunny place.
   ⚠ CAUTION: Be careful if using glass thermometers.
2. Cover one thermometer with black construction paper and the other with white construction paper.
3. After 15 minutes, check the temperatures of both thermometers.

Practicing Your Skills

4. **OBSERVE:** What were the temperature readings of the two thermometers?
5. **COMPARE:** Which thermometer had the higher reading?
6. **RELATE:** Which color takes in more heat energy from the Sun, black or white?
7. **CONCLUDE:** What color do you think is used in solar collectors? Why?

▲ **STEP 2** Cover the thermometers with paper.

15-5 How can natural resources be conserved?

Objective

Describe ways to conserve natural resources.

Key Term

recycling: using a natural resource over again

Recycling Natural resources can be conserved by **recycling,** or by using them over again. Aluminum, glass, paper, and plastics can all be recycled. For example, when paper is recycled, fewer trees need to be cut down. Recycling also uses less energy than finding new resources. This conserves fossil fuels.

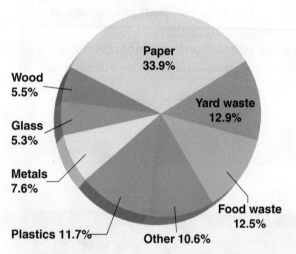

▲ **Figure 15-12** Types of household waste

Another way to conserve resources is to use other materials in their place. For example, some iron and aluminum parts in engines can be replaced with plastic. Some steel cables can be replaced by nylon ones.

1 DESCRIBE: How does recycling conserve natural resources?

New Mineral Sources Mineral resources on land are running out. However, the oceans may be a new source of minerals. Many minerals, such as sodium, sulfur, potassium, magnesium, and bromine, are dissolved in ocean water. Scientists are looking for less expensive ways to take minerals from the ocean.

Another new source of minerals might be space. Moon rocks contain aluminum, magnesium, titanium, and silicon. Asteroids may contain billions of tons of nickel and iron. Spacecraft have been sent to study asteroids with this in mind. Astronomers use special instruments to determine an asteroid's mineral makeup.

2 LIST: What are some possible new sources of minerals?

Water Conservation The supply of clean, fresh water on Earth is limited. One way to conserve water is not to waste it. Do not run the water when you brush your teeth. Take showers rather than baths because showers use less water. Fix leaky faucets quickly.

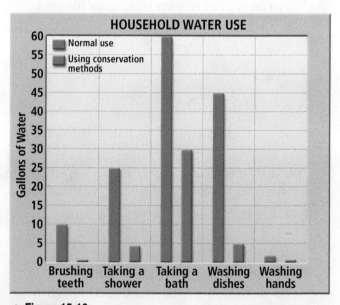

▲ **Figure 15-13**

3 STATE: What are two ways to conserve water?

Soil Conservation Some farming methods help conserve soil. For example, in contour farming, farmers plow across the slope of the land. In terracing, flat areas, or terraces, are created on the side of a hill. Both these methods help prevent water from washing away soil. In strip-cropping, grasses are planted between rows of crops to hold water and help stop erosion.

▲ **Figure 15-14** Strip-cropping can help conserve soil.

Windbreaks such as rows of trees help stop wind from blowing soil away. Fertilizers can replace the nutrients used up by plants. So can planting legumes.

 NAME: What farming methods help conserve soil?

✓ CHECKING CONCEPTS

1. What process reuses natural resources?
2. How can iron and aluminum engines be updated to conserve resources?
3. What do fertilizers add to soil?
4. What farming methods help stop water from washing away soil?

💡 THINKING CRITICALLY

5. **EXPLAIN:** How does recycling reduce waste?
6. **CALCULATE:** About 90 new aluminum cans can be made from 100 recycled cans. If each person in your class recycled one can each day, how many new cans could be made from what your class recycled in a month?

INTERPRETING VISUALS

Use Figure 15-13 to answer the following questions.

7. **IDENTIFY:** Which household activity uses the most water?
8. **INFER:** What could you do to save water while doing this activity?
9. **IDENTIFY:** Which household activity shows the biggest difference between normal use and conservation use?
10. **INFER:** What do people do that might cause the difference mentioned in Question 9?

Real-Life Science
COMPOSTING

One way to help conserve natural resources is by composting. Composting turns food waste into fertilizer. It also reduces the amount of solid waste that must be put in landfills.

Composting is usually done outdoors, in a shaded area. In a compost pile, scraps of plant materials, such as peels and rinds, are mixed with soil. Microbes in the soil break down the plant material. This releases nutrients. These microbes eat both "brown" and "green" plant materials. Brown materials, such as straw and mulch, are from dead or dried plants. The microbes use them for energy. Green materials, such as leaves and other plant parts, provide nitrogen and other nutrients. As the microbes break down the plant materials, heat is given off. This warms the surrounding soil.

▲ **Figure 15-15** Composting helps the environment by recycling food waste. It also reduces the need for commercial fertilizers.

Thinking Critically What plant wastes from your dinner last night could you have used for composting?

15-6 What is wildlife conservation?

INVESTIGATE

Observing the Effects of Detergent on Wildlife

HANDS-ON ACTIVITY

1. Pour one cup of tap water into a medium-size mixing bowl.
2. Add 1 teaspoon of vegetable oil. Observe the surface of the water.
3. Sprinkle 2 teaspoons of laundry detergent powder over the surface of the water. Gently stir with a spoon to mix, but try not to produce bubbles. Again, observe the surface of the water.

STEP 3

THINK ABOUT IT: The oil on birds' feathers makes them waterproof. This helps the birds stay afloat. What could detergent do to bird feathers? How does this endanger the birds?

Objectives

Identify the main threat to wildlife today.
Describe two ways to conserve wildlife.

Key Term

wildlife: all the plants and animals that live in an area

Endangered Wildlife All of the plants and animals that live in an area make up the area's **wildlife.** Over the past few centuries, hundreds of plant and animal species have died out, or become extinct. Many more are endangered, or moving toward extinction. Once a species becomes extinct, it will never return. The African elephant is an endangered animal. There are very few African elephants left. Other species have been identified as threatened. This means their numbers are going down, although they are not yet considered to be endangered.

▶ DEFINE: What is wildlife?

Loss of Habitat Loss of habitat is the main threat to wildlife. As the number of people on Earth increases, there is less space for other species. Land that was once covered with forest is now used for cities, farms, roads, and industry. The tropical rain forests are rapidly disappearing. More than half of all plant and animal species that live on Earth today live in tropical rain forests.

▲ **Figure 15-16** African elephants, though endangered, are still hunted for their ivory tusks.

▶ IDENTIFY: What is the biggest threat to wildlife today?

Laws and Wildlife One way to conserve wildlife is to pass laws that protect it. Some of these laws regulate hunting and fishing. In recent years, some countries have passed laws stopping the use of certain pollutants. There are also new laws to stop the destruction of wildlife habitats.

▶ DESCRIBE: How do laws help protect wildlife?

Wildlife Refuges A wildlife refuge is an area, like a national park, where animals and plants are protected. Setting up wildlife refuges helps conserve wildlife. Some zoos also help conserve wildlife. Breeding programs at these zoos have helped save some endangered species from extinction. In some cases, members of some species are returned to their natural environment.

▲ **Figure 15-17** Whooping cranes are an endangered species. This pair is at a national wildlife preserve in Arkansas.

In the United States, the National Wildlife Refuge System operates more than 550 wildlife refuges across the country. One example is Klamath Basin in Oregon and California. This vast region of shallow lakes and marshes protects many species of water birds and plants. Alaska has sixteen refuges, making up 83 percent of the entire National Wildlife Refuge System. On its 77 million protected acres are caribou, bears, moose, and wolves, among others.

 STATE: What are two ways to conserve wildlife?

☑ **CHECKING CONCEPTS**

1. Wildlife in danger of extinction is called _____.

2. To conserve wildlife, many different countries have passed laws that include rules for fishing and _____.

3. Once a kind of plant or animal becomes _____, it will never return.

4. A wildlife _____ is an area where wildlife is protected.

 THINKING CRITICALLY

5. INTERPRET: What does the statement "Extinct is forever" mean?

6. CONCLUDE: Is it important to save the rain forests? Why?

BUILDING SCIENCE SKILLS

Researching and Writing The dodo bird is an extinct animal. So is the passenger pigeon. Find out about five other animals or plants that once thrived but are now extinct. In which countries did they live? When? What were they like? How did their loss affect the environment in which they lived? Write a report with your findings.

◈ *Integrating Life Science*

TOPICS: habitats, endangerment, biodiversity

ENDANGERED ANIMALS

You have read about the northern spotted owl. Unfortunately, this owl is not the only endangered animal. There are hundreds of others. The main causes of endangerment are loss of habitat, hunting, and animals captured for the pet trade.

In recent years, there has been a big conservation effort to save the giant panda, which is native to China. For example, trees in panda habitats are no longer being cut down. However, some scientists fear that only a thousand or so pandas are left. Some other well-known animal species facing possible extinction are elephants, tigers, manatees, gorillas, whales, tortoises and marine turtles, rhinoceroses, and condors.

▲ **Figure 15-18** The giant panda, which is endangered, is native to China.

Thinking Critically How is saving species an act of conservation?

15-7 What causes air pollution?

Objectives

Identify causes of air pollution. Explain how air pollution harms the environment.

Key Terms

smog: mixture of smoke, fog, and chemicals

acid rain: rain containing acids produced by water chemically combining with certain gases

Air Pollution The burning of fossil fuels is the major cause of air pollution. When these fuels are burned, harmful substances enter the atmosphere. Thick, black smoke from chimneys contains dust and soot. Dust and soot are pollutants that can remain in the air for a long time. They can irritate eyes, throat, and lungs. Many cities have a smog problem. **Smog** is a mixture of smoke, fog, and chemicals. Smog also irritates the lungs of people, especially those with breathing problems.

▲ **Figure 15-19** Smog over a city pollutes the air.

▶ **1** IDENTIFY: What is the major cause of air pollution?

Acid Rain Cars and factories burn fossil fuels. This releases large amounts of carbon dioxide and other gases into the air. Some of these gases mix with water in the air and form acids. The acids then fall to Earth as **acid rain.** Acid rain is harmful to both living and nonliving things.

Acid rain that falls into lakes and streams kills fish. Acid rain also harms trees and causes brick, stone, and metal structures to weather, or break apart.

▲ **Figure 15-20** Scientists study trees affected by acid rain.

▶ **2** EXPLAIN: How does acid rain form?

Temperature Inversions Some large cities are ringed by mountains. As cool air flows into a valley, it pushes the warm air upward. This warm air becomes caught between two layers of cold air. The warm air cannot rise farther because of the cooler air pushing down on it. The mountains block the warm air from leaving the area. This potentially dangerous condition is known as a temperature inversion.

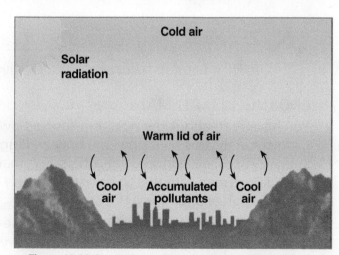

▲ **Figure 15-21** A temperature inversion traps polluted air.

During a temperature inversion, smog will continue to build up until a new weather system pushes the warm air up over the mountains. The cool air below can then circulate, reducing pollution.

▶ **3** DESCRIBE: What is a temperature inversion?

Carbon Dioxide Levels Fuels need oxygen to burn. When fossil fuels burn, they give off the gas carbon dioxide. The carbon dioxide traps heat energy produced by the Sun's rays. This is called the greenhouse effect. Carbon dioxide is a greenhouse gas.

Some scientists think that the increase of carbon dioxide in the air is causing the average air temperature to rise around the world. This rising temperature may cause dramatic climate changes.

 RELATE: How can an increase of carbon dioxide in the air cause air temperature to rise?

Protecting the Air Many countries have laws to help control or reduce air pollution. In the United States, most vehicles must have antipollution devices. Factories, too, must have filters on their smokestacks. The filters reduce the number of solid particles, called particulates, released into the air. However, using less fuel is still the best way to reduce air pollution.

 EXPLAIN: How do laws help reduce air pollution?

 CHECKING CONCEPTS

1. Smoke contains tiny pieces of dust and _____.
2. Smog is a mixture of smoke, fog, and _____.
3. Carbon dioxide traps _____ energy.
4. Some pollutant gases combine with _____ in the air to form acid rain.

THINKING CRITICALLY

5. **PREDICT:** The rising heat in Earth's atmosphere could cause glaciers to melt. How could this affect sea level and coastal cities?
6. **HYPOTHESIZE:** Is acid rain more of a problem in wet or dry climates? Explain.
7. **INFER:** What two words form the word *smog*?

HEALTH AND SAFETY TIP

Cities with air pollution problems often warn residents when smog levels are very high. Find out why people in these cities should not exercise outdoors on these smog-alert days.

 Hands-On Activity

OBSERVING AIR POLLUTANTS

You will need a hand lens, a microscope slide, a toothpick, and petroleum jelly.

1. Use the toothpick to coat one side of a glass slide with a thin layer of petroleum jelly.
2. Place the slide on a window ledge overnight.
3. Examine the slide with a hand lens the next day.

Practicing Your Skills

4. **OBSERVE:** What are some of the things you observed on your slide?
5. **INFER:** What do you think these particles are?
6. **IDENTIFY:** Where do you think these particles came from?
7. **HYPOTHESIZE: a.** Where in your neighborhood do you think you could place your slide to trap fewer pollutants? **b.** Where in your neighborhood do you think you could place your slide to trap more pollutants?
8. **ANALYZE:** How could you prove both of your hypotheses?

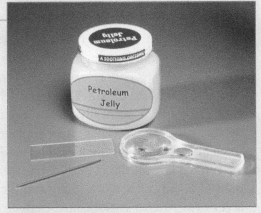

▲ **STEP 1** Coat one side of the slide with petroleum jelly.

THE Big IDEA

How can chemical reactions make air deadly?

If you live in a large city, you have probably observed skies darkened by a blanket of smoke and fog. This is smog. Smog is a colloid. In a colloid, particles remain in suspension and do not settle out. Smog contains several chemical compounds, fog, and soot. If you have respiratory problems, smog might make you feel uncomfortable. Usually, it is not deadly.

The smog that blanketed London, England, in 1952 was a thick, gray haze that smelled like coal smoke. Then the haze turned yellow and quite deadly. The air smelled terrible. Taking even the smallest breath caused a sharp pain in the lungs. When the smog finally began to lift, nearly 4,000 Londoners were dead.

The cause of this deadly smog has been traced to the coal-burning plants around the city. The plants had released coal smoke, containing sulfur dioxide, and particles of soot into the air. Ordinarily, air contaminated by this mixture would soon be replaced by fresh air moving into the area. However, the air mass surrounding London remained in place for almost a week. Above the city, a layer of warm air was trapped between two layers of cool air. This stopped the normal air circulation.

Fuel oils burned for heat increased the amount of sulfur dioxide in the air. Eventually, the air became more acidic than lemon juice. With each breath, residents of the city drew sulfuric acid into their bodies.

Look at the illustrations that appear on these two pages. Then, follow the directions in the Science Log to find out more about "the big idea." ✦

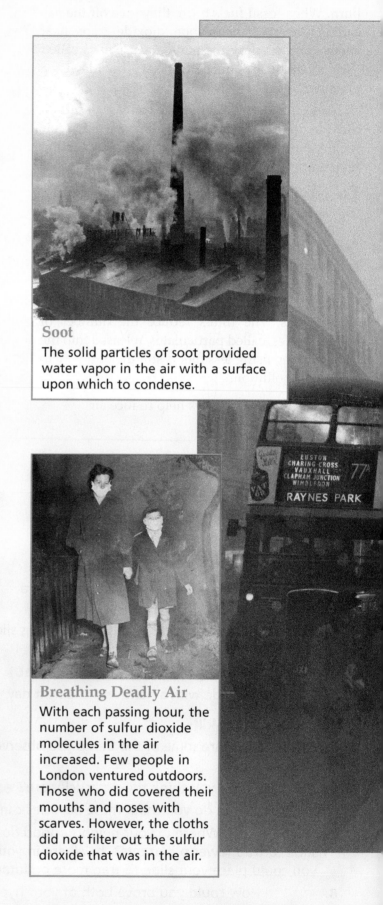

Soot
The solid particles of soot provided water vapor in the air with a surface upon which to condense.

Breathing Deadly Air
With each passing hour, the number of sulfur dioxide molecules in the air increased. Few people in London ventured outdoors. Those who did covered their mouths and noses with scarves. However, the cloths did not filter out the sulfur dioxide that was in the air.

science Log

WRITING ACTIVITY

The Environmental Protection Agency (EPA) provides daily information about air quality. Do research to find out what the current conditions are where you live. Start your search for information at www.conceptsandchallenges.com. Then, write a script for a radio news broadcast explaining these conditions. Include facts such as smog levels and whether there is currently a temperature inversion.

Colloid   Solution

Colloids Scatter Light

As the days passed, visibility dwindled to zero. The particles of the colloid scattered light from the headlights of cars. In the photo of beakers, you can see that light passes through a solution but is scattered by a colloid.

▲ **Figure 15-22** Except for the soot it contains, smog, like most colloids, cannot be separated by filtering. In London, the smog contained molecules of sulfur dioxide from coal smoke. These molecules dissolved in the water droplets making up the fog and formed sulfuric acid.

15-8 What causes water pollution?

INVESTIGATE

Observing Water Pollution
HANDS-ON ACTIVITY

1. Pour $\frac{1}{2}$ cup of tap water into a one-gallon glass container.
2. Add and stir in two drops of red food coloring.
3. Add 1 cup of tap water at a time to the jar until the red food coloring disappears from view.

THINK ABOUT IT: How many cups of water did it take to make the red food coloring disappear? Is the red food coloring gone entirely just because it can no longer be seen? What does this tell you about the effects of pollution on streams and wildlife?

Objective
Describe the major sources of water pollution.

Key Term
sewage: wastes usually flushed away in water

Water Pollution Water pollution occurs when harmful substances enter water sources. Some pollutants dissolve in the water. Others float. Many lakes and rivers were once used for drinking and swimming. Today, many of these are polluted. Not even fish can live in some of these waters.

▲ **Figure 15-23** The foam in this river is from detergents.

▶ EXPLAIN: Why are many lakes and rivers not used for drinking water today?

Sewage Wastes that usually are flushed away in water, such as biological wastes, are called **sewage.** Sewage is a source of water pollution. Bacteria and other disease-causing organisms live in sewage. Sewage also contains soaps and chemicals.

▶ DESCRIBE: What harmful things are in sewage?

Chemical Pollutants Many different chemicals pollute the water. Fertilizers are chemicals that help plants grow. Pesticides are used to kill animal pests and weeds. Farmers use fertilizers and pesticides on their food crops.

Many of the chemicals that make up fertilizers and pesticides are poisonous to living things. They can be washed off farm fields and seep into the groundwater. This water is then carried to lakes and rivers. The chemicals in the water may harm organisms that live in the water.

FRESHWATER POLLUTANTS		
Kinds of Pollutants	**Examples**	**Sources**
Disease-causing organisms	*Giardia, Cryptosporidium,* bacteria	Human wastes, runoff from livestock pens
Pesticides and fertilizers	DDT, nitrates, phosphates	Runoff from farm fields, golf courses
Industrial chemicals	PCBs, carbon tetrachloride, dioxin	Factories, industrial waste, disposal sites
Metals	Lead, mercury, copper	Factories, waste disposal sites
Radioactive wastes	Uranium, carbon-14	Medical and scientific disposal sites, nuclear power plants
Petroleum products	Oil, gasoline	Road runoff, leaking underground storage tanks

▲ **Figure 15-24**

Chemical pollutants also come from industry. Some industries illegally bury their wastes in barrels, or metal drums, in the ground. If the drums rust or break apart, the wastes can leak into the groundwater.

Industries also dump chemical wastes directly into water. These wastes are harmful to fish living in the water. They are also harmful to people who eat the fish.

Mercury is a poisonous element that is sometimes found in polluted water. Many fish cannot be eaten because they contain mercury. Figure 15-24 contains examples of different types of freshwater pollutants, including chemical pollutants.

 NAME: What are two sources of chemical pollutants?

Protecting the Water Sewage treatment plants have been built in many cities and towns. These plants change sewage into less-harmful materials.

Laws also help fight water pollution. These laws require industries to clean their wastes before dumping them into lakes and rivers. Laws have also banned the use of certain pesticides and soaps.

 EXPLAIN: What happens to sewage at sewage treatment plants?

✓ CHECKING CONCEPTS

1. What are pesticides used for?
2. What causes water pollution?

3. What happens when metal drums storing industrial wastes rust?
4. Where do fertilizers and pesticides that seep into groundwater end up?
5. Why is sewage potentially harmful?

💡 THINKING CRITICALLY

6. MODEL: Draw a flowchart that shows how a pesticide could end up in a person's body.
7. EXPLAIN: How could you help stop water pollution?
8. PREDICT: What might happen if drums containing harmful chemicals were buried on a beach? Explain your answer.

DESIGNING AN EXPERIMENT

Design an experiment to solve the following problem. Include a hypothesis, variables, a procedure with materials, and a type of data to study. Also, tell how you would record your data.

PROBLEM: Sewage increases the amount of algae in water. Algae are plantlike organisms. As algae die and decay, they use up the oxygen in the water. How can you show what will happen to fish living in the water as the oxygen in the water is used up?

 Integrating Life Science

TOPICS: ecology, environment

EUTROPHICATION

Runoff carries nutrients into lakes. Farming, the cutting of timber, and sewage treatment plants can also change the chemical balance in lakes. The buildup of nutrients in lakes is called eutrophication (yoo-troh-fuh-kay-shuhn). It can turn lakes into swamps and then into dry land.

▲ **Figure 15-25** A buildup of nutrients caused the green algae to grow out of control in this body of water.

In nature, plants eventually die and add organic sediment to a lake's bottom. This sediment may combine with silt from erosion. Over time, the lake may gradually be filled in. However, this natural process can be speeded up by eutrophication from certain farming practices and the treatment of sewage in sewage plants. Healthy lakes can become choked with vegetation. Eutrophication is a widespread problem in U.S. lakes today.

Thinking Critically What human practices cause eutrophication?

LAB ACTIVITY
Saving Water and Energy

BACKGROUND

A leaky faucet can result in a big waste of water and energy. Each drop, though small, adds up. Over time, a lot of water can be wasted down the drain. If hot water is coming from the faucet, energy is wasted along with the water. Fixing a leaky faucet can help save valuable resources.

PURPOSE

You will calculate how much water and energy a leaky faucet wastes.

PROCEDURE

1. Turn on the cold water tap just enough to create a steady drip. Adjust the tap until the rate of drip is about 10 to 20 drips per minute. Place a large glass under the drip.

2. Copy the chart shown in Figure 15-26.

3. Predict how many liters of water you think will be wasted if the faucet drips for an hour. Write down your prediction in your data chart, as shown in Figure 15-26.

4. Collect the water dripping from the faucet for 10 minutes. Use the graduated cylinder to measure the amount. In your data chart, record in milliliters (mL) the amount of water collected.

5. To find out how many liters of water are wasted in one year, carry out the calculations in the chart as shown in Figure 15-27.

Materials

Safety goggles, lab aprons, watch with second hand, graduated cylinder, thermometer, paper, cup, pencil, calculator, large glass

▲ **STEP 1** Adjust the tap until the rate of drip is correct.

▲ **STEP 4** Measure how much water was lost by pouring it into the graduated cylinder.

6. When a hot water faucet leaks, both water and energy are wasted. Heat energy is used to heat water. A calorie is the amount of heat energy needed to raise the temperature of 1 mL of water by 1°C. A kilocalorie is the amount of heat needed to raise the temperature of 1 L (1,000 mL) of water by 1°C. The water from the hot water tap is 40°C.

7. Take the temperature of the water coming from the cold water tap. Find out how much the temperature of the cold water has been raised.

▲ **STEP 7** Measure the temperature of the cold water.

8. To estimate the amount of heat energy wasted by a leaky hot water tap, multiply that number by the number you calculated would be lost in a year. Record this number in your data table.

My Data

My prediction	
Amount of water collected	
Volume of water per year	
Temp. of cold water	
Energy to heat 1 L of water	
Amount of energy (in kilocalories) wasted per year	

▲ **Figure 15-26** Use a copy of this table to record your observations.

How to Find Volume of Water Wasted

To get mL per hour	__ mL × 6 = __ mL/hr
To get mL per day	__ mL/hr × 24 = __ mL/day
To get mL per year	__ mL/day × 365 = __ mL/yr
To get liters per year	__ mL/yr ÷ 1,000 = __ L/yr

▲ **Figure 15-27** Use a copy of this table to do your calculations.

CONCLUSIONS

1. CALCULATE: Burning one barrel of fuel oil produces about 23,000,000 kilocalories of heat energy. How many barrels of oil would be wasted by a leaky faucet dripping hot water for a year?

2. CALCULATE: How many 2-liter bottles of water would be wasted in a year?

3. ANALYZE: What can you do to limit the amount of water that is wasted?

4. ANALYZE: Why is it important to conserve resources such as oil and water?

15-9 How is water purified?

Objectives

Explain why water must be purified. Identify five ways to purify water.

Key Terms

hard water: water containing a lot of minerals, especially calcium and magnesium

soft water: water containing few or no minerals

desalination: process of getting freshwater from salt water

▲ **Figure 15-29** A water treatment plant

Drinking Water Drinking water comes mostly from reservoirs, springs, or wells. A reservoir is a lake made by people. Reservoirs store large amounts of freshwater. Pipelines carry the water to homes and businesses.

Some water contains dissolved minerals such as calcium and magnesium. Water that has high levels of calcium and magnesium in it is called **hard water.** It is difficult for soap to form suds in hard water. Water with few or no minerals in it is called **soft water.**

▶ **IDENTIFY:** What are two minerals in hard water?

Purifying Water Water for drinking and bathing must be purified, or cleaned. Water is usually purified in water treatment plants. Water can be purified in the following ways.

- **Sedimentation** (sehd-uh-muhn-TAY-shuhn): The water is allowed to stand for long periods of time. Heavy particles, such as sand and dirt, settle to the bottom and are removed.

- **Coagulation** (koh-ag-yoo-LAY-shuhn): Alum and other chemicals that cause particles to clump together are added to the water. The clumps of particles settle to the bottom. The particles are then removed from the water.

- **Filtration** (fihl-TRAY-shuhn): Water is passed through a filter to remove small particles.

- **Aeration** (air-AY-shuhn): Water is sprayed into the air. Oxygen from the air dissolves in the water. The oxygen kills some of the harmful microorganisms in the water.

- **Chlorination** (klawr-uh-NAY-shuhn): Chlorine is added to the water. This chemical kills any harmful microorganisms that are in the water.

▶ **NAME:** What are five ways to purify drinking water?

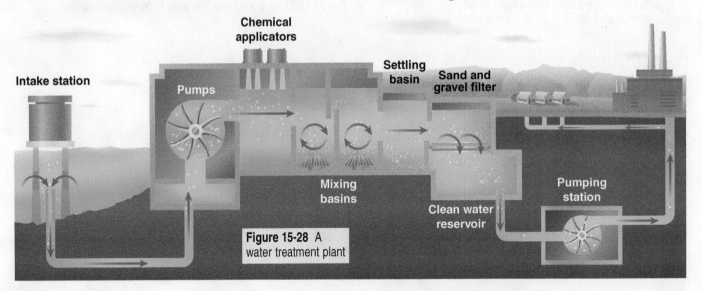

Intake station
Chemical applicators
Pumps
Settling basin
Sand and gravel filter
Mixing basins
Clean water reservoir
Pumping station

Figure 15-28 A water treatment plant

Desalination The process of getting freshwater from salt water is called **desalination.** One method of desalination is to distill the salt water. The water is boiled until it evaporates. This leaves the salt behind. The water vapor is then condensed to produce liquid freshwater. Another method involves freezing the water. This also leaves the salt behind. A third method is to pump ocean water at high pressure through a fine filter. The filter separates out much of the salt in the water. Water still containing too much salt is returned to the ocean.

Desalination is a very costly operation. It uses large amounts of energy and a lot of equipment. However, some nations, such as those in the Middle East, do it anyway. These nations have very limited freshwater resources.

 DESCRIBE: What are three ways to desalinate water?

 CHECKING CONCEPTS

1. Hard water contains high levels of calcium and _____.

2. A human-made lake that stores freshwater is called a _____.

3. Desalination means to _____ salt from water.

 THINKING CRITICALLY

4. ANALYZE: Explain the water purification method described in each statement.
   a. Chemicals that cause particles to clump together are added to water. **b.** Water is sprayed into the air. **c.** Water stands for long periods of time.

INTERPRETING VISUALS

Use Figure 15-28 to complete the following questions.

5. IDENTIFY: What materials are used for filtration?

6. ANALYZE: Where does the water in reservoirs come from?

7. INFER: What substance is added to water to kill microorganisms?

HEALTH AND SAFETY TIP

Many "safe-looking" products found around the home are really dangerous chemicals. They can contaminate water supplies. Examples of such products are bleaches, detergents, and other cleaning agents. Read the labels on products you find around your home and see how to safely dispose of them.

 People in Science

WATER PURIFICATION TECHNICIAN

A water purification technician works at a water treatment plant. He or she controls and maintains the equipment at the plant and also takes water samples during the purification process. The water samples are tested for impurities. The technician also checks the amount of chemicals in the water. It is part of the technician's job to make sure that the proper amounts of chlorine and other chemicals are being used.

To become a water purification technician, you must have a high school diploma. Water purification technicians may learn their trade through on-the-job training. Some water purification technicians take two-year programs in water purification technology.

Thinking Critically What is the purpose of a water treatment plant?

▲ **Figure 15-30** A water purification technician tests water samples.

15-10 What causes land pollution?

Objective
Describe the causes of land pollution.

Key Terms
litter: materials that are carelessly thrown away
biodegradable: material that breaks down easily

Litter and Garbage Have you ever seen cans, bottles, papers, and plastic materials that were thrown on the ground? These carelessly thrown-away materials are called **litter.** Litter is one of the causes of land pollution. Litter harms the land and destroys the beauty of many areas.

Garbage, mainly paper wastes, also causes land pollution. Each year people create billions of tons of garbage. The garbage builds up at dumps or is put in landfills. There, the garbage is buried between layers of soil. Many materials in garbage are **biodegradable.** This means they break down easily. Some, though, take many years to break down. Other materials contain harmful substances that may seep into the soil.

▶ **IDENTIFY:** What are two causes of land pollution?

Industrial Wastes Chemical wastes from industry pollute the water. They also pollute the land.

Some industrial wastes are buried in drums in the ground. Many of these toxic wastes contain harmful metals such as mercury and lead. In many places, these wastes are leaking from the drums into the ground. They then pollute the land and can harm living things.

▲ **Figure 15-31** Toxic waste site in Houston, Texas

▶ **DESCRIBE:** How are some industrial wastes disposed of?

Protecting the Land Getting rid of garbage and chemical wastes is a growing problem. Cities have taken some steps to reduce land pollution. Garbage is collected regularly. Streets are cleaned of litter. However, much more needs to be done.

Go Online
active art

For: Sanitary Landfill activity
Visit: PHSchool.com
Web Code: cep-5042

◀ **Figure 15-32**
Overflowing trash cans ruin the landscape of city streets.

One solution to the problem of land pollution is to make use of certain wastes. Some wastes can be used as fertilizers. Others can be burned as energy sources. Still other wastes, such as plastics, glass, paper, bottles, and cans, can be recycled.

The cleanup of chemical wastes that leak into the soil is a more difficult problem. Cleaning up these wastes is expensive and takes years.

 ANALYZE: What are some solutions to the problem of land pollution?

✓ CHECKING CONCEPTS

1. Materials that are carelessly thrown away are called _____.

2. Some wastes can be burned to produce _____.

3. Garbage put between layers of land creates a _____.

4. Cleaning up chemical wastes from the _____ is expensive and takes a lot of time.

5. **ANALYZE:** What are some steps you can take to reduce the amount of litter in your neighborhood?

6. **APPLY:** How can industrial wastes pollute both land and water?

DESIGNING AN EXPERIMENT

Design an experiment to solve the following problem. Include a hypothesis, variables, a procedure with materials, and a type of data to study. Also, include a way to record your data.

PROBLEM: Laws have been passed in many locations around the country that place a small deposit, such as a dime, on beverage containers. If the containers are taken back to a store, deposits are returned. Besides promoting recycling, deposits may reduce litter. Design an experiment that would prove whether deposits do reduce litter. Put your findings in a report. Include a graph or chart.

 Real-Life Science

GETTING RID OF GARBAGE

The United States produces over 250 million tons of garbage each day. For years, solid waste was put into landfills. Most of that waste was made up of biodegradable compounds. As it decayed, more room became available in the landfill. However, in the last 50 years, new, longer-lasting materials have been put in landfills. Our landfills are becoming full.

What can we do with our garbage? Some common disposal methods are incineration, or burning, and ocean dumping. Incineration saves landfill space and can be used to produce heat and electricity. However, it also adds pollutants to the air. Special filters must be used to trap these pollutants. The dumping of sewage and other wastes in the ocean threatens ocean environments.

▲ **Figure 15-33** A landfill is one way to get rid of waste. However, our landfills are rapidly filling up.

Reusing and recycling can reduce our waste problem. So can composting. In composting, decayed organic waste is used as a natural fertilizer.

Thinking Critically Only a small percentage of our solid waste that can be recycled is recycled. Why do you think this is so?

What are some global effects of pollution?

Objective
Explain how pollution spreads across borders.

A World with No Borders The lines that divide countries on maps do not exist in reality. From space, you see just one world, with large areas of land surrounded by even larger areas of ocean.

Pollution does not stay in just one place. Fumes from automobiles, homes, and factories are carried by the wind around the globe. Pollutants dumped into rivers gradually make their way into the oceans. Ocean currents carry them around the world. Pollution is not just one country's problem. It is a global problem.

▶ 1 ANALYZE: Why is pollution a global problem?

Acid Rain All rainwater is slightly acidic. Certain gases, such as sulfuric oxide and nitric oxide, can mix with rainwater. This makes the drops more acidic. These gases are produced by power plants, industries, and motor vehicles. Global winds spread the gases across borders. There they mix with rainwater. Many countries other than the ones producing the gases are affected by acid rain.

Acid rain damages forests. It also collects in lakes and rivers, poisoning fish and water plants. It breaks down rock and mud and releases harmful chemicals into the water. About 10,000 lakes in Sweden contain so much mercury that the government has discouraged people from eating fish caught there. Some bodies of water contain so much dissolved copper that the hair of persons drinking the water turns green.

▶ 2 HYPOTHESIZE: How does acid rain affect the lives of people?

Radiation In 1986, a poorly designed nuclear reactor in Chernobyl, Ukraine, exploded. The explosion and fires that followed released huge amounts of radiation into the atmosphere. It was the world's worst nuclear energy accident.

Thirty people working near the reactor died shortly after the accident. Ten more people died later from thyroid cancer brought on by the accident. Winds and water carried radioactive dust around the world. The worst affected areas were near the plant. However, Poland, Hungary, and Sweden were also affected. The dust destroyed rich farmlands, contaminated cow milk, and exposed up to 600,000 people to radiation.

▲ **Figure 15-34** Chernobyl in the Ukraine was the site of the world's worst nuclear reactor accident to date.

▶ 3 IDENTIFY: How is radioactive dust spread around the world?

Ozone Holes Ozone is a special form of oxygen. Ozone is created from oxygen by lightning and ultraviolet (UV) light from the Sun. Most of this ozone ends up in a thin layer about 35 km above Earth's surface. Ozone is very important to life on Earth because it absorbs most of the UV light coming from the Sun. Large amounts of UV light cause eye damage and skin cancer in humans.

Some industrial chemicals, such as CFCs, release gases that rise into the upper atmosphere. These gases destroy the ozone layer, creating holes in it. In recent years, satellites have found lower than normal levels of ozone above Earth's poles, particularly in the South Pole region.

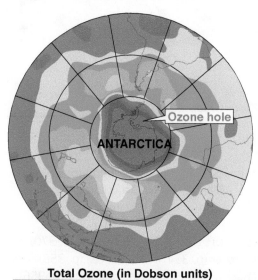

Total Ozone (in Dobson units)

150 180 210 240 270 300 330 360 390

▲ **Figure 15-35** An enhanced satellite image of the ozone hole over the South Pole. The thinnest part is shown in red.

More ultraviolet light is reaching Earth's surface than in the past. Many industries have begun using ozone-safe chemicals. However, the damage already done may take decades to repair.

4 **EXPLAIN:** Why is the chemical known as ozone important to people?

1. Why are various kinds of pollution considered to be a global problem?
2. How does pollution spread around the world?
3. How is acid rain spread?

 THINKING CRITICALLY

4. **INFER:** How will population increases affect global pollution?
5. **APPLY:** What can individuals do to reduce global pollution?

INTERPRETING VISUALS

Use Figure 15-35 to answer the following questions.

6. What part of Earth are you looking at?
7. Where is the ozone hole the thinnest?
8. What does the yellow represent?
9. What does this map reveal to us about ozone in the atmosphere?

 Science and Technology

USING SPACE TO TRACK POLLUTION

Looking at Earth from space, astronauts can see thousands of square kilometers at a time. This gives them a special view of Earth's surface.

From space, astronauts can see smoke from forest fires set in South America to clear land for farming. The smoke stretches out for thousands of kilometers across the Atlantic Ocean. During the Desert Storm conflict in the Middle East in 1991, astronauts saw giant black, smoky smudges from the burning of Kuwaiti oil fields. The smoke spread out for 60 km southward over the Persian Gulf.

▲ **Figure 15-36** Smoke from the burning Kuwaiti oil fields spread out for many kilometers.

Astronauts are not the only ones to use space to track pollution. Orbiting satellites use cameras and computers to map changes in world temperatures. They also track ozone levels over the poles. Data collected by satellites and astronauts are made available to scientists who study pollution. Noting changes in the world environment year after year helps scientists predict the future. Currently, they are predicting a worsening trend in global pollution.

Thinking Critically Why is space a good place to study global pollution?

Chapter Summary

Lessons 15-1 and 15-2

- The **environment** is everything that surrounds a living thing. Oxygen, nitrogen, and carbon dioxide cycle through the environment. **Pollution** harms the environment.

Lessons 15-3 and 15-4

- The main sources of energy are oil, coal, and natural gas. Fossil fuels are nonrenewable.
- **Hydroelectric power** is produced from quickly flowing water.
- The splitting and combining of atoms produces **nuclear energy.** Nuclear energy has serious drawbacks.
- **Solar energy** can heat homes and provide electricity.
- **Solar cells** convert solar energy to electricity.
- **Geothermal energy** is energy from heat within Earth. Tidal energy comes from tides. Wind, too, is used to produce electricity.

Lessons 15-5 and 15-6

- **Natural resources** are materials from Earth used by living things. Some can be reused or replaced. Others cannot. **Recycling** allows resources to be reused.
- Many kinds of **wildlife** are becoming extinct due to loss of living space.

Lesson 15-7

- Burning fossil fuels causes air pollution and increases the amount of carbon dioxide in the air. Dust and soot are air **pollutants. Smog** is a mixture of smoke, fog, and chemicals.
- **Acid rain** harms both living and nonliving things.

Lessons 15-8, 15-9, and 15-10

- **Sewage** and industrial waste produce water pollution.
- Drinking water comes from reservoirs, wells, or springs. Water contains dissolved minerals.
- **Litter,** garbage, and chemicals from farms and industry pollute land. Cleaning up chemical wastes from land is very difficult.

Lesson 15-11

- Pollution spreads around the world by wind and ocean currents. Acid rain, radiation, and ozone holes are some global pollution issues.

Key Term Challenges

acid rain (p. 362)
biodegradable (p. 372)
conservation (p. 352)
desalination (p. 370)
environment (p. 350)
geothermal energy (p. 356)
hard water (p. 370)
hydroelectric power (p. 354)
litter (p. 372)
natural resource (p. 352)

nuclear energy (p. 354)
pollutant (p. 350)
pollution (p. 350)
recycling (p. 358)
sewage (p. 366)
smog (p. 362)
soft water (p. 370)
solar cell (p. 356)
solar energy (p. 356)
wildlife (p. 360)

MATCHING **Write the Key Term from above that best matches each description.**

1. everything that surrounds a living thing
2. mixture of smoke, fog, and chemicals
3. waste that is usually flushed away in water
4. water that contains many minerals
5. heat energy from inside Earth
6. plants and animals living in nature
7. electricity produced from moving water
8. energy produced by splitting atoms
9. anything that harms the environment
10. wise use of natural resources

FILL IN **Write the Key Term from above that best completes each statement.**

11. Gases in the air mix with water and fall to Earth as _____.
12. Materials, such as paper and cups, that are left on the ground are called _____.
13. Materials that come from Earth and are used by living things are called _____.
14. The use of natural resources over and over again is called _____.
15. Water with few or no minerals is called _____.

Content Challenges TEST PREP

MULTIPLE CHOICE Write the letter of the term or phrase that best completes each sentence.

1. Oil, coal, and natural gas are three different kinds of
   a. fossil fuels.
   b. water pollutants.
   c. acid rain.
   d. nuclear fuels.

2. Soap, chemicals, and bacteria are commonly part of
   a. acid rain.
   b. litter.
   c. garbage.
   d. sewage.

3. Sedimentation and coagulation are two kinds of
   a. water purification methods.
   b. farming methods.
   c. energy resources.
   d. air pollutants.

4. Pesticides and fertilizers are two kinds of
   a. sewage.
   b. natural resources.
   c. chemical pollutants.
   d. farming methods.

5. A species of plant that is no longer found alive is
   a. threatened.
   b. extinct.
   c. endangered.
   d. polluted.

6. Devices that convert sunlight into electricity are called
   a. nuclear reactors.
   b. solar cells.
   c. fossil fuels.
   d. geothermal panels.

7. The major threat to wildlife is
   a. air pollution.
   b. water pollution.
   c. loss of living space.
   d. overhunting.

8. Minerals and fossil fuels are examples of
   a. air pollutants.
   b. nonrenewable resources.
   c. renewable resources.
   d. land pollutants.

9. Electricity produced from heat inside Earth is
   a. geothermal energy.
   b. solar energy.
   c. nuclear energy.
   d. tidal energy.

TRUE/FALSE Write _true_ if the statement is true. If the statement is false, change the underlined term to make the statement true.

10. The burning of <u>wood</u> is the major cause of air pollution.

11. Acid rain can cause brick to <u>weather</u>.

12. More carbon dioxide in the air may drive temperatures <u>down</u>.

13. Soap does not form suds easily in <u>hard</u> water.

14. Industrial wastes cause both water and <u>land</u> pollution.

15. Aluminum cans and newspapers are <u>replacement</u> materials.

16. Contour farming prevents water from <u>eroding</u> soil.

17. Farmers plant rows of trees on their land to prevent <u>water</u> from carrying away soil.

18. Uranium is a common fuel for <u>nuclear</u> energy.

19. <u>Geothermal</u> energy comes from the rising and falling of tides.

20. A species that is <u>endangered</u> is gone forever.

Concept Challenges *TEST PREP*

WRITTEN RESPONSE **Answer each of the following questions in complete sentences.**

1. EXPLAIN: How can burning wastes both reduce land pollution and conserve fossil fuels?

2. ANALYZE: How does the growth of cities affect wildlife?

3. ANALYZE: How does water pollution affect the fishing industry?

4. INFER: Why is flat land in less danger of erosion by water than hilly land?

5. ANALYZE: Would wind energy be a good energy source in your area? Explain.

6. INFER: What cycle provides us with fresh supplies of drinking water?

7. LIST: What are three natural resources that are not renewable?

8. INFER: What alternative energy source might be good for coastline cities? Why?

9. HYPOTHESIZE: How does the destruction of a habitat affect a wildlife population living there?

10. ANALYZE: What forms of pollution other than acid rain, radiation, and ozone depletion could spread around the globe? How would they be spread?

INTERPRETING VISUALS **Use Figure 15-37 to answer each of the following questions.**

11. What energy resource accounts for the most energy use?

12. What percentage of the world's energy use do fossil fuels make up?

13. What percentage of the world's energy use do other fuels make up?

14. Which type of fuel accounts for more energy use, all nonfossil fuels combined or natural gas?

15. About what percentage of fossil fuel use does coal account for?

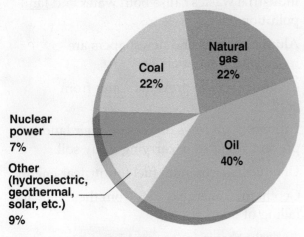

▲ **Figure 15-37** Energy resources

Chapter 16 The Exploration of Space

▲ **Figure 16-1** The space shuttle lifts off from its launch pad in Cape Canaveral, Florida.

The space shuttle is made up of an orbiter, a fuel tank, and booster rockets. The orbiter carries the crew and cargo into space and lands back on Earth like an airplane. The space shuttle is the world's first reusable spacecraft. It can fly missions and return home, then return to space later for more missions. The first shuttle mission, with the orbiter *Columbia*, was launched on April 12, 1981.

▶What do you think are the advantages in having a reusable spacecraft system?

Contents

16-1 What is astronomy?

INVESTIGATE

Calculating the Length of a Light-Year
HANDS-ON ACTIVITY

1. Light travels about 300,000 km per second. How many kilometers does light travel per minute? Write this number down.

2. How many kilometers does light travel per hour? Multiply your number from Step 1 by 60. Write this number down.

3. How many kilometers does light travel in a day? Multiply the number you got in Step 2 by 24. Write this number down.

4. Multiply the number you got in Step 3 by 365, for the number of days in a year. This will give you the distance in kilometers that light travels in one year.

THINK ABOUT IT: Why would knowing the speed of light be important to astronomers?

Objective
Explain what is meant by astronomy.

Key Terms
astronomy (uh-STRAHN-uh-mee): study of stars, planets, and other objects in space

solar system: Sun and all the bodies that orbit it

Ancient Astronomy People have wondered about the skies for thousands of years. The study of space and all the objects in it is called **astronomy.** Astronomy is one of the oldest sciences. Ancient records predicting eclipses of the Sun date back to the first century B.C.

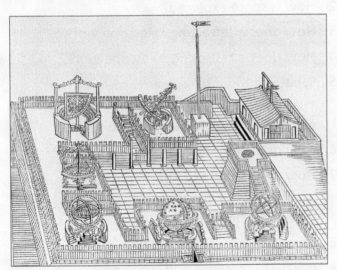

▲ **Figure 16-2** Ancient astronomers studied the skies with special tools.

The planets Mercury, Venus, Mars, Jupiter, and Saturn were all known more than 5,000 years ago. No new planets were found until 1781, when Uranus was discovered.

 LIST: Which planets did the ancients know?

Uses of Astronomy Ancient peoples solved many problems using astronomy. Most ancient societies depended on the changing of the seasons. Farmers had to know when to plant their crops. Astronomers were able to predict the coming of spring for them. Sailors, too, used the positions of the stars to navigate at sea.

2 EXPLAIN: How did the ancients use astronomy?

Modern Astronomy Ancient astronomers made observations using only their eyes. Over time, new tools helped astronomers to see farther into space. In 1609, the Italian scientist Galileo (gal-uh-LAY-oh) Galilei used a simple telescope to look at the Moon and other objects. Today, astronomers use telescopes, satellites, and space probes to observe the planets and study stars many trillions of kilometers from Earth.

What do modern astronomers study? They study the universe. The universe is everything that exists. Astronomers called planetologists study the solar system. The **solar system** includes the Sun and all of the bodies in space that orbit it. Astronomers called cosmologists study how the universe began and how it will end.

▲ **Figure 16-3** Telescopes help astronomers study objects in space.

 DESCRIBE: What are two kinds of astronomers?

✓ CHECKING CONCEPTS

1. Five thousand years ago, there were _____ known planets, not including Earth.
2. Sailors found their way using the _____.
3. The universe is _____ that exists.

4. Ancient astronomers made observations using only their _____.
5. Astronomers called _____ study how the universe began.
6. The first astronomer to use a telescope to view the Moon was _____.

THINKING CRITICALLY

7. **INFER:** Early astronomers observed that the planets changed their positions in the night sky. However, the stars kept the same positions. Why did sailors use the stars and not the planets to find their way at sea?

BUILDING READING SKILLS

Vocabulary On a sheet of paper, list the names of the following stars: Vega, Sirius, Aldebaran, Polaris, Algol, Capella, Betelgeuse, and Proxima Centauri. Find out what each name means in its original language. Write the meaning and identify the original language next to each name. Also, find out how the names are pronounced.

How Do They Know That?

EARLY IDEAS ABOUT EARTH

Astronomy is an ancient science. Records dating back to before 2000 B.C. show that there was a calendar based on movements of the Sun and Moon. At that time, most people believed Earth was flat, with the stars inside a giant sphere that moved around Earth.

In the sixth century B.C., Pythagoras (pih-THAG-uh-ruhs), a Greek mathematician, challenged the view that Earth was flat. He noted that the masts of ships disappeared below the horizon. He also saw that Earth's shadow on the Moon during a lunar eclipse was curved. From these observations, Pythagoras reasoned that Earth must be round. In the fourth century B.C., the Greek philosopher Aristotle (AR-ihs-taht-uhl) claimed that Earth was at the center of the universe. This claim

▲ **Figure 16-4** Nicolaus Copernicus

went mostly unchallenged for almost 2,000 years. Then, in the early sixteenth century, the Polish mathematician Nicolaus Copernicus (koh-PUHR-nih-kuhs) suggested that the Sun, not Earth, was the center of the solar system. Later observations by Tycho Brahe, Johannes Kepler, Galileo, and Sir Isaac Newton supported Copernicus. This was the beginning of modern astronomy.

Thinking Critically What change in thinking led to modern astronomy?

16-2   How is space explored?

Objective

Explain how space exploration helps scientists learn about Earth and the universe.

Key Term

galaxy (GAL-uhk-see): huge collection of stars, gas, and dust that travels together through space

Answers from Space

The Space Age really began in 1957 with the launch of the Russian satellite *Sputnik*. A year later, the United States launched *Explorer 1*. Since then, humankind has sent spacecraft all around the solar system and people to the Moon. Scientists hope that these missions will answer questions about the universe. They want to know, for example, how the solar system formed and whether intelligent life exists elsewhere in the universe.

▲ **Figure 16-5** *Explorer 1* was the first U.S. spacecraft to be successfully launched.

 INFER: Why do scientists explore space?

How the Universe Formed

Space exploration may provide clues as to how the universe was formed. Scientists think that the universe began about 13 billion years ago in a huge explosion called the Big Bang.

Soon after the Big Bang, galaxies began to form. A **galaxy** is a huge collection of stars, gas, and dust that travels together through space as one body. The most distant galaxies were probably formed soon after the Big Bang.

 DEFINE: What are galaxies?

Hubble Space Telescope

Astronomers are learning more about the universe by using a telescope that is orbiting Earth. The Hubble Space Telescope was launched into space in 1990. It is named after the American astronomer Edwin Hubble. This telescope has observed and taken pictures of many of the planets and distant galaxies that are hard or even impossible to see clearly from Earth.

When the Hubble began operating in space, it did not work properly. Images from deep space were blurry. The problem was corrected several years later during a mission of the space shuttle *Endeavour*.

 INFER: How can the Hubble Space Telescope see so far into space?

◄ **Figure 16-6** The Hubble Space Telescope orbits Earth. It has provided images of many galaxies, such as the Large Magellanic Cloud, seen above.

✔ CHECKING CONCEPTS

1. Space exploration really began in the year _____.

2. Scientists think that the universe began about _____ years ago.

3. The explosion that scientists think might have started the universe is called the _____.

4. The _____ Telescope, which orbits Earth, is able to see very distant galaxies.

5. The space shuttle _____ fixed the Hubble's imaging problem.

💡 THINKING CRITICALLY

6. HYPOTHESIZE: How might traveling deeper into space help scientists answer some of their questions about space?

7. INFER: Why is it easier for telescopes in orbit to view stars?

8. CONCLUDE: How has the Hubble Space Telescope increased our knowledge of space?

Web InfoSearch

Astrolabes The most common astronomical instrument until about 1650 was the astrolabe. It was used to observe the altitude of stars and to guide sailors. The Greek astronomer Hipparchus probably refined the first one. Astrolabes were often made of brass. The Adler Planetarium and Astronomy Museum in Chicago has the largest collection of astrolabes in North America.

▲ **Figure 16-7** Astrolabe from the seventeenth century

SEARCH: Use the Internet to find out more about astrolabes. Are they still being made today? Start your search at www.conceptsandchallenges.com. Some key search words are **astrolabe instrument** and **Hipparchus astrolabe.**

Real-Life Science

SPINOFFS FROM SPACE

How can space exploration help people on Earth? It produces spinoffs. A spinoff is a benefit or product that results from an unrelated activity or process.

Sending spacecraft into space is very costly. One way to save costs is by developing smaller, lighter equipment. Smaller radios, computers, and televisions made for use in space travel are now used on Earth. Many foods sent into space with the astronauts are freeze-dried to make them lighter and last longer. Many of these foods are available in supermarkets today. Lightweight, fireproof, durable clothing, nonstick cookware, and sunglasses that adjust to changes in light are all spinoffs from space.

Other spinoffs help us recover from illnesses. Doctors on Earth need to check on astronauts in space. To meet this need, scientists developed tiny monitoring, recording, and transmitting devices now used on Earth.

Thinking Critically Why is freeze-dried food good for any type of travel?

▲ **Figure 16-8** Improvements in fireproof clothing are a spinoff from space exploration.

16-3 How does a refracting telescope work?

Objective
Explain how a refracting telescope works.

Key Terms
refracting (rih-FRAKT-ing) **telescope:** telescope that uses convex lenses to produce an enlarged image

convex (kahn-VEHKS) **lens:** lens that is thicker in the middle than it is at the edges

Galileo's Telescope Galileo was the first person to look at objects in space through a telescope. Have you ever looked through a telescope? If you have, you know that a telescope makes faraway objects appear much nearer than they are. If you look at the Moon through a telescope, you can see many features on its surface that you cannot see with your eyes alone. Galileo looked at the Moon soon after the telescope was invented. He was the first person to see that the Moon's surface is not smooth. Galileo saw craters, plains, and hills on the Moon.

▲ **Figure 16-9** Galileo's telescope, with Italy in the background

▶ **1** NAME: What features did Galileo see on the surface of the Moon?

Refracting Telescopes Galileo used a **refracting telescope.** It consisted of a tube with two lenses inside. A lens is a piece of glass or plastic that refracts, or bends, light.

The telescope shown in Figure 16-10 is a simple refracting telescope. The lenses in a refracting telescope are convex lenses. **Convex lenses** are lenses that bulge outward. They are thicker in the middle than they are at the edges.

When light passes through a convex lens, the light appears to bend inward, as shown in Figure 16-10. The light produces an image that is larger than the image you would see with your eyes alone.

▶ **2** DESCRIBE: What kinds of lenses are used in a refracting telescope?

How the Lenses Work Each of the lenses in a refracting telescope has a special job to do. The lens at the far end of the tube is called the objective lens. The objective lens collects light and brings the image into focus. The lens at the other end of the tube is called the eyepiece. This lens enlarges, or magnifies, the image formed by the objective lens.

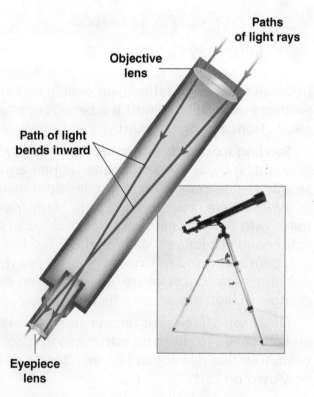

Paths of light rays

Objective lens

Path of light bends inward

Eyepiece lens

▲ **Figure 16-10** A simple refracting telescope

The objective lens and the eyepiece lens work together. They can produce a sharp, clear image of a distant object.

 NAME: What are the two lenses in a refracting telescope called?

✓ CHECKING CONCEPTS

1. A telescope makes the Moon appear _____.

2. Galileo saw _____, hills, and plains on the Moon.

3. The _____ in a refracting telescope contains two convex lenses.

4. A convex lens appears to bend, or _____, light.

5. The lenses in a refracting telescope are _____ lenses.

6. The two lenses that are used in a refracting telescope are the objective lens and the _____ lens.

 THINKING CRITICALLY

7. COMPARE: Which surface features of the Moon are also found on Earth?

8. INFER: Why does the image that is formed by a telescope appear to be nearer than the object really is?

9. HYPOTHESIZE: If light did not bend when it was passed through a lens, would the refracting telescope still work? Why or why not?

BUILDING SCIENCE SKILLS

Observing Many objects that you use every day contain convex lenses. Make a list of common objects that contain convex lenses. List as many of them as you can. Briefly describe how the lenses are used in these objects. Hint: What part of your body has a convex lens?

 Hands-On Activity

MAKING A SIMPLE TELESCOPE

You will need 2 convex lenses or magnifying glasses.

1. Look at a distant object through a convex lens.

2. Move the lens back and forth slowly. Stop when you see the object clearly through the lens.

3. Without moving the first lens, hold a second convex lens close to your eye.

4. Move the second lens back and forth slowly. Stop when you can see the distant object clearly through both lenses.

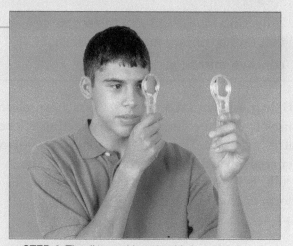

▲ **STEP 4** The distant object should show clearly through both lenses.

Practicing Your Skills

5. IDENTIFY: What part of a telescope does the first lens represent?

6. OBSERVE: How does the image appear through the first lens?

7. IDENTIFY: What part of a telescope does the second lens represent?

8. OBSERVE: How does the image appear when you look through both lenses?

9. ANALYZE: Would a telescope with a large objective lens be better than one with a small objective lens? Explain.

16-4 How does a reflecting telescope work?

INVESTIGATE

Modeling the Way Light Travels
HANDS-ON ACTIVITY

1. Cut three 15- by-15 cm cards from cardboard. On each card, in the middle of one side, cut a 2- by-2 cm notch. Use modeling clay to place the cards about 10 cm apart. Line up the notches so they are in a straight line with each other.

2. Shine a flashlight behind the cards. Use the modeling clay to hold up a large index card at the other end of the row of cards.

3. Darken the room. Observe any light on the index card.

4. Move the cards so that the notches are not in a straight line. Observe the light on the index card.

THINK ABOUT IT: When did light appear on the index card? What does this tell you about how light travels?

STEP 2

Objectives
Explain how a reflecting telescope works. Compare it with a refracting telescope.

Key Terms
reflecting (rih-FLEHKT-ing) **telescope:** telescope that uses a concave mirror to collect light
concave mirror: mirror that curves inward

Using Mirrors to See A refracting telescope uses lenses to collect light. A **reflecting telescope** uses a mirror. This mirror is a **concave mirror.** It curves inward. In a reflecting telescope, the mirror collects light from distant objects and focuses it to form an image.

▶ DEFINE: What is a reflecting telescope?

Newton's Telescope In 1668, Isaac Newton, an English scientist, made the first reflecting telescope. He used a concave mirror to collect the light and a convex lens as an eyepiece to magnify the image. He also used a flat mirror to reflect light from the concave mirror to one side. This prevented the eyepiece from blocking the incoming light.

Some reflecting telescopes have the eyepiece to one side of the telescope tube. A camera can then be attached to it to take pictures.

▲ **Figure 16-11** Newton uses his reflecting telescope.

▶ EXPLAIN: Why is the eyepiece that is used in a reflecting telescope sometimes found on one side of the tube?

Modern Reflecting Telescopes Modern reflecting telescopes have very large mirrors. The Hale Telescope on Mount Palomar in California has a mirror 5 m across.

The twin Keck telescopes that sit on the summit of Mauna Kea in Hawaii have 36 mirrors that together measure about 10 m across. This gives a light-collecting area almost half the size of a tennis court. Composite telescopes are being developed today that will have mirrors of up to 16 m across.

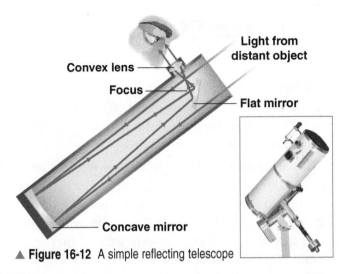

Light from distant object

Convex lens

Focus

Flat mirror

Concave mirror

▲ **Figure 16-12** A simple reflecting telescope

 EXPLAIN: What is the benefit of larger mirrors in telescopes?

✓ CHECKING CONCEPTS

1. What kind of telescope uses a mirror to collect and focus light?
2. Who made the first reflecting telescope?
3. What kind of lens is used as an eyepiece in a reflecting telescope?

4. Where is a reflecting telescope's eyepiece sometimes found?
5. Where are two modern reflecting telescopes with very large mirrors found?

💡 THINKING CRITICALLY

6. CONTRAST: How do refracting and reflecting telescopes differ?
7. ANALYZE: Why is a reflecting telescope with a large concave mirror better than a reflecting telescope with a small mirror?
8. INFER: What might the pictures taken by a reflecting telescope be used for?

BUILDING SCIENCE SKILLS

Researching An observatory is a building or group of buildings with large telescopes. Find out what kinds of telescopes are used in the following observatories: Kitt Peak, Mauna Kea, Yerkes, and Mount Wilson. Write a report.

Integrating Environmental Science

TOPICS: pollution, overdevelopment

LIGHT POLLUTION

Because of streetlights, the night sky near cities and towns is never very dark. This is true even when there is no Moon showing and clouds hide the stars. The lights reflect off water droplets and other particles in the air. So much light makes it difficult for astronomers to observe stars and other objects using optical telescopes. Astronomers call this interference light pollution.

Street lamps cause a large percentage of light pollution. Businesses that leave on electric signs all night contribute, too. Many people keep lights on around their homes for safety and security. All of these lights brighten the nighttime sky and make viewing difficult. They can also upset the natural cycles of plants and animals in the area. Fewer lights, shields on streetlights that direct light down, and lights that are activated only when needed can all help reduce light pollution.

Thinking Critically What could you do to cut down on light pollution?

▲ **Figure 16-13** Satellite photos from 20 years ago (top) and today (bottom).

16-5 What is a radio telescope?

Objective
Explain how a radio telescope works.

Key Term
radio telescope: telescope that can receive radio waves from sources in space

Star Search Stars are usually not visible during the day. They are there, but you cannot see them because of the Sun.

The Sun is also a star. It is the star closest to Earth. The bright light of the Sun outshines the dimmer light from the distant stars. On rainy nights, clouds hide the light from the stars. Not even a refracting or reflecting telescope can help you see the stars on a cloudy night.

1 EXPLAIN: Why are the stars not visible in daylight?

Radio Waves from Space Stars not only send out visible light. They also send out all forms of electromagnetic radiation.

A **radio telescope** can receive radio waves from space. It can find stars during the day or when there are clouds.

In 1932, an American engineer, Karl Jansky, heard the first radio signals from space. He found that the radio waves were coming from the center of our galaxy, the Milky Way Galaxy.

In 1937, Grote Reber built a radio telescope with a 9.5-m reflector dish, or antenna. With this, Reber was able to make the first radio map of the Milky Way Galaxy.

The antenna of a radio telescope works like a mirror does in a reflecting telescope. The antenna collects and focuses radio waves given off by stars and other objects in space. The radio waves are transmitted to a receiver. An astronomer can actually "listen" to the stars this way.

2 COMPARE: How is a radio telescope like a reflecting telescope?

Advantages of Radio Telescopes There are three main advantages to using radio telescopes. First, a radio telescope can detect some objects that refracting and reflecting telescopes cannot see. Many objects in the universe give off strong radio waves but very little visible light.

Second, a radio telescope can be used in any kind of weather. Radio waves can travel through clouds in Earth's atmosphere. Reflecting or refracting telescopes cannot be used on very cloudy nights.

Third, a radio telescope can be used during the day, when stars other than the Sun are not visible. Reflecting or refracting telescopes can only be used at night, when the Sun's light does not drown out the light from other, more distant stars.

3 EXPLAIN: How is a radio telescope able to function on a cloudy night?

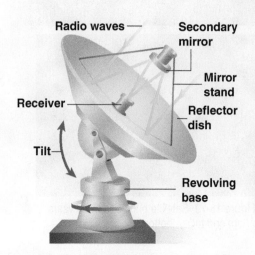

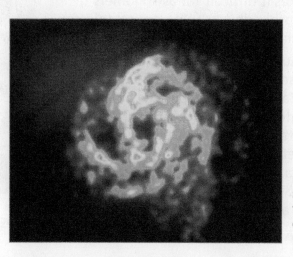

◀ **Figure 16-14** Left: The antenna system of a radio telescope. Right: A false-color image produced by a radio telescope.

1. The star closest to Earth is _____.
2. You cannot see stars on a _____ night.
3. A _____ telescope can be used during the day.
4. The first radio map of the Milky Way Galaxy was made by _____.
5. The _____ of a radio telescope works like the mirror of a reflecting telescope.

💡 THINKING CRITICALLY

6. CONTRAST: How do radio telescopes differ from reflecting and refracting telescopes?
7. LIST: What are three advantages of radio telescopes over optical telescopes?
8. INFER: How do you think astronomers can identify that a sound picked up by a radio telescope is from space?

Web InfoSearch

Interferometry A radio interferometer is two or more radio telescopes linked electronically. This greatly increases their power. Radio interferometers, such as the Very Large Array, can make much more detailed pictures than single radio telescopes can.

▲ **Figure 16-15**
The Very Large Array

SEARCH: Use the Internet to find out more about this. Where is the Very Large Array found? What is it used for? Start your search at www.conceptsandchallenges.com. Some key search words are **radio telescope, interferometer,** and **Very Large Array radio telescope.**

Science and Technology

THE SEARCH FOR LIFE ELSEWHERE

Exobiology is a branch of biology that deals with the search for life, including intelligent life, outside of the solar system. In the 1950s, American scientists realized that radio signals could come from or be sent across the galaxy. The signals were, therefore, perfect for communicating with aliens, should any be talking or listening.

▲ **Figure 16-16** The radio telescope at Arecibo in Puerto Rico

Project SETI (Search for Extraterrestrial Intelligence) was formed in 1959 to listen for radio signals. In 1974, the radio telescope at Arecibo in Puerto Rico sent the first human message to the stars. It was made up of 1,679 on-off pulses aimed 25,000 light-years away, at a cluster of stars known as M13.

SETI was canceled in 1993 without having received any alien signals. However, in 1995, a new program was formed called Project Phoenix. Based in Greenbank, West Virginia, Phoenix used radio telescopes from all over the world to listen for artificial radio signals from space.

Thinking Critically If you could contact an alien, what would you tell it about Earth?

THE Big IDEA

How do telescopes detect electromagnetic waves in space?

A rainbow shows the colors of the visible spectrum. Each color of the visible spectrum forms from light rays that have a particular wavelength. Violet has the shortest wavelength of the visible spectrum. Red has the longest wavelength.

Rays of light can have wavelengths shorter than violet and longer than red. We cannot see light at these wavelengths with our unaided eyes. However, special telescopes and other instruments are able to detect this light. Using these tools, scientists know that the visible spectrum is just one small part of the entire electromagnetic spectrum.

Astronomers use the invisible parts of the electromagnetic spectrum to study light rays with shorter or longer wavelengths than those of the visible spectrum. Using these tools, astronomers have gathered a great deal of information about distant stars and galaxies.

Note that infrared light, microwaves, and radio waves all have wavelengths longer than the colors of the visible spectrum. These invisible parts of the electromagnetic spectrum are used in everyday life. Microwaves cook foods. Infrared light keeps foods warm. Radio waves broadcast movies and music around the world. Ultraviolet light, X-rays, and gamma rays all have wavelengths shorter than the colors of the visible spectrum. Tanning booths use ultraviolet rays to darken the skin. X-rays take pictures of bones and teeth. Gamma rays can kill cancer cells.

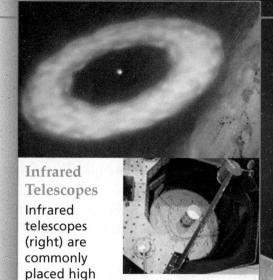

Infrared Telescopes

Infrared telescopes (right) are commonly placed high on satellites that travel through space. One infrared telescope detected rings of dust around the star Vega (shown above) and other nearby stars. Scientists believe these rings might be newly forming solar systems.

Gamma Ray Telescopes

The Compton Gamma Ray Observatory (above right) spent four years in space compiling an image of the Milky Way. The halo effect shown (above left) was made by gamma rays emitted from space.

Figure 16-17 ▶
Electromagnetic spectrum

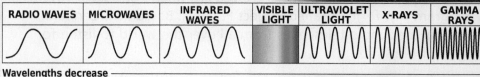

RADIO WAVES	MICROWAVES	INFRARED WAVES	VISIBLE LIGHT	ULTRAVIOLET LIGHT	X-RAYS	GAMMA RAYS

Wavelengths decrease ⟶

Look at the illustrations that appear on these two pages. Then, follow the directions in the Science Log to learn more about "the big idea." ✦

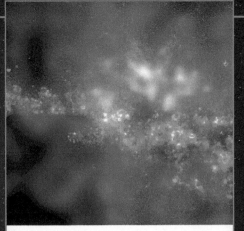

X-Ray Telescopes

Most X-ray telescopes, like the Chandra Observatory shown below, contain a reflector made up of a series of curved mirrors. Astronomers use X-ray telescopes to study hot gases (shown above), black holes, comets, and quasars.

Ultraviolet Light Telescopes

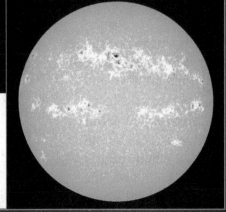

Ultraviolet telescopes are often located aboard satellites like the one shown here. The telescopes have gathered information about very hot space objects such as the Sun (right), quasars, and white dwarfs.

16-6 How do astronomers measure distance?

Objective

Identify two methods astronomers use to measure distances in space.

Key Terms

light-year: unit of measurement equal to about 10 trillion km

parallax (PAR-uh-laks)**:** apparent change in the position of a distant object when seen from two different places

astronomical (as-truh-NAHM-ih-kuhl) **unit (AU):** unit of measurement based on the Sun's distance from Earth and equal to about 150 million km

Measuring Distance Most distances on Earth can be measured in meters or kilometers. How would you measure the distance from Earth to the stars? You might try to use kilometers. However, astronomers have found that the distances to stars are so great that the numbers are too large to work with easily.

For example, the star called Proxima Centauri (PRAHK-suh-muh sen-TAW-ree) is the closest star, other than the Sun, to Earth. Proxima Centauri is 40,000,000,000,000 km from Earth. As you can see, this is a very large number. Astronomers had to create special units to measure distances in space.

▶ **1** EXPLAIN: Why did scientists create special units to measure distances in space?

Light-Years Astronomers often measure the distance to an object in space using light-years. A **light-year** is equal to the distance light travels in one year.

Light travels through space at a speed of about 300,000 km per second. A light-year is equal to almost 10 trillion km. Light from the Sun reaches Earth in a little more than 8 minutes. Light from the North Star, Polaris, reaches Earth in about 431 years.

▶ **2** INTERPRET: How far, in light-years, is Polaris from Earth?

Parallax Astronomers can use parallax to find out distances to the closer stars. **Parallax** is the apparent change in the position of a distant object when seen from two different places.

Figure 16-18 shows how a nearby star seems to move against a background of more distant stars. By measuring how much the nearby star appears to move, astronomers can calculate how far away the star actually is. Nearby stars have a larger angle of parallax than distant stars do.

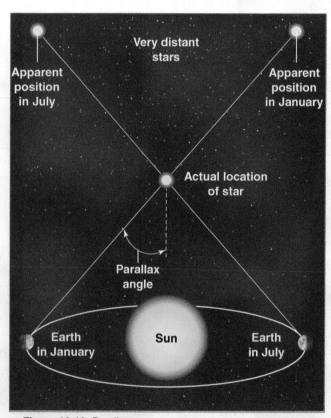

▲ **Figure 16-18** Parallax

Astronomical Units Although it varies, the average distance from Earth to the Sun is about 150 million km. Astronomers call this distance an astronomical unit. One **astronomical unit**, or 1 **AU**, is equal to 150 million km. An astronomical unit can also be used to measure distances in space, especially distances between the planets in the solar system. Figure 16-19 shows the distances of the planets from the Sun in astronomical units.

DISTANCES OF PLANETS FROM THE SUN			
Planet	Distance	Planet	Distance
Mercury	0.4 AU	Jupiter	5.2 AU
Venus	0.7 AU	Saturn	9.5 AU
Earth	1.0 AU	Uranus	19.2 AU
Mars	1.5 AU	Neptune	30.1 AU

▲ **Figure 16-19**

 OBSERVE: In astronomical units, how far from the Sun is Venus?

☑ CHECKING CONCEPTS

1. Why do astronomers not measure the distances to stars in kilometers?
2. What is the name of the star, other than the Sun, closest to Earth?
3. What is the average distance from Earth to the Sun in kilometers?
4. What is an astronomical unit?

5. What is the speed of light in space?
6. What is a light-year?

💡 THINKING CRITICALLY

7. **CALCULATE:** Convert each of the distances shown in Figure 16-19 into kilometers.
8. **SEQUENCE:** Put the planets in order based on distance to each other, from greatest distance to least distance.

BUILDING MATH SKILLS

Calculating One light-year is equal to the distance light travels in one Earth year, or 10 trillion km. The diameter of Earth is only 13,000 km. The star known as Alpha Centauri is 4.4 light-years away. Figure out how many Earths would have to be placed side by side to reach Alpha Centauri. Procyon is 11.4 light-years away. How many Earths would be needed to reach the star known as Procyon?

 Hands-On Activity

OBSERVING PARALLAX

You will need three sheets of continuous-feed computer paper, a metric ruler, a drinking straw, and tape.

1. Remove one of the side edges from the computer paper. Tape this strip horizontally to the wall.
2. Tape the straw upright on a metric ruler at the 15-cm mark.
3. Stand about 3 m from the wall. Hold the ruler level with the floor. Close your left eye and line up the straw with the left end of the paper strip.
4. Open your left eye and close your right eye. Count the number of holes the straw appears to move along the strip.
5. Move the straw to the ruler's 30-cm mark and repeat Steps 3 and 4.

▲ **STEP 3** Close your left eye and line up the straw with the left end of the paper strip.

Practicing Your Skills

6. **IDENTIFY:** What does the strip of paper with the holes represent?
7. **OBSERVE: a.** At the 15-cm mark, how many holes did the straw appear to move? **b.** How many did it move at the 30-cm mark?
8. **ANALYZE:** Why does the straw appear to change position?
9. **COMPARE:** Which has a greater parallax, a nearby star or a faraway star? Why?

16-7 How does a rocket work?

Objective
Describe how a rocket works.

Key Term
thrust: forward force produced in a rocket engine

Newton's Third Law of Motion The Chinese invented rockets almost 800 years ago. They used them for fireworks and weapons.

To understand how a rocket works, you must know Newton's third law of motion. This law says that for every action, there is an equal and opposite reaction. For example, suppose you are sitting in a rowboat on a lake. You throw a rock into the lake. This is the action. At the same time, the rowboat moves backward slightly. This is the reaction.

1 STATE: What is Newton's third law of motion?

Rocket Engines The force that pushes a rocket forward is called **thrust.** The greater the thrust, the higher and faster the rocket will travel. What causes thrust? Fuel is burned inside a rocket engine. The fuel can be a solid or a liquid. As the fuel burns, inside the engine it produces hot gases that begin to expand. The expanding gases create pressure inside of the engine. This pressure forces the hot gases out of the back of the rocket. This is the action force. The rocket moves forward, in the opposite direction. This is called the thrust, or reaction force.

2 DEFINE: What is thrust?

▲ **Figure 16-20** The *Saturn V* rocket was much more powerful than earlier rockets. It was used to launch the *Apollo* astronauts to the Moon.

Escaping Earth's Gravity A lot of thrust is needed for a rocket to escape Earth's gravity. To get into Earth orbit, a rocket must reach a speed of more than 40,000 km/h. Large amounts of fuel are needed to produce enough thrust to reach this speed.

Rocket engines need oxygen to burn fuel. In space, there is no air to supply the oxygen. Rockets must carry their own.

As a rocket moves farther away from Earth, the pull of Earth's gravity on the rocket becomes weaker. Once the rocket is in space, there is little to slow it down. The rocket does not need to burn fuel to keep moving. It keeps moving in the same direction at a constant speed. Fuel is needed in space only to change the rocket's speed or direction.

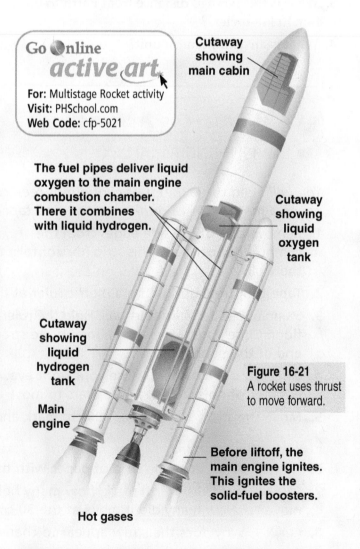

Go **O**nline
active art

For: Multistage Rocket activity
Visit: PHSchool.com
Web Code: cfp-5021

Cutaway showing main cabin

The fuel pipes deliver liquid oxygen to the main engine combustion chamber. There it combines with liquid hydrogen.

Cutaway showing liquid oxygen tank

Cutaway showing liquid hydrogen tank

Main engine

Figure 16-21
A rocket uses thrust to move forward.

Before liftoff, the main engine ignites. This ignites the solid-fuel boosters.

Hot gases

3 EXPLAIN: Why must rockets carry oxygen?

✓ CHECKING CONCEPTS

1. Rockets were invented by the _____ people.

2. Newton's third law of motion says that for every action, there is an equal and _____ reaction.

3. The force that pushes a rocket forward is called _____.

4. Rocket fuel needs _____ to burn.

5. As a rocket moves farther away from Earth, the pull of gravity becomes _____.

THINKING CRITICALLY

6. ANALYZE: What is fuel needed for in space?

7. PREDICT: Could a rocket traveling at a speed of 10,000 km/h get into space? Explain.

8. INFER: Why is thrust also known as the reaction force?

9. EXPLAIN: Why does a rocket not need to burn fuel to keep moving once it is in space?

BUILDING MATH SKILLS

Calculating Thrust is a force. The unit of force in the metric system is the newton (N). One newton (1 N) is equal to 4.5 lb. Below is a list of rockets and their thrusts at launch. The thrust is given in pounds. Convert each thrust into newtons. Then, list the rockets in order, from least thrust to greatest thrust.

Delta	205,000 lb
Saturn V	7,570,000 lb
Mercury-Atlas	367,000 lb
Space shuttle	6,925,000 lb
Vanguard	28,000 lb

For example:

$$1 \text{ N} = 4.5 \text{ lb}$$
$$105,000 \text{ lb} \div 4.5 \text{ lb/N} = 23,333 \text{ N}$$

Hands-On Activity

DEMONSTRATING ACTION AND REACTION FORCES

You will need about 3 m of fishing line, a 3-cm piece of a drinking straw, tape, a balloon, and a twist tie.

1. Inflate a balloon. Close the end with a twist tie.

2. Thread the fishing line through the straw. Tape the straw across the top of the balloon.

3. Tie one end of the string to a chair. Hold the other end.

4. Move away from the chair. Hold the string tight. Remove the twist tie from the balloon and observe what happens.

▲ **STEP 2** Tape the straw to the balloon after you thread the fishing line through it.

Practicing Your Skills

5. EXPLAIN: What happened to the air in the balloon when you removed the twist tie?

6. OBSERVE: Where did the balloon go?

7. INFER: In which direction did the air from the balloon move?

8. IDENTIFY: **a.** What was the action force? **b.** What was the reaction force?

LAB ACTIVITY
Modeling Newton's Third Law of Motion

Materials
Safety goggles,
35-mm film canister
with inner-locking cap,
sheet of paper,
cellophane tape,
scissors, fizzing
antacid tablet, water,
tablespoon

BACKGROUND

The only way to reach space is to ride a rocket. The force driving most rockets is produced when rocket fuel burns. Hot gases shoot out from the engines of the rocket, and the rocket travels upward into space. However, not all rockets have to burn fuel to work. Thrust can be produced in many ways.

PURPOSE

In this activity, you will construct and fly a rocket.

PROCEDURE

1. Copy the chart in Figure 16-22.

2. Using half a sheet of paper, roll and tape a snug tube around a film canister. Make sure the cap end of the canister sticks out 12 mm. Tape the tube to the canister.

3. Cut out and tape rocket fins to the lower end of the tube. The fins can be of any shape. Make three or four fins. Cut out a half-circle of paper. Roll it into a nose cone. CAUTION ⚠ Be careful when using scissors.

4. Tape the nose cone to the upper end of the tube. Your rocket is now ready. Draw a diagram of the rocket in your chart.

5. Put on your safety goggles. Take your rocket to a launch site. Put a tablespoon of water inside the canister. Drop in one-half of an antacid tablet that fizzes when dropped into water.

▲ **STEP 2** Roll the paper around the film canister.

▲ **STEP 3** Tape rocket fins to the lower end of the tube. Prepare a nose cone.

▲ **STEP 5** Drop half of your antacid tablet into the canister.

▲ **STEP 6** Set your rocket on the launch pad and step away.

6. Quickly snap the film canister cap in place. Set the rocket right side up on the launch pad and step away. Record your observations in your chart.

Diagram of your rocket	How well did your rocket perform?
Diagram of someone else's rocket	How well did that rocket perform?

▲ **Figure 16-22** Draw a diagram of your rocket and someone else's rocket. Record your observations.

CONCLUSIONS

1. OBSERVE: How high did your rocket go?

2. OBSERVE: Did any other rockets fly higher than yours?

3. ANALYZE: What do you think made some rockets fly higher than others?

4. COMPARE: Write a report comparing the two rockets you observed. Say why you think one worked better than the other.

What is the space shuttle?

Objective

Explain how the space shuttle works.

A Reusable Spaceship In the 1960s and 1970s, all spaceflights were made with spacecraft that could be used only once. This was very expensive and wasteful. The National Aeronautics and Space Administration (NASA) decided to build a spacecraft that could go into space and return to Earth many times. This new kind of spacecraft was known as the Space Transportation System, or the space shuttle.

 INFER: How was the space shuttle an improvement over earlier spacecraft?

Design of the Shuttle The space shuttle has three main parts. Two of the parts are needed to get the shuttle into space. These are the solid-fuel booster rockets and the liquid-fuel tank. The third part is the shuttle orbiter. The orbiter is the only part that stays in space after launch.

How does the shuttle get into orbit? At launch, both the booster rockets and the orbiter's rocket engines are fired. After launch, the boosters separate from the orbiter. They fall back into the ocean and can be hauled out to be used again.

The large liquid-fuel tank provides fuel for the orbiter's engines. The tank drops away before the orbiter reaches orbit. It is not reusable.

Once the orbiter is in space, the engines are turned off. They are fired again to change the orbiter's speed and direction when it is ready to return to Earth. When its mission is over, the orbiter glides to a landing on a runway.

◄ **Figure 16-24** The orbiter uses a parachute to help slow its speed upon landing.

2 **LIST:** What are the three main parts of the space shuttle?

Uses of the Shuttle The shuttle's cargo bay is designed to carry between 10,000 and 50,000 kg of equipment into orbit. The weight depends partly on the shuttle's altitude in space. Satellites and space probes can be launched from the shuttle.

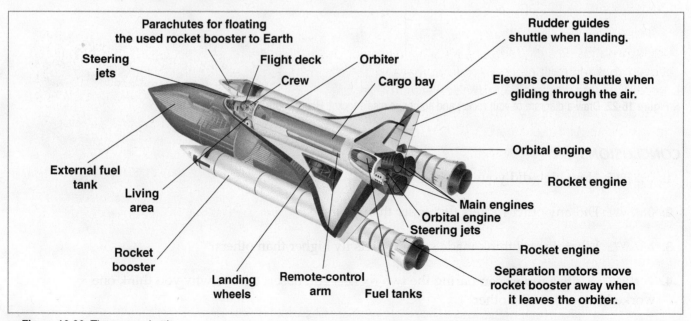

▲ **Figure 16-23** The space shuttle

Shuttle astronauts can repair satellites in orbit. Satellites can also be returned to Earth for repair.

▲ **Figure 16-25** Spacelab is used for experiments aboard the space shuttle.

The shuttle will sometimes carry a flying laboratory called Spacelab in its cargo bay. In this laboratory, a variety of science experiments are performed. The shuttle is also used to ferry people and supplies into space.

 NAME: What is the laboratory carried by the shuttle called?

CHECKING CONCEPTS

1. Another name for the space shuttle is _____.

2. The shuttle orbiter lands like an airplane on a _____.

3. Satellites are carried in the shuttle's _____.

4. Spacelab is a flying _____.

💡 THINKING CRITICALLY

5. ANALYZE: How is the space shuttle useful to people on Earth?

6. INFER: Why is it important for the boosters to be separated from the orbiter before going into orbit?

INTERPRETING VISUALS

Use Figure 16-23 to answer the following questions.

7. IDENTIFY: How many main parts does the space shuttle have?

8. INFER: What part of the shuttle actually goes into space?

9. ANALYZE: How does the design of the shuttle make it a kind of space plane?

Science and Technology

THE NATIONAL AERONAUTICS AND SPACE ADMINISTRATION

The National Aeronautics and Space Administration, or NASA, started operations in 1958. NASA is a government agency that supports research. It also develops vehicles and programs for exploring Earth's atmosphere and space.

Over the years, NASA has achieved many technological breakthroughs. Project Mercury, NASA's first major project, proved that technology could help humans to survive in space. The *Apollo* missions put people on the Moon.

Space shuttles today are helping to build the International Space Station. Spacecraft are being sent to Mars and beyond. The Hubble Space Telescope takes pictures of the solar system and the stars beyond. Satellites are being launched into space for many different purposes. NASA technology has also been used to improve our health. *Apollo* technologies led to computerized aerial tomography, or CAT scans, and better kidney dialysis machines. Space shuttle technologies led to a new pump used in artificial hearts.

▲ **Figure 16-26** NASA technicians work on Earth and in space.

Thinking Critically What types of vehicles has NASA built?

What are satellites and space probes?

Objective

Explain how artificial satellites and space probes are used to explore space.

Key Terms

satellite (SAT-uhl-eyet): natural or artificial object orbiting a body in space

orbit: curved path of one object around another object in space

Artificial Satellites

A **satellite** is any object, natural or artificial, that follows a curved path around another object in space. The curved path of the object is its **orbit**.

▲ **Figure 16-27**
An *Intelsat VI* satellite

For thousands of years, astronomers were only able to study the skies from the surface of Earth. Then, on October 4, 1957, the Space Age began. On that day, the Soviet Union launched the first artificial satellite. It was called *Sputnik*. *Sputnik* circled Earth every 96 minutes.

Most satellites are launched into one of four main orbits. Nearly circular orbits are usually about 250 km above Earth's surface. Polar orbits are usually about 800 km high.

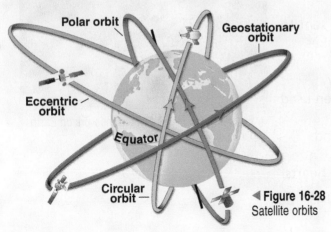

Polar orbit

Geostationary orbit

Eccentric orbit

Equator

Circular orbit

◀ **Figure 16-28**
Satellite orbits

The height of a highly elliptical, or eccentric, orbit depends on where the satellite is in its orbit. A geostationary orbit is 36,000 km above Earth's surface. A satellite in geostationary orbit stays above the same spot on Earth. This is because it travels at the same speed as the planet rotates.

1 ▶ NAME: What is the curved path of a satellite called?

Uses of Satellites Since *Sputnik*, thousands of artificial satellites have been placed in orbit around Earth. These collect information about Earth, the Sun, the stars, other planets, comets, and other bodies in the solar system.

For example, the Global Positioning System (GPS) is a radio navigation system of about 24 satellites operating in circular orbits. GPS is a guidance service provided by the U.S. Air Force Space Command unit.

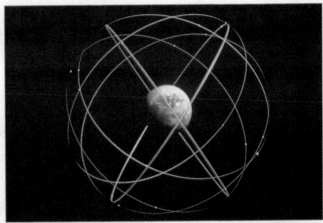

▲ **Figure 16-29** The 24 GPS satellites circle Earth using six different orbits.

The system relays positions on Earth's surface in degrees of latitude and longitude. GPS receivers with computers have improved surveying techniques. Surveyors are now able to monitor changes of Earth's crust caused by tectonic motion. Meteorologists are able to use GPS signals to measure the temperature and water content of the atmosphere. Geologists can accurately map changes in the Greenland ice sheet to help them understand climate changes.

Computers are essential in turning satellite data or measurements into meaningful information. For example, computers help meteorologists translate weather satellite data into current temperatures, pressures, humidity readings, and wind speeds. This information is used to create a weather report.

 DESCRIBE: What are satellites used for?

Space Probes Astronauts have been sent to the Moon to explore it and have returned safely to Earth. Space can also be explored by space probes, which do not carry people. In fact, many kinds of space exploration are best done with space probes. Space probes can go places that would be too far or too dangerous for astronauts to travel to.

For example, part of the *Galileo* space probe sent to Jupiter entered its atmosphere in 1995. It radioed important information to Earth before being destroyed by high temperatures and pressure. *Cassini*, launched in 1997, reached Saturn in 2004. It was scheduled to orbit the planet and its moons until June 2008.

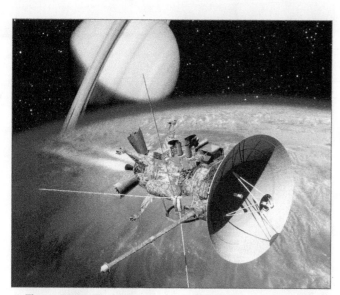

▲ **Figure 16-30** The *Cassini* probe explored Saturn from orbit when it got there in 2004.

Space probes are usually sent on one-way missions. They do not return to Earth. Some space probes to the outer planets, such as *Voyagers 1* and *2*, have even been sent out of the solar system.

The *Voyager* space probes were launched in 1977. In 1989, *Voyager 2* became the first spacecraft from Earth to reach Neptune. Both space probes sent back stunning images of all the giant planets.

Scientists believe that *Voyager 2* will continue traveling for thousands of years. They hope to continue receiving signals from both space probes until at least the year 2020.

 IDENTIFY: What are two planets that have been visited by space probes?

☑ **CHECKING CONCEPTS**

1. What is a satellite?
2. What was *Sputnik*?
3. What was the first space probe to reach Neptune?
4. What did *Cassini* do when it got to Saturn?

💡 **THINKING CRITICALLY**

5. NAME: What are two advantages that space probes have over spaceships and human crews?
6. INFER: *Telstar* was one of the first artificial satellites. It was launched in 1962. *Telstar* was a communications satellite. What do you think was the function of *Telstar?*
7. INFER: How does GPS help ships and aircraft?

BUILDING SCIENCE SKILLS

Classifying Below is a list of some important artificial satellites. Find out the function of each. Then, classify each according to its function. On a piece of paper, write the words *Communications Satellite, Weather Satellite, Navigation Satellite,* and *Scientific Satellite.* Place each satellite under its correct heading.

Early Bird	*Explorer I*	*Intelsat*	*Tiros*
Echo	*Landsat*	*Nimbus*	*Transit*

◄ **Figure 16-31**
Tiros

How are space stations used?

Objective

Explain the role of space stations.

Space Stations Artificial satellites and space probes are very useful in space exploration. They can gather information and send it back to scientists on Earth. The scientists do not have to leave Earth. Sometimes, however, scientists prefer to make their observations directly. In a space station, scientists can live and work in space for long periods of time.

▶ **EXPLAIN:** What is a space station useful for?

Early Space Stations In 1971, the former Soviet Union launched the first space station, *Salyut* ("salute"). The first U.S. space station, *Skylab*, was launched in 1973. It was about the size of a small house. Three teams of astronauts visited *Skylab*. Eventually, *Salyut* and *Skylab* wandered from their orbits, causing them to fall to Earth. They had shown, though, that people could safely live and work in space.

▲ **Figure 16-32** *Skylab* was the first U.S. space station.

The former Soviet Union later constructed in space its second space station, called *Mir* ("peace"). The first part of *Mir* was launched in 1986. Some Russian cosmonauts stayed on *Mir* for more than a year, setting new records. *Mir* fell out of orbit and back to Earth in 2001.

▶ **NAME:** What was the first U.S. space station?

The International Space Station The United States and Russia launched the first parts of a new space station, called the International Space Station, or ISS, in 1998. Other countries are involved in this project, as well. The ISS may be complete by 2010. Many parts have already been carried into orbit by space shuttles or other rockets.

People have been working and living on the ISS since the year 2000. They use the space shuttle to travel to and from Earth. The completed ISS will have laboratories, living quarters, docking bays for shuttles, and solar panels for energy. It will also have a satellite repair shop.

▲ **Figure 16-33** The International Space Station (ISS) is scheduled to be finished by the year 2010.

▶ **DESCRIBE:** What are some parts of the ISS?

Living in Space Astronauts on the ISS must live and work in conditions that are very different from those on Earth. Life-support systems on board must provide oxygen and remove carbon dioxide. The air has to be pressurized. Food and water must be supplied from Earth. The water must be recycled.

Because of the very low gravity in space, the body does not have to work as hard in space as it does on Earth. Muscles tend to weaken. Therefore, exercise is essential to keep the astronauts' bodies in shape. Also, sleeping areas in space must have straps to prevent astronauts from floating off. Eyeshades must be worn because the Sun rises and sets every hour and a half on a spacecraft in near-Earth orbit.

 HYPOTHESIZE: What are some other problems astronauts might have living in space?

☑ CHECKING CONCEPTS

1. In a _____, scientists can live and work in space.
2. The first space station was called _____.

3. Parts for the ISS are carried into orbit mostly by the _____.
4. The ISS will be used to repair _____.

THINKING CRITICALLY

5. INFER: Astronauts living on a space station have to adjust to the weightlessness of space. Ordinary chores are often more complicated than they are on Earth. Identify three things that you do every day on Earth, such as take a shower, that might be very difficult to do on a space station.

DESIGNING AN EXPERIMENT

Design an experiment to solve the following problem. Include a hypothesis, variables, a procedure with materials, and a type of data to study. Also, tell how you would record your data.

PROBLEM: Earth's climate may be getting warmer partly because of the burning of fossil fuels. This could melt polar ice caps and create new deserts. How can scientists study this problem from the ISS?

 People in Science

AEROSPACE WORKER

Space probes, satellites, and space stations are manufactured by the aerospace industry. This industry employs about one million workers. About half of the people in the aerospace industry actually work on putting spacecraft together. Many inspectors check the quality of each job as it is completed.

Because the aerospace industry uses the latest technologies, many aerospace workers have a background in science and engineering. The aerospace industry also employs lawyers, accountants, and clerical workers. If you are a high school graduate and a graduate of a technical school or college, you might want to find a job in the aerospace industry.

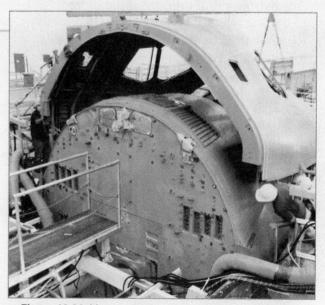

▲ **Figure 16-34** Many aerospace workers help assemble rockets.

Thinking Critically Why is it important to have many inspectors checking spacecraft?

Chapter Summary

Lessons 16-1 and 16-2

- **Astronomy** helped ancient societies solve practical problems. Modern astronomers use telescopes, satellites, and space probes to study the **solar system** and the rest of the universe.

Lessons 16-3 and 16-4

- Galileo used an early **refracting telescope** to look at the Moon. A refracting telescope uses two **convex lenses.**
- A **reflecting telescope** usually uses a **concave mirror** to collect light. Newton made the first reflecting telescope.

Lesson 16-5

- A **radio telescope** picks up radio waves from objects in space.

Lessons 16-6 and 16-7

- **Light-years** are used to measure distances in space. One light-year is the distance light travels in one year, or about 10 trillion km.
- One **astronomical unit,** the distance from Earth to the Sun, is equal to 150 million km.
- Newton's third law of motion explains how rockets work. **Thrust** pushes a rocket forward.
- Rocket engines carry oxygen to burn fuel in space for changing speed or direction.

Lesson 16-8

- The space shuttle is reusable. Both the booster rockets and the liquid-fuel tank drop off before the orbiter reaches space. The orbiter returns to Earth and lands on a runway.
- The shuttle has many uses, including the launching and repairing of satellites.

Lessons 16-9 and 16-10

- Thousands of artificial **satellites** are in **orbit** today around Earth.
- Space probes can go to dangerous places. They can be sent on one-way missions.
- A space station allows scientists to live and work in space for long periods of time.
- The ISS is being built in orbit from parts carried by space shuttles. It will have a full-time research laboratory and satellite repair station.

Key Term Challenges

astronomical unit (p. 392)	parallax (p. 392)
astronomy (p. 380)	radio telescope (p. 388)
concave mirror (p. 386)	reflecting telescope (p. 386)
convex lens (p. 384)	refracting telescope (p. 384)
galaxy (p. 382)	satellite (p. 400)
light-year (p. 392)	solar system (p. 380)
orbit (p. 400)	thrust (p. 394)

MATCHING Write the Key Term from above that best matches each description.

1. curved path of an object around another object
2. force that pushes a rocket forward
3. distance of 150 million km
4. mirror that curves inward
5. lens thicker in the middle than at its edges
6. large system of stars
7. the Sun and all the bodies that circle the Sun
8. natural or artificial object that orbits a body in space

FILL IN Write the Key Term from above that best completes each statement.

9. The study of stars, planets, and other bodies in space is called _____.
10. A telescope that uses two convex lenses to produce an enlarged image of an object is a _____.
11. A telescope that is used to study radio waves coming from space is a _____.
12. A unit of distance equal to 10 trillion km is the _____.
13. A telescope that uses mirrors to form an image is a _____.
14. An apparent change in the position of a distant object when seen from two different places is called _____.
15. To measure distances to the planets, astronomers usually use _____.

Content Challenges TEST PREP

MULTIPLE CHOICE **Write the letter of the term or phrase that best completes each sentence.**

1. The first artificial satellite launched into space was
   a. *Apollo.*
   b. *Voyager.*
   c. *Telstar.*
   d. *Sputnik.*

2. A concave mirror
   a. curves inward.
   b. curves outward.
   c. is flat.
   d. curves inward and outward.

3. The telescope used by Newton was a
   a. refracting telescope.
   b. reflecting telescope.
   c. radio telescope.
   d. scanning telescope.

4. The closest star to Earth, other than the Sun, is
   a. Io.
   b. Proxima Centauri.
   c. Polaris.
   d. *Voyager.*

5. An astronomical unit is equal to the distance from
   a. Earth to the Moon.
   b. the Sun to the Moon.
   c. Earth to the Sun.
   d. Earth to Pluto.

6. To get into space, a rocket must reach a speed of more than
   a. 3,000 km/h.
   b. 4,000 km/h.
   c. 30,000 km/h.
   d. 40,000 km/h.

7. The space station that is currently in orbit is called
   a. the space shuttle.
   b. *Saturn V.*
   c. *Apollo.*
   d. the ISS.

8. Muscles can weaken in space because of the
   a. high temperatures.
   b. low air pressure.
   c. low gravity.
   d. change of diet.

TRUE/FALSE **Write *true* if the statement is true. If the statement is false, change the underlined term to make the statement true.**

9. The first <u>artificial</u> satellite was launched in 1957.

10. Scientists think that the universe began when a huge explosion called the <u>Big Bang</u> occurred.

11. The telescope used by Galileo was a <u>radio</u> telescope.

12. The first person to study the surface of the Moon with a telescope was <u>Newton</u>.

13. The lens in a refracting telescope that collects light and focuses the image is the <u>objective</u> lens.

14. A telescope that uses mirrors instead of lenses is a <u>refracting</u> telescope.

15. Stars can be studied on a cloudy night with a <u>radio</u> telescope.

16. The *Galileo* space probe is studying the atmosphere of <u>Earth</u>.

17. The only part of a space shuttle that goes into space is the <u>liquid-fuel tank</u>.

18. Newton's <u>third</u> law of motion states that for every action, there is an equal and opposite reaction.

Concept Challenges TEST PREP

WRITTEN RESPONSE **Answer each of the following questions in complete sentences.**

1. EXPLAIN: Why is space exploration important?

2. CONTRAST: What is the difference between a refracting telescope and a reflecting telescope?

3. INFER: What are the advantages of unmanned space probes?

4. EXPLAIN: How do scientists use parallax to calculate the distances to stars?

5. EXPLAIN: How does Newton's third law of motion describe how a rocket works?

6. ANALYZE: What is the advantage of the space shuttle over earlier spacecraft?

7. INFER: How are space probes able to travel to the outer reaches of our solar system without a huge fuel reserve?

8. INFER: Before the discovery of the planet Uranus, no planets had been discovered for 5,000 years. Why did it take such a long time for astronomers to discover Uranus?

9. ANALYZE: If you were an astronomer today, what types of tools could you use to explore space?

10. INFER: How many natural satellites orbit Earth?

11. CALCULATE: One astronomical unit is equal to 150 million km. One light-year is equal to 10 trillion km. How many astronomical units are in one light-year?

INTERPRETING VISUALS **Use Figure 16-35 to answer each of the following questions.**

12. Which of these star systems is closest to Earth?

13. Which of these star systems is farthest from Earth?

14. How many stars are in the Alpha Centauri star system?

15. Can you tell from this chart how close these stars are to one another? Explain your answer.

16. How could two stars that are about the same distance from Earth be far apart from each other?

| NEAREST STARS AND STAR SYSTEMS ||
Name of Star or Star System	Distance (in light years)
Alpha Centauri A, B, C	4.4
Barnard's Star	5.9
Lalande 21185	8.3
Sirius A, B	8.6
Ross 154	9.7
Epsilon Eridani	10.5
HD 217987	10.7
Ross 128	10.9
61 Cygni A, B	11.4
Procyon	11.4

▲ Figure 16-35

Chapter 17 The Solar System

▲ **Figure 17-1** Saturn's majestic rings, shown here in false colors, were first seen by Galileo in 1610.

Saturn is the second largest planet in our solar system. Its beautiful rings make it the easiest planet to recognize. Like Jupiter, Saturn is a huge ball made mostly of gas. It is surrounded by clouds. Saturn is ten times farther from the Sun than Earth is. To the naked eye, it looks bright yellow. Computers often enhance the images taken of Saturn using false colors. This allows its atmosphere and its many individual rings to be seen.

▶ What do you think Saturn's rings might be made of?

Contents

17-1 What is the solar system?

Objectives

Name the planets that make up the solar system. Describe how they are grouped.

Key Terms

solar system: the Sun and all the objects that orbit the Sun

nebula (NEHB-yuh-luh)**:** cloud of gas and dust in space

orbit: curved path of one object around another object in space

Formation of the Solar System The **solar system** is the Sun and all the objects that orbit it. Scientists are not sure how the solar system formed. However, several theories have been developed. One popular theory states that the solar system formed from a spinning cloud of gas and dust called a **nebula.**

Scientists think that gravity caused the nebula to shrink, or contract, to form the Sun. After the Sun formed, the leftover gas and dust in the nebula formed the other objects in the solar system. This took many millions of years.

The Sun contains more than 99.8 percent of the mass in our solar system. The planets make up most of the rest of the mass.

A planet is a body in orbit around the Sun. It must have enough mass to assume a round shape and have an orbit that is clear of other bodies.

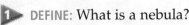 **DEFINE:** What is a nebula?

The Sun's Family The Sun's family consists of eight planets with at least 162 moons. There are four inner planets: Mercury, Venus, Earth, and Mars. These planets are small and rocky. There are four outer planets: Jupiter, Saturn, Uranus, and Neptune. These planets are large and composed of gases. They are often called the gas giants. There are also three dwarf planets: Ceres, Pluto, and Eris. They have a total of four moons. Together these objects exist on a plane that is over 10 trillion km in diameter.

The inner and outer planets are separated by the Main Asteroid Belt. The belt lies between Mars and Jupiter and is composed of hundreds of thousands of small rocky bodies. These are often called planetoids.

Beyond the orbit of Neptune is another region called the Kuiper Belt. It is a disk-shaped region containing many small icy bodies. Many comets come from this belt. Far beyond the Kuiper Belt is another vast cloud of comets called the Oort Cloud.

 IDENTIFY: Which planets are known as the gas giants?

Planet Pathways Ancient peoples observed that the planets changed their positions among the stars. The planets seemed to wander in the sky. The word *planet* comes from a Greek word meaning "wanderer."

Neptune
Uranus
Saturn
Jupiter
Mars Earth Venus Mercury

▲ **Figure 17-2** The solar system contains eight planets. They are divided into the inner planets and the outer planets.

Earth is one of the eight planets in the solar system. Like the other planets, Earth moves in a curved path around the Sun. This path is the planet's **orbit.** All of the planets orbit the Sun in the same direction.

 CLASSIFY: Which are the inner planets?

☑ CHECKING CONCEPTS

1. The solar system may have formed from a _____.
2. The solar system contains _____ planets.
3. A nebula is a _____.
4. The path of a planet around the Sun is the planet's _____.
5. The planets can be divided into two groups, the inner planets and the _____ planets.
6. The _____ separates the inner and outer planets.

💡 THINKING CRITICALLY

7. **SEQUENCE:** List the planets in order from nearest to the Sun to farthest from the Sun.
8. **HYPOTHESIZE:** Why is the solar system often referred to as the Suns family?

BUILDING SCIENCE SKILLS

Researching As seen from Earth, some planets seem to have unusual motions in their orbits. For example, early astronomers were puzzled to discover that for part of the year, Mars and some other planets seemed to move backward in their orbits compared with the movements of Earth. Do research to find out why Mars and some other planets seem to sometimes exhibit these retrograde motions. Draw a diagram of these motions and write a report explaining them.

▲ **Figure 17-3** Mars, along with some other planets, exhibits retrograde motion.

 ## How Do They Know That?

PLANETS BEYOND THE SOLAR SYSTEM

Are there planets going around other suns? Are there other solar systems? Planets located outside our solar system are known as extra solar planets.

It isn't easy to find planets around other suns. Planets are very small compared with stars and usually have less than one-billionth the brightness. Still, it is possible to find planets orbiting other stars. Today, powerful telescopes may be able to detect other extrasolar planets if they are large enough.

Planets have a gravitational effect on stars the same way that stars have a gravitational effect on planets. Planets cause a star to wobble. Telescopes can detect this wobble. Using this method, a planet was discovered in orbit around the star 51 Pegasi in 1995. More than 300 extrasolar planets have been discovered so far.

Thinking Critically Why are planets that orbit other stars called extrasolar planets?

▲ **Figure 17-4** An artist's drawing of 51 Pegasi and some of its planets.

What do we know about orbits?

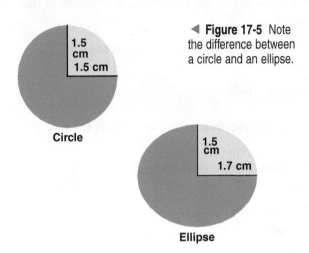

◀ **Figure 17-5** Note the difference between a circle and an ellipse.

Objective

Describe the shape of Earth's orbit.

Key Terms

ellipse (eh-LIPS): flattened circle, or oval

perihelion (per-uh-HEE-lee-uhn): point in a planet's orbit at which it is closest to the Sun

aphelion (uh-FEE-lee-uhn): point in a planet's orbit at which it is farthest from the Sun

Gravity Every object in the universe pulls on every other object. This pull is the force of gravity, or gravitational attraction. There is gravitational attraction among all objects in the universe. For example, there is gravitational attraction between the Sun and the planets. This gravitational attraction pulls the planets toward the Sun as they move through space. Instead of flying off into space, the planets move in orbits around the Sun. Gravity also pulls all objects on Earth toward the center of the planet.

▶ 1 STATE: What force pulls all nearby objects toward the center of Earth?

Earth's Orbit A circle is perfectly round. All lines drawn from the center of the circle to its rim are the same length. An **ellipse** looks like a slightly flattened circle or oval. Lines drawn from the center to different points on its rim are different lengths.

Earth and all the other planets travel around the Sun in elliptical orbits. This means the planet is not always the same distance from the Sun. In January, for example, Earth reaches its perihelion. **Perihelion** is the point at which a planet is closest to the Sun. Earth is about 147 million km from the Sun at perihelion. In July, Earth reaches its aphelion. **Aphelion** is the point at which a planet is farthest from the Sun. Earth is about 152 million km from the Sun at aphelion.

▶ 2 DESCRIBE: What is the shape of Earth's orbit?

Orbital Velocity The speed at which a planet travels in its orbit is called its orbital velocity. The closer a planet is to the Sun, the greater is its orbital velocity. A planet moves fastest at perihelion. It moves slowest at aphelion.

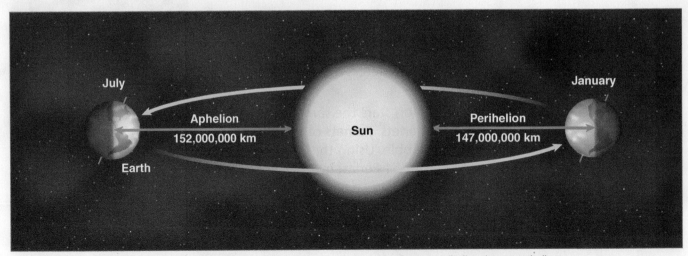

▲ **Figure 17-6** Earth travels in an elliptical orbit around the Sun. It is closer to the Sun at perihelion than at aphelion.

The closer two objects are to each other, the greater the gravitational attraction between them. As a planet gets closer to the Sun, the gravitational attraction between the planet and the Sun increases. As a result, the planet moves faster in its orbit.

As a planet moves farther from the Sun, the gravitational attraction between the planet and the Sun decreases. The planet slows down. This is why a planet moves fastest at perihelion and slowest at aphelion. The difference in gravitational attraction also explains why the planets closer to the Sun move faster than those farther from the Sun.

3 ▶ STATE: When does Earth move fastest in its orbit?

☑ CHECKING CONCEPTS

1. An ellipse has an _____ shape.
2. Earth's path around the Sun is its _____.
3. Earth moves in an _____ orbit.

4. The point at which Earth is closest to the Sun is _____.
5. A planet's speed in its orbit is its _____.

THINKING CRITICALLY

6. HYPOTHESIZE: The planets are different distances from the Sun. Mercury is closest to the Sun. Neptune is farthest from the Sun. Which of the two planets has the greater orbital velocity? Explain.

INTERPRETING VISUALS

Use Figure 17-6 to answer the following questions.

7. ANALYZE: What month is it when Earth is closest to the Sun?
8. ANALYZE: What month is it when Earth is farthest from the Sun?
9. CALCULATE: How much farther from the Sun is Earth at aphelion than at perihelion?

Hands-On Activity

DRAWING THE SHAPE OF EARTH'S ORBIT

You will need paper, cardboard, two pins, string, a pencil, and a metric ruler.

1. Place a sheet of paper on the cardboard. Draw a horizontal line 1 cm long near the center of the paper.
2. Stick one pin through the paper and cardboard at the end of each line. Label one of the pins Sun.
3. Tie the ends of a piece of string together to make a loop about 10 cm long. Place the loop around the pins.
4. Hold a pencil point inside of and against the string. At the length of the string loop, move the pencil around the pins, marking the paper.

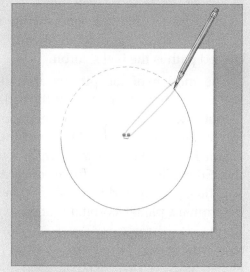

▲ **STEP 4** Hold your pencil inside of the string and move it around.

Practicing Your Skills

5. INFER: You have created a slight ellipse. Why do people assume Earth's orbit is a circle?
6. IDENTIFY: Label the points of aphelion and perihelion.
7. IDENTIFY: Measure and label the distances to aphelion and perihelion.
8. IDENTIFY: Label the months Earth reaches aphelion and perihelion.

THE Big IDEA

What keeps the planets and moons in orbit?

When you throw a ball, you give it a forward motion. At the same time, gravity pulls the ball toward the center of Earth. As a result, the ball has two motions. It has a forward and a downward motion. These two motions cause the ball to follow a curved path.

Suppose that you tied a string around the ball and swung the ball around your head. You would feel an outward pull on the string. If you were to let go of the string, the ball would fly away from you. However, as long as you hold onto the string, the ball will keep moving in a curved path around your head. This curved path is the ball's "orbit."

The motion of the planets around the Sun is similar to the motion of the ball. The planets, which are in motion, keep moving forward in a straight line. However, there is also a force pulling them inward, toward the Sun. This is the force of gravity. Together, gravity and forward motion help determine a planet's orbital motion.

When you hear the word *gravity*, you probably think of the force that pulls objects toward Earth. However, gravity is not limited to our planet. It happens in space, too. Every object in space pulls on every other object. That means that gravity occurs between the Sun and each planet. This attraction toward the Sun keeps the planets from spinning off into space. Gravity also keeps moons orbiting planets.

Look at the illustrations that appear on these two pages. Then, follow the directions in the Science Log to learn more about "the big idea." ✦

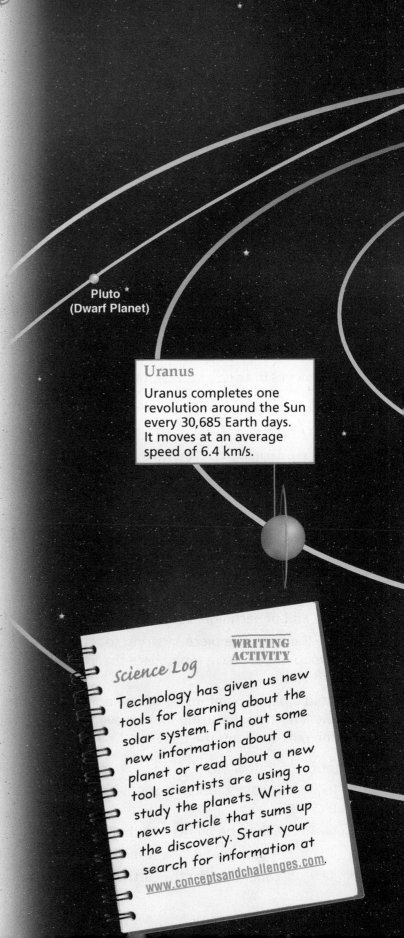

Pluto
(Dwarf Planet)

Uranus

Uranus completes one revolution around the Sun every 30,685 Earth days. It moves at an average speed of 6.4 km/s.

Science Log

WRITING ACTIVITY

Technology has given us new tools for learning about the solar system. Find out some new information about a planet or read about a new tool scientists are using to study the planets. Write a news article that sums up the discovery. Start your search for information at www.conceptsandchallenges.com.

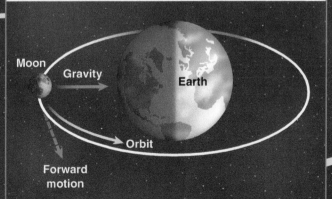

Mercury

Mercury orbits the Sun at an average speed of 48 km/s. At this rate, it completes one revolution every 88 Earth days.

Neptune

Moving at a rate of 6.81 km/s, Neptune completes one trip around the Sun every 60,188 Earth days.

Mars

Mars completes one trip around the Sun every 687 Earth days. It travels at an average speed of 24 km/s.

Venus

The second planet from the Sun, Venus moves at an average speed of 35 km/s. Venus completes one revolution every 225 Earth days.

Sun

Asteroid Belt

Saturn

Traveling at a rate of 9.6 km/s, Saturn completes one trip around the Sun every 10,759 Earth days.

Jupiter

The largest planet of the solar system, Jupiter moves at an average rate of 13 km/s.

Earth

Earth is moving at an average rate of 30 km/s around the Sun. At the same time, Earth's Moon is orbiting Earth. As with Earth and the Sun, the Moon is moving forward, away from Earth. However, the force of gravity is also pulling it toward Earth. This creates the Moon's orbital path.

Moon — Gravity — Earth

Orbit

Forward motion

Figure 17-7 The solar system

17-3 What do we know about Earth's Moon?

Objective
Describe some features of the Moon.

Key Terms
mare (MAH-ray), *pl.* **maria:** broad, flat plain on the Moon's surface

crater (KRAYT-uhr): round hole on the Moon's surface

Moon Landing On July 20, 1969, an American astronaut, Neil Armstrong Jr., stepped onto the surface of the Moon. He was the first human to do so. He and his crew had traveled 384,000 km from Earth to the Moon. The trip took five days. Since 1969, 12 astronauts have been to the Moon and returned to Earth. *Apollo 17* in 1972 was the last mission to send astronauts to the Moon.

▲ **Figure 17-8** Astronauts walked on the Moon for the first time in 1969.

 STATE: When did the first person walk on the Moon?

Moon Facts Earth has only one natural satellite, called the Moon. The Moon is much smaller than Earth. It has a diameter of about 3,400 km. Because the Moon has less mass than Earth does, its gravity is less than Earth's gravity.

The gravity on the Moon's surface is only one-sixth as strong as the gravity on Earth. The Moon's weaker gravity means that you can jump much higher on the Moon than you can on Earth.

The Moon has no liquid water, and it has an extremely thin atmosphere. Temperatures on the Moon can range from over 100°C to below –200°C. Astronauts need to wear space suits to survive on the Moon.

 NAME: What are three important facts about the Moon?

The Moon's Surface Galileo saw and named the three main types of features on the Moon's surface. He named the smooth, dark areas that he saw **maria.** The word *maria* means "seas" in Latin. The first astronauts to land on the Moon landed in the Sea of Tranquility. Today, scientists know that the Moon's maria are not seas but broad, flat plains. Galileo also saw light areas on the Moon. These light areas are mountains, or highlands. Some mountains on the Moon are higher than the highest mountains on Earth.

▲ **Figure 17-9** The Moon has no water to drink and no air to breathe. Visitors must bring their own supplies.

The third feature Galileo saw on the Moon's surface were its many **craters.** Large objects striking the Moon's surface caused most of the craters. Erupting volcanoes may have caused the rest.

▲ **Figure 17-10** Craters on the Moon

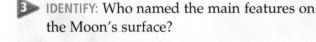

3 ▶ IDENTIFY: Who named the main features on the Moon's surface?

 CHECKING CONCEPTS

1. The distance from Earth to the Moon is _____ km.
2. The Moon has a _____ of 3,400 km.
3. The word *maria* means _____ .
4. Three features on the Moon's surface are maria, _____, and highlands.

 THINKING CRITICALLY

5. **CALCULATE:** How much would a 120-lb person weigh on the Moon?
6. **CALCULATE:** How much would you weigh on the Moon?
7. **INFER:** Astronauts left their footprints on the Moon's surface. These footprints may remain unchanged for millions of years. Why?
8. **ANALYZE:** Why did the astronauts who walked on the Moon have to wear boots with lead weights in them?

BUILDING SCIENCE SKILLS

Observing Many features on the Moon are visible to the unaided eye. Others can be seen clearly through binoculars. Observe a full Moon. First use only your eyes. Then use binoculars. Compare how well you are able to see certain features with your unaided eyes and with binoculars. Make a drawing of the features you were able to identify and label those features.

Hands-On Activity

MODELING CRATER FORMATIONS

You will need a shoebox, plaster of Paris, a metric ruler, and three rocks of different sizes.

1. Mix the plaster of Paris according to the directions. Make enough to fill the shoebox one-third of the way up.
2. Pour the plaster of Paris into the shoebox. Just before the plaster hardens, drop one of the rocks into the box from a height of 25 cm. Then, drop the other rocks from the same height.
3. Remove the rocks and drop them from a height of 10 cm.
4. Remove the rocks and let the plaster of Paris harden. Measure the rocks and craters in as many ways as you can.

Practicing Your Skills

5. **EXPLAIN:** What do the rocks represent?
6. **COMPARE:** Which rock made the deepest crater? Which rock made the widest crater?
7. **APPLY:** How do you think craters were formed on the Moon?

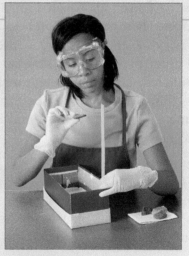

▲ **STEP 3** Drop the rocks a second time from a lower height.

17-4 What are the other moons in the solar system?

Objective

Compare the moons of the different planets in the solar system.

Key Term

satellite (SAT-uhl-eyet): natural or artificial object orbiting another body in space

Natural Satellites A **satellite** is any natural or artificial object that orbits another object in space. People have observed the only natural satellite of Earth, the Moon, since ancient times.

For thousands of years, Earth was believed to be the only planet in the solar system to have a moon. Then, in 1610, Galileo discovered four of the moons of Jupiter. Today, astronomers know that six of the planets (Earth, Mars, Jupiter, Saturn, Uranus and Neptune) have moons.

Until the late 1970s, almost all of the known moons had been discovered using Earth-based telescopes. Then, two space probes, called *Voyager 1* and *Voyager 2*, traveled beyond the Asteroid Belt to the outer planets. They sent back to Earth the first detailed, close-up photographs of the many moons that orbited Jupiter, Saturn, Uranus, and Neptune. Together, *Voyagers 1* and *2* discovered at least 35 new moons.

▶ DESCRIBE: What planets have natural satellites?

Moons of the Inner Planets Mercury and Venus are the only planets in the solar system without at least one moon. Earth has only one moon.

Mars has two moons, named Deimos and Phobos. These were discovered in 1877. They are made of dark, carbon-rich rock. Because of their makeup, both reflect very little light from their surface. Both moons are small and lumpy. Deimos has a peanut shape. Both moons also have many craters. One crater on Phobos is 10 km across.

Both moons orbit close to Mars. Phobos takes less than a Martian day to go once around the planet. Deimos takes a little more than a day.

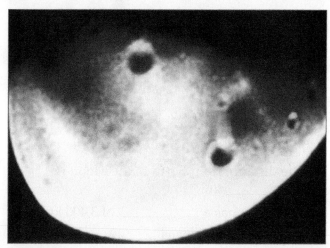

▲ **Figure 17-11** Mars's moon Deimos is shaped like a peanut.

▶ IDENTIFY: Which of the inner planets have one or more moons?

Moons of the Outer Planets Jupiter has at least 63 known moons. Jupiter and its moons have been described as a minisolar system.

Jupiter's moons are very varied. Some are rocky. Others are icy. The four moons first viewed by Galileo are often referred to as the Galilean moons. They are the largest of Jupiter's moons.

The Galilean moons travel around Jupiter in a nearly circular orbit, almost exactly around the planet's equator. It is possible to track the movements and positions of these moons using a good pair of binoculars.

The Galilean moons played an important role in the history of astronomy. When their orbits were first observed, it was proven that not everything in space revolved around Earth.

In 1995, a space probe, appropriately named *Galileo*, arrived at Jupiter to study the Galilean moons. The largest Galilean moon is Ganymede, followed by Callisto, Io, and Europa. Ganymede is the largest moon in the solar system, with a diameter of 5,268 km. Callisto has a dark, icy surface with many white craters. Impacts from asteroids and other bodies probably exposed clean ice beneath the dirtier top layer. Io has active volcanoes on it. Europa is covered with ice that may have liquid water below the surface.

◀ **Figure 17-12** Io is a large, volcanically active moon of Jupiter.

Saturn has 59 known moons. Five of these moons are very large. Saturn's largest moon is Titan. Titan is the second largest moon in the solar system.

Huygens is a probe sent to Titan by the European Space Agency. It arrived there in 2004, as part of the *Cassini* mission to Saturn. It parachuted toward the surface and reported on conditions beneath the moon's orange clouds.

▲ **Figure 17-13** This is an artist's concept of Saturn and six of its moons as seen from a seventh moon.

Uranus has 27 known moons. Titania is the largest, with Oberon second. The moons of Uranus are very varied. Some have deep canyons and long scars on their surface. Others have large, smooth areas between areas riddled with craters. Miranda may have more types of landforms than any other body in the solar system. Ten of Uranus's moons were discovered by *Voyager 2* in 1986.

Neptune has 13 known moons. Only two, Triton and Nereid, are visible from Earth. Triton orbits in the opposite direction from the rest of Neptune's moons. It has the coldest surface in the solar system, at –235°C. Scientists think Triton is covered with frozen nitrogen and methane.

The dwarf planet Pluto has three moons. The largest is Charon. It was discovered in 1978. Charon is about half the size of Pluto. Some scientists suspect its surface to be covered with water ice and impact craters. One theory suggests that an icy fragment of Pluto was knocked off when Pluto collided with another object. This fragment could be Charon.

The dwarf planet Eris has one natural satellite.

3 IDENTIFY: Which outer planet has the most moons?

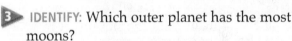

✓ CHECKING CONCEPTS

Match each planet or dwarf planet with its correct moon.

1. Jupiter   **a.** Charon
2. Mars   **b.** Triton
3. Uranus   **c.** Io
4. Pluto   **d.** Titania
5. Neptune   **e.** Titan
6. Saturn   **f.** Phobos

💡 THINKING CRITICALLY

7. SEQUENCE: List the planets in order from the one with the most moons to the ones with the fewest. Include planets that have no moons.

8. INFER: Why are the four largest moons of Jupiter called the Galilean moons?

BUILDING SCIENCE SKILLS

Researching The names given to moons are chosen by the International Astronomical Union. Newly discovered moons are numbered first, with the year they are discovered, then named later. The names chosen come from many different sources. For example, recently discovered moons of Uranus were named after characters in the plays of Shakespeare. Choose the moons of one planet. Find the source of each moon's name. Write a report of your findings.

LAB ACTIVITY
Looking Back in Time

Materials
Safety goggles
2 Plastic petri dishes
Dry sandbox sand
Dropper bottle
Water
Pictures of craters on the Moon

▲ **STEP 1** Fill the petri dish with sand and the dropper bottle with water.

▲ **STEP 3** Move your dish around as you squeeze out drops of water from the bottle.

BACKGROUND

The solar system has more than 90 moons. Meteorite impacts have altered the terrain of most of these moons by creating craters. Many moons, such as Earth's Moon and Jupiter's Callisto, are heavily pitted with meteor craters. If a plain on the surface of a moon has craters, it is likely that the plain formed first and was later altered by impacts. The number of impacts helps scientists estimate the age of the plain. If the plain has very few or no craters, it probably formed very recently. If the plain is heavily cratered, the plain is probably ancient. Scientists can often determine the sequence of when the impacts occurred that created the craters. They do this by looking for overlapping craters.

PURPOSE

In this activity, you will create a moon with many craters on its surface and infer its history.

PROCEDURE

1. Put on your safety goggles. Fill one petri dish almost to the top with sand. Fill the dropper bottle with water.

2. Copy the chart in Figure 17-14. Hold the dropper bottle about 25 cm above the dish and squeeze out a drop of water. Observe what happens when the water strikes the surface of the sand. Record your observations in your chart.

3. For the next minute, squeeze a drop from the bottle every second. Move the dish around as you release the drops every second. Have some drops fall by themselves. Have other drops fall on top of each other or close together. Observe the raindrop pattern you produced on the sand. Record your observations.

4. Trade your dish for a dish made by another group. Try to determine the sequence in which the craters were made. Record your observations.

5. In your chart draw a picture of the dish with circles to represent the craters. Look at the overlapping craters. Mark older craters with the number 1. Mark newer craters with the numbers 2, 3, and so on.

6. Fill a second petri dish with sand. Use your thumb to make a large crater in the center.

7. Squeeze drops from the bottle in and around the big crater. Observe and record what happens.

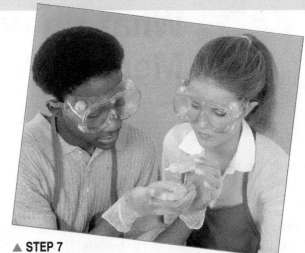

▲ STEP 7
Squeeze drops of water around the large crater you made with your thumb.

8. Look at pictures of the craters on the Moon. Can you tell which craters are younger and which are older? Note down your comments below the chart.

Step	What You Observe	Written Description
1		
2		
3		

▲ **Figure 17-14** Use a copy of this chart to write down your observations and draw your pictures.

CONCLUSIONS

1. OBSERVE: What happened when the first drop of water hit the sand?

2. ANALYZE: How can you tell which crater is newer when two craters overlap?

3. OBSERVE: What happened to the large crater you created with your thumb when it was hit with more drops of water?

4. ANALYZE: What is the difference between an old crater and a young one?

5. INFER: How do craters tell scientists if the surface of a moon is very young or very old?

What do we know about Mercury, Venus, and Earth?

Objective

Identify the basic features of the three innermost planets.

Mercury Mercury is the planet closest to the Sun. Of all the planets, Mercury travels the fastest around the Sun. However, it rotates slowly on its axis. This dry, rocky planet has no atmosphere. Temperatures on Mercury range from 430°C during daylight hours to –170°C during Mercury's night. Because Mercury is so close to the Sun, astronomers cannot see it easily from Earth. However, astronomers learned a lot when, in 1974, the space probe *Mariner 10* visited Mercury and sent back photographs. In the 1990s, radar was used to study Mercury's surface. We now know that the surface of Mercury is covered with craters.

▲ **Figure 17-15** Mercury is very similar to Earth's Moon. It has no atmosphere, and its surface is covered with impact craters.

 DESCRIBE: What is Mercury like?

Venus The planet Venus is similar to Earth in size, mass, and density. However, Venus is a very hostile world. Its average temperature is higher than the average temperature of any other known planet. The air pressure on Venus is 90 times more crushing than that of Earth's air at sea level.

Astronomers think these conditions are related to Venus's carbon dioxide atmosphere and thick clouds of sulfuric acid. From Earth, we can only see Venus's cloudtops.

Venus has retrograde rotation. This means that it spins slowly in the opposite direction from most of the other planets.

▲ **Figure 17-16** The pressure on the surface of Venus, seen here, is equal to that of the pressure on Earth deep down in the ocean.

Many space probes have orbited Venus or landed on it. These probes have revealed smooth plains, mountains, and valleys. Like the Moon, Venus goes through phases. We see only varying amounts of its sunlit side.

2 INFER: Why was Venus once called Earth's twin?

Earth The third planet from the Sun and the fifth largest in the solar system is Earth. Earth is the only planet known to have oceans of liquid water. It is also the only planet known to support life. Life occurs on Earth because of moderate temperatures, an atmosphere containing oxygen, and liquid water.

Earth has a magnetic field around it because of the iron in its core. Electrically charged particles from the Sun, mostly electrons and protons, bounce around in the atmosphere above Earth. They are trapped in Earth's magnetic field.

Occasionally, some of these particles escape from the magnetic field and rain down on Earth. They strike atoms and molecules in the upper atmosphere and cause them to glow. In the Northern Hemisphere, this glow is known as the aurora borealis, or the northern lights. In the southern hemisphere, it is the aurora australis, or southern lights.

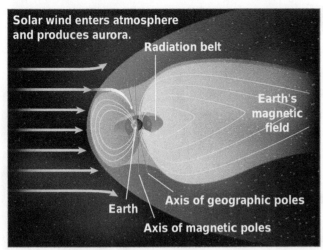
Solar wind enters atmosphere and produces aurora.

Radiation belt

Earth's magnetic field

Earth

Axis of geographic poles

Axis of magnetic poles

▲ **Figure 17-17** Charged particles from the Sun are trapped in Earth's magnetic field.

 LIST: What conditions make life on Earth possible?

✓ CHECKING CONCEPTS

1. What are the three innermost planets?
2. What does the surface of Mercury look like?
3. What gas in the atmosphere makes the surface of Venus so hot?
4. Which inner planet has liquid water?

💡 THINKING CRITICALLY

5. **COMPARE:** How is the surface of Mercury similar to the surface of Earth's Moon?
6. **ANALYZE:** Venus has rocks similar to basalt. On Earth, these rocks are usually found near volcanoes. What does this suggest?

Web InfoSearch

More About Venus Sunlight striking the surface of a planet warms the ground. This releases heat radiation. Like glass in a greenhouse, the atmosphere traps some of the heat. In some places, such as on Venus, the heat keeps building up. This is called a runaway greenhouse.

SEARCH: Use the Internet to find out what the temperature is on Venus and why. Could Earth someday become like Venus? How could it? Start your search at www.conceptsandchallenges.com. Use the key search words **runaway greenhouse effect, Venus, planet profile,** and **carbon dioxide.**

 Integrating Life Science

TOPICS: origin of life, molecular biology

HOW LIFE ON EARTH BEGAN

Nobody knows for sure how life on Earth began. Scientists think they know when it happened—about 3.5 billion years ago.

Many scientists think that the first living things were certain molecules, or strings of atoms. These molecules floated in water, alongside billions of unattached atoms. As these molecules bumped into other molecules, they traded atoms. Eventually, a chain of atoms came together that could actually make copies of itself using the free-floating atoms.

How can a chain of atoms make copies of itself? It happens all the time, right inside your body. It is how your body grows. Molecules inside your body grab onto atoms to create more molecules. When molecules first did this billions of years ago, they began to show some of the characteristics of living things.

Over time, life forms that were especially good at making copies of themselves outnumbered other life forms. These life forms were our very distant ancestors.

Thinking Critically What parts of your body can make copies of themselves?

▲ **Figure 17-18** Stromatolites are among the oldest fossils. They were formed in sedimentary rock by blue-green algae.

What do we know about Mars?

INVESTIGATE

Seeing Mars in 3-D
HANDS-ON ACTIVITY

STEP 2

1. Make a viewer by cutting out two eyeholes from a rectangle of stiff paper. The holes should match your eye positions.

2. Tape a piece of red filter over one hole. Tape a piece of blue filter over the other hole.

3. Hold the viewer in front of your eyes so that your right eye looks through the blue filter and your left eye looks through the red filter. Examine pictures of Mars's surface taken by the *Pathfinder* mission supplied by your teacher.

THINK ABOUT IT: Why might scientists find 3-D pictures useful for studying Mars?

Objective
Describe features on the planet Mars.

Key Term
rift: valley caused by a crack in the crust of a planet

The Red Planet Mars is the fourth planet from the Sun. Its orbit period is 687 days. Its rate of rotation is 24 hours and 37 minutes. Therefore, the lengths of a day on Mars and on Earth are almost the same. Mars has seasons similar to Earth's seasons because of the similar tilt of its axis. However, Mars is half the diameter of Earth. Its surface is reddish in color. Mars has volcanoes, valleys, polar ice caps, craters, and river channels. It has a thin carbon dioxide atmosphere.

The air pressure on Mars is about the same as the air pressure on Earth at an altitude of 35 km. Except for some icy spots at the poles, no water is visible on the Martian surface. Mars is a dry world. It can be colder than Antarctica in winter and as warm as a spring day in the American Midwest.

▶ **CONTRAST:** How do Mars and Earth differ?

The Martian Surface Many space probes, including two *Viking* landers, have studied Mars. Photographs show that the surface has many craters and is covered with loose rocks. Winds of up to 100 km/h raise giant dust storms that cover the planet. Scientists think that Mars probably once had rivers or lakes on its surface.

▶ **IDENTIFY:** What spacecraft visited Mars?

▲ **Figure 17-19** The surface of Mars was photographed by the *Viking* lander. It showed a landscape with rocks scattered all around.

Giant Volcanoes and Canyons The largest known volcano in the solar system is called Olympus Mons. Olympus Mons is found on Mars. It is 21 km high. Had Olympus Mons formed on Earth, it would not have been nearly as high. This is because Earth's gravity is stronger. At the summit of the volcano is a large crater. Mars has many other large volcanoes. Mars also has a large **rift,** or crack, in its crust that forms a complex canyon system. The canyon, called Vallis Marineris, stretches 4,000 km. On Earth, this canyon would reach across the United States.

 EXPLAIN: Why are volcanoes on Mars much larger than volcanoes on Earth?

Water on Mars Scientists have used robot spacecraft to search for water on Mars. Finding water could mean that Mars has life. There is some water ice at the Martian south pole. There are also many dry channels on Mars that look as though they were carved by running water. Where is the water today? It may be frozen beneath the surface or have boiled away in the thin atmosphere.

 INFER: Where might water be on Mars?

☑ CHECKING CONCEPTS

1. What causes the huge dust storms on Mars?

2. How are Mars and Earth similar?

3. How do the Vallis Marineris on Mars and the Grand Canyon on Earth compare in size?

4. Why do we think water might exist on Mars?

💡 THINKING CRITICALLY

5. INFER: If Mars once had water, what might have happened to it?

6. APPLY: Could humans live on Mars? How?

Web InfoSearch

Martian Canals In 1877, an Italian astronomer said that he had seen "channels" on Mars. This word became "canals" when the report was translated into English. Some people, including the astronomer Percival Lowell, assumed that the canals must have been built by Martians.

SEARCH: Use the Internet to find out more about the "canals" on Mars. Do they exist? Start your search for information at www.conceptsandchallenges.com. Use the key search words **Martian canals, Mars canals Lowell,** and **Percival Lowell.**

 Integrating Life Science

TOPICS: bacteria, fossils

FOSSILS FROM MARS?

In 1984, a meteorite was found in Antarctica that scientists think came from Mars. Like other planets, Mars has been struck by asteroids often in its past. Mars was struck by one such asteroid about 16 million years ago. Pieces of the surface broke off and went flying into space. Scientists believe a meteorite from this asteroid strike eventually fell to Earth.

▲ **Figure 17-20** Possible bacteria fossils (right) were found on an Antarctic ice sheet similar to the one above.

Some scientists studying the rock found unusual, rodlike structures in it. They suggested that these tiny structures might be bacteria fossils. If the rodlike structures are from Mars, it could mean that life existed on Mars many years ago. However, these structures might have become part of the meteorite as it fell through the atmosphere to Earth.

Thinking Critically What evidence of possible life was in the meteorite?

What are asteroids and meteoroids?

Objective

Compare asteroids, meteoroids, meteors, and meteorites.

Key Terms

asteroid (AS-tuhr-oid): large chunk of rock or metal that orbits the Sun

meteoroid (MEET-ee-uhr-oid): small piece of rock or metal that travels through space

meteor (MEET-ee-uhr): rock or metal that enters Earth's atmosphere

meteorite (MEET-ee-uhr-eyet): piece of rock or metal that falls on a planet or moon's surface

Asteroids There is a large gap in the solar system between the orbits of Mars and Jupiter. For many years, astronomers thought the gap must contain a planet. They searched the gap but did not find the missing planet. Then, in 1801, an Italian astronomer spotted a tiny dot of light that orbited the Sun, like the planets. The astronomer had discovered the first asteroid. Ceres, as it was named, is 940 km across. It is now considered a dwarf planet.

▲ **Figure 17-21** The Asteroid Belt is found between Mars and Jupiter. At left is a computer illustration of Ceres.

Ceres and other **asteroids** are leftover debris from the formation of the solar system. They are made up of pieces of rock or metal or a combination of rock and metal. Today, thousands of asteroids are known. Most orbit the Sun in the so-called Asteroid Belt between Mars and Jupiter.

▶ **1** LOCATE: Where is the Asteroid Belt?

Meteoroids Asteroids can collide, breaking off small pieces from both asteroids. These pieces, called **meteoroids,** scatter around the solar system. Most pieces are smaller than a sand grain. If a meteoroid enters a planet's atmosphere, friction will cause all or some of the meteoroid to burn. A bright streak will then be seen in the sky. Meteoroids that produce that bright streak are called **meteors**. Large pieces of meteoroids that reach a planet's surface are called **meteorites.** A crater can result from the impact.

◀ **Figure 17-22** A meteorite much bigger than the one below struck Arizona. It formed the crater known as Meteor Crater, seen at left.

▶ **2** NAME: What is a meteoroid that enters Earth's atmosphere called?

Meteor Showers Sometimes many meteor flashes will be seen in a night. These displays are called meteor showers. The meteoroids that fall in meteor showers are tiny, dust-sized particles from comets. Comets travel in long orbits that regularly take them close to the Sun. As a comet approaches the Sun, some of the ice in it melts. This releases trapped dust particles. When Earth passes through the dust left by a passing comet, the dust burns up in the atmosphere. A meteor shower occurs.

▶ **3** EXPLAIN: How are meteor showers produced?

Meteorites on Earth More than 30,000 meteorites have been found on Earth's surface. However, most meteorites fall into the sea. Some meteorites have crashed through the roofs of houses and slammed into cars. Fortunately, these events are very rare.

Once in a while, a large meteorite strikes Earth's surface. One such impact took place in Arizona 50,000 years ago. A 1-km-wide crater, shown in Figure 17-22, was produced when the meteorite struck.

The best place to look for meteorites today is in Antarctica. When meteorites fall on ice, they are easy to see. Some four-billion-year-old meteorites have been found there.

 IDENTIFY: Where are meteorites easy to spot?

☑ CHECKING CONCEPTS

1. Where are meteoroids found?
2. What is a meteoroid?
3. How big are the particles in a meteor shower?
4. Where do most meteorites land on Earth?
5. What particles are burned up in meteor showers?

THINKING CRITICALLY

6. **CONTRAST:** How are meteoroids, meteorites, and meteors different?
7. **INFER:** How might the surface of a meteorite look after going through Earth's atmosphere?

Web InfoSearch

How the Moon Formed One thing scientists wanted to learn from the *Apollo* program was how the Moon was created. Moon rocks provided scientists with important clues. Today, some scientists believe that the early Earth was struck by a very large object, very likely an asteroid. Some of the debris from the collision flew off into space. Eventually, this debris came together to become the Moon.

SEARCH: Use the Internet to find out what evidence led scientists to this theory. Go to www.conceptsandchallenges.com to begin your search. Some key search words are **Moon rocks** and **asteroids.**

 Real-Life Science

NEAR-EARTH OBJECTS

Not all asteroids are in the Asteroid Belt. Thousands cross or come close to Earth's orbit every year. These are named near-Earth objects (NEOs). About 918 NEOs are considered a possible danger to Earth. These objects are all being monitored by several groups.

About 65 million years ago, an asteroid about 10 km wide struck Earth. The huge crater it is believed to have formed, called Chicxulub, is found in the Gulf of Mexico and on Mexico's Yucatán peninsula. This is the impact that many scientists now think might have ended the rule of the dinosaurs. However, no known NEO is currently a serious threat to Earth.

▲ **Figure 17-23** Artist's concept of an asteroid hitting Earth

What if such an object should appear? Can anything be done to stop a catastrophe? Some people have suggested blowing the object up with a nuclear bomb. However, this might create many small pieces that could strike with the same deadly force. It would be better to nudge the asteroid in another direction. However, no one knows exactly how to do this yet.

Thinking Critically How might you force an asteroid to change direction?

What do we know about Jupiter and Saturn?

Objective

Identify some features of Jupiter and Saturn.

A Gas Giant Jupiter is the largest planet in the solar system. It is the fifth planet out from the Sun. Because of its size, Jupiter can be seen without a telescope. Its mass is twice that of all the other planets combined. Jupiter has a diameter of 143,000 km. Earth's diameter is less than 13,000 km.

Jupiter is a gas giant with a rocky core. It is made up mostly of the light gases hydrogen and helium. Its density is only one-fourth that of Earth's. Colorful bands of clouds cover the entire planet.

All of the gas giants, including Jupiter, have rings around them. These rings are made up of small particles of dust and ice. Each particle is a tiny satellite. The rings circle the planet around the equator. A thin, faint ring around Jupiter was discovered by *Voyager 1* in 1979.

▲ **Figure 17-24** The planet Jupiter (upper right) is big enough to hold more than 1,300 Earths. The other objects in the picture are four of Jupiter's moons.

▶ NAME: What two gases make up most of Jupiter?

The Great Red Spot The largest and best-known feature of Jupiter is its Great Red Spot. Astronomers believe this is a huge storm, similar to a cyclone. It was probably created by steam and ammonia rising from the atmosphere below Jupiter's cloudtops.

In 1994, Jupiter was hit by comet Shoemaker-Levy 9. The comet was pulled apart by Jupiter's gravity. Twenty-one pieces crashed into the thick atmosphere of Jupiter. Astronomers studied the impacts to learn more about Jupiter's atmosphere.

▲ **Figure 17-25** The Great Red Spot is a huge storm on Jupiter.

▶ DESCRIBE: What is the Great Red Spot?

The Ringed Planet The second largest planet in the solar system and the sixth out from the Sun is Saturn. The diameter of Saturn is about 121,000 km.

Like Jupiter, Saturn is a gas giant made up mostly of hydrogen and helium. Saturn has colorful bands of clouds like Jupiter. However, Saturn is less dense than Jupiter is. It is even less dense than water.

Saturn's rings are its most distinctive feature. Galileo thought they were ears or handles when he saw them through his telescope. There are three main rings. Many thousands of smaller rings orbit inside the main rings. There is a large gap between two rings called the Cassini division. The *Cassini* probe began studing Saturn's rings in 2004.

▲ Figure 17-26 The orange bands in this picture are really clouds racing from east to west around Saturn.

3 ▸ IDENTIFY: What is Saturn mostly made up of?

CHECKING CONCEPTS

1. The largest planet in our solar system is _____.

2. The second largest planet in our solar system is _____.

3. Jupiter's mass is more than _____ the mass of the other planets put together.

4. Jupiter is made up mostly of _____ and helium.

5. The Great Red Spot is caused by steam and _____ rising into Jupiter's atmosphere.

THINKING CRITICALLY

6. COMPARE: What are two ways in which Jupiter and Saturn are alike?

7. INFER: What makes Jupiter and Saturn gas giants?

BUILDING SCIENCE SKILLS

Researching and Modeling Two small moons of Saturn, Pandora and Prometheus, orbit on either side of what is called the F ring. These moons are known as shepherds. *Pioneer 11* first saw them in 1979. Find out what these moons do and how they do it. Report your findings. Then, draw a sketch of Saturn's ring system and label the shepherd moons and the F ring.

Science and Technology
PROBING THE SECRETS OF JUPITER

The *Voyagers* gave us incredible images of Jupiter and its moons as the probes flew by. Then, in December 1995, the space probe *Galileo* went into orbit around Jupiter. This began a lengthy and still ongoing scientific exploration of Jupiter and its moons.

Galileo's first task involved separating a smaller probe and releasing it. This probe, slowed by a parachute, fell through Jupiter's atmosphere. Instruments on the probe measured the amounts of gases. Scientists found much less helium and water vapor than they had expected. They were also surprised to learn that the winds grew stronger instead of weaker as the probe descended.

▲ Figure 17-27 The *Galileo* space probe

Galileo also provided new information about Jupiter's largest moons. For example, it appears that sections of ice covering Europa are moving away from each other. This movement might be caused by water beneath the ice. Another surprising discovery was a magnetic field around Ganymede.

Thinking Critically Why might finding water on Europa be exciting to scientists?

What do we know about Uranus, Neptune and the dwarf planets?

Objective

Identify some features of Uranus, Neptune and the dwarf planets.

Key Terms

dwarf planets: small, planetlike objects that orbit the Sun and share their orbits with similar objects

Uranus The seventh planet from the Sun and the third largest planet in the solar system is Uranus. The diameter of Uranus is about 51,000 km.

In 1781, Uranus became the first planet to be discovered by using a telescope. Very little was known about Uranus until 1986, when the *Voyager 2* space probe flew past it. *Voyager 2* sent back many images and discovered ten new moons.

◀ **Figure 17-28** Uranus may have collided with another large body early in its history and been knocked over. This image was taken by an infrared camera. The planet's real color is blue-green, and its ring is very thin.

Uranus is made mostly of hydrogen and helium. The blue-green color of the clouds shows that the atmosphere also contains methane.

Oddly, the axis of Uranus is horizontal. The planet appears to be lying on its side. Its poles point toward the Sun. This unusual tilt may have been caused by a collision with another planet-size body early in its history.

Uranus spins fast and has a very strong magnetic field. It also has a faint ring.

▶ **LIST:** What are three gases found in the atmosphere of Uranus?

Neptune The eighth planet from the Sun is Neptune. Neptune is similar to Uranus in size and mass. Its diameter is about 49,500 km, and it also has a faint ring around its equator. Neptune is so far from the Sun that it takes 165 Earth years to revolve once around it.

Neptune was discovered in 1846. It was the last planet to be visited by *Voyager 2*. Photographs taken by *Voyager 2* show that Neptune has a Great Dark Spot, similar to Jupiter's Great Red Spot. Neptune is also a gas giant. Its upper atmosphere is made mostly of clouds of frozen methane, which gives the planet its blue-green color. The lower atmosphere contains mostly hydrogen and helium. Neptune is the windiest planet. Winds can blow east to west at over 1,500 km/h.

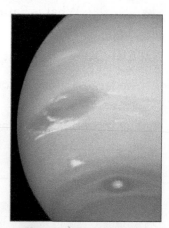

▲ **Figure 17-29** Through a telescope, Neptune is blue-green and shows few features.

▶ **IDENTIFY:** When was Neptune discovered?

Dwarf Planets In 2006, the International Astronomical Union decided on a new definition of a planet. Pluto no longer fit that definition, so scientists reclassified Pluto as a dwarf planet. **Dwarf planets** are planetlike objects that orbit the Sun. Unlike planets, however, dwarf planets share their orbits with other, similar objects. For example, Pluto has an irregular orbit that overlaps the orbit of Neptune. Ceres and Eris are other dwarf planets. Dwarf planets are smaller than the other planets in the solar system.

▲ **Figure 17-30** The Sun looks very small from Pluto's orbit.

Pluto has a frozen surface of methane, nitrogen, and carbon dioxide. In 2006, NASA launched the *New Horizons* spacecraft. It will travel to Pluto and its moon, Charon. It should arrive in 2015, becoming the first spacecraft to visit there.

 IDENTIFY: What is the definition of a dwarf planet?

The Kuiper Belt Between Neptune and the outer regions of the solar system is the Kuiper Belt. This belt was discovered in 1992. It was named after the Dutch astronomer who suggested that it might exist. The Kuiper Belt may contain as many as 100 million fragments of ice and rock. These fragments could be from a planet that never formed. Pluto, Eris, and their moons are classified as Kuiper Belt objects.

EXPLAIN: What kinds of objects are in the Kuiper Belt?

✓ CHECKING CONCEPTS

1. What is the most unusual feature of Uranus?
2. How is Neptune similar to Uranus?

3. How long does Neptune take to complete one orbit around the Sun?
4. Which was the last planet that *Voyager 2* visited?

💡 THINKING CRITICALLY

5. **HYPOTHESIZE:** Pluto may have once been a moon of Neptune. What might have caused Pluto to go into its own orbit?

Web InfoSearch

Neptune's Wobble A century ago, astronomers thought they observed a strange wobble in Neptune's orbit. Many thought the wobble was caused by a distant, unseen planet. Today, we know that the wobble does not exist at all.

SEARCH: Use the Internet to find out more about this. How did the search for another gas giant lead to the discovery of Pluto? Start your search at www.conceptsandchallenges.com. Some key search words are **Clyde Tombaugh**, **discovery of Pluto**, and **Pluto Charon**.

 People in Science

JET PROPULSION LAB WORKER

The Jet Propulsion Laboratory (JPL) in Pasadena is run by the California Institute of Technology for NASA. Since 1960, it has been involved in exploring the solar system using space probes. Today, it serves as command center for missions such as *Voyager*, *Magellan*, and *Galileo*.

JPL employs many scientists, engineers, and technicians. They are involved in the launching and tracking of satellites, as well as space probes. The satellites study the oceans, the ozone, and other physical features of Earth. Scientists at JPL constantly analyze the data sent back to Earth. They must also check that the instruments are working and try to fix them remotely if they are not. JPL instruments also scan the skies for near-Earth objects that might collide with Earth. Most JPL scientists have a strong background in science and mathematics.

▲ **Figure 17-31** Jet Propulsion Lab scientists test the robotic arm of NASA's Mars rover *Curiosity*

Thinking Critically What are some activities engineers at JPL might take part in?

What is a comet?

Making a Scale Model of a Comet
HANDS-ON ACTIVITY

1. Using a pen, put a dot in the center of a 5-inch paper plate. This dot represents a comet's nucleus. Glue a cotton ball to the plate to cover the dot. The cotton ball represents the gas cloud that surrounds the nucleus of a comet. This is called the coma.

2. Attach five streamers to the back of the plate with tape. The streamers represent the comet's tail. Make sure all the streamers face in the same direction.

3. Compare your comet with a whole peppercorn or a small pea, which can represent Earth.

4. Compare your comet with a 10-inch paper plate, which can represent the Sun.

THINK ABOUT IT: How does your comet model compare to the size of Earth? How does it compare to the size of the Sun?

Objectives
Define comet and identify the features of a comet.

Key Terms
comet: lump of ice, frozen gas, and dust that orbits the Sun

nucleus: head or solid part of a comet

coma: gas cloud that surrounds the nucleus of a comet

tail: long, ribbonlike trail of comet dust and gas

Comet Parts Like planets and asteroids, comets are also members of the solar system. A **comet** is a lump of ice, frozen gas, and dust that orbits the Sun. Comets orbit the Sun in very long ellipses that often take them beyond the orbit of Pluto.

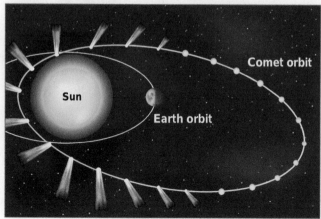

▲ **Figure 17-32** A comet's orbit typically takes it near the Sun and then back to the outer reaches of the solar system.

A comet has three parts. The core, or **nucleus**, is basically a dirty ice ball. It is made of water ice, frozen gas, and dust. The cloud of gas that surrounds the nucleus is called the **coma**. Stretching out from the coma is one or more **tails**. A stream of particles coming from the Sun pushes the tail or tails away from the center of the solar system.

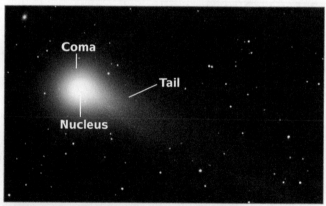

▲ **Figure 17-33** The structure of a comet

1 DESCRIBE: What are comets made of?

Ghostly Travelers Comets travel in deep space, where it is very cold. For most of their trip around the Sun, they are invisible. As a comet approaches the Sun, it begins to warm up. Some of the ice begins to melt. Gas and dust are released from the nucleus and spread out to form the coma. Soon, the tail begins to form. Tails can stretch out for millions of kilometers.

From Earth, a comet looks like a ghostly patch in the sky. It suddenly appears one night as sunlight begins reflecting off it.

Over time, the coma expands, and the tail stretches out into space. After rounding the Sun, the comet moves back into deep space and disappears from view.

 EXPLAIN: What causes a comet's tail to grow?

Where Comets Come From Astronomers think that many comets come from the Oort Cloud. This cloud, named after the Dutch astronomer Jan Oort, is far beyond Neptune's orbit. The Oort Cloud may contain trillions of inactive comets. A second cloud of comets or cometlike material called the Kuiper Belt exists beyond the orbit of Neptune.

Comets were formed billions of years ago when the solar system was young. After the Sun formed, gas and dust surrounding the new Sun formed into small pieces of ice, rock, and metal. These pieces eventually stuck together to form larger objects. The largest bodies became planets and moons. The smaller bodies became asteroids and comets.

 INFER: What materials became comets?

☑ CHECKING CONCEPTS

1. The parts of a comet are the nucleus, the coma, and the _____.

2. Comets orbit the Sun in long, _____ orbits.

3. The Oort Cloud is found outside the orbit of _____.

4. The heaviest materials, such as rock and _____, formed the planets, moons, comets, and asteroids.

💡 THINKING CRITICALLY

5. **INFER:** Why are scientists interested in comets?

6. **INFER:** What happens to the size of the nucleus of a comet each time it orbits the Sun?

DESIGNING AN EXPERIMENT

Design an experiment to solve the following problem. Include a hypothesis, variables, a procedure with materials, and a type of data to study. Be sure to also include a way to record your data.

PROBLEM: Astronomers believe that the nucleus of a comet begins melting as the comet nears the Sun. Design an experiment that will prove this. Your experiment will be carried on a spacecraft that will travel with the comet as it orbits the Sun.

 How Do They Know That?
PREDICTING COMETS

Scientists know that comets are coming days or months before they become visible to the naked eye. The comets appear in the sky right where scientists predict they will be. How do they do that?

▲ **Figure 17-34** Halley's comet as seen in 1960

Most comets travel around the Sun many times before they melt or leave the solar system. British astronomer Sir Edmund Halley was the first person to predict a comet's return, in 1758. The comet was later named after him.

Old comets, ones that have passed by the Sun before, are easy to predict. Today, comet orbits are calculated by computers. To find new comets, astronomers take pictures of the same regions of the night sky several days apart. If one of the stars in the first picture is in a different place in the second picture, it could be a comet. Powerful telescopes are then trained on the object. Eventually, astronomers identify it as a comet or some other object, like an asteroid. If it is a comet, it will begin releasing gas as it nears the Sun.

Thinking Critically Why do comets become visible as they get closer to the Sun?

Chapter Summary

Lessons 17-1 and 17-2

- The **solar system** may have formed from a spinning cloud of gases and dust called a **nebula.** There are eight planets in the solar system. The planets can be divided into inner and outer planets.

- An **ellipse** has an oval shape. Most planets travel around the Sun in elliptical **orbits.**

- Earth's orbital velocity is greatest at **perihelion** and least at **aphelion.**

Lesson 17-3

- The Moon is Earth's only natural **satellite.** Humans first landed on it in 1969. There is no air or water on the Moon. The Moon has **maria,** highlands, and **craters.**

Lessons 17-4 and 17-5

- Mercury and Venus have no moons. Mars has 2, Jupiter has at least 28, Saturn 30, Uranus 21, and Neptune 8.

- Mercury is the closest planet to the Sun. It has many craters. Venus has a blanket of sulfuric acid clouds. Earth supports life.

Lessons 17-6 and 17-7

- Mars is reddish. It might have had running water in the past.

- **Asteroids** orbit the Sun in a belt between Mars and Jupiter. Space objects called **meteoroids** may enter Earth's atmosphere. If they burn up, they are called **meteors.** If they strike Earth's surface, they are **meteorites.**

Lessons 17-8 and 17-9

- Jupiter is the largest, most massive planet. It is a gas giant. Its Great Red Spot is a huge storm. Saturn is the least dense planet and has distinctive rings. Rings are particles of ice and dust that orbit a planet around its equator.

- Uranus is a gas giant that appears to be lying on its side. Neptune, also a gas giant, has an upper atmosphere of frozen methane.

Lesson 17-10

- **Comets** are dirty ice balls. They have long, elliptical orbits.

Key Term Challenges

aphelion (p. 410)	meteoroid (p. 424)
asteroid (p. 424)	nebula (p. 408)
coma (p. 430)	nucleus (p. 430)
comet (p. 430)	orbit (p. 408)
crater (p. 414)	perihelion (p. 410)
ellipse (p. 410)	rift (p. 422)
mare (p. 414)	satellite (p. 416)
meteor (p. 424)	solar system (p. 408)
meteorite (p. 424)	tail (p. 430)

MATCHING Write the Key Term from above that best matches each description.

1. curved path of one object around another object in space

2. flattened circle, or oval

3. lump of dust and ice that orbits the Sun and has a gaseous tail

4. natural or artificial object orbiting another body in space

5. cloud of gas and dust in space

6. valley caused by a crack in the crust of a planet

7. rock or metal that enters Earth's atmosphere from space

8. head or solid part of a comet

9. Sun and all the objects that orbit the Sun

10. point in a planet's orbit at which the planet is farthest from the Sun

APPLYING DEFINITIONS **Explain the difference between the words in each pair. Write your answers in complete sentences.**

11. asteroid, meteoroid

12. meteor, meteorite

13. aphelion, perihelion

14. craters, maria

15. nebula, solar system

16. satellite, moon

Content Challenges TEST PREP

MULTIPLE CHOICE **Write the letter of the term or phrase that best completes each statement.**

1. The planet closest in size to Earth is
   a. Venus.
   b. Mercury.
   c. Uranus.
   d. Jupiter.

2. The Great Red Spot is the best-known feature of
   a. Mercury.
   b. Neptune.
   c. Uranus.
   d. Jupiter.

3. The planet that is the farthest from the Sun is
   a. Venus.
   b. Neptune.
   c. Uranus.
   d. Jupiter.

4. The only planets in the solar system without at least one moon are
   a. Jupiter and Mars.
   b. Earth and Venus.
   c. Jupiter and Mercury.
   d. Mercury and Venus.

5. American astronauts first set foot on the Moon in
   a. 1957.
   b. 1969.
   c. 1972.
   d. 1975.

6. Earth is closest to the Sun in
   a. July.
   b. September.
   c. March.
   d. January.

7. The gas giants of our solar system are Jupiter, Saturn, Uranus, and
   a. Earth.
   b. Venus.
   c. Neptune.
   d. Mars.

8. The light-colored areas on the Moon are
   a. mountains.
   b. rivers.
   c. plains.
   d. oceans.

9. The first planet to be discovered by using a telescope was
   a. Jupiter.
   b. Uranus.
   c. Mars.
   d. Mercury.

TRUE/FALSE **Write *true* if the statement is true. If the statement is false, change the underlined term to make the statement true.**

10. Some scientists think a nebula <u>expanded</u> to form the solar system.

11. The <u>core</u> of a comet is made of dust and ice.

12. Earth moves <u>fastest</u> at perihelion.

13. The largest planet in the solar system is <u>Neptune</u>.

14. Earth has only one <u>ring</u>.

15. <u>Uranus</u> is tipped on its side.

16. The region between Mars and Jupiter is called the <u>Meteoroid</u> Belt.

17. Saturn's density is <u>less</u> than the density of Jupiter and even water.

18. The first asteroid found was named <u>Ceres</u>.

Concept Challenges TEST PREP

WRITTEN RESPONSE **Answer each of the following questions in complete sentences.**

1. INFER: Why is the term *wanderer* inaccurate for describing a planet?

2. INFER: Why do rocks on the Moon not weather or erode as rocks on Earth do?

3. ANALYZE: What is one trait that the inner planets have in common? The outer planets?

4. HYPOTHESIZE: What are some reasons astronauts may go back to the Moon?

5. INFER: Why are scientists looking for water on Mars?

6. ANALYZE: Why was Galileo's discovery of four moons orbiting Jupiter important to the history of astronomy?

7. EXPLAIN: How can a comet passing through Earth's orbit cause a meteor shower?

8. INFER: Why does a comet's tail always point away from the Sun?

9. EXPLAIN: Why does Earth's orbital velocity change as it orbits the Sun?

10. COMPARE/CONTRAST: How are the inner planets and outer planets alike and how are they different?

INTERPRETING VISUALS **Use Figure 17-35 to answer each of the following questions.**

11. How many moons does Neptune have?

12. How many planets have no moons?

13. What planet has the most known moons?

14. Do any of the inner planets have rings?

PLANETS, MOONS, AND RINGS		
Planets	**Number of Known Moons**	**Rings**
Mercury	0	No
Venus	0	No
Earth	1	No
Mars	2	No
Jupiter	63	Yes
Saturn	59	Yes
Uranus	21	Yes
Neptune	8	Yes

▲ Figure 17-35

Chapter 18 The Sun and Other Stars

▲ **Figure 18-1** The Eagle Nebula is also known to astronomers as M16.

These dark structures may look like cave formations or undersea coral. However, they are actually columns of cool hydrogen gas and dust in a nebula. Nebulae are the birthplaces of new stars. The Eagle Nebula, above, is 6,500 light-years away from Earth. The tallest column is about one light-year tall. This picture was taken with a camera on the Hubble Space Telescope. The image reveals the various elements that make up the matter in the nebula.

▶ What do you think are some of the elements that make up stars?

Contents

18-1 How are stars formed?

Objectives

Describe how stars form. Name some characteristics of stars.

Key Terms

star: ball of gases that gives off light and heat

nebula (NEHB-yuh-luh)**:** cloud of gas and dust in space

protostar: dense material in the center of a nebula that is about to become a star

binary stars: two stars that revolve around each other

star cluster: large group of stars that travel together through space

Tiny Points of Light The Sun is a star. A **star** is a big ball of gases that gives off heat and light. The Sun is only one of billions of stars that make up our galaxy, and there are billions of galaxies. Between the stars and galaxies are vast stretches of nearly empty space.

On a clear night, you can see thousands of stars in the sky. Most of these look to us like tiny points of light. This is because they are so far away. Most stars appear white to the unaided eye. However, a closer look reveals that stars come in different colors. For example, Rigel is a blue star. Betelgeuse (BEET-uhl-jooz) is red. The Sun, of course, is yellow. Stars also show a huge range in size, brightness, and surface temperature. How large and massive a star is determines what will eventually happen to it.

▲ **Figure 18-2** The Sun is only one of billions of stars. However, the unaided eye sees only a few thousand stars.

Different stars have different elements. Most stars are made up of the gases hydrogen and helium. Other elements often found in stars include sodium, calcium, and iron. The most common element in stars is hydrogen. All of these elements are found in varying amounts in stars.

1 NAME: What is the most common element in stars?

Formation of Stars A star forms from a cloud of gas and dust in space called a **nebula.** Gravity causes the nebula to contract and start spinning. This flattens the nebula into a disk. Material at the center of the disk forms a **protostar.**

As the nebula continues to contract, temperature and pressure build. Eventually, nuclear reactions begin, and the protostar starts to give off light and heat. A new star is born.

2 NAME: What is the first stage in star formation?

▲ **Figure 18-3** A star begins as a cloud of gas and dust that forms into a protostar. When it begins to give off light and heat, the protostar has become a true star.

Double Stars and Star Clusters Unlike the Sun, most stars are double, or binary, stars. **Binary stars** are pairs of stars that travel through space together and revolve around each other.

Some stars are part of multiple-star systems. They contain three or more stars. Many stars move through space in large groups called **star clusters.** Some clusters are globular, or round, in shape. Others are open, or loosely arranged.

▲ **Figure 18-4** A globular cluster can contain millions of stars.

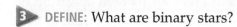 **DEFINE:** What are binary stars?

☑ **CHECKING CONCEPTS**

1. What is the star closest to Earth?
2. What two gases make up most stars?
3. What is a nebula?
4. What causes a spinning nebula to contract?
5. What two shapes do star clusters form?

💡 **THINKING CRITICALLY**

6. SEQUENCE: What are the stages in the formation of a star?
7. INFER: Why are rounded clusters called globular clusters?

BUILDING SCIENCE SKILLS

Classifying Stars are grouped according to color, or spectral classes. The letters *O, B, A, F, G, K,* and *M* represent spectral classes. Blue stars are in spectral class O or B. Red stars are M stars. Do some research on the following stars: Canopus, Arcturus, Sirius, Rigel, the Sun, Betelgeuse, Altair, and Capella. Then, put them in their correct spectral class.

Science and Technology

OBSERVATORIES

Most professional astronomers today work at observatories. Instead of using just their eyes to look through telescopes, they use sensitive electronic cameras to build up an exposure over many minutes or hours. Then, computers analyze the data. Astronomers study the pictures and the computer data.

Most observatories use reflecting telescopes with large mirrors. The Special Astrophysical Observatory in Russia has a mirror 6 m in diameter. However, large mirrors often sag under their own weight, blurring the image. This has led scientists to build reflecting telescopes that use many small mirrors acting as one. The Keck Telescope at Mauna Kea, in Hawaii, has a mirror made of 36 thin glass segments. Together, these segments make a mirror 10 m in diameter.

▲ **Figure 18-5** Kitt Peak National Observatory

Many observatories in the United States, such as Palomar near San Diego, California, are run by cities or nonprofit groups. Kitt Peak National Observatory, near Tucson, Arizona, is the largest U.S. observatory.

Thinking Critically What activities are conducted inside observatories?

18-2 How is spectroscopy used to study stars?

Objective

Describe how astronomers use spectroscopy to study stars.

Key Terms

spectrum, *pl.* **spectra:** pattern of different colors of light coming from an object

spectrograph (SPEHK-truh-graf)**:** device that measures the spectrum of an object

spectroscopy (spehk-TRUH-skohp-ee)**:** study of light coming from objects in space

Colors of Starlight White light is a mixture of different colors of light. When you aim a beam of white light at a prism, the prism separates or spreads out the light into its colors. This pattern of colors is called a **spectrum.**

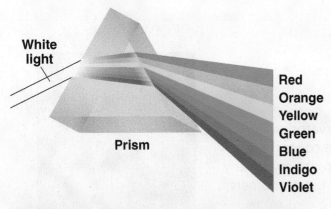

White light — Prism — Red Orange Yellow Green Blue Indigo Violet

▲ **Figure 18-6** A prism breaks up white light into a spectrum.

The spectrum of white light contains red, orange, yellow, green, blue, indigo, and violet. These are the colors you see in a rainbow.

Astronomers learn about stars by studying their light. They use a **spectrograph,** which contains a prism that separates light from the star into bands of colors. The spectrograph also contains a camera to focus the spectrum and record it on photographic or electronic film. The study of light coming from objects in space is called **spectroscopy.**

1 DEFINE: What is a spectrum?

Color and Composition A spectrum reveals the chemical makeup of a star. Stars are very hot. When elements are heated enough, they give off light. Each element gives off its own spectrum of light. Astronomers can study this spectrum to find out what elements make up the star.

2 EXPLAIN: What does a spectrum reveal?

Color and Temperature The surface temperature of a star is related to its color. Stars come in different colors. Blue stars are the hottest, at around 29,000°C to 40,000°C. Red stars, at around 2,100°C to 3,200°C, are the coolest. A yellow star, like our Sun, is about 6,000°C. Scientists are able to determine the approximate temperature of a star from its spectrum.

3 APPLY: If a star is medium hot, what would be its color?

Hydrogen

Helium

◄ **Figure 18-7** The spectra for hydrogen and helium

✓ CHECKING CONCEPTS

1. Different colors of light make up a _____.

2. When an element is _____, it gives off a spectrum of light.

3. Each _____ in a star gives off its own spectrum.

4. The _____ of a star is related to its color.

5. The hottest stars are the color _____.

💡 THINKING CRITICALLY

6. ANALYZE: A star has a very high surface temperature. What color does this star appear?

7. CALCULATE: What is the difference in degrees Celsius between the hottest stars and the coolest stars?

Web InfoSearch

The Doppler Effect Have you ever noticed that a siren moving toward you sounds different from one moving away from you? This is known as a Doppler effect. Both sound and light waves are affected by the Doppler effect.

SEARCH: Use the Internet to find out more about the Doppler effect. How is it important in astronomy? What are redshift and blueshift? How can scientists find out how fast an object is moving from its Doppler effect? Begin your search at **www.conceptsandchallenges.com**. Some key search words are **Doppler effect astronomy**, **Doppler redshift**, and **Doppler blueshift**.

Hands-On Activity

MAKING A SPECTROSCOPE

You can use a spectroscope to separate white light into a band of colors. You will need a cardboard tube, a diffraction grating, a sheet of black construction paper, scissors, tape, a light bulb, and colored crayons.

1. Tape a diffraction grating to one end of a cardboard tube.

2. Cut a thin slit in the center of a sheet of black construction paper. ⚠ CAUTION: Be careful when using scissors.

3. Cover the other end of the cardboard tube with the sheet of black paper. Use tape to hold the paper in place.

▲ **STEP 4** Look through your tube at a light bulb.

4. Hold the end of the tube with the diffraction grating up to your eye. Look through the tube at a light bulb. Slowly turn the tube until you see a spectrum. Draw the spectrum.

5. Use your spectroscope to look at other light sources, such as a fluorescent tube. ⚠ CAUTION: Do not look at the Sun with your spectroscope.

Practicing Your Skills

6. DESCRIBE: What does a spectroscope do?

7. COMPARE: **a.** Were the spectra from different light sources the same or different? **b.** How can you explain the similarities or differences of the spectra?

18-3   What is magnitude?

Objective

Compare apparent magnitude and absolute magnitude.

Key Term

magnitude (MAG-nuh-tood): way to measure a star's brightness

Brightness of Stars In some places you can see about 2,000 stars in the night sky without a telescope. Some stars appear brighter than others. One way to measure a star's brightness is by **magnitude.**

How bright a star appears to us depends on its temperature, size, and distance from Earth. A hot star is usually brighter than a cool star. A large star is usually brighter than a small star. The closer a star is to Earth, the brighter it usually appears to us.

▶ **NAME:** What is the measure of a star's brightness called?

Apparent Magnitude The brightness of a star as seen from Earth is called the star's apparent magnitude. Planets can be classified this way, too, although they shine only with reflected light.

Astronomers have developed a scale for apparent magnitude. On this scale, a star with a low number appears brighter than a star with a high number. Bright stars usually have an apparent magnitude of 1. These are called first-magnitude stars. Very bright stars can have negative magnitudes. The dimmest stars you can see without a telescope are sixth-magnitude stars. You can see the magnitudes of some stars and other bodies in Figure 18-8 below.

▶ **COMPARE:** Which appears brighter, a third-magnitude star or a sixth-magnitude star?

Absolute Magnitude Astronomers can also find the absolute magnitude of a star. The absolute magnitude of a star is its actual brightness. Absolute magnitude describes how bright a star would appear to us if all the stars were the same distance from Earth.

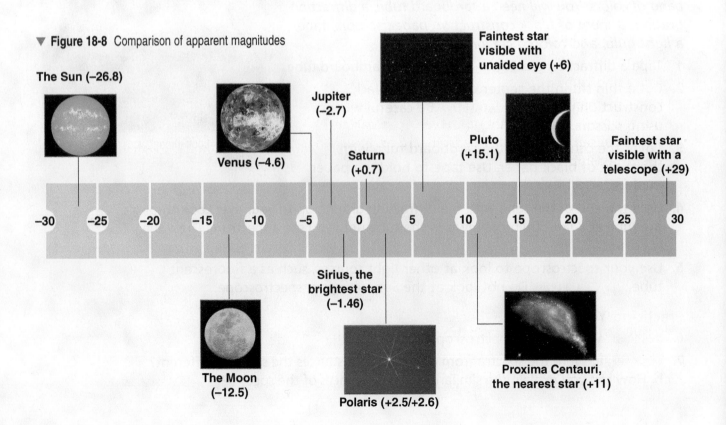

▼ **Figure 18-8** Comparison of apparent magnitudes

The Sun (−26.8)

Venus (−4.6)

Jupiter (−2.7)

Saturn (+0.7)

Faintest star visible with unaided eye (+6)

Pluto (+15.1)

Faintest star visible with a telescope (+29)

−30 −25 −20 −15 −10 −5 0 5 10 15 20 25 30

The Moon (−12.5)

Sirius, the brightest star (−1.46)

Polaris (+2.5/+2.6)

Proxima Centauri, the nearest star (+11)

For example, the Sun appears very bright to us because it is so near Earth. If the Sun were farther away, it would not appear as bright to us. A dim star that is close to Earth may appear brighter than a bright star that is far away. All stars have both an apparent magnitude and an absolute magnitude.

 DESCRIBE: What is absolute magnitude?

✓ CHECKING CONCEPTS

1. Magnitude is a measure of a star's _____ .

2. Magnitude depends on a particular star's size, _____ , and distance from Earth.

3. A fourth-magnitude star appears _____ than a first-magnitude star.

4. The brightness of a star as seen from Earth is its _____ magnitude.

5. The actual brightness of a star is its _____ magnitude.

THINKING CRITICALLY

6. **HYPOTHESIZE:** Two stars have the same absolute magnitude but different apparent magnitudes. Explain how this can be true.

7. **COMPARE:** The Sun is the star closest to Earth. It has an absolute magnitude of 5.4. The star Altair has an absolute magnitude of 2.2. Which star is really brighter? Explain.

BUILDING MATH SKILLS

Calculating First-magnitude stars are about 2.512 times brighter than second-magnitude stars. These are about 2.512 times brighter than third-magnitude stars, and so on. Using this information, you can figure out how faint a star is compared to some other star. If two stars are five magnitudes apart, you would multiply 2.512 to the fifth power (2.512^5) to get 100. This means that a first-magnitude star is 100 times brighter than a sixth-magnitude star. Use this formula and a calculator to compare a star with a magnitude of 25 to a star with a magnitude of 5.

 Hands-On Activity

OBSERVING MAGNITUDE

You will need one large flashlight and one small flashlight.

1. Work in groups of three.

2. Have one partner hold a large flashlight and another partner hold a small flashlight. Have both partners stand the same distance away from you and turn on their flashlights.

3. Compare the brightness of the two flashlights.

4. Now, have the person holding the small flashlight move closer to you. Compare the brightness of the two lights.

▲ **STEP 2** Have your partners stand the same distance away from you and turn on their flashlights.

Practicing Your Skills

5. **COMPARE: a.** When they were the same distance away, which appeared brighter, the large flashlight or the small flashlight? **b.** Which had the greater apparent magnitude? **c.** Which had the greater absolute magnitude?

6. **OBSERVE: a.** What happened when the small flashlight was moved closer? **b.** Which had the greater apparent magnitude? **c.** Which had the greater absolute magnitude?

18-4 How are stars classified?

The H-R Diagram In the early 1900s, astronomers Ejnar Hertzsprung and Henry Russell each made a separate but similar discovery about stars. They found that there is a relationship between a star's absolute magnitude and its surface temperature and color. Together, Hertzsprung and Russell developed a chart called the Hertzsprung-Russell, or H-R, diagram. The H-R diagram shows that the brightness of most stars increases as the star's surface temperature increases.

▶ 1 DESCRIBE: What does the H-R diagram show?

Main Sequence Stars A star's position on the H-R diagram depends on its absolute magnitude and its surface temperature, or color. Temperature is in degrees Kelvin (K). Suppose that a star has a blue color and a low absolute magnitude. This star would be placed in the upper left corner of the diagram. A red star with a high absolute magnitude would appear in the lower right corner. Most stars fall in a narrow diagonal band that runs from the upper left to the lower right corner of the diagram. Stars that fall in this band are called **main sequence stars.** The Sun and most stars that you can see at night are main sequence stars.

▶ 2 CLASSIFY: What kind of star is the Sun on an H-R diagram?

Other Stars Some stars do not fall within the main sequence. They may be bright but not very hot. Many of these stars are red, orange, or yellow in color. Because they are not very hot, they should not be very bright. However, because these stars are very large, they give off a great deal of light. They have large absolute magnitudes. These stars are called **red giants.** Red giants appear in the upper right corner of an H-R diagram.

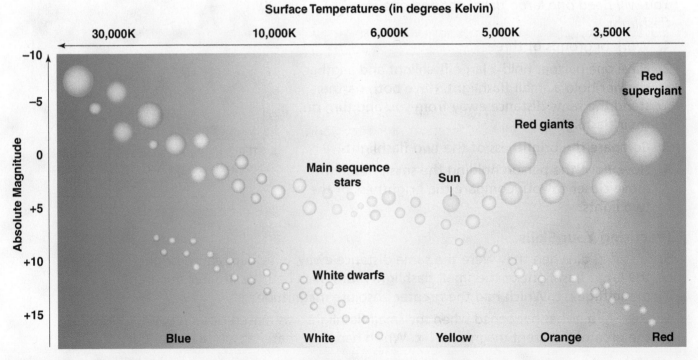

▲ **Figure 18-9** An H-R diagram shows the relationship between the brightness of stars and their surface temperatures.

442

Some stars are even larger and brighter than red giants. These stars are called **supergiants.**

Other stars that fall outside of the main sequence are hot but very small. These stars are blue or white. They are called **white dwarfs.** White dwarfs are found in the lower part of an H-R diagram, below the main sequence stars.

 DEFINE: What are white dwarfs?

✔ CHECKING CONCEPTS

1. The H-R diagram shows the relationship between _____ magnitude and temperature.

2. The Sun is a _____ sequence star.

3. A very large, bright star is a red _____.

4. Red giants are found in the upper _____ of an H-R diagram.

5. White dwarfs are small, _____ stars.

💡 THINKING CRITICALLY

Use Figure 18-9 to answer the following questions.

6. **COMPARE:** Which star has a higher absolute magnitude, a red giant or a white dwarf?

7. **COMPARE:** Which star has a greater surface temperature, a red giant or a white dwarf?

8. **ANALYZE:** What is the average surface temperature of a white dwarf?

9. **IDENTIFY:** What stars are even larger than red giants?

BUILDING MATH SKILLS

Graphing Create a line graph that shows where each kind of star appears on the H-R diagram. Plot the absolute magnitude along the vertical axis. Plot the temperature along the horizontal axis. Label each point with the kind of star it represents. Do the points form a pattern? Write a few sentences describing how the pattern formed compares to the pattern in Figure 18-9.

 ## *How Do They Know That?*

DISTANCES TO THE STARS

How do astronomers measure distances to stars? The distance of close stars can be found by observing the star's parallax. Parallax is based on how the star seems to shift position over time. However, the distances to stars that are very far away seemed almost impossible to measure. Then, an American astronomer discovered a way to find the distances to stars in other galaxies.

Henrietta Swan Leavitt (1868–1921) was born in Lancaster, Massachusetts. She graduated from what is now Radcliffe College and soon went to work at the Harvard Observatory. She was studying a kind of star called a Cepheid (SEHF-ee-id) variable. A Cepheid variable is a star that changes its brightness in a regular pattern over a set period of time.

In 1912, Leavitt identified 25 Cepheid variables in a nearby galaxy. She observed the period of each star, or how long the star took to go from bright to dim and back to bright again. She showed that the longer the period of a star is, the brighter the star. A star's brightness is related to its distance. Astronomers used this relationship to calculate the distance to faraway stars.

▲ **Figure 18-10** Henrietta Swan Leavitt used Cepheid stars to show that a star's brightness is related to its distance.

Thinking Critically Why do you think parallax is not useful for measuring all stars?

Objective

Describe the stages in the life cycle of a star.

Key Terms

nova: explosion where the outer layers of a star are blown off

supernova: violent explosion where a star is blown apart

Life Cycle of a Star Stars change over time. This is called a life cycle. A star's complete life cycle takes many millions of years. As time passes, the star changes its mass into energy. The energy is given off as light and heat. Eventually, most of the mass is used up, and the star dies. By studying many different stars, astronomers have learned how stars change during their life cycles.

▶ 1 EXPLAIN: Where does a star's energy come from?

Protostar to Giant Stars are formed from nebulae. Gravity pulls the dust and the gas in the nebula together, forming a protostar. If the protostar becomes hot enough, nuclear reactions start to take place. In these reactions, hydrogen is changed into helium. Large amounts of energy are produced. These reactions turn the protostar into a star.

Now the star is on the main sequence. During this stage, hydrogen at the star's center continues to change into helium. When this process ends, small stars will stop shining and contract to become white dwarfs. Larger stars, however, will start new nuclear reactions that turn helium into carbon. The energy produced by these reactions expands the star and makes it cooler. It is now a red giant.

▶ 2 DESCRIBE: What is the main sequence stage?

Death of a Star The next stage in a star's life cycle depends on the star's mass. A medium-size star loses mass and begins to contract. The outer parts create a glowing cloud called a planetary nebula. The core of the star becomes a white dwarf. For a brief time, the white dwarf becomes very hot. The end stage of a white dwarf is thought to be a small, cold, dark object called a black dwarf. Scientists think it takes a trillion years for a black dwarf to form.

Sometimes a white dwarf will blow off its outer layers in a huge, bright explosion. This explosion is called a **nova.** A very massive star may blow itself apart in a **supernova.** During a supernova, or right after it, the star may collapse to become a neutron star or a black hole.

▶ 3 DESCRIBE: What happens when a medium-size star runs out of hydrogen?

Go **Online**
active art

For: The Lives of Stars activity
Visit: PHSchool.com
Web Code: cfp-5043

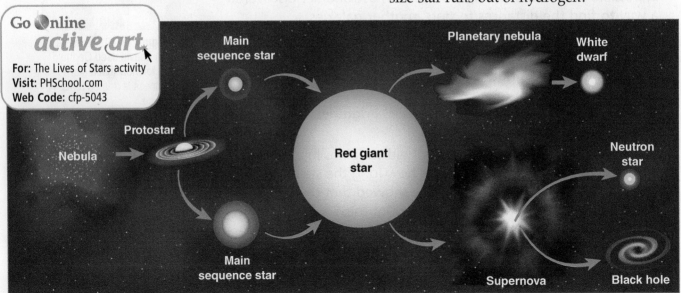

▲ **Figure 18-11** The life cycle of a star

Supernova 1987A On February 24, 1987, a supernova was seen in the Large Magellanic Cloud. This is more than 160,000 light years from Earth. The so-called Supernova 1987A was the first to be seen by the naked eye from Earth in almost 400 years. Astronomers studied the light coming from the supernova as it slowly dimmed. Viewing the supernova helped them to learn more about the evolution of stars.

 INFER: What was the likely energy source of Supernova 1987A?

☑ CHECKING CONCEPTS

1. A star changes _____ into energy.
2. The _____ stage is the briefest in a star's life cycle.
3. A main sequence star becomes a red giant or _____ when _____.
4. A white dwarf may blow off its outer shell in an explosion called a _____.
5. A supernova may occur in a very _____ star.

THINKING CRITICALLY

Use Figure 18-11 to complete the following exercise.

6. **SEQUENCE:** A flowchart shows a sequence of events. Create a flowchart showing the stages in the life cycle of a star. Begin with a protostar.

Web InfoSearch

Tycho Brahe Tycho Brahe was a 16th-century Danish astronomer. After studying law all day, he would go out at night to observe the stars. Brahe found that most of the astronomical information of the time was not accurate. He decided to devote his life to making accurate observations of the stars.

SEARCH: Use the Internet to find out more about Tycho Brahe's achievements. What did the king of Denmark give Brahe and why? Start your search at www.conceptsandchallenges.com. Key search words are **Tycho Brahe, Brahe King Denmark,** and **Tycho Brahe biography.**

How Do They Know That?

PULSARS

After a very massive star explodes, its core collapses. This collapse squeezes protons and electrons together until they become neutrons. This is how a neutron star is formed.

Neutron stars are incredibly dense. One teaspoonful of neutron star material would weigh over 2 billion tons. As they rotate, neutron stars send out radio waves and light that reach Earth in pulses. This is how pulsars got their name. Pulsars spin like the light atop a lighthouse. They emit radio or light waves or both that appear and then disappear in a regular pattern. The radio waves can be detected using a radio telescope.

The pulse of a pulsar tells us how fast the pulsar is spinning. The fastest pulsars discovered so far spin about 642 times per second. Some pulsars spin much more slowly, only once every few seconds.

Pulsars were first discovered in 1967 by Anthony Hewish and his graduate student, Jocelyn Bell. Hewish later received a Nobel Prize for identifying pulsars as a new class of stars.

Thinking Critically How did neutron stars get their name?

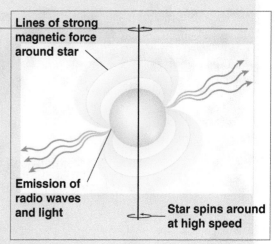

▲ **Figure 18-12** A pulsar spins like a light on a lighthouse.

18-6 What kind of star is the Sun?

Objective
Describe the parts of the Sun.

Key Terms

core: center of the Sun

photosphere (FOHT-oh-sfeer)**:** inner layer of the Sun's atmosphere

chromosphere (KROH-muh-sfeer)**:** layer of the Sun's atmosphere above the photosphere

corona (kuh-ROH-nuh)**:** outer layer of the Sun's atmosphere

Structure of the Sun The Sun is one of about 100 billion stars in our part of the universe. However, it is the only one close enough for us to study in detail. The Sun is an average star in size, mass, and temperature. Its diameter is 1,400,000 km. Because the Sun is made mostly of gases, it has no distinct boundaries. However, it has two main parts. These parts are the core and the atmosphere.

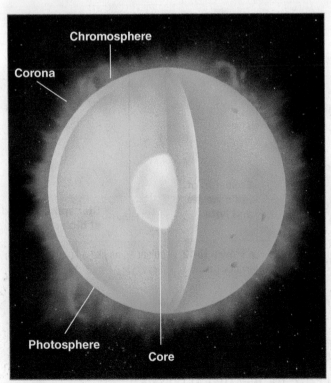

▲ **Figure 18-13** The atmosphere of the Sun is made up of the photosphere, the chromosphere, and the corona.

 NAME: What are the two main parts of the Sun?

The Sun's Core The center and hottest part of the Sun is the **core.** The core makes up about 10 percent of the Sun's diameter. It is where the Sun's energy is produced. The temperature of the core is about 15,000,000°C.

 IDENTIFY: Where is the Sun's core?

The Sun's Atmosphere Since the Sun is made up almost entirely of gas, its atmosphere takes up most of its volume. There are three thin layers at the outer edge of the atmosphere. One layer is the **photosphere,** or light sphere. The photosphere is the visible surface of the Sun. The gas in the photosphere glows and gives off light.

Above the photosphere lies another layer of the atmosphere, called the **chromosphere,** or "color sphere." This part of the Sun gives off a weak red glow that can be seen only under special conditions, such as during a solar eclipse. The chromosphere extends for thousands of kilometers.

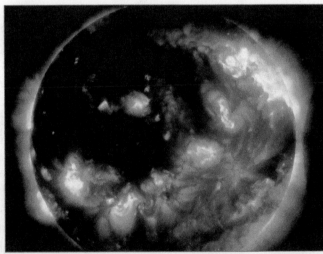

▲ **Figure 18-14** The chromosphere is seen more clearly in this photograph of the Sun taken by a special telescope.

The **corona** is the outermost layer of the Sun's atmosphere. This envelope of gases normally extends 1 million km from the Sun. It produces a glow about half as bright as a full Moon. The temperature of the corona is about 1,500,000°C. Like the chromosphere, the corona can usually be seen only during a solar eclipse.

3 LIST: What are three layers of the Sun's atmosphere?

1. What is at the center of the Sun?

2. What is the approximate temperature of the Sun's core?

3. Which part of the Sun is the source of the Sun's energy?

4. How many layers make up the Sun's atmosphere?

5. Which layers of the Sun's atmosphere can be seen only during a solar eclipse?

6. DESCRIBE: What is the basic structure of the Sun?

7. COMPARE: Which is the hottest part of the Sun?

8. INFER: Why is the part of the Sun you named in Question 7 the hottest?

9. ANALYZE: The word *corona* comes from a Latin word meaning "crown." Why do you think the outer layer of the Sun is called the corona?

Earth's atmosphere filters out most of the harmful rays the Sun produces. However, some of the rays that get through can be harmful. For example, the Sun is far too bright to look at directly without damaging your eyes. Astronomers use special telescopes to study the surface of the Sun. Also, you know that sunlight can cause sunburn and can damage skin. Some kinds of skin cancer are caused by overexposure to the Sun. You should always take care to protect your skin and your eyes from overexposure to sunlight.

 Hands-On Activity

OBSERVING THE SUN

You will need a ring stand, a clamp, a 20- by 28-cm sheet of cardboard, binoculars, and a sheet of white paper.

1. Clamp a pair of binoculars to a ring stand.

2. Cut a hole in the cardboard so that it fits over one eyepiece; the other eyepiece is covered. Tape the cardboard on securely.

3. Point the binoculars toward the Sun.
   ⚠ CAUTION: Never look directly at the Sun. Looking directly at the Sun could damage your eyes.

4. Hold the sheet of white paper a short distance from the eyepiece. An image of the Sun should appear on the sheet of white paper. Move the paper back and forth until your image of the Sun comes into sharp focus.

5. Quickly trace your image of the Sun onto the paper. Then, move the paper away to prevent scorching it. ⚠ CAUTION: If you hold the paper there for too long, it may ignite. Be sure to quickly remove it and the binoculars after you have drawn your image.

▲ STEP 4 Hold the paper a short distance from the eyepiece and look for an image of the Sun on it.

Practicing Your Skills

6. IDENTIFY: When you look at your image of the Sun, what layer are you seeing?

7. INFER: Why do you think you cannot see the other layers of the Sun's atmosphere?

8. INFER: Why is this a good method to use to observe a solar eclipse?

18-7 What is the surface of the Sun like?

Objective

Describe sunspots, prominences, and solar flares.

Key Terms

sunspot: dark, cool area on the Sun's surface

prominence (PRAHM-uh-nuhns)**:** stream of gas that shoots high above the Sun's surface

solar flare: eruption of electrically charged particles from the surface of the Sun

Sunspots Some areas on the surface of the Sun are cooler than the areas around them. The gases in these cooler areas do not shine as brightly as the areas around them. As a result, these areas appear dark. The dark, cooler areas on the Sun's surface are called **sunspots.** Sunspots usually appear to move in groups across the Sun in the same direction. The appearance of movement is caused by the spinning of the Sun on its axis. Sunspots may last for days or even months.

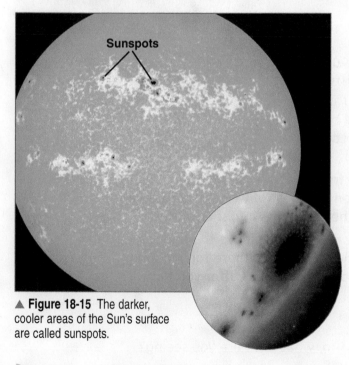

▲ **Figure 18-15** The darker, cooler areas of the Sun's surface are called sunspots.

1 EXPLAIN: Why do sunspots all appear to move in the same direction?

Prominences Streams of flaming gas shoot out from the surface of the Sun. These streams of gas are called **prominences.**

Prominences most often form in the chromosphere or photosphere. They can reach many thousands of kilometers above the Sun's surface. Then, they fall back into the Sun, forming huge arches. Prominences are best seen during a solar eclipse. They can last for weeks or months.

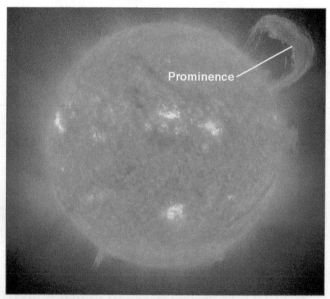

▲ **Figure 18-16** Prominences form in the chromosphere or photosphere.

2 DEFINE: What are prominences?

Solar Flares Energy sometimes builds up in the Sun's atmosphere. This buildup of energy usually happens near a group of sunspots. If the energy is given off suddenly, a **solar flare** is formed.

Solar flares usually do not last for more than an hour. Some may last for only a few minutes. In that time, though, they release enormous amounts of energy.

Solar flares send streams of electrically charged particles out into space. When these particles reach Earth's surface, they can cause electrical outages and disrupt communications. Solar flares are also the cause of the auroras, also called the northern and southern lights, on Earth.

▲ **Figure 18-17** Solar flares send streams of charged particles out into space.

 DESCRIBE: How do solar flares affect Earth?

CHECKING CONCEPTS

1. Sunspots appear dark because they are _____ than surrounding areas.

2. Streams of gas from the surface of the Sun are _____.

3. Solar flares release streams of _____ particles.

THINKING CRITICALLY

4. **MODEL:** Draw and label a picture of the Sun. Show all of the features of the Sun that were discussed.

Web InfoSearch

Sunspots and Ice Ages Astronomers have found that sunspot activity seems to build up and decrease in an 11-year cycle. This cycle has been linked to climate changes on Earth. For example, the Little Ice Age of the 1600s has been associated with a long period of low sunspot activity.

SEARCH: Use the Internet to find out more about sunspots. Why do they move across the Sun in an 11-year cycle? Could magnetic activity be a part of it? If so, how? Start your search for information at www.conceptsandchallenges.com. Some key search words are **sunspots**, **sunspots magnetic**, and **sunspot ice ages**.

Integrating Physical Science

TOPICS: magnetism, solar energy, ions

THE SOLAR WIND

Electrons and charged particles called ions move off the surface of the Sun. They slip through gaps in the magnetic fields of the Sun's corona and travel through space in all directions. This movement of charged particles through space is called the solar wind. It is not related to the air that blows across Earth's surface.

The ions heading toward Earth are drawn to Earth's magnetic poles. As the solar wind passes Earth, the charged particles that are moving at very high speeds may interact with the magnetic field of Earth. Once in Earth's atmosphere, they react with the oxygen and nitrogen atoms there. This reaction causes the light shows in the sky known as the auroras, or the northern and southern lights.

The tail of a comet also shows evidence of the solar wind. The solar wind sweeps the gases evaporating from the comet nucleus into a tail. Because of the solar wind, a comet's tail always points away from the Sun.

Thinking Critically Why do you think ions are drawn toward the magnetic poles of Earth?

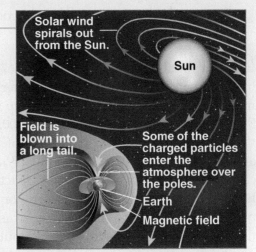

▲ **Figure 18-18** The solar wind spirals out from the Sun and enters the atmosphere over the poles.

18-8 How does the Sun produce energy?

Objective

Describe the process by which energy is produced in the Sun.

Key Terms

nucleus (NOO-klee-uhs), *pl.* **nuclei** (NOO-klee-eye): center, or core, of an atom

fusion (FYOO-zhuhn): reaction in which atomic nuclei combine to form larger nuclei

Solar Energy The Sun gives off energy in many forms, including heat and light. Where does this energy come from? You know that burning produces heat and light. However, burning does not produce the heat and the light of the Sun. The Sun produces energy by nuclear reactions. The **nucleus** is the center of an atom. In a nuclear reaction, the nuclei of atoms are changed.

▶ DESCRIBE: What kind of reaction produces the heat and the light of the Sun?

Nuclear Fusion The Sun is about 71 percent hydrogen and 27 percent helium. Other elements make up the remaining 2 percent. Deep inside the Sun, the temperature is more than 15,000,000°C. At these high temperatures, the nuclei of hydrogen atoms combine, or fuse. This kind of reaction is called hydrogen **fusion**. In this reaction, four hydrogen nuclei combine to form one helium nucleus. The mass of a helium nucleus is less than the mass of all four hydrogen nuclei put together. The missing mass has been changed into energy.

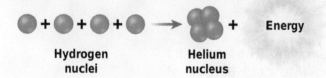

Hydrogen nuclei   **Helium nucleus**   **Energy**

▲ **Figure 18-19** Hydrogen fusion

▶ EXPLAIN: What happens in a fusion reaction?

Matter and Energy Albert Einstein helped explain how the Sun produces its energy. Einstein said that matter could be changed into energy. His equation $E = mc^2$ explains how a small amount of matter can be changed into a large amount of energy.

▲ **Figure 18-20** Albert Einstein

In this equation, E is energy, m is mass, or the amount of matter, and c is the speed of light. The speed of light is 300,000 km/s. Astronomers have used Einstein's equation to calculate how much energy the Sun produces.

▶ STATE: What is Einstein's equation?

Fusion Energy Fusion energy is one possible alternative source of nuclear energy. Fusion reactors may someday be a source of economical, clean, and safe energy. Hydrogen atoms can be combined in a fusion reaction to produce helium plus a great deal of energy. Because water contains hydrogen, the oceans could be an almost unlimited source of fusion energy.

▲ **Figure 18-21** A technician performs maintenance inside a Tokamak fusion reactor.

Extremely high temperatures and pressures are needed for fusion reactions to take place. Scientists are experimenting with different ways to bring about these reactions.

One experimental fusion reactor uses a magnetic trap, or "magnetic bottle," to hold the fusion reaction. It also uses high-powered laser beams.

 IDENTIFY: What would be the main fuel for fusion reactors?

✓ CHECKING CONCEPTS

1. What are two forms of solar energy?
2. What is the core of an atom called?
3. What two elements make up 98 percent of the Sun?
4. What happens to the missing mass in a hydrogen fusion reaction?
5. What does *E* stand for in Einstein's equation?

💡 THINKING CRITICALLY

6. INFER: Why are the nuclear reactions that take place in the Sun called fusion reactions?
7. ANALYZE: Explain how $E = mc^2$ shows that a small amount of matter can be changed into a very large amount of energy.

INTERPRETING VISUALS

Ordinary hydrogen nuclei contain one proton. Heavy hydrogen nuclei contain one proton and one neutron. Two pairs of heavy hydrogen nuclei fuse with two stray protons to form two light helium nuclei. These then fuse to form one ordinary helium nucleus. This reaction releases two protons, or ordinary hydrogen nuclei, and energy. Use Figure 18-22 to answer the following questions.

8. IDENTIFY: What kinds of atoms are produced during the Sun's fusion reactions?
9. ANALYZE: What symbol in the diagram represents the energy released?

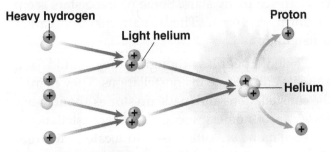
▲ **Figure 18-22** Fusion

 Integrating Life Science

TOPICS: photosynthesis, food chain

FOOD FROM THE SUN

The Sun's energy reaches Earth as heat and light. This energy causes water on Earth to evaporate and rise into the air. The water then falls to Earth as rain. Rain helps plants to grow. Green plants use sunlight to make food. Without rain and sunlight, green plants would die. People and other animals could not survive.

▲ **Figure 18-23** All animals depend on photosynthesis for food.

The foodmaking process in green plants is called photosynthesis. The plants take in carbon dioxide and water. Sunlight supplies the energy needed by plants to make food. Some of the food is then used by the plants. The rest is stored. People and other animals use the stored food in plants when they eat the plants. Animals that eat other animals are taking in the energy from plants stored in the cells of the animals that are eaten.

During photosynthesis, plants give off oxygen. The oxygen goes into the air. People, other animals, and plants need oxygen to survive. Not all animals breathe air, but they do respire and get their oxygen this way. Without plants covering Earth and releasing oxygen, animals could not breathe.

Thinking Critically How is the oxygen produced by plants a kind of food animals must take in to survive?

What are constellations?

Objectives

Explain what constellations are. Name some familiar constellations.

Key Term

constellation (kahn-stuh-LAY-shuhn): group of stars that form a pattern in the sky

Star Patterns When you look at the night sky, you can see many stars. Some of these stars seem to form patterns. These patterns are called **constellations.**

Ancient peoples thought they could see animals and people in constellations. They named the constellations and made up stories about them. Today, astronomers recognize 88 constellations. Constellations are often used to locate individual stars.

Stars seem to move slowly across the sky. Different constellations and star groups appear overhead at different times of the year. The constellations visible in the Northern Hemisphere are different from those visible in the Southern Hemisphere. However, the stars are relatively stationary. It is the movements of Earth that are making it look like the stars are changing position in the sky.

▶ **1** DEFINE: What is a constellation?

Orion the Hunter In the Northern Hemisphere, Orion the Hunter is a constellation seen in the evening sky from November to March. It rises in the east.

Three bright stars make up Orion's belt. Betelgeuse, a red giant star, is under Orion's arm. Rigel, a giant blue-white star, is in Orion's knee.

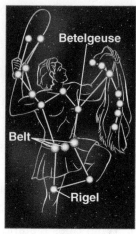

▲ **Figure 18-25** Orion

▶ **2** NAME: What are two stars in Orion?

The Bear Constellations One of the easiest constellations to find in the northern sky is Ursa Major. Its name means "big bear."

Ancient peoples thought they could see the shape of a large bear in the constellation. The Big Dipper is part of Ursa Major. It is made up of seven stars, three in the handle, four in the cup. Two bright stars in the cup of the Big Dipper are called the pointers. They point to Polaris, which is also known as the North Star.

Ursa Minor, meaning "little bear," is another constellation in the northern sky. Ursa Minor is also called the Little Dipper. Polaris is the first star in the handle of the Little Dipper.

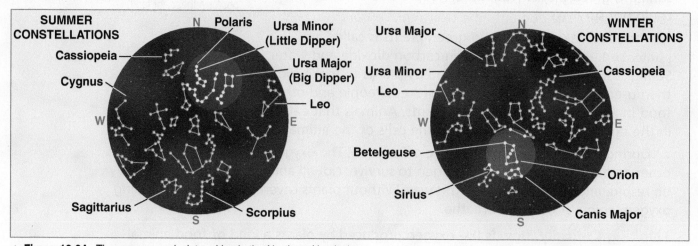

▲ **Figure 18-24** The summer and winter skies in the Northern Hemisphere

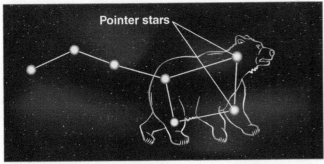
▲ **Figure 18-26** The Big Dipper is in the constellation Ursa Major.

 NAME: What does the name Ursa Major mean?

CHECKING CONCEPTS

1. What are patterns of stars called?
2. How many constellations are there?
3. What is the Big Dipper?
4. What is the name of the North Star?
5. What is the name of the red star in Orion?

THINKING CRITICALLY

6. INFER: Why are the two bright stars in the cup of the Big Dipper called the pointers?
7. INFER: Although other stars appear to rotate in the night sky, Polaris does not seem to change position over the North Pole. Why do you think this is?
8. ANALYZE: Why do stars in constellations appear close even though they may be very far apart?

BUILDING SCIENCE SKILLS

Researching The zodiac is a band of constellations that lie along the ecliptic. Over a year's time, the Sun seems to trace a path in the sky along the ecliptic. What is the ecliptic? How many different constellations make up the zodiac? Do research on one of the constellations. What is the story behind it? Write your findings in a report.

Real-Life Science

IDENTIFYING THE CONSTELLATIONS

The oldest known astronomical texts were written by the ancient Sumerians. They recorded the names of constellations still known today as the lion, the bull, and the scorpion. The ancient Greek and Chinese peoples had different names for some of the same constellations. The ancient Egyptians named about 25 constellations, including the crocodile and the hippopotamus.

▲ **Figure 18-27** The constellation called Leo is in the zodiac between Cancer and Virgo. Its brightest star is called Regulus.

Astronomers continued naming the constellations right up until the twentieth century. In 1930, an official listing of 88 constellations was published by the International Astronomical Union. One of these is Leo the Lion.

To find the constellations, go out on a dark night and scan the sky. If you do not already know geographical directions in your area, learn them. This will help you use the sky charts published in books and magazines. To orient yourself, try to find the brightest stars and identify them. They can help you locate other star groups.

Orion is one of the easiest constellations to see in the winter sky. Look for Betelgeuse and Rigel. The three stars in Orion's belt point to Sirius in Canis Major (the Dog Star) and Aldebaran in Taurus, the bull constellation.

Thinking Critically How could you find out geographical directions in your area?

18-10 What are galaxies?

Objective

Describe the three main types of galaxies.

Key Terms

galaxy (GAL-uhk-see): huge collection of stars, gas, and dust that travel together through space

elliptical galaxy: galaxy shaped like a ball or slightly flattened ball

irregular galaxy: galaxy with no definite shape

spiral galaxy: galaxy shaped like a flattened disk with spiral arms

Galaxies Stars appear as small points of light. Among these points of light, you can also see some fuzzy patches. Some of these patches are nebulae, or clouds of gas and dust. Others are galaxies. A **galaxy** is a huge collection of stars, gas, and dust that travel together through space. Using the newest telescopes, astronomers can see billions of galaxies. Galaxies are the building blocks of the universe.

Galaxies have different shapes. Astronomers classify, or group, galaxies based on shape. There are three kinds of galaxies: elliptical, irregular, and spiral.

▶ **DEFINE:** What are galaxies?

Elliptical and Irregular Galaxies Some galaxies have rounded shapes. These galaxies are known as **elliptical galaxies.** Elliptical galaxies can also look like slightly flattened balls. The stars in an elliptical galaxy are usually older than the stars in other kinds of galaxies. Elliptical galaxies are larger than irregular galaxies but smaller than spiral galaxies.

Galaxies with no regular shape are called **irregular galaxies.** Irregular galaxies are smaller and fainter than elliptical and spiral galaxies. They may be the most common kind of galaxy.

▶ **COMPARE:** Which is more common, an elliptical galaxy or an irregular galaxy?

Spiral Galaxies **Spiral galaxies** are shaped like flattened disks. They usually have one or more spiral arms that branch out from their centers. One type of spiral galaxy is called the barred spiral. The arms of barred spirals branch out from the end of a short bar made up of stars and gas.

▶ **DESCRIBE:** What special feature do spiral galaxies have?

The Milky Way Galaxy All the stars you can see in the night sky with your unaided eye are part of our home galaxy, called the Milky Way Galaxy. Our solar system is in the Milky Way Galaxy.

Elliptical

Irregular

Spiral

▲ **Figure 18-28** Galaxies come in three basic shapes: elliptical, irregular, and spiral.

The Milky Way Galaxy is part of a group of more than 20 other galaxies. Together, these galaxies are known as the Local Group.

The Milky Way Galaxy is a spiral galaxy. It contains about 100,000 billion stars. At its center is a huge bulge of stars about 10,000 light-years across. The distance from edge to edge of the spiral arms is about 100,000 light-years. The Sun is in a spiral arm about two-thirds of the way from the center of the Milky Way Galaxy.

▲ **Figure 18-29** The Milky Way Galaxy

 CLASSIFY: What kind of galaxy is the Milky Way Galaxy?

The Milky Way Band There is a band of stars stretching across the sky. Ancient peoples called this band the Milky Way. They thought it looked like a river of milk. When you look at the Milky Way band of stars, you are seeing the flattened disk of the Milky Way Galaxy, where the spiral arms lie.

▲ **Figure 18-30** Part of the Milky Way band of stars in the sky

5 IDENTIFY: What is the Milky Way band?

Galactic Neighbors Most galaxies are millions of light-years from Earth. For example, the great spiral galaxy in the constellation Andromeda, seen on the far right in Figure 18-28, is 2 million light years away. The Andromeda Galaxy is much larger than our own galaxy. You can see it without a telescope.

The closest galaxies to Earth are the Large Magellanic Cloud and the Small Magellanic Cloud. These irregular galaxies are 160,000 and 200,000 light years away, respectively.

6 IDENTIFY: Which galaxies are closest to the Milky Way Galaxy?

✓ CHECKING CONCEPTS

1. Galaxies are made up of billions of _____.

2. Astronomers classify galaxies on the basis of their _____.

3. There are _____ main types of galaxies.

4. The oldest stars are found in _____ galaxies.

5. Stretching across the sky is the _____ band of stars.

💡 THINKING CRITICALLY

6. LIST: What are the three main types of galaxies?

7. CALCULATE: If all the galaxies in the Local Group have about the same number of stars, about how many stars are in the Local Group?

INTERPRETING VISUALS

Use Figure 18-31 to complete the following exercise.

8. CLASSIFY: Classify each of the galaxies shown as spiral, elliptical, or irregular.

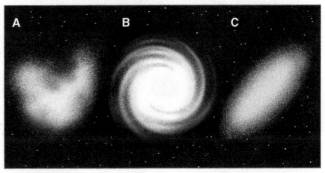

▲ **Figure 18-31**

LAB ACTIVITY
Counting Galaxies

Materials
Hubble Deep Field
picture
Calculator

BACKGROUND

The universe is very large. It has a vast number of galaxies that are each home to billions of stars like our Sun. The Hubble Deep Field picture represents only a tiny part of the whole sky. More than 30 million of these pictures would be needed to cover the entire sky.

PURPOSE

In this activity, you will estimate how many galaxies are found in a tiny fragment of the sky.

PROCEDURE

1. Your teacher will divide you into four groups. Examine the picture given to your group by your teacher. It was taken by the Hubble Space Telescope.

2. Copy the chart in Figure 18-33. Then, count the number of galaxies in your picture and record the number in your chart.

3. Your picture is a part of a larger picture. The larger picture is four times the size of your picture. The other groups are looking at the other three parts. How many galaxies do you think the entire picture contains? Estimate how many and record this number in your chart.

4. Trade the number of galaxies you counted in your picture with numbers arrived at by the groups that are counting the other three pictures. Record the numbers in your chart.

STEP 1 Examine the picture given to you by your teacher.

▲ **Figure 18-32** The Hubble Deep Field image

My Data Chart	
Number of galaxies in your picture	
Estimate the total number of galaxies. (Your number times 4.)	
Number of galaxies in group 2's picture	
Number of galaxies in group 3's picture	
Number of galaxies in group 4's picture	
Total of all pictures	

▲ **Figure 18-33** Use a copy of this chart to record your calculations.

CONCLUSIONS

1. **OBSERVE:** How many galaxies did you count?

2. **ESTIMATE:** How many galaxies are there in the total picture?

3. **COMPARE:** How did your estimate compare with the actual count when you totaled the counts from the four groups?

4. **INFER:** For what other things might you use this estimating technique?

18-11 What else do we know about the universe?

INVESTIGATE

Modeling the Expanding Universe
HANDS-ON ACTIVITY

1. Partially inflate a round balloon. Twist the opening and hold it shut with a paper clip or a rubber band.

2. With a marking pen, draw four dots on the surface of the balloon in a square pattern. Label them *A, B, C, D.*

3. Using a string, measure the distance between each of the four dots (*A* to *B, A* to *C, A* to *D, B* to *C, B* to *D,* and *C* to *D*). Hold the string next to a ruler and record each measurement in a table.

4. Inflate the balloon to its fullest and tie the end.

5. Repeat your measurements and record the distances.

THINK ABOUT IT: What happened to the distances between the dots as you inflated the balloon? Did some dots move farther apart than others did? Why? Suppose the balloon represents the universe. How does this activity show what is happening to the universe and to the galaxies in it?

Objective
Describe some unusual features of the universe.

Key Terms

Big Bang: explosion that may have begun the universe about 14 billion years ago

black hole: massive star that has collapsed and whose gravity is so powerful that it pulls in everything, even light

quasar: continuous burst of brilliant light and enormous energy from a very massive black hole

How Big Is the Universe The universe is everything, including the Sun, its solar system, and the many billions of stars in all the galaxies. It is everything that exists in space, even space itself. The distances between stars and galaxies are vast. If you could travel at the speed of light (300,000 km/s), it would take you more than 10 billion years to cross the part of space astronomers can see with their telescopes.

 EXPLAIN: What does the universe include?

The Big Bang Scientists think that the entire universe was once contained in a single, very hot, very dense point. About 14 billion years ago, a huge explosion caused it to start expanding rapidly. This explosion is called the **Big Bang.**

As the universe expanded, it cooled. Atoms and molecules formed. Gradually, the atoms and molecules collected into the objects that make up today's universe, which is still expanding.

▲ **Figure 18-34** The radio waves caused by the Big Bang are represented in this picture by the pink ripples. These waves can still be detected today.

EXPLAIN: What is the Big Bang?

Black Holes and Quasars The universe is filled with many strange objects. For example, a black hole can form when a very massive star collapses in on itself. A **black hole** is an object so dense that nothing pulled into it by gravity can come out.

A black hole appears black because not even light can escape from its surface. All of the matter at the center of a black hole is squeezed into an infinitely tiny point.

Black holes are often found at the centers of galaxies. These black holes can be millions of times heavier than stars. When matter falls into these extremely massive black holes, tremendous bursts of light and energy are released. Astronomers call these bursts **quasars.** Quasars glow brighter than the light of a thousand galaxies.

 ANALYZE: How are black holes and quasars related?

Colliding Galaxies The whole universe is in motion. Planets swirl around stars. Stars swirl around galaxies. Galaxies spread out into deep space. Sometimes two or more galaxies approach each other like colliding cars. The distance between stars is so great that the two galaxies pass right through each other like ghosts. However, gravity will sometimes pull galaxies like these together. They form into a single, bigger galaxy.

 EXPLAIN: How can galaxies merge?

✔ CHECKING CONCEPTS

1. About how many stars are in the universe?
2. What happens when stars fall into a black hole?
3. What are colliding galaxies?
4. How long ago did the universe form?

💡 THINKING CRITICALLY

5. EXPLAIN: Why are the galaxies moving outward?
6. INFER: Do you think the galaxies will continue to move outward?
7. ANALYZE: If you had a spaceship that could travel at the speed of light, could you visit another galaxy?

DESIGNING AN EXPERIMENT

Design an experiment to solve the following problem. Include a hypothesis, variables, a procedure with materials, a type of data to study, and a way to record your data.

PROBLEM: The gravity field near a black hole is very strong. Any matter that gets near the black hole is sucked in by its powerful gravity. Design an experiment that models what might happen to matter as it passes near a black hole. Will it fall straight in or spiral around it first? Indicate why you chose one or the other.

 ## *Integrating Physical Science*

TOPICS: forces, waves

GRAVITATIONAL WAVES

Energy travels freely across the universe. We only see light waves, but scientific instruments can see radio waves, X-rays, ultraviolet light, and other forms of radiation. The energy in gravity also travels across the universe. Unless you are very close to an object, the gravity, or the attraction, you feel from it is very faint. Very massive objects have a stronger gravitational attraction than less massive objects do.

▲ **Figure 18-35** A gravitational wave spreads out a little like ripples in a pond.

If all objects in the universe stayed still, the attraction of gravity would remain the same at all times. However, stars and galaxies do not stand still. When they move, they are believed to produce ripples in the gravitational field that travel across the universe as gravity waves. The waves would spread out in a manner similar to the water waves in a pond when a pebble is thrown in. However, instead of just moving across a flat surface like the pond waves, gravity waves would likely move in all directions.

Thinking Critically How could gravitational attraction cause waves?

THE Big IDEA

How can we estimate the size of the universe?

The universe has been expanding since the Big Bang. It is not expanding into anything, however. Instead, space itself is stretching out, and carrying the galaxies with it. The American astronomer Edwin Hubble was the first to present this idea. In 1929, he showed that the galaxies were rushing away from each other.

Hubble studied the brightness of a class of stars known as Cepheid stars. Using these stars, he was able to measure how far away certain galaxies were. He was also able to figure out how fast the galaxies were moving by examining their redshift. Hubble discovered that the galaxies closest to us are moving slower than the galaxies farther away. He also discovered that a galaxy's speed, or velocity (V), is directly related to its distance (D) from us. This relationship can be expressed using a number called the Hubble constant (H).

Knowing that the universe is expanding is very useful to astronomers. By measuring the velocity of a distant galaxy, they can determine its distance. Since the universe must be large enough to hold every galaxy, astronomers can use the most distant galaxies known to estimate the size of the universe.

However, astronomers have discovered that it is very difficult to give an exact value for Hubble's constant. This number could be as low as 15 and as high as 30 km/s/mly (kilometers per second per million light-years). Unless we can determine this value exactly, we can only give a range of possible sizes for the universe.

Look at the photos on these two pages. Then, follow the directions in the Science Log to learn more about "the big idea." ✦

The Milky Way

Earth and the other planets of our solar system are located about 50,000 light-years from the center of the Milky Way Galaxy, on one of its spiral arms.

The Small Magellanic Cloud

About 200,000 light years from Earth lies the Small Magellanic Cloud. By the 1920s, astronomers had realized that this fuzzy cloud of light was actually a distant galaxy.

The Large Magellanic Cloud

The Large Magellanic Cloud is an irregular galaxy visible only in the Southern Hemisphere. It is named after Portuguese explorer Ferdinand Magellan. Magellan's crew were the first Europeans to describe this cluster of stars that is more than 160,000 light-years from Earth.

Andromeda

The Andromeda Galaxy is the most distant galaxy that can be seen from Earth without a telescope. This spiral galaxy lies about 2 million light-years from Earth.

With the **Big Bang** explosion, the universe was created and began to expand outward.

WRITING ACTIVITY

Science Log

How would you like to take a trip through the universe and visit other parts of the Milky Way Galaxy, the neighboring Magellanic Clouds, and the Andromeda Galaxy? Research these terms online at www.conceptsandchallenges.com. Write a story for a travel magazine. Tell others how to prepare for the trip and what to look for on the way.

DO THE MATH!

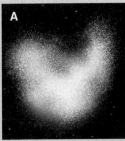 

▲ **Figure 18-36**

The two galaxies shown in Figure 18-36 appear to be the same size. They are not. One is simply farther away. You can tell which galaxy is bigger than the other by measuring how far each galaxy is from Earth.

STEP 1 Use the following formula to determine each galaxy's distance:

$$D = \frac{V}{H}$$

Distance (D) is equal to the velocity (V) of the galaxy divided by the Hubble constant. (H). Velocity, or speed, is measured in kilometers per second (km/s). Let Hubble's constant here be as 20 km/sec/mly.

STEP 2 Find out how far Galaxy A is from Earth. The velocity for Galaxy A is 1,000 km/s.

Galaxy A:

$$D = \frac{1,000 \ km/s}{20 \ km/s/mly} = \underline{\hspace{2cm}} \ mly$$

STEP 3 Find out how far Galaxy B is from Earth. The velocity for Galaxy B is 4,000 km/s.

Galaxy B:

$$D = \underline{\hspace{2cm}} = \underline{\hspace{2cm}} \ mly$$

So, which galaxy is farther from Earth, A or B? Explain your choice.

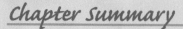

Chapter Summary

Lesson 18-1

- Most stars are hot, glowing balls of hydrogen and helium gases. The Sun is one of many billions of stars. A star forms from a **protostar** in a cloudy **nebula.**

Lessons 18-2 and 18-3

- **Spectroscopy** is the study of light from objects in space. A **spectrum** helps us identify a star's elements.
- The measure of a star's brightness is its **magnitude.** There is apparent magnitude and absolute magnitude.

Lessons 18-4 and 18-5

- An H-R diagram shows how a star's absolute magnitude is related to its surface temperature.
- Most stars, like the Sun, are **main sequence stars** on the H-R diagram.
- **Red giants** and **supergiants** are huge, bright stars. **White dwarfs** are small, hot stars.
- Stars begin life as protostars. Then, they enter the main sequence stage. Small and medium-size stars become white dwarfs, then black dwarfs. Very massive stars explode as **supernovas** and become neutron stars or black holes.

Lessons 18-6, 18-7, and 18-8

- The Sun has a **core** and an atmosphere. The Sun's atmosphere consists of the **photosphere,** the **chromosphere,** and the **corona.**
- **Sunspots** are dark, cooler areas on the Sun's surface. **Prominences** are streams of gas that arch above the Sun's surface. **Solar flares** send out energy and charged particles.
- The Sun has nuclear reactions called **fusion.** During fusion, hydrogen atoms combine to form helium.

Lessons 18-9, 18-10, and 18-11

- **Constellations** are groups of stars that form patterns in the sky.
- **Galaxies** are **elliptical, irregular,** or **spiral** in shape. The Milky Way Galaxy is a spiral galaxy.
- The Milky Way band of stars is in the Milky Way Galaxy.
- The universe is all that exists. **Black holes** pull in even light. **Quasars** emit tremendous energy.

Key Term Challenges

Big Bang (p. 458)
binary stars (p. 436)
black hole (p. 458)
chromosphere (p. 446)
constellation (p. 452)
core (p. 446)
corona (p. 446)
elliptical galaxy (p. 454)
fusion (p. 450)
galaxy (p. 454)
irregular galaxy (p. 454)
magnitude (p. 440)
main sequence star (p. 442)
nebula (p. 436)
nova (p. 444)
nucleus (p. 450)

photosphere (p. 446)
prominence (p. 448)
protostar (p. 436)
quasar (p. 458)
red giant (p. 442)
solar flare (p. 448)
spectrograph (p. 438)
spectroscopy (p. 438)
spectrum (p. 438)
spiral galaxy (p. 454)
star (p. 436)
star cluster (p. 436)
sunspot (p. 448)
supergiant (p. 442)
supernova (p. 444)
white dwarf (p. 442)

MATCHING **Write the Key Term from above that best matches each description.**

1. inner layer of the Sun's atmosphere

2. grouping of stars that form a pattern in the sky

3. cloud of dust and gas in space

4. measure of a star's brightness

5. dark, cooler areas on the Sun's surface

6. large group of stars in a galaxy

7. very small, hot star

8. center, or core, of an atom

9. device that measures the spectrum of an object

10. galaxy with no definite shape

IDENTIFYING WORD RELATIONSHIPS **Explain how the words in each pair are related. Write your answers in complete sentences.**

11. nova, supernova

12. star, protostar

13. binary star, star cluster

14. red giant, white dwarf

15. elliptical galaxy, spiral galaxy

Content Challenges TEST PREP

MULTIPLE CHOICE Write the letter of the term or phrase that best completes each statement.

1. The Sun is only one of billions of
   a. nebulas.
   b. stars.
   c. galaxies.
   d. constellations.

2. In Einstein's equation $E = mc^2$, c is
   a. energy.
   b. mass.
   c. the speed of light.
   d. the amount of matter.

3. The Milky Way Galaxy is
   a. a spiral galaxy.
   b. an elliptical galaxy.
   c. an irregular galaxy.
   d. a spherical galaxy.

4. The hottest stars are
   a. red.
   b. blue.
   c. yellow.
   d. orange.

5. The Sun's energy is produced in the
   a. corona.
   b. photosphere.
   c. chromosphere.
   d. core.

6. Supernova 1987A occurred in
   a. the Milky Way Galaxy.
   b. the Large Magellanic Cloud.
   c. the Andromeda Galaxy.
   d. the star cluster M13.

7. The actual brightness of a star is its
   a. apparent magnitude.
   b. first magnitude.
   c. sixth magnitude.
   d. absolute magnitude.

8. The spinning of the Sun on its axis causes
   a. solar flares.
   b. sunspot movement.
   c. prominences.
   d. fusion.

9. The outermost layer of the Sun's atmosphere is the
   a. photosphere.
   b. chromosphere.
   c. corona.
   d. core.

10. Betelgeuse is a star found in
    a. the Big Dipper.
    b. the Little Dipper.
    c. Ursa Major.
    d. Orion.

TRUE/FALSE Write *true* if the statement is true. If the statement is false, change the underlined term to make the statement true.

11. The gravity of a black <u>dwarf</u> is so great that nothing can escape.

12. The main features of the universe are <u>galaxies</u>.

13. The most common element in most stars is <u>helium</u>.

14. Sunspots are dark, <u>cooler</u> areas on the surface of the Sun.

15. The brightness of most stars increases as the star's surface temperature <u>decreases</u>.

16. The Sun and all the planets in the solar system are in the <u>Milky Way Galaxy</u>.

17. Each <u>element</u> gives off its own spectrum of light.

18. To separate white light into the colors of the rainbow, scientists can use a <u>prism</u>.

19. Galaxies with no regular shape are called <u>elliptical</u> galaxies.

20. Streams of gas shooting from the Sun's surface are called <u>prominences</u>.

Concept Challenges TEST PREP

WRITTEN RESPONSE Answer each of the following questions in complete sentences.

1. COMPARE: How is a nova similar to a supernova?

2. EXPLAIN: What happens to material in the center of a nebula?

3. INFER: What forces cause streams of gases to shoot high above the Sun's surface?

4. INFER: What holds the stars together in a galaxy?

5. INFER: How does the Sun produce energy?

6. ANALYZE: Where are the electrically charged particles that stream out from the Sun created?

7. CONTRAST: What is the difference between a red giant star and a supergiant star?

8. INFER: Which is the densest part of the Sun?

9. ANALYZE: How do astronomers find out the chemical makeup of a star?

10. INFER: What is meant by the "birth" and "death" of a star?

11. INFER: Why can fossil fuels be called "stored sunlight"?

12. ANALYZE: Why is an old main sequence star made up of a larger percentage of helium than a young main sequence star?

INTERPRETING VISUALS Use Figure 18-37 to answer the following questions.

13. What is the center part of the Sun called?

14. What three layers make up the Sun's atmosphere?

15. What is the temperature of the corona?

16. About how many degrees Celsius hotter is the chromosphere than the photosphere?

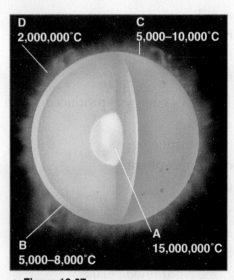

D 2,000,000°C

C 5,000–10,000°C

B 5,000–8,000°C

A 15,000,000°C

▲ Figure 18-37

Appendix A Metric System

The Metric System and SI Units

The metric system is an international system of measurement based on units of ten. More than 90% of the nations of the world use the metric system. In the United States, both the English system and the metric system are used.

The *Système International*, or SI, has been used as the international measurement system since 1960. The SI is a modernized version of the metric system. Like the metric system, the SI is a decimal system based on units of ten. When you want to change from one unit in the metric system to another unit, you multiply or divide by a multiple of ten.

- When you change from a smaller unit to a larger unit, you divide.
- When you change from a larger unit to a smaller unit, you multiply.

METRIC UNITS		
LENGTH	SYMBOL	RELATIONSHIP
kilometer	km	1 km = 1,000 m
meter	m	1 m = 100 cm
centimeter	cm	1 cm = 10 mm
millimeter	mm	1 mm = 0.1 cm
AREA	SYMBOL	
square kilometer	km^2	$1\ km^2 = 1,000,000\ m^2$
square meter	m^2	$1\ m^2 = 1,000,000\ mm^2$
square centimeter	cm^2	$1\ cm^2 = 0.0001\ m^2$
square millimeter	mm^2	$1\ mm^2 = 0.000001\ m^2$
VOLUME	SYMBOL	
cubic meter	m^3	$1\ m^3 = 1,000,000\ cm^3$
cubic centimeter	cm^3	$1\ cm^3 = 0.000001\ m^3$
liter	L	1 L = 1,000 mL
milliliter	mL	1 mL = 0.001 L
MASS	SYMBOL	
metric ton	t	1 t = 1,000 kg
kilogram	kg	1 kg = 1,000 g
gram	g	1 g = 1,000 mg
centigram	cg	1 cg = 10 mg
milligram	mg	1 mg = 0.001 g
TEMPERATURE	SYMBOL	
Kelvin	K	
degree Celsius	°C	

▲ Figure 1

COMMON METRIC PREFIXES			
micro-	0.000001 or 1/1,000,000	deka-	10
milli-	0.001 or 1/1,000	hecto-	100
centi-	0.01 or 1/100	kilo-	1,000
deci-	0.1 or 1/10	mega-	1,000,000

▲ Figure 2

METRIC-STANDARD EQUIVALENTS	
SI to English	English to SI
LENGTH	
1 kilometer = 0.621 mile (mi)	1 mi = 1.61 km
1 meter = 1.094 yards (yd)	1 yd = 0.914 m
1 meter = 3.28 feet (ft)	1 ft = 0.305 m
1 centimeter = 0.394 inch (in.)	1 in. = 2.54 cm
1 millimeter = 0.039 inch	1 in. = 25.4 mm
AREA	
1 square kilometer = 0.3861 square mile	$1\ mi^2 = 2.590\ km^2$
1 square meter = 1.1960 square yards	$1\ yd^2 = 0.8361\ m^2$
1 square meter = 10.763 square feet	$1\ ft^2 = 0.0929\ m^2$
1 square centimeter = 0.155 square inch	$1\ in.^2 = 6.452\ cm^2$
VOLUME	
1 cubic meter = 1.3080 cubic yards	$1\ yd^3 = 0.7646\ m^3$
1 cubic meter = 35.315 cubic feet	$1\ ft^3 = 0.0283\ m^3$
1 cubic centimeter = 0.0610 cubic inch	$1\ in.^3 = 16.39\ cm^3$
1 liter = 0.2642 gallon (gal)	1 gal = 3.79 L
1 liter = 1.06 quarts (qt)	1 qt = 0.946 L
1 liter = 2.11 pints (pt)	1 pt = 0.47 L
1 milliliter = 0.034 fluid ounce (fl oz)	1 fl oz = 29.57 mL
MASS	
1 metric ton = 0.984 ton	1 ton = 1.016 t
1 kilogram = 2.205 pounds (lb)	1 lb = 0.4536 kg
1 gram = 0.0353 ounce (oz)	1 oz = 28.35 g
TEMPERATURE	
Celsius = 5/9(°F − 32)	Fahrenheit = 9/5°C + 32
0°C = 32°F (Freezing point of water)	72°F = 22°C (Room temperature)
100°C = 212°F (Boiling point of water)	98.6°F = 37°C (Human body temperature)
Kelvin = (°F + 459.67)/1.8	Fahrenheit = (K × 1.8) − 459.67

▲ Figure 3

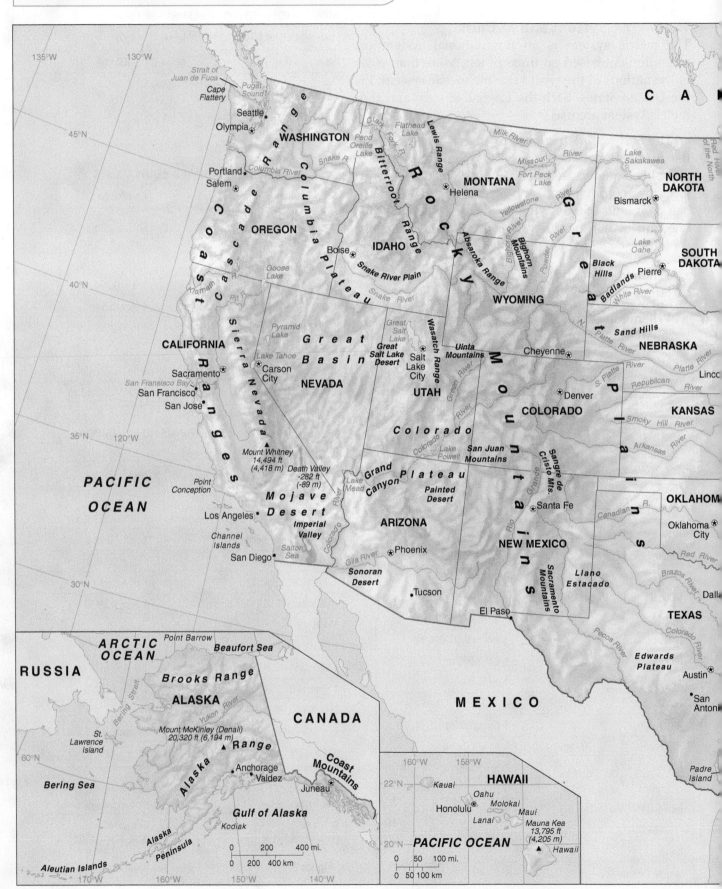

▲ Figure 4

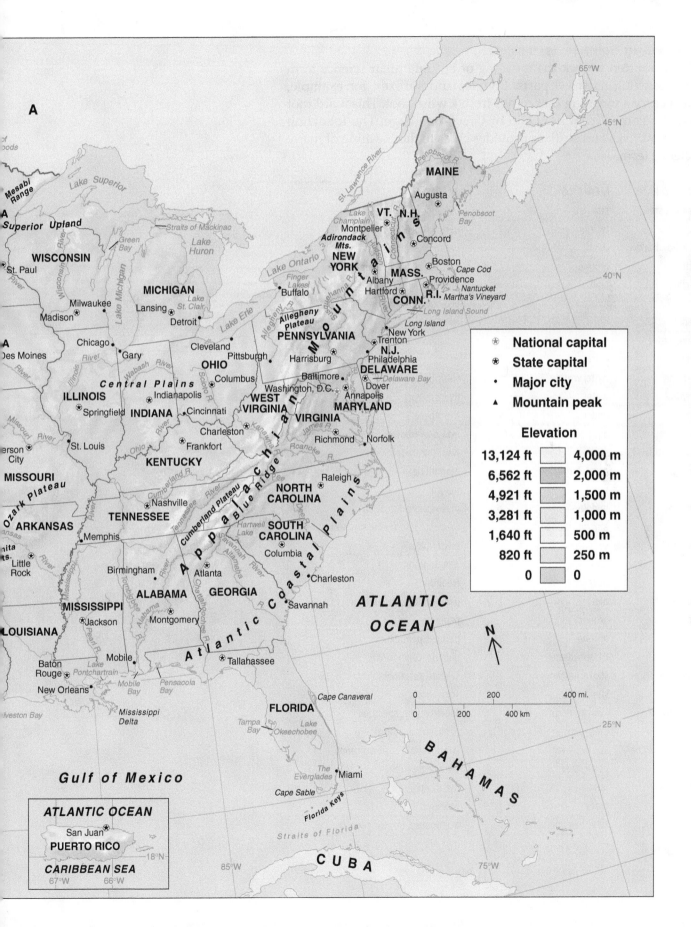

A

Mesabi Range

Lake Superior

Superior Upland

Straits of Mackinac

Green Bay

Lake Huron

Lake Michigan

WISCONSIN

St. Paul

Milwaukee

Madison

MICHIGAN

Lansing

Lake St. Clair

Detroit

Lake Erie

St. Lawrence River

MAINE

Augusta

Lake Champlain

VT. N.H.

Montpelier

Concord

Penobscot R.

Penobscot Bay

Adirondack Mts.

NEW YORK

Finger Lakes

Lake Ontario

Buffalo

Albany

Hartford

MASS.

Boston

Cape Cod

Providence

Nantucket

R.I.

Martha's Vineyard

CONN.

Long Island Sound

New York

Long Island

Chicago

Gary

Cleveland

Pittsburgh

Allegheny Plateau

PENNSYLVANIA

Harrisburg

N.J.

Philadelphia

DELAWARE

Des Moines

OHIO

Columbus

Baltimore

Washington, D.C.

Dover

Delaware Bay

ILLINOIS

Indianapolis

INDIANA

Cincinnati

WEST VIRGINIA

MARYLAND

Annapolis

Springfield

VIRGINIA

Central Plains

Wabash River

Scioto R.

St. Louis

Charleston

Frankfort

Richmond

Norfolk

MISSOURI

KENTUCKY

Ozark Plateau

Roanoke R.

Cumberland R.

Raleigh

Jefferson City

Nashville

NORTH CAROLINA

Blue Ridge

TENNESSEE

Cumberland Plateau

ARKANSAS

Memphis

Tennessee River

Hartwell Lake

SOUTH CAROLINA

Appalachian Mountains

Little Rock

Birmingham

Atlanta

Columbia

ALABAMA

GEORGIA

Charleston

Savannah

MISSISSIPPI

Montgomery

ATLANTIC OCEAN

Jackson

LOUISIANA

Tallahassee

Atlantic Coastal Plains

Baton Rouge

Mobile

Lake Pontchartrain

New Orleans

Mobile Bay

Pensacola Bay

Mississippi Delta

Cape Canaveral

FLORIDA

BAHAMAS

Gulf of Mexico

Tampa Bay

Lake Okeechobee

The Everglades

Miami

Cape Sable

Florida Keys

Straits of Florida

ATLANTIC OCEAN

San Juan

PUERTO RICO

CARIBBEAN SEA

CUBA

Legend:
- ⊛ National capital
- ⊛ State capital
- • Major city
- ▲ Mountain peak

Elevation

13,124 ft	4,000 m
6,562 ft	2,000 m
4,921 ft	1,500 m
3,281 ft	1,000 m
1,640 ft	500 m
820 ft	250 m
0	0

N

0   200   400 mi.

0   200   400 km

45°N

40°N

65°W

25°N

75°W

18°N

67°W   66°W

85°W

Appendix C Science Terms

Analyzing Science Terms

You can often unlock the meaning of an unfamiliar science term by analyzing its word parts. Prefixes and suffixes, for example, each carry a meaning that comes from a word root. This word root usually comes from the Latin or Greek language. The following list of prefixes and suffixes provides clues to the meaning of many science terms.

WORD PART	MEANING	EXAMPLE
astr-, aster-	star	astronomy
bar-, baro-	weight, pressure	barometer
batho-, bathy-	depth	batholith, bathysphere
circum-	around	circum-Pacific, circumpolar
-cline	lean, slope	anticline, syncline
eco-	environment	ecology, ecosystem
epi-	on	epicenter
ex-, exo-	out, outside of	exosphere, exfoliation, extrusion
geo-	earth	geode, geology, geomagnetic
-graph	write, writing	seismograph
hydro-	water	hydrosphere
hypo-	under	hypothesis
iso-	equal	isoscope, isostasy, isotope
-lith, -lithic	stone	Neolithic, regolith
magn-	great, large	magnitude
mar-	sea	marine
meso-	middle	mesosphere, Mesozoic
meta-	among, change	metamorphic, metamorphism
micro-	small	microquake
-morph, -morphic	form	metamorphic
neo-	new	Neolithic
paleo-	old	paleontology, Paleozoic
ped-, pedo-	ground, soil	pediment
peri-	around	perigee, perihelion
-ose	carbohydrate	glucose, cellulose
seism-, seismo-	shake, earthquake	seismic, seismograph
sol-	sun	solar, solstice
spectro-	look at, examine	spectroscope, spectrum
-sphere	ball, globe	hemisphere, lithosphere
strati-, strato-	spread, layer	stratification, stratovolcano
terra-	earth, land	terracing, terrane
thermo-	heat	thermosphere
top-, topo-	place	topographic
tropo-	turn, respond to	tropopause, troposphere

▲ Figure 5

Appendix **D** Guide to Common Rocks and Minerals

COMMON ROCKS		
Rock Name	**Rock Type**	**Comments**
Anthracite coal	Sedimentary	Dark brown to black in color; shiny, hard, scaly, and dense; used as fuel; also used in producing coal gas and in the iron, steel, synthetic rubber, and dye industries
Basalt	Igneous	Fine-grained; dark in color; often rings like a bell when struck with a hammer; used for road paving
Compact limestone	Sedimentary	Fine-grained, soft, and porous; normally pale in color; used in building stones and in making lime
Conglomerate	Sedimentary	Very colorful; texture varies; consists of pebbles cemented together; often contains useful mineral grains; used as a building stone
Gneiss	Metamorphic	Coarse-grained; layers of different minerals often give a banded appearance; some varieties used as building material, both rough and polished
Granite	Igneous	Coarse-grained; mostly light in color, in shades of pink, gray, and white; important building stone, either polished or rough
Marble	Metamorphic	Coarse-grained; reacts with acid; color varies; often patterned; important building stone
Mica schist	Metamorphic	Medium- to coarse-grained; sparkly gray to black in color; contains important minerals
Obsidian	Igneous	Light to dark in color; glassy luster; sometimes translucent; brittle; used industrially as raw material; in ancient times was used for tools and sculptures
Pumice	Igneous	Light to dark in color; spongy appearance; many holes; lightweight, may float in water; used as building insulation
Sandstone	Sedimentary	Coarse-grained; usually sand color; often contains deposits of oil and gas; used for building
Shale	Sedimentary	Microscopic grains; clay composition; smooth surface, hardened mud appearance; some varieties, when processed, yield oil
Slate	Metamorphic	Find-grained; cleaves into thin flat plates; shiny dark gray color; used as shingles for roofing, for flooring, and blackboards

▲ Figure 6

MINERALS			
Mineral	Chemical Formula	Color	Streak
Apatite	$Ca_5(F,Cl)(PO_4)_3$	Green, brown, red	White
Augite	$(Ca,Na)(Mg, Fe, Al)(Si,Al)_2O_6$	Dark green, black	Green to gray
Beryl	$Be_3Al_2Si_6O_{18}$	White, yellow, blue, green	White
Biotite (Mica)	Complex substance containing Fe, Mg, Si, O and other elements	Black, brown, dark green	White to light brown
Calcite	$CaCO_3$	Gray, white	White
Chalcopyrite	$Cu_2Fe_2S_4$	Brass, yellow	Greenish black
Copper	Cu	Copper red to black	Copper red
Corundum	Al_2O_3	Various colors	White
Diamond	C	Colorless to black	Colorless
Dolomite	$CaMg(CO_3)_2$	Pink, white, gray, green, brown, black	White
Feldspar	$(K, NA, CA)(AlSi_3O_8)$	Colorless, white, various colors	Colorless, white
Fluorite	CaF_2	Light green yellow, bluish green, and other colors	White
Galena	PbS	Lead gray	Lead gray
Gold	Au	Gold	Gold
Graphite	C	Black to gray	Black
Gypsum	$CaSO_4 \cdot 2H_2O$	Whitish gray	White
Halite	$NaCl$	Colorless and various colors	Colorless
Hematite	Fe_2O_3	Reddish brown to black	Light to dark red
Hornblende	Complex substance containing Ca, Na, Mg, Ti, and Al	Dark green, black, brown	Colorless
Magnetite	Fe_3O_4	Iron black	Black
Olivine	$(Mg,Fe)_2SiO_4$	Olive green	White
Pyrite	FeS_2	Brass, yellow	Greenish, brownish, black
Quartz	SiO_2	Colorless, white, any color when not pure	White
Serpentine	$Mg_3Si_2O_5(OH)_4$	Green, yellow, brown, or black	White
Silver	Ag	Silver, black	Silver
Sphalerite	ZnS	Brown, black, red, and other colors	White, yellow, brown
Sulfur	S	Yellow	White
Talc	$Mg_3Si_4O_{10}(OH)_2$	Gray, greenish white	White

▲ Figure 7

Appendix D Guide to Common Rocks and Minerals (continued)

MINERALS				
Mineral	**Luster***	**Hardness**	**Specific Gravity**	**Fracture/Cleavage**
Apatite	Vitreous	5	3.1–3.2	Fracture
Augite	Vitreous	5–6	3.2–3.6	Cleavage
Beryl	Vitreous	8	2.65–2.90	Fracture
Biotite (Mica)	Vitreous	2.5–6	2.8–3.2	Cleavage
Calcite	Vitreous	3	2.7	Cleavage
Chalcopyrite	Metallic	3.5–4	4.1–4.34	Fracture
Copper	Metallic	2.5–3	8.5–8.93	None
Corundum	Vitreous to adamantine	9	4.02	Fracture
Diamond	Adamantine	10	3.52	Cleavage
Dolomite	Vitreous to pearly	3.5–4	2.85	Cleavage
Feldspar	Vitreous	6	2.55–2.75	Cleavage
Fluorite	Vitreous	4	3.18	Cleavage
Galena	Metallic	2.5	7.4–7.6	Cleavage
Gold	Metallic	2.5–3	15.3–19.3	None
Graphite	Metallic	1–2	2.3	Cleavage
Gypsum	Silky	2	2.3–2.4	Cleavage
Halite	Vitreous	2.5	2.1–2.6	Cleavage
Hematite	Metallic	5–6	5.26	Fracture
Hornblende	Vitreous	5–6	3.2	Cleavage
Magnetite	Metallic	6	5.18	Fracture
Olivine	Vitreous	6.5–7	3.2–4.2	Fracture
Pyrite	Metallic	6–6.5	4.9–5.2	Fracture
Quartz	Vitreous	7	2.65	Fracture
Serpentine	Vitreous	2–5	2.5–3.2	Fracture
Silver	Metallic	2.5–3	10.0–12.0	None
Sphalerite	Metallic, submetallic, adamantine, resinous	3.5–4	3.9–4.1	Cleavage
Sulfur	Adamantine	1.5–2.5	2.0–2.1	Cleavage
Talc	Vitreous	1	2.7–2.8	Cleavage

*Luster is the appearance of the light reflected from the surface of a mineral. This is another aid to identifying minerals. Adamantine describes a mineral that has a brilliant diamondlike luster. Vitreous describes a mineral that has a glassy luster.

▲ Figure 8

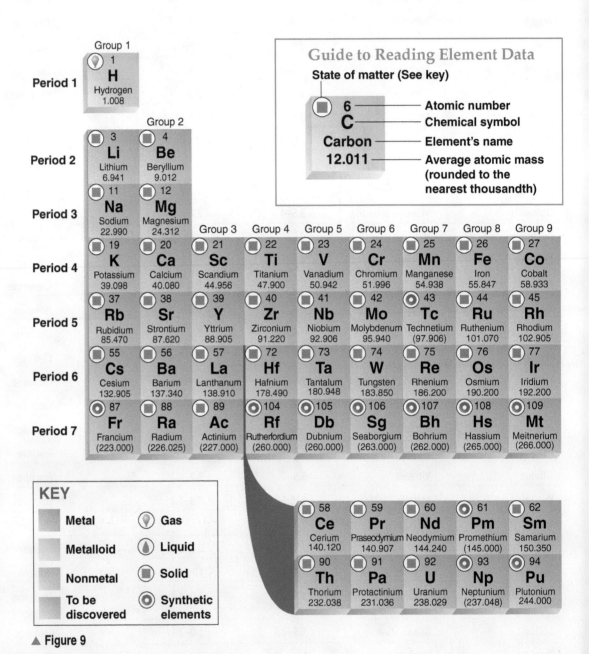

▲ Figure 9

Group 18

						2 He Helium 4.003

	Group 13	Group 14	Group 15	Group 16	Group 17	
	5 B Boron 10.811	6 C Carbon 12.011	7 N Nitrogen 14.007	8 O Oxygen 15.999	9 F Fluorine 18.998	10 Ne Neon 20.183
	13 Al Aluminum 26.982	14 Si Silicon 28.086	15 P Phosphorus 30.974	16 S Sulfur 32.064	17 Cl Chlorine 35.453	18 Ar Argon 39.948

Group 10	Group 11	Group 12							
28 Ni Nickel 58.710	29 Cu Copper 63.540	30 Zn Zinc 65.370	31 Ga Gallium 69.720	32 Ge Germanium 72.590	33 As Arsenic 74.922	34 Se Selenium 78.960	35 Br Bromine 79.909	36 Kr Krypton 83.800
46 Pd Palladium 106.400	47 Ag Silver 107.870	48 Cd Cadmium 112.400	49 In Indium 114.820	50 Sn Tin 118.690	51 Sb Antimony 121.750	52 Te Tellurium 127.600	53 I Iodine 126.904	54 Xe Xenon 131.300
78 Pt Platinum 195.090	79 Au Gold 196.967	80 Hg Mercury 200.590	81 Tl Thallium 204.370	82 Pb Lead 207.200	83 Bi Bismuth 208.980	84 Po Polonium (209.000)	85 At Astatine (210.000)	86 Rn Radon (222.000)
110 Ds Ununnilium (269)	111 Rg Unununium (272)	112 Uub Ununbium (277)	113 Uut (284)	114 Uuq Ununquadium (296)	115 Uup (288)	116 Uuh (298)	117 Uus (not yet recognized)	118 Uuo (294)

63 Eu Europium 151.960	64 Gd Gadolinium 157.250	65 Tb Terbium 158.924	66 Dy Dysprosium 162.500	67 Ho Holmium 164.930	68 Er Erbium 167.260	69 Tm Thulium 168.934	70 Yb Ytterbium 173.040	71 Lu Lutetium 174.970
95 Am Americium (243.000)	96 Cm Curium (247.000)	97 Bk Berkelium (247.000)	98 Cf Californium (251.000)	99 Es Einsteinium (254.000)	100 Fm Fermium (257.000)	101 Md Mendelevium (258.000)	102 No Nobelium (259.000)	103 Lr Lawrencium (262.000)

*Atomic masses in parentheses are of the most common form of the atom.

Appendix F   Meteorological Scales

Saffir-Simpson Hurricane Scale

The Saffir-Simpson scale measures the wind speed of hurricanes. The category number tells the wind speed and amount of damage a hurricane can cause. Since the 1970s, the National Hurricane Center in the United States has used this scale to classify hurricanes. The scale was developed by Herbert Saffir, an engineer, and Robert Simpson, a former director of the National Hurricane Center. The National Hurricane Center is located on the campus of Florida International University, Miami, Florida. The Center is part of NOAA, the National Oceanic and Atmospheric Administration.

CATEGORY	WIND SPEED (mph)	DAMAGE
1	74–95	Minor
2	96–110	Moderate
3	111–130	Strong
4	131–155	Very Strong
5	More than 155	Devastating

◀ Figure 10

Beaufort Wind Speed Scale

This scale is named for the nineteenth-century British naval officer who devised it. The Beaufort Scale classifies wind speed according to its effects. It was originally used in 1806 as an aid for sailors. It has since been adapted for use on land. The scale has been modified through the years.

CODE	SPEED (MPH)	DESCRIPTION	EFFECTS ON LAND
0	Below 1	Calm	Smoke rises vertically
1	1–5	Light air	Smoke drifts slowly
2	6–11	Light breeze	Leaves rustle
3	12–19	Gentle breeze	Leaves and twigs move
4	20–28	Moderate breeze	Small branches move
5	29–38	Fresh breeze	Small trees sway
6	39–49	Strong breeze	Large branches sway
7	50–61	Near gale	Walking difficult
8	62–74	Gale	Twigs snap off trees
9	75–88	Strong gale	Minor damage
10	89–102	Whole gale	Significant damage
11	103–114	Storm	Widespread damage
12	Above 117	Hurricane	Widespread destruction

◀ Figure 11

The Fujita Intensity Scale

This scale provides a measure of the strength of a tornado. It was developed by tornado specialist Dr. Tetsuto Theodore Fujita, of the University of Chicago.

CATEGORY	WIND SPEED (mph)	DAMAGE
F0	40–71	Light
F1	72–112	Moderate
F2	113–157	Considerable
F3	158–206	Severe
F4	207–260	Devastating
F5	261–318	Incredible

◀ Figure 12

Appendix G Astronomy Tables

PLANETARY DATA				
Planet	Diameter (km)	Time for One Spin on Axis	Time for One Orbit of the Sun	Average Distance From the Sun (km)
Mercury	4,880	58.65 days	87.97 days	57.9 million
Venus	12,103.6	243.0 days	224.70 days	108.21 million
Earth	12,756	23.93 hours	365.26 days	149.6 million
Mars	6,794	24.66 hours	686.98 days	227.9 million
Jupiter	142,984	9.93 hours	11.86 years	778.57 million
Saturn	120,536	10.66 hours	29.4 years	1.43 billion
Uranus	51,118	17.24 hours	84.01 years	2.87 billion
Neptune	49,528	16.11 hours	164.78 years	4.5 billion

▲ Figure 13

KEY ROBOT PROBES TO PLANETS, COMETS, AND ASTEROIDS				
Probe	Type	Target	Encounter	Achievements
Pioneer 10	Flyby	Jupiter	1973	First to cross Asteroid Belt; took close-up photos of Jupiter
Mariner 10	Flyby	Mercury	1974–1975	Only probe to Mercury
Venera 9	Orbiter/lander	Venus	1975	First views of surface
Viking 1 and 2	Orbiters/landers	Mars	1976	Photographed surface; searched for life
Pioneer 11	Flyby	Saturn	1979	First detailed views
Voyager 1 and 2	Flybys	Jupiter	1979	Details of all four planetary systems; Voyager 2 was first probe to Uranus and Neptune
		Saturn	1980–1981	
		Uranus	1986	
		Neptune	1989	
Giotto	Flyby	Comet	1986	First close-up view of nucleus
Galileo	Flyby/orbiter	Gaspra	1991 and	First flyby of an asteroid; first orbit of Jupiter
		Jupiter	1995	
Mars Global Surveyor	Orbiter	Mars	1997	Mapped surface and searched for water
Mars Odyssey	Orbiter	Mars	2001	Mapped surface and searched for water
Cassini	Flyby/orbiter	Saturn	2004	Detailed studies of the planet and its rings

▲ Figure 14

SOLAR ECLIPSES THROUGH THE YEAR 2030		
Date	Duration of Totality (minutes)	Location
Nov. 23, 2003	4.4	Central America
April 8, 2005	0.7	South Pacific Ocean
March 29, 2006	4.1	Africa, Asia Minor, Russia
August 1, 2008	2.4	Arctic Ocean, Siberia, China
July 22, 2009	6.6	India, China, South Pacific
July 11, 2010	5.3	South America
Nov. 13, 2012	4.0	Australia, South America
Nov. 3, 2013	1.7	North and South America, Africa
March 20, 2015	2.78	Europe, Africa
March 9, 2016	4.15	Asia, Australia
August 11, 2018	2.7	Europe, Asia
July 2, 2019	4.5	Pacific Ocean, Chile, Argentina
Dec. 14, 2020	2.2	Pacific and Atlantic oceans, South America
Dec. 4, 2021	0.38	Antarctica, Southern Africa
April 20, 2023	1.3	Asia, Australia
April 8, 2024	4.5	North and Central America
August 12, 2026	2.3	North America, Europe
August 2, 2027	6.4	Africa, Asia
July 22, 2028	5.1	Asia, Australia
Nov. 25, 2030	3.7	Botswana, S. Africa, Australia

◀ Figure 15

Regularly Occurring Meteor Showers

Occasionally, 60 or more meteors flash across the sky in a single hour or two. These light displays are called meteor showers. They occur when Earth crosses a comet's orbit and groups of meteoroids from the comet's tail collide with Earth's atmosphere. The dates in the table below are peak dates. For most showers, the meteors can be seen for a few weeks, but the peak occurs somewhere around the middle of the time period.

METEOR SHOWERS		
Shower	Approximate Peak Dates	Associated Comet
Quadrantids	January 4–6	—
Lyrids	April 20–23	Thacher
Eta Aquarids	May 3–5	Halley's comet
Delta Aquarids	July 30	—
Perseids	August 12	Comet 1862 III
Draconids	October 7–10	Comet Giacobini-Zinner
Orionids	October 20	Halley's comet
Taurids	Nov. 3–13	Encke's Comet
Leonids	Nov. 18	Temple-Tuttle
Geminids	Dec. 4–16	3200 Phaeton

◀ Figure 16

Appendix **H** Star Charts

Spring Sky

To use this chart, hold it up in front of you and turn it so that
the direction you are facing is at the bottom of the chart. This
chart works best at 34° north latitude and at the following times:
10:00 P.M. on March 1; 9:00 P.M. on March 15; 8:00 P.M. on March
30. However, it can be referenced at other times and latitudes
within the United States.

NORTHERN HORIZON

Cepheus

Cassiopeia

Draco

Ursa Minor
(Little Dipper)

Andromeda

Polaris
(North Star)

Triangulum

Bootes

Perseus

Aries

Ursa Major
(Big Dipper)

Capella

Arcturus

Auriga

Pleiades

Castor

Taurus

**EASTERN
HORIZON**

Cancer

Gemini

Aldebaran

**WESTERN
HORIZON**

Pollux

Virgo

Leo

Procyon

Eridanus

Spica

Regulus

Canis
Minor

Betelgeuse

Orion

Corvus

Rigel

Hydra

Sirius

Canis
Major

Lepus

Columba

Vela

SOUTHERN HORIZON

Summer Sky

To use this chart, hold it up in front of you and turn it so that
the direction you are facing is at the bottom of the chart. This
chart works best at 34° north latitude and at the following times:
10:00 P.M. on June 1; 9:00 P.M. on June 15; 8:00 P.M. on June 30.
However, it can be used at other times and latitudes within the
United States.

NORTHERN HORIZON

Cassiopeia

Cepheus

Polaris
(North Star)

Gemini

Castor

Ursa Minor
(Little Dipper)

Pollux

Deneb

Draco

Cygnus

Cancer

Delphinus

Vega

Ursa Major
(Big Dipper)

Lyra

Altair

Corona
Borealis

Leo

**EASTERN
HORIZON**

Hercules

Bootes

**WESTERN
HORIZON**

Aquila

Regulus

Acturus

Serpens Caput

Serpens Cauda

Ophiuchus

Virgo

Hydra

Sagittarius

Libra

Spica

Corvus

Scorpius

Antares

Centaurus

SOUTHERN HORIZON

Appendix **H**   Star Charts (continued)

Autumn Sky

To use this chart, hold it up in front of you and turn it so that the direction you are facing is at the bottom of the chart. This chart works best at 34° north latitude and at the following times: 10:00 P.M. on September 1; 9:00 P.M. on September 15; 8:00 P.M. on September 30. However, it can be used at other times and latitudes within the United States.

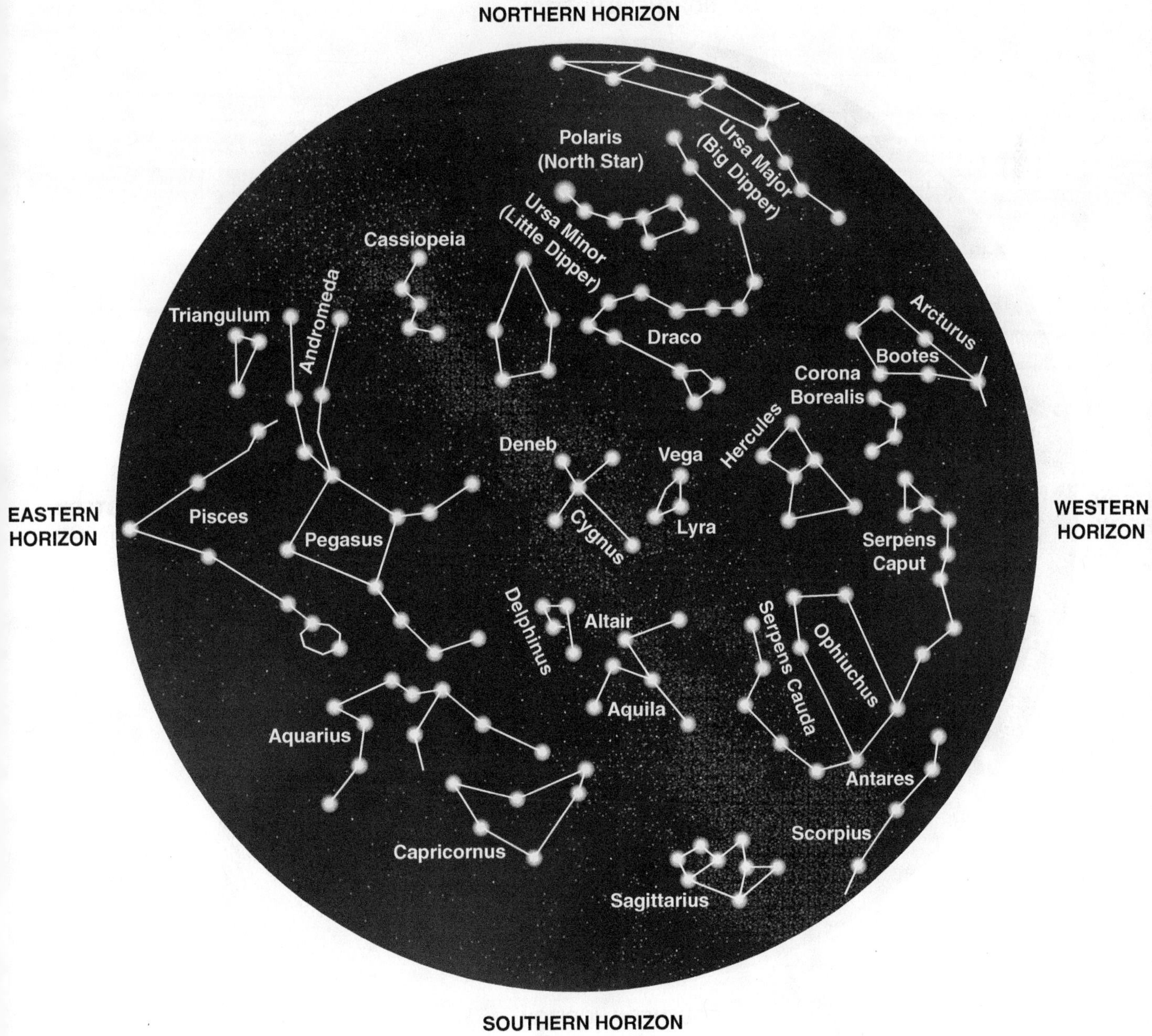

NORTHERN HORIZON

Polaris
(North Star)

Ursa Major
(Big Dipper)

Ursa Minor
(Little Dipper)

Cassiopeia

Andromeda

Arcturus

Triangulum

Draco

Bootes

Corona
Borealis

Deneb

Vega

Hercules

**EASTERN
HORIZON**

Pisces

Cygnus

Lyra

**WESTERN
HORIZON**

Pegasus

Serpens
Caput

Delphinus

Altair

Serpens Cauda

Ophiuchus

Aquila

Aquarius

Antares

Capricornus

Scorpius

Sagittarius

SOUTHERN HORIZON

Winter Sky

To use this chart, hold it up in front of you and turn it so that the direction you are facing is at the bottom of the chart. This chart works best at 34° north latitude and at the following times: 10:00 P.M. on December 1; 9:00 P.M. on December 15; 8:00 P.M. on December 30. However, it can be used at other times and latitudes within the United States.

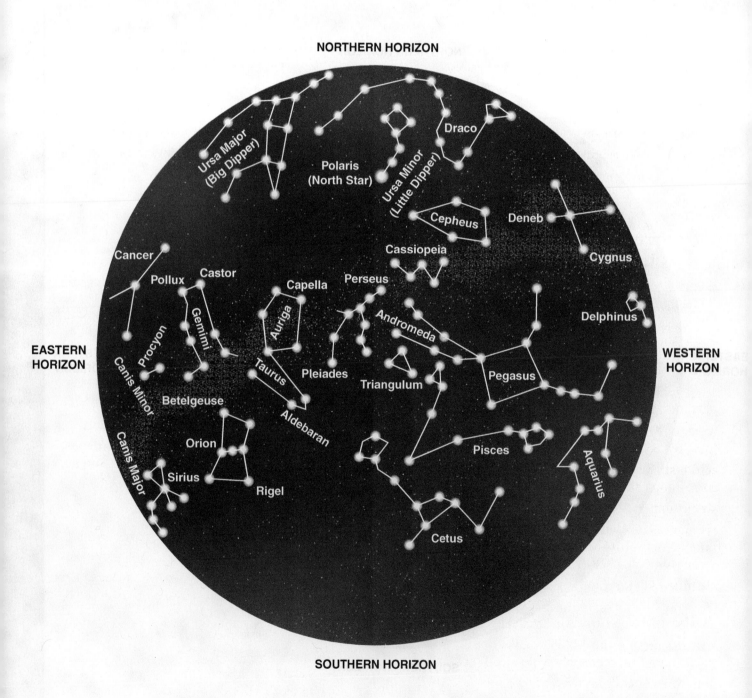

NORTHERN HORIZON

Ursa Major (Big Dipper)
Draco
Polaris (North Star)
Ursa Minor (Little Dipper)
Cepheus
Deneb
Cassiopeia
Cygnus
Cancer
Pollux
Castor
Capella
Perseus
Gemini
Auriga
Andromeda
Delphinus
Procyon
Taurus
Pleiades
Pegasus
Canis Minor
Triangulum
Betelgeuse
Aldebaran
Pisces
Orion
Aquarius
Canis Major
Sirius
Rigel
Cetus

EASTERN HORIZON

WESTERN HORIZON

SOUTHERN HORIZON

Glossary

Pronunciation and syllabication have been derived from *Webster's New World Dictionary*, Second College Edition, Revised School Printing (Prentice Hall, 1985). Syllables printed in capital letters are given primary stress. (Numbers in parentheses indicate the page number, or page numbers, on which the term is defined.)

		PRONUNCIATION KEY			
Symbol	Example	Respelling	Symbol	Example	Respelling
a	transpiration	(tran-spuh-RAY-shuhn)	oh	biome	(BY-ohm)
ah	composite	(kuhm-PAHZ-iht)	oi	asteroid	(AS-tuhr-oid)
aw	atoll	(A-tawl)	oo	altitude	(AL-tuh-tood)
ay	abrasion	(uh-BRAY-zhuhn)	ow	compound	(KAHM-pownd)
ch	leaching	(LEECH-ing)	s	satellite	(SAT-uhl-yt)
eh	chemical	(KEHM-i-kuhl)	sh	specialization	(spehsh-uhl-ih-ZAY-shuhn)
ee	equinox	(EE-kwih-nahks)	th	thermocline	(THUR-muh-klyn)
f	hemisphere	(HEHM-ih-sfeer)	th	weathering	(WEHTH-uhr-ing)
g	galaxy	(GAL-uhk-see)	uh	volcanism	(VAHL-kuh-nihzm)
ih	anticline	(AN-tih-klyn)	y, eye	anticline, isobar	(AN-tih-klyn), (EYE-soh-bahr)
j	geologic	(jee-uh-LAHJ-ihk)	yoo	cumulus	(KYOOM-yuh-luhs)
k	current	(KUR-uhnt)	z	deposition	(dehp-uh-ZIHSH-uhn)
ks	axis	(AK-sihs)	zh	erosion	(e-ROH-zhuhn)

A

abrasion (uh-BRAY-zhuhn): wearing away of rock particles by wind and water (p. 184)

absolute age: true age of a rock or fossil (p. 98)

acid rain: rain containing acids produced by water chemically combined with certain gases (pp. 164, 362)

acid test: test that helps to identify minerals containing calcium carbonate (p. 50)

air current: up-and-down movement of air (p. 266)

air mass: large volume of air with about the same temperature and amount of moisture throughout (p. 292)

altitude (AL-tuh-tood): height above sea level (p. 310)

amber: hardened tree sap (p. 90)

anemometer (an-uh-MAHM-uht-uhr): instrument that measures wind speed (p. 272)

anticline (AN-tih-klyn): upward fold (p. 110)

aphelion (uh-FEE-lee-uhn): point in a planet's orbit at which it is farthest from the Sun (pp. 332, 410)

apogee (AP-uh-jee): point at which the Moon is farthest from Earth (p. 336)

asteroid (AS-tuhr-oid): large chunk of rock or metal that orbits the Sun (p. 424)

astronomical (as-truh-NAHM-ih-kuhl) **unit (AU):** unit of measurement based on the Sun's distance from Earth and equal to about 150 million km (p. 392)

astronomy (uh-STRAHN-uh-mee): study of stars, planets, and other objects in space (p. 380)

atmosphere (AT-muh-sfeer): envelope of gases surrounding Earth (pp. 18, 252)

atoll (A-tawl): ring-shaped coral reef around a lagoon (p. 244)

atom: smallest part of an element that can be identified as that element (p. 42)

axis (AK-sihs): imaginary line through the center of a planet or other body around which that body spins (p. 326)

barometer (buh-RAHM-uht-uhr): instrument used to measure air pressure (p. 262)

barrier reef: coral reef that forms around a sunken volcanic island (p. 244)

bedrock: solid rock that lies beneath the soil (p. 166)

Big Bang: explosion that may have begun the universe about 14 billion years ago (p. 458)

binary stars: two stars that revolve around each other (p. 436)

biodegradable: material that breaks down easily (p. 372)

biome (BY-ohm): large region with a characteristic climate and plant and animal communities (p. 318)

black hole: massive star that has collapsed and whose gravity is so powerful that it pulls in everything, even light (p. 458)

caldera (kal-DER-uh): large hole that forms when the roof of a magma dome collapses (p. 118)

capacity (kuh-PAS-ih-tee): amount of material something can hold (p. 280)

carbonation (kahr-buh-NAY-shuhn): chemical reaction that occurs when carbonic acid reacts with certain minerals (p. 160)

cave system: series of connected underground caves (p. 186)

cast: mold filled with hardened sediments (p. 90)

cellular respiration (rehs-puh-RAY-shuhn): process by which a cell releases energy from food molecules (p. 252)

chemical formula: formula that shows the elements that make up a compound (p. 44)

chemical (KEHM-ih-kuhl) **symbol:** shorthand way of writing the name of an element (p. 44)

chemical (KEHM-ih-kuhl) **weathering:** weathering that changes the chemical makeup of rocks (p. 158)

chromosphere (KROH-muh-sfeer): layer of the Sun's atmosphere above the photosphere (p. 446)

cinder cone: volcanic cone made up of rock particles, dust, and ash (p. 120)

cirrus (SIR-uhs) **cloud:** light, feathery cloud (p. 286)

clastic (KLAS-tihk) **rock:** sedimentary rock made up of fragments of rock (p. 74)

cleavage (KLEEV-ihj): tendency of some minerals to split along smooth, flat surfaces called planes (p. 52)

climate (KLY-muht): average weather conditions of an area over many years (p. 308)

cold front: forward edge of a cold air mass, formed when a cold air mass pushes under a warm air mass (p. 294)

coma: gas cloud that surrounds the nucleus of a comet (p. 430)

comet: lump of ice, frozen gas, and dust that orbits the Sun (p. 430)

communication: sharing information (p. 8)

composite (kuhm-PAHZ-iht) **cone:** volcanic cone made up of alternating layers of lava and rock particles (p. 120)

compound (KAHM-pownd): substance made up of two or more elements that are chemically combined (p. 42)

concave mirror: mirror that curves inward (p. 386)

condensation (kahn-duhn-SAY-shuhn): changing of a gas to a liquid (pp. 208, 284)

conduction (kuhn-DUHK-shuhn): transfer of heat through matter by direct contact (p. 258)

conservation (kahn-suhr-VAY-shuhn): wise use of natural resources (p. 352)

constant: something that does not change (p. 11)

constellation (kahn-stuh-LAY-shuhn): group of stars that form a pattern in the sky (p. 452)

continental (kahnt-ihn-EHNT-uhl) **drift:** theory that the continents were at one or more times a single landmass that broke apart and eventually moved into the positions they are in today (p. 138)

continental shelf: part of a continent that slopes gently away from the shoreline (p. 242)

continental slope: part of a continent between the continental shelf and the ocean floor (p. 242)

contour interval (KAHN-toor IHN-tuhr-vuhl): difference in elevation between one contour line and the next (p. 34)

contour (KAHN-toor) **line:** line drawn on a map that connects all points having the same elevation (p. 32)

controlled experiment: experiment in which all the conditions except one are kept constant (p. 11)

convection (kuhn-VEHK-shuhn): transfer of heat within a liquid or a gas (p. 258)

convection current: movement of a gas or a liquid caused by changes in temperature (p. 146)

convex (kahn-VEHKS) **lens:** lens that is thicker in the middle than it is at the edges (p. 384)

coprolite (KAHP-roh-lyt): fossilized dung or the stomach contents of ancient animals (p. 94)

coral: small animals found in warm, shallow ocean waters (p. 244)

core: innermost region of Earth (p. 20); center of the Sun (p. 446)

Coriolis effect: bending of Earth's winds and ocean currents by Earth's rotation (p. 232)

corona (kuh-ROH-nuh): outer layer of the Sun's atmosphere (pp. 344, 446)

crater (KRAYT-uhr): pit at the top of a volcanic cone (p. 118); round hole on the Moon's surface (p. 414)

crescent (KREHS-uhnt) **phase:** phase when less than half the Moon is visible (p. 338)

crest: highest point of a wave (p. 234)

crust: solid, thin outer layer of Earth (p. 20)

crystal (KRIHS-tuhl): solid substance with its atoms arranged in a regular, three-dimensional pattern (p. 52)

crystallization: formation of minerals caused by processes such as cooling and evaporation (p. 54)

cumulus (KYOO-myuh-luhs) **cloud:** big, puffy cloud (p. 286)

current: stream of water flowing in the oceans (p. 232)

cycle: series of events that happen over and over again (p. 80)

data (DAYT-uh): information you collect when you observe something (p. 3)

deflation (dee-FLAY-shuhn): removal of loose material from Earth's surface by wind (p. 198)

delta: triangular deposit of sediment located at the mouth of a river (p. 184)

density (DEHN-suh-tee): amount of matter in a given volume (p. 50)

density current: stream of water that moves up and down in ocean depths (p. 232)

deposition (dehp-uh-ZIHSH-uhn): process by which material carried by erosion is dropped in new places (p. 178)

desalination: process of getting fresh water from salt water (p. 370)

dew point: temperature to which air must be cooled to reach saturation (p. 284)

distortion (dih-STOR-shuhn): error in shape, size, or distance (p. 22)

dome mountain: mountain formed when upfolds in rocks created a rounded structure that looks like a bowl turned upside down (p. 114)

drumlin: oval-shaped mound of till (p. 192)

dwarf planet: small, planetlike objects that orbit the Sun and share their orbits with other bodies (p. 428)

E

Earth science: study of Earth and its history (p. 16)

earthquake: sudden, strong movement of Earth's crust (p. 124)

ebb tide: outgoing, or falling tide (p. 238)

element (EHL-uh-muhnt): simple substance that cannot be broken down into simpler substances by ordinary chemical means (p. 42)

elevation (ehl-uh-VAY-shuhn): height of a point on Earth above or below sea level (pp. 32, 112)

ellipse (eh-LIHPS): flattened circle, or oval (p. 410)

elliptical galaxy: galaxy shaped like a ball or slightly flattened ball (p. 454)

environment (ehn-VY-ruhn-muhnt): everything that surrounds a living thing (p. 350)

epicenter (EHP-ih-sehnt-uhr): place on Earth's surface directly above the focus (p. 124)

equator: imaginary line that runs around the middle of Earth's surface and divides it into the Northern and Southern hemispheres (p. 26)

equinox (EE-kwih-nahks): day the Sun shines directly on the equator (p. 332)

erosion (ee-ROH-zhuhn): process by which weathered material is removed and carried from a place (p. 178)

erratic (ih-RAT-ihk): boulder left behind by a retreating glacier (p. 190)

evaporation (ee-vap-uh-RAY-shuhn): process by which a liquid changes into a gas (p. 54); changing of a liquid to a gas (pp. 208, 278)

fault: break in Earth's crust along which movement occurs (p. 110)

fault-block mountain: mountain formed when normal faults uplift a block of rock (p. 114)

floodplain: flat area on the side of a river where sediments are deposited during floods (p. 184)

flood tide: incoming, or rising, tide (p. 238)

focus (FOH-kuhs): point beneath Earth's surface where an earthquake starts (p. 124)

folded mountain: mountain formed by the folding of rock layers (p. 114)

foliated (FOH-lee-ayt-uhd): texture of a metamorphic rock that has mineral crystals arranged in bands (p. 78)

fossil (FAHS-uhl): remains or traces of an organism that lived long ago (p. 90)

fossil fuel (FYOO-uhl): natural fuel that was formed from the remains of living things (p. 102); oil, coal, or natural gas (p. 354)

fracture (FRAK-chuhr): tendency of some minerals to break into pieces with uneven surfaces (p. 52); break in a rock (p. 110)

fringing reef: coral reef that is directly attached to a shore (p. 244)

front: boundary between air masses of different densities (p. 294)

frost: ice formed from condensation below the freezing point of water (p. 284)

fusion (FYOO-zhuhn): reaction in which atomic nuclei combine to form larger nuclei (p. 450)

galaxy (GAL-uhk-see): huge collection of stars, gas, and dust that travel together through space (pp. 382, 454)

gastrolith (GAS-troh-lihth): stone used to grind food (p. 94)

gem: stone that has been cut and polished (p. 58)

geologic (jee-uh-LAHJ-ihk) **time scale:** outline of the major divisions in Earth's history (p. 100)

geothermal (jee-oh-THUHR-muhl) **energy:** energy produced from heat inside Earth (p. 356)

geyser (GY-zuhr): heated groundwater that erupts onto Earth's surface (p. 212)

gibbous (GIHB-uhs) **phase:** phase when more than half the Moon is visible (p. 338)

glacier (GLAY-shuhr): moving river of ice and snow (p. 188)

global winds: large systems of winds around Earth (p. 268)

globe: three-dimensional model of Earth's surface (p. 22)

gram: basic unit of mass (p. 4)

gravity (GRAV-ih-tee): force of attraction that exists among all objects in the universe (p. 410)

groundwater: water that collects in pores in soil and sinks into the ground (p. 210)

guyot (GEE-oh): flat-topped, underwater seamount (p. 242)

half-life: length of time it takes for one-half the amount of a radioactive element to change into a stable element (p. 98)

hanging valley: small glacial valley above a main valley (p. 190)

hard water: water containing a lot of minerals, especially calcium and magnesium (p. 370)

hardness: property of a mineral that relates to how much the mineral resists being scratched (p. 48)

hemisphere (HEHM-ih-sfeer): one-half of a sphere (p. 26)

horizon (huh-RY-zuhn): soil layer (p. 170)

hot spot: place where magma reaches the surface of a tectonic plate (p. 150)

humidity: amount of water vapor in the air (p. 280)

humus (HYOO-muhs): decaying remains of plants and animals (p. 166)

hurricane (HUR-ih-kayn): tropical storm with very strong winds (p. 296)

hydroelectric (HY-droh-ee-LEHK-trihk) **power:** electrical energy produced from moving water (p. 354)

hydrolysis (hy-DRAHL-uh-sihs): chemical reaction that occurs when minerals with little water content react with water (p. 160)

hydrosphere (HY-droh-sfeer): part of Earth that is water (p. 18)

hypothesis: suggested answer to a question or problem (p. 10)

iceberg: large piece of a glacier that enters the ocean (p. 188)

ice cap: large sheet of ice found near Earth's poles (p. 188)

ice wedging: mechanical weathering caused by the freezing and melting of water (p. 158)

igneous (IHG-nee-uhs) **rock:** rock formed by the crystallization of hot melted rock or minerals (p. 66)

index fossil: fossil used to help determine the relative age of rock layers (p. 96)

indicator (IHN-dih-kayt-uhr) **kit:** used to test the acidity of soil; color will change (p. 172)

infer: to form a conclusion (p. 8)

International Date Line: boundary formed where the first and 24th time zones meet (p. 328)

irregular galaxy: galaxy with no definite shape (p. 454)

isobar (EYE-soh-bahr): line on a weather map that connects points of equal air pressure (p. 302)

isotherm: line on a weather map that joins places that have the same temperatures (p. 302)

karst topography: land that has sinkholes, caverns, and underground rivers (p. 186)

kettle lake: lake formed by a retreating glacier (pp. 192, 218)

L-wave: surface wave (p. 126)

lagoon: shallow body of water between a reef and the mainland (p. 244)

lake: low spot in Earth's surface filled with still water (p. 218)

landform: physical feature of Earth's solid surface (p. 112)

latitude (LAT-uh-tood): distance in degrees north or south of the equator in degrees (pp. 26, 310)

lava (LAH-vuh): magma that reaches Earth's surface (pp. 68, 118)

law of superposition: states that each undisturbed sedimentary rock layer is older than the layer above it (p. 96)

leaching (LEECH-ing): removing or washing away the minerals in soil (p. 168)

legend (LEHJ-uhnd): list of map symbols and their meanings (p. 28)

light-year: unit of measurement equal to about 10 trillion km (p. 392)

liter (LEET-uhr): basic unit of liquid volume (p. 4)

lithosphere (LIHTH-oh-sfeer): solid part of Earth (p. 18)

loess (LOH-ehs): thick deposits of windblown dust (p. 198)

longitude (LAHN-juh-tood): measurement in degrees east or west of the prime meridian (p. 26)

longshore current: movement of water parallel to a shoreline (p. 196)

lunar eclipse (ih-KLIHPS): passing of the Moon through Earth's shadow (p. 342)

luster: how a mineral's surface reflects light (p. 48)

magma (MAG-muh): molten rock inside Earth (pp. 68)

magma chamber: underground pocket of molten rock (p. 150)

magnetism (MAG-nuh-tihz-uhm): force of attraction or repulsion associated with magnets (p. 50)

magnitude (MAG-nuh-tood): way to measure a star's brightness (p. 440)

main sequence star: star that falls within a long, narrow, diagonal band across the H-R diagram (p. 442)

mantle (MAN-tuhl): thick layer of Earth below the crust (p. 20)

map: flat model of Earth's surface (p. 22)

map projection (proh-JEHK-shuhn): drawing of Earth's surface, or part of it, on a flat surface (p. 24)

mare (MAH-ray), *pl.* **maria:** broad, flat plain on the Moon's surface (p. 414)

mass: amount of matter in something (p. 4)

mass erosion: downhill movement of weathered materials caused by gravity (p. 180)

matter: anything that has mass and volume (p. 252)

meander (mee-AN-duhr): loop in a mature river (p. 214)

mechanical (muh-KAN-ih-kuhl) **weathering:** weathering in which the chemical makeup of rocks does not change (p. 158)

meniscus: curve at the surface of a liquid in a thin tube (p. 4)

meridian (muh-RIHD-ee-uhn): line on a map or a globe running from the North Pole to the South Pole along Earth's surface (p. 26)

mesosphere (MEHZ-uh-sfeer): third layer of the atmosphere (p. 254)

metamorphic (meht-uh-MOR-fihk) **rock:** rock formed when existing rocks are changed by heat and pressure (p. 66)

meteor (MEET-ee-uhr): rock or metal that enters Earth's atmosphere (p. 424)

meteorite (MEET-ee-uhr-eyet): piece of rock or metal that falls on a planet or moon's surface (p. 424)

meteoroid (MEET-ee-uhr-oid): small piece of rock or metal that travels through space (p. 424)

meter (MEET-uhr): basic unit of length or distance (p. 4)

microclimate (MY-kroh-kly-muht): very small climate zone (p. 314)

mid-ocean ridge: an ocean-floor feature resembling a mountain ridge on land (p. 140)

middle-latitude zone: region between 30° and 60° N and S latitude (p. 312)

millibar (MIHL-ih-bahr): unit of measurement for air pressure (p. 300)

mineral (MIHN-uhr-uhl): naturally occurring, inorganic solid formed from elements or compounds and having a definite chemical makeup and regular atomic structure (p. 46)

model: tool scientists use to represent an object or a process (p. 3)

mold: imprint or hollow in rock that is shaped like and made by an organism (p. 90)

molecule: (MAHL-ih-kyool): smallest part of a substance that has all the properties of that substance (p. 42)

molten (MOHL-tuhn) **rock:** melted minerals (p. 68)

monsoon: wind that changes direction with the seasons (p. 270)

moraine (muh-RAYN): ridge of till deposited by a melting glacier (p. 192)

natural resource: material from the earth that is used by living things (p. 352)

neap tide: tide that is not as high or as low as a normal tide (p. 336)

nebula (NEHB-yuh-luh): cloud of gas and dust in space (p. 436)

nekton (NEK-tahn): free-swimming ocean animals (p. 246)

newton: metric unit of force (p. 260)

nodule (NAHJ-ool): mineral lump found on the ocean floor (p. 240)

nonclastic rock: sedimentary rock made up of dissolved minerals or the remains of living things (p. 74)

nonfoliated: texture of a metamorphic rock that does not have mineral crystals arranged in bands (p. 78)

nonrenewable resource: natural resource that is not easily replaced by nature or human effort (p. 353)

nova: explosion where the outer layers of a star are blown off (p. 444)

nuclear (NOO-klee-uhr) **energy:** energy produced by splitting or combining atoms (p. 354)

nucleus (NOO-klee-uhs): head or solid part of a comet (p. 430); center, or core, of an atom (p. 450)

oceanography (oh-shuh-NAHG-ruh-fee): study of Earth's oceans (p. 226)

ooze: ocean sediment that contains the remains of many ocean organisms (p. 240)

orbit: curved path of one object around another object in space (pp. 400, 408)

ore: mineral that is mined because it contains useful metals or nonmetals (p. 58)

oxbow lake: curved lake formed when a bend in a river is cut off at both ends (p. 214)

oxidation (ahk-sih-DAY-shuhn): chemical change that occurs when oxygen reacts with another substance (p. 160)

P-wave: fastest earthquake wave (p. 126)

Pangaea (pan-JEE-uh): single, giant landmass, or continent, that later broke apart (p. 138)

parallax (PAR-uh-laks): apparent change in the position of a distant object when seen from two different places (p. 392)

parallel (PAR-uh-lehl): horizontal line on a map or globe that circles Earth from east to west at intervals starting at the equator (p. 26)

penumbra (pih-NUM-bruh): light part of a shadow (p. 342)

perihelion (per-uh-HEE-lee-uhn): point in a planet's orbit at which it is closest to the Sun (pp. 332, 410)

pH scale: number scale used to measure acidity (p. 172)

phases (FAYZ-uhz): changing shapes of the Moon (p. 338)

photosphere (FOHT-oh-sfeer): inner layer of the Sun's atmosphere (p. 446)

photosynthesis (foht-oh-SIHN-thuh-sihs): food-making process in green plants (p. 451)

physical property: observable characteristic that describes an object (p. 48)

phytoplankton (fyt-oh-PLANK-tuhn): source of food for floating animals in the ocean (p. 246)

plain: large, flat area just above sea level (p. 116)

plankton (PLANK-tuhn): floating organisms (p. 246)

plate boundary: place where two plates meet (p. 146)

plateau: large, flat area at a high elevation (p. 116)

pluton (PLOO-tahn): large body of igneous rock that can form into different shapes when magma cools inside Earth's crust (p. 68)

polar air mass: air mass that forms over cold regions (p. 292)

polar zone: cold region above 60° N and below 60° S latitude (p. 312)

pollutant (puh-LOOT-uhnt): harmful substance in the environment (p. 350)

pollution (puh-LOO-shuhn): anything that harms the environment (p. 350)

pond: body of water similar to a lake but usually smaller and shallower (p. 218)

pore: tiny hole or space (p. 210)

potable (POHT-uh-buhl): water that is fit to drink (p. 231)

precipitation (pree-sihp-uh-TAY-shuhn): process that occurs when elements and compounds leave a solution and crystallize out as solids (p. 54); water that falls to Earth's surface from the atmosphere (p. 208, 290)

predict: to state ahead of time what you think is going to happen (p. 8)

pressure: amount of force per unit of area (p. 260)

prominence (PRAHM-uh-nuhns): stream of gas that shoots high above the Sun's surface (p. 448)

protostar: dense material in the center of a nebula that is about to become a star (p. 436)

psychrometer (sy-KRAHM-uht-uhr): instrument used to find relative humidity (p. 282)

quasar: continuous burst of brilliant light and enormous energy from a very massive black hole (p. 458)

radiant (RAY-dee-uhnt) **energy**: energy given off by the Sun that can travel through empty space (p. 256)

radiation (ray-dee-AY-shuhn): movement of the Sun's energy through empty space (p. 256)

radio telescope: telescope that can receive radio waves from sources in space (p. 388)

rain gauge (GAYJ): device used to measure rainfall (p. 290)

rapids: part of a river where the current is swift (p. 214)

recycling: using a natural resource over again (p. 358)

red giant: large, bright star that is fairly cool (p. 442)

reflecting (rih-FLEKT-ing) **telescope**: telescope that uses a concave mirror to collect light (p. 386)

refracting (rih-FRAKT-ing) **telescope**: telescope that uses convex lenses to produce an enlarged image (p. 384)

relative (REHL-uh-tihv) **age**: age of an object compared to the age of another object (p. 96)

relative humidity: amount of water vapor in the air compared with the amount of water vapor the air can hold at capacity (p. 282)

renewable resource: natural resource that can be reused or replaced (p. 352)

reservoir: artificial lake (p. 218)

residual (rih-ZIJ-oo-uhl) **soil**: soil remaining on top of the bedrock from which it formed (p. 168)

revolution (rehv-uh-LOO-shuhn): movement of a planet or other body orbiting another body (p. 326)

Richter (RIHK-tuhr) **scale**: scale that measures the energy released by an earthquake (p. 128)

rift: valley caused by a crack in the crust of a planet (p. 422)

rift valley: flat area between two ridges that is formed by spreading plates (p. 140)

Ring of Fire: major earthquake and volcano zone that almost forms a circle around the Pacific Ocean (p. 130)

rock: mixture of minerals, generally cemented together (p. 66)

rock cycle: series of natural processes by which rocks are slowly changed from one kind of rock to another kind of rock (p. 80)

rotation (roh-TAY-shuhn): spinning of a planet or another body on its axis (p. 326)

runoff: water from rain or snow that flows into streams and rivers from surface areas (p. 182)

S

S-wave: second earthquake wave to be recorded at a seismograph station (p. 126)

salinity (suh-LIHN-uh-tee): amount of dissolved salts in ocean water (p. 230)

sand bar: long, offshore underwater deposit of sand (p. 196)

satellite (SAT-uhl-eyet): natural or artificial object orbiting another body in space (pp. 400, 416)

saturated (sach-uh-RAYT-ihd): filled to capacity (p. 280)

scale: feature that relates distances on a map to actual distances on Earth's surface (p. 28)

sea arch: gap formed when waves cut completely through a section of rock (p. 194)

sea stack: column of rock remaining after the collapse of a sea arch (p. 194)

seafloor spreading: process that forms new seafloor (p. 140)

seamount: volcanic mountain on the ocean floor (p. 242)

sediment (SEHD-uh-muhnt): rock particles carried and deposited by water, wind, or ice (pp. 72, 184)

sedimentary (sehd-uh-MEHN-tuh-ree) **rock:** rock formed from pieces of other rocks that are pressed together (p. 66)

seismic (SYZ-mihk) **wave:** earthquake wave (p. 124)

seismograph (SYZ-muh-graf): instrument that detects and measures earthquakes (p. 124)

sewage: wastes usually flushed away in water (p. 366)

shield cone: volcanic cone made up of layers of hardened lava (p. 120)

simulation: computer model that usually shows a process (p. 3)

sinkhole: large hole in the ground formed when the roof of a cavern collapses (p. 186)

sling psychrometer (sy-KRAHM-uht-uhr): instrument used to find relative humidity (p. 282)

smog: mixture of smoke, fog, and chemicals (p. 362)

soft water: water containing few or no minerals (p. 370)

soil: mixture that includes silt, sand, and clay (p. 166)

soil profile (PROH-fyl): all the layers that make up the soil in an area (p. 170)

solar cell: device that converts sunlight into electricity (p. 356)

solar (SOH-luhr) **eclipse:** passing of the Moon between Earth and the Sun (p. 344)

solar energy: energy from the Sun (p. 356)

solar flare: eruption of electrically charged particles from the surface of the Sun (p. 448)

solar noon: time of the day when the Sun is highest in the sky (p. 328)

solar system: Sun and all the bodies that orbit it (p. 380)

solstice (SAHL-stihs): day of the year the Sun reaches its highest or lowest point in the sky (p. 332)

solution: mixture in which the particles of one substance are evenly mixed with the particles of another substance (p. 54)

sonar: echo-sounding system that bounces sound waves off the ocean floor (p. 228)

specialist (SPEHSH-uhl-ihst): person who studies or works on only one part of a subject (p. 16)

specialty: studying or working in only one part of a subject (p. 16)

specific humidity (hyoo-MIHD-uh-tee): actual amount of water in the air (p. 280)

spectrograph (SPEHK-truh-graf): device that measures the spectrum of an object (p. 438)

spectroscopy (spehk-TRUH-skoh-pee): study of light coming from objects in space (p. 438)

spectrum: pattern of different colors of light coming from an object (p. 438)

sphere (SFEER): round, three-dimensional object (p. 18)

spiral galaxy: galaxy shaped like a flattened disk with spiral arms (p. 454)

spit: long, narrow deposit of sand connected at one end to the shore (p. 196)

spring: natural flow of groundwater to Earth's surface (p. 212)

spring tide: tide that is higher or lower than a normal tide (p. 336)

standard time: system whereby all places within a time zone have the same time (p. 328)

star: ball of gases that gives off light and heat (p. 436)

star cluster: large group of stars that travel together through space (p. 436)

station model: record of weather information at a weather station (p. 300)

stratosphere (STRA-tuh-sfeer): second layer of the atmosphere (p. 254)

stratus (STRAY-tuhs) cloud: sheetlike cloud that forms layers across the sky (p. 286)

streak: color of the powder left by a mineral (p. 48)

subduction (suhb-DUHK-shuhn) zone: place where old oceanic crust is forced back down into an ocean trench (p. 142)

submersible (suhb-MUHR-suh-buhl): underwater research vessel (p. 228)

subscript (SUHB-skrihpt): number in a chemical formula that shows how many of each atom are in one molecule of a compound (p. 44)

summit: highest point on a mountaintop (p. 112)

sunspot: dark, cool area on the Sun's surface (p. 448)

supergiant: very large and very bright star (p. 442)

supernova: violent explosion where a star is blown apart (p. 444)

symbol: drawing on a map that represents a real object (p. 28)

syncline (SIHN-klyn): downward fold (p. 110)

tail: long, ribbonlike trail of comet dust and gas (p. 430)

talus: pile of rocks and rock particles that collects at the base of a slope (p. 180)

tectonic plate: large, solid piece of Earth's surface (p. 144)

temperature: measure of the amount of heat energy something contains (p. 4)

texture (TEHKS-chuhr): size of crystals in an igneous rock (p. 70); size of soil particles (p. 168)

theory (THEE-uh-ree): set of hypotheses that have been supported by testing over and over again (p. 10)

theory of plate tectonics (tehk-TAHN-ihks): theory that Earth's crust is broken into plates that float on the upper part of the mantle (p. 144)

thermocline (THUR-muh-klyn): layer of ocean water in which the temperature drops sharply with depth (p. 230)

thermosphere (THUR-muh-sfeer): upper layer of the atmosphere (p. 254)

thrust: forward force produced in a rocket engine (p. 394)

thunderstorm: storm with thunder, lightning, and often heavy rain and strong winds (p. 296)

tide: regular change in the level of Earth's oceans (p. 238)

till: rock material deposited by a glacier (p. 190)

topography (tuh-PAHG-ruh-fee): general form and shape of the land on Earth's surface (p. 32)

tornado (tawr-NAY-doh): small, very violent, funnel-shaped cloud that spins (p. 296)

transpiration (trans-spuh-RAY-shuhn): process by which plants give off water vapor into the air (p. 278)

transported (trans-POR-tihd) soil: soil moved away from the bedrock from which it was formed (p. 168)

trench: deep canyon (p. 142); deep canyon on the ocean floor (p. 242)

tributary (TRIHB-yoo-tehr-ee): smaller stream that flows into the main stream of a river system (p. 182)

tropical (TRAHP-ih-kuhl) air mass: air mass that forms over warm regions (p. 292)

tropical zone: warm region near the equator (p. 312)

troposphere (TROH-puh-sfeer): lowest layer of the atmosphere (p. 254)

trough (TRAWF): lowest point of a wave (p. 234)

tsunami (tsoo-NAH-mee): large ocean wave caused by an earthquake (p. 128)

umbra (UHM-bruh): center or dark part of a shadow (p. 342)

nonfoliated: texture of a metamorphic rock that does not have mineral crystals arranged in bands (p. 78)

unit: amount used to measure something (p. 4)

variable: anything that can affect the outcome of an experiment (p. 11)

vegetation (vej-uh-TAY-shuhn): plants (p. 318)

vent: volcano opening from which lava flows (p. 118)

volcanic mountains: mountains formed from lava or debris, such as ash or rocks, thrown out of a volcano (p. 114)

volcanism (VAHL-kuh-nihz-uhm): movement of magma inside Earth (p. 118)

volcano (vahl-KAY-noh): vent and the volcanic material around it (p. 118)

volume: amount of space an object takes up (p. 4)

warm front: forward edge of a warm air mass, formed when a warm air mass pushes over a cold air mass (p. 294)

water cycle: repeated pattern of water movement between Earth and the atmosphere (p. 208)

waterfall: steep fall of water, as of a stream, from a height (p. 214)

water table: upper layer of saturated rock and soil (p. 210)

wave: regular up-and-down movement of water (pp. 194, 234)

wave-cut terrace: flat section of rock formed by the erosion of a sea cliff (p. 194)

weather: day-to-day conditions of the atmosphere (p. 308)

weathering: breaking down of rocks and other materials on Earth's surface (p. 158)

well: hole dug below the water table that fills with groundwater (p. 212)

white dwarf: very small, hot star (p. 442)

wildlife: all the plants and animals that live in an area (p. 360)

wind: horizontal movement of air (p. 266)

wind vane: instrument that indicates wind direction (p. 272)

world ocean: body of salt water covering much of Earth's surface (p. 226)

Index

mercury barometer, 262, 263

Mercury missions, 337

meridian, 26

Mesosaurus fossils, 138

Mesozoic Era, 100

metal minerals, 47

metamorphic rocks, 67, 78–79, 81, 84–85

meteorites, 218
impacts of, 418

meteoroids, 424, 425,

meteorologists, 16, 281, 293, 300, 401

meteorology, 16

meteors, 424
showers of, 424

methane, 357

mica, 52, 70

microclimates, 314

microwave ovens, 390

Mid-Atlantic Ridge, 130, 143

middle-latitude zones, 312

mid-ocean ridges, 140

migratory animals, 334–335

Milky Way Galaxy, 388, 454–455, 460

millibars, 300

mineral resources, 47

minerals, 46–47, 48–51, 54–55, 58–59, 74–75, 168–169, 353, 358

Miocene Epoch, 100

Miranda, 417

Mir (space station), 402

Mississippi River, 30, 182–183, 215

Missouri River, 183, 215

mistral, 271

Mohave Desert, 257

Mohs, Friedrich, 49

Moh's scale of hardness, 49

mold, 90

molecules, 42, 84, 421

Monarch butterflies, 334–335

monsoons, 271

month, lunar, 339

Monument Valley, 66

Moon, 21, 336, 414–415
craters on, 414, 415
eclipse of, 342–343
facts of, 414
formation of, 425
gravity of, 336
landing on, 414
lighting of, 339
phases of, 338–341
revolution of, 336–337

rocks on, 358
tides and, 238

moonrise, 337

moons
of inner planets, 416
of outer planets, 416–417

moraines, 192

mountain breeze, 270

mountains, 32, 112–113, 114-115, 150, 310

Mount Everest, 113, 242, 263, 287

Mount Fuji, 109

Mount Hood, 120

Mount McKinley, 32

Mount Palomar, 386

Mount Pinatubo, 123

Mount St. Helens, 112, 119, 120, 122–123, 151

Mount Vesuvius, 131

Mount Waialeale, 311

Mount Wilson, 387

mudflows, 180

mussels, 246

mutualism, 167

N

National Aeronautics and Space Administration (NASA), 23, 337, 398, 399

National Oceanic and Atmospheric Administration (NOAA), 296

National Park Service, 353

National Weather Service, 296, 297, 302

natural bridges, 186–187

natural gas, 102–103, 354

natural resources, 350, 352–353
conservation of, 358–359

Natural Resources Conservation Service (NSCS), 169

natural satellites, 416

NavStar, 23

neap tides, 336

near-Earth objects, 425, 429

nebulae, 408, 435

nekton, 246

Neptune, 401, 408, 416, 428
moons of, 417

Nereid, 417

neutrons, 444, 445

Nevado del Ruiz volcano, 147, 181

New Brunswick, 239

New Madrid, Missouri, 131

new Moon, 338, 340

Newton, Isaac, 381, 386
Third Law of Motion of, 394

newtons, 260

Niagara Falls, 219

Niagara River, 214

night, modeling, 326

Nile River, 177, 215

Nile Valley, 177

nitrogen, 19, 42, 252, 350

nitrogen cycle, 350

nitrogen-fixing bacteria, 350

nodules, 240

nonclastics, 74, 75

nonrenewable resources, 352–353

Northern Hemisphere, 26, 233, 268, 332, 420, 452
seasons in, 330–331

northern lights, 420

northern spotted owl, 349, 361

North Pole, 26, 326, 327, 330, 332

North Star, 326, 330, 392

nova, 444

nuclear energy, 355

nuclear fusion, 450

nuclear reactors, 355

nucleus, 450

O

oases, 213

objective lens, 384, 385

observatories, 387, 437

obsidian, 70

occluded fronts, 295

ocean currents, 196, 232–233, 310, 374

Ocean Drilling Program, 228

ocean floor, 242, 243

oceanic crust, 140, 141

ocean landforms, 242–243

oceanographers, 227, 230

oceanography, 16, 227

oceans, 225, 226-227
density of, 230, 232–233
exploration of, 228–229
life in, 246–247
properties of, 230–231

ocean sediments, 240–241

ocean waves, 194–197

Ohio River, 183, 215

oil, 354
formation of, 102–103
products from, 104–105

oil-rig operator, 103

Olduvai Gorge, 95

Oligocene Epoch, 100

Olympus Mons, 423

Oort, Jan, 431

Oort Cloud, 431

ooze, 240–241

opals, 59

orbit, 408
of Earth, 326, 410, 411
satellite, 400

orbital velocity, 410–411

orbiter, 379, 398

Ordovician Period, 100

ores, 58

organic farming, 183

organisms, 19
adaptation to climate of, 320–321
preservation of, in fossils, 90–91

orienteering, 29

Orion the Hunter, 452, 453

outer planets, 408
moons of, 416–417

oxbow lake, 215

oxidation, 160

oxides, 160

oxygen, 19, 42, 46, 252, 350

ozone, 254

ozone holes, 374–375

P

Pacific Ocean, 18, 30, 226

palallax, 443

Paleocene Epoch, 100

paleoclimatologists, 193

Paleozoic Era, 100

palm tree, 320

Palomar, 437

Pandora, 427

Pangaea, 138, 139

Pangaea Ultima, 145

parallax, 392, 393

parallels, 26

Parícutin, 119, 120

partial lunar eclipses, 342

partial solar eclipses, 344, 345

passenger pigeon, 361

peat, 102

pelagic zone, 246

pendulum, 327

penumbra, 342, 345

perigee, 336

perihelion, 332, 410

periods, 101

Permian Period, 100

pesticides, 183, 350, 366
runoff, 183

petrification, 91

petrified fossils, 91

Photo Credits

Photography Credits: All photographs are by Pearson Education, Inc., John Serafin for Pearson Education, Inc., and David Mager for Pearson Education, Inc., except as noted below.

Cover: Earth Science
Galyna Andrushko/Fotolia
Comstock Images/Jupiter Images

Back Cover: Comstock Images/Jupiter Images

Table of Contents: i t Comstock Inc.; v t Comstock Images/Jupiter Images; v b Charles D. Winters/Photo Researchers, Inc.; vi t Comstock Images/Jupiter Images; vi tr ChromoSohm/Photo Researchers, Inc.; vi b Jeff J. Daly/Fundamental Photographs; vii Comstock Images/Jupiter Images; viii t Comstock Images/Jupiter Images; viii tr Alistair Duncan/Dorling Kindersely Limited; viii b PhotoDisc/Getty Images; ix Comstock Images/Jupiter Images; x t Comstock Images/Jupiter Images; x b Philip Coblentz/Brand X/Alamy; xi Comstock Images/Jupiter Images; xii t Comstock Images/Jupiter Images; xii tr C.C. Lockwood/Animals Animals/Earth Scenes; xii b David Ducros/Science Photo Library/Photo Researchers, Inc.; xiii t Comstock Images/Jupiter Images; xiii tr NASA/Science Library/Photo Researchers, Inc.; xiv Comstock Images/Jupiter Images; xv Comstock Images/Jupiter Images; xvi Comstock Images/Jupiter Images; xvii Comstock Images/Jupiter Images; xviii Comstock Images/Jupiter Images; xviii Comstock Images/Jupiter Images

Front Matter P001 t Farrell Grehan/Photo Researchers, Inc.; P001 bl Brand X/Jupiter Images; P001 mr George Ranalli/Photo Researchers, Inc.; P001 br Comstock Images/Jupiter Images; P002 bl Beth Neal/Image Source; P002 br Elliot Hurwitt/Shutterstock; P002 tr AFP/Stringer/Getty Images; P003 Comstock Images/Jupiter Images; P005 Comstock Images/Jupiter Images; P007 Comstock Images/Jupiter Images; P009 t SuperStock, Inc.; P009 bl Brand X/Jupiter Images/Alamy; P009 br Dwayne Newton/Photo Edit; P009 r Comstock Images/Jupiter Images; P010 Imageplus/Corbis Premium RF/Alamy; P011 Comstock Images/Jupiter Images; P013 Comstock Images/Jupiter Images

Chapter 1 P015 PhotoDisc/Getty Images; P016 tl Lloyd Sutton/Alamy; P016 bl Dwayne Newton/Photo Edit; P016 tr SuperStock, Inc.; P016 br Steve bly/Alamy; P017 l NASA/Johnson Space Center; P017 r 123RF; P018 Wildnerdpix/Shutterstock; P021 The Granger Collection; P022 l Jeff Greenberg/Omni-Photo Communications; P022 tr Stephen VanHorn/Shutterstock; P023 CNES; Licensed by SPOT Image Corporation/Photo Researchers, Inc.; P025 Hulton Archive/Getty Images; P029 Chrislofoto/Shutterstock; P030 t PhotoDisc/Getty Images; P030 b The Granger Collection, New York; P031 tl United States Mint; P031 tr Greg and Jan Ritchie/Shutterstock; P031 bl Bettmann/Corbis; P031 br Bettmann/Corbis; P032 U.S. Geological Survey; P033 Ingram Publishing (Superstock Limited)/Alamy; P038 PhotoDisc/Getty Images; P039 PhotoDisc/Getty Images; P040 PhotoDisc/Getty Images

Chapter 2 P041 Jim Zuckerman/Corbis Premium RF/Alamy; P042 l Marcel/Fotolia; P042 r The Natural History Museum/Alamy; P043 tl Martyn F. Chillmaid/Science Photo Library/Photo Researchers, Inc.; P043 tr Lawrence Migdale/Photo Researchers, Inc.; P043 br Bettmann/Corbis; P045 Charles D. Winters/Photo Researchers, Inc.; P046 Kent Foster/Photo Researchers, Inc.; P048 tr Fundamental Photographs; P048 bl Harry Taylor/Dorling Kindersley Limited; P048 bc Harry Taylor/Dorling Kindersley Limited; P048 br Paul Silverman/Fundamental Photographs; P050 l Breck P. Kent/Animals Animals/Earth Sciences; P050 r Gary Retherford/Photo Researchers, Inc.; P051 Gemaldegalerie, Dresden, Germany/Bridgeman Art Library; P051 inset Thessalonika Museum, Greece/Bridgeman Art Library; P052 t Colin Keates/Dorling Kindersley Limited; P052 b Charles D. Winters/Photo Researchers, Inc.; P053 Peter Horree/Alamy; P055 NASA; P058 t Biophoto Associates/Photo Researchers, Inc.; P058 bl Charles D. Winters/Photo Researchers, Inc.; P058 br M. Clayel Jacama/Photo Researchers, Inc.; P059 tl

Bennyartist/Fotolia; P059 tr Colin Keates/Dorling Kindersley Limited; P059 br Tobias Machhaus/Shutterstock; P060-61 bkgd Peter Essick/Aurora & Quanta Productions; P060 Dorling Kindersley Limited; P061 tl U.S. Geological Survey/U.S. Department of the Interior; P061 tm Stephen Oliver/Dorling Kindersley Limited; P061 tr Natural History Museum/Dorling Kindersley Limited; P061 m Ellen Beijers/Shutterstock; P061 b Dane Penland/Smithsonian Institution/AP Wide World Photos; P062 Jim Zuckerman/Corbis Premium RF/Alamy; P063 Jim Zuckerman/Corbis Premium RF/Alamy; P064 Jim Zuckerman/Corbis Premium RF/Alamy

Chapter 3 P065 Pixelite/Shutterstock; P066 Chromosohm/Photo Researchers, Inc.; P067 Jonathan Blair/Corbis; P068 Michael Nicholson/Corbis; P069 John Kay/Corbis; P070 l Phillip Hayson/Photo Researchers, Inc.; P070 r Breck P. Kent/Animals Animals/Earth Scenes; P073 tl Colin Keates/Dorling Kindersley Limited; P073 tr Trevor Clifford/Pearson Education Ltd; P073 b Ric Ergenbright/Corbis; P073 b inset O.S.F./Animals Animals/Earth Scenes; P074 t Joyce Photographics/Photo Researchers, Inc.; P074 m Andrew J. Martinez/Photo Researchers, Inc.; P074 b Farrell Grehan/Photo Researchers, Inc.; P076 tl Phillip Hayson/Photo Researchers, Inc.; P076 tr Grace Davies/Omni-Photo Communications; P076 bl Phillip Hayson/Photo Researchers, Inc.; P076 br Grace Davies/Omni-Photo Communications; P077 Paul Jenkin/Animals Animals/Earth Scenes; P078 tl Andrew J. Martinez/Photo Researchers, Inc.; P078 tr Andrew J. Martinez/Photo Researchers, Inc.; P078 bl Dr Ajay Kumar Singh/Shutterstock; P078 br Andrew J. Martinez/Photo Researchers, Inc.; P079 t PhotoDisc/Getty Images; P079 b Norbert Rehm/Shutterstock; P084 t Michael Nicholson/Corbis; P084 b PhotoDisc/Getty Images; P085 t Chris R. Sharp/Photo Researchers Inc.; P085 m Pixelite/Shutterstock; P085 b Emma Lee/PhotoDisc, Inc.; P086 Pixelite/Shutterstock; P087 Pixelite/Shutterstock; P088 Pixelite/Shutterstock

Chapter 4 P089 Ismael Montero Verdu/Shutterstock; P090 l Jan Kranendonk/Shutterstock; P090 r Paul Maguire/Fotolia; P091 tl Jonathan Blair/Corbis; P091 bl Tom McHugh/Photo Researchers, Inc.; P091 tr Jeff J. Daly/Fundamental Photographs; P094 Tom McHugh/Photo Researchers, Inc.; P095 Des Bartlett/Photo Researchers, Inc.; P099 John Reader/Science Photo Library/Photo Researchers, Inc.; P101 Steve Munsinger/Photo Researchers, Inc.; P102 Dorling Kindersley Limited; P103 PhotoDisc/Getty Images; P106 Ismael Montero Verdu/Shutterstock; P107 Ismael Montero Verdu/Shutterstock; P108 Ismael Montero Verdu/Shutterstock

Chapter 5 P109 Craig Hansen/Shutterstock; P110 Rolf Sziringer/Okapia Bild/Photo Researchers, Inc.; P111 Kevin Schafer/Peter Arnold, Inc.; P112 Jerry McCormick-Ray/Photo Researchers, Inc.; P113 The Granger Collection, New York; P114 t Aleksandr Sadkov/Shutterstock; P114 b Charles Wollertz/123RF; P115 t Georg Gerster/Photo Researchers, Inc.; P115 b Vixit/Fotolia; P116 l Jim Steinberg/Photo Researchers, Inc.; P116 r George Ranalli/Photo Researchers, Inc.; P117 PhotoDisc/Getty Images; P119 t George Gerster/Photo Researchers, Inc.; P119 b David Weintraub/Photo Researchers, Inc.; P121 NASA/Science Source/Photo Researchers, Inc.; P122-123 bkgd David Weintraub/Photo Researchers, Inc.; P122 t D.R. Mullineaux/ZUMApress/Newscom; P122 b Joel W. Rogers/Corbis; P123 t Layne Kennedy/Corbis; P123 b Maslov Dmitry/Shutterstock; P124 Ken M. Johns/Photo Researchers, Inc.; P125 b AFP/Stringer/Getty Images; P128 t David J. Cross/Peter Arnold, Inc.; P128 b Jasper Juinen/AP Wide World Photos; P131 Enrico Della Pietra/Fotolia; P134 Craig Hansen/Shutterstock; P135 Craig Hansen/Shutterstock; P136 Craig Hansen/Shutterstock

Chapter 6 P137 Mikael Eriksson/Shutterstock; P138 The Granger Collection, New York; P141 David Rydevik/Wikipedia; P147 G. Brad Lewis/The Image Bank/Getty Images; P151 Mikael Eriksson/Shutterstock; P152-153 Earth Imaging/Getty Images; P154 Mikael Eriksson/Shutterstock; P155 Mikael Eriksson/Shutterstock; P156 Mikael Eriksson/Shutterstock

Chapter 7 P157 Alistar Duncan/Dorling Kindersley Limited; P158 Kushnirov Avraham/Fotolia; P159 t Russell Ensley/123RF, Inc.; P159 b PhotoDisc/Getty Images; P161 l PhotoDisc/Getty Images; P160 r eDesign/Shutterstock; P161 t Martin Bond/Science Photo Library/Photo Researchers, Inc.; P161 b Vera Bogaerts/Shutterstock; P164 Buddy Mays/Corbis; P165 Popshots/Omni-Photo Communications; P166 C. Allan Morgan/Peter Arnold, Inc.; P168 Sheila Terry/Photo Researchers Inc.; P170 Joy M. Prescott/Shutterstock; P172 t Dorline Kindersley Limited; P172 b Dorling Kindersley Limited; P173 l Dorling Kindersley Limited; P173 r Dorling Kindersley Limited; P174 Alistar Duncan/Dorling Kindersley Limited; P175 Alistar Duncan/Dorling Kindersley Limited; P176 Alistar Duncan/Dorling Kindersley Limited

Chapter 8 P177 NASA; P178 Haveseen/Fotolia; P179 t Dariusz PacioreK/E+/Getty Images; P179 b Doug Steley/Alamy; P180 l Chris R. Sharp/Photo Researchers, Inc.; P180 r Spencer Grant/Photo Researchers, Inc.; P181 G. R. Roberts/Omni-Photo Communication, Inc.; P182 Johnsroad7/Fotolia; P183 Donald Specker/Animals Animals/Earth Scenes; P184 l Beth Neal/Image Source; P184 r Liam Gumley, Space Science and Engineering Center, University of Wisconsin-Madison and the MODIS science team/NASA; P186 t Wildrabbitstudio/Fotolia; P186 b Herb Segars/Animals Animals/Earth Scenes; P187 Rodger Jackman/Oxford Scientific/Getty Images; P188 l Jhumbert0004/Fotolia; P188 r PhotoDisc/Getty Images; P189 t Science Photo Library/Photo Researchers, Inc.; P189 b Marine Biological Laboratory/Mark Marten/Photo Researchers, Inc.; P190 t G. R. Roberts/Omni-Photo Communications; P190 b Popshots/Omni-Photo Communications; P192 Elliot Hurwitt/Shutterstock; P193 Simon Fraser/Science Photo Library/Photo Researchers, Inc.; P194 l Jim Corwin/Photo Researchers, Inc.; P194 r Francois Gohier/Photo Researchers, Inc.; P195 Alex Neauville/Shutterstock; P196 Iofoto /123RF; P197 Padre Island National Seashore, National Park Service; P198 PhotoDisc/Getty Images; P199 t Robert_Ford/iStock/Getty Images; P199 b Christopher Scott/Alamy; P202-203 bkgd AP Wide World Photo; P202 b Library of Congress; P203 t AP Wide World Photo; P203 b USDA/NRCS/NCGC/National Cartography and Geospatial Center; P204 NASA; P205 NASA; P206 NASA

Chapter 9 P207 PhotoDisc/Getty Images; P211 Stephen L. Alvarez/National Geographic Society; P212 PhotoDisc/Getty Images; P213 Sylvain Grandadam/Robert Harding Picture Library Ltd/Alamy; P214 Murray Wilson/Omni-Photo Communications; P215 James Sheffer/Photo Edit; P219 t Spectrumx86/Fotolia; P219 b Worldsat International, Inc./Photo Researchers, Inc.; P222 PhotoDisc/Getty Images; P223 PhotoDisc/Getty Images; P224 PhotoDisc/Getty Images

Chapter 10 P225 Morozova Tatyana/Shutterstock; P226 PhotoDisc/Getty Images; P227 Jeff Rotman/Alamy; P229 t Stuart Westmorland/Photo Researchers, Inc.; P229 b Patricia Jordan/Peter Arnold, Inc.; P231 Yann Arthus-Bertrand/Corbis; P238 t Uzkiland/Fotolia; P238 b Uzkiland/Fotolia; P239 Tom McHugh/Photo Researchers, Inc.; P240 tr Charles D. Winters, Photo Researchers, Inc.; P240 bl Jim Steinberg/Photo Researchers, Inc.; P240 br Jan Hinsch/Science Picture Library/Photo Researchers, Inc.; P243 Pavlovsky/Photo Researchers, Inc.; P244 l David Hall/Photo Researchers, Inc.; P244 r Jean-Marc Truchet/Getty Images; P245 t Douglas Faulkner/Photo Researchers, Inc.; P245 b Mark Doherty/Shutterstock; P246 t Jan Hinsch/Science Photo Library/Photo Researchers, Inc.; P246 b Doc White/Nature Picture Library; P247 Elisei Shafer/Shutterstock; P248 Morozova Tatyana/Shutterstock; P249 Morozova Tatyana/Shutterstock; P250 Morozova Tatyana/Shutterstock

Chapter 11 P251 Philip Coblentz/Brand X/Jupiter Images/Alamy; P253 Lebendkulturen.de/Shutterstock; P255 Michael Giannechini/Photo Researchers, Inc.; P257 David DuCros/Science Photo Library/Photo Researchers, Inc.; P259 Darla Hallmark/Shutterstock; P262 l Bruce Heinemann/PhotoDisc/Getty Images; P262 l inset Charles D. Winters/Science Source; P262 t Leonard Lessin/Peter Arnold, Inc.; P263 t Donna Ikenberry/Animals Animals/Earth Scenes; P263 b The Granger Collection, New York; P266 Bruno Herdt/Getty Image, Inc./Photo Disc/Getty Images; P271 PhotoDisc/Getty Images; P272 tr

David Parker/Science Photo Library/Photo Researchers, Inc.; P272 bl Wil Blanche/Omni-Photo Communications; P272 br Mark C. Burnett/Photo Researchers, Inc.; P274 Philip Coblentz/Brand X/Jupiter Images/Alamy; P275 Philip Coblentz/Brand X/Jupiter Images/Alamy; P276 Philip Coblentz/Brand X/Jupiter Images/Alamy;

Chapter 12 P277 PhotoDisc/Getty Images; P278 l John Anderson/Alamy; P278 r Stuart Westmorland/Photo Researchers, Inc.; P279 Andrew Syred/SPL/Science Photo Library/Photo Researchers, Inc.; P280 Jim Steinberg/Photo Researchers, Inc.; P281 Dwayne Newton/Photo Edit; P284 t Rod Planck/Photo Researchers, Inc.; P284 b Richard Shiell/Animals Animals/Earth Scenes; P285 Hank Morgan/Photo Researchers, Inc.; P286 tr Bruce Watkins/Animals Animals/Earth Scenes; P286 bl John Spragens, Jr./Photo Researchers, Inc.; P286 mr Pavelk/Shutterstock; P286 br Fred Whitehead/Animals Animals/Earth Scenes; P287 t Stephen Ingram/Animals Animals/Earth Scenes; P287 b Inga spence/Alamy; P290 col. 1 Carson Baldwin, Jr./Animals Animals/Earth Scenes; P290 col. 2 Kathy deWitt/Alamy; P290 col. 3 Vvoe/Fotolia; P290 col. 4 C.C. Lockwood/Animals Animals/Earth Scenes; P291 Waldorf27/Fotolia; P293 NASA/Science Photo Library/Photo Researchers, Inc.; P294 John Lemker/Animals Animals/Earth Scenes; p296 OAR/ERL/National Severe Storms Laboratory; P297 t PhotoDisc/Getty Images; P297 b Vstock/Alamy; P298 t Mary Evans Picture Library/Alamy; P298 b Keith Kent/Science Photo Library/Photo Researchers, Inc.; P299 Pasphotography/Shutterstock; P304 PhotoDisc/Getty Images; P305 PhotoDisc/Getty Images; P306 PhotoDisc/Getty Images

Chapter 13 P307 Kenneth Sponsler/Shutterstock; P307 inset Peter Chadwick/Dorling Kindersley Limited; P309 Raldi Somers/123RF; P310 Michael Ellis/Shutterstock; P311 Jacques Jangoux/Alamy; P314 l Jim Schwabel/Index Stock Imagery/Jupiter Images; P314 r Reuters NewMedia Inc./Corbis; P318 Andy Lim/Shutterstock; P319 Robert Lubeck/Animals Animals/Earth Scenes; P319 inset Bjul/123RF; P320 t PhotoDisc/Getty Images; P320 m Francois Gohier/Photo Researchers, Inc.; P320 b L F Stewart/Shutterstock; P321 tl PhotoDisc/Getty Images; P321 tm Charlie Ott/Photo Researchers, Inc.; P321 tr Bios (Compost-Visage)/Peter Arnold, Inc.; P321 b Brad Thompson/Shutterstock; P322 Kenneth Sponsler/Shutterstock; P323 Kenneth Sponsler/Shutterstock; P324 Kenneth Sponsler/Shutterstock

Chapter 14 P325 Jhaz Photography/Shutterstock; P327 The Granger Collection, New York; P332 MyWorld/Fotolia; P333 PhotoDisc/Getty Images; P334 Neil Rabinowitz/Corbis; P335 l Sol Sexto/Photo Disc/Getty Images; P335 r Smari/Getty Images; P337 NASA/Science Photo Library/Photo Researchers, Inc.; P339 Hashim Pudiyapura/Shutterstock; P342 John Chumack/Galactic Images/Photo Researchers, Inc.; P344 Brand X/Jupiter Images; P345 Oversnap/E+/Getty Images; P346 Jhaz Photography/Shutterstock; P347 Jhaz Photography/Shutterstock; P348 t Jhaz Photography/Shutterstock; P348 b John Sanford/Science Photo Library/Photo Researchers, Inc.

Chapter 15 P349 Bob Hosea/Shutterstock; P349 inset U.S. Fish and Wildlife Service; P352 Jeff Greenberg/Omni-Photo Communications; P353 Brandon D. Cole/Corbis; P354 t Falk Kienas/Shutterstock; P354 b Jacques Jangoux/Peter Arnold, Inc.; P355 Joe Sohm/Pan America/Jupiter Images; P356 Chinch Grynieqicz/Ecoscene/Corbis; P357 Nova Scotia Power; P359 Alex S. MacLean/Peter Arnold, Inc.; P361 t C. C. Lockwood/Animals Animals/Earth Scenes; P361 b Mike Flippo/Shutterstock; P362 l Michael Ledray/Shutterstock; P362 r Will McIntyre/Photo Researchers, Inc.; P364-365 bkgd Bettmann/Corbis; P364 t Hulton-Deutsch Collection/Corbis; P364 b Bettmann/Corbis; P365 Bettmann/Corbis; P366 Karla Caspari/Shutterstock; P367 Josh Meyer/Shutterstock; P370 Werner H. Muller/Peter Arnold, Inc.; p371 Steve Allen/Alamy; P372 t Sam C. Pierson, Jr./Photo Researchers, Inc.; P372 b Jeff Greenberg/Alamy; P373 Paul Kern/Omni-Photo Communications; P374 Novosti/Science Photo Library/Photo Researchers, Inc.; P375 Yahya Ahmed/AP Wide World Photos; P376 Bob Hosea/Shutterstock; P377 Bob Hosea/Shutterstock; P378 Bob Hosea/Shutterstock